A year of turmoil all

Last year in our annual we were reflecting principally on the challenges the industry faced as it emerged from the pandemic. The challenges of the pandemic itself are more or less behind us, but at the end of 2022 numerous other issues had joined it to give a somewhat uncertain outlook for the railways at the start of 2023.

Of course, the pandemic's legacy is still with us, not least in the perhaps irreversible changes to working patterns and their impact on the passenger sector. By autumn 2022 this seemed to be settling down – leisure travel was exceeding pre-Covid levels, but commuting and business travel were still well short of where they were before the pandemic. Within that, there are distinct variations – the middle of the week is dominant for commuting, with Mondays and Fridays quieter.

The impact of this change is stark – the railway has been reporting a £2 billion gap between its revenues and costs compared to pre-pandemic conditions. There is general agreement this is unsustainable, and tackling it means growing that revenue or cutting costs – or a combination of both. There have been piecemeal attempts to grow revenue, but the bigger focus seems to be on cost-cutting, with train operators challenged on this front when putting together their business plans for 2023-24. Not helping this is the split between revenue, which accrues to the Treasury, and costs, which are managed by the Department for Transport – another issue that it has been widely agreed must be resolved.

Overlaid on that are the major industrial relations challenges the industry has faced through much of 2022. At the end of the year there was little sign of a resolution, but these issues could hardly have arisen at a less helpful time, when the industry needs every pound of revenue it can get.

Freight has also been hit hard by the industrial action, causing disruption to the sector which has emerged from the pandemic most strongly. The prospects are still positive, but there are warning signs in the wider economic outlook – will a downturn in consumer spending dent intermodal traffic levels, or will the construction boom ease off amid the widely forecast recession the country faces?

The wider economic conditions caused by the Ukraine conflict and other factors place a heavy burden on the industry. In particular, the challenge of soaring inflation affects companies in all areas, and means the cost of projects, replacement rolling stock and much more will be affected. Suppliers' abilities to hold quoted prices may be restricted, and this will not help with tackling the railways' cost burden.

When it comes to reform of the sector, 2022 was a disappointing year. By the end of the year, despite much hard work, the detail of the future structure remained unclear, and it had been confirmed legislation to create the new Great British Railways organisation would not be put before Parliament in the 2022-23 session. This was not helped by wider political turmoil and changes in the ministerial team, and an urgent priority in 2023 must be for the Secretary of State for Transport to confirm his ambitions in this respect.

This is not to say 2022 was all doom and gloom. The highlight of the year must surely have been the opening of London's new Elizabeth Line – aside from a few niggles, the new railway has been operating very well, has proved popular and has drawn widespread attention for the right reasons.

The lessons of the delays and overspend on Crossrail loom large over HS2, the country's next rail megaproject, which put's the capital's new railway firmly in the scale. But HS2 is another bright spot for the railway – huge investment which is now materialising through good construction progress and the huge number of jobs created.

There is much more that could be said about the challenges the sector faces. The biggest ask in 2023 must be for clarity – of direction, in terms of rail reform and the future structure, but also of detail, in terms of plans for decarbonisation, replacement of rolling stock, and projects to enhance the existing network, uncertainty around which all cause issues in the supply chain.

Capturing the state of an industry in flux is not an easy challenge, but is something we attempt to do in the pages that follow. Rail has not lost its will to succeed, even if many people emerge from 2022 somewhat battered and bruised by the tumults and turmoil of the year that has passed. But, if that clarity is provided, there is optimism rail can continue to play its vital role in contributing to a growing and prosperous society. ∎

Philip Sherratt
Editor, *The Modern Railway*

Jobs boost: in a difficult 2022, a bright spot was provided by HS2, which is now supporting nearly 30,000 jobs.

CONTENTS

The scenic West Highland line: ScotRail's No 156458 forms the 10.10 Mallaig to Glasgow Queen Street at Loch Eilt on 6 March 2022. **JAMIE SQUIBBS**

CONTENTS

The Modern Railway

Editor: Philip Sherratt
Design: Matt Chapman
Contributors: Chris Cheek, Keith Fender, Roger Ford, John Glover, Tony Miles, Alan Williams, Julian Worth
Publisher: David Lane
Advertisement Manager: James Farrell
Advertising Production: Rebecca Antoniades

PUBLISHING

Group CEO: Adrian Cox
Publisher, Books and Bookazines: Jonathan Jackson
Head of Design: Steve Donovan
Head of Marketing: Shaun Binnington
Head of Advertising: Brodie Baxter
Head of Operations and E-commerce: Karen Bean
Head of Finance: Peter Edwards

PUBLISHED BY

The Modern Railway is published by:
Key Publishing Limited, PO Box 100, Stamford, Lincolnshire PE9 1XP
Tel: 01780 755131 **Website:** *www.keypublishing.com*

Purchasing additional copies of *The Modern Railway*: Please contact the Key Publishing mail order team on 01780 480404. Corporate and bulk purchase discounts are available on request.

PRINTING:

Printed by Melita Press, Malta

THANK YOU!

We are very grateful to the many individuals from businesses in all sectors of the railway who have kindly provided help in compiling *The Modern Railway*. Information contained in *The Modern Railway* was believed correct at the time of going to press in December 2022. We would be glad to receive corrections and updates for the next edition.

COVER PHOTO: Avanti West Coast Pendolino No 390121 at Headstone Lane on 28 October 2022. **KEN BRUNT**

ISBN 978-1-80282-333-2

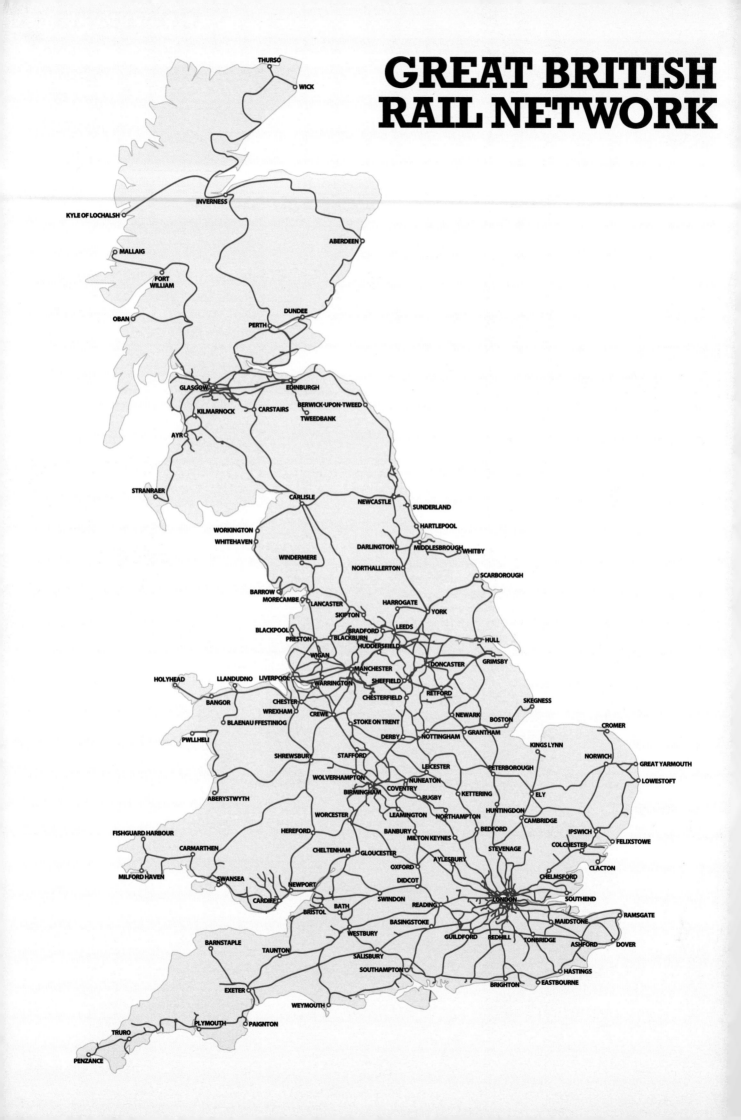

GREAT BRITISH RAIL NETWORK

SETTING THE AGENDA

Government support crucial for a successful 2023

Crossing political boundaries: at the official opening event for the Elizabeth Line at Paddington station on 17 May 2022 were (from left) TfL Commissioner Andy Byford, Mayor of London Sadiq Khan, Transport Secretary Grant Shapps and Prime Minister Boris Johnson. By the end of 2022, of the four men pictured only the Mayor was still in post. **COURTESY CROSSRAIL**

It is hard to believe that at the start of 2022 the coronavirus omicron variant was impacting on people's day-to-day lives and rail passenger numbers were a fraction of what they were before the pandemic.

Yet by August this year passenger numbers on the national network were regularly hitting 85-95% of pre-Covid levels, with revenue figures improving too, hitting 85% and sometimes nudging 90%. This followed the return of freight to 100% levels of the year before. Despite heatwaves and industrial action, the big railway story this year has been the impressive return to rail, although an honourable mention should of course go to the opening of the Elizabeth Line and all the work UK rail suppliers contributed to this fantastic addition to London's transport network.

As 2023 begins, it is important we recognise this bounceback and do all we can to demonstrate to the UK Government that rail needs more capacity both now and in the future, and that rail is a growing industrial sector, supporting 710,000 jobs, £43 billion gross value added,

£14 billion in tax revenues, and (conservatively estimated) £600 to £800 million in rail exports. According to the pan-European railway trade association Unife, the industry will grow globally by 3% every year to 2027. We must all push back against negativity regarding rail's future and any perception of managed decline.

Here in the UK, it is welcome that Chancellor Jeremy Hunt committed to High Speed 2 (HS2), 'core' Northern Powerhouse Rail (NPR) and East West Rail (EWR) in his Autumn Statement. We now need to make the case for investment in the existing network too, whether renewals, enhancements or the necessary rollout of electrification and digitalisation in the months and years to come – even in these difficult economic times. Our message to the Treasury and to Government as we approach Control Period 7 (April 2024 to March 2029) is: don't cut back and don't take your foot off the pedal on railway investment when UK rail is bouncing back from the pandemic.

Whilst we need to be relentlessly positive about the prospects for our industry in 2023, it's only right

we acknowledge the uncertainty we face and remain clear in our six 'asks' of Government as we go into the New Year.

Firstly, rail suppliers need certainty and visibility when it comes to the work pipeline. There needs to be a clear investment plan for Control Period 7, as well as an update of the Rail Network Enhancements Pipeline, fully three years after the last published iteration.

We need more clarity on major rail schemes – despite the Chancellor's announcement, whether the 'full' HS2, NPR and EWR projects, schemes like Midlands Rail Hub and Crossrail 2, or others set out in the Integrated Rail Plan for the North and Midlands will go ahead. And, importantly, there needs to be a commitment to actually deliver them without continually changing the scope once the go-ahead is given.

On rail reform, there needs to be clarity on what the delay in transition to Great British Railways (GBR) means. Who is going to take decisions during the interim between now and the establishment of GBR, and will there be a hiatus in work (the single biggest

concern of rail suppliers when it comes to transition to the new structure)?

In 2023 there needs to be an acceleration of efforts to decarbonise rail if the Government is to hit its objective to get all diesel-only trains off the network by 2040. A rolling programme of electrification and support for hydrogen and battery trains on less intensively used lines is essential to this.

There needs to be support for digitalisation, with 65% of current signalling requiring replacement in the next 15 years, and digital opportunities to improve customer service exploited too.

The Government also needs to invest in research and development and the rollout of innovations, in order to develop cleaner and more efficient ways of operating the railway.

Finally, 2023 should be a year of progression when it comes to the Equality, Diversity & Inclusion (EDI) agenda. 2022 saw the 200th signatory sign up to the EDI Charter. This accolade went to the GBR Transition Team, and it joined 199 other signatories in committing to taking steps both to develop a diverse and inclusive railway industry and to ensure the widest possible talent pipeline is available for employers to develop their workforces.

Despite the economic and industrial relations challenges we are all set to face in 2023, a RIA-commissioned Savanta survey of 160 rail leaders published in November showed rail businesses are optimistic about their own prospects. Only 13% foresaw a contraction, against 87% who expected their business to grow or stay the same compared to this year (with just under 60% expecting their companies to grow). As passengers and freight continue to return to rail, the rail supply sector is ready to play its part in ensuring a challenging time for rail is actually an exciting one, developing in 2023 even more world-class rail infrastructure and rolling stock both for today and for the future. ■

Darren Caplan
Chief Executive,
Railway Industry
Association

Powering a greener Britain: many freight operators are using hydrotreated vegetable oil to power trains in order to cut emissions, including Direct Rail Services with loco No 68006. **COURTESY DRS**

Freight challenges and opportunities

As we enter 2023, the country, and the railways, are beset with problems which cannot help but shape the environment for rail freight. The economy is struggling to keep its head above water, with forecasts suggesting a long and harsh recession. Unemployment is rising, and the cost of living crisis is biting on personal spending. Energy costs are at best volatile and there is no end in sight to the conflict in Ukraine. The aftermath of Covid restrictions is showing both in the NHS and also in business failures, and the impact of extended Government borrowing became all too clear in the Chancellor's Autumn Statement.

This all makes for a fairly gloomy start to 2023. Freight is a derived demand, and when the economy shrinks, so does the need to move goods. Rail has tended to fare better than road in previous downturns, and the early signs are that this is happening again but, even so, you cannot outrun a recession for ever. Maintaining and growing rail freight will inevitably be made harder by the economic outlook.

The railways as a whole are not immune to this either, with spending cutbacks across the board and an uneasy position on industrial relations. Performance and reliability were poor during 2022, and customers have felt the impact of this too often. There is concern over how reduced

funding will affect Network Rail, and its ability to maintain performance for freight customers. 2023 also brings the conclusions of PR23, the Periodic Review for the next Control Period, including new calculations for access charges for all rail freight commodities. Alongside are the questions over rail reform, the commission on access reform, and the Government proposals to repeal EU-derived legislation, all of which brings legal and regulatory uncertainty for freight.

Yet despite the unrelenting bad news, there is still plenty to be positive about. Importantly, customers are still keen to consign more by rail and new businesses are looking to add rail into their supply chains. The drivers for this, in particular sustainability and carbon reduction, remain strong drivers of action, irrespective of the economy. Use of rail is one of the few ways to take carbon out of supply chains right now and we expect that pressure to continue over the year. Equally, the post-Brexit changes to supply chains look set to continue, with an upturn in goods moving in containers through ports rather than on accompanied road trailers on the Dover straits.

There is also continued private investment in rail freight set to deliver over 2023. The third phase of Daventry International Rail Freight Terminal has already had a test train and new rail-linked units are under construction.

Further south, work continues at Northampton Gateway, which should get its main line connection this year. Work continues at West Midlands interchange, and there are expansion and investment plans at other locations too. Meanwhile, a number of sites should submit their planning applications this year.

The Stadler Class 93 locomotives, currently under construction in Spain, are expected to arrive in the UK this year, with the Class 99s set to follow. There are several wagon orders now under way, not least 30 new wagons for Drax to be built by W.H. Davis.

Away from the hard infrastructure there is also ongoing work on sustainability and on digitisation. Use of hydrotreated vegetable oil fuel is increasing for some customers, and the operators and customers are stepping up on actions to reduce carbon, even whilst the longer-term trajectory remains difficult. The recently announced First of a Kind funding had several excellent projects for freight, including tackling auxiliary power on locomotives and improvements to bogie design as well as technology to improve the core systems and processes for freight planning.

The rail freight industry is working hard to deliver growth despite the many challenges ahead. This is not easy – businesses have to balance their ability to grow with financial risk and

the need for stability, yet we should expect to see continued new services over the year. To really help freight flourish, Government and the wider industry has to play its part too. Despite the funding challenges it is essential a pro-growth agenda is allowed to continue, and that new customers are welcomed to rail. The plans for rail reform, however they emerge, must focus on bringing stability for freight operators as well as delivering private sector investment, and any amendments to access policy must work to protect capacity for growth.

No-one expects 2023 to be the easiest year on record, and the early signs show warnings of trouble ahead. Yet the positive messages around rail freight give hope that growth can be achieved, and the investment and commitment already in place give confidence of its delivery. This is good news for the sector, but more importantly it is good news for the economy and the railways too. With continued challenges in the passenger railway, the case for freight is greater than ever, and gives a new sense of being for UK rail. Fewer than 10% of the population use passenger trains, but rail freight touches everyone, be that in supplying supermarkets or generating electricity. More rail freight also helps the economy, providing more productive supply chains and reducing time to market for exporters. Despite the many challenges 2023 has in store, it

may yet be a good year for freight. ■

Maggie Simpson
Director General,
Rail Freight Group

Securing a bright future for rail

As I write this piece for the 2023 *Modern Railways* directory the dust is starting to settle following the delivery of the Chancellor's Autumn Statement. After several months of political turmoil and upheaval, can we now look forward to a period of stability? Or will the new Prime Minister's tenure be relatively short?

From an industry perspective we desperately need some stability so we can move forward from the constant policy changes (or confirmations) to action and real contract opportunities. Whilst government policies set the landscape and environment in which businesses operate, they don't pay the bills – contracts and orders do that. Contracts and orders generate jobs, support economic growth and encourage investment in both skills and technology. The industry needs to see government move from policy to action, and quickly. Suppliers need an assured pipeline of work they can have confidence in to enable them to plan and make those investments.

Yet we face significant challenges. And many of these relate to the perceptions of the industry. Over the last year more than one person and

key stakeholder has described the rail supply chain as 'needy'. The industry has been portrayed as having a sense of 'entitlement' to investment. Do I agree with this view? No, absolutely not – but that's irrelevant, because if that's how the industry is perceived it matters, and we all need to work hard to change those views. So how do we go about this?

One obvious way is to deliver the very best we can despite the ongoing challenges we face. That's why throughout 2023 our focus will be helping our members to understand the changing landscape within which they are working and supporting them to deliver. Suppliers need the contract opportunities to do that, so I reiterate that government moving from policy to action is vital to allowing the rail industry to demonstrate what it can achieve.

A second action is to challenge those perceptions, and that's where organisations like the Rail Forum come in. We need the evidence from the supply chain that demonstrates productivity gains, showcases investments made, highlights carbon reduction and energy-saving actions and so on. Working together, we

can transform some of the current perceptions and use supply chain success and value to drive a different relationship, especially with funding departments within government.

Another way to change perceptions is to evidence the wider impact investing in rail can have. Looking back over 2022, a few standout moments for me have come from our events. For example:

■ our social value event, where I met some of the incredibly passionate people that work for social enterprises that are supplying into rail. The difference working with these organisations makes is humbling and there are so many great stories that the supply chain can tell;

■ the inclusivity panel at our annual conference, that highlighted how far we have come as an industry. The willingness of people to share their views and to open their hearts and minds was great to see and hear (but there's still more to do!);

■ our client conferences demonstrated the clear desire of suppliers to understand customer needs and deliver the best products and solutions to meet those needs;

■ and finally, our collaboration in infrastructure event, which generated a real buzz and sense of opportunity to work better together to deliver low-cost, effective and innovative solutions.

We need to harness these positive stories and again use them to help change those perceptions. If we can work together to demonstrate the major benefits rail brings – be this economic growth or connectivity, reduced carbon emissions or improved air quality – then we can push back on some of the current views and demonstrate the value that the supply chain brings and the critical role we can and do play.

Government desire for change, reduced costs and increased productivity is very real and all projects will be subject to rigorous business cases and review. So, let's demonstrate what we can do and use those positive messages to help us secure a bright future for the industry and our supply chain. ■

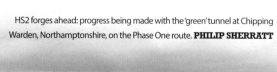

Elaine Clark
CEO, Rail Forum

HS2 forges ahead: progress being made with the 'green' tunnel at Chipping Warden, Northamptonshire, on the Phase One route. **PHILIP SHERRATT**

2023 – Year of ANXIETY

Key decisions deferred in 2022 are a cause for concern, warns *Modern Railways* Industry and Technology Editor **ROGER FORD**

In last year's *The Modern Railway* we characterised 2022 as the 'Year of Waiting'. A year on, and the industry is still waiting for signs of progress on multiple important outstanding decisions. This continuing uncertainty is a widespread cause of concern.

And those decisions taken in 2022 were largely negative. The most significant of these was the Government's failure to find time in this year's Parliamentary legislative programme for the Bill giving Great British Railways (GBR) its powers.

In May 2022, the then Transport Secretary Grant Shapps had told *Modern Railways* it was essential that the Transport Bill, incorporating the GBR legislation, began its Parliamentary journey in September. This would see the legislation become law in 2023, ready for GBR to take up its powers by 1 April 2024.

TIMING

Apart from the obvious need to press ahead with the reforms in the Williams-Shapps Plan (WSP), this date was doubly significant because it would also mark the start of the next regulatory Control Period. Control Period 7 (CP7) will determine the funding required by Network Rail for the five years to March 2029. The Department for Transport's consultation document supporting the proposed Transport Bill had highlighted the modifications to the legislation defining the duties of the Office of Rail and Road (ORR) to accommodate the WSP.

ORR announced the formal start of the Periodic Review for CP7 in June 2022. Periodic Reviews run to

a timetabled series of events, which, in the case of CP7, would culminate in a determination of Network Rail's income in October 2023. Clearly, if GBR was scheduled to take over responsibility for passenger services from April 2024, it would have to be reflected in the Periodic Review.

CRISES

In the event, the political crises during the summer of 2022 meant more-urgent bills would have to take precedence, leaving no time for the GBR legislation. Defending the postponement of the Transport Bill, Ministers have argued many of the benefits claimed for GBR can be achieved without legislation.

Claimed examples include workforce reform, delivering local partnerships, bringing forward a more long-term strategy for rail and reforming how ticketing is used. Who is to be responsible for devising and managing these developments in a fragmented railway remains unclear.

Latest news is that the Bill could be revived in the fourth session of the current Parliament. This could see that Act coming into effect in 2025.

Seeing the fruits of investment: Secretary of State for Transport Mark Harper (right) is shown the completed tunnel bore at Long Itchington Wood on Phase One of HS2 by the company's Chief Executive Mark Thurston. Mr Harper was the third incumbent of the role of Transport Secretary during 2022. **COURTESY HS2 LTD**

Electrification progress: overhead wires being installed east of Manchester as part of the Transpennine Route Upgrade. **COURTESY NETWORK RAIL**

MISALIGNMENT

However, it is the misalignment between the formation of Great British Railways and the start of CP7 which is the main impact of the delayed legislation. Under the original 1993 Railways Act, Periodic Reviews by the rail regulator have determined the income required by the infrastructure operator to fund Operations, Maintenance & Renewals (OMR).

This income is provided by Track Access Charges (TAC) paid by the train operators plus a direct subsidy from Government. However, under the WSP, GBR would be responsible for both infrastructure and the formerly franchised train services. Other than for open access passenger and freight operators, TAC would be redundant.

STATUS QUO

With the delayed legislation, ORR's determination for CP7, including the access charging framework, will have to be based on the current Periodic Review process. ORR claims it will also ensure the framework could eventually be applied by GBR. That said, ORR is 'anticipating' that the charging framework will apply for the duration of CP7, so up to 2029.

With a degree of understatement, ORR adds that it 'recognises there remains some uncertainty around how any transitional arrangements may work as GBR is established'. But that is a long-term concern. The current uncertainty has already interrupted the current Periodic Review process.

TABLE 1: NETWORK RAIL COSTS (£ BILLION)

	2019-20	2020-21
Operations	1.7	2.1
Maintenance	1.7	1.9
Renewals	2.9	3.9
Financing	2.1	1.7

Source: ORR

INCOME

Central to the Periodic Review is the publication by the Department for Transport and the Scottish Ministers of their High Level Output Specifications (HLOS) and Statements of Funds Available (SoFA). The HLOS statements inform Network Rail and ORR on what the governments want from the railway and the SoFA how much they are prepared to pay for it.

DfT was due to provide its HLOS and SoFA by the end of October 2022. With passenger ridership and revenue still recovering from the effects of the pandemic, long-term subsidies for passenger services were already uncertain. Earnings have also been distorted by the long-running industrial disputes affecting both Network Rail, which spends the money, and the train operators, which earn it.

CUTS

At the same time, Network Rail is looking to cut its maintenance expenditure. In November 2022, Chief Executive Andrew Haines told the Railway Industry Association conference that existing maintenance schedules based on fixed periods between attention meant unnecessary work was being done.

A switch to what Mr Haines termed 'reliability-based maintenance', also known as conditioned-based maintenance and already widely applied to traction and rolling stock and in the aviation industry, would cut the amount of work required, saving up to 1,850 jobs. Such job reductions triggered Network Rail's industrial dispute with the RMT union which ran through much of 2022.

A key contribution to the process will be publication, scheduled for February, of Network Rail's Strategic Business Plan (SBP). This will set out, based on the two Governments' HLOS and SoFA, what Network Rail intends to deliver for CP7. The delay to the HLOS and SoFA could put back production of the SBP.

Table 1 shows the latest data available on Network Rail's expenditure. Note that spending on renewals rose by 34% in 2020-21, reflecting ORR's concerns about future asset condition.

This increasing expenditure comes at a time when attempts to

FIGURE 1: INDUSTRIAL ACTION STALLS RIDERSHIP RECOVERY

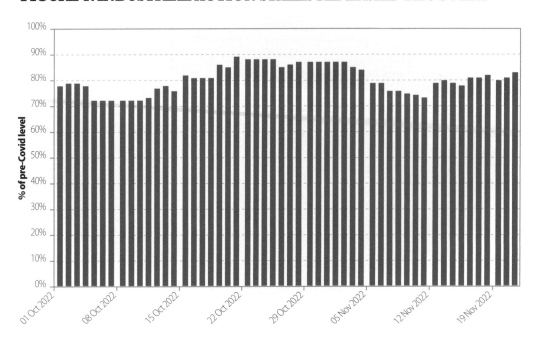

and enable reform and investment in the railways over the period 2024-29'.

ENHANCEMENTS

While Network Rail carries out maintenance in-house, renewals and enhancements are the responsibility of the supply chain, represented by the Railway Industry Association (RIA) and the Rail Forum. While renewals expenditure is the responsibility of the ORR, enhancements are determined by DfT and the Treasury, which provides the necessary funding.

In October 2019, DfT published a preliminary Rail Network Enhancements Pipeline (RNEP) listing schemes scheduled for CP6 (April 2019 to March 2024). An annual update was intended but, as RIA has pointed out through its long-running campaign, the update failed to materialise, despite many claims by ministers that publication was imminent.

Clearly, not knowing the future workload means suppliers and their subcontractors cannot plan investments in recruitment and training, research and development and plant and machinery. Whether 2023 will ease this anxiety remains to be seen.

SLOW IMPLEMENTATION

Current enhancement programmes are also advancing slowly. In his

cut costs have triggered large scale disruption. It should be noted that Periodic Reviews 'lock in' Network Rail's income for the following five years. Reportedly, this is one of the Treasury's concerns about the Government's degree of control over GBR's finances.

FINANCE QUESTIONS

Given all this uncertainty over revenue and funding it is not surprising that, in advance of the Chancellor's Autumn Statement in November 2022, DfT asked for, and was granted, a four-week extension to the deadline for delivering the HLOS and SoFA to ORR, and the documents were eventually published on 1 December. Scottish Ministers had until January 2023. In the event, the Autumn Statement was relatively favourable for transport.

Whether there will be sufficient data for the Periodic Review remains to be seen as the process continues through 2023. However, there is some flexibility to respond to events.

An ORR spokesman told *TMR*: 'We have implemented the statutory Periodic Review process and have control over relevant timescales, and we have the ability to react and adapt to external factors. As such, ORR's Periodic Review 2023 remains on target, and continues to be an important opportunity to support

Passenger return uncertain: passengers disembark a Chiltern Railways service at London Marylebone on 20 April 2022. **TONY MILES**

November 2022 Autumn Statement, the Chancellor confirmed that the Integrated Rail Plan (IRP) would be funded in full, as would High Speed 2 and East West Rail between Oxford and Cambridge.

However, in the case of projects within the IRP and East West Rail, further contracts are unlikely to be let before 2024.

Outside HS2, the major projects in IRP are the Transpennine Route Upgrade (TRU) and extension of the Midland main line (MML) electrification. While funding of £9 to £11.4 billion had been agreed for TRU, the contractors in the alliance have yet to receive further detailed instructions. However, electrification at both ends of the route has started.

Further delaying the TRU completion date – now 2040 – is a late change of policy which will see the route fitted with the European Train Control System (ETCS). This change is to be funded separately, requiring a new procurement process outside the existing alliance.

In the case of the MML, tendering of the electrification to Derby, Nottingham and Sheffield is expected to start in 2023, but with the contract not let before January 2024. Similarly, while good progress is being made on the western end of EWR to Milton Keynes, consultation will continue

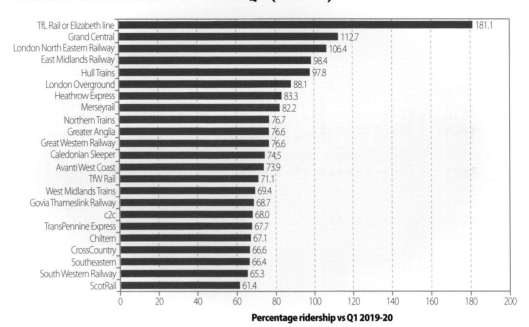

FIGURE 2: RIDERSHIP RETURN Q2 (2022-23)

	Percentage ridership vs Q1 2019-20
TfL Rail or Elizabeth line	181.1
Grand Central	112.7
London North Eastern Railway	106.4
East Midlands Railway	98.4
Hull Trains	97.8
London Overground	88.1
Heathrow Express	83.3
Merseyrail	82.2
Northern Trains	76.7
Greater Anglia	76.6
Great Western Railway	76.6
Caledonian Sleeper	74.5
Avanti West Coast	73.9
TfW Rail	71.1
West Midlands Trains	69.4
Govia Thameslink Railway	68.7
c2c	68.0
TransPennine Express	67.7
Chiltern	67.1
CrossCountry	66.6
Southeastern	66.4
South Western Railway	65.3
ScotRail	61.4

during 2023 on the preferred alignment between Bedford and Cambridge.

NEGATIVE DECISION
Uncertainty within the supply chain was exacerbated by the formal confirmation in 2022 that the Traction Decarbonisation Network Strategy (TDNS), with its rolling programme of electrification, was now unaffordable. In part, this reflected the level of funding allocated to the IRP.

A smaller, phased electrification programme is being developed by the Great British Railways Transition Team (GBRTT). If authorised, the five phases would total 6,900 single track kilometres (stkm) of electrified line added to the network by 2065-70. The TDNS proposed 13,000stkm by 2050.

Later electrification will leave a gap in both suitable rolling stock and rail's contribution to the national target of net zero carbon by 2050. GBRTT is proposing to fill this gap by life-extending existing DMUs and 'buying flexibility' with orders for new electro-diesel bi-modes. As the

revised electrification programme attracts further funding, the bi-modes could be reconfigured, for example to Battery-Electric Multiple-Units.

TRANSITION
That the formal announcement that the TDNS was cancelled, and its replacement, came from the Great British Railways Transition Team and not Network Rail revealed the growing influence of this arm of the DfT. GBRTT is a subsidiary of Network Rail, with a Chair appointed by the Transport Secretary and a Board appointed by the Chair, in consultation with the Secretary of State. It is grant funded by DfT.

As the sole shareholder of GBRTT, the Transport Secretary has appointed a Non-Executive Director to the Board. The GBRTT Board is answerable to the Network Rail Ltd Board but also provides assurance to DfT. GBRTT and the shareholder team works with DfT's own Rail Transformation Programme unit, which monitors GBRTT's performance against the objectives set by DfT.

RIDERSHIP UNCERTAINTY
Initially focused on Network Rail's proposals for cutting maintenance costs, during 2022 industrial action spread across all the rail unions. Action short of a formal dispute also saw drivers declining rest day and weekend working.

Particularly affected by the resulting shortage of drivers have been Avanti West Coast and TransPennine Express. Avanti was forced to cut back services to four trains per hour out of Euston.

While service frequency was gradually being restored, in October 2022 DfT extended Avanti's Emergency Recovery Measures Agreement (ERMA) to 1 April 2023. According to DfT, 'this window is designed to provide Avanti with the opportunity to improve its services. The DfT will subsequently assess Avanti's performance while considering a new National Rail Contract'.

Failure to improve could result in the Inter-city West Coast franchise

TABLE 2: TICKET SALES PRE- AND POST-COVID

	Franchised ordinary ticket: Advance (£ million)	Franchised ordinary ticket: Anytime or Peak (£ million)	Franchised ordinary ticket: Off-Peak (£ million)	Franchised ordinary ticket: Total (£ million)	Franchised season ticket (£ million)	Franchised passenger revenue: Total (£ million)
October to December 2018	439	804	902	2,140	538	2,678
April to June 2022	464	624	859	1,915	166	2,136
Percentage of pre-Covid	106	78	95	89	31	80
Assumed return to pre-Covid (%)	110	80	100	90	35	
Return income per quarter	483	643	902	2,028	188	2,216
Forecast equivalent annual income 2024-25	1,931	2,572	3,608	8,110	753	8,864

Source: ORR

FIGURE 3: SLOW RECOVERY OF FULL FARE TICKETS

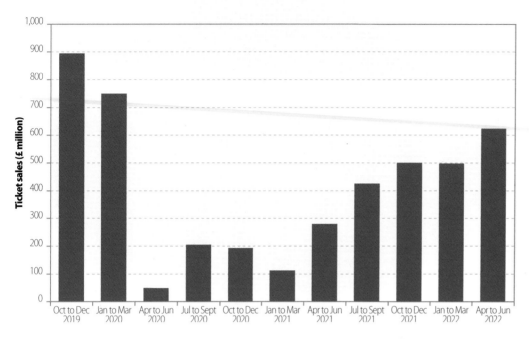

Ticket sales (£ million) — axis 0 to 1,000

Categories: Oct to Dec 2019, Jan to Mar 2020, Apr to Jun 2020, Jul to Sept 2020, Oct to Dec 2020, Jan to Mar 2021, Apr to Jun 2021, Jul to Sept 2021, Oct to Dec 2021, Jan to Mar 2022, Apr to Jun 2022

being added to the Operator of Last Resort's (OLR) three existing failed operators – LNER, Northern and Southeastern. This would be a major decision, because Avanti is also the train operating partner for HS2.

Several other train operators also have depots with the number of drivers available below establishment. In part this has been a hangover from the pandemic, when social distancing requirements meant an instructor and a trainee driver could not share a cab for the supervised driving part of the training course.

RECOVERY UNCERTAIN
As *TMR* went to press talks aimed at resolving the impasse over pay and conditions had broken up. The effects of the disputes will be felt during at least the first half of 2023.

As Figure 1 indicates, overall ridership can return to around 90% of pre-pandemic levels given strike-free services. However, the impact of industrial disputes in October and November is equally clear.

But, as Figure 2 reveals, within the overall return of ridership, data for individual operators varies widely. Similarly, when analysed by ticket type, the contrast between revenues pre- and post-pandemic is equally varied.

Table 2 compares revenue by ticket type for the first quarter of 2022-23 with the final quarter before lockdown. It confirms that advance ticket sales have boomed to exceed pre-pandemic levels – highlighting the strong growth in the leisure market. Off-peak ticket sales are also close to historic levels.

In contrast, season ticket sales remain at just under one-third of their

2018-19 value. Apart from the loss of revenue, the commuter operators are also facing significant changes in travel patterns across the week, as workers are attending offices on, typically, three days a week.

A feature of 2023 is likely to be the progressive change in rolling stock allocations on commuter lines, reflecting demand both across the days of the week and also throughout the day, where peak demand is flattening. The December 2022 timetables saw

the first examples of such changes, and balancing demand and cost will be a challenge to planners and timetablers throughout 2023.

BLACK HOLE
Under the present funding arrangement, DfT covers the costs of train operators, mainly through National Rail Contracts (NRC), in return for a management fee. All passenger revenue is paid to the Treasury.

This separation of costs and revenue lacks an incentive to grow traffic, while in their business plans for the 2023-24 financial year operators have been required to cut costs by a reported 10%.

It is widely assumed that the drop in ridership and revenue has left a £2 billion 'black hole' in the railway's finances. This is confirmed by the *TMR* analysis in Table 2. The estimate of the likely return of revenue during 2023 is based on growth assumptions.

These include continued growth in advance ticket sales and a return to pre-Covid sales of off-peak tickets. The assumption of a return to 80% of previous full fare ticket sales is based on the recovery shown in Figure 4. Expectations for season ticket sales speak for themselves.

With the combination of this revenue 'black hole' and the chilling statement in the Williams-Shapps Plan (below) hanging over the industry, 2023 is undoubtedly set to be a year of anxiety. ∎

UNSUSTAINABLE

'But the current sums being paid to operate and maintain the railways are not sustainable. To truly secure rail's future, there must be radical change. The railways lack a guiding focus on customers, coherent leadership and strategic direction. They are too fragmented, too complicated, and too expensive to run.'
Williams-Shapps Plan 2021

Operating challenges: Avanti West Coast Pendolino No 390121 passes Ledburn Junction with the 14.20 Euston to Manchester Piccadilly on 11 October 2022. **KEN BRUNT**

Now consigned to history: rolling stock withdrawn during 2022 included Govia Thameslink Railway's Class 455 EMUs. GB Railfreight's No 69001 hauls Nos 455804/819 past Twyford en-route from Stewarts Lane to Newport Docks for scrapping on 16 August 2022. **KEN BRUNT**

The rail industry since 1993

PRIVATISATION

British Rail(ways) was a publicly owned and vertically integrated railway, in which the Board provided the infrastructure, owned the trains and operated the services. Under the Railways Act 1993, those functions were separated into around 100 companies, which notably parted operations from the infrastructure. All were privatised.

Running trains on the national network resulted in a track access regime with a charge payable by the operators to the infrastructure company, Railtrack. This included charges for signalling and electrification systems.

The Franchising Director used competitive tendering to let contracts for (initially) 26 passenger train operations, nominally for seven-year terms. Awards took into account what the bidders offered for additional services and investment commitments, and whether they would require a subsidy or pay the government a premium. The independent Rail Regulator plus the Health & Safety Executive undertook the licensing.

Most passenger stations were leased to and then run by the Train Operating Companies (TOCs). Passenger rolling stock was owned by rolling stock companies (ROSCOs), who leased it to the

TOCs. The freight companies (FOCs) mostly owned their locomotives and any wagons not owned by their customers. The Association of Train Operating Companies (ATOC) provided support services.

NEW GOVERNMENT, NEW IDEAS

The 1997 Labour Government wanted some overall direction and planning, creating the Strategic Rail Authority (SRA). But some franchisees were in financial difficulties and rising traffic levels led to performance problems. Following the Hatfield derailment of 2001, caused by poor track condition, Railtrack was replaced by Network Rail.

Over time, many franchises were acquired by bus industry groups and/or by overseas companies.

The cost of the railway to the public purse rose fast. Following the Rail Regulator's 2003 ruling, access charges were funded by government.

The Railways Act 2005 transferred most the SRA's functions to the Department for Transport. Safety policy, regulatory and enforcement functions became the responsibility of the Office of Rail and Road (ORR).

Separately, the government sets out what Network Rail is expected to deliver for the public money it receives in a High Level Output Statement (HLOS) plus

a Statement of Funds Available (SoFA). The present Control Period 6 covers the years 2019-24.

There was political and public faith in the ability of what then seemed to be an ever busier railway to contribute to capacity shortfalls and regional economic growth. The wellbeing of society was growing. The railway was becoming a solution to problems affecting everybody, rather than being a problem in itself.

DEVOLUTION

Devolution has resulted in Network Rail setting up a Regions and Routes structure, while bodies such as Transport for the North are enhancing local decision-making. Transfers of certain powers and budgets to Scotland, Wales, Merseyside and London have also taken place.

What should be determined locally and what centrally? A long-term vision and strategy, together with assured funding, are key requirements, coupled with the recognition that much train operation is on a national, not a local, scale.

Operationally, the big challenge will always be to design a timetable that is economical in resource use, makes good use of the available capacity, enables connections where needed, and is resilient to problems. It must also meet both passenger and freight traffic

needs, if the result is to bring in the revenue. While most passenger traffic is reasonably stable over time, freight flows can alter very quickly.

Is more freedom for TOCs compatible with the aims of public funding and protecting the interests of rail users? How can open access operation be reconciled with the contractual obligations of TOCs?

COPING WITH GROWTH

Coping with growth became a major problem. Platform lengthening and signal repositioning for longer trains is one approach, with the prize being the ability to run (say) 10-car instead of eight-car trains. That raises carrying capacity, but also stock requirements, by 25%.

Advanced signalling systems can allow trains to follow each other more closely, as demonstrated by London Underground on the Victoria Line. With a train every 100 seconds, the time taken to clear the platform of those alighting and refilling it with those wishing to join the next train becomes critical.

The national system challenges are different. Running a stopping service in between fast services on the same track will cause nothing but trouble when capacity is at a premium.

Where does the workforce stand? Some TOCs have still to manage a successful move to Driver Controlled

Operation, despite its widespread use on London Underground and elsewhere in Britain. The sad result has been a series of long running industrial disputes.

PASSENGER VOLUMES

What has actually happened to traffic volumes since privatisation?

Taking the 20 years from 1998-99 to 2018-19, passenger traffic showed sustained growth, as measured in millions of rail passenger kilometres. From a total of 36,300 million, growth of 87% in the ensuing two decades saw the figure reach 67,800 million in 2018-19. That was spread over all three business sectors, with the regional sector doing particularly well. Elsewhere, London Underground showed an 81% gain and light rail patronage more than doubled, but that was on a then fast expanding network.

While the start of passenger growth more or less coincided with the mid-1990s privatisation, this was not necessarily the cause. Factors such as employment levels, economic activity generally, population distribution and its age bands are likely to have been rather more important.

So had the new railway age come about? Sadly, it had not. Huge drops in passenger usage occurred in the first half of 2020 as a result of the Covid pandemic. Suddenly, the train services being provided were vastly in excess of what was needed, even allowing for passengers being spaced out to ensure they were socially distanced.

FREIGHT VOLUMES

A similar measure for rail freight showed more of a variation, ending 2018-19 more or less where it started in 1998-99 as measured in millions of net tonne kilometres. This was the result of the almost total loss of its one time staple traffic of coal. This was offset by vigorous marketing, which resulted in gains, particularly in construction and intermodal traffics.

Since then, Covid effects saw a drop in freight traffic, though nothing like as serious as that for passenger. If the construction industry is brought to a halt, so too is the business of those conveying construction materials. By 2022, the rail freight business seemed to have largely recovered.

WHERE NEXT?

Public attitudes towards the railway seem now to be more confused than ever, due in part perhaps to the ever varying messages emanating from Ministers. Meanwhile, concerns over fare levels generally, how much people travelling only a few days a week will be asked to pay, and the old favourites of overcrowding and system performance, have all been the subject of criticism. Neither, it needs to be said, are such concerns without justification.

Phase One of HS2 to Birmingham now looks secure, with Phase 2a to Crewe also going ahead. Phase 2b on to Manchester is likely to follow, but the eastern leg to Leeds has been curtailed. That will now finish at a junction with the Midland main line in the vicinity of East Midlands Parkway, with HS2 services continuing to either Nottingham, or to Derby, Chesterfield and Sheffield. The situation of services for Leeds is unclear, but all extensions are now linked with the aspirations for Northern Powerhouse Rail and related to Trans-Pennine developments. Completion before the 2040s looks unlikely.

Will the result see HS2 as part of a future, vastly superior rail network, or will the overall vision just wither away? That raises questions about the West Coast Partnership and the poor performance levels being experienced in recent times, let alone how capacity issues are to be tackled.

The Government's devolution agenda also raises a series of questions. Local services for local people is a worthy goal, but how do the much wider interests of longer-distance passenger and, especially, freight operations get taken into account? Are serious improvements to existing routes across the Pennines to be made, including clearance for container traffic, and how does this fit in with a wholly new line? How does any of it relate to the present services, let alone where the funding is coming from?

RAILWAY RESTORATION

Government funds were made available for Restoring your Railway. A successful bid had to demonstrate strategic and socioeconomic benefits, while dealing with any infrastructure complications and land ownership issues. Also required was a description of the proposed services and an estimate of infrastructure and operating costs. Successful bidders would then be awarded funds to develop the business case.

Already under way is the reconsruction and upgrading of the Ashington, Blyth & Tyne line, with its 18 miles of track and six stations. Trains will connect with the Tyne and Wear Metro at Northumberland Park. Total costs are put at arond £470 million, with the opening of a two trains per hour service by 2024.

A further scheme is now under way in Scotland. This is the reopening of a five-mile branch in Fife from Leven and Cameron Bridge to Thornton North Junction. Here, trains will join the Fife Circle, proceding thence to Edinburgh via Kirkcaldy or via Dunfermline. The line was closed to passengers on 6 October 1969, but intermittent freight use continued until 2015. A two trains per hour service is expected to start in 2024.

An earlier reopening was the line from Exeter to Okehampton. This was closed from 5 June 1972, though intermittent use continued on the back of freight movements from Meldon Quarry. These have now ceased, and full passenger operation recommenced from 20 November 2021.

THE PANDEMIC

In the beginning, then Prime Minister Boris Johnson announced on 3 March 2020 'Now is the time to stop all unnecessary travel', to ensure that public transport was available for use by those termed 'key workers'. That focused on NHS staff, but included those working in the transport industry.

On 23 March, the introduction of six-month Emergency Measures Agreements (EMAs) was announced. These superseded franchise agreements. The existing operators continued to run the passenger services, transferring revenue and cost risks to the government. In exchange, they were paid a management fee at a maximum of 2% of their cost base

for the operation. Passenger numbers had already dropped by 70%, with similar reductions in revenues.

From the same date, operators were instructed to run Sunday service level timetables. Service levels were increased, first on 6 July and again subsequently at later dates.

Broadly similar arrangements with slightly different dates were introduced separately for Wales and for Scotland, for London Underground and light rail services.

An important element was the introduction of social distancing, whereby people were expected to leave gaps of two metres between themselves and the next person. Applied to trains, this resulted in the capacity of a vehicle being reduced to perhaps no more than 10% of normal. Together with strong pressure applied by the government to avoid rail use and work from home if at all possible, passenger usage continued to fall.

Face coverings for passengers became compulsory from 15 June 2020.

The effect was a very substantial fall in passenger numbers on the main line network. Compared with the same days in the previous year, spring 2020 saw only 4% to 5% of the travel of a year earlier, improving to 16% by July. On 17 July, the Prime Minister announced that 'anybody may (now) use public transport'. Social distancing rules were relaxed slightly and from 1 August working from home ceased to be encouraged.

Autumn 2020 saw passenger levels of about 33% of pre-Covid levels, but in early 2021 this had fallen back to 15%. From then on, there seems

to have been steady improvement, reaching 45% in June 2021 and 60% in September. It should be stressed that these results were national averages.

Rail freight traffic was much less severely affected, with volumes falling to between 30% and 40% at the low point and largely recovering afterwards.

The Emergency Measures Agreements were replaced in September 2020 by Emergency Recovery Measures Agreements (ERMA), to last for a period of up to 18 months. These ERMAs were a form of management contract. They too reflected the loss in passenger numbers and the general expectation that they would not recover quickly. The ERMAs were generally similar to the EMAs they replaced, but with higher performance requirements and lower (2.0% down to 1.5%) management fees payable by the Government to operators.

The post-Covid situation will need to take into account the levels to which rail traffic has declined, the outlook for its recovery (not necessarily the same for all sectors or in all parts of the country), the timescale over which this might take place, and how the industry is to be funded in the interim. Will serious adjustments to the railway services on offer be needed?

What might the long-term effects on the rail industry be? The key difficulty is that the demand for rail transport is derived. With few exceptions, people travel by rail to get to work, education, shopping, visiting friends and relatives, or whatever. Any enjoyment of the journey itself is only a secondary consideration. Thus travel to or in the course of work is dependent on that work itself existing.

Freight-only – for now: GB Railfreight's No 60002 hauls the 6N19 Lynemouth Power Station to Tyne Coal Terminal working across North Seaton viaduct on the Northumberland line on 13 July 2022. **BILL WELSH**

The key questions revolve around the organisation to take charge, the availability of funding and its sources, and who should take what decisions, together with responsibility for the accompanying risks.

THE WILLIAMS-SHAPPS PLAN FOR RAIL

This White Paper of 20 May 2021 set out the Government's plan for a revolution on the railways in Great Britain. It was based on the shared vision of Keith Williams, the independent Chair of the Rail Review, and Grant Shapps MP, the then Secretary of State for Transport, 'to put rail on the right track to support the levelling up of our towns, cities and regions'.

The summary says the Plan shows 'how the government will make railways the backbone of a cleaner, more environmentally friendly and modern public transport system across the country. By replacing franchising, accelerating innovation and integrating the railways, we will deliver an efficient, financially sustainable railway that meets the needs of passengers and those who rely on rail on a daily basis'.

GREAT BRITISH RAILWAYS

According to the Plan, Great British Railways (GBR) would be the centre of a new public sector organisation and will be 'the single guiding mind that the railways currently lack'. A prime component would be Network Rail, but other duties currently the responsibilities of the Department for Transport or the Rail Delivery Group would be brought in.

Franchises would be replaced by Passenger Service Contracts let by GBR, clearly modelled on the concessions let by Transport for London. GBR would draw up the timetables and set most fares. For the contracts, private companies would be invited to bid a fixed fee to operate them, but would not have to set fares or take the revenue risk. It was hoped this would encourage more private concerns to make operating bids. Operators would, however, have to achieve specified performance levels to earn their payments from GBR. Performance and efficiency would be scrutinised by a reformed Office of Rail and Road.

GBR would bring the railway finances together in a single organisation across track, train and the rail estate. It would manage cost and revenue decisions for the network, with budgets pushed down to regional and even local levels. It would enable the railways to be run

as a public service, with the financial discipline of a modern business.

A 'Whole Industry Strategy Plan' was commissioned by the Secretary of State, to be ready late in 2022, which would become the first 30-year strategy for GBR. This has since been renamed as the 'Long Term Rail Strategy'.

According to the White Paper, GBR would be heavily devolved, and initially based on the five Network Rail Regions. Also promised was empowering of Community Rail Partnerships, reform of Transport Focus, an overhaul of track access and the fares system, a statutory duty within GBR to promote rail freight, and decarbonisation through electrification and the deployment of battery and hydrogen trains.

The cross-industry bodies of the Rail Safety and Standards Board, the Rail Accident Investigation Branch, Rolling Stock Leasing Companies and the British Transport Police are not directly affected by the proposals in the Plan for Rail.

IMPLEMENTATION

There has been little real indication from Government of the form Great British Railways will take.

New legislation is essential, but on 19 October 2022 then Transport Secretary Anne-Marie Trevelyan told the House of Commons Transport Committee the Bill would not be heard during the 2022-23 Parliamentary session. Her successor Mark Harper, addressing the Committee on 7 December, was also non-specific about timescales. Politicians and civil servants have stated there are changes which don't required legislation, although the transfer of franchising powers from the Department for Transport to GBR would.

In any event, it will take time after it becomes law before the new Act is fully operational. That suggests it might be getting very close to the next General Election, which will give the new GBR organisation little time to bed down and find its way. The same will be true for the rest of the rail industry.

A distinct possibility would seem to be to pursue only such items that could be introduced without legislation, or perhaps with minimal legislation for a few uncontroversial issues. The White Paper was based largely on the report written (but not published) by the end of 2019, and situations change.

This would leave the implementation of the rest of the White Paper proposals, in such terms as they might think fit, for the Government that takes office after the next General Election. ∎

Across the industry

DEPARTMENT FOR TRANSPORT

The Department for Transport (DfT) is the civil service body which is responsible for delivering the UK Government's objectives. In matters specific to the rail industry in Great Britain, the Department:

■ sets the strategic direction for the rail industry in England and Wales;
■ funds investment in infrastructure through Network Rail;
■ awards and manages rail contracts;
■ regulates fares.

Some DfT responsibilities are more general, in that they may be common to several transport modes:

■ maintaining high standards of safety and security in transport;
■ providing policy guidance and funding to English local authorities to help them develop new major transport schemes;
■ encouraging the use of new technology such as smart ticketing;

Priorities include the improvement of the existing network, creating new passenger capacity and influencing how the railway should respond to climate change. The DfT's Office of Rail Passenger Services is responsible for delivery.

The onset of Covid effectively led to the end of franchising. From 20 September 2020, Emergency Recovery Measures Agreements (ERMAs) were introduced in which the Government determined the services to be run, becoming responsible for the revenue and costs risks. Companies were given performance targets and received management fees.

As to what follows, see the section on Great British Railways. Some of the DfT's responsibilities will be transferred to the new organisation, while some rail service planning and funding is likely to be devolved to local bodies. For this, new legislation is required.

The Department for Transport published its Transport Decarbonisation Plan in July 2021. Commitments included delivery of a net zero rail network by 2050, the removal of all diesel-only trains by 2040 and support for the development of battery and hydrogen trains.

The West Coast Partnership led by First Trenitalia took over the West Coast main line franchise in December 2019.

Ministerial approval: on 5 December 2022 Scottish Transport Minister Jenny Gilruth MSP officially opened the redeveloped Aberdeen station. Ms Gilruth is pictured (second right) alongside ScotRail's Head of Projects and PMO Kirsty Devlin (second left) and Scotland's Railway MD Alex Hynes (centre), flanked by members of station staff. **COURTESY SCOTRAIL**

The partnership operates the existing services, but is also due to be responsible for the planning and execution of Phase One of HS2 operations (Euston to Birmingham) for a number of years.

Other matters receiving DfT attention are the much heralded reversing of (some) of the Beeching cuts of more than half a century ago, and the establishment of an Acceleration Unit to speed up transport infrastructure projects. These include some Network Rail projects.

In brief, the DfT sets the strategic direction for rail in England, while the Secretary of State has a statutory responsibility for ensuring the continuity of passenger rail services, through franchising or by other means as required.

Secretary of State for Transport Mark Harper
Minister of State for Rail Huw Merriman
Permanent Secretary Bernadette Kelly
Director General, Rail Services & Strategy Conrad Bailey
Director General, Rail Infrastructure Group David Hughes
Director General, High Speed Rail Group Clive Maxwell

TRANSPORT SCOTLAND

Transport Scotland is an agency of the Scottish Government, whose purpose is to increase sustainable economic growth through the development of national transport projects and policies. It is accountable through Scottish Ministers.

Until recently, a total of 93 million passenger journeys have been made annually on ScotRail, most of which were entirely within Scotland. The Glasgow area is the largest commuter operation outside London and users account for about 60% of passenger journeys made on Scottish railways. Other Scottish operations are those of Caledonian Sleeper, while Avanti West Coast, CrossCountry, LNER and TransPennine Express provide services originating in England.

Transport Scotland's Rail Directorate manages the ScotRail and Caledonian Sleeper franchises, the governance of a programme of rail projects, advises ministers on investment priorities and developing future strategies, and liaises with the Office of Rail and Road on Network Rail issues. Safety and the licensing of railway operators remain reserved for Westminster, though Transport Scotland provides input on issues such as cross-border franchises, the Equality Act and safety and standards matters.

Scotland's Rail Directorate is responsible for planning and delivering rail policy, strategy and development. This includes appraisals of capital projects, advice on rail investment decisions, and the specifying of railway outputs the Scottish Government will wish to purchase.

With timetables, the Directorate notes the large number of bodies that are involved and the issues to be resolved. It is recognised timetable development work needs to start around three years before implementation.

With the end of the Abellio franchise, from 1 April 2022 Scotland's railways have been run by Scotrail Trains Ltd, a wholly owned subsidiary of Scottish Rail Holdings Ltd, which itself is wholly owned by the Scottish Government.

A new Temporary Measures Agreement for Caledonian Sleepers has been put in place until 31 March 2023, to ensure service continuity; this contract will now end earlier than planned in June 2023 after the Scottish Government and Serco failed to reach agreement on revised terms for the contract, which had been due to run until 2030.

Scotland's rail services decarbonisation plan foresees the electrification of an average of 130km of single track railway every year until 2035. This would extend the wires to Aberdeen, Carlisle via Kilmarnock, Girvan (but not Stranraer), Inverness via Perth, and Tweedbank (on the reinstated part of the Waverley route). Other more minor schemes such as that to East Kilbride would also be implemented. Aberdeen to Inverness might be electrified in a longer timescale. There would also be important effects on freight traffic.

Other lines such as the West Highland line, that to Kyle and the Far North might use 'alternative traction'.

The key strategic outcomes for Network Rail in Transport Scotland's output statement are:
- improved services;
- improved capacity;
- improved value for money for taxpayers, the farepayer and the rail freight customers alike;
- more effective integration between operations and infrastructure; and
- economic growth.

Cabinet Secretary for Net Zero, Energy and Transport Michael Matheson
Minister for Transport Jenny Gilruth
Director of Rail Bill Reeve

TRANSPORT FOR WALES

It is the duty of the Welsh Assembly Government to promote and encourage integrated transport in Wales. Transport for Wales is a wholly-owned, not-for-profit company, established by the Government in 2015.

The network serves a wide range of markets with significant commuting to both Cardiff and Swansea. There are important cross-boundary flows to Manchester, Birmingham, Cheltenham, Bristol and London, as well as on the borders link between Chester, Shrewsbury, Hereford and Newport. There are also extensive rural services, such as the Central Wales line, services west of Carmarthen, and those to Blaenau Ffestiniog.

The 15-year Operator and Development Partner contract for Wales and Borders was awarded to KeolisAmey, with effect from October 2018. However, due to the fall in passenger numbers caused by the pandemic, a Welsh Government owned company, Transport for Wales Rail Ltd, took over day-to-day operations from 7 February 2021. This company manages 248 stations,

223 of which are within Wales, and operates all main line passenger services wholly within Wales.

TfW has ambitions to develop a 'metro' concept. The South Wales Metro is centred on the Core Valley Lines radiating from Cardiff, which are the subject of an extensive upgrade. An enhanced service on the Wrexham to Bidston line represents an early manifestation of plans for a North Wales Metro.
Deputy Minister for Climate Change Lee Waters
Chief Executive James Price

GREAT BRITISH RAILWAYS TRANSITION TEAM

The Great British Railways Transition Team (GBRTT) was set up to help drive forward reforms and create the railway's new guiding mind, on behalf of government.

Led by Network Rail Chief Executive Andrew Haines, and staffed by a team drawn from the sector and beyond, GBRTT is initially focusing on driving revenue recovery efforts post-pandemic, bringing a whole industry approach to tackling cost and promoting efficiency, and establishing a strategic freight unit to boost the sector. It is also working on a Long-Term Strategy for Rail (formerly the Whole Industry Strategic Plan), aiming to provide a 30-year outlook for the rail sector.

Alongside its leadership team, GBRTT has an Advisory Panel, led by Keith Williams (who led the review which prompted the publication in May 2021 of the Williams-Shapps Plan for Rail), which it says will support the team as it seeks to deliver a more sustainable

railway that better serves the needs of passenger and freight customers.
Transition Team Lead Andrew Haines
Lead Director Anit Chandarana

COVID AND INDUSTRIAL ACTION

Sadly, railway operations in 2022 have been affected by strikes, supported by various unions in respect of a number of disputes. That has been in addition to the problems caused by Covid and the limtations this placed on travel.

This has resulted in the loss of considerable volumes of business traffic, much of which paid full rate fares; as of autumn 2022 business travel was at around 35% of pre-Covid levels. Will online meetings become sufficiently popular that business travel as a whole is likely to decline over time?

A second problem has been the general loss of commuters not wishing to commit themselves to buying annual season tickets; in autumn 2022 commuting had stalled at around 55% of pre-Covid levels. While season tickets are charged at 40 times the appropriate weekly season ticket rate, which represents very good value for money, this becomes much less should the users be regularly working fewer than five days a week in the office. Will a shorter working week become more general, and if so which day(s) might be omitted? This does not result in an economy for the railway, as it is unlikely fewer trains or staff will be required, but revenue will suffer.

More encouragingly, leisure traffic has exceeded pre-Covid levels in much of the country, and its contribution to railway revenues is increasing.

In autumn 2022, the national rail situation could be summarised as

'most of the railway is running most of the services, most of the time'. While passenger volumes in at least some sectors of the business may now be within a reasonable reach of what they were in pre-Covid days, revenues are generally at a much lower level.

It remains to be seen how the industry will respond in terms of services offered and how fares may be adjusted. As matters stand, while the industry awaits the creation of what has been termed the guiding mind of Great British Railways, in whatever form that may take, operators are being encouraged to reduce their operating costs as much as they can. That keeps down the amounts the Department for Transport has to pay them for service provision. However, as fares revenues now accrue directly to the Treasury, there is little incentive for the operating companies to try and grow those revenues, as they do not receive a direct benefit.

On 20 October 2022, the Truss Government announced the Transport Strikes (Minimum Service Levels) Bill, which was a Conservative Party manifesto commitment prior to the 2019 General Election. The legislation will mean a minimum service level must be in place during transport strikes; if this is not delivered, unions will lose their legal protections from damages. Employers will specify the workforce required to meet an adequate service level and unions must take reasonable steps to encure an appropriate noumber of specified workers still work on strike days. Specified workers who still take strike action will lose their protection from automatic unfair dismissal.

Strike action: an RMT union picket line at Nottingham station on 21 June 2022. **PHILIP SHERRATT**

LOCAL GOVERNMENT IN ENGLAND

As the Commons Library 2020 briefing paper on 'The Future of Rail' observed: 'Since 2010 a profusion of local and regional bodies has emerged with different levels of responsibility for transport funding and planning'.

Combined Authorities (CAs) are legal bodies set up using national legislation that enables a group of two or more councils in England to collaborate and take collective decisions across council boundaries. They are responsible for economic development as well as general transport policies.

Passenger Transport Executives (PTEs) in the six former metropolitan areas (Greater Manchester, Merseyside, South Yorkshire, Tyne & Wear, West Midlands, West Yorkshire) were statutory bodies, responsible for setting out policy and expenditure plans for public transport.

They are now responsible to, or have become executive bodies of, the Combined Authorities. Some CAs have a considerably greater geographical coverage than the former metropolitan areas. In general, they are not operators, but Tyne and Wear Metro is operated in-house, while Merseytravel lets and manages the Merseyrail Electrics concession. The CAs are also information providers.

Elsewhere, but not in London, the Local Transport Authority is either the Unitary Authority or the County Council. They are responsible for transport planning, passenger transport and highways.

The Urban Transport Group is a non-statutory body bringing together and promoting the interests of large urban areas.

Local Enterprise Partnerships are voluntary links between local authorities and businesses to help determine local economic priorities. Their Strategic Economic Plans set out priorities for transport investment and bids for funding from the Local Growth Fund.

SUBNATIONAL TRANSPORT BODIES

Excluding Transport for London, there are seven subnational transport bodies in England. The Government's aim is to allow such groups to advise transport ministers on investment priorities in their own areas and on strategic transport schemes to boost growth. These bodies are Transport for the North, Midlands Connect, Transport for the East Midlands, England's Economic Heartland, Transport for the South East, Western Gateway and Peninsula

Industry first: in October 2022 LNER opened the first Family Lounge on the UK network at King's Cross station in London. It has been designed to give families a dedicated space to wait for trains, with activities to keep children entertained. **COURTESY LNER**

Transport. However, only Transport for the North has achieved statutory status; the rest remain in shadow form.

TRANSPORT FOR THE NORTH

Transport for the North (TfN) was accorded statutory status in 2018. It sees its role as to add value, ensuring funding and strategic decisions about transport in the North of England are informed by local knowledge, enterprise and needs. TfN aims to recommend projects which will bring the greatest possible economic and social benefits.

TfN represents the Combined Authorities, Unitary Authorities, County Councils and all 11 Local Enterprise Partnerships from north Lincolnshire and Cheshire to the Scottish border. TfN also works with National Highways, HS2 Ltd and Network Rail.

A Strategic Transport Plan sets out an extensive programme and a number of options are being considered. In general, these include faster and more frequent services between major centres, including ports and airports, and building on the opportunities that HS2 will offer. That includes a new hub station at Manchester Piccadilly.

A variety of potential funding sources has been identified.
Chief Executive Martin Tugwell

TRANSPORT FOR WEST MIDLANDS AND WEST MIDLANDS RAIL EXECUTIVE

The transport arm of the Combined Authority, Transport for West Midlands (TfWM), was set up to co-ordinate infrastructure investment and create a fully integrated, safe and secure network. It also plans for future needs. The extensive area covered includes

that of 10 non-West Midlands local authorities including, for instance, both Herefordshire on the Welsh border and Northamptonshire.

WMRE is a partnership of 14 local authorities within the West Midlands area which was set up with the aim of influencing and eventually managing local rail services within the region. The WMRE membership comprises seven shire and unitary authorities – Herefordshire, Northamptonshire, Shropshire, Staffordshire, Telford and Wrekin, Warwickshire and Worcestershire, and seven metropolitan authorities – Birmingham, Coventry, Dudley, Sandwell, Solihull, Walsall and Wolverhampton.

TfWM and WMRE have co-managed the West Midlands Railway franchise with the Department for Transport and have planned the strategic future of the rail network. They are also developing a light rail network, including West Midlands Metro and Coventry Very Light Rail and wish to maximise the benefits of HS2 across the West Midlands region. In October 2022 WMRE published a draft investment strategy for the years to 2050.
Director of Rail, TfWM and Executive Director, WMRE Malcolm Holmes

TRANSPORT FOR THE EAST MIDLANDS AND MIDLANDS CONNECT

In August 2022, Transport for the East Midlands and Midlands Connect jointly released a paper in which they prioritised three projects. These are the electrification of the remainder of the Midland main line, improved rail links between Nottingham, Leicester and Coventry and delivery of HS2 to the East Midlands and Leeds.

ENGLAND'S ECONOMIC HEARTLAND

This group wishes to see the East West Rail link (Oxford – Bletchley – Bedford – Cambridge) completed in full, including the link to Milton Keynes, the extension beyond Cambridge and the inwards link from Aylesbury.

EUROPEAN UNION (EU)

The UK left the EU's Single Market and Customs Union at the end of 2020. EU decisions which have been incorporated into British law remain in force, unless or until they are specifically revised or revoked by domestic legislation, which may take place through the Retained EU Law Bill brought forward in autumn 2022.

There are four Railway Packages in the common European transport policy. Their objective is to promote the efficiency and competitiveness of railways through gradual liberalisation, and are summarised as follows:

1st Opening the trans-European rail freight market for international services.

2nd Providing a legally and technically integrated European railway.

3rd Revitalising international rail passenger services by extending competition, improving interoperability, and growing rail freight.

4th Standards and authorisation for rolling stock, workforce skills, independent management of infrastructure, liberalisation of domestic passenger services.

EUROPEAN UNION AGENCY FOR RAILWAYS

The Agency contributes to the implementation of the European Union legislation aimed at improving the competitive position of the railways, through interoperability and a common approach to safety. The aim is to make the railway sector work better for society.

To have a more efficient and effective functioning of the railway system, a comprehensive inventory of the basic features of the framework is necessary. This framework would:

■ enhance technical and operational harmonisation;
■ ensure multimodal integration;
■ optimise the railway transport system within the wider economy;
■ accommodate and incorporate research and innovation.

The result will need to take account of the views of passengers, freight users and citizens in general, the providers

Your Way
TO FUTURE MOBILITY

Photo: Kaohsiung Tramway System – CAF Turnkey Project

www.caf.net

Maintaining the network: a track inspection in progress at Sheffield station. **TONY MILES**

of railway services and the supporting industries, and the regulatory bodies.

Executive Director
Josef Doppelbauer

HOUSE OF COMMONS TRANSPORT COMMITTEE

The Transport Committee's purpose is to examine the expenditure, administration and policy of the Department for Transport and associated public bodies.

The Committee decides the topics and requests written evidence from interested parties, who may be called before it. Formal reports are made to the House. These are published, together with a verbatim report of the evidence sessions and the main written submissions.

In July 2022, the Committee's report on the Government's Integrated Rail Plan for the North and Midlands was published. It was not convinced about the lack of an alternative being suggested for the now abandoned Golborne link to the West Coast main line, said the cutting short of the eastern leg of HS2 was not satisfactory for Leeds, and that Bradford would be left out in the cold by the lack of a Northern Powerhouse Rail connection. It criticised what appeared to be the Government's fixation on journey times, noting that line capacity in major upgrades was also very important. It also wanted 'to be sure the benefits (of the Plan) would outweigh the drawbacks'.

Chair Iain Stewart MP

NETWORK RAIL

Network Rail (NR) is the infrastructure management organisation for the national network. The company owns, operates, maintains and develops the national railway infrastructure in Britain. This consists of the track, signalling, bridges, viaducts, tunnels, level crossings and electrification systems, of which it is the monopoly owner (but see also Transport for Wales).

Network Rail owns and operates 20 large stations. With a few minor exceptions, the others are also owned by Network Rail, but the primary responsibility for day-to-day operations is that of the principal train operating company user, to whom the station is leased.

Network Rail Ltd is a public sector company, whose task is the delivery of a safe, reliable and efficient railway network. It is licensed by the Secretary of State for Transport and was allocated £53 billion of public funding for Control Period 6 (CP6, 2019-24). Network Rail retains the commercial and operational freedom to manage the railway infrastructure, but borrowings are constrained by the requirements of HM Treasury.

The company is accountable to its operator customers through access contracts and is regulated by the Office of Rail and Road (ORR). Network Rail is held to account by the ORR for delivering what it promises, at the price agreed, while meeting its operational obligations.

The long-term planning process looks at the network up to 30 years into the future, to enable the company to promote the efficient use of its capability and capacity. Given the political and other uncertainties, what future interventions are likely to be needed, and what are the strategic issues?

From 2019, Network Rail's operations have been devolved to five Regions and 14 Routes (see table).

Each Route has its own managing director and a senior leadership team. The Route businesses operate, maintain and carry out minor renewals to the infrastructure. They are responsible for day-to-day performance and liaison with operators. Their objective is to deliver a safe and reliable railway for all concerned. It is likely these will form the basis of the Great British Railways organisation.

Central functions include matters such as standards and services, where the economies of scale or specialist expertise make it sensible for them to be provided on a national basis.

Network Rail has published a Traction Decarbonisation Network Strategy, in which electrification is seen as well advanced and widely understood. Its main difficulty is a high capital cost, which makes it less suitable for lines with low traffic. The main alternatives are hydrogen and battery, but both are unsuitable for long-distance high-speed and freight services due to their high energy needs. For the 15,400 unelectrified single track kilometres, it suggested 11,700km (76%) should be electrified. However, the plans in the TDNS have been declared unaffordable, and the Great British Railways Transition Team

is now working on an alternative strategy with a phased approach.

Chair Sir Peter Hendy
Chief Executive Andrew Haines

OFFICE OF RAIL AND ROAD

The Office of Rail and Road (ORR) is a non-ministerial government department, funded by the industry for its rail regulatory role. It operates within the legislative framework and is accountable through Parliament and the courts.

ORR is both an economic and safety regulator. Its principal rail functions are in respect of Network Rail's stewardship, the licensing of operators of railway assets and the approval of access arrangements to track, stations and light maintenance depots.

Passenger Train Operators which are franchise or concession holders need to apply to ORR for operating licences, as do freight train operators. The track and station access agreements between these operators and Network Rail require ORR approval.

Similarly, ORR regulates High Speed 1. It also regulates Channel Tunnel operations, in conjunction with the French rail regulator ARAF.

The ORR has concurrent jurisdiction with the Competition and Markets Authority to investigate anticompetitive practices in relation to railways.

The ORR is the independent health and safety regulator for the railway industry, covering both the travelling public and industry workers. HM Railway Inspectorate (HMRI) is part of ORR and its inspectors and policy advisors develop and deliver the safety strategy.

ORR is the enforcing authority for the Health & Safety at Work Act 1974 and various railway specific legislation. It is led by a Board appointed by the Secretary of State for Transport.

Chair Declan Collier
Chief Executive John Larkinson

RAIL DELIVERY GROUP

One of the recommendations of the 2011 McNulty report was that there should be a leadership body for the railway industry. This would develop and issue policies, strategies and

NETWORK RAIL'S REGIONS AND ROUTES

Region	Routes
Eastern	Anglia, East Midlands, North & East, East Coast
North West & Central	North West, Central, West Coast main line South
Scotland's Railway	Scotland
Southern	Kent, Sussex, Wessex, Network Rail High Speed
Wales & Western	Wales, Western

Supporting the supply chain: HS2 Ltd CEO Mark Thurston (second right) on a visit to Booth Industries in Bolton, which is supplying safety doors for HS2's tunnels. **COURTESY HS2**

plans, promoing better alignment on cross-industry matters.

The Rail Delivery Group (RDG) was established in June 2011 by the major passenger and freight train operator groups and Network Rail to fulfil this role, and RDG membership became a licence condition for all operators on the main line network. It also absorbed the work of ATOC, the Association of Train Operating Companies.

The purpose of the RDG is to lead a programme of change, particularly in terms of cost reduction, the industry culture, encouraging more integrated whole-system approaches, and improving the speed and effectiveness of the way it works. A safe, efficient and high quality rail service for users and taxpayers alike is the aim.

The Rail Delivery Group created two distinct divisons within the organisation. The first was Service Delivery, which provided functions such as ticketing systems and online journey planning, to support railway operation. The second, Advocacy and Change, was hived off to a new organisation, Rail Partners, in May 2022.

The RDG acts as a clearing house for passenger transport operators through the Rail Settlement Plan and by providing the National Rail Enquiry Services (NRES), promoting the various Railcards, and administering staff travel.

Many of RDG's functions are expected to be absorbed into the Great British Railways organisation.

Chief Executive Officer
Jacqueline Starr

RAIL PARTNERS

Rail Partners was established in May 2022 and was formerly part of the Rail Delivery Group. There, its purpose was to contribute to the development of

railway policy, while also facilitating cross-industry collaboration.

According to the prospectus of Rail Partners, the railway faces three interrelated and complex challenges. These are:
■ attracting customers back to rail to increase revenue and support economic recovery;
■ reducing the need for taxpayer support by increasing efficiency and cutting costs;
■ developing stronger public-private partnerships focused on delivering for customers.

The company points out that the future growth of passenger revenue in the post-Covid world is crucial to avoiding a spiral of decline, while the stabilisation of the industry's finances is equally important. It is not realistic to think that further government bailouts can or will be forthcoming, given all the other calls on the Exchequer.

That leads to its conclusion that unless the whole industry can change and become more efficient today, it will be impossible to create the conditions for a growing railway tomorrow.

There are five substantial challenges:
■ Great British Railways must be a guiding and not a controlling mind;
■ the new rail contracts are key to an effective public-private partnership;
■ transforming the customer experience is vital;
■ an ambitous target to treble freight volumes by 2050 is needed;
■ decarbonising the railway is critical to achieving net zero.

Chief Executive Officer Andy Bagnall

RAIL SUPPLY GROUP

The Rail Supply Group (RSG) is the leadership body for the supply sector. It works in partnership with the Rail

Delivery Group to set the direction and guidance to industry and government. Formed in 2014, the RSG comprises railway industry business leaders and senior representatives from the Departments for Transport, Business, Energy & Industrial Strategy and International Trade.

The RSG aims to strengthen capability and competitiveness. Its work focuses on digitalisation, data sharing, sustainability and boosting exports and inward investment, all underpinned by efforts to enhance skills, people and productivity.

Chair James Bain

RAIL FORUM

Established in 1993, the Derby-based Rail Forum represents some 300 rail supply businesses from across the UK. It is a not for profit organisation, owned and governed by its members. These include infrastructure and rolling stock consultancies, manufacturers, and a wide range of service providers.

Rail Forum supports its members, enabling them to grow, export and innovate. It has strong links to major rail clients, government and key stakeholders and a vast network of supply chain companies.

Chief Executive Elaine Clark

RAILWAY INDUSTRY ASSOCIATION

The Railway Industry Association (RIA) is the trade association for UK-based suppliers, established more than 140 years ago. It has more than 300 member companies, including manufacturers, maintainers, contractors, consultants, leasing companies and specialist services providers.

RIA represents members' interests to Government, regulators and Network

Rail and offers a forum for member discussions. Key issues are exports, innovation and skills. Information on a wide range of technical, commercial and business issues is circulated.

Like other organisations, RIA has views as to what it would like to see with Great British Railways (GBR). Essentially, these amount to no hiatus in working arrangements, a clear and long-term strategic relationship with suppliers, a partnership that focuses on delivering the best value, but above all a simpler and better railway that works.

RIA offers a one-stop advice service for sourcing equipment, services and expertise from the UK.

Chief Executive Darren Caplan

RSSB

RSSB is a not-for-profit company owned by the major industry stakeholders. Its technical strategy is to deliver a railway fit for the future. The RSSB's principal objective is to lead and facilitate the rail industry's work to achieve continuous improvement in the health and safety performance of the railways in Great Britain.

RSSB has six strategic business areas to support rail organisations:
■ safer rail – to lower the risk from accidents and incidents on and around the railway for passengers, workers and the public;
■ healthier rail – to help create the right environment for employees and make the railway a better place to work;
■ harmonised rail – to bring the industry together to help its many moving parts function as one;
■ efficient rail – to make the railway more reliable and hence more efficient;
■ innovative rail – to see opportunities for new ways of working and help to make smart investment decisions;
■ sustainable rail – to build a coherent industry-wide approach to reduce harmful emissions and improve quality of life for people.

Key activities include the support of cross-industry working groups, the management of system safety, management of an industry-wide programme of research and development in co-operation with the Department for Transport, Network Rail and others, and developing the content of Railway Group Standards and the Rule Book.

This includes identifying all significant risks, including those from train accidents, and ranking the risks of trains passing signals at danger.

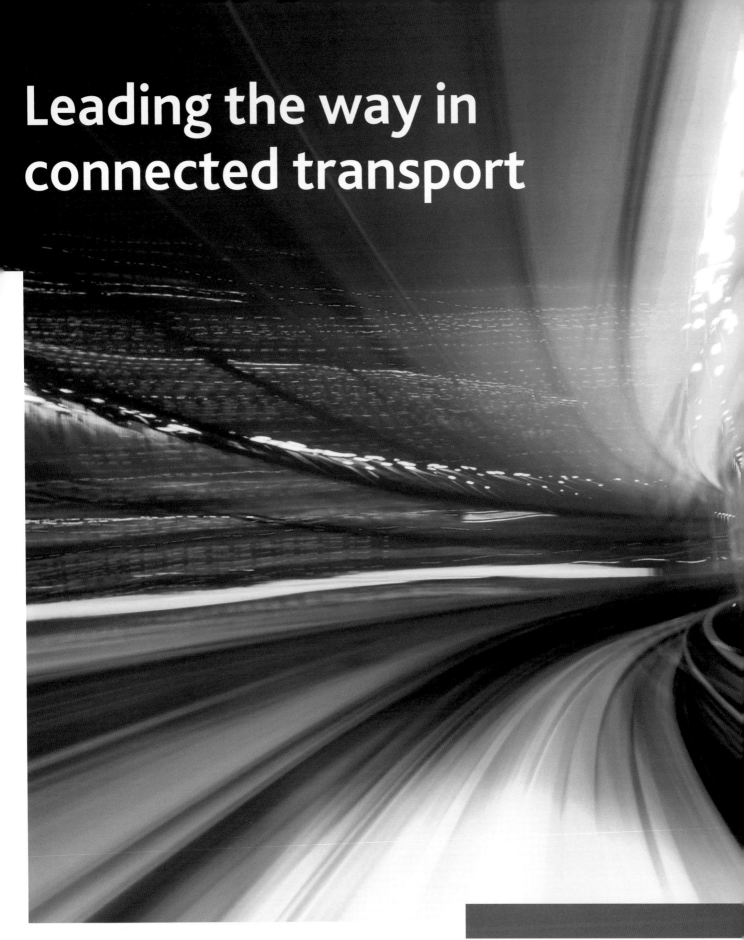

Building Britain's new railway: bored piling works in progress at Wendover Dean viaduct on HS2's Phase One route in July 2022. **COURTESY HS2**

Standards may have the force of law through conditions attached to licences granted by ORR, or by a company through its safety management systems and contracts.

RSSB is registered as the Railway Safety & Standards Board.

Chief Executive Mark Phillips

RAIL ACCIDENT INVESTIGATION BRANCH (RAIB)

RAIB investigates accidents and incidents which occur on the UK main line networks (Network Rail and Northern Ireland Railways), London Underground, other metro systems, tramways, heritage railways and the UK part of the Channel Tunnel.

RAIB was set up as an independent body under the Railways and Transport Safety Act 2003. It employs inspectors and principal inspectors with either a professional railway or investigation background. Including the support team, there is a total staff of 43 people. RAIB Is based in operational centres in Derby and Farnborough. Investigations are focused solely on improving safety.

RAIB is not a prosecuting body and does not apportion blame or liability. The Chief Inspector reports the outcomes of investigations to the Secretary of State for Transport.

RAIB's responsibilities include:
- investigating the causes of railway accidents and incidents where it believes this will bring safety learning to the industry;
- identifying risks which may lead to a similar accident happening again, or make the consequences worse;
- making and publishing recommendations, where appropriate, to improve railway safety.

Chief Inspector Andrew Hall

NATIONAL INFRASTRUCTURE COMMISSION (NIC)

The Commission's task is to enable long-term strategic decision-making by providing a dispassionate and independent assessment of future infrastructure needs. Established as an Executive Agency of HM Treasury in 2017, it aims to be the UK's most credible, forward thinking and influential voice on infrastructure policy and strategy.

The NIC report on Getting Cities Moving was published in June 2022. This affirmed the important and indeed necessary part which public transport systems have to play in this. Essential aspects of such systems are categorised as being accessible, affordable, comfortable, convenient, reliable and safe.

The Commission has already reported in favour of substantial investment in Trans-Pennine services, to be integrated with HS2, and the redevelopment of Manchester Piccadilly.

A National Infrastructure Strategy up to 2050 consists of an in-depth study of the UK's major long-term infrastructure needs, setting out a strategic vision with recommendations to government. There need to be clear goals and plans to achieve them with specific deadlines; a firm funding commitment such as 1.2% of GDP for infrastructure; and a genuine commitment to change.

The Commission has reported in favour of Crossrail 2, but recognises that it is now likely to be delayed indefinitely.

Chairman Sir John Armitt

BRITISH TRANSPORT POLICE

British Transport Police (BTP) is the specialised police service for Britain's railways. BTP provides a service to rail, metro and underground passengers, rail staff and freight customers on the national network throughout Britain, as well as London Underground, Docklands Light Railway, Glasgow Subway, the Sunderland extension of the Tyne and Wear Metro, West Midlands Metro, London Tramlink and IFS Cloud Cablecar (across the Thames in Docklands).

BTP has three operational divisions, with B covering South East England, C the rest of England plus Wales, and D for Scotland. In 2022-23 there were 3,331 Police Officers, 560 Special Officers. 300 PCSOs and 1,651 support staff. Of the £347 million budget for 2022-23, £77 million is for London Underground policing and £270 million for the rest.

The force's Strategic Plan for the years 2022-27 needs to take account of changes in the nature of threats and risks, new travel patterns following the pandemic, the growing importance of rail freight movements, and the need for a long-term net zero delivery strategy. BTP also needs to demonstrate value for money.

The most common crimes remain theft of passengers' property and violence against the person.

Chief Constable Lucy D'Orsi

RAIL FREIGHT GROUP

The Rail Freight Group (RFG) is a trade body representing more than 100 member companies including train operators, ports, terminals, supply chain, infrastructure providers and support services. The Group's aim is to increase the amount of goods moved by rail and to campaign in support of that cause. It does not handle freight directly, but represents the interests of those who do, or who are suppliers of goods and services to the freight industry.

The largest rail freight companies are DB Cargo and Freightliner, with Colas Rail, Direct Rail Services and GB Railfreight accounting for most of the rest. RFG campaigns for a policy environment that supports rail freight, promotes the sector generally and the business growth of members.

What are the principal traffics? In terms of billion net tonne kilometres, in the second quarter of 2022 domestic intermodal traffic, including maritime, accounted for as much as 38.8% of the total freight carried. Construction traffic was quite close behind, with 30.9% of the total. Those two traffics thus accounted for two-thirds of all that carried. Of the rest, metals were 9.0%, oil and petroleum 5.6%, coal 3.0%, international traffic 1.6%, with 11.1% in the miscellaneous category.

The RFG engages with railway organisations, railway authorities and Government at all levels. Its campaigning aims to ensure that politicians and key policy makers are well informed on what rail freight can offer.

Director General Maggie Simpson

HIGH SPEED 1

HS1 Ltd has the 30-year concession to own, operate and maintain High Speed 1 (HS1), at present the UK's only high-speed railway, as well as the stations along the route. These are St Pancras International, Stratford International, Ebbsfleet International and Ashford International.

HS1 is the 109km rail line between St Pancras International in London and the Channel Tunnel, following which it connects with the international high-speed routes. These carry services to Paris, Brussels and Amsterdam. HS1 also carries domestic services from St Pancras to Kent destinations via junctions at Ebbsfleet or Ashford.

In July 2017, HS1 Ltd was acquired by a consortium comprising of funds advised and managed by InfraRed Capital Partners Limited and Equitix Investment Management Limited. Network Rail (High Speed) is the company's contractor for maintaining and operating the railway infrastructure and three of the four stations (not Ashford International).

HS1 Ltd's railway infrastructure has physical connections with Eurotunnel, Dollands Moor freight depot and the Network Rail classic railway at Ashford, Ebbsfleet and Ripple Lane, plus domestic lines north of London.

HS1 has been operating along its entire route length since 2007. The line is signalled for bi-directional operation and the maximum gradient is a stiff 1 in

Fine restoration: the careful and sympathetic restoration of the ironwork at Kettering station on the Midland main line to make space for overhead electrification equipment won Network Rail the Best Overall Entry award at the 2022 National Railway Heritage Awards. This is EMR's Nos 360108/118 arriving on 31 August 2022 with the 16.42 Corby to St Pancras. **PHILIP SHERRATT**

40. Maximum speeds of up to 300km/h are allowed for international services and 230km/h for domestic services. The traffic, signalling and electrical controls and the communications centre for the whole of HS1 are located at the Ashford Area Signalling Centre.

Maximum train lengths on HS1 are 400 metres for international passenger services, 276 metres for domestic passenger and 750 metres (including locomotive) for freight.

The use of the high-speed route by both international and domestic traffic has created technical boundaries, interfaces and interdependencies. These have resulted in contractual relationships with a large number of stakeholders, including regulators, customers, operators, suppliers and others.

Eurostar services run under an open access agreement and Southeastern domestic operations under its own specified requirements. Trains on HS1 must be authorised specifically, to ensure their compatibility with the route.

HS1 Ltd is regulated by the Office of Rail and Road, whose Control Period

3 runs until 2025. The total charges are levied on a per train kilometre basis for freight, and a combination of per train kilometre and per train-minute for passenger services.

The number of revenue earning trains timetabled in the last three years, 2019-20, 2020-21 and 2021-22, in thousands, is shown in the table. Note that this is the number of trains run; what loads they might have been carrying is another matter.

Covid prompted the total number of trains timetabled to run on the HS1 route to fall by one-third compared with 2019-20, with only a slight recovery in 2021-22. International services (Eurostar) were very hard hit, while freight changed little, averaging out at just over one train per day. Domestic Southeastern services via Ashford did better, more or less holding their own, though North Kent line services fell substantially.

In August 2022, Eurostar announced it would be focusing on the core markets of London to Paris and London to Brussels. The service to Disneyland Paris ceases in June 2023 and train calls at Ebbsfleet and Ashford will

not resume until 2025 at the earliest. Also coming into force in 2023 will be new entry rules for visitors to the EU from outside the bloc.
Chief Executive Dyan Crowther

CHARTERED INSTITUTE OF LOGISTICS AND TRANSPORT

The Chartered Institute of Logistics and Transport (CILT) is the professional body for those involved in all aspects of transport and logistics. It is not a lobbying organisation, so it is able to provide considered and objective responses on transport policy to government and others. Through a structure of forums and regional groups, it provides a network for professionals to debate issues and disseminate good practice.

There is an active Strategic Rail Policy Group and another on Rail Freight. CILT includes the Railway Study Forum (formerly the RSA), which provides for the exchange of experience, knowledge and opinion on railway industry issues through meetings or otherwise.
Chief Executive Sharon Kindleysides

RAILWAY CIVIL ENGINEERS ASSOCIATION

Founded in 1921, the Railway Civil Engineers Association (RCEA) is an Associated Society of the Institution of Civil Engineers. It encourages the exchange of knowledge and

experience between its members and continuing professional development. Members are involved in the development, design, construction or maintenance of railway infrastructure, including metros and light rail. Activities aim to foster those interests and achieve a broader understanding of the industry.
Chair Jonathan Buttery

INSTITUTION OF ENGINEERING AND TECHNOLOGY

The Railway Network of the Institution of Engineering and Technology (IET) is focused on engineering. This includes the promotion, construction, regulation, operation, safety and maintenance of railways. This covers also metros, tramways and other forms of guided transport systems. Activities feature lectures, conferences and training courses.

The IET sees transport as a system and that developments in one area will have impacts elsewhere, also that new technology requires a long-term policy goal and incentives for its use.
Chief Executive & Secretary Ed Almond

THE INSTITUTION OF MECHANICAL ENGINEERS

The Railway Division of the Institution of Mechanical Engineers (IMechE) covers research, design, development, procurement,

NUMBER OF TRAINS ON HS1 (THOUSANDS)

	2019-20	2020-21	2021-22
Domestic (North Kent)	26.3	18.5	18.4
Domestic (Ashford)	28.8	26.8	27.3
International passenger	17.6	2.9	5.5
Freight	0.4	0.4	0.4
Total	**73.1**	**48.6**	**51.6**

manufacture, operation and maintenance of traction and rolling stock, also infrastructure, plant and their subsystems and components. This is for all forms of rail-borne guided surface transport, including rapid transit.

The Railway Division hosts an annual Railway Challenge, where teams of contestants each design and build a 10¼-inch gauge locomotive to strict specifications and rules. The results are then evaluated on the (private) Stapleford Miniature Railway. The 2022 event was won by F H Aachen Reuschling. The Chair of the Organising Committee for this event was Simon Iwnicki.

Chair, Railway Division Noel Travers

PERMANENT WAY INSTITUTION

The Permanent Way Institution (PWI) promotes technical knowledge, advice and support about the design, construction and maintenance of every type of railed track on an international basis. Membership is open to those actively engaged in the rail industry and anyone with a general interest.

A series of local events is arranged through its various Sections, as well as on substantial technical learning occasions. Its textbooks, updated from time to time, have been standard works for the industry for many years.

Chief Executive Officer Stephen Barber

CHARTERED INSTITUTION OF RAILWAY OPERATORS

The Chartered Institution of Railway Operators (CIRO) is the UK's leading provider of recognised training opportunities for the railway operations sector. It offers learning opportunities for staff at all points in their career, from the popular Introduction to Rail course to high level academic programmes for senior managers and leaders.

Through its seven Area Councils, there is an ongoing schedule of lively events available locally and nationally, a mentoring programme, interactive online learning modules, and conferences.

Chief Executive Fiona Tordoff

INSTITUTION OF RAILWAY SIGNAL ENGINEERS

The Institution of Railway Signal Engineers (IRSE) was formed in 1912. It aims to advance the science and practice of train control and communications engineering within the industry and to maintain high standards of knowledge and competence within the profession. The over-riding purpose is to help ensure the safe and efficient movement by rail of people and freight, for the public benefit.

A licensing scheme provides assurance about the competence of individuals to carry out technical safety-critical or safety-related work on signalling or railway telecommunications equipment and systems.

Half of the IRSE membership comes from outside the UK.

Chief Executive Blane Judd

YOUNG RAIL PROFESSIONALS

The Young Rail Professionals (YRP) was founded in 2009 to promote the railway industry as a great place to work and to inspire and develop the next generation of railway talent. YRP is open to any young rail professional, whether their interests are in asset management, engineering, franchising, human relations, maintenance, marketing, regulation, rolling stock design, strategic planning, or train operations. YRP now has more than 14,000 members in Britain, spread across nine regions.

For those starting out in their careers, YRP offers networking and professional development opportunities to enhance skills and encourage its members. An ambassadors' programme provides opportunities to attract the next generation into the railway.

Membership is free and there is no charge for events. There is no formal YRP age limit, but activities are aimed at those in their first 10 years in the industry.

National Chair Fi Westcough

REF

The REF (Railway Engineers' Forum) aims to harmonise the various strengths of the constituent institutions in devising and undertaking activities in support of the railway community. The constituent members represent ICE, IET, IMechE Railway Division, CIRO, IRSE, PWI, RCEA and CILT. Associated societies are Young Rail Professionals and the International Council on Systems Engineering (INCOSE).

As a non-political body, the REF can provide a common voice on railway topics from operations to engineering, thus offering a co-ordinated response to requests for professional comment. On its website, the REF also produces a regular listing of professional meetings of its member organisations throughout Britain.

Chair Andrew Simmons (IRSE)

NSAR

The National Skills Academy for Rail is now known as NSAR. It covers the skills needed for engineering, operations, service delivery and the digital railway. The aim is to enable the industry to increase its competitiveness through matching skills and workforce demand to its supply, education and training.

NSAR itself does not deliver training, but works with employers to understand their training needs and with training providers to ensure that they are delivering what the industry needs. Other organisations involved are sector skills and government bodies, to make sure that those in the industry have the right qualifications for the tasks ahead.

How will the newcomers be recruited? Will there be enough of them? When and where will they be needed? At what level of expertise and in which disciplines? Who will train and accredit them? How will this be funded? Are these general industry requirements, or are they related more to specific large projects such as HS2?

NSAR activities include the accreditation of training organisations, course content standardisation, services for employers and training companies, and promoting railway careers. Training companies also need the appropriate capability and capacity.

For the broad categories of infrastructure and rolling stock, there will always be a need for maintenance, renewal and enhancement.

Chief Executive Neil Robertson

INSTITUTE OF TRANSPORT STUDIES, UNIVERSITY OF LEEDS

The aim of the University of Leeds Rail Centre is to enhance understanding of the economics of rail transport demand and supply, rail operation and control, and the economic value of rail technical innovation and investment.

This perspective comes from taking a multidisciplinary approach, in particular combining rail engineering and technical research with economics, such that technical innovations that deliver social welfare gains can be identified.

Key research topics include demand forecasting and travel behaviour, infrastructure cost modelling, efficiency analysis and pricing, project appraisal methodology, off-track and on-track competition, and transport safety.

UKRRIN

The UK Rail Research and Innovation Network (UKRRIN) is designed to create powerful collaboration between academia and industry, aiming to provide a step-change in innovation in the sector and accelerate new technologies and products from research into market applications globally.

The initiative was built on the development of three Centres of Excellence in collaboration with existing industry facilities. These are:
■ digital systems (led by University of Birmingham, in partnership with Lancaster University, Imperial College London, Swansea University and University of Hull);
■ rolling stock (led by University of Huddersfield, in partnership with Newcastle University, Loughborough University, University of Cambridge, University of Bristol, Brunel University and University of Nottingham); and
■ infrastructure (led by University of Southampton, in partnership with the University of Nottingham, the University of Sheffield, Loughborough University and Heriot-Watt University).

Some £92 million of total funding was committed to the centres by the UK Government and leading industrial partners.

UKRRIN offers industry access to purpose built world-leading facilities and skills in a range of areas to support research, development and innovation for new technologies and products. The key aims and objectives are:
■ to support and build UK rail sector capacity and capability to develop, deliver and deploy new technologies;
■ to deliver a step change investment in rail innovation through a world-leading network of UK- based research and testing centres;
■ to increase radically UK rail productivity and performance by delivering transformational innovation and accelerating its uptake; and
■ to develop new strategic relationships with the small to medium sized enterprise supply chain, rail industry and wider transport sector.

TRANSPORT FOCUS

Transport Focus is a non-departmental public body sponsored by the Department for Transport. It is the consumer body for Britain's rail passengers. Transport Focus aims to get the best deal possible for them; its independence is guaranteed by Act of Parliament.

Transport Focus uses research to influence decision-makers on behalf of users, focusing on a number of key issues. These are:
■ performance and disruption;
■ fares and tickets;
■ quality and level of services;
■ investment; and
■ information for passengers.

Of particular concern was the performance of Avanti West Coast, following the company's decision to reduce its timetable at short notice in 2022. From London Euston, this resulted in only one service per hour to each of Glasgow, Liverpool, Manchester and Birmingham, with a two-hourly service to Edinburgh via the West Midlands. Transport Focus found that this was due mainly to staff shortages, with the aim of giving more certainty to passengers as to what would be running.

However, Transport Focus found there was a lack of information throughout and it wasn't always up to date, there were still many short-notice cancellations, many passengers had to stand, and the refund process was cumbersome and slow.

In short, Avanti's operation left much to be desired. It should perhaps be recognised that many other operators were also experiencing problems of this nature but, as Transport Focus said, customers do want to be able to get reliable information, reassurance on what is happening and any rights they might have for compensation.

Chief Executive Anthony Smith

COMMUNITY RAIL NETWORK

Community Rail Network's vision is to help the local partnerships to:
■ enhance the railway's contribution to social inclusion, health and wellbeing;
■ ensure the community has a voice and plays a part in railway development; and
■ communicate the importance of railways to local communities and then promoting them.

There are about 70 Community Rail Partnerships and many more station friends and other organisations. The focus is on practical initiatives to advance the local railway, for which support, advice and information is provided. Community Rail Partnerships try to ensure the importance of the local railway is fully recognised at all levels of decision-making. It also helps to find solutions for common problems, and disseminates examples of good practice.

Chief Executive Jools Townsend

RAILWAY HERITAGE TRUST

The Railway Heritage Trust is an independent company limited by guarantee, which commenced operations in 1985. Its objectives are:
■ to assist operational railway companies in the preservation and upkeep of listed buildings and structures; and
■ to facilitate the transfer of non-operational premises and structures to outside bodies willing to undertake their preservation.

The Trust gives both advice and grants. Grants may cover repair, conservation and restoration works. It supports a wide range of projects, with a balance struck between buildings and structures, and between large projects and small. It does not deal with rolling stock or artefacts.

Network Rail and National Highways (Historical Railways Estate) sponsor the work of the Trust. Recent awards varied from the conversion of rooms at Llandudno station for community use to the restoration of the former Hither Green turntable. The latter has been transported to the Rother Valley Railway, to be returned to full use at Robertsbridge.

Executive Director Tim Hedley-Jones

MINOR AND HERITAGE RAILWAYS

The Office of Rail and Road regulates such railways of 350mm gauge or more for safety. There are well over 200 of them across Britain. Key issues are seen as:
■ leadership and governance;
■ inspection and maintenance of the permanent way, traction & rolling stock, and structures;
■ competence management systems, with particular focus on operating staff;
■ rule book;
■ workshops; and
■ level crossings.

Such railways need to have a safety management system in place that has been adapted to fit the size and nature of the operation. The aim is to ensure the safety of the staff, volunteers, passengers and the public. ■

FINANCE AND LEASING

KEN BRUNT

IN ASSOCIATION WITH **porterbrook**

Track to the future

Angel Trains is investing today, for the future. We're improving the standard of our existing rolling stock, so that passenger journeys are more comfortable, connected and productive. We're trialling new technologies that significantly reduce emissions and drive decarbonisation. And we are supporting the development of innovative systems that can reduce train and infrastructure maintenance costs. Our investments reach beyond rail and support jobs in UK manufacturing and technology industries right across the country.

Above all else we're taking positive action to engineer the brightest future for UK rail.

POWERFUL WAYS TO CUT THE COST OF DECARBONISATION

Decarbonising the rail network is a crucial step to reaching net zero. But the cost and complexity poses significant challenges.

Investment in new power technologies such as hydrogen and batteries can play a part in delivering cleaner, greener travel on parts of the network that may ultimately prove too costly or complex to electrify.

The Zero Emission (ZE) train and hydrogen refueller project proved that hydrogen power can be successfully retrofitted and trains powered by a clean, green fuel. The multi-disciplined team, spanning academia, technical consultancies, hydrogen experts and private finance, worked together to successfully bring cutting-edge green technologies to life. The project not only demonstrated that hydrogen can play a part in a green train future, but highlighted the jobs and skills that are created by an investment of this type. The impact of the ZE train will go far beyond the trial itself, creating opportunities for academic study and research over the coming months and years.

Investment in bi-mode trains, such as our Class 802s, enables trains to bridge the gap between existing overhead wires. And we are investing in both battery retrofit and Hydrotreated Vegetable Oil (HVO) trials so that the entire end-to-end journey can be as clean and efficient as possible.

Working in partnership with Hitachi and First TransPennine Express, our Class 802 battery trial will stress test the capabilities and performance of the system in a challenging real world environment. Our aim is to demonstrate that retrofitting batteries can provide a viable, clean alternative without compromising performance.

Where diesel engines still need to run, our HVO trial in Scotland is demonstrating the benefits of using this renewable liquid fuel. It's worth noting that the technology required to use HVO isn't the constraint to reduced emissions, but the availability of the fuel itself. We're hopeful that our trials will generate wider interest in HVO, helping to increase the supply of the fuel for use in rail at a lower cost.

Through investment in a combination of these technologies we can deliver a cleaner, greener railway faster and more cost-effectively.

INVESTMENT IN INNOVATION CAN HELP DRIVE DOWN COSTS, WITHOUT CROSSING THE LINE ON SAFETY

We have always maintained a focus on bringing innovation to our trains in order to make passenger journeys more comfortable,

Good as new: refurbished interior of the Angel Trains-owned Class 390 Avanti West Coast Pendolino fleet in Standard (left) and First Class (right).

connected and productive. We want passengers to make the most of their journey time and we've had great success with projects such as the digital upgrade of our Northern Class 15x and 333 fleets.

But it's not just passengers who are benefiting from our digital advances. We're also providing our train operating partners with better information, helping to improve the safety, reliability and resilience of train services.

Working with Network Rail, our Lidar scanners are capturing digital images of railway infrastructure. Using these images, we can create digital 3D models that can be used to measure Network Rail's assets to a very high degree of accuracy. This technology can help reduce the need for 'boots on the ballast' and better target improvements, increasing safety and reducing cost.

We are also installing cameras on pantographs so that operators can monitor in-service wear and damage to them. The video footage provides real-time data that enables Network Rail to focus preventative improvements to specific locations.

Investment in technologies such as these are resulting in direct cost savings and improvements to the resilience of the whole network, making maintenance of rail infrastructure cheaper and safer.

Digital upgrade: Northern's fleet of Class 333 EMUs, owned by Angel Trains, has been the subject of improvements to provide better facilities to enable passengers to stay connected during their journeys.

MAKING THE MOST OF EVERY JOURNEY MINUTE

Working and travelling habits may have changed, but high-speed long-distance train travel still offers a viable, and greener, alternative to flying.

The case for taking the train is even stronger when you consider the higher levels of connectivity and productivity over the length of the journey that rail offers. And with tilt technology, our Pendolinos provide the fastest end-to-end journey times possible on the West Coast main line.

The £117 million refurbishment of this iconic fleet provides passengers with an experience that's as good as new. In fact, it's better than new, with the benefits of a proven, reliable product combined with the features and connectivity of a state-of-the-art train.

New ergonomically designed seats, wireless charging, enhanced Wi-Fi connectivity and sockets at every seat mean passengers travelling for leisure or work can make the most of every minute of their journey.

We shouldn't forget that our trains are also a place of work for rail employees, and the reception that the refurbished Pendolinos have received shows that we can all be justifiably proud of what this transformational investment has achieved.

REDUCE, REUSE, RECYCLE

Modernising existing trains is a cost-effective way to avoid the carbon emissions associated with manufacturing new ones. It has all the equivalent benefits of recycling. In addition, train refurbishment often disproportionately benefits UK jobs – the Pendolino refurbishment has enabled us to support the UK supply chain and helped to create over 100 jobs in the Liverpool region.

On Southeastern Railway, the cascade and introduction of our Siemens Class 707 units has brought passengers the immediate benefits of spacious, modern and reliable rolling stock.

Once again, this demonstrates how the deployment of existing rolling stock can quickly meet capacity demands and uplift the passenger travelling experience.

Existing trains, with established supply chains and the specialist knowledge and skills to support them, can provide the capacity and reliability that operators are looking for without the need to procure new trains.

INVESTING FOR THE FUTURE, TODAY

Over the past 15 years, Angel Trains has invested in excess of £5 billion in procuring new trains and modernising our existing ones. We are proud to have directly supported manufacturing and supply chain jobs across the UK during what have been very challenging times.

We'll continue to provide the investment required to create cleaner, greener, more connected journeys and engineer the brightest future for UK rail. ∎

David Jordan
Chief Operation Officer, Angel Trains

Viable decarbonisation opportunity: batteries are being fitted to one of Angel Trains' TransPennine Express Class 802s.

EVERSHOLT
UK RAILS GROUP

Eversholt Rail, a member of Eversholt UK Rails Group, is owned by UK Rails S.A.R.L., a company jointly owned by CK Infrastructure Holdings Limited and CK Hutchison Holdings Limited.

Eversholt Rail owns UK passenger and freight rolling stock and has more than 27 years of experience in the rail industry. Since privatisation Eversholt Rail has invested more than £3 billion in new trains and continues to introduce its newest fleets on the UK network. In late 2020 delivery was completed for the 101 CAF Civity trains supplied to Northern, comprising 58 Class 195 DMUs and 43 Class 331 EMUs.

Eversholt Rail continuously invests in maintaining the quality and reliability of its existing assets through heavy maintenance and major enhancement programmes to deliver better passenger experience and minimise through-life costs.

A Time Based Overhaul of the ScotRail Class 320 EMU fleet has been completed by Brodie Engineering, with a similar project now in progress for the Class 318 fleet. In October 2021 Eversholt Rail completed a Mileage Based Overhaul on its Class 465 Networker EMU fleet.

Eversholt Rail is investing in a £27 million upgrade of Southeastern's 29-strong Class 395 fleet. Work will start in March 2023 at the fleet's home depot at Ashford, and includes provision of LED lighting, USB charging, a live passenger information system, new CCTV and digital infrastructure monitoring technology. Investment in Southeastern's Class 375 fleet includes forward-facing CCTV, On Train Data Recorder replacement, ethernet backbone and passenger information system. This work is in addition to the modifications previously agreed for new at-seat USB charging, energy meters and replacement of existing lighting with LED lights. Eversholt Rail is also contributing towards an investment in an automated vehicle inspection system, which SE Trains plans to deploy on the Class 375 and Class 395 fleets.

Eversholt Rail continues to invest in several innovation workstreams focused on assisting the delivery of the UK Government's decarbonisation commitments.

In November 2021, Alstom and Eversholt Rail announced a Memorandum of Understanding aimed at delivering the UK's first ever brand-new hydrogen train fleet. The two companies have agreed to work together, sharing the technical and commercial information necessary for Alstom to design, build, commission and support a fleet of 10 three-car hydrogen multiple-units (HMUs). These will be built by Alstom in Britain. The contemplated new HMU fleet will be based on the latest evolution of the Alstom Aventra platform. This builds on Alstom and Eversholt Rail's previous partnership to develop the 'Breeze' project for conversion of Class 321 EMUs into Class 600 HMUs.

The development of the Aventra HMUs follows on from the signing of an agreement between hydrogen network operator H2 Green and Eversholt Rail for the companies to work together to determine the production and refuelling infrastructure required to support widescale deployment of hydrogen-powered rolling stock fleets.

Meanwhile, in 2022 Eversholt Rail signed an agreement with Vivarail to develop the Class 321 'Renatus' EMU fleet with battery power and range extension. The companies said the class has the right characteristics, fleet size and availability for conversion to a BEMU. The aim was to develop a design which can operate on battery power for up to 30 miles, although unfortunately Vivarail went into administration in late 2022.

In July 2021 Eversholt Rail unveiled the Class 321 Swift Express Freight train. Converted at Wabtec's Doncaster facility, passenger features have been removed and new flooring and industry standard fixings installed to provide a flexible interior. After a period on trial with GB Railfreight, in October 2022 Eversholt Rail confirmed the unit would be leased to Varamis Rail to operate between Birmingham and Scotland. Conversion of a further four trains by Gemini Rail Services at Wolverton was due for completion by the end of 2022.

The demonstrator vehicle from the Revolution Very Light Rail (RVLR) programme was unveiled in October 2021. Eversholt Rail is part of the RVLR consortium which has set out to meet the challenge of developing an attractive, low-cost rolling stock solution. The demonstrator vehicle, which is equipped with hybrid diesel-electric powerpacks, is based at a purpose-built marketing facility at Ironbridge, on a former passenger line. ■

Battery ambitions: Eversholt Rail's 'Renatus' Class 321s Nos 321305/308 pass Bethnal Green with Greater Anglia's 13.05 Clacton-on-Sea to Liverpool Street on 13 December 2021. **PHILIP SHERRATT**

porterbrook

Porterbrook owns almost one-quarter of the national passenger rail fleet and currently has around 4,000 vehicles on lease or on order. To date it has invested £3 billion in new passenger and freight vehicles and is actively looking to invest a further £1 billion in UK rail in the coming years.

Engineering excellence is central to the company's role as a leading railway asset owner and manager. Porterbrook is a delivery partner, supporting improved industry performance and reliability across operations. Its 30- to 35-year whole life asset management approach optimises value to passengers and taxpayers and aims to minimise environmental impact.

The business has an established reputation for delivering new technologies, such as hybrid and hydrogen-powered trains. These innovations support the Government's commitment to Net Zero by 2050, improve air quality, reduce emissions, and enhance network resilience.

Porterbrook is investing to support future rail freight growth. In addition to its existing freight assets, the company agreed a partnership with GB Railfreight and Greenbrier for 50 new box wagons in 2022 following a deal for 100 new intermodal twin wagons announced in 2021.

Since taking over the Long Marston Rail Innovation Centre in Warwickshire in June 2021, Porterbrook has committed more than £5 million to modernise and enhance the site. The upgraded facilities provide passenger and freight operators, customers and industry partners with an invaluable asset to maintain, upgrade and test rolling stock and new technologies.

In collaboration with industry partners, Porterbrook project manages the delivery of regular upgrades to its rolling stock fleets. Each year the business invests more than £100 million in its existing assets, supporting nearly 100 UK-based companies and supporting around 7,000 jobs.

Around 170 people are employed by the business, of which three-quarters are engineers and project managers. In addition, 33% of the company's workforce is female, including a number of its executive team, which compares favourably to the UK rail industry average of 16%.

Commitment: Porterbrook has invested more than £5 million to modernise and enhance the Long Marston Rail Innovation Centre.

SUPPORTING IMPROVED PERFORMANCE AND DECARBONISATION

Porterbrook is playing a key role in projects that will benefit the whole industry:

- In 2019, Porterbrook introduced 'HydroFLEX', the UK's first hydrogen-powered train. Porterbrook has invested more than £12 million in the project, and a fully productionised version of this innovative train was showcased at Glasgow in November 2021 during COP26. Further testing of HydroFLEX has continued at Porterbrook's Long Marston Rail Innovation Centre throughout 2022 and the company was on course to embark on main line testing in late 2022.
- Porterbrook's HybridFLEX 100mph capable battery-diesel hybrid train was launched into passenger service with Chiltern Railways in early 2022 and has now completed more than 10,000 miles of testing. The train has been retrofitted with a Rolls-Royce powerpack which means quieter and quicker journeys, with 25% less fuel consumption and associated CO_2 emissions, and zero-emissions in and around stations.
- The company is managing the first-in-class European Train Control System (ETCS) project on its Class 43 vehicles for Network Rail, in partnership with Thales UK, which brings digital signalling into the driver's cab. The vehicles successfully completed the second phase of testing in autumn 2022 at the Rail Innovation and Development Centre in Melton Mowbray. The

Supporting freight growth: Porterbrook partnered with GB Railfreight and Greenbrier to order 50 new box wagons.

installation of ETCS on Porterbrook's Class 387 Electrostar fleet, on lease to Govia Thameslink Railway, also commenced in October 2022.
- Porterbrook is working with Network Rail on the Class 153 Visual Inspection Unit (VIU) project, which replaces manual inspections with train-borne monitoring technology and improves workforce safety by reducing the need for maintenance staff to work trackside.
- The business's digital team led a pilot of the Data into Action Reliability Taskforce (DART) which prevented 150 full or part train cancellations over the one-year pilot by proactively using data analytics and targeted engine health checks. The team has also worked with Network Rail to provide Curated Adhesion Data for autumn 2022, delivering a real-time view of track conditions, based

on a combination of wheel slip event recordings and GPS readings taken from Porterbrook trains.
- Porterbrook secured a top score of 100/100 and was named as the Transport Sector Leader in the 2022 GRESB assessment, which assesses and benchmarks the ESG performance of assets worldwide. The result reflected the company's ongoing commitment to sustainability, including emission-cutting initiatives such as HydroFLEX and HybridFLEX.

Porterbrook has been a longstanding part of UK rail for more than 25 years. The industry has an exciting and dynamic future ahead in areas such as the green transition and embracing the potential of digital technology and the company looks forward to supporting this in the coming decades. ■

Delivered for testing: new bi-mode train No 805001 for Avanti West Coast on arrival at the Melton test track in November 2022. **COURTESY AVANTI WEST COAST**

ROCK rail

Rock Rail is an independent developer, investor and asset manager of rolling stock and other rail infrastructure. Established in 2014, Rock Rail has transformed the market for rolling stock funding, leading the way in partnering with major institutional investors (pension funds and insurance companies) and opening up a major new source of funding for the rail industry.

Since 2016 Rock has secured £3 billion of institutional investment in new, state-of-the-art rolling stock fleets. Accounting for around 40% of UK passenger rolling stock orders over the period, it represents over 1,500 modern, technology enabled vehicles that are already transforming passenger journeys, delivering better value for the public sector and supporting a more sustainable railway.

Working closely with its institutional investor, operator and manufacturer partners, Rock provides a complete range of specialist asset management services for its fleets across their full life cycle, managing long-term residual value and ensuring they meet passengers' and rail partners' needs over the long-term.

While Rock's initial focus has been on rolling stock, it is extending its approach to transform the design and delivery of other essential rail infrastructure, including electrification, digital signalling and depots, as well as other new technologies to bring track and train closer together.

NEW APPROACHES

Rock Rail and its investor partners take a long-term view to investment, delivering highly competitive funding over the full life of its trains and contributing to the significant reduction in rolling stock leasing costs since its entry into the market.

Rock is also working with partners across the global supply market to deliver the very best of new technologies from around the world in areas such as decarbonisation, power upgrades, European Train Control System (ETCS) and wider traffic management systems, for the benefit of UK passengers.

Safety assurance is a critical element of Rock's asset management role and it is committed to supporting the rail industry by providing industry-leading safety expertise in existing areas such as 'design for safety' and emerging ones including cyber security.

NEW FLEETS

Rock Rail's first transaction, in February 2016, was for the 25 six-carriage Class 717s built by Siemens for Govia Thameslink Railway's Great Northern route, representing an investment of over £200 million. The rollout of the EMUs was completed in September 2019, replacing mainland Britain's oldest electric trains and seeing passenger satisfaction soar by 22 percentage points.

In October of the same year, Rock Rail secured the £700 million contract for 58 new Stadler BMU and EMU trains for use on Greater Anglia's regional, inter-city and Stansted Express routes (Class 745 and 755). The first trains entered service in July 2019, with the rollout completed in 2020.

Rock Rail went on to secure its largest deal, the £1 billion financing of 90 new Alstom trains (Class 701) for South Western Railway, in June 2017. The 'Arterio' fleet will run across south west London, Surrey and Berkshire.

2019 saw Rock Rail secure its most two recent rolling stock deals. The first of these in August was the £400 million, 33x5-car BMU Hitachi inter-city fleet (Class 810) for East Midlands Railway. The trains are due in service in 2023, making use of existing and future electrification on the Midland main line and replacing the existing diesel-only vehicles. The full fleet is being built in the UK, supporting hundreds of jobs at Hitachi's Newton Aycliffe factory as well as benefitting local suppliers.

In December 2019 Rock secured the £350 million financing for the 135-vehicle Hitachi inter-city fleet for Avanti West Coast. The 10 seven-carriage electric trains (Class 807) and 13 five-carriage bi-modes (Class 805) are due to enter service on the West Coast main line in 2023, serving the West Midlands, North Wales and Liverpool and replacing the current diesel-powered fleet.

SUSTAINABILITY

Rock Rail is committed to delivering responsible investments with sustainable benefits for the environment, local communities and wider society. This strongly aligns with its institutional investor partners, who have at their core a requirement for responsible economic, social and governance-based investment.

Rock's modern fleets are already contributing to a more sustainable railway. They are set to replace many hundreds of diesel vehicles and deliver significant energy efficiencies. In its first year of operation, Rock's Great Northern fleet is estimated to have saved the equivalent of over 4,000 tonnes of CO_2 emissions through the trains' advanced regenerative braking technology.

Rock is also working in partnership with Birmingham Centre for Railway Research and Education and the Technical University of Dresden in Germany, exploring opportunities for greener rail traction solutions.

EUROPE AND BEYOND

Over recent years, Rock Rail has also extended its focus to other markets, setting up operations in Germany and Australia in 2020. It is actively working with local rail partners and global manufacturers on rolling stock and rail infrastructure financing opportunities in Europe and Australia, including the purchase of greener battery and hydrogen powered trains. ∎

Britain's rolling stock
WHO OWNS IT?

Competition to the traditional ROSCOs continues

New rolling stock lessors continue to make inroads into in the UK market, challenging the three major rolling stock leasing companies (ROSCOs).

The three ROSCOs were established at railway privatisation in 1994 to take over ownership of rolling stock from the nationalised British Rail and were sold to the private sector with their initial fleet leases in place.

The aim was for each ROSCO to have a reasonably diversified portfolio, with comparable fleets allocated to each. Larger fleets of a single type were divided, but smaller fleets were allocated to a single ROSCO. This gave each a range of customers and gave most train operating companies (TOCs) a relationship with at least two ROSCOs. At privatisation approximately 38% of passenger rolling stock was allocated to Eversholt, 32% to Angel and 30% to Porterbrook.

A boom in recent orders has seen in excess of 7,000 vehicles ordered since 2014, with Rock Rail the funder for many of these new fleets.

Some passenger rolling stock is owned by train operating groups: FirstGroup owns HST power cars and Mk 3s which form some of GWR's 2+4 'Castle' class HSTs, while Arriva owns Mk 3 vehicles used on Chiltern Railways' London to Birmingham service.

LOCAL OWNERSHIP

Most London Underground rolling stock is owned rather than leased. Crossrail's Class 345 trains were initially owned by Transport for London, before being sold in early 2019 to 345 Rail Leasing, a consortium of Equitix Investment Management Ltd, NatWest and SMBC Leasing, in a 20-year sale and leaseback deal which TfL said released £1 billion to reinvest into the capital's transport network.

The local ownership model has been followed on Merseyside, where the 53 new Stadler-built Class 777 EMUs are owned by Merseytravel (which also led the procurement) on behalf of the Liverpool City Region and leased to Merseyrail.

In 2016 Kilmarnock-based firm Brodie Engineering completed repairs to a Class 156 DMU written off after a 2014 accident. It was leased to ScotRail through a new leasing company, Brodie Leasing Ltd, although it went off lease in 2022.

The Welsh Government initially intended to finance new trains for the Wales and Borders franchise itself, but subsequently received a cheaper offer involving private finance from a consortium of SMBC Leasing and Equitix.

CROSS LONDON TRAINS

A new generation of train owners has steadily established itself. Prominent among them are those providing trains for the Thameslink and Intercity Express Programmes.

Cross London Trains is a consortium comprising Siemens Project Ventures GmbH, Innisfree Ltd and 3i Infrastructure plc, set up (and appointed in 2011) to finance and purchase Class 700 Desiro City trains from Siemens for Thameslink services – a total of 1,140 vehicles in eight- and 12-car sets. In 2019 3i Infrastructure sold its 33.33% stake in the business to a consortium of Dalmore Capital and Equitix Investment Management.

Eversholt Rail was appointed to provide project and asset management services, including project management during the build and delivery of the rolling stock, and then long-term asset management, including both technical and commercial support.

INTERCITY EXPRESS PROGRAMME (IEP)

Agility Trains – a consortium of Hitachi and John Laing – secured the contract (confirmed in 2012) to supply Britain with the next generation of inter-city trains under the Intercity Express Programme (IEP).

Shareholders in Agility Trains West (for the Great Western route's trains) are Hitachi Rail (25%), Apple BidCo 2 Limited (45%), JLIF Holdings (ATW) Limited (15%) and AXA Real Estate Investment Managers (15%). The Apple BidCo 2 Limited shareholder group consists of Dalmore Capital, Equitix, Japan Infrastructure Initiative Company and Rock Rail, while the JLIF Holdings

Product of the Intercity Express Programme: LNER Azuma No 800111 arrives at Newark Northgate with the 07.36 Harrogate to King's Cross on 23 April 2022. **PHILIP SHERRATT**

(ATW) Limited shareholder group consists of Dalmore Capital and Equitix. Shareholders in Agility Trains East (for the East Coast route's trains) are Hitachi Rail (25%), AIP Management (30%), GLIL Infrastructure (30%) and Equitix (15%).

Sources of IEP finance are: European Investment Bank, Japan Bank for International Co-operation, Bank of Tokyo Mitsubishi UFJ, Development Bank of Japan, HSBC, Lloyds, Mitsubishi Trust, Mizuho, Sumitomo Mitsui Banking Corporation (SMBC), Societe Generale and Credit Agricole.

BEACON RAIL

Beacon Rail Leasing Limited was established in January 2009 by BTMU Capital Corporation as its business entity for freight rolling stock leasing in the European market, including the former European portfolio of HSBC Rail (UK). In May 2014, Pamplona Capital Management announced the purchase of Beacon for a consideration of approximately $450 million. In April 2017, Pamplona sold Beacon Rail to institutional investors advised by JP Morgan Asset Management in a transaction valued at around €1 billion.

Headquartered in Luxembourg with additional offices in London and Boston, Beacon Rail's portfolio includes over 200 locomotives, over 1,000 freight wagons, 55 passenger units, 67 double decker coaches and 13 sets of five-car inter-city carriages on lease in the UK, Germany, Denmark, France, Belgium, Norway, Sweden, Austria and the Netherlands.

In Britain, Beacon Rail leases Class 66s to freight operators, including eight to Freightliner. Two Class 66s, transferred from Germany, entered service with GBRf in 2013, and a further nine GBRf Class 66s were sold to Beacon and leased back to GBRf in 2014. In 2018 GBRf agreed a sale and leaseback deal with Beacon for 10 Class 60 locomotives purchased from Colas Rail. Beacon is also the lessor for a series of Class 66s transferred from continental Europe and modified for service in the UK with GBRf.

Beacon Rail has worked with Direct Rail Services (DRS) on the development of Vossloh Eurolight diesel locomotives, with 34 Class 68s now in the UK. These have been followed by 10 electric/diesel dual-mode Class 88 locomotives from Vossloh (now Stadler).

A landmark order was placed in 2022 by GB Railfreight, financed by Beacon Rail, for 30 Stadler electro-diesel Class 99 locomotives. The Co-Co locomotives will have a maximum speed of 75mph and will be powered by overhead catenary or a Stage V low-emission diesel engine. The design is based on Stadler's successful Eurodual six-axle locomotives used in Europe, adapted to the UK loading gauge and specifications. The first of the locomotives is due to be delivered to the UK in 2024, with entry into service from 2025.

Beacon's first passenger trains were acquired in 2012 – 20 three-car Class 313 dual-voltage electric multiple-units, which had been retained by HSBC when it sold rolling stock company Eversholt Rail. Govia Thameslink Railway leases 19 of the Class 313s, and Network Rail leased the 20th as a test train for European Train Control System equipment.

In May 2016 Beacon agreed to purchase 66 Mk 5a carriages, manufactured by CAF, to run in 13 five-car sets for TransPennine Express (TPE). Beacon-owned Class 68 diesel locomotives haul the carriages, which entered service in August 2019 between Liverpool and Scarborough, with a pool of '68s' sub-leased from DRS to TPE.

In July 2017 Beacon purchased 78 Class 220 and 221 Voyager DEMUs from Voyager Leasing, a company established when the fleet was ordered. Of the 352 vehicles, 20 five-car Class 221s work for the West Coast franchise and the remainder of the four- and five-car units with CrossCountry.

In March 2019 Beacon was confirmed as financier for a fleet of 5x5-car Class 803 electric trains built by Hitachi for FirstGroup's Lumo open access service between London King's Cross and Edinburgh, which launched in October 2021. The £100 million deal includes full provision of maintenance for 10 years.

In May 2020 Beacon awarded a contract to British locomotive manufacturer Clayton to build 15 Hybrid+ CBD90 shunting locomotives,

along with options for a period of three years. Designated as Class 18s, in early 2022 one of the locomotives was delivered to GB Railfreight for trial use.

CALEDONIAN RAIL LEASING

Hitachi Rail Europe has built and is maintaining 46 three-car and 24 four-car Class 385 electric multiple-units for ScotRail. The contract is financed by Caledonian Rail Leasing Ltd, a Special Purpose Vehicle created by SMBC Leasing, involving KfW IPEX-Bank of Frankfurt and RBS/Lombard. The order was placed by SMBC Leasing (UK) Ltd.

CALEDONIAN SLEEPERS RAIL LEASING LTD

The fleet of 75 new Mk 5 Caledonian Sleeper coaches was manufactured by CAF. The project was funded with £60 million from Scottish Ministers, with additional financing by Caledonian Sleepers Rail Leasing Ltd, a subsidiary of Lombard North Central plc, part of RBS. The contract was valued at approximately €200 million for CAF, which supplies and manages spares, while the coaches are maintained by Alstom.

CORELINK RAIL INFRASTRUCTURE

West Midlands Trains is introducing new fleets of CAF Civity DMUs (Class 196) and Bombardier Aventra EMUs (Class 730), totalling 404 carriages. Financing of the £680 million investment is by Corelink

Beacon Rail owned: CrossCountry Voyager No 221132 at Haymarket on 3 October 2022 with the 18.13 Edinburgh to Aberdeen. **PHILIP SHERRATT**

Rail Infrastructure Ltd, a ROSCO jointly owned by Infracapital and Deutsche Asset Management.

SMBC LEASING AND EQUITIX LTD

In 2018 SMBC Leasing (UK) Limited and Equitix Limited (SMBC-EQ) together succeeded in securing the financing of an £860 million fleet replacement programme as part of the 15-year Wales and Borders contract, awarded to KeolisAmey. The deal involved procurement of 148 units (421 vehicles) across four different fleet types from two manufacturers and due to enter service from 2021.

CAF is supplying 51x2-car and 26x3-car Class 197 Civity DMUs, while Stadler is building 11x4-car Class 231 Flirt DEMUs, 36x3-car Class 398 tram-trains and 17x4-car and 7x3-car Class 756 Flirt tri-mode multiple-units. The companies say the agreements provide a whole-life asset management approach and a high level of long-term investment security beyond the current lease and usage undertaking terms.

QW RAIL LEASING

QW Rail Leasing, a joint venture between SMBC and National Australia Bank, leases Class 378 electric multiple-

Akiem-owned: Greater Anglia's Nos 379021/009 pass Meridian Water with the 12.09 Hertford East to Liverpool Street on 13 December 2021. This fleet was withdrawn in early 2022 and as of the end of the year was stored out of use. **PHILIP SHERRATT**

units to Arriva Rail London for Transport for London's London Overground concession. It also owns the 57 additional carriages used to increase all the trains to five-car length in 2015.

AKIEM GROUP

In November 2012, Macquarie Group announced that Macquarie Bank Ltd had established a new business, Macquarie European Rail, and agreed to acquire the European rolling stock leasing business of Lloyds Banking Group. In April 2020 the acquisition of Macquarie European Rail by Akiem Group was completed, comprising 137 locomotives, 30 EMUs, 16 DMUs and 110 wagons within the UK and Europe.

UK rolling stock which transferred includes 30 four-car Class 379

EMUs which were operated by Greater Anglia but as of late 2022 were stored out of use, plus a UK rail freight portfolio comprising 19 Freightliner Class 70s, 17 Freightliner Class 66s and 14 Direct Rail Services Class 66s. The acquisition gives Akiem the largest loco fleet on the continent with more than 600 locos operated by 65 customers. ■

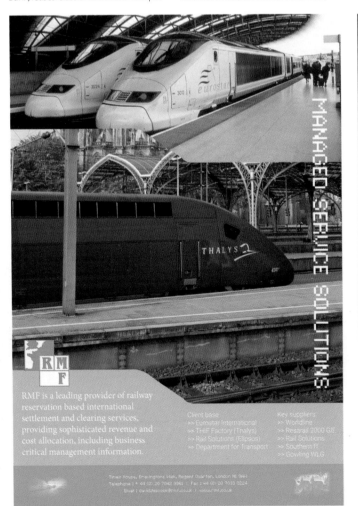

ROSCO fleets

Multiple-unit vehicles, HST power cars and locomotives and their owners

345 RAIL LEASING

Class	Number of vehicles
MTR ELIZABETH LINE	
345	630

AGILITY TRAINS

Class	Number of vehicles
GWR	
800	369
LNER	
800	167
801	330

AKIEM GROUP

Class	Number of vehicles
DIRECT RAIL SERVICES	
66	14
FREIGHTLINER	
66	17
70	19

ANGEL TRAINS

Class	Number of vehicles
AVANTI WEST COAST	
390	574

C2C	
357	112
CHILTERN RAILWAYS	
165	89
CROSSCOUNTRY	
43	7
EAST MIDLANDS RAILWAY	
156	8
158	32
180	20
360	84
GRAND CENTRAL	
180	50
GREAT WESTERN RAILWAY	
43	19
150	6
165	88
166	63
GREATER ANGLIA	
720	425
HULL TRAINS	
802	25
MERSEYRAIL	
507	93
508	69

NORTHERN	
150	140
156	58
158	70
333	64
SCOTRAIL	
43	51
153	5
156	84
SOUTH WESTERN RAILWAY	
444	225
450	508
707	60
SOUTHEASTERN	
465	200
466	86
707	90
TRANSPENNINE EXPRESS	
802	95
TFW RAIL	
158	48
175	70
WEST MIDLANDS TRAINS	
172	24
350	200

BEACON RAIL

Class	Number of vehicles
AVANTI WEST COAST	
221	90
COLAS RAIL	
56	5
66	5
70	7
CROSSCOUNTRY	
220	136
221	116
DIRECT RAIL SERVICES	
68	32
88	10
FREIGHTLINER	
66	8
GB RAILFREIGHT	
60	10
66	27
67	2
GOVIA THAMESLINK RAILWAY	
313	57
LUMO	
803	20
NETWORK RAIL	
313	3

East Midlands Railway electrics: Nos 360102/117 arrive at Luton Airport Parkway with the 17.17 St Pancras to Corby on 31 August 2022. **PHILIP SHERRATT**

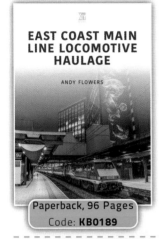

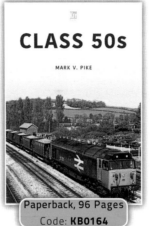

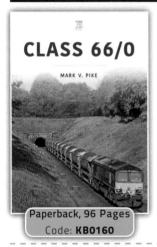

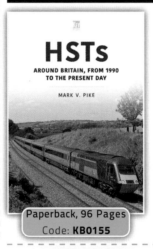

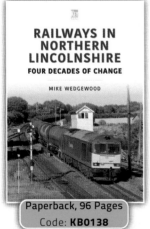
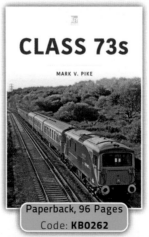

Entry into service awaited: Stadler EMU No 777010 for Merseyrail on test at Southport on 6 July 2021. **TONY MILES**

CALEDONIAN RAIL LEASING

Class	Number of vehicles
SCOTRAIL	
385	234

CORELINK RAIL INFRASTRUCTURE

Class	Number of vehicles
WEST MIDLANDS TRAINS	
196	64

CROSS LONDON TRAINS

Class	Number of vehicles
GOVIA THAMESLINK RAILWAY	
700	1,140

EVERSHOLT RAIL

Class	Number of vehicles
CHILTERN RAILWAYS	
168	9
EAST MIDLANDS RAILWAY	
170	24
222	143
FREIGHTLINER	
66	56
GB RAILFREIGHT	
66	27
GOVIA THAMESLINK RAILWAY	
171	3
GREAT WESTERN RAILWAY	
802	236
GREATER ANGLIA	
321	120
LNER	
91	12
NORTHERN	
158	20
195	149
331	141

SCOTRAIL	
318	63
320	102
334	120
380	130
SOUTHEASTERN	
375	438
376	180
395	174
465	388
TRANSPENNINE EXPRESS	
185	153
397	60

FIRSTGROUP

Class	Number of vehicles
GREAT WESTERN RAILWAY	
43	16

LOMBARD FINANCE

Class	Number of vehicles
COLAS RAIL	
70	10
SOUTH WESTERN RAILWAY	
484	10

MERSEYTRAVEL

Class	Number of vehicles
MERSEYRAIL	
777	68

PORTERBROOK

Class	Number of vehicles
C2C	
357	184
CHILTERN RAILWAYS	
168	76
COLAS RAIL	
43	5
CROSSCOUNTRY	
43	5
170	80

DIRECT RAIL SERVICES	
57	2
EAST MIDLANDS RAILWAY	
156	22
158	20
170	32
FREIGHTLINER	
66	32
86	10
90	10
GB RAILFREIGHT	
66	9
GOVIA THAMESLINK RAILWAY	
171	44
377	902
387	248
GREAT WESTERN RAILWAY	
57	4
150	34
158	41
387	132
HEATHROW EXPRESS	
387	48
NETWORK RAIL	
43	5
NORTHERN	
150	18
155	14
156	54
158	24
170	48
319	44
323	51
769	32
ORION HIGH SPEED LOGISTICS	
326	8
768	4
RAIL OPERATIONS GROUP	
57	4
SCOTRAIL	
158	80
170	102

SOUTH WESTERN RAILWAY	
73	1
158	20
159	90
455	332
458	170
SOUTHEASTERN	
377	60
TFW RAIL	
150	76
153	17
170	24
769	32
WEST MIDLANDS TRAINS	
139	2
170	22
172	69
319	40
323	78
350	148

QW RAIL LEASING

Class	Number of vehicles
LONDON OVERGROUND	
378	285

ROCK RAIL

Class	Number of vehicles
GOVIA THAMESLINK RAILWAY	
717	150
GREATER ANGLIA	
745	240
755	138

SMBC LEASING

Class	Number of vehicles
TFW RAIL	
197	10

Note: information believed correct as at early December 2022. These tables represent a snapshot of a constantly changing situation.

TRAIN FLEET MAINTENANCE AND MANUFACTURE

IN ASSOCIATION WITH

Rail People
Real Expertise

New train reliability improving while replacement fleets sought

Modern Railways Industry & Technology Editor **ROGER FORD** sees uncertain times ahead for the train builders

Despite train operating costs being squeezed, and the return of passenger traffic seeming uncertain, optimistic operators are looking to order replacements for existing train fleets during 2023. Whether budgets constrained by the Department for Transport's National Rail Contracts (NRC), which replaced the Emergency Measures Agreements (EMA) and Emergency Recovery Measures Agreements (ERMA) introduced during the pandemic, will support the additional costs involved remains to be seen.

One unknown is the current cost of new stock. The explosion of orders driven by the change to franchise bid evaluation from 2013 was fuelled by the combination of stable train prices and cheap money.

While infrastructure project costs have soared since privatisation in 1996, the cost of a standard Electric Multiple-Unit vehicle, compared with the last trains ordered by British Rail, has remained effectively constant in real terms at around £1.3 million. However, train manufacturers are warning that rising costs of materials, energy and other inflationary factors mean new train prices are increasing.

FINANCE

At the same time, the international financial crisis means the days of low-cost borrowing are over. When the Rolling Stock Companies (ROSCOs) began procuring trains in the late 1990s, the accepted cost of borrowing was £9,000 per £1 million borrowed per month. By the time the most recent fleets were being ordered, new entrants to the train leasing market were borrowing at rates as low as £5,000 per £1 million.

These rates were reflected in leasing costs, making 'mass extinction' replacement of a train operating companies' (TOCs) entire train fleet affordable. Examples included Greater Anglia and South Western Railway. These saw even relatively recent fleets coming off lease.

However, despite low rental costs for new and replacement fleets, TOC rolling stock costs have increased as new trains have been delivered (Figure 1). Note that the drop in 2021-22 is likely to reflect lower utilisation and fleets being taken out of service and put in store as a result of the pandemic.

Figure 2 shows the change in costs for selected TOCs which have procured significant numbers of new train fleets. ScotRail and Inter-city West Coast are included as examples of TOCs with relatively stable fleets.

Note that Greater Anglia (GA) bucks the trend of increased costs, despite its total fleet replacement over this period. However, deliveries of the much-delayed Alstom Aventra Class 720 fleet will be continuing during 2023. Complete withdrawal of the last of GA's legacy fleets, the Class 321 Renatus, is not scheduled until July, with the final Class 720 due to be delivered in September.

Of particular note in Figure 2 are the dramatic cost increases at London North Eastern Railway (LNER) and Great Western Railway. These reflect the Intercity Express Programme (IEP) train service provision contracts procured by the Department for Transport. The Thameslink Southern & Great Northern (TSGN) replacement stock was also procured by DfT but has a different funding structure.

ASPIRATIONS

Leading the new procurement round is the Scottish Government. Under the current proposal, ScotRail intends to replace around 675 vehicles between 2027 and 2035. Replacement will be linked to end-of-lease or when life extension becomes uneconomic. This implies that only the Siemens Class 380 and Hitachi Class 385 EMUs have a long-term future.

Orders will be driven by Transport Scotland's ambitious electrification programme and commitment to a carbon net zero railway by 2035. First to be ordered will be a new fleet of

Mass extinction nearing completion: Greater Anglia Aventra EMU Nos 720546/521 forming the 14.05 Clacton-on-Sea to Liverpool Street depart from Thorpe-le-Soken and approach Church Path foot crossing on 25 November 2022. **ANTONY GUPPY**

suburban EMUs serving Edinburgh, Glasgow, Perth, Dundee and Aberdeen.

Procurement will run through 2023 for delivery between 2027 and 2030. The requirement is expected to be for a combination of conventional and battery EMUs (BEMUs). The BEMUs will allow the provision of through electric services while electrification progresses.

This order will be followed by the replacements for the current DMUs on rural services. Procurement is expected to start in 2024.

Choice of traction will be critical here. The current expectation is that for the long rural routes, such as the Far North and West Highland lines, only hydrogen fuel cells can provide the necessary range.

Scottish Enterprise and Transport Scotland are funding the conversion of a Class 314 EMU to fuel cell power. The focus of this project is to gain experience of the support system needed for hydrogen traction, rather than development of a prototype train.

Completing the decarbonised fleet will be the replacements for ScotRail's Inter7City IC125 shortened sets linking Scotland's central belt with Aberdeen and Inverness. Procurement should start in 2025.

However, while attractive to the public, these short-formation InterCity 125 sets are expensive to operate and maintain. GWR will be retiring its short 'Castle Class' sets during 2023.

FIGURE 1: TRAIN OPERATOR ROLLING STOCK COSTS 2015-16 VS 2021-22

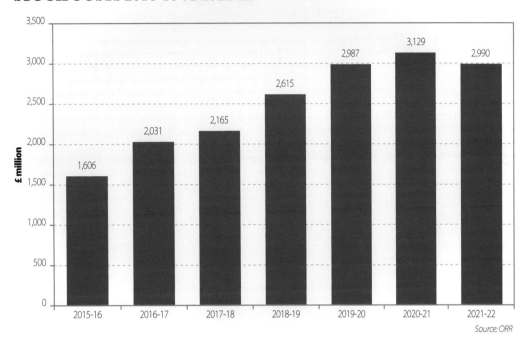

Source: ORR

FIGURE 2: SELECTED TOC ROLLING STOCK COSTS 2016-17 VS 2021-22

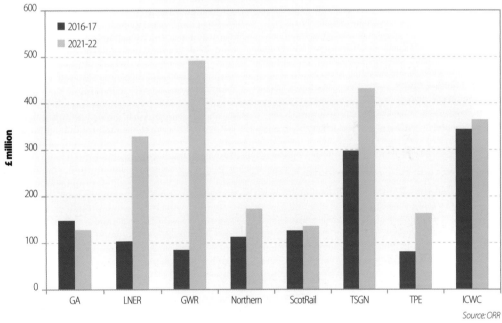

Source: ORR

ORDER BOOKS

ScotRail's suburban replacement fleet will be hotly contested as the manufacturers with UK plants see the end of what have been full order books. The base requirement is put at 64 units/295 vehicles. With options, this increases to around 120 units/550 vehicles.

Hitachi has been the first to warn of an approaching lack of work for its Newton Aycliffe plant. Current workload covers 13x5-car Class 805 bi-modes and 10x7-car EMUs for Avanti West Coast, plus 33x5-car bi-modes for East Midlands Railway (EMR).

Testing on the West Coast main line with the first two Class 805 units is scheduled to start in February. At the end of 2022, factory dynamic testing of the first Class 807 set was imminent. Under the largest of these orders, the first EMR set is due to enter service towards the end of 2023. With a production line 'beat rate' of four to five vehicles a week, this should sustain work at Newton Aycliffe well into 2024.

For Alstom at Derby, estimating the remaining factory workload is complicated by continuing acceptance issues which have meant

deliveries do not necessarily reflect the number of trains already built and in store. As reported above, the Class 720 contract with GA is not due for completion until September 2023.

In addition to UK contracts, Alstom has also been working on the export order of 280 cars for the Cairo Monorail project. The system is expected to open in 2023.

WAITING FOR HS2

Both Alstom and Hitachi have the prospect of the High Speed 2 contract for 54 trains awarded to the joint venture of the two companies in December 2021. Work will be shared between three factories.

Vehicle body assembly and initial fitout will be the responsibility of Newton Aycliffe, with body shells then transferring to Derby for the second stage of fitout and testing. Bogies will be assembled and maintained at Alstom's Crewe facility.

While work on the HS2 fleet is due to start in 2025, the first set is not expected to roll out until 2027. Hitachi Rail CEO Andrew Barr has posted the first warning and is calling on the British Government to make decisions on future rolling stock orders to offer reassurance to the Newton Aycliffe plant.

With no new orders in the pipeline, Mr Barr highlighted the 'good opportunities and business cases' that need to be approved. Warning that Hitachi is a business 'and we can't keep an empty plant there', Andy Barr emphasised: 'We have quite a challenge on our hands'.

SOUTH EASTERN REVIVAL

One of the largest current potential requirements is South Eastern. The replacement of its ex-British Rail fleet of Networker suburban EMUs, originally proposed as part of the 2017 procurement of the replacement franchise, has been revived.

At the time, Siemens was reported to be the preferred bidder before

TABLE 1: NEW TRAIN RELIABILITY, 2022-23 PERIOD 6

Operator	Fleet	Manufacturer	P6 Miles per Technical Incident (MTIN)	P6 MTIN Moving Annual Average
Lumo	Class 803	Hitachi	20,957	67,402
South Western Railway	Class 707	Siemens	77,682	66,416
Hull Trains	Class 802	Hitachi	85,007	60,490
ScotRail	Class 385	Hitachi	55,750	54,233
LNER	Class 801	Hitachi	52,710	46,714
LNER	Class 800	Hitachi	34,262	30,164
Northern	Class 331/0	CAF	34,232	25,671
TransPennine Express	Class 802	Hitachi	182,278	24,523
Govia Thameslink Railway	Class 700	Siemens	19,391	22,817
Great Western Railway	Class 800	Hitachi	31,414	21,533
Govia Thameslink Railway	Class 717	Siemens	22,644	18,113
Greater Anglia	Class 755/4	Stadler	15,590	17,676
Greater Anglia	Class 745/0	Stadler	17,022	17,606
Northern	Class 331/1	CAF	24,478	15,925
Great Western Railway	Class 802	Hitachi	8,613	14,559
Greater Anglia	Class 755/3	Stadler	9,604	14,068
TransPennine Express	Class 397	CAF	10,691	13,513
MTR Elizabeth line (Crossrail)	Class 345 RLU	Alstom	10,034	12,531
Greater Anglia	Class 745/1	Stadler	10,560	11,342
Arriva Rail London	Class 710/3	Alstom	23,075	10,307
Arriva Rail London	Class 710/2	Alstom	10,378	10,216
Northern	Class 195/1	CAF	4,385	9,563
Northern	Class 195/0	CAF	8,260	9,528
Greater Anglia	Class 720/5	Alstom	8,860	8,654
Arriva Rail London	Class 710/1	Alstom	8,340	8,648
TransPennine Express	Nova 3 train set	CAF	2,740	5,291
MTR Elizabeth line (Crossrail)	Class 345 FLU	Alstom	5,991	3,768
South Western Railway	Class 484	Vivarail	10,134	2,904
TfW Rail	Class 769	Porterbrook	1,899	1,621
Northern	Class 769	Porterbrook	1,496	1,445
Chiltern Railways	Class 168	Bombardier/MTU	386	1,005

Note: FLU=full length unit, RLU=reduced length unit

In administration: West Midlands Trains' Vivarail DEMU No 230005 working the 12.55 Bedford to Bletchley at Lidlington on 17 September 2022, before the service was suspended after the rolling stock provider went bust. **JAMIE SQUIBBS**

Out of the box reliability: Lumo's Hitachi EMU No 803005 passes Cramlington on 2 December 2022 with the 09.11 Edinburgh to King's Cross. **BILL WELSH**

franchise procurement, and with it new trains, was terminated. Requiring around 600 vehicles, it would be the largest order which could be met by an existing design, with a timescale ideally timed to fill the pre-HS2 production gap at Hitachi and Alstom.

However, given the cost issues highlighted above, it should be noted that the South Eastern *Official Journal of the European Union Notice* includes the alternative of cascaded existing stock. Nor in competitive tendering can it be certain who will win the contract.

CASCADE PLAN NEEDED

Complicating passenger rolling stock plans is the absence of a national cascade plan. With relatively new stock, released by new trains, owners are faced with the cost of placing them in warm store or scrapping. This has already seen the Class 365 fleet of outer-suburban EMUs go for scrap.

In addition to train operators, the lack of a national cascade strategy is adding uncertainty to the accelerating programme of fitting European Train Control System (ETCS). Without a clear strategy, prioritising fleets for cab fitment runs the risk of trains with only a short remaining life being equipped.

NICHE REQUIREMENTS

Small contracts are also on offer. London North Eastern Railway has evaluated bids responding to its requirement for an additional 10 inter-

city sets to replace the current IC225 legacy fleet. Placement of the order has been deferred pending clarification of future timetable capacity. Meanwhile, following approval of its open access Carmarthen to London service Grand Union Trains will be acquiring four nine-car bi-mode inter-city sets.

LNER's requirement specified 'significant self-power capability' for operation away from the electrified network based on On Board Energy Storage (OBES). This is aimed at reducing diesel power, as is currently the case where LNER's bi-modes are used, and is another example of the growing enthusiasm for battery-electric traction.

VIVARAIL PIVOT

Despite the potential of this emerging market, repurposed train maker Vivarail ran out of finance and on 1 December 2022 called in the receivers. While its diesel-electric multiple-units, converted from London Underground D78 stock, missed their intended Pacer replacement market, a pivot to battery-electric traction was under way.

A combination of the company's fast charge system and advanced battery technology gave its BEMU conversions the potential to handle out-and-back workings of up to 60 miles with a 10-minute recharge at the mid-point. A pilot scheme was planned for the GWR

Greenford branch in 2023 and ways of saving this were being discussed at *TMR* went to press.

After concerns expressed in last year's *TMR*, manufacturers have been getting to grips with the poor reliability of their latest new train fleets. Table 1 records the reliability of all the fleets ordered since 2013. Half of them are now at or above the 15,000 Miles per Technical Incident Moving Annual Average (MTIN MAA) at which train reliability is no longer a significant factor in overall train service performance.

Hitachi, Siemens, CAF and Stadler have all made major improvements in 2022, with Hitachi in the lead. However, fleet reliability overall continues to improve.

Figure 3 shows the overall MTIN MAA, covering all fleets on the network. Note that after the fall in reliability as maintenance depots adopted Covid restrictions, such as social distancing, performance has bounced back and reliability is now even higher than before Covid. The improving reliability of the latest fleets will have contributed to this recovery. ■

FIGURE 3: MTIN MAA ALL FLEETS AT 2022-23 P7

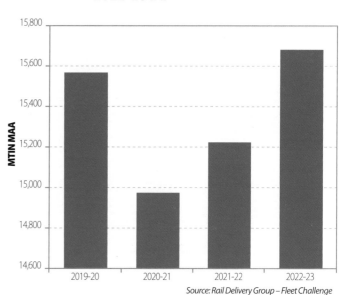

Source: Rail Delivery Group – Fleet Challenge

CAF builds for the future

CAF is a well-established part of the UK rail scene and is now well advanced with the construction of 77 Class 197 DMUs for Transport for Wales at its factory in Newport. The company selected the Celtic Business Park site, on land previously occupied by Llanwern steelworks, because of its good links to road, rail and ports as well as the significant investment in the area which meant local people were available with the right technical and engineering skills. An initial £30 million was invested to get the site up and running, and that figure continues to grow.

INVESTMENT

CAF is looking to its next orders and continues to invest in the Newport site. When the factory was built provision was made for future expansion, with the potential for existing buildings to be extended or for new facilities to be built on the surrounding spare land, thus future-proofing the site.

One significant investment is the construction of a new stores and logistics facility, additional to the current building, because CAF is putting much more emphasis on development of the local supply chain and so requires additional space. This is linked to a company-wide push on social values as CAF looks to become an increasingly socially responsible organisation. Amongst other things, the local procurement team is maximising the amount of UK content in its trains and CAF has also recruited a Social Values Manager to look at how it can further invest in the local area, and more widely across the UK. It is important to CAF to become an integral part of our local communities.

Also coming soon will be a connection from the factory to the South Wales main line. CAF subsidiary BWB Consulting has been providing valuable support on the project. The connection should be in place in 2023, improving the accessibility of the site for future contracts.

The factory has three main parts: the stores facility (with the additional building to follow), the main production workshop with three production lines (a third was added in 2020 for the Class 197 project) and a test house with five roads, capable of accommodating 30 vehicles in total. This latter facility is to be electrified, with designs currently being worked through for how to achieve this, while the possibility of extending the test workshop is also being discussed.

Meanwhile, there have been improvements in the production facility too. As well as the addition of a third production line, gantry cranes have been added for the Class 197 project to allow overhead access, mirroring a facility at CAF's Beasain plant in Spain. There have also been safety improvements, including the provision of moveable platforms and new step boards to improve access for workers during the production process.

UK WORKLOAD

Newport is now into its third manufacturing contract. First

to be built at the site were 44 Class 195 vehicles for Northern, followed by 60 of the 80 vehicles in the order for Class 196 DMUs for West Midlands Trains, which entered service in October 2022.

CAF's other UK fleets include 58 Class 195 Civity DMUs and 43 Class 331 Civity EMUs operating with Northern, 12 Class 397 Civity EMUs and 13 rakes of Mk 5a coaches with TransPennine Express, and 75 Mk 5 carriages for the Caledonian Sleeper overnight service.

CAF has a strong relationship with Northern Irish operator Translink dating back to 2002. CAF has delivered 21 new carriages, which lengthen seven Class 4000 three-car trains to six-car sets, and the final converted set went into passenger service in July 2022.

CAF is also progressing well with the replacement DLR fleet. Testing is well under way and the first units were due to arrive in the UK in early 2023.

New DLR train: one of the CAF-built sets for London's light rail network on test. **COURTESY TFL**

Built in Wales for service in Wales: CAF-built TfW DMU No 197004 at Llandudno on 14 November 2022 on its first day in service on the Conwy Valley line. **TONY MILES**

CLASS 197s

The Newport factory is making good progress with the Class 197 order for Transport for Wales, with the whole fleet being built at Newport. Obviously there is a particular importance to this contract as the fleet is being built in Wales for service in Wales. By late 2022, 32 of the 77 units (predominantly two-car sets) had been moved off site, with some based at Arriva TrainCare at Crewe for driver training activities. Meanwhile, at Newport work had begun on the 60th unit in the build. At present CAF is broadly completing one unit per week.

Of the 77 units, 51 are two-car sets and 26 consist of three carriages. Of the two-car sets, 21 are being fitted with European Train Control System (ETCS) for use on the Cambrian line, with one such unit already being tested; CAF's signalling team has played a pivotal role in supporting the integration of the digital signalling system. From the three-car units, 14 will have First Class – these will be assembled towards the latter end of the build programme. The first train entered service with TfW in November 2022 on the Conwy Valley line, with a gradual rollout planned across North Wales and later across the entire TfW network.

Also significant for CAF is that the Wales and Borders contract is the company's first full maintenance contract for a fleet in the UK. In June 2022 CAF took over operation of Chester depot from Alstom, and this will be the main base for the Class 197 fleet alongside a smaller facility at Machynlleth for the ETCS sub-fleet used on the Cambrian route. CAF is looking to grow the size of its Services business, and with future contracts will be looking to expand its maintenance footprint across the UK.

TECHNOLOGIES

Decarbonisation is high on the agenda within the rail industry, and CAF is also looking towards the potential of battery and hydrogen power.

The Civity UK platform remains its main offer in this country – it has already delivered both 100mph and 125mph diesel and electric variants. There is the potential for battery or hydrogen to be incorporated into the Civity, creating bi-mode or tri-mode trains as dictated by customer requirements.

CAF has strong experience it can call on in both areas, being a market leader in catenary-free battery trams for years, with the technology and integration principles being the same for the main line.

Of note in the UK is CAF's supply of battery trams for the West Midlands Metro, facilitating catenary-free running on extensions to that network – this has involved both the supply of new battery trams and the retrofit of batteries to the existing fleet. Meanwhile, the company has also won a large order to supply battery-electric trains in Germany.

The capability of batteries very much depends on route topography, which CAF engineers can model. For charging, CAF is able to offer a range of solutions, including lineside generators to enable plug-in charging of trains at termini. This aligns with work by sister company BWB to develop a 'modern station' concept, which could create electric transport hubs as part of the journey to net zero.

Meanwhile, CAF is part of a consortium in Continental Europe working to design a hydrogen train prototype by retrofitting a vehicle operated by Spanish company RENFE; it is due to enter passenger service in 2023.

CONTINUED FOCUS ON SUSTAINABILITY

One of CAF Group's main objectives is sustainability. It wants to strike a balance between accomplishing its mission and satisfying both customer and stakeholder requirements and expectations for sustainable long-term value. All of this is unfolded in compliance with both legal obligations and the best practices in these fields. Throughout its history, CAF has had a beneficial impact on environmental, social and corporate governance areas, both in terms of how it carries out its operations and how it develops products and services.

Sustainability – in addition to growth and profitability – is one of the three strategic goals that bolster CAF's 2021-22 Management Plan that sets out specific goals and initiatives. The Sustainability Plan actions include the update of the Materiality Matrix to identify any significant issues in all three areas: the Environment, Social and Corporate Governance (ESG). This Materiality Matrix has provided the basis to draw up CAF's first 'ESG Equity Story', breaking down what sustainability entails for CAF, its governance, major achievements and commitments for the future. Commitments for 2021-22 include participation in the SBTi (Science Bases Targets Initiative) and in the Race to Zero, the first CDP (Carbon Disclosure Project) measurement or the first CO_2 emission measurement with Scopes of 1, 2 and 3. CAF has also set corporate goals to make sustainability indicator improvements, including the main ESG rating indices, with a view towards ensuring CAF ranks above the sector's average. ∎

Stadler in the UK

Since 1942, Stadler has been making trains that are tailored to its customers' requirements and represent smart investment. Following a strategic decision to penetrate the UK, Stadler has secured numerous orders over the last 10 years.

This includes notable success in the metro and light rail sector, and passengers on all underground trains in the UK outside London – in Liverpool, Glasgow and Newcastle-upon-Tyne – will soon be travelling on Stadler trains.

Stadler's first UK order saw Variobahn trams enter service on the Tramlink network in Croydon in 2012. Following two subsequent orders, there are now 12 Stadler Variobahns serving this network.

Stadler delivered seven Class 399 Citylink vehicles for the tram network in Sheffield, the first tram-trains in this country. These operate on the UK pilot tram-train route between Sheffield and Rotherham Parkgate, as well as on the pre-existing Supertram network.

In 2016, Strathclyde Partnership for Transport awarded Stadler the contract to build and supply 17 Metro trains for the Glasgow Subway, in a consortium with Ansaldo (now Hitachi). This project is in the test phase.

In 2017, Stadler signed a contract to manufacture and deliver 52 Class 777 EMUs for the Liverpool City Region

for the Merseyrail network; an extra unit has since been added to take the order size to 53. Testing with the new trains is under way, and in August 2021 the first train was handed over to its owner Merseytravel. Stadler assumed service and maintenance of the legacy fleet in 2017 and will look after the new trains once they are in operation.

In 2021 Stadler and the Liverpool City Region trialled the fitment of a battery to one of the Class 777s. Suitable for operation away from the third rail electrification, the trial was deemed a success, and seven of the '777s' will be fitted with batteries for use on an extension of the Merseyrail network from Kirkby to Headbolt Lane.

In 2020 Stadler signed a contract with Nexus to deliver and maintain 42 new trains for the Tyne and Wear Metro. In 2021 four trains were added to the order as part of Nexus's Metro Flow scheme to increase capacity. Each 60-metre-long train will consist of five carriages and will be able to accommodate up to 600 passengers. Stadler has taken over maintenance of the existing fleet, based at Gosforth depot, and is leading the rebuilding of the depot to suit the new fleet. The first train was delivered to the UK in early 2023, and they will enter service later in the year.

On the main line, in 2016 Stadler won the tender to build 58 new trains

for Greater Anglia. The contract was for 14 Class 755/3 three-car and 24 Class 755/4 four-car bi-modes, 10 12-car Class 745/0 electric and 10 12-car Class 745/1 electric trains. All are now in service, with Stadler providing full service and maintenance from Crown Point depot in Norwich.

In 2019, Stadler was awarded the contract to supply 71 trains for the Wales and Borders operation. This major contract is for 36 three-car Class 398 Citylink tram-trains and 35 Flirt trains (Class 231 and Class 756).

The tram-trains will operate from Cardiff to Treherbert, Aberdare and Merthyr Tydfil. These trains will be able to take power from overhead wires and on-board batteries, supporting plans for intermittent electrification of the Core Valley Lines.

Of the 35 Flirts, 11 Class 231s are diesel-powered and will be used on South Wales Metro services to Maesteg, Ebbw Vale and Cheltenham. The 24 '756s' (7x3-car and 17x4-car) will be tri-modes, capable of running on diesel, overhead electric wires and battery power.

In January 2021 Stadler confirmed an order from Rail Operations (UK) Ltd to supply 30 Class 93 tri-mode locomotives. The Class 93 is a Bo-Bo mixed traffic locomotive based on Stadler's Class 68 and 88 locomotives. However, it has a higher top speed

of 110mph and is able to operate under electric, diesel and battery power. In electric mode, it can run under 25kV AC overhead lines with a power of 4,000kW. The Caterpillar C32 diesel engine will have a nominal power of 900kW and meets EU Stage V emission requirements. Two Lithium Titanate Oxide (LTO) traction battery packs will provide 400kW of extra power to supplement the engine when the locomotive is running in diesel/battery hybrid mode, as well as for last mile carbon-free shunting operation. The first locomotive is due to be delivered to the UK in spring 2023.

In April 2022 Stadler confirmed an order from GB Railfreight and Beacon Rail to supply 30 Class 99 electro-diesel bi-mode locomotives. The design is based on Stadler's successful Eurodual six-axle locomotives used in Europe, adapted to the UK loading gauge and specifications. The Co-Co locomotives will have a maximum speed of 75mph and will be powered by 25kV overhead catenary or a Stage V low emission diesel engine for non-electrified routes. They will have a maximum tractive effort of up to 500kN, and under electric operation the locomotives will offer power at rail of 6,000kW. Construction is due to begin in summer 2023, with the first loco due to be completed in summer 2024. After delivery to the UK later that year, it is due to be accepted into traffic in the second half of 2025, with the full fleet to be in service in 2026. ∎

Tram-train for Wales: Class 398 Citylink vehicle on the test track at Stadler's Valencia factory. **COURTESY STADLER**

LIFTING   **SERVICING**   **TRAINING**

 TOTALKARE
POWERED BY **EMANUEL**

LIFTING JACKS & BOGIE LIFTS

Lifting and inspection equipment you can rely on for all maintenance of rail vehicles.

With **40 years' experience** on heavy duty lifting solutions, Totalkare combines world class products with industry leading support to facilitate effective maintenance and repair.

BOGIE LIFTS

+ **6,000 - 14,000KG**

+ **COMPLIANT WITH DIFFERENT RAIL GUAGE SYSTEMS**

+ **HYDRAULIC LIFT PLATFORM**

MOBILE LIFTING JACKS

+ **HEAVY DUTY**

+ **SYNCHRONISED**

+ **RELIABLE**

REQUEST A QUOTE

CALL 0121 585 2724
WEB WWW.TOTALKARE.CO.UK

Alstom in the UK

Alstom is the UK and Ireland's leading supplier of new trains, train services and signalling equipment. Alstom has built, or is building, just under 40% of the UK main line train fleet, as well as many London Underground trains and all Dublin Luas trams. Alstom provides the widest range of smart solutions in the rail market, from innovative high-speed rolling stock, metros and trams to maintenance, modernisation, infrastructure and signalling.

In January 2021 Alstom completed the acquisition of Bombardier Transportation (BT), including the iconic Litchurch Lane facility in Derby, the heart of one of the largest cluster of rail-connected businesses anywhere in the world. Employing 6,000 people in the UK and Ireland, Alstom designs and build trains at Derby, the UK's largest train factory, one of the largest in Alstom globally and the only UK train rolling stock factory able to design, develop, manufacture, test and service trains for UK and export markets.

Alstom also operates the Widnes Technology Centre – currently delivering the largest ever UK train refurbishment project, that of the entire Pendolino fleet for Avanti West Coast; the first refurbished unit entered passenger service in April 2022. This is in addition to major

sites at Crewe, Ilford and Plymouth, plus around 30 train services depots across the UK and Ireland. Around two-thirds of the UK main line fleet is supported in some way by Alstom.

Alstom's Derby site is nearing the end of its order book for 2,660 Aventra Electric Multiple-Unit cars for the Elizabeth Line, London Overground, and the East Anglia, South Western, West Midlands and Essex Thameside rail franchises. The Aventras have been designed and built in Britain and the Aventra platform remains class-leading – one of the fastest, smartest and most economical trains in modern rail. Derby is also currently building 280 Innovia monorail cars for the Cairo Monorail project, the first UK rolling stock export by any company in 13 years – since Derby's export order for Gautrain in South Africa.

In December 2021 a joint venture of Alstom and Hitachi was awarded the contract to build 54 200-metre-long 225mph trains for HS2 Phase One and 2a services. Body assembly and initial fitout will take place at Hitachi's Newton Aycliffe facility and final fitout and testing by Alstom at Litchurch Lane. The bogies will be assembled and maintained at Alstom's Crewe site. The first train is expected to be completed in around 2027, and will enter service between 2029 and 2033.

Also in December 2021, Alstom won an order from Irish Rail to supply trains for the Dublin Area Rapid Transit network in a €270 million (approximately £230 million) deal. The initial order is for 6x5-car EMUs and 13x-5car BEMUs, based on the X'trapolis platform, and in late 2022 a further 18x5-car BEMUs were added to the order. The battery trains will be able to run for 80km beyond the DART electrified network, with charging provided at terminus stations and via regenerative braking. Subject to funding, the order could rise to 750 vehicles in a contract which includes a 15-year support contract. The trains will be built at Katowice in Poland and commissioned at Inchicore depot. The first trains are due to enter traffic in 2025.

Alstom's Digital and Integrated Solutions business provides signalling and infrastructure solutions across the UK&I, with major sites at Plymouth, Hatfield and York. It is the leading signalling contractor in Control Period 6. For example, Alstom supported the Bristol Area Signalling Renewals – stage four of which was Network Rail's largest ever signalling commissioning. Alstom has been installing its Atlas European Train Control System on the Great Western Railway between Paddington and Airport Junction, the

UK's first Baseline 3 ETCS trackside installation, alongside the Victoria and Feltham resignalling schemes.

The acquisition of Bombardier Transportation (BT) in January 2021 has created a global mobility leader committed to respond to the increasing need for greener transportation worldwide. This includes the most comprehensive product portfolio, unparalleled research and development innovation capabilities, the many complementarities of the two groups – for example, Alstom's leading position in hydrogen and BT's expertise in battery technology.

Decarbonisation is also Alstom's global corporate mission: to support the transition towards global sustainable transport systems that are inclusive, environmentally friendly, safe and efficient. Transport accounts for almost one-third of global energy consumption. Alstom is committed to supporting carbon neutrality in transport by building innovative, sustainable mobility solutions with a lower carbon footprint while actively contributing to the public debates on sustainable development policies.

On a global level Alstom develops and markets mobility solutions that provide the sustainable foundations for the future of transportation. Alstom's product portfolio ranges from high-speed trains, metros, monorails and trams to integrated systems, customised services, infrastructure, signalling and digital mobility solutions. ∎

New trains for Dublin: visual of the X'Trapolis units Alstom will supply for the Dublin Area Rapid Transit.

Siemens Mobility Ltd

Siemens Mobility manages the movement of people, goods and services sustainably, economically and effectively. The company is constantly developing intelligent mobility solutions that increase availability of infrastructure, optimise throughput and improve the passenger experience.

This enables train operators to shape today's and tomorrow's transportation needs, with Siemens Mobility offering trains, infrastructure, automation, electrification solutions and turnkey systems as well as related services. The company has a strong focus on digitalisation, bringing together the very best innovation, data science, analytics and software development.

In the UK, the company has over 4,500 employees and supports over 22,000 jobs in the UK supply chain. It operates from some 70 locations nationwide, including eight purpose-built rail maintenance depots and manufacturing facilities in Chippenham and Ashby-de-la-Zouch (for signalling, control and communications equipment), as well as Poole (train cab radio and communications equipment manufacture). These facilities serve overseas needs as well as domestic requirements.

Desiro City in service: Southeastern's Nos 707011/013 arrive at New Cross on 20 April 2022. **PHILIP SHERRATT**

THE FUTURE OF UK RAIL MANUFACTURING

Much progress has been made on the company's latest rail manufacturing site in Goole, East Riding of Yorkshire. This will play a pivotal role in supplying 94 new underground trains for London's Piccadilly Line. Due to open in 2023, the £200 million investment will create up to 700 permanent, skilled jobs in engineering and manufacturing, with a further 250 during the construction phase and up to 1,700 indirect jobs throughout the UK supply chain.

In addition to the main facility, Siemens Mobility is also creating a railway and supplier 'village' with shared warehousing and logistics and space for small and medium-sized enterprises. This will have a key focus on research and development for the UK. The Rail Accelerator and Innovation Solutions Hub for Enterprise (RaISE) was opened in May 2022, and provides 3,200 square metres of commercial floor space comprising office and workshop accommodation. The space is available to let to small and medium sized enterprises in any sector

and is not exclusive to rail, as well as including office space for Siemens Mobility. A second phase comprises a £50 million centre of excellence for rail research and innovation developed between Siemens Mobility and the University of Birmingham.

DEVELOPING AND DECARBONISING THE RAIL INDUSTRY

Siemens Mobility continues to lead the way on building technologically advanced and cost-effective trains that shape the future of commuter and regional services, helping to connect communities and level up the economy.

The company's record in train development is clear. The trailblazing Desiro trains frequently top industry reliability tables and are firm favourites with passengers. The Desiro City, the UK's first second generation train, has now celebrated five years in service, increasing capacity and improving the traveller experience on Thameslink routes.

In addition to providing commuter trains and maintenance, Siemens Mobility has extensive experience in building high-speed rolling stock and infrastructure globally, including providing 17 trains for Eurostar.

Decarbonisation of the industry is a key priority. The company is developing low-emission alternatives, with bi-mode options using battery and hydrogen technologies and greener rail infrastructure options.

This includes offering Mobility as a Service (MaaS) solutions to address the complete journey, from the first to the last mile. As part of this, Siemens Mobility has urged UK Government to go further and faster to meet Net Zero targets, highlighting a potential 10-year discrepancy for railway decarbonisation plans and identifying a number of major routes for upgrade.

Viewing the railway as a whole system – including trains, track and signalling – and using the latest innovations is essential. This also includes digitalisation and better use of data, using cloud-based application suites such as Railigent.

Railigent enables better understanding of rail data and the generation of valuable information. This allows train operators to increase the efficiency and reliability of their fleets and operations, with the ability for third party data platform integration, to drive decarbonisation and whole life savings.

FOCUSED ON UK RAIL INFRASTRUCTURE

Siemens Mobility is a global leader in the design, supply, installation and commissioning of digital signalling, control and rail communications solutions. It is the only company to have full research and development, manufacturing, testing and delivery capabilities for signalling in the UK.

The company develops, designs and deploys a range of world-class technology to deliver safe, efficient

railway operation. This includes cab radios and communication systems for trains. It also includes the technology which equips Thameslink trains with a combination of Automatic Train Operation (ATO) and European Train Control System (ETCS) to enable automatic operation through the London core, and London Underground to achieve a world class 36 trains per hour service on the Victoria Line. These systems deliver significant performance and capacity benefits to passengers and operators.

Siemens Mobility has been a key partner in the delivery of the Elizabeth Line, providing a state-of-the-art signalling system as well as the communications and control systems for the central section of the railway.

Opening up new routes and increasing capacity and performance also requires state-of-the-art rail electrification. Siemens Mobility's products and services cover the complete spectrum of requirements for AC and DC electrified railways, including an innovative lightweight catenary system and technologies that remove the need for large construction projects and help reduce the cost of electrification. The company is fully committed to driving the delivery of sustainable electrification solutions and helping to design alternative solutions – such as discontinuous electrification in conjunction with bi-mode trains – as either and interim or long-term solutions. ■

Hitachi Rail

Hitachi Rail's vision is that every passenger, customer and community can enjoy the benefits of more seamless, sustainable journeys, and the company believes it can deliver it by transforming mobility. Hitachi now employs around 3,000 people in the UK, in its factory at Newton Aycliffe in County Durham and in depots across the country.

Hitachi now has more than 200 inter-city trains operating in Great Britain with Great Western Railway, LNER, Hull Trains, TransPennine Express and Lumo. The Lumo Class 803 fleet has been the company's most reliable out-of-the-box fleet. Also recently delivered were the Class 385 EMUs for ScotRail. The longstanding Class 395 'Javelin' fleet used on Southeastern Highspeed services will be refreshed from March 2023 under a contract agreed with the operator and owner Eversholt Rail, the work taking place at Ashford depot.

Following the discovery of cracks on Hitachi's 800 Series units, all Class 800 to 803 vehicles are to have fatigue cracks in their yaw damper brackets repaired at Arlington Fleet Services, Eastleigh in a programme which is expected to run until 2028. The cracks were discovered in spring 2021 in both the yaw dampers and the lifting plates on Hitachi-built '80x' trains, causing all the trains to be temporarily withdrawn from service. In 2022 the Office of Rail and Road released a report describing lessons learned from the incident. Repairs will also be undertaken on Class 385 and 395 vehicles.

Currently under construction at Hitachi's Newton Aycliffe factory are

10 Class 807 EMUs and 13 Class 805 bi-mode trains for Avanti West Coast, and 33 bi-mode Class 810 trains for East Midlands Railway. The EMR fleet is the first for which Hitachi is welding car bodies at Newton Aycliffe following an £8 million investment in the site.

In December 2021 a joint venture of Alstom and Hitachi was awarded the contract to build 54 200-metre-long 225mph trains for HS2 Phase One and 2a services. Body assembly and initial fitout will take place at Hitachi's Newton Aycliffe facility and final fitout and testing by Alstom at Litchurch Lane. The bogies will be assembled and maintained at Alstom's Crewe site. The first train is expected to be completed in around 2027, and will enter service between 2029 and 2033.

In 2021 Hitachi agreed to acquire the Thales Ground Transportation Systems business. This enhances its pedigree as an innovator and provider of digital railway solutions. The acquisition will help the business to further grow its presence in Germany, Canada and the Asia Pacific market.

In a similar vein, Hitachi completed the acquisition of Perpetuum in 2021. The British rail technology firm is pioneering digital solutions that dramatically improve train reliability and performance, including live monitoring of critical parts, preventative maintenance and identifying rough ride on the UK rail network. Hitachi's 93 Intercity Express Trains in service with Great Western Railway are to be fitted with 'Perpetuum Onboard' wireless technology to monitor wheelset and bogie parts in a move which Hitachi

Built in the North East: a Class 810 bi-mode for East Midlands Railway taking shape at Hitachi's Newton Aycliffe plant. **COURTESY EMR**

says will boost fleet availability by over 100 days per year. Hitachi and its Perpetuum subsidiary have also been awarded a contract by Network Rail to develop the first real-time digital solution that monitors, and eventually predicts, sections of track that affect ride quality and require maintenance, using sensors on-board trains.

In the UK, Hitachi has begun a new signalling contract for the Gloucester area for Network Rail. The 1960s signalling infrastructure will be replaced with the latest in digital signalling solutions to help reduce passenger disruption and improve safety during trackside maintenance. This growth is founded on Hitachi's existing signalling expertise in the

UK, which includes the framework Wales & Western signalling framework and successfully testing European Train Control System technology on the Cambrian main line in Wales.

Hitachi is trialling battery technology on numerous fleets. It is working with Eversholt Rail to fit batteries to a Class 802 operated by Great Western Railway, and with Angel Trains to similarly fit a Class 802 operated by TransPennine Express. The company says the tri-mode train will cut carbon emissions by at least 20% and reduce fuel consumption. Trains would operate on battery rather than diesel power when entering and exiting stations to cut noise pollution and emissions in those areas. ∎

Battery trial planned: TransPennine Express Class 802 at Manchester Victoria; one unit will be fitted with batteries as a trial. **PHILIP SHERRATT**

Connected transport: Nomad Digital is leading the industry in the development of innovative intelligent solutions.

Nomad Digital

Nomad Digital is a world-leading provider of passenger, fleet management and monitoring solutions to the transport industry.

Partnering with train and freight operators, rolling stock owners and train builders to facilitate a significantly enhanced service from passenger Wi-Fi to infrastructure monitoring, Nomad Digital brings its systems architecture and integrator capabilities to provide modern processing, monitoring and connectivity solutions to trains.

Understanding the potential unlocked value of data collected from rail journeys, Nomad Digital also supports operators with achieving operational efficiencies through real-time fleet monitoring, utilising the latest approaches: Artificial Intelligence (AI) and machine learning expertise.

This includes supporting the development of proactive rail maintenance strategies with robust rail connectivity and edge processing at the core. Providing operators with in-depth fleet intelligence for data-driven decision-making can help tackle operations and maintenance challenges early, thus preventing costly fleet downtime.

Nomad Digital also offers an extensive range of infrastructure monitoring solutions, with its powerful Onboard Data Centre (ODC) providing edge processing capabilities to report on 'events' detected by on-board monitoring systems.

Keeping connected: Nomad Digital provide a range of solutions that facilitate a significantly enhanced passenger experience with seamless connectivity, real-time journey information and on-board entertainment.

MORE THAN A TO B

As passengers continue to seek more than just a journey that gets them from A to B, seamless connectivity and other value-added services, all easily accessible in a safe, connected environment, are now simply part of an expected service that passengers want to feel comfortable and in control when using public transport.

With this in mind, Nomad Digital continues to have one eye trained on the future to develop innovative, AI supported solutions to meet ever-evolving industry demands for a fully connected, end-to-end passenger experience, as well as supporting Mobility as a Service (MaaS) initiatives.

CONNECTING EVERYTHING FOR AN INTELLIGENT JOURNEY

The modern-day landscape of rail services with connectivity at the heart of everything is where Nomad

Digital comes in. The integration of Nomad's products and services into the on-train environment improves the passenger journey and delivers efficient technology, both operating on one common platform. Nomad Digital's aim is to add intelligence to what were once passive fleet sensors, eradicating the need to rip and replace.

INTEGRATED AND SCALABLE SOLUTIONS

Among all of the available solutions within Nomad's portfolio, its offerings include:
- fleet and rail connectivity;
- trackside networks;
- real time reporting;
- real time fleet management;
- security-as-a-service;
- Wi-Fi and internet access;
- remote online condition monitoring;
- Onboard Data Centre;
- CCTV;
- engage infotainment portal;

- passenger and on-board information systems;
- mobile engineering applications; and
- infrastructure monitoring solutions.

THE TRAIN FUTURE

Improved utilisation of available data and extracting more value from existing on-board and wayside sensors is key to the future of rail and public transport. Being able to harness more insights from existing data sources and fill any gaps with AI techniques will help build passenger and operator confidence. From a passenger perspective, they will be alerted when issues have arisen along their journey and will be aware of alternative options which may not necessarily be using a traditional mode of travel ie e-scooters. Operators will have the ability to detect potential issues with their rolling stock or the infrastructure they operate on and be able to act before service-affecting failures occur.

Increased edge processing will make the reliance on data transmission less demanding, with only event data being sent. Connectivity will improve with the rollout of 5G and eventually 6G networks, but it will also see satellite connectivity become a viable alternative with the development of new phased array antennas, LEO satellite constellations and falling data costs.

The latest innovative communication solutions, which include trackside radio networks, can revolutionise the rail industry by providing a flawless, uninterrupted connection for the end consumer, with rail operators benefiting from the savings in long-term use.

Every indicator is pointing to an increasing demand and higher expectation from rail passengers for fast, consistent and reliable Wi-Fi communications during their journeys. With the introduction of 5G technology for the train to ground link, some of these measures will be met, however, there is still a strong argument for a private trackside radio network for when the digital experience of passengers becomes priority.

LEADING THE WAY IN CONNECTED TRANSPORT

As rail industry requirements continue to evolve, Nomad Digital is committed to innovation and the development of industry-leading solutions to champion the digital train becoming a reality. ∎

Sector specialists

TALGO

Spanish manufacturer Talgo has set up a UK division and established a head office at Barrow Hill Roundhouse in Chesterfield.

The company says the move reaffirms its commitment to the UK, 'true manufacturing' and an 'all Britain' strategy. In June 2019 it submitted a bid for the contract to build new trains for HS2, but after it was eliminated from the process it launched a legal challenge against HS2 before reaching a mutual resolution in 2021.

Talgo has also entered into a framework agreement with Chesterfield Borough Council, with plans to develop an Innovation Centre, co-located with Barrow Hill Roundhouse. Also planned as part of the company's UK presence is a manufacturing facility on the site of the former Longannet power station in Fife.

VIVARAIL

Vivarail was set up in 2015 with the aim of producing low-cost, low maintenance rolling stock. After being based for five years at the Quinton Rail Technology Centre at Long Marston, in October 2019 the company announced it would relocate to Southam, near Leamington Spa. It also established a production facility at Seaham in County Durham, specialising in genset manufacture and overhaul. Sadly, in November 2022 the company announced its intention to appoint administrators, which it duly did the following week.

The company was established by industry veteran Adrian Shooter and had been developing new technologies which were mostly installed on new trains rebuilt from former London Underground 'D' stock trains. While the aluminium bodyshells and bogies of the tube trains were reused, the traction equipment was all new.

In April 2019 Vivarail's first rebuilt Class 230 entered passenger service as part of a contract to deliver 3x2-car diesel-electric multiple units to West Midlands Trains for the Bedford to Bletchley line. South Western Railway ordered 5x2-car Class 484 EMUs powered by third rail for the Island line between Ryde and Shanklin on the Isle of Wight. The trains were part of a wider £26 million investment in the island's railway and, after delays including software challenges, entered service in November 2021. Vivarail has also supplied 5x3-car diesel/battery hybrid units for Transport for Wales Rail Services for the Wrexham to Bidston line, although technical challenges and crew training issues have delayed entry into service.

Two battery-powered Class 230s were exported to Pennsylvania to

perform demonstration runs for Vivarail's former parent company Railroad Development Corporation to showcase the pop-up metro concept. The idea, promoted by RDC Chairman Henry Posner III, is to introduce passenger services on lightly-used freight lines, with the promise that for less than the cost of a consultancy study a trial service can be operated for a year to establish demand.

In November 2021 Vivarail showcased a battery-powered Class 230 at the COP26 climate change conference in Glasgow. The unit performed demonstration runs for delegates between Glasgow Central and Barrhead.

Over time, Vivarail's focus has switched to battery power. It created a prototyped fast charge system for battery units, based on the London Underground four-rail system, and also hoped to supply battery systems for retrofit to existing trains. To test

Island line: one of South Western Railway's five Vivarail Class 484s on the Ryde to Shanklin route on the Isle of Wight. Although the Class 230s on the Marston Vale line were withdrawn after Vivarail went into receivership, the Island line units remained in service. **COURTESY SWR**

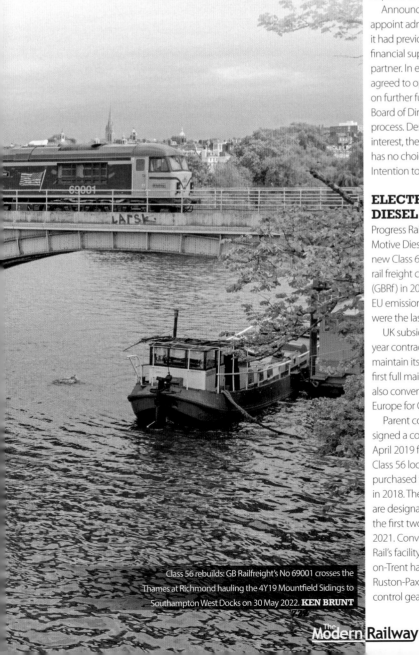

Class 56 rebuilds: GB Railfreight's No 69001 crosses the Thames at Richmond hauling the 4Y19 Mountfield Sidings to Southampton West Docks on 30 May 2022. **KEN BRUNT**

the technology, Vivarail agreed a contract with Great Western Railway for the battery-powered Class 230 deployed at COP26 to be used on the West Ealing to Greenford branch, taking charge from a fast charge system installed at West Ealing. It is hoped this trial will still go ahead.

Announcing the move to appoint administrators, Vivarail said it had previously benefited from the financial support of a sole investment partner. In early 2022 the company agreed to operate without reliance on further funding, so Vivarail's Board of Directors approved a sale process. Despite a positive level of interest, the company said its board has no choice but to file a Notice of Intention to appoint administrators.

ELECTRO-MOTIVE DIESEL TECHNOLOGY

Progress Rail company Electro-Motive Diesel delivered a final seven new Class 66 locomotives to UK rail freight company GB Railfreight (GBRf) in 2016. Due to changes in EU emissions standards, the locos were the last Class 66s to be built.

UK subsidiary EMDL signed a 10-year contract with GBRf in 2012 to maintain its Class 66s – the company's first full maintenance contract. It has also converted '66s' from continental Europe for GBRf for service in the UK.

Parent company Progress Rail signed a contract with GBRf in April 2019 for the repowering of 16 Class 56 locomotives the operator purchased from UK Rail Leasing in 2018. The repowered locos are designated as Class 69s, with the first two unveiled in summer 2021. Conversion work at Progress Rail's facility at Longport, Stoke-on-Trent has seen the locos' Ruston-Paxman RK3 engines and control gear upgraded to EMD 12-710 Series engines, rated for EU Stage IIIA emissions certification, with updated electronic controls, based on the Class 66.

GEMINI RAIL GROUP

Gemini Rail Group comprises the former Knorr-Bremse Rail Services and Kiepe Electric UK businesses. This included the transfer of the former KB facilities at Springburn near Glasgow and Wolverton near Milton Keynes, branded as Gemini Rail Services, although the company has since closed the Springburn works. The Kiepe Electric business is now known as Gemini Rail Technology and is based in Birmingham.

The Wolverton works continues to operate, although the company has sought alternative uses for the wheelshop. Traditional renovation contracts have included installation of new traction equipment on 18 Class 442 EMUs for South Western Railway (before this contract was abandoned in March 2021), a C6 heavy overhaul on Class 150s and refurbishment of Class 323 EMUs. Gemini also won a contract from Eversholt Rail to convert Class 321 EMUs to carry parcels and other light freight.

Gemini has set up a new sub-brand, GemEco, which is working on developing decarbonisation projects including hybrid technology and alternative propulsion.

Property developer St Modwen, which owns Wolverton works, has obtained outline planning consent to demolish most of the buildings in favour of housing. The lifting shop is planned to be extended and another two bays added, creating a four-track modern fleet maintenance

Clayton loco: one of the company's CBD90 locomotives in use by Tata Steel.

facility. This, along with the Royal Train shed, incident repair and high-voltage test bay, will be the focus of Gemini's future operations.

Knorr-Bremse has retained its UK component and aftermarket business and plans to focus on connected on-board railway subsystems and related services.

WABTEC FAIVELEY UK

The combined resources of Wabtec and Faiveley Transport have created one of the world's largest public rail equipment companies, with a presence in all key rail freight and passenger markets worldwide. In February 2019 Wabtec completed its merger with GE Transportation, formerly a business unit of GE.

The company's transit segment designs, manufactures, markets and services a large range of high added-value components, systems and services which the company believes help customers build and maintain trains that are safe, reliable and cost efficient throughout their life cycle.

Wabtec has refocused its traditional refurbishment business in the UK following changes within the market. The aim has been to bring its UK subsidiaries together under the 'One Wabtec' brand. This has involved the creation of centres of excellence: for products

and systems at Faiveley Transport (Birkenhead), for vehicles and bogies at Doncaster, and for powertrains at LH Group (Barton-under-Needwood).

The restructure resulted in the closure of the wheelset and vehicle overhaul facility at Kilmarnock, which Wabtec acquired in 2011; the facility has since been taken over by Brodie Engineering. This was followed in 2021 by the closure of the production facility at Brush Traction in Loughborough. The company has consolidated its operations at its Doncaster site, although here too the size of the workforce has been reduced significantly.

The group undertakes the construction, refurbishment and maintenance of railway rolling stock, locomotives, passenger trains and freight wagons. Recent major refurbishment contracts undertaken include the conversion of Class 319 EMUs to bi-mode Class 769s for Porterbrook and upgrades to HSTs for CrossCountry, Great Western Railway and ScotRail, where modifications have included provision of power doors. Both projects faced technical and resource challenges but were completed during 2021. Conversion of a Class 321 passenger unit for freight purposes for owner Eversholt Rail's 'Swift Express Freight' concept was completed in summer 2021.

BRODIE ENGINEERING

Brodie Engineering is a Kilmarnock-based rolling stock engineering business employing around 100 staff at its offices and workshops. The design and project office is immediately adjacent to the four-road, 14-vehicle capacity workshop.

In mid-2020 the company supplemented its Bonnyton Rail Depot facility by taking over the former Wabtec plant, a 100,000 square foot facility which originally opened in 1840. The two sites are the last remaining independent overhaul facilities in Scotland.

Having traditionally focused on specialist work such as corrosion and collision damage repairs, Brodie Engineering has broadened its portfolio to include longer-term overhaul programmes and mobile engineering, dispatching teams to outside locations to support customers in delivery of current projects. A headline project was the conversion of five Class 153s for ScotRail into carriages for cycles and large sporting equipment, which were introduced from July 2021 on the West Highland line. A programme of time-based overhauls on ScotRail's Class 320 EMUs has been followed by a similar programme on the Class 318 fleet; both are owned by Eversholt Rail.

LORAM UK

The business formerly known as Railway Vehicle Engineering Ltd (RVEL) was acquired by American firm Loram in July 2016. The company maintains and overhauls infrastructure, freight and passenger vehicles, allowing the railway to enhance and extend the life of rolling stock assets. Its Derby workshops can also undertake bespoke re-engineering projects, vehicle repaints and repowering of rolling stock.

CLAYTON EQUIPMENT

The Clayton Equipment Company Ltd was founded in 1931. Numerous changes of ownership followed before the company came under the control of Rolls-Royce. In March 2005, after 50 years as a subsidiary of major British organisations, Clayton Equipment once again became an independent company and immediately entered a highly successful period of independent trading. It relocated its office and factory to a new facility in Burton-upon-Trent in 2006.

Today the company specialises in mining and tunnelling locomotives along with metro and shunting locomotives, locomotive conversions and rail equipment. Its current work includes the construction of 15 CBD90 hybrid locomotives for Beacon Rail, designated as Class 18s. ∎

PASSENGER TRAIN OPERATORS

TONY MILES

IN ASSOCIATION WITH

New rail contracts dominate

By the end of 2022 nearly all passenger operators contracted by the Department for Transport were operating under National Rail Contracts (NRCs). These are intended to pave the way for future Passenger Service Contracts (PSCs), although little information has been provided about when or how these may be implemented.

The Covid-19 pandemic forced the Government to suspend all franchises and introduce Emergency Measures Agreements (EMAs) in March 2020. EMAs saw DfT take revenue and cost risk, with a management fee of up to 2% paid to operators.

In September 2020 the Government declared traditional franchises were at an end as it planned a pathway to introduction of concessions. The EMAs mostly transitioned into Emergency Recovery Measures Agreements (ERMAs), described as 'transitional contracts' with a lower management fee of a maximum of 1.5% of the cost base of the franchise and a stronger weighting towards performance delivery. Only Avanti West Coast now remains on an ERMA, this having been extended by six months rather than an NRC being awarded on account of the operating challenges the company faced during 2022.

CrossCountry was an exception, with a new Operating Contract Franchise Agreement (OCFA) starting in October 2020 for three years, while GWR and Southeastern both remained on EMAs which had begun in April 2020. Of the latter two, GWR has moved to an NRC while Southeastern joined the Operator of Last Resort portfolio in October 2021.

Exceptions to this rule within England were Transport for London's London Overground and Crossrail concessions and the Liverpool City Region's Merseyrail concession, all of which continued under pre-existing terms.

The Scottish Government introduced EMAs for the ScotRail and Caledonian Sleeper franchises in April 2020. ScotRail transferred from Abellio to the Scottish Government's Operator of Last Resort in April 2022, and Serco's Caledonian Sleeper contract will come to an end in June 2023.

The Welsh Government took a slightly different approach for the Wales and Borders contract, initially retaining pre-existing contract terms but providing short-term support before moving to a six-month EMA running from May to November 2020, with total support amounting to up to £105 million. In October 2020 it confirmed a further extension of the EMA to February 2021, after which operations became the responsibility of a publicly-owned subsidiary of Transport for Wales.

The table below sets out the status of all franchises and concessions in the UK, showing both their pre-pandemic franchise status and emergency measures status at the time of going to press. ∎

INDEX OF TRAIN OPERATING COMPANIES

COMPANY	OWNING GROUP	PRE-EXISTING FRANCHISE STATUS	CURRENT ARRANGEMENT	PAGE
Avanti West Coast	FirstGroup/Trenitalia	West Coast Partnership to March 2026, option to 2031	ERMA extended to March 2023	73
Great Western Railway	FirstGroup	Direct award franchise to March 2023, option to 2024	NRC to June 2025	74
South Western Railway	FirstGroup/MTR	Franchise to August 2024	NRC to May 2023	76
TransPennine Express	FirstGroup	Franchise to April 2023	NRC to May 2023	77
Hull Trains *	FirstGroup	Open access agreement to 2032	n/a	78
Lumo *	FirstGroup	Open access agreement to 2031	n/a	79
Merseyrail * (a)	Serco/Abellio (e)	Concession to July 2028	Pre-existing contract continues	80
Caledonian Sleeper * (b)	Serco	Franchise to April 2030	Contract to terminate in June 2023	80
East Midlands Railway	Abellio (e)	Franchise to August 2027	NRC to October 2030	82
Greater Anglia	Abellio (e)/Mitsui	Franchise to October 2025	NRC to September 2026	83
West Midlands Trains	Abellio (e)/Mitsui	Franchise to March 2026	NRC to September 2026	84
London North Eastern Railway	Operator of Last Resort	Direct award contract to June 2023, option to 2025	n/a	86
Northern	Operator of Last Resort	Direct award contract to February 2024, option to 2027	n/a	87
Southeastern	Operator of Last Resort	Contract tbc		88
Transport for Wales Rail * (c)	TfW subsidiary			90
ScotRail * (b)	Scottish Rail Holdings			91
c2c	Trenitalia	Franchise to November 2029	NRC to July 2023	93
Chiltern Railways	Arriva	Franchise to December 2021	NRC to December 2027	94
CrossCountry	Arriva	Operating Contract Franchise Agreement to October 2023		95
Grand Central *	Arriva	Open access contract to 2026	n/a	96
London Overground * (d)	Arriva	Concession to November 2024	n/a	98
Govia Thameslink Railway	Govia	Management contract to September 2021	NRC to April 2025	100
MTR Elizabeth line * (d)	MTR	Concession to May 2025	n/a	102
Heathrow Express *	FirstGroup (GWR)	Management contract to 2028	n/a	103
Getlink (Eurotunnel) *	n/a	n/a	n/a	103
Eurostar *	n/a	n/a	n/a	104

*Notes: * not contracted by the Department for Transport; (a) concession agreement with Liverpool City Region; (b) devolved to Scottish Government; (c) devolved to Welsh Government; (d) concession agreement with Transport for London; (e) Abellio management buyout due to be completed, with takeover by Transport UK Group*

Pandemic prompts subsidy rise

Unsurprisingly, train operating companies received increasing levels of government support during 2020-21, as **CHRIS CHEEK** explains

As time moves on from the events that destabilised our world in a way few had foreseen, the consequences of almost two years of disruption, uncertainty and unprecedented change are still working their way through our lives. Nowhere is this truer than in our public transport industries, where pre-Covid levels of patronage and revenue – especially from commuters – remain unmatched.

We still do not know whether the economic and social changes brought about by Covid are permanent or whether, given time, life will return to what in 2019 we thought of as 'normal'. The virus is still with us and, as I write, a new surge in the winter of 2022-23 is widely expected, with unknown consequences for working habits and public attitudes.

There always was going to be a revival in demand in 2021-22 from the depths of collapse during the three lockdowns in the previous year. The question was how far the bounceback would take things.

In the end, patronage in 2021-22 was 990 million, 43.5% down on 2019's record total of 1,744 million. The sharpest fall was on the London commuter routes at 44.7% with 668 million journeys. The regional services lost 41.1% of their passengers, carrying a total of 230.6 million.

Long-distance inter-city routes were down 39.1% to 87.4 million.

On the revenue front, the total recovered to £5,840 million, but still down from £10,241 million in 2019. London and the South East revenue was 45% down at £2,816 million. Inter-city services were 42% short of pre-Covid levels, earning £1,986 million, whilst regional services recovered best, to within 33.6% of 2019 levels on £1,058 million.

INCREASE IN SUBSIDY

The full impact on the rail industry's finances for 2021-22 had yet to be published at the time of writing, but information published by the Department for Transport shows it paid out £3,279 million in support to train operators in England between March and October 2021, bringing the total since the start of the pandemic to £11,900 million.

Looking at the wider figures for the whole industry, the total public sector passenger railways bill grew by over £1 billion in 2020-21. Revenue support for passenger services took up the lion's share of this with £10,216 million – £8,359 million from DfT in direct subsidies and another £96 million via PTE grants. The Scottish Government chipped in £899 million, Transport for London £526 million and the Welsh Government £367 million.

This spending was then supplemented by another £6,641 million in grants to Network Rail. Add in £20 million worth of freight grants, and total revenue support was £16,908 million, compared with £6,489 million in 2019-20.

With the transition to the various types of emergency agreement between the DfT and the train operators, tracking the financial performance of the industry has become more difficult. Under the new arrangements, passenger revenue is now paid to the government, whilst the DfT funds the cost of operations plus a small profit margin – effectively a 'cost plus' deal.

The Office of Rail and Road's publication on the finances of the passenger operators puts them on to a common basis for financial year end and cost headings. It measures movements in costs, revenue and subsidy for each operator, but the 'profit' or 'loss' shown for each rests with the public sector – whether DfT, Transport Scotland, Transport for London or Transport for Wales – rather than the private sector operator. This is of course a complete change from the regime prevailing in 2019-20, so year-on-year comparisons on profits must be treated with much caution. It is nevertheless a useful and fascinating snapshot of the financial health of the passenger railway during the pandemic.

According to analysis of these figures by specialist analysts Passenger Transport Intelligence Services, the operations as a whole saw an increased surplus in 2020-21. Overall, the figures show that, after subsidy, there was a surplus of £164.5 million at a margin to passenger revenue of 6.7%. This will have helped offset the other expenditure on support.

Across the all the 'franchised' train operating companies, passenger and other income fell by 78.4% to £2,468 million (previous year: £11,417 million), to which must be added government support of £10,215 million (£1,190 million). Operating costs were virtually unchanged at £12,519 million, within 0.1% of the previous year's total.

LOSS AND SURPLUS

Despite the intervention of the DfT in changing agreements, there were still sharp variations between different rail industry sectors and between train operators. Overall, seven of the 20 trading TOCs made an operating loss on these figures, up from six last year. Caledonian Sleeper recorded a loss of 56.5%, down from 64.1% the year before. Merseyrail saw a sharp deterioration to record a 26.6% loss, and next came Chiltern in the red by 17.9%. They were followed by Abellio's ScotRail operation on 15.8%. c2c Rail saw a loss of 9.3% (improved from last

No Government support during Covid: Merseyrail's losses increased sharply in 2020-21. No 508123 arrives at Chester on 29 August 2022. **PHILIP SHERRATT**

Revenues suppressed: CrossCountry's No 170618 calls at Cambridge with the 16.27 Stansted Airport to Coleshill Parkway (terminating short of Birmingham due to engineering work) on 23 February 2022. **PHILIP SHERRATT**

year). The Welsh operations of TfW saw a 4.1% deficit, whilst CrossCountry slipped into deficit by 0.9%.

Inter-city operators returned a cash surplus of 10.5% of passenger and other income. Total turnover amongst the companies before support fell by 83% to £732 million. The loss was offset by DfT funding of £3,214 million. Operating costs, meanwhile, fell by 3.9% to £3,862 million, leaving a surplus of £76 million.

Operators in London and the South East earned a surplus between them of just over £100 million. Passenger and other income collapsed by 75.8% to £1,427 million, whilst operating costs rose by 1.6% to £5,945 million. Government support during the year was £4,618 million.

Amongst the regional TOCs, passenger and other income across the sector was down by 75.8% to £317.5 million, whilst operating costs rose by 3% to £2,711 million. Even after total subsidy receipts of £2,382 million, an operating deficit of £12 million was recorded at a margin to passenger and other income of -3.8%.

Individually, the best result was achieved by East Midlands Railway, which returned an operating margin of 20.4%. Next came Great Western on 15.3%, whilst TfL Rail earned 13.4%. Four other businesses earned surpluses of more than 10% of passenger and other income, being Avanti West Coast, Govia Thameslink Railway, Northern and West Midlands Trains.

In the summaries below, figures are extracted from ORR Table 7223, Franchised Train Operator Finances and 7233 Non-Franchised Train Operator Finances, with additional information from statutory accounts. As already noted, the collapse of revenues during and between the Covid lockdowns meant much greater reliance was placed on government support.

Therefore, the operating margins shown in 2020-21 do not represent private sector profits, but the surplus accruing to the public sector of revenue over costs and revenue support.

LONG-DISTANCE OPERATORS

CALEDONIAN SLEEPER

The troubled history of Serco's Caledonian Sleeper contract continued during the year, with multi-million-pound losses continuing to be incurred. Consequently, the announcement in October 2022 of an early termination of the contract in June 2023 following a failure to agree a new financial settlement came as little surprise. During the year, services were severely restricted during the lockdowns, and as a result revenue was 79% down. Operating costs fell by 7% overall, but track access charges rose slightly, whilst rolling stock charges increased by one-quarter following the delivery of the new fleet. The net subsidy payable by Transport Scotland more than trebled but there was still a deficit of £3.2 million.

PERIOD TO	31/03/2021	31/03/2020
	£000	£000
Turnover	5,725	27,307
Operating Costs	(54,612)	(58,731)
Operating Profit before grant/premium	(48,888)	(31,424)
Net subsidy/premium	45,656	13,911
Operating Profit	(3,232)	(17,513)
Margin	(56.5%)	(64.1%)
COST HIGHLIGHTS		
Track access	4,967	4,889
Rolling stock	8,693	6,866
Staff	9,779	10,580

CROSSCOUNTRY

The operation saw a small deficit of £0.7 million (0.9%) during the

year. Revenue loss was higher than many at over 86%. Operating costs were cut by 1.7% overall, despite an increase in track access charges. Revenue support almost exactly matched the deficit. Existing operator Arriva was awarded a new direct award contract during the financial year, running for three years until October 2023.

PERIOD TO	31/03/2021	31/03/2020
	£000	£000
Turnover	76,070	547,654
Operating Costs	(505,052)	(513,798)
Operating Profit before grant/premium:	(428,982)	33,856
Net subsidy/premium	428,296	(6,936)
Operating Profit	(686)	26,920
Margin	(0.9%)	4.9%
COST HIGHLIGHTS		
Track access	137,699	135,585
Rolling stock	41,454	45,092
Staff	113,912	114,835

EAST MIDLANDS

Having only taken over in August 2019, Abellio's new East Midlands Railway business was less than 40 weeks old when the pandemic struck. The original eight-year franchise agreement was replaced by the emergency agreements

PERIOD TO	31/03/2021	31/03/2020
	£000	£000
Turnover	88,162	423,800
Operating Costs	(420,890)	(414,360)
Operating Profit before grant/premium	(332,728)	9,440
Net subsidy/premium	350,751	27,436
Operating Profit	18,023	36,875
Margin	20.4%	8.7%
COST HIGHLIGHTS		
Track access	91,588	105,457
Rolling stock	63,092	48,817
Staff	132,023	132,441

devised by the DfT. This in turn was replaced by a new eight-year National Rail Contract in October 2022, running until 2030. Revenue fell by 79% during the year, whilst operating costs rose by 1.6%, thanks largely to increased rolling stock charges. Government support totalled £332.7 million, resulting in an £18 million surplus.

GREAT WESTERN RAILWAY

The FirstGroup-owned company reached agreement with DfT on a new National Rail Contract in June 2022, lasting until June 2025 but with the option of a further three years. The company had also become responsible for the operation of the Heathrow Express service (qv) in 2019. During the year, the operator saw revenue drop by 76.9%, whilst operating costs were reduced by 6.2%, thanks mainly to a 3.6% fall in labour costs. Government support totalled £1,049 million, giving a £40.3 million surplus (15.3% of passenger and other income).

PERIOD TO	31/03/2021	31/03/2020
	£000	£000
Turnover	263,285	1,138,746
Operating Costs	(1,312,176)	(1,399,058)
Operating Profit before grant/premium	(1,048,891)	(260,312)
Net subsidy/premium	1,089,148	313,890
Operating Profit	40,257	53,578
Margin	15.3%	4.7%
COST HIGHLIGHTS		
Track access	191,532	189,656
Rolling stock	494,971	473,009
Staff	353,368	366,551

INTER-CITY EAST COAST

The DfT-owned London North Eastern Railway (LNER) took over the services in June 2018, and completed the introduction of the new 'Azuma' fleet from May 2019 onwards. Revenue was down by almost 85% during the year,

PERIOD TO	31/03/2021	31/03/2020
	£000	£000
Turnover	127,982	838,664
Operating Costs	(702,105)	(727,367)
Operating Profit before grant/premium	(574,123)	111,296
Net subisdy/premium	575,453	(105,784)
Operating Profit	1,330	5,512
Margin	1.0%	0.7%
COST HIGHLIGHTS		
Track access	74,832	94,117
Rolling stock	332,777	203,421
Staff	149,923	157,325

and operating costs fell by 3.5%. Savings in track access and staff costs were offset by a hefty 63% increase in rolling stock leasing costs as the new fleet of trains was fully introduced. Public support of £575 million enabled a surplus of £1.3 million to be earned.

INTER-CITY WEST COAST

This was another business that had changed hands shortly before the onset of the pandemic, with FirstGroup/Trenitalia's Avanti West Coast taking over from Virgin Trains on 7 December 2019. At the time of writing, industrial relations problems and a severe shortage of drivers has placed the future of the business in jeopardy, being awarded a six-month extension of its contract in October 2022 as opposed to the expected 10-year deal. During 2020-21, the operator saw revenue fall by almost 87%, whilst operating costs were 4.1% lower, with reduced staff costs offsetting increases in track access and leasing charges. Support of £725 million helped to deliver a £20.5 million surplus at a margin of 12.6% of passenger and other income.

PERIOD TO	31/03/2021	31/03/2020
Turnover	162,611	1,234,334
Operating Costs	(867,286)	(903,965)
Operating Profit before grant/premium	(704,675)	330,370
Net subsidy/premium	725,238	(284,381)
Operating Profit	20,563	45,988
Margin	12.6%	3.7%
COST HIGHLIGHTS		
Track access	182,617	157,070
Rolling stock	358,778	354,611
Staff	195,522	216,394

LONDON AND SOUTH EAST OPERATORS

CHILTERN

The Arriva-owned business achieved a new agreement with DfT in December

PERIOD TO	31/03/2021	31/03/2020
	£000	£000
Turnover	38,013	251,512
Operating Costs	(201,296)	(211,675)
Operating Profit before grant/premium	(163,283)	39,837
Net subsidy/premium	156,470	(46,189)
Operating Profit	(6,813)	(6,352)
Margin	(17.9%)	(2.5%)
COST HIGHLIGHTS		
Track access	46,986	48,277
Rolling stock	9,667	9,824
Staff	55,348	57,199

2021, which will see the company remain in charge until at least March 2025. During the year, passenger and other income was 84.9% down, whilst operating costs were cut by 4.9%, with savings in all three main cost components. Government support of £156.4 million was insufficient to wipe out the deficit, though, leaving a shortfall of £6.8 million.

EAST ANGLIA

The Abellio/Mitsui-owned company signed a new operating contract with Government in September 2021, running for five years until September 2026. During 2020-21, the business lost 75% of its revenue, but saw its operating costs rise by 2.5%, despite savings in staff costs and rolling stock charges. Government support of £429.9 million offset the deficit and left the operation with a £10.8 million surplus.

PERIOD TO	31/03/2021	31/03/2020
Turnover	193,067	773,069
Operating Costs	(612,106)	(597,225)
Operating Profit before grant/premium	(419,039)	175,844
Net subsidy/premium	429,876	(154,639)
Operating Profit	10,837	21,205
Margin	5.6%	2.7%
COST HIGHLIGHTS		
Track access	107,141	97,149
Rolling stock	138,596	152,466
Staff	167,607	173,260

ESSEX THAMESIDE (C2C RAIL)

The Italian-owned company signed a new contract with Government in July 2021, but only for two years until July 2023. This predominantly commuter railway saw revenue fall by 72.6% during the year, but operating costs increased by 19.3% thanks to rises in track access charges and staff costs. Government support

of £110.5 million was insufficient to cover the loss fully, and a deficit of £4.7 million was recorded.

PERIOD TO	31/03/2021	31/03/2020
	£000	£000
Turnover	50,940	185,654
Operating Costs	(166,185)	(139,314)
Operating Profit before grant/premium	(115,246)	46,339
Net subsidy/premium	110,517	(66,149)
Operating Profit	(4,728)	(19,809)
Margin	(9.3%)	(10.7%)
COST HIGHLIGHTS		
Track access	24,137	22,668
Rolling stock	28,394	30,886
Staff	52,086	46,123

LONDON OVERGROUND

This concession operation is effectively the template for the Government's new operating contracts for the railway. Transport for London takes revenue risk and specifies the timetable, whilst Arriva takes responsibility for delivering the service. During the year, the operation saw revenue fall by 64.3% whilst operating costs rose by 3%, mainly driven by increases in staff costs, rolling stock leasing and track access charges. The Overground operation received £238 million in support from TfL, in turn enabling it to earn a surplus of £5.9 million.

PERIOD TO	31/03/2021	31/03/2020
	£000	£000
Turnover	96,264	269,682
Operating Costs	(328,586)	(318,610)
Operating Profit before grant/premium	(232,322)	(48,928)
Net subsidy/premium	238,200	56,600
Operating Profit	5,878	7,672
Margin	6.1%	2.8%
COST HIGHLIGHTS		
Track access	53,641	35,968
Rolling stock	35,258	32,427
Staff	120,646	110,831

MTR ELIZABETH LINE

An MTR Corporation-owned company holds the concession to operate Crossrail until 2023, recently extended until 2025. Prior to the opening of the Elizabeth Line in May 2022, the company ran the TfL Rail operation comprising Great Eastern suburban routes from Liverpool Street and the Heathrow to Paddington Heathrow Connect service. The company expanded its operations during the year as work began on the testing of the new infrastructure ahead of opening for service. During the year, the TfL Rail operation saw revenue fall by 57%, whilst operating costs were reduced by 4.6% – thanks largely to a hefty cut in rolling stock charges. Financial support from TfL was already over £200 million a year but rose by 39% to £287.7 million. This generated a £10 million operating profit.

PERIOD TO	31/03/2021	31/03/2020
	£000	£000
Turnover	74,949	174,468
Operating Costs	(352,609)	(369,678)
Operating Profit before grant/premium	(277,660)	(195,210)
Net subsidy/premium	287,700	206,795
Operating Profit	10,040	11,585
Margin	13.4%	6.6%
COST HIGHLIGHTS		
Track access	117,822	102,697
Rolling stock	21,241	70,635
Staff	90,990	97,512

SOUTH EASTERN

Following the discovery of accounting irregularities, the Govia joint venture was stripped of its contract in October 2021, being transferred to the DfT-owned SE Trains. The business had seen a 75.1% loss in revenue during 2020-21, whilst operating costs had risen by 3.2% to £1,085 million.

Surplus earned: a GWR 'Castle Class' HST powered by Nos 43160/016 calls at Newport with the 05.40 Penzance to Cardiff Central on 26 July 2022. **PHILIP SHERRATT**

Costs reduced: Govia Thameslink Railway's Southern-branded Nos 377707/708 at Battersea Park on 16 September 2021 with the 10.55 Victoria to Dorking. **PHILIP SHERRATT**

DfT support totalled £879 million, giving a surplus of £18.8 million.

PERIOD TO	31/03/2021	31/03/2020
Turnover	224,833	901,759
Operating Costs	(1,085,008)	(1,051,039)
Operating Profit before grant/premium	(860,175)	(149,280)
Net subsidy/premium	878,968	184,960
Operating Profit	18,792	35,680
Margin	8.4%	4.0%
COST HIGHLIGHTS		
Track access	456,621	424,233
Rolling stock	240,284	222,011
Staff	242,355	238,908

SOUTH WESTERN RAILWAY

The FirstGroup/MTR Corporation joint venture signed a new National Rail Contract for the operation in May 2021, running until May 2023, but with an option to extend by a further two years. During 2020-21, the business saw revenue fall by 80.2%, whilst operating costs rose by a hefty 14.6% – driven by an increase of 9.5% in staff costs and 14.7% in track access charges. DfT support totalled £755.2 million, meaning the business saw a surplus of £6.8 million.

PERIOD TO	31/03/2021	31/03/2020
	£000	£000
Turnover	214,613	1,086,367
Operating Costs	(962,985)	(840,206)
Operating Profit before grant/premium	(748,373)	246,160
Net subisdy/premium	755,199	(300,554)
Operating Profit	6,826	(54,393)
Margin	3.2%	(5.0%)
COST HIGHLIGHTS		
Track access	216,475	188,676
Rolling stock	179,452	190,208
Staff	315,577	288,138

THAMESLINK, SOUTHERN & GREAT NORTHERN

Government was already taking revenue risk on this mega-business before the onset of the pandemic, paying operator Govia its operating costs plus a small margin whilst keeping the revenue. The operation saw revenue fall by 76.8% during the year, whilst costs were reduced by 5.3%, thanks to falls in track access charges and rolling stock costs. This meant the DfT's support bill was just over £1,310 million, enabling the operation to generate a surplus of £47.3 million.

PERIOD TO	31/03/2021	31/03/2020
	£000	£000
Turnover	416,687	1,792,712
Operating Costs	(1,680,001)	(1,774,899)
Operating Profit before grant/premium	(1,263,314)	17,813
Net subsidy/premium	1,310,614	10,979
Operating Profit	47,300	28,792
Margin	11.4%	1.6%
COST HIGHLIGHTS		
Track access	475,923	487,061
Rolling stock	448,454	452,482
Staff	497,446	496,852

WEST MIDLANDS TRAINS

The joint venture of Abellio and Mitsui signed a new five-year National Rail Contract in September 2021. The business saw revenue fall by 74.4% during 2020-21, whilst there was a 1.5% rise in operating costs as both staff costs and track access charges increased, offset to some extent by a 2.2% cut in rolling stock charges. The net subsidy paid by Government increased to £451.2 million, resulting in a £12.2 million surplus.

PERIOD TO	31/03/2021	31/03/2020
	£000	£000
Turnover	117,637	458,624
Operating Costs	(556,599)	(548,125)
Operating Profit before grant/premium	(438,962)	(89,501)
Net subsidy/premium	451,156	111,692
Operating Profit	12,194	22,191
Margin	10.4%	4.8%
COST HIGHLIGHTS		
Track access	115,580	112,126
Rolling stock	94,309	96,408
Staff	172,439	169,487

REGIONAL OPERATORS

MERSEYRAIL ELECTRICS

The 25-year concession agreement with the Serco/Abellio joint venture has an expiry date of 2028. Progress was made in the summer of 2022, with agreement being reached with trade unions over the introduction of the new Stadler-built train fleet and plans for driver-only operation dropped. The business saw income fall by 43.4% during the year, with a 4.9% reduction in costs. However, there was no additional financial support from DfT, whilst payments from Merseytravel fell by almost £6 million. As a result, there was a shortfall of £10.9 million.

PERIOD TO	31/03/2021	31/03/2020
	£000	£000
Turnover	41,018	72,496
Operating Costs	(151,183)	(158,933)
Operating Profit before grant/premium	(110,165)	(86,437)
Net subsidy/premium	99,270	105,748
Operating Profit	(10,895)	19,311
Margin	(26.6%)	26.6%
COST HIGHLIGHTS		
Track access	27,441	28,017
Rolling stock	12,674	12,753
Staff	58,595	59,255

NORTHERN

The operation changed hands at the start of the pandemic, with a new state-owned company taking over from the heavily loss-making Arriva franchise on 1 March 2020. During 2020-21, the business saw passenger and other income fall by 71.7%, whilst operating costs were also reduced, by 4.7%. This was covered by DfT support of £757.1 million, providing a surplus of £12.6 million.

PERIOD TO	31/03/2021	31/03/2020
	£000	£000
Turnover	112,399	396,589
Operating Costs	(856,956)	(898,914)
Operating Profit before grant/premium	(744,557)	(502,326)
Net subsidy/premium	757,115	386,816
Operating Profit	12,558	(115,510)
Margin	11.2%	(29.1%)
COST HIGHLIGHTS		
Track access	150,366	151,944
Rolling stock	163,837	136,744
Staff	356,744	349,903

SCOTRAIL

The ScotRail business was taken back into public ownership in April 2022, but the operation remained in the hands of Abellio until then under an emergency agreement. Revenue fell by 80.4% in 2020-21, whilst operating costs rose by 3.6%, driven largely by a 4% increase in track access charges. The net subsidy payment made by Transport Scotland amounted to £853.6 million, but was insufficient to cover these costs, meaning a further deficit of £12.3 million was incurred.

PERIOD TO	31/03/2021	31/03/2020
Turnover	77,606	396,544
Operating Costs	(943,529)	(911,005)
Operating Profit before grant/premium	(865,923)	(514,461)
Net subsidy/premium	853,661	515,803
Operating Profit	(12,262)	1,342
Margin	(15.8%)	0.3%
COST HIGHLIGHTS		
Track access	341,300	328,166
Rolling stock	135,338	136,758
Staff	252,546	261,907

TRANSPENNINE EXPRESS

The FirstGroup-owned company began a two-year National Rail Contract in May 2021. A further such contract has been proposed, running for up to eight years and covering the period of the Transpennine Route Upgrade modernisation works. During 2020-

21, revenue fell by 80.8%, whilst operating costs rose significantly, up 26.7%. This was the result of a £27.5 million increase in rolling stock charges following the completion of deliveries of the new fleet. Support from DfT increased to £336.9 million, meaning the business just broke even.

PERIOD TO	31/03/2021	31/03/2020
	£000	£000
Turnover	52,069	271,814
Operating Costs	(388,942)	(307,087)
Operating Profit before grant/premium	(336,873)	(35,273)
Net subsidy/premium	336,876	35,273
Operating Profit	3	(0)
Margin	0.0%	(0.0%)
COST HIGHLIGHTS		
Track access	59,903	62,897
Rolling stock	145,579	118,050
Staff	89,417	88,488

WALES AND THE BORDERS

After just over two years in charge, the Keolis/Amey joint venture ended its operation of the business in February 2021, as Covid had meant the franchise agreement was financially unsustainable. The operation was taken over by a new Welsh Government-owned company, though Amey retains a role in delivering infrastructure upgrades. Revenue in 2020-21 fell by 80.4%, whilst costs of operation rose by 3.8%, thanks largely to a 6.6% increase in staff costs. The net subsidy paid by TfW increased to £335.6 million, but was insufficient to cover the costs, leaving a further deficit of £1.4 million.

PERIOD TO	31/03/2020	31/03/2019
	£000	£000
Turnover	34,372	175,802
Operating Costs	(371,365)	(357,929)
Operating Profit before grant/premium	(336,993)	(182,127)
Net subsidy/premium	335,582	185,568
Operating Profit	(1,410)	3,441
Margin	(4.1%)	2.0%
COST HIGHLIGHTS		
Track access	52,641	60,999
Rolling stock	56,727	62,983
Staff	148,238	138,999

NON-FRANCHISED OPERATIONS

GRAND CENTRAL

The onset of the pandemic in 2020-21 saw services suspended between 3 April and 26 July, and again during subsequent national lockdowns. No Government support was provided, meaning the Arriva-owned business incurred very heavy losses of over £42 million as revenue collapsed by 84.2% whilst operating costs rose by 11.4%. As a consequence, it was announced in September 2020 that plans to introduce a service between Blackpool and London Euston had been abandoned.

PERIOD TO	31/03/2021	31/03/2020
	£000	£000
Turnover	8,158	51,496
Operating Costs	(50,515)	(45,347)
Operating Profit before grant/premium	(42,357)	6,150
Net subsidy/premium	0	0
Operating Profit	(42,357)	6,150
Margin	(519.2%)	11.9%
COST HIGHLIGHTS		
Rolling stock	245	4,888
Staff	9,623	9,238
Diesel fuel	2,737	4,765
Other (incl track access)	37,910	26,456

HULL TRAINS

The FirstGroup-owned business launched a new fleet of five-car bi-mode high-speed 'Paragon' trains built by Hitachi a few weeks before the onset of the pandemic. Services were suspended during the three national lockdowns in the absence of Government support, though the company did receive some Government assistance during the year, in the form of a £2.1 million grant from the Coronavirus Employment Retention Scheme (known as 'the furlough'). Revenue loss was 88.5% but the service suspensions meant costs were 45.8% lower, leaving a loss after grant of £10.2 million

compared with the previous year's £2.9 million operating profit.

PERIOD TO	31/03/2021	31/03/2020
	£000	£000
Turnover	3,736	32,540
Operating Costs	(16,072)	(29,661)
Operating Profit before grant/premium	(12,336)	2,879
Net subsidy/premium	2,131	0
Operating Profit	(10,205)	2,879
Margin	(273.2%)	8.8%
COST HIGHLIGHTS		
Rolling stock	4,558	2,519
Staff	5,451	7,033
Diesel fuel	107	3,379
Other (incl track access)	5,956	16,730

Figures from company accounts rather than ORR.

EUROSTAR INTERNATIONAL

Remarkably, no financial support was available to Eurostar from any of the three main governments involved, so additional funds had to be raised from lenders and shareholders to keep the business afloat during the pandemic. Revenue fell by 75.3% during the year, but significant 41.7% savings were made in operating costs as services were sharply reduced. The

PERIOD TO	31/03/2021	31/03/2020
	£000	£000
Turnover	254,469	1,028,779
Operating Costs	(546,100)	(936,440)
Operating Profit before grant/premium	(291,631)	92,339
Net subsidy/premium	0	0
Operating Profit	(291,631)	92,339
Margin	(114.6%)	9.0%
COST HIGHLIGHTS		
Track Access and Tunnel Charges*	181,650	368,775
Staff	75,600	113,417
Other (incl rolling stock)	288,850	454,248

* from annual accounts (apportioned)

result was a huge £292 million loss. The plans announced during 2020 to merge Eurostar and Thalys (operator of trains between Paris, Brussels and destinations in Holland and Germany) were approved and a new holding company was launched in May 2022.

HEATHROW EXPRESS/ CONNECT

The ORR figures provide an insight into the economics of the premium-priced Heathrow Express operation. This was not available in past years as they were originally integrated with the finances of BAA, later Heathrow Airport Limited (HAL). Since December 2019, the operation has been contracted to FirstGroup's Great Western company, though HAL retains control of branding and takes revenue risk. The Heathrow Connect stopping service between Paddington and Heathrow became part of the TfL Rail operation in May 2018 in anticipation of the opening of the Elizabeth Line. In 2020-21, the railway suffered a 95% drop in revenue as airport traffic plummeted. Costs were reduced, yielding savings of 21.5%. No financial assistance was available from DfT, so the £40.5 million losses were borne by Heathrow Airport.

PERIOD TO	31/03/2021	31/03/2020
	£000	£000
Turnover	5,253	110,383
Operating Costs	(45,792)	(58,330)
Operating Profit before grant/premium	(40,539)	52,054
Net subsidy/premium	0	0
Operating Profit	(40,539)	52,054
Margin	(771.7%)	47.2%
COST HIGHLIGHTS		
Rolling stock	9,502	10,924
Staff	2,398	10,171
Other (incl track access)	33,892	37,234

Now in the public sector: TfW's No 150255 calls at Ninian Park on 24 March 2022 with the 17.36 Cardiff Central to Radyr via the City line. **PHILIP SHERRATT**

Train operator owning groups

ARRIVA

Arriva is the division of the German state rail group Deutsche Bahn (DB) responsible for regional passenger transport outside Germany. UK Trains operating profit (EBITDA adjusted) in 2021 was €34 million (2020: €38 million). DB had previously stated its intention to divest its Arriva subsidiary, but it appears the UK Trains division will now remain part of its core business for the foreseeable future.

Arriva operates four UK rail contracts: the Arriva Rail London concession was launched in 2016; the CrossCountry franchise was won prior to 2010; and Arriva has run Chiltern Railways since acquiring its parent Laing Rail in 2008. Open access train company Grand Central was acquired in 2011. Arriva operated the Northern franchise until March 2020, when it transferred to the Department for Transport's Operator of Last Resort.

The company was a bidder for the East Midlands franchise before being disqualified in April 2019; it initially brought a legal challenge against this decision but settled out of court just before the trial began.

The train maintenance, overhaul and servicing company Arriva TrainCare (formerly LNWR) is based in Crewe, with other locations at Bristol, Eastleigh, Cambridge and Tyne Yard.
MD, Arriva UK Trains: David Brown

FIRSTGROUP

FirstGroup holds four UK passengers contracts and runs open access operations Hull Trains and Lumo.

In August 2019 the company (in a joint venture with Trenitalia) was awarded the West Coast Partnership franchise, running from December 2019, which is planned to include initial operation of high-speed services when HS2 opens. The South Western Railway franchise (in

a joint venture with MTR) began in September 2017. The TransPennine Express franchise launched in April 2016, having previously been operated in a joint venture with Keolis. The company has operated Great Western Railway under a series of direct award agreements.

The new Lumo open access service between London and Edinburgh launched in October 2021. Hull Trains has an open access agreement running until 2032. First also operates London Trams on behalf of Transport for London.

FirstGroup's other major focus is the UK bus market. Revenue in FirstGroup's rail division was £3,881.4 million in 2021-22 (2020-21: £3,619 million). Adjusted operating profit of £87.8 million (2020-21: 108.1 million) represents a margin of 2.3% (2020-21: 3.0%).
UK Rail Managing Director: Steve Montgomery

GOVIA

Govia is a joint venture partnership between British company The Go-Ahead Group and Keolis. Go-Ahead, the 65% majority partner, is a major bus operator with contracts in Singapore and Ireland as well as the UK. In August 2022 Go-Ahead accepted a joint venture takeover offer from Australian bus company Kinetic and Spanish transport company Globalvia. Keolis – in which French Railways (SNCF) is a major shareholder – operates trains, buses and metros across the world.

Govia now has only one UK rail operation, Govia Thameslink Railway, after Southeastern was transferred to the Operator of Last Resort in October 2021 following what the Department for Transport described as a 'breach of good faith' concerning an undisclosed £25 million payment. Govia had operated Southeastern since 2006. In April 2022 GTR began a National Rail Contract running for up to six years.
Go-Ahead Group Chief Executive: Christian Schreyer

GRAND UNION TRAINS

Grand Union is an open access operator founded by former Alliance Rail Managing Director Ian Yeowart with the aim of providing 'a new customer-focused standard of train service.' In December 2022 the company was awarded rights by the Office of Rail and Road to operate

Last Stagecoach UK Rail operation: a Supertram vehicle at the Cathedral stop on 27 October 2018. When the current concession ends, the intention is to transfer operation to a public sector company. **PHILIP SHERRATT**

new services between London and Carmarthen via the Great Western main line, which are due to start in 2025. It also has an application with ORR for services between London and Stirling via the West Coast main line. For the Great Western service Grand Union is working with Spain's national operator RENFE and private equity firm Serena Industrial Partners. Services on both routes would be operated by new electro-diesel trains; a previous proposal to initially using Mk 4 coaches has been abandoned as none are available within the timeframe required.

KEOLIS AMEY

Keolis, in which French Railways (SNCF) is a major shareholder, formed a joint venture with infrastructure firm Amey to successfully bid for the 15-year Operator and Development Partner (ODP) contract for the new Wales and Borders franchise, which began in October 2018. However, in October 2020 the Welsh Government announced that day-to-day operations would transfer in-house to an agency of Transport for Wales in February 2021. Amey remains a partner of TfW as infrastructure manager leading on the Core Valley Lines upgrade.

The same partnership of Keolis and Amey operates the Metrolink light rail network in Manchester under a concession arrangement with Transport for Greater

Manchester and the Docklands Light Railway under a Transport for London concession, while Keolis is a partner in the consortium which operates the Nottingham Express Transit light rail system.

Keolis UK Chief Executive: Alistair Gordon

MITSUI

Mitsui is a Japanese company which operates across a range of sectors, including machinery and infrastructure. In March 2017 Mitsui completed the acquisition of a 40% stake in the Greater Anglia franchise. It also holds a 15% stake in the West Midlands franchise; upon its launch in December 2017 Abellio (now Transport UK Group) held a 70.1% stake, with Japanese railway company JR East and Mitsui sharing the remaining stake equally, but JR East has divested its share so the balance is now 85% Transport UK Group and 15% Mitsui.

MTR

The MTR Corporation was established in 1975 as the Mass Transit Railway Corporation with a mission to construct and operate an urban metro system to help meet Hong Kong's public transport requirements. MTR has an average weekday patronage of about 5.6 million passengers.

In the UK, MTR's first involvement in rail operations was as a partner with Arriva subsidiary Laing in London Overground Rail Operations Ltd (LOROL), which ran the London Overground concession from 2007 until November 2016. In May 2015 the company began operating TfL Rail services as part of its concession to operate Elizabeth Line services, with the operating company now named MTR Elizabeth line; this concession was initially let to 2023 but has been extended to May 2025.

MTR joined with FirstGroup in a successful bid for the South Western franchise, which commenced operation in August 2017, MTR holding a 30% stake in the venture. However, it was unsuccessful as lead partner in a bid for the West Coast Partnership franchise, losing out to FirstGroup and Trenitalia.

Chief Executive Officer, MTR UK: Steve Murphy

OLR HOLDINGS

DfT OLR Holdings Ltd (DOHL) is the Department for Transport subsidiary which provides an operator of last resort function, maintaining continuity of passenger rail services if

a passenger rail franchise terminates and is not immediately replaced, fulfilling the Secretary of State's requirements under the Railways Act.

Following the termination of the Virgin Trains East Coast franchise in June 2018, DOHL took over the East Coast franchise through wholly owned subsidiary London North Eastern Railway (LNER). A new three-year deal began in June 2020, with the option of a further two-year extension.

OLR added Northern to its portfolio in March 2020 following the early termination of the Arriva Rail North franchise due to financial difficulties.

A third operation joined the OLR portfolio in October 2021 when DfT opted not to issue a new contract to Govia for the Southeastern franchise following an issue with an undeclared £25 million payment.

The Welsh and Scottish Governments have separate Operator of Last Resort arrangements, through which the Transport for Wales and ScotRail operations were taken over in 2021 and 2022 respectively.

Chair, DfT OLR Holdings Limited: Richard George

SERCO

Serco is a 'business to government' company with transport as one of its five specialist sectors. Since March 2015 it has operated the Caledonian Sleeper franchise under a 15-year contract to the Scottish Government; however in October 2022 it was announced that the contract would terminate early in June 2023 after the Scottish Government declined to accept a rebasing proposal from Serco. Serco also holds a 50% share alongside Transport UK Group in Merseyrail, a 25-year concession running to 2028. Serco Rail Technical Services offers services including vehicle testing and condition monitoring.

STAGECOACH AND VIRGIN

Stagecoach Group operates across three main divisions – UK Bus (regional operations), UK Bus (London) and UK Rail, having sold its North American division. In April 2022 a company managed by DWS Infrastructure assumed control of Stagecoach Group.

The only remaining business within the UK Rail division is now the Supertram light rail network in Sheffield, which Stagecoach operates in a concession running to 2024. Local politicians have agreed that when the concession expires it will not be retendered and operation will transfer to a public sector company.

Stagecoach was previously a major player in the UK rail scene, but its involvement ended after the conclusion of the Virgin Trains franchise in December 2019, in which it held a 49% stake. The East Midlands Trains franchise had concluded in August 2019.

Stagecoach Group Chief Executive: Martin Griffiths

TRENITALIA

Trenitalia is the primary train operator in Italy and is owned by Ferrovie dello Stato Italiane, itself owned by the Italian Government. The company entered the UK rail market in February 2017 when it acquired the c2c franchise from National Express for a total consideration of £72.6 million. The franchise had been awarded to National Express starting from November 2014 for a 15-year term.

Trenitalia holds a 30% stake in the joint venture with FirstGroup which took over the West Coast franchise in December 2019. The companies originally formed a similar venture for the East Midlands franchise but subsequently withdrew from the competition, while Trenitalia was also shortlisted for the South Eastern franchise but again withdrew; in the event that competition was cancelled anyway.

MD, Trenitalia UK: Ernesto Sicilia

TRANSPORT UK GROUP

Transport UK Group Ltd was set to acquire what was Abellio's UK portfolio in autumn 2022 through a management buyout led by then Abellio UK Managing Director Dominic Booth. Abellio was a subsidiary of Dutch national passenger operator NS, but NS opted to divest its UK portfolio.

The transferring portfolio comprises Greater Anglia (operated in a 60/40 joint venture with Mitsui), West Midlands Trains (in an 85/15 joint venture with Mitsui), East Midlands Railway (wholly owned) and a 50/50 joint venture with Serco for the 25-year Merseyrail concession running to 2028. Greater Anglia and West Midlands Trains both transitioned to National Rail Contracts in September 2021, each running for up to five years, with EMR following in October 2022 in a deal which could run until 2030.

Abellio operated the ScotRail franchise from April 2015 until March 2022, when it transferred to the Scottish Government's Operator of Last Resort.

MD, Transport UK Group: Dominic Booth

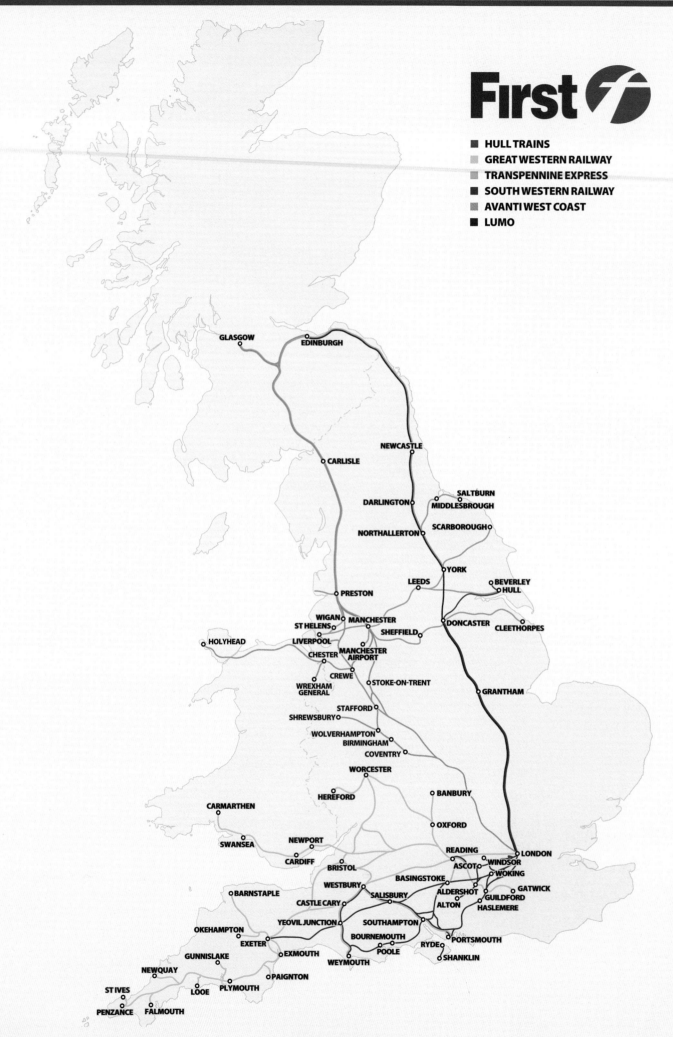

First 7

- HULL TRAINS
- GREAT WESTERN RAILWAY
- TRANSPENNINE EXPRESS
- SOUTH WESTERN RAILWAY
- AVANTI WEST COAST
- LUMO

AVANTI WEST COAST

West Coast Partnership – ERMA contract to March 2023

Avanti West Coast, a joint venture of FirstGroup (70% majority partner) and Trenitalia, became the new operator of the West Coast Partnership franchise on 8 December 2019, taking over from Virgin Trains.

At its launch the Department for Transport explained that the contract would be in two phases, although with ongoing uncertainty over HS2 the exact date for the switch between the phases remains unclear. The initial timescale showed the joint venture operating Inter-city West Coast services until March 2026, before the second phase, running to March 2031, would see First Trenitalia operating HS2 services alongside reshaped conventional services on the West Coast main line. DfT had the option to extend the first phase, which should also see Avanti acting as shadow operator for HS2, providing a range of design, development and mobilisation services, for up to five years. The second phase had the option of an extension period of up to three years.

Following the impact of the coronavirus pandemic the West Coast Partnership franchise was moved onto an Emergency Recovery Measures Agreement which was set to last until 16 October 2022, after which DfT was expected to agree a direct award contract with Avanti that would run for up to 10 years. However, following operational challenges through the summer of 2022 DfT opted to extend the ERMA to 1 April 2023 whilst demanding

WEST COAST PARTNERSHIP DEVELOPMENT

Under the original contract awarded prior to the pandemic First Trenitalia was set to be a key partner to HS2 Limited, the Department for Transport and other stakeholders to develop world-class high-speed services and maximise the benefits of the new high-speed line.

The West Coast Partnership will be a 'shadow operator' for the design and development of the new HS2 services. Work will include advising on the design of the new trains and developing options for a new fares system for HS2 services with tickets that are integrated with the wider rail ticket system. It has been tasked with developing a 'passenger-focused timetable' making best use of the capacity and speed of the new infrastructure and deliver the smooth launch of the HS2 services along with the redesigned Inter-city West Coast services that will run after HS2 is launched. It will also advise on setting up the future structure for the next contract after the initial five years of HS2 operation.

significant improvements before a longer-term contract could be agreed.

At present Avanti is operating services from London Euston to Glasgow, Liverpool, Manchester and Birmingham with the existing fleet of 35 11-car and 21 nine-car Class 390 Pendolino electric tilting trains, and 18 five-car Class 221 diesel Super Voyager units.

In July 2021 work began on the £117 million project to refurbish and transform the Pendolino fleet. Work includes fitting new Standard Class seats, with leather headrests in Standard Premium and First; conversion of one First Class carriage on each of the 35 11-car Pendolinos to provide more than 2,000 extra Standard Class seats; the introduction of a new café-bar; improved lighting and new interior carpets; greater use of technology with customer-friendly passenger information screens; additional luggage space; power points at every seat; and refurbished toilets. The changes to the seating mean a refurbished 11-car Pendolino has 607 seats: 508 Standard Class, up from 444 (an increase of 9.6%), with the remaining 99 split across First and Standard Premium. The first refurbished set, No 390125, returned to service on 25 April 2022 and by the end of the year around one-third of the fleet had been completed.

Standard Premium is the new additional class of travel introduced by Avanti in May 2021; available on all its Pendolino services, it sits between Standard and First Class and offers passengers better seats, greater space and a guaranteed table. They will also have the option to purchase refreshments via Avanti's new 'At-Seat Order' feature, where items are delivered to them without moving from their seat. An enhanced First Class offering with improved catering and more bespoke customer service was introduced in 2021 and is now available seven days a week.

In June 2022, two of Avanti's Class 221 Super Voyagers, Nos 221142/143, went off lease ahead of the programme to replace them all with 13 five-car bi-mode

SENIOR PERSONNEL
AVANTI WEST COAST

Managing Director vacant

Executive Director, Commercial Sarah Copley

Executive Director, Customer Experience, Onboard Philippa Cresswell

Executive Director, HR Helen Diksa

Executive Director, Finance Craig Forster

Executive Director, Customer Experience, Stations Clare Kingswood

Executive Director, Operations Barry Milsom

Executive Director, Partnerships and Strategy Richard Scott

Executive Director, Technology Rob Tyler

Executive Director, Projects Michael Weston

WEST COAST PARTNERSHIP DEVELOPMENT

Managing Director Shamit Gaiger

Train Services Director Russell Evans

Customer Experience Director Joost Noordewier

Finance & Contracts Director Gary Miller

PMO Director Eileen Abbess

Rolling Stock Director Adriano Scapati

Business Design & Organisation Director Sue Whaley

Pendolinos still going strong: Avanti West Coast's No 390128 heads south through Winwick Junction with the 08.36 Glasgow Central to London Euston on 5 July 2022. **TONY MILES**

Class 805 units and 10 seven-car electric Class 807 sets which are being assembled at Hitachi's Newton Aycliffe facility in the North East. Funded by Rock Rail and ASI in a £350 million deal, the '807s' will operate between London Euston, the West Midlands and Liverpool Lime Street, while the '805s' will run from Euston to North Wales. The first '805' began dynamic testing in late 2022 with acceptance expected in June 2023 ahead of staff training and introduction into passenger service.

Following a significant reduction in services through the pandemic, services were stepped up in September 2021. However in the summer of 2022 shortages of drivers and other crew members, along with the impact of the disputes with all the trade unions, forced Avanti to reduce services significantly, running as few as four trains per hour from Euston instead of the planned seven services an hour. With a recruitment plan for an additional 100 drivers in place, DfT agreed a service improvement plan with Avanti that included a commitment to increase services as these new drivers became available and to continue to deliver on its traincrew recruitment plans to reduce reliance on rest day working. An improved timetable from December 2022 was planned to no longer rely on any rest day working, an industry first. Avanti launched a campaign to help recruit 40 new train drivers at locations throughout the UK in early 2022; the initiative aims to encourage more people, especially women, to consider the role as a realistic career to pursue. ■

KEY STATISTICS
AVANTI WEST COAST

	2020-21	2021-22
Punctuality (on time)	61.8%	53.0%
Cancellations	2.0%	3.9%
Passenger journeys (millions)	6.2	21.6
Passenger kilometres (millions)	1,155	4,226
Passenger train kilometres (millions)	25.6	25.7
Route kilometres operated	1,310.0	1,310.0
Number of stations managed	16	16
Number of employees	3,326	3,278

GWR

National Rail Contract to 2025

FirstGroup runs the Greater Western franchise, which was rebranded from First Great Western to Great Western Railway (GWR) in 2015. A series of short-term contracts followed, and in March 2020 it was confirmed that a further direct award contract to 31 March 2023 had been agreed, with an option to extend this to by another year at the Department for Transport's discretion. On 30 March 2020 Covid-19 saw the company move to a six-month Emergency Measures Agreement with DfT, and this was subsequently extended several times to June 2022, when GWR was awarded a National Rail Contract to continue operating the Great Western network. This runs to 21 June 2025, with the potential for a further three years at the Secretary of State's discretion.

GWR has completed the introduction 36 Class 800/0 five-car and 21 nine-car Class 800/3 bi-mode Hitachi Intercity Express trains (IETs) procured by the DfT; these are supplemented by 22x5-car and 14x9-car Class 802 bi-mode sets procured by GWR, primarily for operation between London Paddington and the South West. The '802s' are designed for use over the more demanding terrain into Devon and Cornwall, with higher power available when working in diesel mode. Problems with cracking detected on several vehicles saw a number of sets taken out of service in May 2021 before a programme to return many of them to service was approved. A long-term programme of repair is being developed with manufacturer Hitachi.

GWR has retained 35 Class 43 HST power cars along with 63 modified and refurbished Mk 3 coaches, which are formed into 14 2+4 Class 255 sets branded 'Castle Class' trains. These sets work the longer-distance services in the West Country; however, with costly overhauls required shortly these are all planned to be withdrawn by December 2023, with IETs and DMUs covering for them instead.

Class 387 EMUs have taken over most local services out of Paddington, with the majority of services onto branch lines in the Thames Valley provided by diesel-powered shuttles from main line stations. In July 2021 GWR operated a 12-car Class 387 formation through the Severn Tunnel to Cardiff and these trains are now being used to provide extra capacity for major events at the Principality Stadium and other venues in the city.

Testing of the Class 769 tri-mode units has continued with the 19 sets, which will be able to work on overhead and third rail power as well as under their own diesel power, to be used on services between Reading and Basingstoke, Reading, Redhill and Gatwick, and on the Henley and Bourne End lines; reliability issues have delayed entry into service but further testing and improvement work should see them enter service shortly.

GWR is also expected to bring forward proposals for the replacement

Taking Pride: GWR's IET No 800008, with rainbow flashes, passes Hanwell on 31 October 2022 with the 14.28 Paddington to Cheltenham Spa. **PHILIP SHERRATT**

SENIOR PERSONNEL
GREAT WESTERN RAILWAY

Managing Director Mark Hopwood (in photo)
Customer Service & Operations Director Richard Rowland
Interim Commercial Director Lee Edworthy
Engineering Director Simon Green
Business Assurance Director Joe Graham
Human Resources Director Ruth Busby

of its Class 150 and 158 DMUs, and to look at options to replace the current overnight fleet of sleeping cars and, in particular, the locomotives used to work the trains. Work to refurbish London – Penzance 'Night Riviera' sleeper vehicles was completed in mid-2018; the sleeper trains feature a redesigned lounge bar, and each service has one accessible cabin and an accessible toilet next to each other.

GWR signed a deal with Vivarail to trial new battery-charging technology on its network; supported by Network Rail, the trial was planned to take place on the 2.5-mile Greenford branch and test Vivarail's trackside fast charging equipment in an operational setting for the first time, although Vivarail went into receivership in December 2022. No 230001, converted from an ex-London Underground 'D' stock set, has a claimed range of up to 62 miles on battery power,

with off-network tests indicating the fast charge system can recharge the batteries in only 10 minutes. The trial was being supported by £2.15 million in funding from DfT's Rail Network Enhancement Pipeline, while Innovate UK helped fund development of the fast charge technology.

The Dartmoor line from Exeter to Okehampton, which reopened in November 2021, has seen passenger numbers exceeding expectations, with more than 250,000 journeys made in the first year after services returned to the restored line. From May 2022 service frequency was doubled to hourly.

Platform improvements at St Ives have been delivered in order to handle the large numbers of visitors to the town who choose to travel there by rail from the large car park at St Erth, whilst three new stations are due to open shortly on the GWR

network: Marsh Barton, Portway Parkway and Reading Green Park.

In August 2022 GWR launched a new pay-as-you-go smartcard on routes radiating from Bristol, which rolls payments and tickets into one and ensures customers get the best value on the day of travel. Responding to the change in customer travel habits, GWR launched a new Long Weekender ticket in September 2022,

which offers savings of more than 60% to leisure travellers. With Sundays having become particularly busy, GWR has sought to free up services on that day so customers using the Long Weekender will depart at any time on a Friday or Saturday and return at any time on a Monday. The offer is initially being trialled on routes from London Paddington to the wider Bristol area and South Wales. ■

KEY STATISTICS
GREAT WESTERN RAILWAY

	2020-21	2021-22
Punctuality (on time)	80.3%	70.8%
Cancellations	1.5%	3.0%
Passenger journeys (millions)	17.9	55.1
Passenger kilometres (millions)	1,106	3,804
Passenger train kilometres (millions)	35.9	42.4
Route kilometres operated	1,997.2	1,997.2
Number of stations managed	194	194
Number of employees	6,408	6,230

South Western Railway

National Rail Contract to May 2023

FirstGroup and MTR began operating the new South Western franchise as South Western Railway (SWR) on 20 August 2017. The 70:30 joint venture was due to hold the franchise for seven years, to 18 August 2024, with an extension option of up to 11 months. Following the impact of the coronavirus pandemic the SWR franchise was placed on an Emergency Measures Agreement and then an Emergency Recovery Measures Agreement, before agreement was reached for a move to a two-year National Rail Contract; this runs until 30 May 2023 with an optional extension of two years.

SWR provides commuter services from London Waterloo to south west London, suburban and regional services in the counties of Surrey, Hampshire and Wiltshire as well as regional services in Devon, Somerset, Berkshire and Wiltshire. Its subsidiary Island Line operates services on the Isle of Wight. SWR manages 184 stations; after carrying 203.7 million passengers in 2019-20, the pandemic prompted a fall to just 45.7 million passengers in 2020-21 before recovering to 108.5 million in 2021-22. Since May 2022, overall passenger numbers have stabilised at around 69% of pre-pandemic levels, with peak travel at around 53%. In December 2021 SWR ceased running between Salisbury and Bristol Temple Meads.

SWR's December 2022 timetable features reductions in high peak and off-peak services into London Waterloo compared to pre-Covid levels; however, the company says the revised timetable 'provides sufficient capacity to cover current and forecast demand, while making a series of changes to improve customer journeys'. The company suggests the timetable broadly maintains current service levels across the network while delivering a more consistent and efficient service for customers, based on close scrutiny of current travel patterns. SWR adds that it will continue to monitor changes in customer flows to adapt with agility where funding can be secured.

SWR continues to deliver improvements under the National Rail Contract including the introduction of new trains, pioneering next-generation on-board 5G Wi-Fi from evo-rail, investment in stations and depots and further steps to improve the accessibility of the railway. SWR also continues to deliver its enhanced apprenticeship programme, being the only organisation in the world to have been awarded all three types of accreditation that

SENIOR PERSONNEL
SOUTH WESTERN RAILWAY

Managing Director Claire Mann (in photo)
Chief Operating Officer Stuart Meek
Safety & Security Director Jane Lupson
Engineering & Infrastructure Director Neil Drury
Projects & Change Director Alex Foulds
Finance & Strategy Director Jonathan Roberts
Commercial, Customer & Community Director Peter Williams
Performance & Planning Director Steve Tyler
Service Delivery Director (interim) Christian Neill
Train Service Director (interim) Andy Penrose
People & Culture Director Sharon Johnston

KEY STATISTICS
SOUTH WESTERN RAILWAY

	2020-21	2021-22
Punctuality (on time)	82.0%	74.4%
Cancellations	1.9%	2.8%
Passenger journeys (millions)	45.7	108.5
Passenger kilometres (millions)	1,111	3,058
Passenger train kilometres (millions)	28.4	32.9
Route kilometres operated	997.8	998.0
Number of stations managed	187	187
Number of employees	5,643	5,265

Refurbishment and replacement beckon: SWR services pass at Mortlake on 20 December 2021. At left Nos 458503/530 form the 10.50 Waterloo to Reading, as Nos 455859/735 work the 10.23 Windsor & Eton Riverside to Waterloo. The '458s' are due to be refurbished and reconfigured for longer-distance services, but the '455s' will be withdrawn as new Class 701 EMUs are introduced. **KEN BRUNT**

Investors in People offer: people, wellbeing and apprenticeships.

Introduction of the new Alstom Aventra Class 701 'Arterio' EMUs has been impacted by Covid and delays in Alstom's production lines. Drivers' union ASLEF declared the cabs not fit for purpose on a number of counts and remedial work has been required to part of the fleet. SWR has worked through a number of challenges and software updates to help Alstom deliver a fleet of trains that performs consistently and that the operator is confident to bring into passenger service. In order to make sure the effect on current services was minimalised, SWR has been sub-leasing 12 of the 30 Class 707 trains it has released back from Southeastern to provide additional capacity. SWR has an extensive programme of testing, training, safety validation and mobilisation in place to ensure the Class 701s are ready to deliver safe, comfortable and reliable services; the fleet will be introduced as early as possible in 2023.

The refurbishment programme for 28 Class 458 EMUs has now begun and is due to continue throughout 2023. With work being carried out at its Widnes facility, Alstom plans to revamp the passenger saloons to meet the needs of long-distance passengers, reforming the sets back to four-car formations and reconfiguring the units to operate at a top speed of 100mph. The lease period for the sets has been extended to 2027 to allow SWR to make full use of the refurbished units.

The £26 million investment plan agreed with DfT for the 13.7km Island Line, linking Ryde to Shanklin, saw an upgrade to power supplies and platforms and track improvement work, which includes a new passing loop at Brading. This was complemented by the replacement of the fleet of Class 483 EMUs dating from 1938 with five Class 484 two-car EMUs from Vivarail. Slower than expected progress with the infrastructure work and technical problems with the Class 484 sets saw reopening of the line, which closed for the upgrade on 4 January 2021, delayed until 1 November 2021. The section of the Island Line between Ryde Esplanade and Ryde Pier Head closed from 30 October 2022 until spring 2023 to allow Network Rail to carry out a complex programme of vital maintenance and improvements on Ryde Pier; work to strengthen the pier should extend its life by up to 60 years. ∎

Nova 2: TPE's No 397010 arrives at Wigan North Western with the 16.12 Liverpool Lime Street to Glasgow Central on 27 August 222. **PHILIP SHERRATT**

National Rail Contract to 2023

Awarded to FirstGroup, the TransPennine Express (TPE) franchise was due to run from 1 April 2016 for seven years, with a possible two-year extension. Delivery is co-managed by the Department for Transport and the Rail North Partnership, which brings together representatives from 29 local transport authorities. Following the impact of the coronavirus pandemic TPE was moved onto an Emergency Recovery Measures Agreement, and in May 2021 a new two-year National Rail Contract (NRC), which runs until 30 May 2023 with an optional extension of up to two years, was agreed with the DfT.

The Department has since indicated that it proposes to agree a direct award National Rail Contract with FirstGroup for the continued operation of TransPennine Express rail services covering up to eight years, with the first four of those fixed and the following four flexible and based on the Secretary of State for transport's discretion. Key features of this direct award will be an obligation to support delivery of the Transpennine Route Upgrade (TRU) programme and to comply with, support, stand behind and drive the delivery of both rail services and workforce reform. The TRU element was a key factor in deciding the length of the contract as DfT wanted 'stewardship and service continuity' during this complex project.

Around 75% of the company's revenue has come from leisure passengers, with 15% derived from regular commuters and 10% from business travellers; TPE carried 28.6 million passengers in 2019-20, but the impact of Covid-19 saw this fall to just 5.4 million in 2020-21 before recovering to 16.2 million in 2021-22.

TPE focuses on running inter-city services in the North of England and between Manchester and Scotland, having agreed to deliver investment of more than £500 million in order to transform services, with new and refurbished trains supporting a series of timetable improvements which were due to see a 55% increase in the number of services connecting the largest cities in the North of England and Scotland.

The May 2018 timetable change saw Manchester – Leeds local trains transferred to TPE from Northern and changes to the routing of services from the North East to Manchester Airport via Manchester Victoria station and over the Ordsall Chord. Congestion on several parts of the network saw punctuality fall significantly, and from December 2019 a number of changes were made to TPE's timetables. Positive changes included the introduction of a new service between Liverpool and Glasgow via the West Coast main line, the extension of Liverpool to Newcastle services onwards to Edinburgh and the extension of Manchester Airport to Middlesbrough services to Redcar Central. Problems with crew training and availability, connected to the delayed introduction of the new train fleets, saw some of these timetable improvements deferred into early 2020; however, the pandemic meant many of the changes were not fully implemented before services were cut back in line with other operators.

Continuing problems with crew availability have seen a high level of cancellations during 2022, with a number of trains removed from the timetable or only running for part of the route in order to provide a more reliable service. This has included the Liverpool to Edinburgh service via the East Coast main line being cut back to Newcastle and a separate Newcastle to Edinburgh service introduced from December 2021; in May 2022 these trains began to call at the newly opened station at Reston in Berwickshire.

SENIOR PERSONNEL
TRANSPENNINE EXPRESS

Managing Director Matthew Golton (in photo)
Finance Director Carolann James
Commercial Director Darren Higgins
Fleet, Safety & Service Delivery Director Paul Staples
Major Projects Director Chris Nutton
Operations Director Paul Watson
Customer Service & Operations Director Kathryn O'Brien
Service Planning & Performance Director Jerry Farquharson
Strategy Director Louise Ebbs
HR Director Nicola Buckley
Business Development Director George Thomas
Business Assurance Director Fran Barrett

As passenger numbers have returned TPE has retained some of the service pattern changes introduced during the pandemic. On its North Pennine route of the parts of the Manchester Airport – Newcastle timetable have been combined with the Liverpool Lime Street – Newcastle – Edinburgh service, permanently reducing the number of trains running over the congested Ordsall Chord, albeit with most Class 185 workings using pairs of units to retain capacity.

Most Liverpool – Scarborough services have also been reduced to a shuttle service between York and Scarborough. December 2022 was set to see a further raft of changes, with Manchester to Hull services extended to Liverpool via Manchester Victoria and the Manchester Airport to Cleethorpes service re-routed to start at Liverpool and running via the Cheshire Lines Committee route through Warrington to Manchester Piccadilly; this service allows Northern to reduce its services over the CLC route at the same time. Some of the Cleethorpes trains are worked by the Nova 3 Mk 5a and Class 68 sets, whilst some services on the West Coast main line to Scotland continue to be worked by Nova 1 Class 802 bi-mode units alongside the more usual Class 397 EMUs.

All 51 Class 185 three-car DMUs have been fully refurbished; at least 36 of the units are due to remain

KEY STATISTICS
TRANSPENNINE EXPRESS

	2020-21	2021-22
Punctuality (on time)	70.8%	62.9%
Cancellations	2.2%	3.0%
Passenger journeys (millions)	5.4	16.2
Passenger kilometres (millions)	398	1,186
Passenger train kilometres (millions)	13.4	15.7
Route kilometres operated	1,252.9	1,252.9
Number of stations managed	19	19
Number of employees	1,428	1,570

with the business, although this number could increase in the light of changed passenger demand and possible alterations to the services the company operates.

In October 2022 TPE welcomed its first qualified female driver at Liverpool Lime Street depot, whilst earlier in the year it won the Social Inclusion award at the annual Women in Rail Awards. ■

Open access agreement until 2032

Open access operator Hull Trains launched in September 2000 when three daily return services operated between Hull and London Kin'gs Cross. Progressive increases in service frequency have seen it run up to 92 direct services a week from Hull and the Humber region direct to the capital, with two of its five services a day in each direction extended to serve Beverley.

Improvements in the company's train fleet culminated in the introduction in December 2019 of the first of a fleet of five Class 802 bi-mode 'Paragon' trains in a £60 million investment that has provided additional capacity for services whilst helping reduce Hull Trains' carbon footprint by approximately 60%. The company obtained approval in 2019 for a further 10-year open access agreement which runs until 2029, subsequently extended by a further three years to 2032.

KEY STATISTICS
HULL TRAINS

	2020-21	2021-22
Punctuality (on time)	56.5%	60.1%
Cancellations	2.9%	2.1%
Passenger journeys (millions)	0.1	0.8
Passenger kilometres (millions)	15	177
Passenger train kilometres (millions)	0.3	1.3
Route kilometres operated	344.4	344.4
Number of employees	98	101

The company's 21st birthday was celebrated on 8 October 2021, when a Paragon unit was unveiled in a new commemorative livery at Hull Paragon station. At the time Hull Trains reported that from its first year,

when it carried just 80,000 passengers, to the time it was forced to suspend services due to Covid-19, it was carrying over one million passengers a year.

The lengthy disruption caused by the pandemic saw services suspended several times, with the company ending 2021 running a reduced timetable as customer demand changed due to Covid-19 and concerns over a possible future lockdown; sadly this was just two weeks after the business had introduced its 94th weekly service, the highest service level ever offered in the company's history. In the year 2020-21 Hull Trains saw around 0.1 million passenger journeys, equating to 7.4% of journeys made in 2019-20. The full timetable was reintroduced in stages during 2022.

Hull Trains has consistently ranked among the top performing operators in the UK according to customers, with a recent National Rail Passenger Survey scoring it above the industry average for passenger satisfaction. The company says its customer-focused ethos, building a strong relationship with its customers, has been key to its success, consistently demonstrating values which has seen it ranked highly among customers and winning awards along the way.

Hull Trains has a strong local identity, and in 2022 a public vote on the name of one its 'Paragon' train fleet led to a train being named *Jean Bishop (The Bee Lady)* after a Hull local who spent 30 years fundraising in her hometown, raising more than £125,000 for charity dressed as a bee. The other fourv trains in the Paragon fleet are named *Amy Johnson*, *William Wilberforce*, *The Humber Bridge* and *The Land of Green Ginger*, the latter named after a famous street. ∎

Electric blue: Lumo's No 803005 passes Newark Northgate with the 14.49 Edinburgh to King's Cross on 23 April 2022. **PHILIP SHERRATT**

lumo

New open access service from October 2021

The new open access service over the East Coast main line between Edinburgh and London King's Cross branded 'Lumo' began operating on 25 October 2021. Operated by FirstGroup under an initial 10-year contract, the operator is allowed to run five services a day in each direction, with all trains calling at Morpeth and Newcastle and a small number calling additionally at Stevenage. In November 2022 Lumo carried its millionth passenger, having run over 2,500 services, as data showed rail has overtaken air travel to become the preferred mode of transport between Edinburgh and London.

Lumo uses a new fleet of 5x5-car Class 803 sets manufactured by Hitachi, which offer single class accommodation and operate in electric mode only. Financed by Beacon Rail in a £100 million order which includes maintenance, the trains are fitted with a battery which can maintain on-board 'hotel' power if the 25kV overhead supply fails. FirstGroup says the trains 'are ergonomically designed for comfort and ease, helping passengers to work or play'; the custom-designed seats have been 'ergonomically designed and tested for longer journeys', with an adjustable tray table, privacy wings and personal lighting.

The fare strategy for Lumo mimics that of the airline industry, a market FirstGroup is keen to challenge, with advance tickets available well ahead of the traditional 12-week timeframe. With long-distance coach travellers also targeted by the new service, Lumo's average ticket price is £37, whilst business travellers taking the first service of the day from London can arrive in Edinburgh by 10.00, more than one hour earlier than was previously possible.

As part of the marketing drive, emphasis is being placed on the environmental credentials of rail travel, with FirstGroup emphasising that the train will be 'at least six times greener than flying'. Lumo estimates it could have saved the equivalent CO_2 emissions of 21,000 homes' electricity use for an entire year by virtue of its passengers choosing its 100% electric trains rather than flying. ∎

Paragon: Hull Trains unit No 802304 crosses Retford viaduct with the 09.48 King's Cross to Hull on 12 February 2022. **JOHN WHITEHOUSE**

SENIOR PERSONNEL
HULL TRAINS AND LUMO

In September 2022 FirstGroup announced that Hull Trains and Lumo would operate under a single Managing Director with many head office functions combined.

Managing Director Martijn Gilbert (in photo)
Commercial & Revenue Director (First Rail) Stuart Jones
Head of Commercial Development (Hull Trains) Tom McFall

Batteries included: Stadler's No 777140 for Merseyrail on display at the InnoTrans trade fair in Berlin in September 2022. **KEITH FENDER**

KEY STATISTICS
MERSEYRAIL

	2020-21	2021-22
Punctuality (on time)	85.3%	78.8%
Cancellations	1.2%	1.1%
Passenger journeys (millions)	9.0	21.0
Passenger kilometres (millions)	165	382
Passenger train kilometres (millions)	4.3	5.4
Route kilometres operated	120.7	120.7
Number of stations managed	66	66
Number of employees	1,129	1,149

 Merseyrail

25-year concession to 2028

The 25-year contract to run the Merseyrail Electrics network, with a total value of £3.6 billion, was awarded in 2003 to a Serco and Abellio joint venture, subject to five-yearly reviews. Merseytravel, the transport executive body of Liverpool City Region Combined Authority (CA), manages the unique operating concession for this self-contained 750V DC third rail electrified railway.

Liverpool City Region provides funding to Merseyrail Electrics through a devolved special rail grant from the Department for Transport to deliver rail services under the concession agreement. This has continued throughout the pandemic; however, these payments do not make up all of Merseyrail Electrics' income, which also comes from ticket sales and other commercial income, and this fell significantly through 2020-21 as passenger numbers dropped to nine million from over 30 million in 2019-20, before recovering to 21 million in 2021-22. The LCRCA worked alongside Merseyrail to ensure services were kept at optimum levels to match local demand and needs whilst considering the available resources and government guidelines.

Merseyrail normally operates over 600 regular services per day and serves 68 stations over its 75-mile network. It has been the most heavily-used urban railway network in the UK outside London. The Northern line links Southport, Ormskirk and Kirkby to Hunts Cross, and the Wirral line serves West Kirby, New Brighton, Chester and Ellesmere Port. A 6.5-mile central Liverpool loop line runs through a tunnel, with four

 CALEDONIAN SLEEPER

15-year contract to end early in 2023

The 15-year franchise for overnight services between London Euston and Scotland, awarded to Serco Caledonian Sleepers Limited, began operation on 31 March 2015. At its launch Serco said the franchise was expected to deliver revenue of up to £800 million over 15 years. The impact of the pandemic saw the Scottish Government move the contract onto an Emergency Measures Agreement (EMA) which, following extensions, ran until 28 February 2022. At that point,

with continued significant ongoing impact from the pandemic on sleeper services, a further Temporary Measures Agreement (TMA) was agreed until March 2023.

The contract that was signed in 2014 included a 'rebase clause' which meant that, after seven years of the 15-year franchise, Serco could present to the Scottish Government with alternative financial arrangements for the remaining years of the contract. It was announced in October 2022 that the Government and Serco had not been able to reach agreement on these revised terms, and accordingly the contract will now end in June 2023, at which point, unless other arrangements can be agreed, Serco

will hand back the management of the sleeper to the Scottish Government. It is unlikely that the Sleeper operation will be merged with ScotRail and there remains the possibility that a new management contract could still be agreed with Serco. On announcing the decision, the Scottish Government stated: 'It is worth noting that Serco Caledonian Sleepers Limited has, broadly, delivered well and significantly improved Caledonian Sleeper services over the last seven years.'

Trains run nightly except on Saturday nights on two routes from London: the Lowland Sleeper to/from Glasgow and Edinburgh; and the Highland Sleeper to/from

Aberdeen, Inverness and Fort William. In total the Caledonian Sleeper serves 48 stations overall – 43 in Scotland and five in England.

A new fleet of 75 coaches, built by CAF, was introduced from 2019; valued at approximately £150 million, the new fleet is part-funded by a £60 million grant from the Scottish Government. The vehicles offer different accommodation types including berths with an en-suite shower and WC, double, twin and single bed variants as well as reclining seats. There is also a brasserie-style Club Car.

The reservation system offers a broad range of fares to help growth in passenger numbers, and the

SENIOR PERSONNEL
CALEDONIAN SLEEPER

Managing Director Kathryn Darbandi (in photo)
Operations Director Magnus Conn
(Interim) Head of Operations Dale Williams
Head of Guest Experience Service Delivery Scott Fraser
Commercial and Procurement Director Graham Kelly
Finance Director Chris Gemmell
Head of Sales & Marketing Steven Marshall

KEY STATISTICS
CALEDONIAN SLEEPER

	2020-21	2021-22
Punctuality (on time)	74.4%	68.3%
Cancellations	3.8%	5.5%
Passenger journeys (millions)	0.1	0.2
Passenger kilometres (millions)	58	150
Passenger train kilometres (millions)	0.9	1.3
Route kilometres operated	1,470.9	1,470.9
Number of employees	184	187

underground stations in Liverpool and one in Birkenhead. Average fares are among the cheapest in the country and rises are capped at the Retail Price Index level.

The operator has modernised significantly in recent years and 180 platform smart card validators have now been installed at 66 stations across the Liverpool City Region; tap-in tap-out for passengers will be introduced in 2023. The network has also received an additional £66 million in funding from the Liverpool City Region Combined Authority Transforming Cities Fund.

City centre stations have undergone refurbishment in recent years; a new station (Maghull North) was opened on the network in June 2018 whilst the reopening of Ainsdale station the same year, following an extensive refurbishment, saw it become Merseyrail's most eco-friendly station.

In 2022 work started on a new station at Headbolt Lane, due to open in 2023, which will be reached by a 1.2km extension from the current terminus at Kirkby, whilst the new station at Liverpool Baltic could open in 2025. Lifts have been installed at other stations to make Merseyrail more accessible, with work recently undertaken at Birkenhead Park, Hillside and Hunts Cross. Full accessibility was due to be

achieved in December 2022 once work at St Michael's was completed. A Merseyrail Accessibility Forum has been launched to engage with passengers with accessibility needs and organisations that represent them.

A £460 million project to replace the legacy fleet of 59 three-car Class 507 and Class 508 trains, which date back to the 1970s, was approved by the CA in December 2016. Stadler is supplying a fleet of 53 Class 777 trains, which have been designed specifically for the Merseyrail network and feature pioneering sliding step technology which will play a part in making Merseyrail the most accessible heavy rail network in the country. They will also provide Wi-Fi connectivity and improve passenger security through on-board CCTV which will be viewable in real time at the network control centre. Merseytravel owns the trains and leases them to the operator, with the project financed through a reserve fund and loans, including from the Public Works Loan Board and European investment Bank.

The 65-metre-long four-car EMUs are three metres longer than the existing trains and able to carry 60% more passengers (486 per train), while retaining the same number of seats. Power supply, track and station upgrades are also part of the

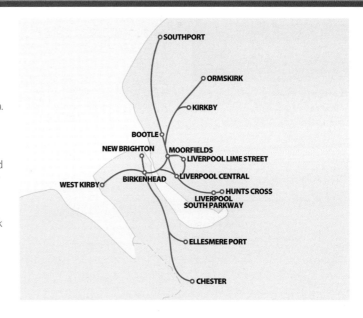

programme. The fleet is based at a new depot at Kirkdale as well as the refurbished Birkenhead North facility.

Successful trials with batteries temporarily installed on No 777002 prompted the decision to fit seven '777s' with batteries during

manufacture. Their deployment on services to Headbolt Lane will avoid the need for the extension to be electrified, and the proof of concept paves the way for the proposed Merseyrail network expansion across Liverpool City Region and beyond. ∎

SENIOR PERSONNEL
MERSEYRAIL

Managing Director Andy Heath (in photo)
People Director (Deputy MD) Jane English
Finance Director Christopher Maher
Chief Operating Officer Zoe Hands
Commercial Director Suzanne Grant

ability to book 12 months ahead has proved popular. Serco says it markets the service as a high quality hotel experience, with its fares reflecting the uplift in quality it aims to deliver.

The Covid-19 pandemic saw a reduced timetable in operation alongside the temporary closure of the Club Car and removal of the seated vehicles, the latter meaning Caledonian Sleeper trains were

unable to provide their usual daytime services on the Fort William line and from Kingussie, Aviemore and Carrbridge on the Inverness line.

Improving the sustainability of day-to-day operations has become a priority for Caledonian Sleeper; the company regularly points out that its overnight services represent a low-impact way to travel up and down the UK. It notes that waste from

trains is either recycled or recovered by depots into another operation.

Rolling stock maintenance is carried out under contract by Alstom, whilst traction and train crew are provided by GB Railfreight. GBRf has a refurbished fleet of 10 Class 92 locomotives for the main legs of the journey over the West Coast main line to Glasgow/Edinburgh, with six rebuilt Class 73/9 locomotives for non-electrified sections to Fort

William, Aberdeen and Inverness; their new R43 4000 V8 engines represent one of the most efficient diesel engines for fuel consumption on the network today. Class 66 locomotives are regularly paired with a Class 73/9 on the Inverness and Fort William portions; however, GBRf has purchased two Class 67 locomotives, Nos 67023/027, which will also be used on these services. ∎

Highland Sleeper: No 92006 heads the southbound working at Old Linslade on 16 April 2021. **KEN BRUNT**

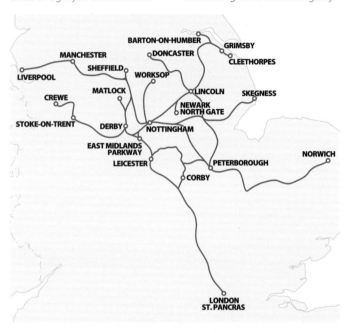

EMR

National Rail Contract to 2030

The East Midlands franchise was awarded to Abellio, a wholly-owned subsidiary of the Dutch railway company Nederlandse Spoorwegen, under an eight-year contract which began on 18 August 2019 and was due to run until 21 August 2027, with an optional extension of two years at the discretion of the Secretary of State. East Midlands Railway replaced East Midlands Trains, which had been run by Stagecoach from 11 November 2007.

Following the impact of the coronavirus pandemic the EMR franchise was moved onto Emergency Measures Agreement and Emergency Recovery Measures Agreement contracts which ran until October 2022. In early October Abellio announced it had been awarded a National Rail Contract for EMR which runs until 17 October 2026, with an option for the DfT to extend it by up to four more years to 2030 at its discretion.

EMR operates inter-city services from London St Pancras over the Midland main line to Leicester, Nottingham, Derby and Sheffield. Local and inter-regional services include trains between Liverpool and Norwich as well as services to Crewe, Matlock, Worksop, Skegness and Cleethorpes. Trains on the Barton-on-Humber branch transferred to EMR from Northern in 2021, whilst links to Nottingham have been improved through the extension of the Crewe to Derby service to the city and on to Newark along with the introduction of an hourly Sunday service to Matlock. Other improvements have been delivered across the EMR Regional network and in May 2021 the new EMR Connect service between Corby and St Pancras via Luton Airport Parkway, operated by the company's first electric fleet, the Class 360 EMUs released by Greater Anglia, began operating.

A £600 million project to replace much of the rolling stock fleet with new or refurbished trains, including 33 Hitachi bi-mode Class 810 Aurora trains and the 21 Class 360s, upgraded to 110mph operation, is underway. The plan includes the transfer of the Etches Park depot in Derby to Hitachi as the maintenance base for the new bi-mode trains. Due for introduction into service in 2023, the Class 810 EMR 'Aurora' units will be an evolution of the AT300 design supplied to other UK operators, with 24-metre vehicles rather than 26 metres and a slightly modified nose profile. Each five-car set will have four underfloor diesel generator modules rather than the three used in the Class 800s and 802s. The units will operate 'regularly' in 10-car formations, providing increased seating capacity. The air-conditioned trainsets will have Wi-Fi and at-seat charging facilities, as well as enhanced passenger information displays. In June 2022 EMR released a documentary which showcased the ongoing project to build its new Aurora fleet.

The four five-car Class 180 Adelante sets were introduced on EMR's inter-city services after being released by Hull Trains in early 2020; they enabled EMR to withdraw its

Skegness summer special: EMR's No 180111, normally deployed on the Midland main line, heads away from Hubberts Bridge with the 11.42 Skegness to Derby on 6 August 2022. **PHILIP SHERRATT**

HST sets and are due to be used until the new Class 810s have entered service. From July to September 2022 the Class 180s operated EMR's seasonal summer Saturday services between Derby and Skegness.

Other rolling stock coming into the franchise includes a total of 43 Class 170 DMUs released by ScotRail, TfW Rail and West Midlands Trains, some of which have already entered service, and a number of Class 171 DMUs from GTR which will be converted to Class 170s for long-term use with EMR. The first three '171s' transferred to EMR in September 2022 and were temporarily numbered as Class 170/9 sets until work to replace their Dellner couplers with the BSI type used on Class 170s is completed. They initially entered service with EMR in Southern livery ahead of a repaint scheduled for early 2023. Three ex-TfW Rail sets followed in October 2022, joining one two-car unit which had already transferred.

Now that it is retaining the Nottingham – Liverpool service EMR will have to resource additional trains for that route; as Class 170s have begun to enter service several sets have been seen on these services, replacing four-car Class 158 formations. Whilst the long-term impact on timetables following the pandemic is still to be evaluated, the December 2022 timetable saw EMR restore additional services and it intends to continue with plans to improve connectivity across its network as well as running more trains later in the evening and at weekends on local and long-distance routes. ∎

SENIOR PERSONNEL
EAST MIDLANDS RAILWAY

Managing Director Will Rogers (in photo)
Operations Director Paul Barnfield
Fleet Director Neil Bamford
Customer Services Director Neil Grabham
Commercial Director Simon Pready
Finance Director Tim Gledhill
HR Director Kate Holden
Transition & Projects Director Lisa Angus

KEY STATISTICS
EAST MIDLANDS RAILWAY

	2020-21	2021-22
Punctuality (on time)	75.2%	58.2%
Cancellations	1.7%	2.9%
Passenger journeys (millions)	5.1	18.0
Passenger kilometres (millions)	410	1,488
Passenger train kilometres (millions)	19.2	22.9
Route kilometres operated	1,549.8	1,501.5
Number of stations managed	90	102
Number of employees	2,504	2,294

greateranglia

National Rail Contract until 2026

The Greater Anglia franchise awarded to Abellio was due to run from October 2016 to October 2025, with the option of an additional year. In March 2017 a 40% stake was sold to Mitsui. Following the impact of the coronavirus pandemic the Greater Anglia franchise was transferred onto an Emergency Recovery Measures Agreement contract to September 2021, after which the company moved to a new National Rail Contract which will run for up to five years, although DfT has the option to end the agreement two years early in line with changes planned for the industry.

Greater Anglia provides the majority of commuter/regional services from London Liverpool Street to Essex, Suffolk, Norfolk and parts of Hertfordshire and Cambridgeshire, as well as many regional services throughout the East of England. It also operates long-distance trains from London to Norwich via Ipswich and the Stansted Express service. Passenger journeys in 2019-20 were 84.9 million, but fell significantly in the first phase of the pandemic to just 19 million in 2020-21 before rising again to almost 50 million in 2021-22. Passenger numbers have passed 80% of pre-pandemic levels, with regional and West Anglia inner-suburban services at above pre-pandemic levels. Greater Anglia's inter-city and Stansted Express numbers are close to previous levels, however Great Eastern peak London commuting is at around 70%, although it continues to rise. The post-Covid timetable being operated by Greater Anglia sees approximately 90% of pre-pandemic services being operated, with only the Stansted Express markedly different at half-hourly, although these services are now worked by 12-car rather than

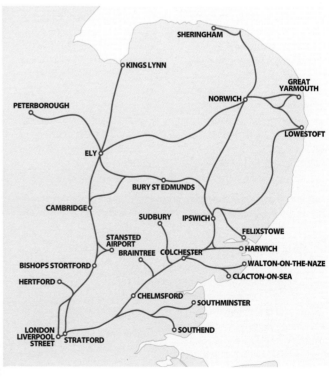

Level access boon: Greater Anglia's No 755335 calls at Cambridge with the 15.37 Stansted Airport to Norwich on 23 February 2022. **PHILIP SHERRATT**

eight-car sets so demand is still being catered for. Options for the May 2023 timetable are still being reviewed.

Improved performance from the new trains has already helped the operator to deliver record-breaking punctuality levels (reaching a new annual Public Performance Measure result of 95.03% in February 2022). New trains should enable some journey time reductions in the next few years; this will primarily be seen on the inter-city route, where a reduction of five minutes is already in place on some services between Norwich and London.

The company continues to deliver on a commitment to replace its entire train fleet in a £1.5 billion programme that is seeing 1,043 new carriages introduced. All its fleets of inter-city trains (10x12-car Class 745/0), Stansted Express trains (10x12-car Class 745/1) and regional bi-mode trains (24x4-car Class 755/4 and 14x3-car Class 755/3) manufactured by Stadler are in service. The accessible features of the Stadler units, including ramps which deploy at doorways, were developed with the support of accessibility groups and stakeholders and have set a new benchmark for accessible trains in the UK.

By October 2022 80 of the 133x5-car Class 720 Aventra EMUs from Alstom (formerly Bombardier) were

KEY STATISTICS
GREATER ANGLIA

	2020-21	2021-22
Punctuality (on time)	85.5%	85.8%
Cancellations	1.9%	1.8%
Passenger journeys (millions)	19.0	49.6
Passenger kilometres (millions)	757	2,102
Passenger train kilometres (millions)	24.9	25.7
Route kilometres operated	511.0	511.0
Number of stations managed	133	134
Number of employees	2,867	2,799

in service. Complete rollout of this fleet is expected to take until summer 2023. All services in West Anglia are now worked by new trains. Of the legacy Greater Anglia fleets, by October 2022 only 30 refurbished 'Renatus' Class 321s remained, whilst many of the other trains withdrawn from use by Greater Anglia have transferred to new operators.

Greater Anglia has continued with major investment in depots and servicing facilities (including carriage washers to suit the new fleet) at Crown Point, Ilford, Clacton, Orient Way, Southend and Cambridge depots (the latter in a joint scheme with Govia Thameslink Railway).

All stations are being refreshed or refurbished in a £60 million programme which includes new

customer information screens, more ticket machines and more parking for cars and cycles. Some work, such as recent platform extensions on the Hertford East branch, is linked to the introduction of new trains. A major scheme has been completed at March, Bury St Edmunds has a new entrance plus car and cycle parking, whilst the new station at Soham opened in December 2021.

Greater Anglia has moved season ticket issuing onto more durable plastic smartcards and continues to make more tickets available via mobile and online channels.

Greater Anglia will continue its close partnership working with Community Rail Partnerships, station adopters and other local stakeholders to promote and develop rail in line with local needs, alongside further work on sustainability, environment, energy efficiency and biodiversity consistent with the decarbonisation agenda. The company's station adoption programme has reached 126 of its 135 stations, with over 300 adopters (the highest levels yet in both respects), and Greater Anglia has launched a pioneering Wildlife Friendly Station accreditation scheme in conjunction with local wildlife trusts. ■

SENIOR PERSONNEL
GREATER ANGLIA

Managing Director Jamie Burles (in photo)
Train Service Delivery Director Jay Thompson
Franchise and Programmes Director Andrew Goodrum
Engineering Director Martin Beable
Commercial and Customer Service Director Martin Moran
Asset Management Director Simone Bailey
HR and Safety Director Katy Bucknell
Finance Director Michael Robertson

wmtrains
National Rail Contract to 2026

West Midlands Trains replaced London Midland on 10 December 2017 in a franchise which was due to run to March 2026. The franchise was awarded to a consortium of Abellio (70%), JR East (15%) and Mitsui (15%). Following the impact of the coronavirus pandemic the franchise was moved onto an Emergency Recovery Measures Agreement contract which ran to September 2021, after which the company moved onto a directly awarded National Rail Contract which runs until 2026, although the Department for Transport has the option to end the agreement two years early in line with changes planned for the industry. JR East has exited the consortium, and its 15% share passed to Abellio.

Trains are operated under two distinct brand names, each with a unique livery. London Northwestern Railway is the identity used for longer-distance services on the West Coast main line, including those running between London Euston and Crewe and between Birmingham New Street and Liverpool as well as the Watford to St Albans and Bletchley to Bedford branch lines and commuter services into London Euston.

Trains in the Birmingham and West Midlands region carry the West Midlands Railway brand; services include suburban trains centred around Birmingham, some regional services from Birmingham to Shrewsbury and Hereford and local services on the Nuneaton – Coventry – Leamington line. The Stourbridge Town branch is operated on behalf of WMT by Pre Metro Operations using the unique Parry People Mover railcars.

Services operating in the West Midlands area are jointly managed by the DfT and the West Midlands Rail Executive, a partnership of 16 Metropolitan District, Shire and Unitary local transport authorities. The creation of the two separate operating units within WMT was designed to enable the West Midlands Railway service group to be let separately in the future, with an option for this process to be managed locally rather than from London via the DfT.

During 2022 WMT was particularly pleased with the successful delivery of a robust train service during the 2022 Commonwealth Games in Birmingham. Ahead of the Games the rebuilt station at Perry Barr was opened in May, and work to rebuild

KEY STATISTICS
WEST MIDLANDS TRAINS

	2020-21	2021-22
Punctuality (on time)	74.3%	66.1%
Cancellations	2.2%	4.7%
Passenger journeys (millions)	13.6	42.4
Passenger kilometres (millions)	536	1,712
Passenger train kilometres (millions)	20.4	22.3
Route kilometres operated	899.6	899.6
Number of stations managed	149	149
Number of employees	2,886	2,901

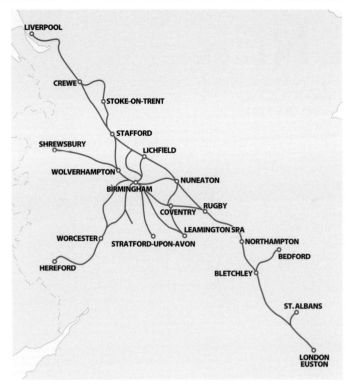

University station is expected to be completed in spring 2023.

From May 2019 a number of timetable and service initiatives saw additional trains operating between Birmingham and Shrewsbury and the linking up of London Euston – Birmingham and Birmingham – Liverpool/Rugeley Trent Valley (Chase Line) services as through trains. The Trent Valley stopping service was altered to run directly from Stafford to Crewe, significantly reducing journey times. Many Cross City line services were extended from Longbridge to the new Bromsgrove station and the hourly shuttle between Leamington Spa and Coventry began serving the new station at Kenilworth, which opened in April 2018.

Whilst the aim of the West Coast timetable was to reduce the number of services terminating at Birmingham New Street and to provide more journey opportunities for passenger crossing the city, the timetable proved difficult to manage and punctuality fell significantly. Shortly before the arrival of Covid-19 changes were made which saw services split at Birmingham New Street once again and following further service reductions due to the pandemic a significant improvement in performance led to a decision to retain many of the timetable changes in the long-term. This will include retaining the four trains per hour service (previously six) on the Cross City line, instead running longer trains.

The new December 2022 timetable has been designed around a robust, reliable framework allowing for additional services to be added as/ when passengers return. Services on the congested Coventry corridor have been thinned out to boost performance and create paths into New Street for the new half-hourly Camp Hill line service to King's Norton calling at Moseley Village, Kings Heath and Pineapple Road, which is due to start in December 2023. WMT services between Birmingham and both Liverpool and Shrewsbury will remain hourly, again with longer trains provided. The commuter service into London Euston is amended to deliver an all-day standard pattern timetable, overlaid with additional services in the peaks. In May 2023 the Snow Hill line timetable will be revised, moving to a 30-minute interval pattern on the lines towards Whitlocks End and Dorridge in place of the uneven 20/40-minute timetable introduced during the pandemic.

WMT has worked hard to recruit additional drivers; in the 12 months to October 2022 the company achieved a 25% increase in crew numbers; with the driver establishment standing at a highest-ever level of 672.

The £680 million order for 110 new trains is progressing. The first of the 12 two-car and 14 four-car Class 196 CAF Civity DMUs entered service between Birmingham and Shrewsbury in October 2022, ahead of deployment on services to Hereford in spring 2023; they will also be used later on the new Camp Hill service and the Coventry to Leamington service.

Progress with the Alstom Class 730 EMUs has been slower, with a number of technical issues delaying entry into service. The first Class 730/0 three-car Aventra sets should enter service on London Northwestern routes into London Euston in early 2023, albeit in WMR livery, ahead of transfer to the West Midlands once five-car '730s' are available. WMT has confirmed a change to the original order, which was to have seen 36x3-car and 45x5-car units delivered; the fleet will now comprise 48x3-car and 36x5-car units. ∎

SENIOR PERSONNEL
WEST MIDLANDS TRAINS

Managing Director Ian McConnell (in photo)
Engineering Director John Doughty
Finance Director David Lindsay
HR Director Jo MacPhail
HSSE Director Angela Prescott
Client & Contracts Director Max Taylor
Operations Director Darren Ward
Customer Experience Director Jonny Wiseman

New DMUs now in service: West Midlands Trains' CAF unit No 196107 at Wolverhampton on 14 October 2022. **PHILIP SHERRATT**

LNER
LONDON NORTH EASTERN RAILWAY

Operator of Last Resort since 2018

Run by the Government's Operator of Last Resort, LNER took over from Virgin Trains East Coast on 24 June 2018 when Stagecoach and Virgin confirmed they would be unable to meet their financial obligations to the Department for Transport. Initially the Department for Transport suggested the company would operate services until a new public-private partnership was established in 2020, however in June 2020 the DfT announced LNER had been given a direct award contract to continue running services beyond 28 June 2020 for three years with an optional extension period of up to 26 rail periods (equivalent to two years). Following the ending of franchising and with the prospect of significant reform for passenger services in September 2022 the DfT confirmed the services agreement dated 24 June 2018 had been updated and extended until June 2023, with an option to extend further to June 2025. When the company was launched the Secretary of State also confirmed LNER would be the long-term identity for the Inter-city East Coast franchise.

LNER operates long-distance inter-city services on the East Coast main line from London King's Cross to North East England and Scotland. It manages 11 stations itself and its trains call at 55 stations in total. Principal services operate between London and Aberdeen, Edinburgh, Newcastle and Leeds, with less frequent trains serving Inverness, Glasgow, Skipton, Bradford, Harrogate, Hull, Lincoln and Middlesbrough.

In September 2020 LNER completed the project to introduce the 65 new Hitachi 'Azuma' trains made up of 10x5-car and 13x9-car Class 800 bi-mode multiple-units and 12x5-car and 30x9-car Class 801 EMUs. The discovery of cracks in some vehicles in May 2021 has had an impact on fleet availability, but Hitachi has now developed a long-term solution to the problem.

Whilst Covid has created some uncertainty over future levels, LNER had previously indicated it expected to procure additional new trains, and currently eight sets of Mk 4 coaches along with 12 Class 91 locomotives have been retained to provide additional capacity. In June 2022 LNER unveiled a new and distinctive livery for its InterCity 225 fleet, which features its trademark colours of red, oxblood, grey and white, along with its iconic logo, bringing a new look to the trains while also giving a nod to its proud past. The full fleet is receiving the new livery as part of its scheduled essential maintenance programme.

A planned major change to the East Coast main line timetable from May 2022 was deferred in August 2021 after a range of problems including power supply issues and the cracks on the train fleet as well as other issues including negative public reaction to changes, the time needed to rewrite the timetable, and the operational feasibility of the timetable itself. Network Rail advised that the new timetable should be deferred to at least May 2023, but it seems unlikely it will be implemented then.

LNER has, however, introduced additional services to Lincoln and Harrogate and launched a new daily service between Middlesbrough and London, also serving Thornaby, from December 2021. In May 2022 LNER launched direct Azuma services from the new station at Reston in the Scottish Borders.

KEY STATISTICS
LNER

	2020-21	2021-22
Punctuality (on time)	79.3%	70.3%
Cancellations	2.4%	3.1%
Passenger journeys (millions)	4.2	17.7
Passenger kilometres (millions)	1,066	4,388
Passenger train kilometres (millions)	17.0	22.2
Route kilometres operated	1,480.6	1,514.5
Number of stations managed	11	11
Number of employees	3,005	3,017

Smart new livery: wearing it's new LNER oxblood colours, No 91127 heads the 19.33 to Leeds at King's Cross on 28 July 2022. **PHILIP SHERRATT**

As with other operators, future timetable developments will depend on passenger recovery; in 2019-20 LNER carried 21.2 million passengers; this fell to just 4.2 million in 2020-21 before recovering to 17.7 million in 2021-22. In October 2022 the company reported it was leading the way with post-pandemic passenger recovery after results published by the Office of Rail and Road showed it had seen more customers return to its services when compared with pre-pandemic usage than any other 'franchised' operator, topping the table for a record fifth consecutive quarter. Its own data showed that by October passenger numbers for the year were more than double those for the same period the previous year; LNER the reported passenger numbers had actually exceeded pre-Covid levels.

In May 2022 LNER announced an investment of £800,000 into station waiting rooms across the East Coast route in the most comprehensive renovation in almost 20 years. The refurbished rooms will boast a new contemporary colour scheme of white and silver combined with new anthracite coloured flooring, whilst furniture includes new leather seating which has built-in USB and plug socket charging points for phones and laptops.

In July 2022 LNER appointed Dr Linda Wain as its first female Engineering Director whilst earlier in the year the company was recognised as a Top Employer in the UK by the Top Employers Institute for the third year running; the company was praised for its excellent work in areas including employee health and wellbeing, diversity and inclusion, work environment and performance development.

During the pandemic LNER trialled the operation of 'reservation-only' services for all passengers, even those catching a train at short notice or with 'walk-up' tickets. As restrictions were lifted the approach was adapted and branded 'Seat Sure'; LNER continues to recommend customers reserve a seat, whilst increased flexibility is offered for those who want to travel without making a reservation, with some coaches set aside for unreserved seats. ∎

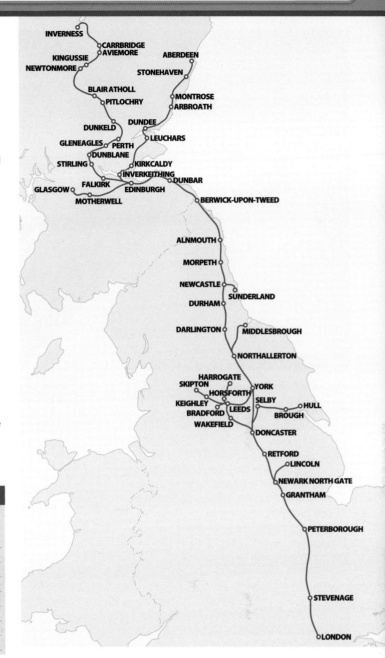

SENIOR PERSONNEL
LNER

Managing Director David Horne (in photo)
Commercial Director David Flesher
Communications Director Kate McFerran
Engineering Director Linda Wain
Chief Digital & Innovation Officer Danny Gonzalez
People & Customer Experience Director Claire Ansley
Safety & Operations Director Warrick Dent
Finance Director James Downey

 NORTHERN

Operator of Last Resort since March 2020

Northern Trains has been under the control of the Government's Operator of Last Resort since 1 March 2020. This replaced Arriva's nine-year contract which had begun on 1 April 2016, with an option for an additional year dependent on performance. At the time, the Secretary of State announced that the Northern franchise was 'no longer financially viable'.

Northern is now jointly managed from Leeds by the Department for Transport and Rail North, which represents 29 local authorities across the region.

Whilst many of the commitments made by the previous operator are continuing, including the fleet transformation project, Northern is focusing on improvements to train performance and customer satisfaction. The withdrawal of the Pacer fleets, seen by many as a key target for the company, was finally completed on 27 November 2020 following a stay of execution through the pandemic where the sets were used to provide additional capacity to maintain social distancing on Northern's services.

On 17 May 2021 the first services were worked by Northern's Class 769 'Flex' bi-mode units, eight of which have been converted from Class 319 EMUs with the addition of two MAN D2876 diesel engines each capable of generating up to 523hp (390kW). In December 2020 Northern announced that the final Class 195 DMU had been accepted, completing the delivery of its new CAF fleets, totalling 58 Class 195 DMUs and 43 Class 331 EMUs.

In a change to its original plans, Northern will be retaining its 17 Class 323 EMUs and taking on 17 of the 26 sets due to be released by West Midlands Trains in preference to the Class 319 units it originally planned to use. This decision has seen Northern's Class 323 sets refurbished and modified to make them compliant with accessibility regulations.

All existing trains which will remain with the company, including those joining the Northern fleet, are being fully refurbished and fitted with free customer Wi-Fi, improved passenger information systems and at-seat power sockets. In order to provide additional capacity on routes where four-car sets cannot be accommodated Northern has reformed four Class 150/1 two-car sets with the addition

KEY STATISTICS
NORTHERN

	2020-21	2021-22
Punctuality (on time)	76.3%	67.0%
Cancellations	1.3%	3.3%
Passenger journeys (millions)	21.9	67.5
Passenger kilometres (millions)	591	2,001
Passenger train kilometres (millions)	39.8	48.7
Route kilometres operated	3,196.7	3,158.0
Number of stations managed	477	465
Number of employees	6,666	6,854

To be joined by units from the West Midlands: Northern's No 323230 at Hadfield on 29 August 2022 with the 11.44 to Manchester Piccadilly. **PHILIP SHERRATT**

SENIOR PERSONNEL
NORTHERN

Managing Director Nick Donovan (in photo)
Chief Operating Officer Tricia Williams
Safety & Environment Director Mike Roe
People Director (interim) Andy Ward
Customer and Commercial Director Mark Powles
Strategic Development Director Rob Warnes
Engineering Director Jack Commandeur
Finance Director Matt Williams
Programmes Director Emma Yates

of a vehicle from two disbanded Class 150/2 units to create new three-car Class 150/0 sets. Along with the two prototype units, Nos 150001/002, this has given the company a six-strong fleet of three-car trains.

Following successful trials on two Class 319 sets Northern is fitting new 'leaf-busting' technology 'Water-Trak' to 16 of its Class 170 units that operate through areas most affected by poor autumn conditions.

In October 2022 Northern marked the one-year anniversary of its takeover of Neville Hill depot on the outskirts of Leeds. Since becoming sole operator, Northern has completed a site-wide clean-up, integrated teams for more efficient working, improved security, refurbished facilities for staff and improved safety with the installation of illuminated walkways.

The problems encountered with the May 2018 timetable and a recognition that capacity is not available for all the proposed services without infrastructure improvements, particularly around Manchester and Leeds, has led to a rethink of the major timetable uplift programme proposed under the original franchise

agreement with Arriva. The advent of the pandemic and the subsequent reduction in services brought a significant improvement in punctuality and this provided useful research for

the development of plans for a more robust timetable via a taskforce that involved DfT, Network Rail, Transport for the North and train operators. From Sunday 11 December 2022 a new timetable involved some areas seeing more trains running where they have been reduced since the start of the year whilst others have seen services reduced or calls provided by other operators. A number of significant changes have been made to services running into and through Manchester and the North West aimed at improving reliability across this very busy area of the rail network; this includes a changes in calling patterns or starting and destination points. ∎

southeastern.

Operator of Last Resort from October 2021

Having been operated by Govia since April 2006, in October 2021 operation of Southeastern services transferred to the Department for Transport's Operator of Last Resort. The decision was made by the Department for Transport after it uncovered evidence that since 2014 Southeastern had not declared over £25 million of historic taxpayer funding which should have been returned. The business now trades as SE Trains Limited, although the Southeastern brand name has been retained across stations and trains. Govia had operated services under a series of direct award contracts since 2014.

Southeastern serves Kent, south east London and part of East Sussex and operates high-speed domestic services on High Speed 1 (HS1). It operates on three main routes: the South Eastern main line from London Cannon Street and London Charing Cross to Dover via Sevenoaks; the Chatham main line between London Victoria and Dover/Ramsgate via the Medway Towns; and High Speed 1 from London St Pancras. It runs a completely electric train fleet and is committed to managing its traction energy, with over 70% of its main line and metro fleets fitted with regenerative braking. Southeastern operates 164 stations, with services calling at 182 stations in total.

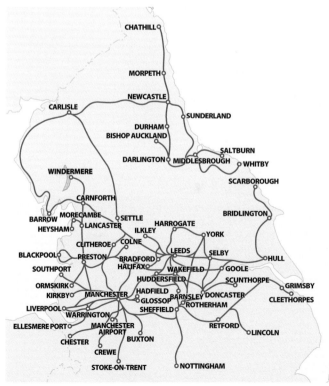

KEY STATISTICS
SOUTHEASTERN

	2020-21	2021-22
Punctuality (on time)	78.2%	71.4%
Cancellations	1.8%	2.3%
Passenger journeys (millions)	40.2	97.8
Passenger kilometres (millions)	995	2,543
Passenger train kilometres (millions)	25.8	26.6
Route kilometres operated	748.3	748.3
Number of stations managed	164	164
Number of employees	4,480	4,556

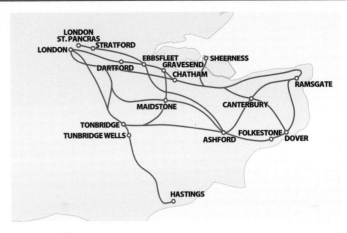

Southeastern Highspeed services call at Stratford International and Ebbsfleet International. Trains from London to the Medway towns and Faversham leave the high-speed line at Ebbsfleet and continue via the North Kent line and Chatham main line. Trains for Dover Priory and Margate leave the high-speed line at Ashford International. A limited peak-hour service operates between St Pancras and Maidstone West via Ebbsfleet and Strood. In October 2022 Southeastern announced a £27 million upgrade for the Class 395 Javelin trains that are used on the Highspeed services; the initial phase of the project will take seven months and include design, engineering and procurement, with the upgrade to the first of the 29 trains commencing in March 2023 at Southeastern's Ashford depot. The scope of the programme includes: full interior refresh, including new seating layouts to assist people with reduced mobility, as well as LED lighting, USB charging and a live passenger information system.

In December 2022 a wholesale change to Southeastern's timetable was made which is expected to provide more space on trains where it's most needed, a more consistent timetable throughout the day and improved punctuality. At the same time, following a fall in demand, Southeastern removed First Class accommodation from its main line trains.

In September 2021 Southeastern introduced the first of the Class 707 units which are transferring from South Western Railway for use on Metro services; with the leases of all 30 sets having transferred to Southeastern, 12 remain sub-leased back pending the introduction of SWR's new Class 701 EMUs.

A number of Class 465/466 Networker EMUs are in store because of a lack of stabling space on the network and the sets remain on lease, with their future still to be determined. In November 2022 Southeastern published a contract notice seeking expressions of interest in replacement of the Networker fleet.

Under a Kent County Council-led project a new station is currently under construction at Thanet Parkway, expected to open in May 2023, on the Ashford – Canterbury – Ramsgate line, which will be served initially by Highspeed services. A Medway Council-led project is examining the extension of Gravesend services over the freight-only line to a proposed station at Sharnal Street, on the Isle of Grain. ■

SENIOR PERSONNEL
SOUTHEASTERN

Managing Director Steve White (in photo)
Engineering Director Mark Johnson
Passenger Services Director David Wornham
Commercial Director Alicia Andrews
Operations and Safety Director Scott Brightwell
HR Director Steve Foster
Finance Director Paul Barlow
Communications and Stakeholder Director (interim) Ben Ruse
Head of Safety and Environment Steve Lewis

Electrostars on duty: Southeastern's No 375706/822 pass New Cross with the 15.40 Charing Cross to Ramsgate on 20 April 2022. **PHILIP SHERRATT**

TRAFNIDIAETH CYMRU TRANSPORT FOR WALES
Gwasanaethau Rheilffyrdd Rail Services

Operator of Last Resort from February 2021

The Wales and Borders franchise was awarded by Transport for Wales on behalf of the Welsh Government to KeolisAmey, starting on 14 October 2018, and was due to run for 15 years. However, the impact of the Covid-19 pandemic and the subsequent collapse in passenger numbers saw the Welsh Government move the TfW Rail contract onto an Emergency Measures Agreement (EMA) before announcing in October 2020 that it would take full ownership of Transport for Wales Rail from 7 February 2021, since when operation has been under a new Government-owned subsidiary. The Welsh Government said this would provide longer-term financial stability, necessary to secure plans for infrastructure improvements and deliver future improvements for passengers.

TfW says it will continue to deliver key aspects of the original contract, including the £800 million rolling stock plan that will see the vast majority of journeys made on brand new rolling stock and the remainder on extensively refurbished trains brought into the company.

Having taken the Core Valley Lines north from Cardiff to Treherbert, Merthyr Tydfil, Aberdare and Rhymney into local control in 2020, work is under way to electrify the routes as part of the creation of the 'Central Metro'. Other routes to Maesteg and Ebbw Vale are not being electrified, and whilst ownership will remain with Network Rail they will be part of the wider South Wales Metro. The CVL wiring is described as 'smart electrification'; trains will switch between electric and battery power through unpowered sections of overhead line equipment where otherwise expensive, time-consuming work such as raising bridges and adjusting historic station canopies would have been needed. Commonly referred to as 'discontinuous electrification', this has been made possible by improvements in battery technology. One other important feature of the CVL upgrade is the aim of maximising use of renewable energy to provide traction power, for stations and at other locations.

New trains have been ordered from CAF and Stadler. The CAF fleet comprises 51x2-car and 26x3-car Civity DMUs. The first of these entered service in November 2022 on the Conwy Valley line, and the rollout of this fleet will continue through 2023. They are being assembled at

CAF's facility at Newport, with the manufacturer branding them 'trains made in Wales for the people of Wales'.

Three Stadler fleets have been ordered. 11x4-car Class 231 Flirt DEMUs will work on the Maesteg, Cheltenham Spa and Ebbw Vale services, as well as initially to Rhymney, whilst 24 tri-mode Class 756 variants (7x3-car and 17x4-car), which can work on diesel, 25kV AC and battery power, will cover services on routes linking the Vale of Glamorgan and destinations north of Cardiff. With a battery range of around 40 miles, they will run on AC mode north of Cardiff and diesel to the south, providing a cross-city connection. On the Rhymney line it is expected that they will switch to battery power beyond Bargoed, however the area around Rhymney station, where trains will

be stabled, is also to be electrified. The third fleet is 36x3-car Class 398 Citylink tram-trains, capable of 25kV and battery operation, which will operate from Cardiff to Treherbert, Aberdare and Merthyr Tydfil once the lines are electrified. Services will run through to a rebuilt station at Cardiff Bay, with the single-track section upgraded with double-tracking and a new intermediate station built near Loudoun Square.

TfW also operates loco-hauled trains: 12 Mk 4 coaches and four driving van trailers released by LNER were acquired for the long-distance North to South Wales services and entered service in June 2021. The acquisition of further vehicles means TfW has a total of eight five-car rakes, used on Cardiff to Holyhead and (from December 2022) on South

KEY STATISTICS
TFW RAIL

	2020-21	2021-22
Punctuality (on time)	80.7%	67.0%
Cancellations	1.8%	4.0%
Passenger journeys (millions)	5.0	17.6
Passenger kilometres (millions)	187	735
Passenger train kilometres (millions)	17.9	20.6
Route kilometres operated	1,826.6	1,827.0
Number of stations managed	248	248
Number of employees	2,585	2,769

New trains on test: Stadler Flirt DEMU Nos 231005/003 for TfW at Cardiff Central on 26 July 2022. **PHILIP SHERRATT**

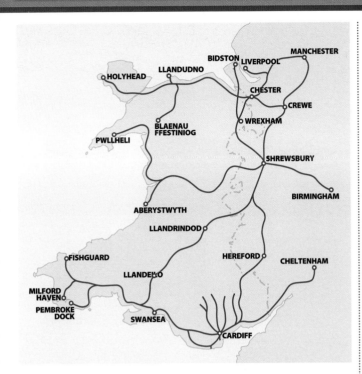

Operator of Last Resort from April 2022

ScotRail services moved into Scottish Government ownership from 1 April 2022, as a subsidiary of Scottish Rail Holdings, in turn a subsidiary of Transport Scotland. This replaced Abellio, which had operated the franchise since April 2015. The seven-year contract included the option for a three-year extension contingent on performance criteria being met, but in December 2019 the Scottish Government announced that the 'break clause' would be activated and the franchise would conclude on 31 March 2022. During the Covid pandemic an Emergency Measures Agreement was introduced. In the follow-up to the transfer Abellio noted that far from being profitable it had needed to pay money into the business throughout its tenure.

The Scottish Government has indicated the transfer to the public sector will involve a core Operator of Last Resort period of three to five years, 'although Ministers' ability to award a contract for up to 10 years (the maximum award duration available) is preserved'.

Abellio established a 'deep alliance' with Network Rail, aimed at delivering improved performance and efficiencies, and the two parties are led by a single MD; this arrangement continues. ScotRail serves more than 350 stations on a network which is vital to Scotland's communities, and to the country's booming tourist industry. However, the damage done by the pandemic has had a deep impact in Scotland; in 2020-21 ScotRail saw 14.4 million passenger journeys, a very significant fall from the 96.4 million in 2019-20 and with recovery in 2021-22 only showing an uplift to 46.7 million journeys the return of passengers is lagging well behind most English operators. Industrial relations issues have had a significant impact on

ScotRail throughout 2022, and with many calls on Government funds as the cost of living crisis continues this will continue to be a significant challenge for the devolved administration.

As the country emerged from the pandemic a consultation was launched over the future timetables ScotRail should operate; the consultation noted that prior to the pandemic, on a number of routes across the country, significantly more seats were being provided than were required for the number of passengers travelling. On a typical weekday just 23% of the available seats were occupied, and the consultation concluded: 'Returning to a pre-pandemic timetable would result in trains operating 26 million more vehicle miles each year for little customer benefit'. As well as increased emissions, that would increase ScotRail costs to the taxpayer by tens of millions of pounds annually. The proposals put forward for 'a new, better performing timetable' were to operate around 2,100 services each weekday with some additional services, others combined and some journey times extended to allow services to make additional calls. When introduced in May 2022 ScotRail stated: 'This timetable will be a new starting point for future timetable development. We will deliver a timetable that is sustainable in the short- to medium-term, whilst continuing to react to the changes that will see in the future as customer behaviours continue to evolve.'

The completion of a number of infrastructure projects, particularly the electrification of key routes, allowed ScotRail to replace many diesel trains with new, more reliable electric units. ScotRail says it is fully committed to making rail more environmentally friendly and is working hard to help decarbonise the railway by 2035. The most recently introduced new fleet comprises 70 Hitachi Class 385 EMUs, whose introduction helped ScotRail reach the milestone of 75% of its customers travelling on electric or zero emission trains. ScotRail is also examining how new technologies

Wales to Manchester services. The sets, hauled by Class 67s leased from DB Cargo, have First Class carriages, free Wi-Fi, accessible toilets and provide an enhanced food offering.

Another fleet being retained by TfW alongside new trains is its Class 153s. Refurbishment to Persons with Reduced Mobility compliance of 26 '153s' was completed in July 2022, with a further four sets purchased since. TfW will retain 13 '153s', all of which it owns directly, of which six will be reconfigured to provide enhanced cycle storage on the Heart of Wales line, with the other seven units having full PRM modifications. The retention of Class 153s, along with changes to the deployment of the Class 197s, is allowing TfW Rail to release the Class 170s it took on from Greater Anglia.

The first of eight Class 769 trains, procured for Valley Lines services until they are electrified, entered passenger service on the Rhymney line on 15 December 2020, although TfW now intends to withdraw these sets in 2023 to create space for its new fleets at Cardiff Canton depot.

Five three-car Class 230 Vivarail diesel/battery hybrid units for the Borderlands line between Wrexham

and Bidston are due to enter service during 2023, somewhat later than planned as the new design has required far more development and testing than originally envisaged.

TfW is spending £194 million on station improvements, including the modernisation of all 247 existing stations on the network and the building of five new stations, four in Cardiff itself. On 15 February 2021 the new Bow Street station at Ceredigion in mid-Wales opened.

More than 170 stations in Wales have been fitted with a Welsh language information system called 'Geraint' which can provide clear Welsh language journey announcements and up to the minute changes. Transport for Wales has launched a new WhatsApp number for customer enquiries, as a key step in its commitment to transform the customer experience for the Wales and Borders rail service. In August 2020 TfW confirmed the start of a programme to install new ticket vending machines and operating smartcards on many of its routes; the new machines have improved Welsh Language components and include raised pictograms for visually impaired customers. ∎

SENIOR PERSONNEL
TFW RAIL

Chief Operations Officer Jan Chaudhry-Van de Velde (in photo)
Operations Director Martyn Brennan
Engineering Director Ryan Williams
Planning and Performance Director Colin Lea
Onboard Director Bethan Jelfs
Stations Director Lisa Cleminson

KEY STATISTICS
SCOTRAIL

	2020-21	2021-22
Punctuality (on time)	77.7%	71.2%
Cancellations	2.1%	2.8%
Passenger journeys (millions)	14.4	46.7
Passenger kilometres (millions)	397	1,474
Passenger train kilometres (millions)	35.9	38.6
Route kilometres operated	3,120.5	3,120.5
Number of stations managed	355	355
Number of employees	5,211	4,926

Electric ambitions: ScotRail's No 385113 calls at Haymarket with the 18.00 Edinburgh to Glasgow Queen Street on 3 October 2022. **PHILIP SHERRATT**

for its trains, offices and worksites can help reduce its carbon footprint. This includes hybrid, battery powered and hydrogen trains and solar-powered generators for track maintenance work.

A tender notice published in August 2022 outlined ScotRail's plans to purchase new trains which would replace all but the current Class 380 and 385 fleets, including the withdrawal of all diesel trains. The number of sub-fleets will be consolidated from the current 11 to, ideally, five types. First up will be a new fleet of suburban trains to enter service between 2027 and 2030, expected to comprise around 120 units and 550 vehicles, with a minimum core order for 64 units and 295 vehicles. A mix of EMUs and battery-electric units (BEMUs) is planned. This will be followed by new fleets for rural routes and for inter-city routes.

Station improvement projects have continued, with a £5 million redevelopment of Stirling station and an £8 million renovation of Aberdeen station under way and

a £14.5 million scheme to expand the station concourse, improve the forecourt and create a new transport hub at Motherwell also progressing. The £14.5 million project to build a new two-platform, fully accessible station on the Inverness – Aberdeen line to serve Inverness Airport was due for completion by the end of 2022. In October 2022 ScotRail announced that Dunfermline Town railway station would be renamed Dunfermline City, after its historic status was officially recognised by King Charles III.

With the post-pandemic reintroduction of an on-board food and drink service ScotRail announced a £918,000 programme to recruit 29 new on-train hospitality stewards as part of plans to reintroduce and improve the food and drink offering on board trains across its network. The company also announced a recruitment drive for 24 Travel Safe Officers, three Travel Safe Supervisors and one Safeguarding Manager, creating a permanent 28-strong team which will work closely with British

Transport Police to support customers and colleagues in the promotion of a safe railway environment, both on trains and in stations. The team has the ability to focus quickly on emerging hotspots, actively engaging with and educating individuals and groups

on the impact of unsafe behaviours when on or around the railway. Since its introduction, the Travel Safe team has targeted a number of stations and routes, and ScotRail has seen a drop in reported events during, and after, the anti-social behaviour exercises. ∎

SENIOR PERSONNEL

SCOTRAIL

Managing Director, Scotland's Railway Alex Hynes (in photo)
Chief Operating Officer Joanne Maguire
Interim Finance Director James Griffin
Safety, Engineering and Sustainability Director David Lister
Service Delivery Director David Simpson
Commercial Director Lesley Kane
Interim Communications Director David Ross
Interim HR Director Marie-Thérèse Weighton

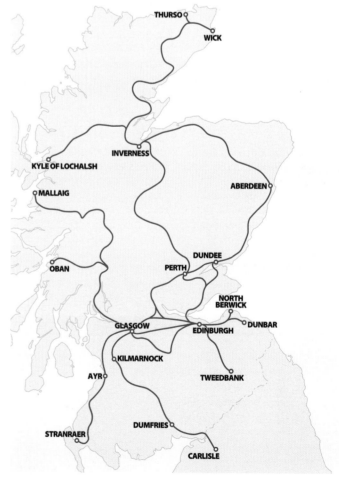

c2c

National Rail Contract to July 2023

c2c provides commuter services from its London terminus Fenchurch Street, and on occasions from Liverpool Street, to the northern Thames Gateway area of southern Essex, with the main service groups being from Fenchurch Street to Shoeburyness via Basildon, to Southend Central via Ockendon and to Grays via Rainham.

The c2c Essex Thameside franchise was acquired by Trenitalia UK from National Express Group (NX) on 10 February 2017. NX had operated the franchise since 2000 and won a new 15-year term starting on 9 November 2014. Following the impact of the coronavirus pandemic c2c was moved onto an Emergency Recovery Measures Agreement contract which took it through to March 2021 and, after an extension, to July 2021. Subsequently Trenitalia agreed a National Rail Contract with the Department for Transport which runs until July 2023, with an optional two-year extension at the Secretary of State's discretion.

In 2015 the company managed demand for additional capacity by converting 20% of its fleet of 74 Class 357 EMUs to a 'metro' style layout, with two seats either side of the aisle instead of the previous 3+2 seating. This improved capacity by increasing the amount of available standing space.

Further capacity was provided with the arrival of six four-car Bombardier Class 387 trains on a short-term lease, whilst a new timetable from January 2017 included faster journeys between Southend and London and longer trains for many stations. The '387s' have now transferred to other operators, but extra capacity will soon be provided by a new fleet of 12 five-car Alstom Aventra Class 720/6 trains. The new units will provide capacity for 5,000 additional passengers, with 20% more seats. Work is under way at East Ham depot to accommodate the new sets, with the first unit having been delivered in April 2022 for testing and training on the trains to begin.

During the pandemic c2c reduced its timetable to focus on serving key workers; this was followed by a step-up in services in April 2021. In September 2021 this was consolidated, with the company operating around 85% of its pre-Covid timetable on weekdays and a full service at weekends. All services are now operated with eight-car sets, this having been made possible by the reduction in the overall timetable. Use of trains continues to be monitored and other trains may be reinstated should demand increase, although few changes were made for the December 2022 timetable. The impact of the pandemic was significant at c2c, with annual passenger numbers falling from 47.3 million in 2019-20 to 15 million in 2020-21 and 28.1 million in 2021-22.

In October 2022 Transport Focus announced that c2c passengers were again the most satisfied commuters in the country. This followed a survey which interviewed rail passengers across all operators; c2c topped the league with a 96% overall satisfaction rate among passengers surveyed. c2c also comes in first place among train operators for punctuality/reliability, with 96% of passengers saying they were satisfied with this and 91% saying they were satisfied in terms of the level of crowding.

In June 2021 c2c launched its Accessible Travel Policy, which includes a new commitment to making the railway more accessible to everyone and to improving the railway experience for disabled and elderly customers. Information has been provided about station and train facilities, ticketing and fares, and travelling using a wheelchair, mobility scooter, assistance dog or companion. Since April 2022 Passenger Assistance at stations can be booked two hours before travelling. In addition, all c2c staff received Disability Awareness and Inclusive Customer Service training by July 2021; created and delivered by Inclusion London, an organisation run by and for deaf and disabled people set up to promote equality and inclusion, all the trainers that delivered the bespoke c2c course have lived experience as disabled people, which made the training particularly successful.

During the COP26 climate change conference c2c celebrated the 60th anniversary of the introduction of electric trains on its route, with British Rail having operated the first electric train on the c2c route on Tuesday 7 November 1961; the last steam trains were phased out on the c2c line by June 1962. ∎

KEY STATISTICS
C2C

	2020-21	2021-22
Punctuality (on time)	84.9%	83.4%
Cancellations	1.0%	1.3%
Passenger journeys (millions)	15.0	28.1
Passenger kilometres (millions)	329	622
Passenger train kilometres (millions)	6.0	6.0
Route kilometres operated	125.5	125.5
Number of stations managed	25	25
Number of employees	648	633

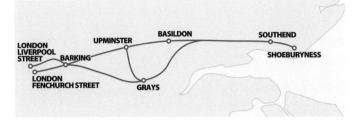

SENIOR PERSONNEL
C2C

Managing Director Rob Mullen (in photo)
Delivery Director Laura McEwen
Commercial Director Claire McCaffrey
Engineering Director Jeff Baker
Finance Director Phil Leney
Head of Communications Alice Shimali

New c2c train on test: Nos 720607/605 pass Old Linslade with a Wembley to Crewe run on 11 October 2022. **KEN BRUNT**

Chilternrailways
by arriva

National Rail Contract to 2027

Having operated the franchise since July 1996, Chiltern Railways' unique 20-year franchise ran from March 2002 until December 2021, conditional on various investments being made. The company is owned by Arriva UK Trains. Following the impact of the coronavirus pandemic the Chiltern franchise was moved onto an Emergency Recovery Measures Agreement contract through to December 2021, after which the company was awarded a new National Rail Contract which can run to 2027 and has a guaranteed core term of 3.25 years.

Chiltern Railways operates trains via the Chiltern main line between Birmingham Snow Hill and London Marylebone and the second main line route between Aylesbury and the capital, along with branch lines linking Princes Risborough with Aylesbury, Leamington Spa with Stratford-upon-Avon and Bicester with Oxford. The latter became a new through route between London Marylebone and Oxford in December 2016 when the £259 million Evergreen 3 project was completed. Some London to Birmingham services are extended to serve Kidderminster in the morning and evening peaks, including at weekends. The company serves 62 stations and manages 35; in 2019-20 it carried 28.4 million passengers, but the pandemic saw this fall to just 4.6 million journeys in 2020-21 before recovering to 14.3 million in 2021-22.

The May 2019 timetable saw the number of direct trains between Stratford-upon-Avon and London Marylebone increased in both directions, and in 2019 Chiltern announced a significant spend on improving Warwick Parkway and Leamington Spa stations. Passenger surveys regularly see Chiltern receive high approval ratings from customers. The company introduced Delay Repay 15 in May 2022.

After reducing services significantly in response to the pandemic, Chiltern's May 2021 timetable increased capacity and improved connectivity on weekend trains between London Marylebone and Birmingham and London Marylebone and Oxford, whilst the May 2022 timetable saw extra carriages added to the busiest morning peak services into Marylebone to aid recovery as passenger numbers continued to rise.

Chiltern operates an all-diesel train fleet of 39 Class 165/0 DMUs, 28 Class 168 DMUs and a small number of loco-hauled Mk 3 coaches powered by Class 68 locomotives; four two-car Class 172 units acquired in 2010 transferred to West Midlands Trains in 2021. With London Marylebone the only non-electrified main line terminus in London, this has highlighted the fact Chiltern needs to address its environmental impact rapidly. This is exacerbated by calls for it to cease operation of the Mk 3 sets as soon as possible both because of the cost of retaining them and because of the excessive noise levels created by the Class 68 locomotives.

In February 2022 Chiltern unveiled two-car unit No 168329 which had been fitted with a Hybrid PowerPack; the HybridFlex is the product of a collaboration between rolling stock owner Porterbrook and engineering giant Rolls-Royce. As well as offering zero emissions and near silent operation at stations, the HybridFlex reduces fuel consumption and cuts CO_2 emissions by up to 25%, Nitrous Oxide (NOx) emissions by over 70% and particulate emissions by over 90% compared to the engines it replaces.

In 2022 Chiltern announced it was seeking proposals for the supply of

KEY STATISTICS
CHILTERN RAILWAYS

	2020-21	2021-22
Punctuality (on time)	80.1%	74.2%
Cancellations	1.5%	2.0%
Passenger journeys (millions)	4.6	14.3
Passenger kilometres (millions)	214	751
Passenger train kilometres (millions)	8.7	9.2
Route kilometres operated	349.2	349.2
Number of stations managed	35	35
Number of employees	850	896

battery-electric multiple-units as part of an assessment of its rolling stock strategy and, in particular, how it can achieve non-diesel operation. In the absence of a significant change in government policy, the Chiltern network is unlikely to be electrified in the medium-term. Through two parallel requests for proposals, Chiltern is looking at options to either manufacture or convert between 30 and 70 BEMUs and test and certify them. A contract for new trains would have an estimated value of £400 million, whilst remanufactured units could be purchased or leased under a contract with an estimated value of £200 million.

The 2022 Commonwealth Games was a major event for Chiltern, with the operator working to improve several stations ahead of the event. At Birmingham Moor Street station Chiltern was assisted by The Friends of the Shakespeare Line, which built custom-made 'platform-scale' garden planters and installed them at the station, as well as refreshing the existing planters and reviving the station gardens between the platforms. In addition, facilities management company Mitie took part in a thorough deep clean of the station whilst refreshing painted platform markings and vintage benches. Down the line at Leamington Spa, almost £2 million was spent ahead of the start of the Games on the renewal and refurbishment of the station entrance and forecourt along with enlarged and upgraded public spaces and new seating areas, improved wayfinding and signage, enhanced lighting, new CCTV, renewal of paintwork and the installation of new artwork in the pedestrian underpass.

In August 2022 a nine-foot bronze statue and plinth of Chiltern Railways founder Adrian Shooter was unveiled at London Marylebone station, paying tribute to his contribution to the Chiltern operation over many years. At the same event Chiltern Turbostar No 168001, the first train ordered by any private sector railway operator following privatisation, was named *Adrian Shooter CBE*. ∎

Stay of execution: a Chiltern Railways loco-hauled set with No 68015 at Birmingham Moor Street on 22 April 2022 awaiting departure with the 12.55 to Marylebone. **PHILIP SHERRATT**

crosscountry

Franchise contract to October 2023

The CrossCountry (XC) network is the most extensive of any UK operator. Owned by Arriva UK Trains, it operates inter-city long-distance services between the South of England and the North of England or Scotland via Birmingham, and medium-distance, stopping or semi-fast services between Birmingham and other cities in the Midlands, as well as some longer runs to Wales and West Anglia.

Having started on 11 November 2007, Arriva's franchise was initially due to run until 31 March 2016. In September 2016, the Department for Transport announced a new directly awarded contract, extending the contract to December 2019, and subsequent extensions took the franchise through to October 2020. The arrival of the pandemic saw the company move to an Emergency Measures Agreement before a new contract was agreed with DfT in the autumn of 2021 running until October 2023, with an option to extend the agreement for an additional year at DfT's request. Uniquely this is branded an 'Operating Contract Franchise Agreement'.

Stretching from Scotland to Cornwall, Manchester to the south coast of England, and Wales to Stansted Airport, the CrossCountry franchise serves seven out of the 10 major cities in Great Britain but does not serve London. Its 3,860km (2,400-mile) network includes many university towns and airports, with approximately 300 services each weekday, enabling it to carry over 40 million passengers a year. The impact of the pandemic saw this fall to just 6.7 million in 2020-21 before rising to 20.6 million in 2021-22.

CrossCountry's inter-city services are typically operated by four-car and five-car Voyager DEMUs or seven-car HST sets, whilst its regional services based on Birmingham

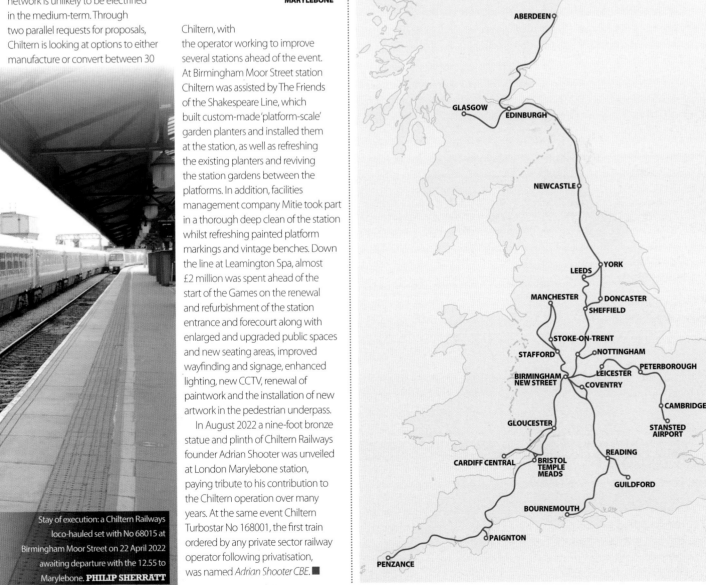

are usually operated by two-car and three-car Turbostar DMUs.

CrossCountry does not manage any stations, although it serves many across Great Britain; the vast majority of its services serve Birmingham New Street and in common with other operators the company has seen a growing trend towards leisure travel as the country recovers from the impact of the pandemic. The reduced timetable through the pandemic saw many services operated by pairs of Class 220 and 221 units, ensuring capacity was maintained and at key times social distancing was made easier. Whilst many trains that were suspended have been restored, some services have not been fully reinstated, with trains to the extremes of the CrossCountry network and frequencies on other routes reduced. Discussions over the future timetable and which services will be reinstated in the longer-term have continued, with a handful of trains restored as demand has increased.

CrossCountry and DfT are still working to understand what the demand for services will be in the future and the timetables that this will require.

Negotiations over the future of the operation have continued; prior to the coronavirus pandemic it had been accepted by DfT that much-needed improvements in capacity through

Open access contract to 2026

Grand Central Rail (GC) has been operating for almost 15 years, and its extended open-access contract runs until 2026; a series of ownership changes culminated in GC becoming part of Arriva in November 2011.

GC's first open access service, from Sunderland to London King's Cross, was launched in December 2007, and by 2012 the company was providing five return journeys. The West Riding service started in May 2010, offering three trains a day between Bradford Interchange and King's Cross. A fourth West Riding service was introduced in December 2013, and in April 2017 all West Riding trains began calling at the new Low Moor station. From May 2022 an additional daily service began running between Sunderland and King's Cross, bringing Grand Central's weekday offering to six return journeys (five on Sundays).

Grand Central operates a 10-strong fleet of five-car Class 180 'Adelante' units, with sufficient sets to allow a capacity boost on the busiest trains by running 10-car formations. A £9 million refresh of the trains, with revamped catering facilities and the first leather-trimmed Standard Class seats in a UK fleet, has been completed, whilst the company has worked with Alstom, Angel Trains and Network Rail to fit the latest European Train Control System (ETCS) equipment – the first in service since the mid-Wales project in 2010. Grand Central is also trialling dual-fuel technology on a Class 180 with the use of liquified natural gas (LNG); the practical demonstration, undertaken in conjunction with G-volution, has seen one of the vehicles within No 180112 modified to work on a mix of LNG and diesel with the aim of reducing fuel costs, particulate matter, and CO_2 emissions.

As the open access operator gets no Government support, Grand Central was forced to suspend all services three times during the worst lockdown periods of the Covid-19 pandemic; services were

SENIOR PERSONNEL
GRAND CENTRAL

Chief Operating Officer Sean English
Head of HR Angela Newsome
Head of Drivers Colin Barker
Head of Customer Service Delivery Leanne Maskell
Head of Commercial Nick Clarke
Finance and Business Development Director (Arriva UK Trains) Alex Scott

KEY STATISTICS
GRAND CENTRAL

	2020-21	2021-22
Punctuality (on time)	69.3%	56.5%
Cancellations	2.8%	2.7%
Passenger journeys (millions)	0.2	1.0
Passenger kilometres (millions)	43	283
Passenger train kilometres (millions)	0.8	2.1
Route kilometres operated	518.5	518.5
Number of employees	163	164

Anniversary special: CrossCountry power car No 43184, in InterCity Executive livery and with a *Modern Railways* headboard, awaits departure from Leeds on 27 September 2022 with the 'Severn Valley Adventurer' HST special to Kidderminster and Bridgnorth. **TONY MILES**

KEY STATISTICS
CROSSCOUNTRY

	2020-21	2021-22
Punctuality (on time)	69.2%	60.0%
Cancellations	1.6%	2.8%
Passenger journeys (millions)	6.7	20.6
Passenger kilometres (millions)	560	1,814
Passenger train kilometres (millions)	19.5	21.5
Route kilometres operated	2,710.1	2,710.1
Number of stations managed	0	0
Number of employees	1,961	1,914

On 27 September 2022 CrossCountry celebrated 40 years of HSTs on its North East to South West route, alongside 60 years of *Modern Railways* magazine, when the 'Severn Valley Adventurer' HST special ran from Leeds to Kidderminster via Wakefield Westgate, Doncaster, Sheffield, Derby and Birmingham New Street. The southbound working was led by power car No 43184, recently repainted into InterCity Executive livery, carrying a *Modern Railways* headboard, whilst on arrival at Kidderminster the other power car, No 43366, which as No 43166 was one of the first power cars to be used on CrossCountry services in the early 1980s, was named *HST 40*. ∎

SENIOR PERSONNEL
CROSSCOUNTRY TRAINS

Managing Director Tom Joyner (in photo)
Finance Director Gillian Ingham
Head of Corporate Affairs Sally Gillespie
Industry Projects and Planning Director Jo Davey
Service Delivery Director Mark Goodall
Customer Director Colette Casey
HR Director Wendy Smith
Regional Director – North East & Scotland Ben Simkin
Regional Director – West Midlands & NW Nick Chadwick
Regional Director – E Midlands & E Anglia John Robson
Regional Director – West & Wales Huw Margetts

the leasing of additional rolling stock would have to be delivered in the next contract period, whilst the ageing HST fleet will need to be replaced. However, in February 2020 CrossCountry gained two extra HST power cars to enable four of the five seven-car HST sets to be diagrammed to work regularly, with the fifth set on standby as a 'hot spare'; this is planned to be the case from May 2023.

With suitable rolling stock due to be released by other operators in the next few years, DfT and CrossCountry are understood to be assessing options for some of these trains to be used to provide a much-needed capacity uplift for the business.

finally restored on 1 March 2021. The company reported it 'had to make a number of difficult but necessary decisions and implement some painful changes in response to the impact of the Covid crisis'. As a result, Grand Central has continued to receive financial and practical support from parent company Arriva.

Passenger data shows that from a high of 1.5 million journeys in 2018-19 ridership fell to 0.2 million in 2020-21 before recovering to one million journeys in 2021-22.

In October 2022 Grand Central announced it was topping the table as the train operator with the highest relative increase in numbers since the start of the Covid pandemic. ∎

Dual-fuel trial: Grand Central's No 180112 passes Brookmans Park with the 08.53 Sunderland to King's Cross on 1 November 2022. The green stripe denotes the vehicle which has been modified to work on a mix of liquified natural gas and diesel. **KEN BRUNT**

Eight-year concession to 2024

Arriva has operated the London Overground on behalf of Transport for London (TfL) since November 2007, initially in a partnership with MTR and as a wholly-owned subsidiary called Arriva Rail London since 2016. Known locally as the Overground, the suburban rail network celebrated its 15th anniversary on 11 November 2022.

Working in partnership, TfL and ARL strive to deliver improvements for London Overground passengers through more frequent services, new trains, better facilities and improved interchanges. The nature of the contract means that TfL takes revenue risk, setting fares, buying rolling stock and defining service levels. Each period, ARL receives a fixed concession payment with adjustments based on performance across a number of measures: operating performance; revenue protection; customer satisfaction; staff behaviour and presentation; and 'KPIs' (station, train quality standards, staff, and equipment availability).

In common with other TfL services, the Overground is denoted by its own colour, a vivid orange which was inherited from the former East London line prior to its transfer from Underground to Overground. Other services from the launch operated over the North and West London lines and Gospel Oak to Barking line. In May 2015 the Liverpool Street to Enfield Town, Cheshunt (via Seven Sisters) and Chingford services, as well as trains between Romford and Upminster, transferred from Greater Anglia to TfL to become part of the London Overground network. Trains serve 113 stations, and whilst the company saw 186 million passenger journeys in 2019-20 the impact of Covid-19 brought this down by 68.2% in 2020-21 to 59.2 million.

Initially services were all operated by a 57-strong fleet of Class 378 electric trains, all extended to five-cars in 2015. Thirty-seven dual-voltage AC/DC units cover the Stratford to Richmond and Willesden Junction to Clapham Junction routes, with 20 DC-only units working on services over the East London line and between Euston and Watford Junction.

A £260 million order for 45 four-car Class 710 Bombardier (now Alstom) Aventra EMUs was placed by TfL in July 2015, for use on the West Anglia routes and the Watford DC, Gospel Oak to Barking and Romford to Upminster lines; they are from the same family as the Class 345s ordered for the Elizabeth Line. Nine additional units were ordered in February 2018: three four-car Class 710/2 units and six five-car Class 710/3 units, the latter to allow Class 378 units to be cascaded to strengthened East London line services. Services out of Liverpool Street were initially worked by a mix of legacy Class 315 and 317 EMUs until the arrival of the Class 710 units enabled the withdrawal of the older sets. The new trains offer interconnected walk-through carriages, free Wi-Fi, real-time information screens, USB charging points and more wheelchair spaces to make accessible travel easier.

Overground night services operate on Friday and Saturday nights between New Cross Gate and Highbury & Islington, enabling passengers to connect into the Victoria and Jubilee Line Night Tube services. Boxing Day services on London Overground ran for the first time on 26 December 2019, with trains running from Highbury & Islington to West Croydon and Clapham Junction to Hackney Wick.

Towards the end of 2021 London Overground completed the rollout of 129 upgraded customer information screens; the screens were installed at 35 stations and included a 4m x 2.5m flagship screen at Shepherd's Bush station. In April 2022 Project Adiona, an initiative to refresh some of the more tired looking stations on the network, was completed, focusing on Bruce Grove, Hackney Central, West Croydon, Willesden Junction and Edmonton Green.

In June 2022 a second entrance opened at Imperial Wharf station to support growing passenger numbers, while in early July 2022 the major station improvement scheme at Hackney Central was completed, including a new second entrance and easier interchange to Hackney Downs station.

On 18 July 2022 the extension to the new Barking Riverside station opened, adding 4.5km of railway to the Gospel Oak to Barking line and marking the first extension to the London Overground network since 2015. ■

KEY STATISTICS
LONDON OVERGROUND

	2020-21	2021-22
Punctuality (on time)	83.2%	79.4%
Cancellations	2.3%	2.8%
Passenger journeys (millions)	59.2	126.9
Passenger kilometres (millions)	402	864
Passenger train kilometres (millions)	7.9	9.1
Route kilometres operated	167.4	167.4
Number of stations managed	81	81
Number of employees	1,534	1,529

SENIOR PERSONNEL
ARRIVA RAIL LONDON/LONDON OVERGROUND

Managing Director Paul Hutchings (in photo)
Customer Experience Director Charlotte Whitfield
Operations Director Matt Pocock
Engineering Director Kate Marjoribanks
Finance Director Steve Best
HR Director Oli Gant

Capitalstar: London Overground's No 378150 at Brockley with the 16.10 Highbury & Islington to Crystal Palace on 20 April 2022. **PHILIP SHERRATT**

GTR

National Rail Contract until April 2025

At its inception Govia Thameslink Railway (GTR) was the largest rail franchise in the UK in terms of passenger numbers, trains, revenue and staff. It has been operated by Govia, a joint venture between the British Go-Ahead Group (65%) and French company Keolis (35%), since 14 September 2014 on a management contract with the Department for Transport. In August 2022 Go-Ahead accepted a joint venture takeover offer from Australian bus company Kinetic and Spanish transport company Globalvia.

The nature of the contract means Govia has passed ticket revenue directly to the Government and received a payment for the operation of services; the arrangement was chosen because of the extensive work being carried out on the Thameslink route through the centre of London.

A similar process was adopted by the Department for Transport for all operators as it took control of railway financing at the outbreak of Covid-19. At the start of the pandemic the franchise was moved onto an Emergency Measures Agreement until 20 September 2020; subsequently GTR was moved to an Emergency Recovery Measures Agreement which ran until the end of the original franchise contract in September 2021 before being extended further to 31 March 2022. Shortly before this date DfT announced it had awarded a National Rail Contract (NRC) to GTR to continue operating the Thameslink, Southern and Great Northern rail services from 1 April 2022 until at least 1 April 2025, with up to a further three years at the Secretary of State's discretion. The NRC is also a management contract which has extremely limited exposure to changes in passenger demand and no substantial cost risk to GTR; on its award it was confirmed GTR will earn a fixed management fee of £8.8 million per annum (equivalent to a margin of 0.5% of its cost base) to deliver the contract, with a performance fee equivalent to an additional 1.35% margin subject to the achievement of performance targets set by DfT. The contract also allows for individual project fees to be earned by GTR on the delivery of additional initiatives as directed by DfT.

GTR replaced the previous Thameslink & Great Northern franchise held by First Capital Connect (FCC). From 26 July 2015, GTR incorporated Southern and Gatwick Express, which had previously been operated as a separate franchise by Govia. Separate branding is used for Thameslink, Great Northern, Southern and Gatwick Express.

The Thameslink and Great Northern routes connect regional centres north and south of London such as Peterborough, Cambridge, Bedford, Luton and Brighton. They provide rail links to Gatwick and Luton airports, and to Eurostar at St Pancras International. Farringdon station provides an interchange between Thameslink and the Elizabeth Line and has created a connection for trains to Heathrow airport, Canary Wharf and central London. Southern services operate into London Bridge and London Victoria from south London and the south coast, and between Watford Junction and Croydon via the West London line.

On 30 March 2020 the massive downturn in flights from Gatwick airport due to the global pandemic saw the suspension of the Gatwick Express service until April 2022. Notwithstanding the temporary timetable changes due to Covid-19, the two-year £150 million programme to rebuild Gatwick Airport station has continued and is due to be completed in 2023; the project has required a reduction in services through the station since 17 May 2020, although the reduced demand for travel, particularly at peak times, has reduced the number of passengers whose journeys have been disrupted quite considerably.

In October 2019 GTR completed its five-year £2 billion fleet transformation programme as the last of its 42-year-old Great Northern Class 313 EMUs was withdrawn, whilst on 14 May 2021 the last Great Northern service to be worked by a Class 365 Networker left King's Cross for Peterborough at 18.12.

In May 2022 a farewell tour around the GTR network marked the retirement of the company's 40-year-old Class 455 units; the trip began and ended at London Victoria, meandering through south London, Surrey and Sussex for nearly 10 hours. The itinerary took the train through more than 70 stations and included a lunch stop at Brighton. Operated during Mental

Thameslink: No 700060 arrives at Luton Airport Parkway with the 17.46 Luton to Rainham on 31 August 2022. **PHILIP SHERRATT**

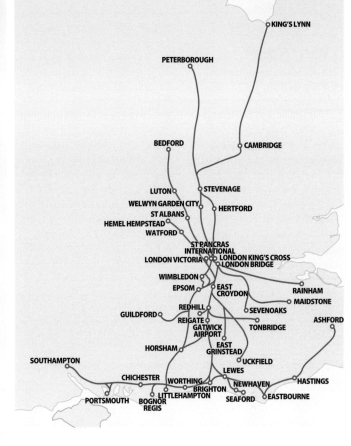

KEY STATISTICS
GOVIA THAMESLINK RAILWAY

	2020-21	2021-22
Punctuality (on time)	79.9%	74.7%
Cancellations	3.4%	5.7%
Passenger journeys (millions)	76.1	179.0
Passenger kilometres (millions)	1,777	4,696
Passenger train kilometres (millions)	59.7	57.4
Route kilometres operated	1,287.5	1,268.0
Number of stations managed	235	235
Number of employees	7,481	7,413

Health Awareness week, the train carried representative of the local Mind association for Croydon along with over 500 enthusiasts, with over £26,000 being raised for the charity.

The Siemens Class 700 EMUs work under European Train Control System Level 2 Full Supervision and Automatic Train Operation (ATO) through the central London core of the Thameslink route, a first for main line trains in the UK.

A £27 million programme, funded by DfT, to increase capacity on the busy Fen line route between Cambridge and King's Lynn, with improvements to the power supply and platform extensions at Waterbeach and Littleport stations, enabled eight-car formations to begin running on the route from 13 December 2020 with calls at these intermediate stations.

The pandemic has seen a number of timetable changes at GTR, with services being reduced and restored a number of times in response to Government restrictions and passenger demand as lockdowns eased. As with other operators, passenger numbers on GTR services have been seriously impacted; in 2019-20 the operator saw 348.9 million passenger journeys, but this fell to 76.1 million in 2020-21 before recovering to 179.0 million in 2021-22. In February 2022 changes to timetables focused on providing more

services, with 12,000 additional seats for passengers travelling in and out of London at peak times; from May 2022 the Great Northern, Southern and Thameslink timetable changes were again targeted mostly at supporting commuters returning to the workplace, although reduced demand at weekends saw some short distance routes reduced on Saturdays. On Great Northern in particular more trains were introduced in the morning and evening rush hours to and from Moorgate in the City of London. From September 2022 frequencies were further increased at busy times on several Southern routes, with 45 additional weekday train services overall.

Many members of staff at GTR have undergone training to help them better assist passengers with accessibility needs, and improvements have been made to the provision of passenger assistance across the GTR network. From April 2022 passengers with Great Northern, Thameslink, Southern and Gatwick Express have been able to book assistance for their journey just two hours in advance of catching a train, at any time of the day. GTR's driver recruitment programme is also continuing to focus on attracting more women to the industry, as well as a diverse range of candidates from all ages and walks of life that may have never considered a career in rail before.

The pandemic saw GTR introduce measures to enable passengers to socially distance more easily by using smartphone eTickets at more stations on its network; the completion of a two-year project allows GTR's passengers to scan eTickets at 60 stations bought via the company's OnTrack app or website and displayed on their smartphone or printed out at home. Despite being driven by the pandemic, it was recognised that eTickets offer an improved journey experience for many passengers anyway; the company notes that barcode eTicket sales increased in the UK from 25% of UK rail ticket revenues pre-Covid to 33% as passengers realised the benefits of non-contact travel. ∎

SENIOR PERSONNEL
GOVIA THAMESLINK RAILWAY

Chief Executive Officer Patrick Verwer (in photo)
Chief Operating Officer Angie Doll
Chief Financial Officer Ralph Pidsley
Managing Director, Great Northern & Thameslink Tom Moran
Managing Director, Southern & Gatwick Express vacant

ELIZABETH LINE

Crossrail concession to May 2025

Constructed under the Crossrail project, the Elizabeth Line, which links Reading and Heathrow Airport to the west of London with Stratford, Shenfield and Abbey Wood to the east, finally opened for passenger services on 24 May 2022. Prior to the opening of the central section services which had transferred from Great Western Railway, Heathrow Connect and Greater Anglia were operated with legacy fleets and then new Class 345 units into Paddington and Liverpool Street stations.

Services are operated under a concession awarded to the MTR Corporation by Transport for London which began in 2015. This was originally due to run to May 2023, but TfL has exercised the option of a two-year extension to May 2025.

The Elizabeth Line name, with the purple colour scheme, was announced in February 2016; the colour became closely associated with Queen Elizabeth II, featuring strongly in her Platinum Jubilee celebrations. Following the opening of the Elizabeth Line the TfL Rail brand, which had been used for the interim services out of Paddington and Liverpool Street, was discontinued. The line was formally opened by the late Queen on 17 May 2022 in what was one of her final public engagements.

The full route, which stretches for some 100km and uses newly constructed tunnels to link tracks to the west and east of London, was due to open in 2018; the total length of tunnelled sections is approximately 42km (26 miles). A series of problems, including delays to the completion of the infrastructure but most significantly issues around the on-board software on the train fleet and the way it interfaces with different signalling systems over the route, saw opening delayed by around four years.

The Elizabeth Line is electrified at 25kV AC and the tunnels, at 6.2m diameter, are significantly larger than traditional tube or underground tunnels to allow for the overhead wiring, the larger size of the Class 345 trains and to allow for a passenger walkway throughout which means that trains can be evacuated via the side doors rather than through the cabs and onto the track. Trains in the central section are driven automatically using the Communications Based Train Control (CBTC) system. Stations through the core section feature platform screen doors which only open once trains have come to a halt at the correct locations.

All services are worked by the fleet of 70 nine-car 90mph Class 345 EMUs manufactured by Alstom (formerly Bombardier), with the final legacy Class 315 units which operated out of Liverpool Street retired in December 2022.

All 41 stations are equipped with CCTV and offer step-free access; 13 of these (the central and Heathrow stations) have level access between trains and platforms.

The Elizabeth Line opened on 24 May 2022 with a passenger service between nine new London stations from Paddington to Abbey Wood, through the new tunnels under central London. Bond Street station opened later than the other new Elizabeth line stations, on 24 October 2022. Services began with a frequency of 12 trains per hour in each direction from 06.30-23.00 Monday to Saturday. On most Sundays, services were suspended for further testing and integration work.

On 6 November 2022, the next phase of opening the Elizabeth Line integrated services from the east and west into the new central tunnels and stations, with Sunday services also starting.

The final timetable across the entire railway is due to be in place no later than May 2023; at that point frequency in the central section between Paddington and Whitechapel will be up to 24 trains per hour during the peak and 20 trains per hour off-peak. At this point direct services will also be introduced from Shenfield to Heathrow Airport. ■

KEY STATISTICS
MTR ELIZABETH LINE

	2020-21	2021-22
Punctuality (on time)	88.5%	84.3%
Cancellations	1.7%	2.2%
Passenger journeys (millions)	18.0	37.4
Passenger kilometres (millions)	222	460
Passenger train kilometres (millions)	5.9	6.6
Route kilometres operated	98.8	98.8
Number of stations managed	24	24
Number of employees	1,425	1,255

SENIOR PERSONNEL
MTR ELIZABETH LINE

Managing Director	Nigel Holness (in photo)
Train Service Delivery Director	Marcus Jones
Engineering Director	Kevin Jones
Concession Director	Nick Arthurton
Customer Experience Director	Paul Parsons
Safety, Quality & Environment Director	Mark Starkey
Driver Operations Director	Paul Groves
People & Culture Director	Claire Metcalfe
Finance & Business Systems Director	Ben Milway

TFL ELIZABETH LINE

Director, Elizabeth line	Howard Smith
Deputy Director Operations	Danny Fox
Infrastructure Director	Stewart Mills

Great Western suburban service: No 345035 calls at West Ealing with the 15.02 Paddington to Heathrow Airport on 31 October 2022. **PHILIP SHERRATT**

Heathrow Express

GWR management contract to 2028

Heathrow Express launched in 1998; the non-franchised service is the fastest rail link from London to Heathrow Airport, with trains departing every 15 minutes for most of the day from two platforms at London Paddington. Journey times are 15 minutes between Paddington and Heathrow Central (for Terminals 2 & 3) and 21 minutes to Terminal 5.

Trains reach the airport on a specially constructed line, principally in a tunnel from Stockley near Hayes & Harlington on the Great Western main line, for about 3.5km to Heathrow Terminals 2 & 3. A 1.8km branch from Terminals 2 & 3 to Terminal 5 opened in 2008 and Terminal 4 (opened in 1998) can be reached by transferring to an Elizabeth Line service from Terminals 2 & 3. In 2019 Heathrow Express installed ticket barriers at Paddington, enabling customers to use pay-as-you-go Oyster and contactless ticketing.

In March 2018 it was announced that operation of the service would be outsourced to the Great Western franchise, currently operated as GWR by FirstGroup, under a contract running from August 2018 until 2028.

Heathrow Airport Ltd continues to own the service and is responsible for managing the stations at the airport; Heathrow Express also retains the commercial aspects including marketing, ticket pricing and revenue and it is expected the operating arrangement will transfer to any future holder of the Great Western contract.

Prior to the outbreak of Covid-19 Heathrow Express reported that approximately 55% of its customers were business passengers. As the pandemic developed, the significant reduction in air passengers saw the service frequency reduced to every 30 minutes for several months.

In the run-up to the pandemic almost 6.5 million journeys were taken on Heathrow Express every year, but this fell to just 0.3 million in 2020-21. As air travel has recovered so have passenger numbers, with 1.8 million journeys taken in 2021-22 when demand was still supressed.

Heathrow Express is focusing on encouraging people out of their cars and back onto public transport; it is working with Heathrow Airport to meet its goal of ensuring that 45% of airline passengers travel by public transport by 2026. Since July 2022, Business First passengers have been given access to airport fast track security when departing from Heathrow and in 2023 Heathrow Express will upgrade its customer app, adding further

new languages whilst improving functionality and accessibility to allow speedier booking.

Having been operated since its start by a fleet of 14 Class 332 EMUs, these were replaced in December 2020 by a new sub-fleet of 12 Class 387 four-car Electrostar units manufactured by Bombardier. The dedicated fleet has been specially converted so customers continue to enjoy a premium airport experience complete with First Class accommodation, high speed Wi-Fi, additional luggage racks and on-board entertainment. The trains have regenerative braking, which reduces wear and tear as well as reducing

overall energy consumption. Heathrow Express has also become one of the first train operators to run the ETCS (European Train Control System) signalling system.

Heathrow Connect, which was operated jointly by Heathrow Express and GWR, transferred to TfL Rail on 20 May 2018 and is now part of the Elizabeth Line. When services on the new Crossrail route are at full strength, rail services to Heathrow will step up from 18 to at least 22 trains per hour, although Heathrow Express will remain the only non-stop and fastest connection between London Paddington and Terminals 2 & 3. ∎

SENIOR PERSONNEL
HEATHROW EXPRESS

Business Lead Daniel Edwards
Head of Commercial Strategy Mark Eastwood
Head of Customer Experience Mike Morgan-Batney

KEY STATISTICS
HEATHROW EXPRESS

	2020-21	2021-22
Punctuality (on time)	89.0%	84.2%
Cancellations	2.0%	3.8%
Passenger journeys (millions)	0.3	1.8
Passenger kilometres (millions)	7	46
Passenger train kilometres (millions)	0.6	1.1
Route kilometres operated	29.0	29.0
Number of stations managed	3	3
Number of employees	163	183

Channel Tunnel Group

The 50.45km (31.35-mile) Channel Tunnel carries cars, coaches and lorries on shuttle trains between terminals at Folkestone and Coquelles. It has twin railway tunnels and a service tunnel and is operated by Getlink under a 100-year concession signed in 1986 with the French and British Governments; 2019 marked the 25th anniversary of the cross-Channel Fixed Link. In November 2017 the operator of the trains and the tunnel itself, Groupe Eurotunnel, announced it had changed its name to Getlink.

Eurostar and freight train operators also run long-distance international trains through the Tunnel; Eurotunnel has nine passenger shuttles for cars and coaches and 18 for trucks or lorries, each powered by two

locomotives; the Truck Shuttles carry either 31 or 32 heavy goods vehicles of 44 tonnes whilst the Passenger Shuttles can transport up to 120 cars and 12 coaches.

As Eurotunnel recovered from the Covid-19 pandemic, almost 1.4 million trucks were carried on board Le Shuttle freight services in 2021 and more than 960,000 passenger vehicles on Passenger Shuttles. This was despite the Group reporting that it was 'a year marked by travel restrictions (no unrestricted days in 2021) and the implementation of the Brexit agreement'.

The impact of new border rules has been managed well by Getlink with a new 'Eurotunnel Border Pass' launched; this is a virtual wallet which communicates with Eurotunnel infrastructure, allowing import and export documents to be automatically sent to the UK and French authorities when arriving at the Tunnel terminals. New border services facilities involve

a dedicated Eurotunnel team which welcomes truck drivers and assists them to complete customs formalities. At Calais the complete train scanner, operated by French Customs, enables the inspection of up to 30 750 metre-long freight trains per day in the Fréthun yard.

On publication of its results for the first half of 2022 Getlink reported that the gradual lifting of travel restrictions and the effective management of the re-establishment of EU to UK customs controls had led to a significant recovery in traffic during the first

weeks of 2022 compared to the same period in 2021, 'with a notable return of passenger customers in line with the trends expected by the European shorthaul airline market'.

In the 2021 financial year the Group's consolidated revenues were €774 million, with trading profit at €108 million, down 28% compared to 2020. This resulted in a net result for the 2021 financial year of a loss of €229 million. As a result, the Group announced it was considering options for the refinancing of the C2a tranche of Eurotunnel's Term Loan. ∎

SENIOR PERSONNEL
GETLINK (EUROTUNNEL)

Chairman of the Board of Governors Jacques Gounon
Chief Executive Officer, Getlink Yann Leriche
Chief Operating Officer, Eurotunnel Guillaume Rault
Chief Communication Officer Anne-Sophie de Faucigny
Director of Public Affairs John Keefe
Chief Financial Officer, Getlink Géraldine Périchon
Chief Commercial Officer Deborah Merrens

Channel Tunnel inter-city trains

Eurostar runs trains through the Channel Tunnel to link St Pancras International with Paris, Brussels, Rotterdam, Amsterdam, Lille and Calais. 2019 marked the celebration of 25 years of Eurostar, with over 190 million passengers carried since services began in 1994.

Launched by state railway companies, the British interest was sold to London & Continental Railways (LCR) by the Government in 1996. As it prepared to sell the Channel Tunnel Rail Link (HS1), the Government took control of LCR in 2009, and in 2010 a new standalone joint venture company, Eurostar International Limited (EI), replaced the unincorporated joint venture of the three national companies. In 2015 the UK Government sold its entire interest in EI for £757 million. A consortium comprising Caisse de dépôt et placement du Quebec (CDPQ) and Hermes Infrastructure acquired the Government's 40% stake in Eurostar for £585.1 million.

In May 2022 Eurostar concluded a merger with Thalys, which operated high-speed services in the Netherlands, Belgium and France, and announced that the Thalys brand would be discontinued. All services now operate under the Eurostar name but with the two different liveries retained; Eurostar Group was established as the holding company for what is now one of the biggest high-speed operators in Europe.

Eurostar Group is owned by the French national railway's SNCF Voyages Développement (55.75%), Canadian investor CDPQ (19.31%), Belgian national passenger operator SNCB (18.50%) and funds managed by Federated Hermes Infrastructure (6.44%). The company operates a mixed fleet of 12 e300 trainsets constructed by Alstom between 1992 and 1996 and 17 e320 EMUs built by Siemens between 2011 and 2018.

A twice-daily service between London and The Netherlands launched on 4 April 2018 using the new e320 (Class 374) trains which are compatible with the Netherlands high-speed infrastructure; a third daily train was launched on the route in June 2019 with the service increasing to four a day from September 2022. Initially a stop for security checks in Brussels was needed on the return trip to London, but this requirement ended on 26 October 2020.

The Covid-19 pandemic, which saw almost all services withdrawn and draconian travel restrictions imposed, had a devastating effect on Eurostar's finances and passenger numbers, with the company forced to agree a £250 million refinancing agreement with its shareholders and banks in May 2021. Service frequencies are now significantly improved, but the additional border checks when entering the Schengen area following Brexit have resulted in a significant increase in processing times for passengers. Eurostar has upgraded the French passport gates in London and more UK gates are going into Paris, and an extra French control booth is to be installed in London. Despite this, peak capacity through the stations is now 30% lower than pre-Brexit, and even with all booths staffed St Pancras can currently process a maximum of 1,500 passengers per hour, compared to 2,200 in 2019. As a result, Eurostar says it may be several years before services are fully restored and its services will not stop at Ebbsfleet or Ashford International stations until at least 2025 whilst security processes are developed and improved. In August 2022 Eurostar also announced that it was suspending its direct trains to Disneyland Paris, preferring instead to focus on 'core routes'.

Financial results showed a loss before tax of £305.4 million for the year ended 31 December 2021, with 1.6 million passengers carried against 2.5 million the previous year, when losses before tax amounted to £427.8 million. This fall in ridership is significant when it is remembered that in 2019 passenger volumes stood at 11 million journeys. In its financial statements at the end of 2021, Eurostar indicated increasing optimism that the severe dampening of demand would be short-term and hoped for increased numbers from the February half-term and Easter holidays in particular. The company reported a 'significant uptick' in business travel in the first half of 2022, with passenger numbers at around 70% of pre-Covid levels despite the reduced service frequency. With sustainability reported to be a key factor in many business travel policies and as more than 20% of Eurostar's corporate customers are mandating train travel whenever possible, the operator points out that a flight between London and Paris is equivalent to 13 Eurostar journeys in terms of its carbon footprint. ■

SENIOR PERSONNEL

EUROSTAR

Chief Executive Officer	Gwendoline Cazenave (in photo)
Deputy CEO, Chief Operations & Travel Experience Officer	Bertrand Gosselin
Chief People Officer	Nele De Brabandere
Chief Commercial Officer	François Le Doze
Chief Technology & Process Optimisation Officer	Laurent Bellan
Chief Health & Safety Officer	Simon Lejeune
Chief Financial Officer	David Sitruk
General Secretary & Chief Strategic Partnerships Officer	Gareth Williams
Chief Business Development & Integration Officer	Mattieu Quyollet

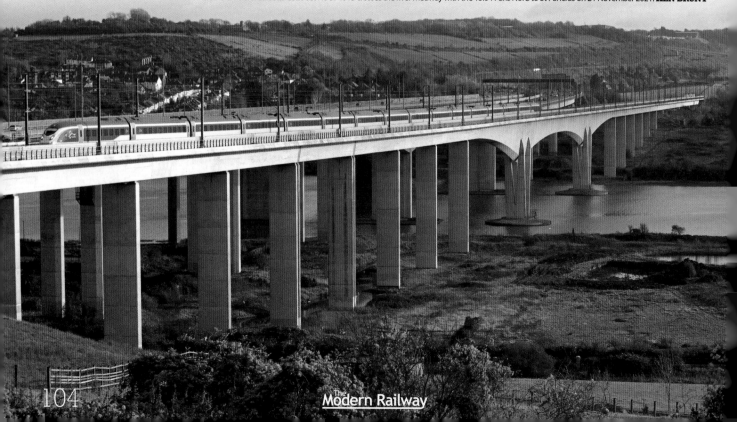

Siemens Velaro: Eurostar e320 set No 374013 crosses the river Medway with the 13.04 Paris Nord to St Pancras on 21 November 2021. **KEN BRUNT**

FREIGHT AND HAULAGE

Freight operator losses double

CHRIS CHEEK reports on another difficult year for FOCs

Generally speaking, rail freight volumes held up well during the pandemic, with the volume of freight lifted falling by 6.4% in 2020-21, rather less than the previous year's 7.4% drop. There was, however, a strong recovery in 2021-22, with volumes up to 79.9 million tonnes, a rise of 16.4%.

Despite this, the rail freight industry's run of losses continued into 2020-21, with four of the 'big five' players recording increased losses and only one operator, GB Railfreight, turning a profit. The industry's combined losses more than halved during the year, according to analysis undertaken by consultant PTIS in *Rail Industry Monitor* (RIM).

Cash operating losses virtually doubled, from last year's £14.1 million to £27.1 million, with margins going from -1.5% to -3.1%. The combined turnover of the companies analysed was 5.1% down at £876.7 million, whilst operating costs fell by a smaller 3.6%. taking the total to £903.9 million.

RIM also reports on market share, as measured by turnover. DB Cargo's share remained unchanged at 34.3%, still the lowest by some margin since privatisation. It is interesting to reflect that this figure stood at over 80% in the late 1990s. Freightliner was next but slipped back from 33.4% last year to 31.2% this. The winner once again was the post-privatisation new entrant GB Railfreight, now owned by Infracapital, which inched upwards from 21.6% to 22.9%. Meanwhile, the Nuclear Decommissioning Authority's rail arm Direct Rail Services advanced slightly from 9.1% to 9.3%.

In the summaries that follow, information is taken from the statutory accounts lodged at Companies House for the period shown, apportioned where possible to the fiscal year.

GB RAILFREIGHT

The company saw further revenue growth during the year, despite the pandemic, and improved profit levels as costs were reduced very slightly. New contracts from both existing and fresh customers saw 84 new wagons introduced, and new offices and intermodal sidings were opened in Peterborough and the company increased its workforce once more. The company remained profitable and recorded an increased margin.

PERIOD TO	31/03/2021	31/03/2020
	£000	£000
Turnover	201,055	199,277
Operating Costs	(190,686)	(190,865)
Operating Profit/(Loss)	10,369	8,412
Operating Margin	5.2%	4.2%

DIRECT RAIL SERVICES

The company's finances deteriorated once again during the year, as revenue fell by 3.2%, This was attributed by the directors to lower than expected revenue growth as a result of Covid and the deferment of a new nuclear contract. Losses were mitigated by tight control of costs, which only rose by 0.4%.

PERIOD TO	31/03/2021	31/03/2020
	£000	£000
Turnover	81,695	84,364
Operating Costs	(87,712)	(87,363)
Operating Profit	(6,017)	(2,999)
Operating Margin	-7.37%	-3.55%

DB CARGO

The UK and international companies recorded increased operating and pre-tax losses during the year, as revenue fell by 5.1%. There were savings of 3.7% in operating costs, but even so loss margins widened. In addition to the losses shown, there were also exceptional items in both years representing writebacks of previous impairment and restructuring charges. These mitigated the losses.

PERIOD TO	31/03/2021	31/03/2020
	£000	£000
Turnover	300,412	316,720
Operating Costs	(315,471)	(327,521)
Operating Profit	(15,059)	(10,802)
Operating Margin	-5.0%	-3.4%

FREIGHTLINER

The company had another difficult year, as revenue fell back by a hefty 18.3%. Operating costs were cut by 12.5%, but this could not prevent increased operating losses. The directors report that further downturns in volumes followed the imposition of national lockdowns. Turnover included £0.84 million in Covid support grant and £10.3 million (last year: £7.8 million) in government grants under the Mode Shift Revenue Support Scheme – Intermodal.

PERIOD TO	31/12/2020	31/12/2019
	£000	£000
Turnover	181,166	221,638
Operating Costs	(202,606)	(231,454)
Operating Profit	(21,440)	(9,816)
Operating Margin	-11.8%	-4.4%

FREIGHTLINER HEAVY HAUL

The group's trainload freight business saw results deteriorate further during the year, despite revenue growth of over 6%. However, operating costs rose by a higher 6.9%, resulting in the increased losses shown.

PERIOD TO	31/12/2020	31/12/2019
	£000	£000
Turnover	92,113	86,718
Operating Costs	(107,402)	(100,436)
Operating Profit	(15,289)	(13,718)
Operating Margin	-16.60%	-15.82%

West Coast containers: GB Railfreight's No 66740 passes Wigan North Western with the lightly loaded 4S57 Hams Hall to Mossend intermodal on 27 August 2022. **PHILIP SHERRATT**

porterbrook

Supporting freight growth

Porterbrook is committed to investing in rail freight for the long-term and to bringing sustainable, innovative and affordable rolling stock options to the UK supply chain.

GB Railfreight's new box wagons support modal shift and cut carbon and congestion by moving freight from road to rail.

www.porterbrook.co.uk
Linkedin Porterbrook
Twitter @PorterbrookRail

Positive long-term prospects for freight

Rail freight faces short-term challenges, but its long-term prospects are still good, suggests **JULIAN WORTH**

A school report on rail freight for autumn term 2022 might contain the headmaster's summary 'has considerable potential in the medium- and long-term but faces significant short-term challenges'. The fundamentals of rail freight remain strong and the need to decarbonise supply chains is driving – and will continue to drive – modal shift from road to rail. However, rail freight is a bellwether of the UK economy and thus faces some choppy water over the next year or two.

To put this in context, 2021-22 was an excellent year for rail freight. Volumes not only exceeded pre-Covid levels, but non-coal freight recorded the highest tonne kilometres since 1970 – and was within a whisker of being the highest since 1960. Rail freight thus had the best year for well over 50 years, which comes as a surprise to those who still perceive it as struggling and in terminal decline.

Star of the show was construction which, buoyed by high demand for aggregates from HS2 and general construction activity, had its best year on record. Nearly 24% up on the previous year, this was a full 10% higher than the previous record – and could have been higher still, but for some performance problems in the autumn leaf-fall season, when the operation of Rail Head Treatment Trains (RHTTs) put Freight Operating Company (FOC) resources under considerable pressure.

Petroleum was also 24% up on the previous year, but this was from a very low level caused by Covid travel restrictions, and the sub-sector has still to fully recover. The 'Other' category, which includes biomass, domestic waste, industrial minerals and automotive, had its best year since 2005-06 and was 11% up on the previous year, which – unlike petroleum – was largely unaffected by Covid. This was driven by greater use of biomass in electricity generation and by high

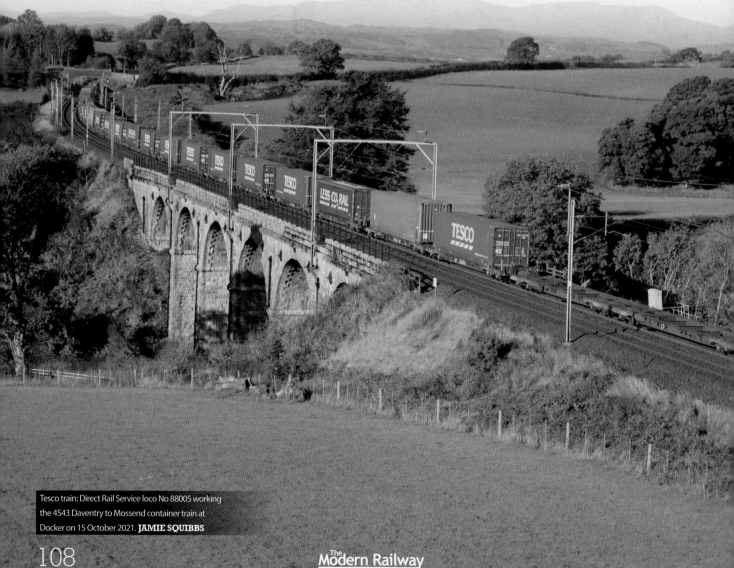

Tesco train: Direct Rail Service loco No 88005 working the 4S43 Daventry to Mossend container train at Docker on 15 October 2021. **JAMIE SQUIBBS**

levels of domestic waste, buoyed by large numbers of home deliveries and disposal of all that packaging.

GLOBAL SHOCKS

Sadly, as we moved into 2022-23, external events meant the economy turned down and rail freight's customers in almost every sector have faced much tougher times. Transport is a classic 'derived demand' and rail freight is no exception – it is dependent entirely on what customers require moving. If their sales are down, fewer raw materials are needed and fewer products are despatched, so the demand for logistics services such as rail freight inevitably drops.

Global events are largely to blame for this, notably Putin's invasion of Ukraine and the subsequent energy crisis, plus the ongoing effects of Covid on world trade and supply chains. At root is a lack of confidence about future economic prospects – businesses have reined in capital spending and corporate investors have adopted a much less bullish view. As a result, there is a marked reduction in

Coal revival: GB Railfreight's No 66708 *Glory to Ukraine* hauls an Immingham to Ratcliffe coal train through Beeston on 20 April 2022. **PHILIP SHERRATT**

construction activity, which reduces demand not only for aggregates and cement, but also for steel products such as tubes, cladding and sections.

Consumers are much less inclined to splash out on a new car, new furniture or new clothes. This quickly impacts on automotive and intermodal traffic as it is the latter products – and many others – that fill the containers which rail moves from the deep sea ports of Felixstowe, London Gateway and Southampton to inland warehouses and distribution centres. The problem is exacerbated by consumers delaying the purchase of new cars as they wait to see how electric vehicles and charging facilities will develop.

With consumers buying fewer goods, warehouses are full to the brim and cannot accept further deliveries of products they ordered many months ago, in better times. Containers sit at intermodal terminals, which rapidly run short of space, meaning trains from ports are cancelled or run lightly loaded. Ports, in turn, clog up with containers awaiting movement inland. Meanwhile, as containers are not being emptied and returned to China, there is a shortage of boxes for current orders – which may be very different to what is sitting in stock – and so it goes on.

The resurgence of Covid in China – and the stringent precautions taken by the authorities in enforcing lockdowns – mean factories are closed for several weeks and then try desperately to catch up with orders, generating further volume surges which inevitably lead to more congestion and delays. Some experts believe it will take years for this disruption of global supply chains to settle down and for the system to regain the efficiency and equilibrium it had prior to Covid.

Bringing this back to UK rail freight, the last thing FOCs want to do is operate part-loaded container trains, as intermodal margins are very tight in any event, but this is

happening all too often on some routes. Ironically, although customers want to make more use of rail and there is space on trains, congestion in warehouses and terminals sometimes means a box is moved by road. This can often be because a consignment has been delayed at sea or sat in a stack at the port and is needed quickly to fulfil an order.

COAL REVIVAL

So, where does this leave us? The first three months of 2022-23 have seen rail freight down by around 8% on the record year of 2021-22. RMT strikes at Network Rail (the FOCs were not in dispute with RMT or the other unions) and extra bank holidays for the Platinum Jubilee were partly responsible, but most traffic would probably have been moved on non-strike days and a relatively small tonnage is likely to have been sent by road instead. It is inescapable that the economic downturn was the main driver, with intermodal and construction both down by 8% and metals by 16%.

There were some smaller compensating improvements in automotive, which doubled as supply chain difficulties eased, and coal, which was up a whopping 3.5 times on the previous year. High gas prices and increased purchases of coal to provide resilience in electricity supplies through the winter lay behind this. Wind and solar energy now provide baseload generation for the grid, topped up by nuclear and gas. With the risk of insufficient gas being available and nuclear stations suffering ongoing technical issues, a cold, calm, foggy winter's day – with high demand but

little wind or solar generation – could see the UK seriously short of electricity.

To reduce the risk of the lights going out, National Grid contracted with the owners of the three remaining coal-fired power stations (Ratcliffe, West Burton and Drax) to purchase significant tonnages of coal and be ready to generate when required through the winter. West Burton and Drax had stopped burning coal over a year ago and had cleared their stocks in expectation of never using coal again. It is no small exercise to reactivate a coal handling system, boilers and turbines that were thought to be redundant, so would have received little or no maintenance in readiness for decommissioning. Drax, in particular, was actively planning to convert its last two coal-fired units to biomass and would not have been enthusiastic at resuming the use of coal.

It remains to be seen how long this coal 'insurance policy' will be needed. In the absence of a solution to the crisis in Ukraine, it has to be assumed Putin will continue to restrict gas supplies to Western Europe. Investment in renewables is proceeding apace and new nuclear will, eventually, come

on stream, but it is not at all clear that these will fill the gap left by gas shortages in winter 2023-24 or even 2024-25. It may be, therefore, that coal will continue to be required for a few more years, which would probably not present too many difficulties for Ratcliffe and West Burton, but Drax seems unlikely to want to continue using coal after winter 2022-23.

There is no small irony in the fact that carbon capture and storage (CCS) is now close to becoming a reality since, had this been developed at pace in the 1990s and 2000s, Britain could have continued burning coal for many decades. The UK is blessed with huge voids under the North Sea from which oil and gas have been extracted over the last 50 years. These would allow captured carbon to be sealed underground for millennia, but a lack of will by UK governments, of all colours, to seize this strategic opportunity meant we became dangerously over-reliant on gas for electricity generation. A more rational approach would have been to continue using coal, with CCS fitted to eliminate carbon emissions, whilst developing renewable sources of power.

INTERMODAL DENTED

Notwithstanding the unexpected boost from coal, it is clear that the short-term prognosis for rail freight is not what was hoped a year ago. Intermodal, in particular, may yet see further falls as consumers tighten their belts to pay sky-high energy bills. Logisticians were not expecting the 2022 pre-Christmas surge in consumer goods to be anything like a normal year and some were forecasting no surge at all. Imports through the deep sea container ports could well be significantly reduced in consequence. Southampton may see the biggest impact, as the shipping lines have switched the UK call on several of their routes to Felixstowe or London Gateway. The latter overtook Southampton in 2022 in terms of containers handled, an impressive statistic for a port that didn't exist 10 years ago.

HS2 construction is likely to keep construction at a higher level than might otherwise be the case, and continued housebuilding generates demand for aggregates in the bread-and-butter market. Metals is a worry, as the steel industry and its customers are

vulnerable to economic fluctuations. In late 2022 South Wales, at around 10% down and exporting significant tonnages through South Wales and East Coast ports (plus an occasional train through the Channel Tunnel), appeared to be holding up better than Yorkshire and Humberside, which was more than 20% down on 2021-22. Scunthorpe is fortunate to have the rail rolling mill as a good business stream, although this may be affected by Network Rail spending cuts. Its other businesses, along with those of the Sheffield area plants, are less secure, and doubts remain about Liberty Steel's operations at Rotherham and Stocksbridge.

ALTERNATIVES TO RAIL

For all this, there are bright spots in both bulk and consumer goods that point to a much healthier medium- and long-term prognosis. Businesses' drive to reduce their carbon footprint shows no sign of abating and long-distance haulage remains one of the biggest – and most intractable – sources of carbon in the supply chain. The solution for short- and medium-distance haulage

Biomass working: DB Cargo's No 66136 forms the 4R53 Drax to Immingham at Walden Stubbs on 8 March 2022. **JAMIE SQUIBBS**

is emerging rather faster than had been envisaged – in late 2021 Tesco started using battery-powered HGVs to move swap bodies from Wentloog intermodal terminal, near Cardiff, to its regional distribution centre (RDC) at Magor, a distance of about 20 miles.

These 37-tonne gross laden weight (glw) HGVs have a range of around 200km (125 miles), which would cover a significant proportion of UK local and regional distribution – around 60% of HGV tonne kilometres are generated by trips of 100km or less. If charging were available at supermarket loading docks and other major delivery points, to top up a truck's battery for the return to base whilst it was being unloaded, almost all local and regional distribution trips could be decarbonised in this way.

Truck manufacturers are putting huge effort into increasing the carrying capacity and range of battery trucks, but it seems unlikely that a 44-tonne gross laden weight HGV with a range of 300km or more will be available in the foreseeable future. Long-distance battery-powered vehicles could stop to recharge every 200-250km or so, but this would seriously hamper operational efficiency and push up

Toyota train: a boost for automotive freight was the launch of a new service moving Toyotas to and from continental Europe. The service, operated by DB Cargo, links Toton yard with Valenciennes in France, conveying hybrid Corollas for export from Toyota's Derby plant and importing Yaris and Aygo models. Preparations for the new service included the construction of a new automotive transfer facility at Toton and investment by vehicle logistics provider Groupe CAT in a specialist wagon fleet. On 24 October 2022 DB Cargo's No 66051 *Maritime Intermodal Four* crosses over Crofton Road Junction approaching Peckham Rye with the 6X11 Toton to Dollands Moor working. **ANTONY GUPPY**

costs – even if relatively fast high-capacity HGV charging was available at motorway service stations en-route.

Trials with motorway electrification (the Electric Road System – ERS) and HGVs fitted with pantographs are under way in Germany and Sweden, with the M180 near Scunthorpe being considered for a UK trial. However, whilst technically feasible, there are huge operational, safety and funding challenges in moving from a carefully managed small-scale trial, with specially maintained trucks and handpicked drivers, to a viable operation in the rough and tumble of the real world. There is a distinct lack of enthusiasm from hauliers about fitting trucks with pantographs and the very different maintenance regime that goes with electric power. Crucially, as well as an enormous outlay to electrify the motorway and trunk road system from scratch (as against the railway, which is already 40% electrified), the economics of ERS do not even start to work unless a very high proportion of trucks use the system and draw power from the overhead line equipment.

Hydrogen is touted as the solution in some quarters but, unlike batteries, there are very few examples of hydrogen being used in HGVs, even on a trial basis. The apparent attractions of a fuelling operation akin to diesel, with only water vapour emitted from the tail pipe, start to fade when the cost of producing green hydrogen is considered.

Where hydrogen is available as a by-product from local industry, such as on Teesside and Merseyside, it makes complete sense to use it – probably

in local buses, refuse trucks and so on. However, manufacturing clean hydrogen from wind or solar power requires three times as much energy as using the electricity in its prime form. Even hydrogen proponents agree it is better to use electricity as a direct power source where possible. Coupled with the challenges of transporting hydrogen efficiently and safely (existing pipelines are not suitable without substantial modification) and on-vehicle tankage, this suggests hydrogen is unlikely to be more than a niche transport fuel.

MODAL SHIFT

This leaves electrified rail freight as the proven, most viable solution for decarbonising trunk haulage. In the short-term, in advance of near-full electrification of the core freight network, modal shift from HGVs to diesel-hauled rail is one of the easiest and most effective ways of reducing carbon emissions from a supply chain. Notwithstanding improved HGV engine efficiency and allowing for some local road mileage from rail terminals, modal shift to rail is likely to save 60-70% of carbon emissions compared with HGV trunking.

This fact is not lost on many businesses and lies behind the decisive move to rail by companies such as Coca-Cola, Highland Spring, Tesco and Maritime Transport. Coca-Cola has switched around 30% of its HGV tonne kilometres to rail, with two nightly trains from Yorkshire, one

Slate boost: the freight yard at Llandudno Junction has been revived to support a new service transporting Welsh slate aggregate to Luton. Operated by GB Railfreight, the first train ran in July 2022. The Welsh Government provided match funding to Breedon Group for the enhancements at Llandudno Junction freight sidings via the Freight Facilities Grant scheme. **COURTESY NETWORK RAIL**

to Mossend for the Scottish market and one to Tilbury for London and the South East. Both are operated by GB Railfreight, in conjunction with Culina Stobart and Maritime Transport respectively, and the Tilbury train returns north with product from a Coca-Cola factory in North Kent. By 2023, Highland Spring will be despatching 40% of its production by rail, from a new siding at Blackford near Gleneagles, to Daventry for final

distribution to retailers in the South, the Midlands and East Anglia.

It is hard to imagine two better examples of fast-moving consumer goods than Coca-Cola and Highland Spring, and both companies have committed themselves firmly to rail trunking. The UK's biggest retailer, Tesco, has used rail for the last decade but continues to expand and now has 14 trains a day on five routes, with an intention of adding an extra service

every six months. Many other retailers and manufacturers use rail on a daily basis, but do so via the eight daily multi-customer trains operated between Daventry and Central Scotland by Russell Logistics and Malcolm Logistics.

THIRD PARTY LOGISTICS

Maritime Transport's move into rail is particularly significant, since the company is the UK's largest road container haulier. John Williams, its

far-sighted Chairman, is clear that the days of long-distance road movements are coming to an end and that rail is the future for trunking, allied to regional distribution by his road fleet. To this end, he is investing over £50 million in intermodal terminals as the hubs in a multimodal supply chain network. The investment is already paying back as, at a time when many road hauliers are struggling, Maritime has increased its turnover and profit, which John Williams attributes in no small measure to his rail activities.

Crucially, these are now extending beyond ports to inland terminal container movements to domestic trunking between terminals across Britain – such as the Coca-Cola business mentioned above. Mr Williams sees this as the company's major growth opportunity in the future, providing end-to-end zero carbon logistics services which use rail for the trunk haul. This model, superficially similar to the old domestic Freightliner operation, lends itself much more to being Third Party Logistician (3PL)-led rather than FOC-led. 3PLs have the knowledge and experience of working closely with customers on the fine detail of fast-moving consumer goods supply chain operations, a skill set FOCs do not have and would find it hard to acquire and sustain. Far better that FOCs partner with 3PLs like Maritime, Russell and Malcolm to provide an

Aggregates to North Blyth: in summer 2022 GB Railfreight started a new service moving aggregates from Shap Summit Quarry to Battleship Wharf in North Blyth for Breedon to be used for the foundations of a BritishVolt gigaplant, but uncertainty over the scheme led to the service being suspended in autumn 2022. On the morning of 5 July 2022, No 66798 hauls the empty wagons from the first working with the return move to Shap, here passing Freemans Crossing. **BILL WELSH**

integrated service to the end customer, as GBRf has done with Coca-Cola through Maritime and Culina Stobart.

Multi-customer trains assembled by 3PLs from a wide variety of customers are critical to the expansion of rail in the consumer goods market, since very few customers have the volume to run their own trains in the way Tesco and Coca-Cola do. Even these majors do not always use all the capacity on a train and sell slots to other companies to maximise utilisation, particularly on the return leg. An example of this is the use of Tesco's train from Inverness to Mossend, and thence to Daventry, to move fibreboard produced in the Highlands to markets in the South. In addition, many supply chains require deliveries to be spread through the day so, even if there is sufficient daily volume for a train, loads may need to be despatched at four- or six-hourly intervals – this is frequently the case with chilled and fresh produce. In such circumstances, a spread of multi-customer trains across the 24 hours can bring the business to rail in a way one dedicated customer train cannot.

NEW TERMINALS

John Williams is not alone in seeing the crucial importance of terminals to the development of rail and decarbonising supply chains. Commercial property investors, such as Prologis and SEGRO, are pumping

Cambrian timber: the first freight train on the Cambrian line for many years operated on 29 April 2022, when Colas Rail hauled timber from forests in Ceredigion and Powys by rail from Aberystwyth to the Kronospan factory in Chirk. In fading evening light ETCS-fitted Network Rail loco Nos 97304/303 head east with the inaugural working. **COURTESY NETWORK RAIL**

hundreds of millions of pounds into Strategic Rail Freight Interchanges (SRFIs), where an on-site intermodal terminal allows containers and swap bodies to be moved between a train and warehouses without using public roads. The ability to use shunt tractors and dolly trailers instead of HGVs and scarce Class 1 drivers saves £80 to £100 on every load – a huge saving over the 20-year life of a warehouse.

The 'Golden Triangle of Logistics' in the Midlands, where many major National Distribution Centres (NDC) are located, is the fulcrum of SRFI development. Daventry International Rail Freight Terminal (DIRFT) was the first such facility, established in 1994 for Channel Tunnel traffic, and has gone from strength to strength, with the opening of DIRFT III – a continental-scale terminal alongside the M1 – now imminent. This kilometre-long behemoth has five tracks, surrounded by acres of concrete for container handling and storage, capable of dealing with around 30 775-metre trains a day. Alongside the main terminal an 800,000 square foot NDC hub for Royal Mail, with its own station platform for handling express logistics/mail trains, is being commissioned – around 12 arrivals/departures per day are envisaged.

Other well-established SRFIs are located at Hams Hall and Birch Coppice to the north east of Birmingham and have continued to grow. East Midlands Gateway has been in operation for only three years but, such is its success, it is being doubled in size seven years earlier than expected. Further north, in Yorkshire, iPort at Doncaster has been similarly successful and is also to be doubled in size. Next in line is Northampton Gateway, which is in build and is expected to open in 2023-24. This will be followed by West Midlands Interchange (WMI) near Penkridge, for which construction contracts have been awarded. A Development Consent Order (DCO) application for Hinckley National Rail Freight Interchange is likely to be submitted in 2023 and other proposals are being developed for Stanton, near Ilkeston and Etwall, south of Derby.

Other SRFI proposals are being worked up 'under the radar'. Some of these are located in the Golden Triangle and others in the RDC clusters around the UK. These are key locations for trunking and it is important SRFIs are forthcoming to facilitate the use of rail for flows into these clusters. Parkside, near Warrington, at the heart of the North West cluster, is at the early (non-rail) stage of development and there are also proposals for a rail terminal to serve the South West cluster at Avonmouth.

The Scottish cluster is reasonably well served by terminals at Mossend (two), Coatbridge and Grangemouth, but a full-blown SRFI is being developed by P.D. Stirling and partners – Mossend International Railfreight Park (MIRP) – and the J.G. Russell Group is planning to create a major SRFI on part of the former Ravenscraig steelworks. Anglo-Scottish trunking is already rail's strongest domestic consumer goods route and the 300km-plus distance from markets in England makes it the best prospect for early and sizeable modal shift. The apparent proliferation of terminal capacity in the Scottish central belt is thus entirely logical and is to be welcomed.

MODAL TRANSFER FACILITIES

Two further types of terminal will need to be developed in due course, both much smaller than SRFIs and consisting of simple modal transfer facilities – essentially a siding with hard standing and road access for HGVs. The first is to serve remote areas such as the far South West, where stores are a long road haul from RDCs at Avonmouth. Mid-Cornwall is further from Avonmouth than Inverness is from Central Scotland, so a Tesco-type operation would be logical. It was thought for many years that the restricted loading gauge beyond Exeter precluded intermodal operations to

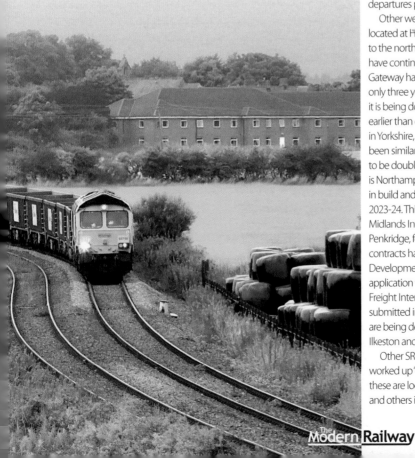

Machen revived: in March 2022 DCRail instigated new aggregates flows from Machen quarry, near Newport, South Wales to Oxford Banbury Road terminal, and from Newton Abbot Hackney yard to Hitchin. On 11 August 2022 No 60046 slows to collect the token from the signaller at Park Junction, Newport with a working of empties from Oxford to Machen. **KEN BRUNT**

Plymouth and Cornwall, but it has now been established that low-floor wagons will allow most types of containers and swap bodies to be conveyed – there is optimism that an initial service might start in 2023.

The second type of terminal is edge-of-city transfer points where smaller swap bodies (20 to 30 feet long, refrigerated as necessary) could be lifted from trains loaded with picked product at a central distribution centre onto purpose-built battery city logistics trucks for delivery to stores across the city. This is a different and parallel market to express logistics trains into city centre stations for final delivery by e-vans, e-bikes and couriers. The latter is a parcels market, whereas the 20 to 30 foot swap bodies are geared to volume consumer goods, which are currently delivered to stores by HGVs.

Although online shopping has grown substantially, most home deliveries are from supermarkets and follow the standard retail supply chain from RDC to store, before being delivered in a van to customers' homes. It is a common and serious misconception that online shopping equates to parcels operations: far from it – for all Amazon's success, the volume of goods routed via stores is substantially greater than that moved as parcels. Edge-of-city intermodal terminals are thus likely to be more important for urban logistics than city centre stations, but the two are complementary and in no sense mutually exclusive.

STEEL PROSPECTS

Away from consumer goods, the steel industry is also very focused on decarbonisation and Tata, which already sends close to 80% of its output from South Wales by rail, is keen to find rail/intermodal solutions for finished products from plants in North Wales, the Midlands and the North East. A more far-reaching impact of decarbonisation would be seen if Tata Port Talbot and British Steel Scunthorpe switched from blast furnace production to electric arc furnaces. This would see inbound flows of iron ore and coking coal replaced by large tonnages of scrap metal. Most scrap generated in the UK is currently exported, with only a small proportion moved to ports by rail. Significant new rail flows could be expected to emerge on routes such as the South East and the Midlands to South Wales, amounting to possibly three to four million tonnes a year.

A number of scrap terminals already exist in the urban areas, albeit some are mothballed, but more will be needed to supply such volumes. Scrap could be a mirror image of aggregate movements into urban areas and could employ a similar modus operandi, with portions of trains from a series of relatively compact urban terminals combined into a large train for the trunk haul to the steel works. We thus have a further imperative for urban terminals to add to the growing demand for aggregates and the consumer goods opportunities outlined above. Strategic land use planning for urban areas needs to recognise this need and protect the small number of suitable sites along rail lines against residential development, which is always seen as the top priority.

CONSTRUCTION A BRIGHT SPOT

The biggest bright spot in bulk remains construction materials – cement and blocks/bricks as well as aggregates,

Containers from Felixstowe: Freightliner's No 90006 *Modern Railways magazine/Roger Ford* is partially reflected in the river Stour estuary at Cattawade during high tide on 15 July 2022 while powering the 4M87 Felixstowe to Trafford Park intermodal. **ANTONY GUPPY**

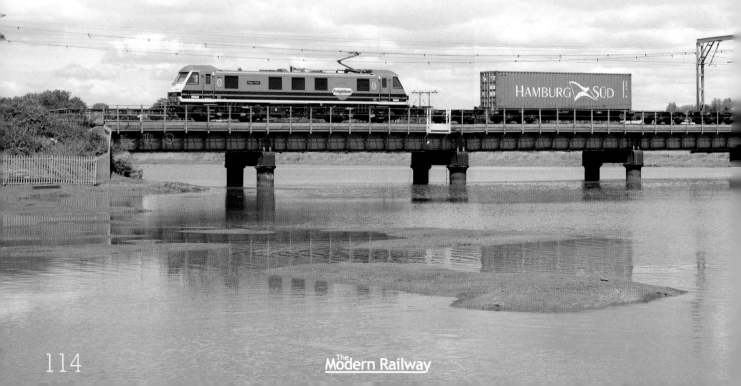

although the latter is where the big tonnages lie. This is partly driven by decarbonisation but even more so by economies of scale of production and progressive exhaustion of local sources close to urban areas.

The Mineral Products Association published its updated Minerals Strategy in October 2022, which highlighted that demand for aggregates was likely to increase by 20-30% over the next 20 years but that permitted reserves of land-won sand and gravel are rapidly being consumed. More use can be made of secondary aggregates like slag and slate waste, but greater use of crushed rock and/or sea-dredged sand and gravel will be inevitable if demand is to be met.

Producers are agreed that investment in both material sources will be concentrated at large facilities (quarries or landing points) which, because of their scale and supply chain economics, will almost certainly be rail-connected. This is very likely to result in a substantial increase in rail movements, with one producer alone expecting the rail market share of its output to double or even treble. The last year has seen a host of new terminals opened around Birmingham plus several more in London, whilst volumes continue to increase through the established terminal network.

Already, the growing demand for rail-borne aggregates has outstripped capacity of the established quarries and the aggregate majors are actively developing additional sources. Tarmac has reopened long-dormant quarries

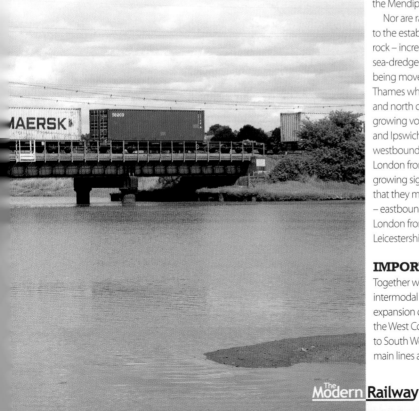

Mendips heavy haul: No 59205, unbranded but now owned by Freightliner, heads west of Newbury powering the 7C77 Wembley reception sidings to Merehead on 18 October 2022. **JAMIE SQUIBBS**

at Hindlow and Hillhead in the Peak District and has opened a new loading facility for seaborne aggregates at Tilbury. It has also reactivated loading facilities and run trains from Ferryhill quarry in County Durham. Hanson has reopened Tytherington quarry, north of Bristol, with increased capacity, and reactivated mothballed rail loading facilities at Penmaenmawr in North Wales, Machen (near Newport) and Shap.

Aggregate Industries is using significant tonnages of Scottish granite shipped into the Thames and moved by rail to terminals in the South East. Cemex is forwarding increasing tonnages from its Dove Holes quarry in the Peak District and Breedon is doing likewise from its Dow Low quarry

nearby. Breedon has also started to send slate waste from a new terminal at Llandudno Junction to depots in the Midlands and the South East. Another secondary aggregate seeing increased use is steelworks slag, with Tarmac sending several trains a week from Port Talbot to the South East.

As can be seen, the Peak District has taken off as a source of aggregates and is getting close to the output of the Mendips. Both now dwarf the output of the Leicestershire quarries, which are in relative decline. Peak District limestone is now moving as far south as Battersea, Barking and west London, as well as supplying large tonnages into the West and South Midlands. South Wales and North Wales are emerging as important sources to supplement the Mendips and the Peak District.

Nor are rail movements restricted to the established flows of crushed rock – increasing tonnages of sea-dredged sand and gravel are being moved by rail, mostly from Thames wharves to depots west and north of London, but with growing volumes from Newhaven and Ipswich. In consequence, westbound movements across London from the Thames are growing significantly, to the point that they match – or even exceed – eastbound movements across London from quarries in the Mendips, Leicestershire and the Peak District.

IMPORTANCE

Together with the growth of intermodal on the same routes, expansion of aggregates traffic means the West Coast, East Coast, North East to South West and Great Western main lines are seeing significant

freight growth, as is the Hope Valley. With W12 gauge clearance now added to the Transpennine Route Upgrade, with accelerated delivery, and East West Rail shortly to deliver a new direct route from Southampton and the South West to the Golden Triangle, rail freight is expanding its presence on the network.

It is to be hoped the Treasury will recognise the importance of rail freight to the UK economy, as well as for Net Zero 2050, and allow the Department for Transport to approve some of the pressing schemes that are needed. Capacity enhancement on the Felixstowe branch and the cross-country route via Ely is the number one priority, as is progress with freight electrification – starting with the two-mile London Gateway branch. This, and a small number of other infill schemes, would reduce the use of diesel locos for long distances under the wires, avoiding substantial and unnecessary carbon emissions.

The extreme pressure on public finances is likely to mean major projects are off the agenda for much of the next decade, but these small rail freight schemes should be much more affordable. They would also allow ministers to demonstrate they were making progress towards Net Zero 2050 where possible – a not insignificant consideration with a general election looming in the next couple of years, if not sooner. ■

Julian Worth has spent 43 years in the rail freight industry in a wide variety of roles, including Managing Director, Transrail Freight and Marketing Director, English Welsh & Scottish Railway. He is Chairman of the Chartered Institute of Logistics and Transport's Rail Freight Forum.

Collaborating for a good cause: DB Cargo was the operator of the UK Rail for Ukraine aid train, working with partners from across the industry.

DB Cargo UK is part of a large international network of rail freight companies run by Deutsche Bahn. Operating in 16 different countries, DB is Europe's number one provider of rail logistics solutions.

Based in Doncaster, DB Cargo UK is the largest rail freight company operating in Great Britain. With more than 2,000 employees, the company provides freight haulage services to a variety of sectors.

The company's core markets are metals, waste, automobiles, chemicals and aggregates. DB Cargo UK is the biggest mover of metal products in the UK, providing a continuous pipeline of raw materials to local manufacturers. Specially adapted trains transport 90% of UK car manufacturers' finished vehicles, taking them fresh from the production line to UK and international markets. A highlight in 2022 was the launch of a new service for Toyota, with loaded workings in both directions between Toton and Valenciennes in Northern France. Preparations included investment in a new £2.6 million automotive transfer facility at Toton as well as a £3 million investment by logistics provider Groupe CAT in a specialist wagon fleet.

The company also transports fuels and chemicals from UK refineries to the frontline, as well as moving huge volumes of aggregates and building materials to support some of the UK's largest construction projects. DB Cargo's intermodal services connect ports, terminals and distribution centres, ensuring the speedy delivery of some of Britain's biggest High Street brands to Britain's consumers.

Recent contract wins have included biomass transport from the ports of Immingham and Hull to Drax power station and a 10-year contract with Brett Aggregates to move sea-dredged products from Brett's terminals in Ipswich, Cliffe and Newhaven. HS2 has also been a significant source of work – DB Cargo and Hanson operated the first freight train for HS2, which delivered aggregates to the Calvert railhead.

In addition, DB Cargo UK also provides track maintenance to Network Rail and a rail breakdown recovery service to other operators, along with charter and steam services for passengers. Among the latter, DB Cargo has the charter to operate the Royal Train.

DB Cargo was the operator of the one-off UK Rail for Ukraine humanitarian aid train in April 2022. This conveyed more than 1,500 tonnes of aid, including non-perishable food, hygiene and medical products, basic living equipment, and other much-needed supplies. The 500-metre train consisted of 24 containers. The UK Rail for Ukraine consortium was established in February 2022 and was led by a project team including Network Rail, Symposium Consulting, DB Cargo UK, LNER, Avanti West Coast, MTR Elizabeth line and The Veterans Charity.

In October 2018, UK manufacturing was given a major boost with the opening of DB Cargo UK's new steel logistics centre in the West Midlands. Construction took more than 12 months and saw the German-owned freight operator more than double the size of its existing facility in Knowles Road, Wolverhampton, which receives imported steel from as far afield as Holland and Sweden. In June 2021 the terminal was the destination for the first revenue-earning train from Sunderland Docks for two decades, when No 60015 hauled 21 wagons of steel coil imported by customer Marcegaglia. This was followed in 2022 by a new flow of steel from Scunthorpe to the Port of Sunderland for British Steel.

In April 2019 DB Cargo UK announced a major new agreement with road haulier Maritime Transport Ltd which saw two of the UK's largest freight operators combine their expertise to increase rail freight capacity and competition in the intermodal market. Under the terms of the proposed agreement, DB Cargo UK was contracted to run Maritime Intermodal's rail operations out of Felixstowe and Southampton, while Maritime Intermodal took on responsibility for DB Cargo UK's terminals in Trafford Park, Manchester and Wakefield in West Yorkshire, thus strengthening the road haulier's national network of strategic hubs. In October 2021 the lease of Mossend EuroTerminal also transferred from DB Cargo to Maritime in a similar agreement.

Maritime Intermodal also took responsibility for DB Cargo UK's existing intermodal customers on its Felixstowe and Southampton services. The number of intermodal services being operated by Maritime Intermodal continues to grow; in 2021 the company added a fifth service from the Port of Felixstowe, running to East Midlands Gateway, while a two-year contract with Maersk covers movements from Felixstowe to Wakefield and East Midlands Gateway and from London Gateway to Wakefield and Trafford Park.

DB Cargo has experimented extensively with the use of Hydro-treated Vegetable Oil (HVO) as a locomotive fuel, offering better environmental credentials than traditional diesel fuel. The fuel has been used in Class 60, 66 and 67 diesel locomotives; it is synthetically made through the hydro-treatment process from vegetable oils or animal fats, which significantly reduces harmful carbon dioxide (CO_2) and nitrogen oxide (NOx) emissions when used in diesel vehicles and machinery in place of traditional red diesel. One HVO-powered Class 66, No 66004, received a distinctive green 'I am a Climate hero' livery. ∎

a Genesee & Wyoming Company

Freightliner, a subsidiary of Genesee & Wyoming Inc. (G&W), is an established, award-winning freight transportation provider, specialising in rail, with businesses in the United Kingdom and Continental Europe. Offering customers a wide range of rail freight solutions to cater for the requirements of a diverse market sector, Freightliner provides a safe, reliable and cost-effective rail freight partnership.

As a leading provider of intermodal and bulk freight haulage, with depots and terminals spread nationwide, Freightliner operates services across the entire UK rail network as well as offering rolling stock and infrastructure maintenance solutions.

Running more than 100 services daily, the company moves more than 770,000 maritime containers per year from the deep-sea ports of Felixstowe, Southampton and London Gateway to all major conurbations in the UK, offering total coverage of the UK network.

Through deep sea and inland terminals, third party sites and road depots, Freightliner provides customers with the choice of booking a rail only or a rail/road solution, enhancing the efficiency and effectiveness of their transport operations.

As a leading UK rail freight company with more than two decades' experience transporting bulk freight, Freightliner has set new standards of reliability, flexibility and customer service whilst continuing to invest in innovative solutions for every business need.

Freightliner operates 270 bulk trains per week, moving 23 million tonnes of bulk freight annually, offering haulage solutions for rail infrastructure maintenance, cement, aggregates, waste, industrial minerals, rail industry services and more.

Freightliner is the largest user of electric locomotives to haul freight, and in 2021 the company acquired 13 Class 90 locomotives from Porterbrook to complement its pre-existing 10 electric locomotives. Other environmental initiatives include the trial of a composite fuel comprising hydrogenated vegetable oil and fossil-derived fuel, which reduces emissions, and a project with sustainability specialist Clean Air Power to demonstrate a Class 66 running on hydrogen power.

Supporting this is Freightliner's in-house Maintenance Division with specialist facilities located around the country offering packages for the repair and maintenance of rolling stock and track, including diesel locomotive maintenance in Leeds and electric locomotive maintenance at a purpose-built facility in Crewe, a wagon maintenance facility in Southampton and a wagon overhaul facility in Manchester.

Freightliner has also invested in a new, state-of-the art railroad locomotive and wagon maintenance and fuelling facility in Ipswich, in close proximity to the Port of Felixstowe.

Sister company Pentalver Transport has terminals at Southampton, Felixstowe and London Gateway; Phase 3 expansion at the latter has been completed, increasing overall site capacity from 4,000 to 7,400 twenty-foot equivalent units (TEU).

Freightliner is also rightly proud of its industry-leading safety performance in the UK. Safety is at the heart of everything it does, and all aims, actions and activities are focused on the goal of 'zero injuries'. Since the G&W acquisition, Freightliner's safety performance has improved dramatically from an already industry-leading position on almost every safety metric. ∎

SENIOR PERSONNEL
FREIGHTLINER GROUP

CEO – UK/Europe (interim) Becky Lumlock (in photo)	
Chief Financial Officer Will Wright	
Chief Commercial Officer Andrew Daly	
HR Director Glynis Appelbe	
Managing Director, Intermodal Logistics Chris Lawrenson	
General Counsel Geraint Harries	
Managing Director, UK Rail Blake Jones	
Safety & Sustainability Director Louise Ward	
Strategy & Transformation Director Gideon Rutherford	

Double-headed aggregates working: Freightliner's Nos 59204/206 lead the 6A09 Merehead to Acton yard at Hungerford on 18 November 2022. **JAMIE SQUIBBS**

Rebuilt from '56s': GBRf's Nos 69005/001 haul the 4Z69 Tonbridge West Yard to Acton Lane at Imperial Wharf on 13 May 2022. **JAMIE SQUIBBS**

GB Railfreight

Founded in 1999, in the post-privatisation era unlike other freight operators which date from British Rail days, GB Railfreight (GBRf) has grown and expanded into one of the largest rail freight companies in the UK. Since September 2019 the company has been owned by Infracapital, having been sold by EQT.

Intermodal operations remain at the core of GBRf's business, supporting its commitment to furthering sustainability by facilitating the reduction of carbon emissions and consumption across the UK. Partnerships include a five-year deal with the Mediterranean Shipping Company (UK) (MSC), which GBRf has provided rail services for since 2002, with a volume-based agreement for services from Felixstowe and London Gateway to the Midlands and Yorkshire. Prior to this, GBRf and MSC UK had already launched a new intermodal service towards the end of 2020 operating to the Port of Liverpool from the East Midlands, running five times a week.

GBRf has partnered with Maritime Transport, with new services in 2022 including an intermodal service connecting Maritime's Birmingham Intermodal Freight Terminal with the Port of Felixstowe, and a service for Coca-Cola between Wakefield Europort and the Port of Tilbury.

In construction, GBRf is committed to the development of HS2, moving construction materials, spoil and aggregates and contributing to logistics operations at HS2's logistics hub at Willesden. A new service moving aggregates from Shap Summit Quarry to North Blyth for the foundations of a BritishVolt gigaplant began in summer 2022, but was suspended after the gigaplant project ran into financial trouble.

GBRf has continued to develop its fleet plans. The highlight of 2022 was the confirmation of an order for 30 Class 99 electro-diesel bi-mode locomotives from Stadler, funded by Beacon Rail. The Co-Co locomotives will have a maximum speed of 75mph and will be powered by 25kV overhead catenary or a Stage V low emission diesel engine for non-electrified routes. The design is based on Stadler's successful Eurodual six-axle locomotives used in Europe, adapted to the UK loading gauge and specifications. Construction is due to begin at Stadler's factory in Valencia in summer 2023. The first loco is due to be completed in summer 2024, and will be delivered to the UK later that year before being accepted into traffic in the second half of 2025. The remaining locos will follow at a rate of two or three per month, with the final loco in the order for 30 due to be accepted in 2026.

The operator has also continued to augment its Class 66 fleet – it

Electro-diesels ordered: visual of the GBRf Class 99, built by Stadler and financed by Beacon Rail.

has leased five Beacon Rail locos formerly owned by Direct Rail Services and has continued to import '66s' from Continental Europe. The programme to rebuild former Class 56 locos as Class 69s continues, with 16 '69s' being built by Electro-Motive Diesel, the first examples of which are now in service.

Meanwhile, the wagon fleet has continued to grow, and in late 2022 GBRf took delivery of 50 JNA-X box wagons, financed by Porterbrook and built by Greenbrier in Romania. The three companies also partnered to produce 100 Greenbrier '60 intermodal twin wagons, the first of which arrived in the UK in late 2022.

GBRf has a contract with Network Rail for operation of the Rail Innovation & Development Centre (RIDC) Melton at the facility in Melton Mowbray, Leicestershire, and has several contracts to haul new multiple-units around the network. GBRf also holds the contract to operate the maintenance trains on London's Elizabeth Line, which opened to passengers in 2022.

GBRf is based in Peterborough in a new headquarters building which was opened in 2021. It features a 24-hour control centre, training operations departments and an asset management team. ■

SENIOR PERSONNEL
GB RAILFREIGHT

Managing Director John Smith (in photo)
Finance Director Karl Goulding-Davis
Production Director Ian Langton
Commercial Director Liam Day
Business Development Director Tim Hartley
Asset Director David Golding

COLAS RAIL FREIGHT

Colas Rail Freight is part of the Colas Group, a subsidiary of the French-based multinational Bouygues, a prominent provider of railway infrastructure construction and maintenance services.

The company has won haulage contracts within Network Rail's Control Period 6 (CP6) portfolio, including network, bulk ballast and possession trains and rail head treatment trains (RHTTs). In December 2018 Colas won a deal from Network Rail for operation of rail grinding trains.

Freight flows include cement workings for Tarmac from Dunbar (Oxwellmains) to Aberdeen, Inverness, Viewpark (Uddingston), Seaham and West Thurrock; a flow of cement from Aberthaw (south Wales) to Moorswater in Cornwall ceased at the end of 2020. Flows from Lindsey oil refinery convey bitumen to Total UK's Preston production plant, to Colnbrook in west London and Rectory Junction, Nottingham, and in 2022 Colas took over the oil flow from Lindsey to Kingsbury. Colas also moves aviation fuel from the Ineos refinery at Grangemouth to Prestwick Airport and petroleum products from this plant to Dalston in Cumbria. Trains of timber for building materials manufacturer Kronospan

are operated to Chirk from Baglan Bay in south Wales and Carlisle, to which in 2022 was added a new flow from Aberystwyth. A new flow of stone from Ravenstruther freight terminal to Carlisle commenced in August 2022; the terminal is a former opencast mining site that has been repurposed to serve a nearby granite quarry.

The Colas Rail group holds various infrastructure contracts, including track and rail systems alliance and signalling deals for CP6 from Network Rail, and Colas is part of the Midland Metro Alliance which is developing and building extensions to the light rail network in the West Midlands.

The Pullman Rail rolling stock overhaul and engineering facility in Cardiff was part of the Colas Rail group, but in 2021 Transport for Wales signed a deal to purchase the business.

DIRECT RAIL SERVICES

Direct Rail Services is a subsidiary of Nuclear Transport Solutions, part of the Nuclear Decommissioning Authority. The business was established to provide British Nuclear Fuels Limited with a strategic rail transport service. The company is also active in general rail freight, mainly in retail distribution.

Intermodal is a key market for DRS, and in early 2022 the operator signed a new three-year deal with Tesco

covering a range of flows: Daventry to Mossend, Tilbury, Wentloog, and Teesport via Doncaster; Mossend to Teesport and Inverness; and Tilbury to Coatbridge. The latter flow hosted Tesco's first refrigerated rail service, which launched in December 2021. The deal extends a long-running partnership between the companies – Tesco has used rail to transport goods since 2008.

A new service for Forth Ports in partnership with Eddie Stobart began in June 2019 linking Tilbury and Grangemouth, followed in 2021 by an Aberdeen to Grangemouth service, while in 2020 DRS won a new contract to transport cars from the Ford factory at Dagenham to the rail terminal at Garston, near Liverpool.

Haulage contracts for Network Rail in Control Period 6 include network, bulk ballast and possession trains, rail head treatment trains and seasonal winter treatment trains. In the passenger sector the company provides support and traction for franchised and charter passenger operators.

Fleet modernisation has been led by Stadler (formerly Vossloh) locomotives, with 34 diesel-powered Class 68s. Some are used for passenger services, including sub-leases to Chiltern Railways

and TransPennine Express. These have been supplemented by 10 bi-mode Class 88 locomotives. Rated at 5,360hp under 25kV AC supply and at 900hp in diesel mode from a Caterpillar 12-cylinder engine, they offer 'last mile' operation on non-electrified lines. As it modernises its fleet, DRS has put a large proportion of its heritage locos up for sale.

DRS won the 2022 'Golden Whistle' award for best performing freight operator at the event organised by *Modern Railways* and the Chartered Institution of Railway Operators for the ninth consecutive year.

RAIL OPERATIONS (UK) LTD

Rail Operations Group (ROG) began operation in 2015, handling train movements relating to rolling stock delivery, testing, maintenance, modification and refurbishment programmes. Clients include rolling stock companies, passenger operators and the supply industry. Now under the Rail Operations (UK) Ltd banner, the company has expanded with subsidiaries Traxion, focusing on storage regimes for stock, and Orion, the high-speed logistics business.

In January 2021 Star Capital acquired a majority stake in the business. This in turn triggered the

Railhead treatment train: DRS loco Nos 68017/002 'top and tail' a Nunthorpe to Carlisle Kingmoor working at Metrocentre on 13 October 2021. **BILL WELSH**

Leased by Varamis Rail: Eversholt Rail's converted 'Swift Express Freight' Class 321 No 321334 is being used for a new high-speed logistics service. **COURTESY EVERSHOLT RAIL**

signing of a framework agreement with Stadler for the supply of 30 Class 93 tri-mode locomotives. An initial batch of 10 locos is due to for delivery in 2023. The Class 93 is a Bo-Bo mixed traffic locomotive based on Stadler's Class 68 and 88 locomotives. However, it has a higher top speed of 110mph and is able to operate under electric, diesel and battery power. In electric mode, it can run under 25kV AC overhead lines with a power of 4,000kW. The Caterpillar C32 diesel engine will have a nominal power of 900kW and meets EU Stage V emission requirements. Two Lithium Titanate Oxide (LTO) traction battery packs will provide 400kW of extra power to supplement the engine when the locomotive is running in diesel/battery hybrid mode, as well as for last mile carbon-free shunting operation.

In the meantime, ROG principally uses Class 37 and 47 locomotives leased from Europhoenix, equipped with Dellner drophead couplers and electrical translating equipment to eliminate the use of barrier/translator vehicles for electric multiple-unit haulage. The company is also diversifying into infrastructure testing, and worked with Network Rail and Data Acquisition and Testing Services on the test programme for the overhead wires on the Midland main line between Bedford and Corby. It has also been successful in winning contracts as test operator for a range of new passenger fleets.

The Orion business is based on the transport of parcels and light freight by using converted Class 319 EMUs. A mixed fleet of 10 Class 768 bi-modes and nine Class 326 EMUs is planned, which can

Tri-mode takes shape: the first car body for one of Rail Operations (UK)'s Stadler Class 93s in July 2022; the first loco is due to arrive in the UK in spring 2023.

be used in combination depending on customer requirements.

ROG has entered into a long-term service contract with Loram UK for the provision of vehicle maintenance, which includes inventory management, storage and service. The two Derby-based companies began working on an ad-hoc basis in 2020.

WEST COAST RAILWAYS

With its main base at Carnforth and a subsidiary depot at Southall, west London, WCR specialises in operating charter trains both on its own account and for other tour operators, using diesel and steam traction.

In addition to an extensive programme of tours throughout the year, WCR runs the regular seasonal steam-hauled trains over the West Highland extension from Fort William to Mallaig, branded as the 'Jacobite'. Traction is also occasionally provided for stock and plant moves.

The registered diesel fleet includes Classes 33, 37, 47 and

57, not all operational. WCR also manages the operation of steam locomotives belonging to various owners. Its pool of coaching stock includes four main line registered rakes – one of Metro-Cammell 1960s-built Pullman carriages.

VICTA RAILFREIGHT

Victa Railfreight has been providing a wide range of support services to rail freight customers, operators and suppliers since 1995. It operated its first trains over Network Rail infrastructure in January 2015, soon after award of its train operator licence.

In November 2021 Victa began operating a new intermodal shuttle between Immingham and Doncaster as a six-week trial. Planned to run twice daily to make productive use of assets over a short distance, the trial was launched by iPort in Doncaster in conjunction with DFDS.

Other recent contracts wins have included a deal with Cemex UK

which sees Victa provide shunting services at Dove Holes in the Peak District, working in conjunction with freight operators providing trunk haulage. Victa is also providing 'last mile' services within the Port of Tilbury for Direct Rail Services in connection with a new service from the Port to Daventry and Mossend, launched by Stobart Rail in September 2018.

As well as providing shunting and train preparation for freight operating companies and a number of train operating companies at locations across the country, Victa supplies operations staff on an ad-hoc basis to perform similar duties on engineering possession sites.

INTERCITY RAILFREIGHT

InterCity RailFreight provides for deliveries of goods to and from London using high-speed passenger trains. The first service launched between Nottingham and London, latterly carrying bio samples, and shellfish and other seafood have been transported from Cornwall to London. In 2020 ICRF said it had access to more than 100 125mph daily rail services across the East Midlands, Great Western and CrossCountry networks. The model is based on a door-to-door service, with local couriers using electric vehicles and cargo bikes to connect to trains.

DEVON AND CORNWALL RAILWAYS

Formerly a subsidiary of British American Railway Service Ltd and now part of the Cappagh Group of companies, Devon and Cornwall Railways Ltd (DCRail) is a freight operator based in Derby. Services provided include operation of bulk freight trains and terminals in London. The company recently introduced four Class 60 locomotives to supplement its fleet. In 2022 DCRail began operating a new flow of aggregates from the revived terminal at Chessington South.

VARAMIS RAIL

Varamis Rail is a new freight operating company which is aiming to deliver a new concept in parcel delivery and provide huge environmental benefits to the country. In 2022 the Doncaster-based company leased Eversholt Rail's converted 'Swift Express Freight' Class 321 unit. Having gained its operator licence, it launched a new service between Birmingham International and Mossend, operating five nights per week. ∎

INNOVATION AND ENVIRONMENT

Seeking sustainability: engineers inspect Porterbrook's HydroFLEX hydrogen train.

How rail can support the path to Net Zero

The British rail network can play a significant role in achieving the target of Net Zero by 2050 by encouraging modal shift from road transport to rail. Investment in rail infrastructure can have a substantial economic and environmental impact which can positively support economic growth through the transition to green jobs.

Many private sector businesses, including Porterbrook, have both the finance and expertise to assist the Government in delivering this policy objective.

The Net Zero transition is a huge opportunity for the railway to reaffirm its economic and social value to the country across infrastructure, operations and rolling stock. With the right vision, strategy and delivery plan, we could be on the brink of a golden age for rail as the catalyst of economic growth and backbone of tomorrow's integrated and decarbonised transport system.

For asset owners like Porterbrook there is a need to demonstrate adaptability as environmental expectations evolve. Competition plays a vital role in this respect: to mitigate residual value risk, we are incentivised to continuously invest in higher levels of safety, passenger experience and operational performance including sustainability.

These investments have included a £100 million investment to upgrade our Electrostar fleet at Govia Thameslink Railway, a £25 million contract with Alstom to upgrade our Class 458 fleet operated by South Western Railway and a £20 million investment in air quality and decarbonisation initiatives covering hydrogen, battery, hybrid and synthetic fuel technologies.

Initiatives such as those cited above can provide significant economic and employment opportunities in the future for rail and the wider Net Zero transition across operations, infrastructure and the wider supply chain. Research by Oxford Economics for the Railway Industry Association (RIA) in 2021 showed that every £1 invested in rail generated £2.50 of value elsewhere in the economy.

In the years ahead, many thousands of new employees will be needed on the railway. Research by the National Skills Academy for Rail (NSAR) predicts significant workforce shortages in the future of between 5,000 and 15,000 people per annum. The industry must at least double its annual intake of apprentices, which is currently around 2,500 a year. The research also found that a more strategic approach to skills in the workforce could also save up to £800 million a year, around 2.5% of industry costs.

STRATEGY

Porterbrook is contributing to the development of the industry's Sustainable Rail Strategy, led by RSSB, which is due to be published in early 2023. We support the advice and evidence that has already been provided to the Long-Term Plan for Rail through the Situation Reports issued in November 2021, which set out proposed goals and roadmaps for issues including carbon, air quality, biodiversity and the circular economy.

A clear strategy from Government on the pathway to Net Zero can support and incentivise businesses to better plan and deliver investment. In this respect, we support the Committee on Climate Change's recommendation that 'a comprehensive delivery plan is now needed, outlining which lines will be electrified and when and providing guidance on investment in new technologies and procurement of zero-emission trains'.

We believe a long-term system of contracting, and a circular economy based approach, would allow rail asset owners to take whole life asset responsibility. In turn, this could improve the reliability and performance of rolling stock and ensure we can use rail resources for as long as possible and get the maximum value out of them.

In collaboration with industry partners from across the rail supply chain, we continue to project manage the delivery of regular upgrades to our rolling stock fleets. This equates to annual investment of over £100 million in our existing assets, which supports over 100 UK-based companies and around 7,000 jobs.

Moreover, our shareholders have set out a very clear investment strategy and wish for the business to advance our environmental, social and governance (ESG) disclosures over the coming years. In 2022, we secured a top score of 100/100 and were named as the Transport Sector Leader in the annual Global Real Estate Sustainability Benchmark (GRESB) assessment. The result reflects the company's ongoing commitment to sustainability and key project initiatives such as the development of alternatively powered trains HydroFLEX and HybridFLEX.

The railway can be a significant catalyst for moving towards net zero across the transport system through modal shift from road. Investment in rail is prominent within the Government's infrastructure ambitions and can be an enabler of green economic growth by boosting jobs and skills on the road to net zero. Private sector finance and expertise can play an important role in supporting the delivery of these targets. ■

Dartmoor line wins top innovation prize

Industry gathers to celebrate achievements in 2022

The Restoring your Railway project to reintroduce regular passenger services on the Dartmoor line from Exeter to Okehampton won the top Major Project prize at the 2022 Railway Innovation Awards, recognising its achievement in cutting cost and time from the original plan. There was stiff competition for the prize, with Highly Commended certificates awarded for the reconstruction of Bletchley flyover, the completion of Midland main line electrification to Corby and the launch of the new Lumo open access service.

The 2022 awards, held in partnership with the Railway Industry Association and part of the *Modern Railways* Fourth Friday Club, took place on 1 July. The keynote speaker was HS2 Ltd CEO Mark Thurston, who highlighted how innovation is opt-out not opt-in for the company building Britain's new high-speed line.

Prizes were presented in seven other categories, with winners ranging from the environmental mitigations introduced by the East West Rail Alliance to Whoosh and Grand Central's Journey Central concept to a project to demonstrate a moveable overhead conductor bar for use in freight terminals. There was also a Special Award recognising the work of the UK Rail for Ukraine collaboration which organised a special train conveying humanitarian aid for those impacted by the war which began in the early months of 2022.

GOLDEN SPANNERS REWARD MAINTENANCE EFFORTS

The efforts of the rolling stock sector were recognised at the annual Golden Spanner Awards, held on 25 November 2022. The awards celebrate the achievements of rolling stock depots in increasing the reliability of their fleets. Awards are made in categories based on the type and age of train concerned, with awards for the most reliable and most improved fleets plus the fleet generating the fewest delay minutes per incident. Overall, fleet reliability

Top innovation: the restoration of regular passenger services over the Dartmoor line picked up the Major Project prize at the 2022 Railway Innovation Awards. Pictured (left to right) are prize presenter Philip Sherratt, Editor of *Modern Railways* and a member of the judging panel; Mike Parker-Bray (Devon and Cornwall Rail Partnership); Christian Irwin (Network Rail); Matt Barnes (GWR); Carla Watts (Network Rail); Ian Mundy (GWR).

Coming together to celebrate 60 years of *Modern Railways*: at the reception in the House of Commons in June 2022 organised by the magazine's team are (from left) Philip Sherratt, Editor of *Modern Railways*; Lee Rowley MP, then Minister at the Department for Business, Energy and Industrial Strategy; Anna Ince, CEO at event sponsor Resonate; Network Rail Chief Executive Andrew Haines; Shadow Rail Minister Tan Dhesi MP; Rail Minister Wendy Morton MP; Chris Loder, MP for West Dorset and sponsoring MP for the event; Adrian Cox, CEO of *Modern Railways*' owner Key Publishing.

is improving as new trains bed in and the restrictions of the pandemic ease – a creditable effort by rolling stock engineers across the country.

GOLDEN WHISTLES FOR BEST PERFORMERS

Skilful operators can make the trains run safely and on time – and the best operators deserve recognition.

For this reason, the Chartered Institution of Railway Operators and *Modern Railways* magazine joined forces to launch the Golden Whistle Awards. These awards acknowledge best practice and congratulate railway operators and infrastructure managers (including passenger and freight operators, Network Rail and Irish Rail) that have done a good job by rewarding them with that ultimate symbol of smart operating – a whistle.

Based on objective data, awards are presented for best and most improved performance in categories including on time performance and minimising delays. Awards for outstanding operator are also given out, based on nominations judged by a panel of senior figures from the CIRO.

The 2022 awards returned to an in-person format, with LNER Managing Director David Horne giving the keynote speech. A morning conference featured topical presentations about operating issues.

THE FOURTH FRIDAY CLUB

The *Modern Railways* Fourth Friday Club provides a unique networking forum for executives from all sectors in the railway industry. As well as the three awards events, four regional conferences focus on developments in the Midlands, the North of England, Scotland, and Wales and the West. Since the first meeting in 2003, the growing reputation of the club for attracting senior policy makers and top railway managers as guest speakers has seen membership expand rapidly. For more information visit *www.modernrailways.com/fourth-friday-club*. ■

EXPO BRINGS THE INDUSTRY TOGETHER

Hundreds of visitors from across the rail industry converged on Milton Keynes on 22-23 November 2022 for the first ever Modern Railways EXPO show. Under the banner of the theme 'The Future of Britain's Railway', exhibitors from all industry sectors showcased their products and services. Network Rail had a major presence, with representatives of the SPEED, Commercial & Procurement and Research & Development teams hosting stands and holding popular seminars across the two days of the show. The Rail Forum Zone hosted the CrossTech Hubble Conference, Sustainable Supply Chain drop-in sessions and a session on Rail Cybersecurity, all of which were well attended. The Future of Britain's Railways conference brought together leading industry speakers across the show's two days, with sessions on Rail Reform, Train Service Delivery and Revenue, Fares and Ticketing.

The show also formed the culmination of *Modern Railways* magazine's 60th birthday celebrations. Earlier events to mark this milestone included a reception at the House of Commons and a railtour with a CrossCountry HST to the Severn Valley Railway.

Our 2023 Programme

- **Friday 27 January 2023**
RAIL IN THE MIDLANDS
Held in Derby, this year's Midlands Rail Conference will once again look at key rail opportunities and issues within the region.

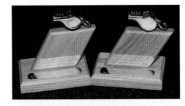

- **Friday 3 March 2023**
THE GOLDEN WHISTLE AWARDS & CONFERENCE
Our collaboration with the Institution of Railway Operators, industry operating veteran Dick Fearn hands out the awards for excellence in railway operating.

- **Wednesday 8 March 2023**   **NEW EVENT!**
RAIL IN SCOTLAND

With the high levels of interest in the future of Scotland's rail network we are staging our first conference discussing key developments. Held in Glasgow at the Grand Central Hotel, the rail conference forms day one of a two-day focus on Scotland's transport development. Day two will have a bus and coach agenda.

- **Wednesday 29 March 2023**
RAIL IN WALES AND THE WEST

This all-day conference returns to Bristol for 2023. With considerable investment in infrastructure and services across the region, this will be a popular event.

- **Friday 23 June 2023**
RAILWAY INNOVATION AWARDS

The longest established awards event in the UK rail calendar, celebrating the best in innovative thinking.

- **Wednesday 27 September 2023**
RAIL IN THE NORTH OF ENGLAND

Now established as a regular fixture, this all-day conference this year takes place at Manchester's Museum of Science and Industry.

- **Friday 24 November 2023**
THE GOLDEN SPANNER AWARDS & CONFERENCE

The 'must-attend' event for the rolling stock maintenance sector. Modern Railways' Industry & Technology Editor Roger Ford hands out his coveted Golden Spanners.

For more information please contact:
- Coordinator & Conference Manager: **DAVID LANE**
Mob: **07795 031051** Email: **david.lane@keypublishing.com**

- Membership Sales: **JAMES FARRELL**
Tel: **01780 755131 ext: 152** Mob: **07741 264791**
Email: **james.farrell@keypublishing.com**

Key Publishing Ltd,
Gwash Way Ind. Estate,
Ryhall Road,
Stamford,
Lincolnshire
PE9 1XP

KEY Publishing

the *Modern Railways* website:
/fourth-friday-club

558/22

BEYOND BOUNDARIES
or now just more of the same?

Community Rail Partnership Chairman **ALAN WILLIAMS** is concerned that changes many in the movement wish to see may be abandoned if proposals in the 'Plan for Rail' do not now proceed

As everywhere, Covid came as a great shock to community rail. Almost all activities were turned on their head. Overnight, the drive to get more people out and about using our trains became 'stay at home, do not travel unless absolutely necessary'. Our stations were silent, out of bounds. The usual gatherings of our volunteers were banned.

But unlike much of industry and commerce across the country, at Government behest, the railway didn't close, and a reduced service was provided for essential workers. On my line, as on many others, relieved of our usual promotional tasks, we were able to concentrate more on the community aspects of our role, providing information, organising transport, obtaining and distributing masks, supporting foodbanks and so on.

And when we emerged from the worst of the pandemic, it soon became clear things had changed. The numbers of people commuting stayed far below pre-Covid levels –

and still are. In contrast, demand for leisure travel roared back – on several lines, including ours, on some days exceeding pre-pandemic levels. But what should have been an ideal opportunity to promote rail travel again was constrained by the inability of many Train Operating Companies (TOCs) to restore full services because of an acute shortage of drivers.

Then came the strikes. The railway was again in disarray. Suddenly the 'do not travel' message, usually the last resort of a railway operator,

was not only back but worse than at the height of the pandemic. Because this time there were plenty of people wanting to travel, but on many lines fewer trains and on some, including ours, none at all.

Emergency timetables, sometimes changing from day to day, were in operation and bore little resemblance to those published. For many on the community rail frontline it was and remains confusing and disheartening. The welcome co-operation between TOCs that

developed during the Covid shutdowns evaporated. Once again, nobody seemed to be in charge.

Government says it wants us to promote leisure rail travel to reduce the cost of the railway for the taxpayer. But how do you promote a service which is at best unreliable and on some days doesn't appear at all?

Likewise, ministers say they want rail to be greener, a policy which community rail enthusiastically endorses. But Government continues to delay further rail electrification and other elements of rail decarbonisation. And while it says it wants to encourage modal shift from road to rail, it has announced plans for major new road construction but continues to freeze road fuel duty while allowing rail fare increases year on year.

A WASTE OF TIME?

Are we, some confused community rail supporters are beginning to ask, all wasting our time?

The answer is emphatically no. Much very good community rail work

Great idea: two of ScotRail's Class 153 Highland Explorer carriages at Glasgow Queen Street. **PHILIP SHERRATT**

continues. But there is a dire need for clear, sustained direction. Ever since Government abolished the Strategic Rail Authority in 2005, there has been no apparent overall rail strategy.

So when, in the midst of everything else, the Department for Transport published the 'Plan for Rail' White Paper in May 2021, including the creation of a whole new organisation, Great British Railways, followed by an invitation to contribute to WISP, the Whole Industry Strategic Plan, it seemed an ideal opportunity for Community Rail Network to set out its stall, the need for change founded on solid experience. Supported by 74 CRPs around the country, the movement enthusiastically took up the challenge. These represent almost 100 lines and include around 1,200 station friends groups across the country, together actively supporting almost half of all of Britain's stations, many in rural areas which are otherwise unstaffed – and often uncared for. And there is plenty of evidence that growth of ridership on community supported lines consistently outstrips that on lines which are not.

Together, the numbers involved are far greater than those of any one TOC and represent a huge pool of talent which supports the rail industry mainly for free, a resource most industries can only dream of but which remains underappreciated and therefore underutilised.

The current confusion in the industry is an opportunity for this to change, because based on years of sitting on the sidelines as observers free of political dogma, community rail really does know some of the answers.

A KEY COMMITMENT

A key commitment in the DfT 'Plan for Rail' is that 'Community Rail Partnerships will be empowered to strengthen rail's social and economic impact'. This chimes with the widely held view across the community rail network that, to succeed in the post-pandemic environment, the rail industry will need to go beyond its traditional boundaries, to reach way beyond simply trying to restore something like its traditional passenger base so as to engage with and serve communities as a whole, in many of which rail is currently simply not part of or relevant to everyday life.

We know that nationally one in four households do not have access to a car. On some parts of my line, the figure is as much as 40%, yet contracts with operators continue to encourage the status quo with expansion of car parks, which do nothing to encourage modal shift and merely add to pollution around stations.

There has been a huge increase in cycling, both for leisure and to offset increasing fuel costs, yet current rail policy and thus provision still actively discourages people from bringing their bikes on trains. My line passes through a national park, and with the support of that authority and two other CRPs we proposed that serviceable single-car Class 153s going off-lease and possibly destined to be scrapped should instead be adapted and added to existing trains to both alleviate overcrowding and act as bike carriers to meet the undoubted demand. The idea was subsequently taken forward in Scotland, and such trains are now in use, while similar proposals are being

progressed in Wales, but frustratingly neither our operator nor the DfT were supportive. Without this support, the third party funding which would have been necessary was not forthcoming, and on a daily basis people with bikes are being turned away.

ENGAGE WITH US

In its detailed and comprehensive response to the Whole Industry Strategic Plan, Community Rail Network stressed the need for a specific requirement for the rail industry to engage with, and to be responsible and accountable to, the communities it serves. Although it was a key theme of the 'Plan for Rail' White Paper, the community rail experience is that it still remains a 'nice to have' in many parts of the industry, with little actual commitment.

Community engagement and strong local relationships are vital to understanding and responding to local needs. This might seem obvious, but my experience and that of colleagues over and over again is that input on such things as timetables, fares or the condition of station facilities is consistently ignored. Unless the industry is prepared to drill down and listen to the needs of the community, it will never be able to adequately provide the services they want. Community rail is almost always the only conduit to achieve the deep dives that are necessary but which would otherwise be impossible, or at least prohibitively costly.

It needs to be clear that providing this voice for the community, as already required in the DfT's Community Rail Development

Splendidly kept station: Northern's No 158758 speeds through Hindley with the 13.18 Leeds to Wigan Northern Western on 27 August 2022. **PHILIP SHERRATT**

Taking care: station adopters at Bures, on Greater Anglia's Sudbury branch, with a Class 755 bi-mode train in the background. **COURTESY GREATER ANGLIA**

Strategy, will require Network Rail and operators to commit to a participatory, empowering approach to community rail and the communities it supports. This requires a substantial change of attitude in many quarters, providing a seat around the table, or at least a significant opportunity to input, when policy is being developed and decisions made, not just presented as a fait accompli after the event.

It is clear, too, that in some parts of the industry, even where the work of community rail is acknowledged and supported, it is viewed as just another part of the railway to be managed. It is not. It is an independent part of the voluntary sector tasked to be the 'critical friend' of the railway industry and the relevant parts of local and national government. It is this independence that enables it to provide the breadth of local knowledge and connections which often remote railway management cannot have and which provides its strength and its ability to act as that critical friend.

NEW RESPONSIBILITIES

However, in asking that the WISP recognises community rail as a partner and its involvement in business planning and decisions,

the movement has to recognise that this new role would bring new responsibilities and the need for itself to address change.

There is no single specification for a Community Rail Partnership or station adoption team and as a result there is a wide spectrum of size, commitment, activity and funding. Some are driven by representatives of the local community while others are more 'top down' and guided by local authorities, some of whom also seem to think community rail activity is a social service to be managed rather than encouraged and facilitated. Likewise, to be brutal, the degree of professionalism can vary.

However, the funding, scope and performance of each CRP is largely dictated not by any of these but by the policy of the TOC with which it works and the degree of support from its local authority. In reality, lip service to the DfT in contractual commitments aside, some TOCs are much more supportive than others. For example, in my own area, Northern, despite having more CRPs on its patch than any other train operator, nevertheless financially supports all of them and provides free travel on its network for community rail officers. In contrast, the TOC which manages the station

at which my line joins the rest of the network does neither. Not exactly the spirit of 'one railway'.

There is clearly much to do if community rail is to achieve its potential as the railway works towards the 'Plan for Rail' proposal that the main community rail relationship should switch from the 15 or so individual train operators to one of the divisions of the new Great British Railways, or possibly now one of the current Network Rail Regions.

At the moment CRPs have to work with each of the marketing departments of the TOCs relevant to their line, which in some cases can be up to five. On my line it is four, which is both time-consuming for us and confusing for the intending passenger, because each train operator has its own agenda and priorities.

It was originally intended that revenue risk would in future sit with whatever GBR becomes rather than the National Rail Contracts which are replacing franchises, and that GBR would also be responsible for marketing and branding across the national network. Likewise, it was proposed that station management should in future be integrated rather than as now the domain of one particular operator, which at

present is not always even the main user. Such proposals would imply major changes in relationships for community rail but seemed likely to be welcomed by the public.

IS IT WANING?

But, with two changes of both Prime Minister and Secretary of State for Transport since the 'Plan for Rail' was published in 2021, support for it now seems to have waned, with no commitment to either content or timescale for the primary legislation required.

There is therefore real concern across the community rail movement that the changes it regards as necessary and on which many have devoted so much of their time to develop will also be shelved and the present unsatisfactory aspects instead allowed to drift.

The first public railway, the Stockton and Darlington, opened in 1825, triggering huge changes in society. It will be a great pity if the 200th anniversary is remembered not for two centuries of progress but for a continuing refusal to recognise and embrace necessary further change. ∎

Alan Williams is Chairman of the Esk Valley Railway Development Company and a Vice President of Railfuture.

MAJOR PROJECTS

IN ASSOCIATION WITH

HS2 breaks records

Jobs boost and construction progress for new high-speed line – but there are still challenges ahead

HS2 is a huge project. By autumn 2022, nearly 30,000 people were working at 350 sites across the route. Some 2,760 suppliers are involved. The cost range for Phases One, 2a and 2b western leg is £53 to £71 billion (at 2019 prices, at which all costs are currently stated).

Main construction work on Phase One between London and the West Midlands began in 2020. Phase 2a from the West Midlands to Crewe achieved Royal Assent in February 2021, and main construction work is set to begin in the second half of 2023. And with the Government's commitment to Phase 2b from Crewe to Manchester, the Bill had its second reading in June 2022 and the aim is to achieve Royal Assent in 2025.

The Government's Integrated Rail Plan, published in November 2021, confirmed plans for the eastern leg of HS2, which will comprise a new section of high-speed railway from the West Midlands to the East Midlands, but the full eastern leg has been abandoned in favour of upgrades to the East Coast and Midland main lines. Development of HS2 East is being carried out by HS2 Ltd and Network Rail in conjunction with work to electrify the Midland main line. That the plans set out in the IRP would be progressed was confirmed by Chancellor Jeremy Hunt in the Government's Autumn Statement in November 2022.

COST AND SCHEDULE

Phase One from London to the West Midlands remains on schedule to open between 2029 and 2033. A phased opening is planned, with passenger services running first between Birmingham Curzon Street and Old Oak Common before they run through to Euston.

While it remains within its overall budget of £44.6 billion, in an update to Parliament in October 2022 Transport Secretary Mark Harper highlighted that HS2 Ltd is at risk of exceeding its final delivery cost of £40.3 billion. Of this, £18.3 billion had been spent, with an additional £1 billion for land and property provisions and £10.6 billion

contracted and not spent. HS2 Ltd was predicting around £1.9 billion of net additional cost pressures on Phase One.

Phase 2a is due to be delivered between 2030 and 2034, with a cost range of £5.2 to £7.2 billion.

For the Phase 2b western leg, delivery into service is due between 2035 and 2041, the estimated cost range was £15 to £22 billion. The removal of the Golborne link from the Western Leg Bill scheme has reduced the overall estimated cost range to £13 to £19 billion; the Golborne link was the proposed connection north from Crewe to join the West Coast main line, but Sir Peter Hendy's Union Connectivity Review recommended the Government should investigate alternative solutions, including a connection which could join the WCML further north near Preston.

MAIN WORKS MOBILISED

The issuing of Notice to Proceed for Phase One in April 2020 granted formal approval for the main design and construction phases of HS2 to get underway. HS2 Ltd awarded four main works civils contracts to joint venture organisations in July 2017 covering the route from London to

the West Midlands, and having initially focused on scheme design and site preparation these have transitioned to full detailed design and construction.

The four contracts are together valued at £12 billion. Beginning at the south end of the route, SCS Railways (Skanska, Costain and Strabag) has the contracts covering Euston Tunnels and Approaches and Northolt Tunnels, valued together at £3.298 billion.

The contract for the Chiltern Tunnels and Colne Valley viaduct (package C1) is held by the Align JV comprising Bouygues Travaux Publics, Sir Robert McAlpine and VolkerFitzpatrick, valued at £1.6 billion. This section starts around 20km west of central London and features 21.6km of high-speed line, including the 3.37km viaduct across the Colne Valley and the 16.04km twin-bored Chiltern Tunnel.

EKFB JV, comprising Eiffage, Kier, Ferrovial Agroman and Bam Nuttall, is the contractor for lots C2 and C3, covering the North Portal Chiltern Tunnels to Brackley and Brackley to South Portal of Long Itchington Wood Green Tunnel sections, totalling 80km in length. The section includes 15 viaducts, 5km of green tunnels, 22km of road diversions, 67 overbridges and 30

Getting ready to go again: TBM *Dorothy* is reassembled at the north portal of Long Itchington Wood Tunnel ready to start the second tunnel bore. **COURTESY HS2**

million cubic metres of excavation, with a total contract value of £2.269 billion.

The fourth contractor, and most significant by value, is the BBV JV of Balfour Beatty and Vinci. Valued at £4.8 billion, it holds the contracts covering Long Itchington Wood Green Tunnel to Delta Junction and Birmingham Spur and the Delta Junction to West Coast main line tie-in (Handsacre Junction), totalling 90 route kilometres.

TUNNELS

Tunnelling has been a major area of progress for HS2 so far. Construction work on Phase One will require 10 Tunnel Boring Machines (TBMs) in total, six of them to work in the London area.

HS2 celebrated its first tunnelling breakthrough in July 2022 when TBM *Dorothy* completed the first of two bores to create a one-mile tunnel at Long Itchington Wood, having been launched in December 2021. The TBM was then returned to the north portal to start work on the second of the two bores, which began in November 2022.

The longest tunnel on Phase One is through the Chilterns, running for 10 miles. Two TBMs, *Florence* and *Cecilia*, were launched in summer 2021 and by October 2022 had completed four miles of excavation. At Chalfont St Giles they met one of four ventilation shafts in the tunnel; there is also a fifth shaft for emergency access only. The tunnels are being lined with 56,000 segments from a precast factory at the Chiltern

Longest bridge: the first spans of the Colne Valley viaduct in place at the west end of the structure, with the 'launching girder' used to construct the viaduct behind, on 20 September 2022. **PHILIP SHERRATT**

Tunnels South Portal site, just inside the M25 motorway. In August 2022 the first of 38 cross passages connecting the northbound and southbound tunnels was completed. The two TBMs are due to complete their excavations in 2024.

Meanwhile, the first TBM in the London area was launched in October 2022 from West Ruislip. *Sushila* was followed later that month by *Caroline* in starting work on a five-mile tunnel to Greenford, which will take 22 months to excavate. Two further TBMs will be launched in 2023 from Greenford to the Victoria Road site, just west of Old Oak Common station, creating a further 3.4-mile twin bore tunnel. Completing the London tunnels will be a 4.5-mile twin-bore from Old Oak Common to Euston, on which work is due to start in 2024.

Contractor SCS is masterminding a major logistics operation, with as much material as possible moved by rail. In September 2021 a logistics hub was inaugurated at the former Willesden Euroterminal site, from where material excavated during the construction of the London tunnels will be removed by rail and tunnel segment rings will be delivered. In November 2022 Minister Huw Merriman launched a 1.7-mile network of spoil conveyors, which serve the Old Oak Common station site, Victoria Road crossover box and Atlas Road site. These will transport spoil excavated during the construction of the station, the crossover box, Northolt Tunnel East and a logistics tunnel.

Not all HS2 tunnels are bored using TBMs, and contractor EKFB is building three 'green' tunnels using the 'cut and cover' method. The first, which will run for 2.5km, is under construction at Chipping Warden in Northamptonshire. After a cutting is excavated, tunnel segments made by Stanton Precast

in Nottinghamshire are installed before the structure will be covered by earth to fit in with the surrounding countryside. The construction method, developed by EKFB, applies lessons from the construction of

French high-speed lines. Similar green tunnels will be built at nearby Greatworth as well as Wendover in Buckinghamshire, both by EKFB, and there are shorter green tunnels on other route sections at Burton Green

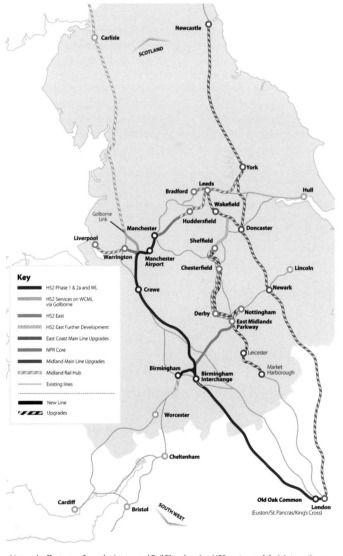

Key

▬▬	HS2 Phase 1 & 2a and WL
▬▬	HS2 Services on WCML via Golborne
▬▬	HS2 East
▨▨	HS2 East Further Development
▬▬	East Coast Main Line Upgrades
▬▬	NPR Core
▬▬	Midland Main Line Upgrades
▨▨	Midland Rail Hub
····	Existing lines
▬▬	New Line
▨▨	Upgrades

Network effect: map from the Integrated Rail Plan showing HS2 routes and their interactions with Northern Powerhouse Rail and proposed upgrades to the existing network.

in Warwickshire and at Copthall, near Hillingdon in north west London.

VIADUCTS AND CUTTINGS

Excavation is not just about building tunnels, and in October 2022 contractor EKFB started earthworks to create two long cuttings. One runs for 2.5 miles from Barton Hartshorn to Mixbury and the other runs for 2.1 miles at Calvert in Buckinghamshire. A total of 1.9 million cubic metres of material will be excavated to create the two cuttings. Material from the excavation will be reused elsewhere on the project to help create embankments, noise barriers and landscaping. In total, there will be 70 cuttings on the Phase One route.

In addition to the longest cuttings, work has begun on the longest viaduct on HS2 across the Colne Valley. The 3.4km structure will stretch across a series of lakes and waterways between Hillingdon and the M25. In May 2022 then HS2 Minister Andrew Stephenson launched a 700-tonne 'launching girder' which is lifting concrete deck segments to place the viaduct's arches into position. Originally built in 2004, the launching girder was first used during the construction of the Hong Kong East Tsing Yi Viaduct. Specially designed to handle complex viaduct construction, the machine is named *Dominique* in memory of Bouygues engineer Dominique Droniou, who played a leading role in its design and development. Some 1,000 deck segments are being built

at a factory at the Chiltern Tunnel South Portal site by contractor Align. These will sit on 56 piers, each weighing around 370 tonnes.

In July 2022 work began on the 450-metre Wendover Dean viaduct in Buckinghamshire. It will be the first major railway bridge in the UK to be built with a 'double composite' structure, which HS2 says will use significantly less carbon-intensive concrete and steel in comparison to a more traditional design.

In June 2022 planning approval was received from Birmingham City Council for Curzon Viaduct No 3 and Lawley Middleway Viaduct. These will form part of the Curzon Street Station Approach area, which is made up of four connected viaducts between Duddeston Junction Viaduct and Curzon Street station in central Birmingham. The other viaducts are Curzon Street No 1 Viaduct (furthest from the station) and Curzon Street No 2 Viaduct.

One of the earliest milestones on HS2 was the installation of the first permanent structure in August 2020 – a bridge over the M42 near Solihull in the West Midlands. This is part of work on the delta junction towards the northern end of Phase One where the line into central Birmingham will diverge from that continuing northwards towards Crewe and to Handsacre, where trains can join the West Coast main line. The delta junction will be 9.5km long and consists of seven bridges and viaducts spanning three rail lines,

eight roads, five rivers and canals and the M6 motorway. The 2,742 segments to create this complex of bridges and viaducts are being built at a site at Kingsbury in Warwickshire.

STATIONS

Work is also progressing on the four stations on Phase One.

At Euston, the joint venture of Mace and Dragados appointed by HS2 as construction partner in March 2019 moved onto the site to begin work in July 2020.

In March 2022 HS2 Ltd published updated designs for the high-speed terminus at Euston. The designs are based on a 10-platform station which can be built in a single stage; this replaces the previous plan for an 11-platform station built in two stages. There will be 10 450-metre-long sub-surface platforms and a 300-metre-long ground level concourse, with the station hall set to become the largest station concourse in the UK and also functioning as a sheltered north-south route across the site. Retail and station facilities will be on the ground and first floors, underneath a dramatic top-lit station roof. There will be entrances to the north, south and west of the station, plus internal entrances to the adjacent Network Rail station and direct links to the London Underground stations at Euston and Euston Square. Master development partner Lendlease is leading on plans for oversite development.

Another major project at Euston is the relocation of a London

Underground traction substation for the Northern Line which sits on the HS2 station site. Mace Dragados is building a new 'box' that will house the relocated equipment and provide ventilation to the tube line, connected to the current underground site by a new tunnel. The building for the new TSS has been dubbed the 'sugar cube' on account of its design.

The Old Oak Common site in west London was handed over to station construction partner BBVS (a joint venture of Balfour Beatty, Vinci and Systra) in July 2020, following enabling works by a joint venture of Costain and Skanska. The station will have a total of 14 platforms serving the high-speed line and the Great Western main line and is expected to be used by 250,000 passengers per day. Planning approval for the high-speed station was received in May 2020 from the Old Oak and Park Royal Development Corporation (OPDC).

Construction is under way on both the station box and the Victoria Road crossover box to the west of the station and in March 2022 contractor SCS JV completed the base slab construction for the Victoria Road ancillary shaft, which will provide ventilation and emergency access to Northolt Tunnels.

The contract for Birmingham Curzon Street station was awarded in 2021 to a joint venture of Mace and Dragados. In April 2020 the station received planning approval from Birmingham City Council based on designs developed by Grimshaw Architects and WSP. The two-stage

Station box: view of the site of Old Oak Common station looking east on 22 November 2022. At left is the Crossrail depot used to maintain Class 345s for the Elizabeth Line, while out of shot to the right is the Great Western main line. The green girder bridge carries the railway line from Kensington Olympia to Willesden over the Great Western main line and the Grand Union Canal. **KEN BRUNT**

New trains for HS2: visual of the winning design from Alstom/Hitachi.

main contract starts with detailed design, followed by construction. In September 2021 work began on the refurbishment project for the Grade One listed Old Curzon Street station in Birmingham, undertaken by KN Circet on behalf of enabling works contractor LMJV (Laing O'Rourke and J Murphy & Sons).

HS2's final station construction contract, for Interchange station near Solihull, was awarded in summer 2022 to Laing O'Rourke, with a value of up to £370 million. The construction site for the station covers an area of 150 hectares within a triangle of land formed by the M42, A45 and A452. Significant progress has already been made on the site, including construction of modular bridges over the M42 and A446 as part of a remodelled road network in the area to facilitate access to the new station. BBV, the main works contractor for this part of the route, is preparing the site for the new station. In 2023, after an initial 12-month planning stage, Laing O'Rourke will start the detailed design, ahead of construction starting in 2024. The station is due for completion in 2027 in advance of the railway opening between 2029 and 2033.

CONTRACT OPPORTUNITIES

HS2 has continued to award contracts, with many more to come in 2023.

The landmark award came in December 2021 with the £2 billion contract to supply 54 200-metre-long 225mph trains for Phase One and 2a services, which will be able to run on both the new high-speed line and the conventional network, awarded to a joint venture of Alstom and Hitachi. Body assembly and initial fitout will take place at Hitachi's Newton Aycliffe facility and final fitout and testing by Alstom at Litchurch Lane. The bogies will be assembled and maintained

at Alstom's Crewe site. The first train is expected to be completed in around 2027 and will enter service between 2029 and 2033. This followed a competition which included legal challenges from losing bidders.

Separately, a shortlist of three bidders has been announced for the £275 million contract to build the depot and control centre at Washwood Heath, Birmingham. This comprises Turkish firm Gulermak; Vinci Construction/Keltbray; and VolkerFitzpatrick/VolkerRail. The first design images for the depot were unveiled in June 2022.

Three companies have been shortlisted for the contract to supply signalling and control systems across Phases One and 2a: Alstom, Hitachi and Siemens. With a combined value of £540 million, the contract covers European Train Control System (ETCS) signalling and Traffic Management (TM) technology, with the potential for the extension of TM to cover Phase 2b as well. Contract award is planned for quarter two of 2023.

In December 2020 HS2 Ltd announced four shortlists for suppliers of Track Systems for Phases One and 2a, each covering separate stretches of route. The Track Systems contractors will co-ordinate the design, logistics and installation of rail, switches and crossings and precast slab track.

In October 2020 HS2 awarded a contract to PORR UK Ltd and Aggregate Industries UK to design and manufacture the modular track system for Phases One and 2a. Valued at £260 million, the companies will use a system known as Slab Track Austria, with track manufactured at a purpose-built factory at Shepton Mallet in Somerset and then transported to site. A separate contract worth up to £156 million was launched in December 2020 for a provider of around 180 switches and crossings.

In January 2022 HS2 Ltd awarded a framework contract to design, deliver and maintain more than 160 lifts and 130 escalators at HS2's four stations, to TK Elevator, with a final value of between £207 and £316 million.

Alstom and Costain are competing for the £498 million Tunnel and Lineside M&E package, while Siemens is competing with a Thales/Telent joint venture for the contract to deliver telecommunications systems across Phases One and 2a. There is a shortlist of four for the contract to deliver high voltage power supply systems for HS2, valued at £523 million: a Colas/Eiffage joint venture; a Siemens Mobility/Siemens Energy/Costain joint venture; an SSE Enterprise Contracting/Linxon/Arcadis joint venture; and UK Power Networks Services (Contracting) Ltd.

Four bidders are competing for the contract to deliver overhead catenary for Phases One and 2a: Colas Rail, Rapide JV (SPL Powerlines/INEO/Keltbray), a China Railway Electrification Engineering Group Co Consortium; and Balfour Beatty/ETF/TSO. HS2 will use the V360 design range under licence from SNCF Reseau, the first system in Europe to be certified for speeds of up to 360km/h.

Beyond Phase One, three bidders were shortlisted for the £500 million contract to become design and delivery partner for Phase 2a: 2 Connect JV (Aecom/Costain); AMS JV (Atkins/Mace Consult/Systra); and Jacobs UK. Bam Nuttall, Galliford Try, Laing O'Rourke and Skanska were shortlisted for the advanced civils works contract for Phase 2a. ■

HS2 PHASE ONE: MAIN CONTRACTORS

STATIONS

Euston	
Master Development Partner	Lendlease
Design	Over Arup and Partners/Grimshaw
Construction	Mace/Dragados

Old Oak Common	
Design	WSP/Wilkinson Eyre
Construction	Balfour Beatty/Vinci/Systra

Interchange	
Design	Ove Arup and Partners/Arup/Wilkinson Eyre
Construction	Laing O'Rourke

Birmingham Curzon Street	
Design	WSP/Grimshaw
Construction	Mace/Dragados

CIVILS WORKS

Area South (Euston Tunnels and Approaches and Northolt Tunnels)	SCS Railways (Skanska/Costain/Strabag)
Area Central (Chiltern Tunnels and Colne Valley Viaduct)	Align JV (Bouygues Travaux Publics/VolkerFitzpatrick/Sir Robert McAlpine)
Area Central (North Portal Chiltern Tunnels to Brackley and Brackley to South Portal of Long Itchington Wood Green Tunnel)	EKFB JV (Eiffage/Kier/Ferrovial Agroman/Bam Nuttall)
Area North (Long Itchington Wood Green Tunnel to Delta Junction and Birmingham Spur and Delta Junction to West Coast main line tie-in)	BBV JV (Balfour Beatty/Vinci)

TRANS-PENNINE
upgrade under way

Up to £11 billion to improve Manchester to York route

Many would say it has been a long time coming, but improvement of the Manchester – Leeds – York Trans-Pennine route is under way. Government has confirmed it will spend more than £9 billion to upgrade the route, but completion will take many years.

TRU spans the 76-mile route between Manchester Victoria, Leeds and York. While initially launched as a £3 billion scheme featuring only partial electrification, the scope has increased significantly and now includes electrification throughout, capacity and linespeed increases and the rollout of digital signalling across the whole route.

The upgrade has been broken down into a series of projects by geographical area, which are at varying stages of maturity. Two alliances have been appointed to deliver the upgrades: for the route of west of Leeds this comprises Network Rail with Amey, Bam Nuttall, Arup and Siemens, while east of Leeds NR has partnered with VolkerRail, J Murphy and Sons and Siemens.

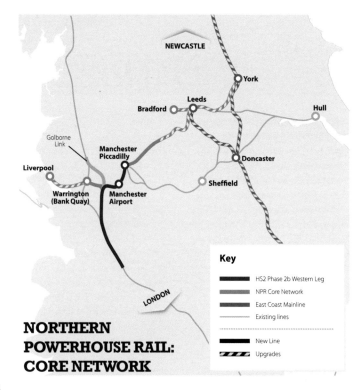

NORTHERN POWERHOUSE RAIL: CORE NETWORK

Key

▬▬▬	HS2 Phase 2b Western Leg
▬▬▬	NPR Core Network
▬▬▬	East Coast Mainline
───	Existing lines
▬▬▬	New Line
▬▬▬	Upgrades

The most advanced areas, which are currently in delivery, are at the outer ends: these are area W1 between Manchester Victoria and Stalybridge and E1 between Church Fenton and Colton Junction. In area W1, electrification is in progress, bridges are being rebuilt and the tracks at Miles Platting are being realigned to increase linespeeds.

In area E1, overhead wires are being installed between Church Fenton and Colton Junction, where the Trans-Pennine route meets the East Coast main line. Work began in October 2019, but will not be completed until 2024 as two Christmas closures will be needed to connect the new equipment to the existing OLE on the ECML. Energisation is due in March 2024, with the full scheme including a linespeed increase due for completion by December 2024.

A major milestone in 2022 was the granting of a Transport and Works Act Order for upgrades on the Huddersfield to Westtown (near Dewsbury) stretch, which includes four-tracking and electrification. This upgrade (section W3), the largest TWAO Network Rail has ever been granted, includes four-tracking, electrification and improvements at four stations, including remodelling at Huddersfield, the rebuilding of Mirfield station and relocation of Ravensthorpe station to permit grade separation at Thornhill Junction, where the lines heading east to Leeds and Wakefield diverge.

Diversionary routes will play a key role, in particular during the major works on this stretch, and enabling works are in progress on the Calder Valley and Castleford routes. The Hope Valley upgrade to the Manchester to Sheffield route, also in progress, is a standalone project, but this route will also be used for diversions during TRU works.

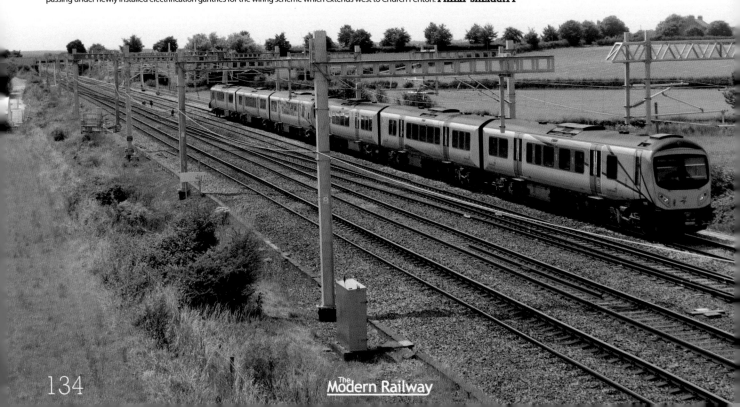

Signs of TRU progress: TransPennine Express's Nos 185118/146 approach Colton Junction with the 11.40 Manchester Airport to Redcar Central on 11 July 2022, passing under newly installed electrification gantries for the wiring scheme which extends west to Church Fenton. **PHILIP SHERRATT**

ON TO NPR

The Transpennine Route Upgrade now forms the first phase of Northern Powerhouse Rail, as set out in the Government's Integrated Rail Plan, published in November 2021, and this has prompted the approval of an enhanced version of TRU. Work being developed by Network Rail therefore includes additional capacity through Dewsbury, east of Leeds and west of Huddersfield. In the Autumn Statement in November 2022, the Chancellor reiterated the Government's commitment to the schemes in the IRP.

The IRP committed to 40 miles of new high-speed railway between Warrington and Marsden, east of Standedge Tunnel, sharing HS2 infrastructure through Manchester; this is likely to include a surface level terminus station at Manchester Piccadilly, rather than the underground through station favoured by Transport for the North. Continuing east from Marsden, trains would then re-join the existing Trans-Pennine route through Huddersfield, and thus the plan falls short of TfN's ambitions for a full new build NPR route via Bradford.

The IRP outlined the three NPR options TfN considered. The option it has selected, Option 1, is the cheapest of the three with a cost of £22 billion, but according to the IRP all three would deliver similar journey times and all offered low to poor value for money.

Assessing the merits of a route via Bradford or via Huddersfield, the IRP concluded that it is not feasible to serve both on a fast Manchester to Leeds

line. It ruled out a through route via Bradford on the basis that areas outside the city would not be best served by a new line, it being quicker for residents in those areas to travel to Leeds.

However, in an attempt to ensure the city does not miss out, the line between Bradford and Leeds via New Pudsey is proposed to be electrified and to be the subject of linespeed improvements, potentially cutting the non-stop journey time to as little as 12 minutes.

West of Manchester, TfN favoured a full new line to Liverpool with an underground station at Warrington and a new station at Liverpool. However, the IRP said this would cost around £6 billion more than its recommended option, which is for the high-speed line to serve reinstated low-level platforms at Warrington Bank Quay and for trains to then use the disused Fiddlers Ferry line, which would be upgraded and electrified, to reach the existing station at Liverpool Lime Street, which would be upgraded and expanded. The Fiddlers Ferry option had previously been criticised as a 'cheap and dirty' solution by local politicians.

According to the timeline within the IRP, Manchester to Stalybridge electrification will be completed first in the mid-2020s, followed by Huddersfield to Leeds by 2030 and

Leeds to York in the early 2030s. The Phase Two upgrades with sections of new build line would follow, with work stretching into the 2040s.

NORTH OF YORK

The East Coast main line north of York is capacity constrained, with a maximum of six long-distance high-speed trains able to operate each hour. This was a key stumbling block in the proposed recast of the ECML timetable, as Newcastle to Leeds/Manchester services would have been cut from two to one per hour.

The IRP favoured a significant upgrade of the ECML, both south and north of York. North of York, this would aim to increase the number of paths for long-distance high-speed trains to seven or eight per hour. Improvements planned include extending the four-track railway through to north of Northallerton, an additional through platform on the east side of Darlington station, an upgrade of the Stillington route for freight services, restoration of a third track north of Chester-le-Street and of the Bensham curve just south of Newcastle, and lengthening of bay platforms at Newcastle. Proposals for reopening the 21-mile Leamside line, however, are suggested as being best considered as part of a future city region settlement.

HOPE VALLEY

Plans to improve connections between Manchester and Sheffield will focus on the existing Hope Valley line, building on the present capacity scheme for which funding of £137 million was approved in 2021 and on which work is in progress.

The scheme will provide capacity for a third fast service per hour between the cities by the December 2023 timetable change. The main enhancements are doubling of the single-track section through Dore & Totley station, where a second platform is being built, and provision of a loop east of Bamford station to allow eastbound passenger services to overtake slower freight workings.

According to the IRP, Network Rail analysis suggests three NPR trains per hour could run between Manchester and Sheffield via the Hope Valley line, with targeted investment permitting them to run via Stockport. This would likely require the doubling of the Hazel Grove chord (to enable the three trains to be evenly spaced at 20-minute intervals) and restoration of a third line between Dore and Sheffield. This infrastructure could support four trains per hour on the Hope Valley line itself, but interventions would be needed in the Manchester area to provide capacity into Piccadilly. ∎

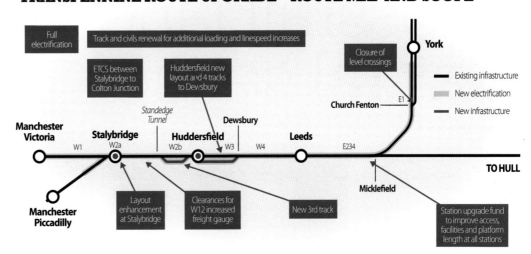

TRANSPENNINE ROUTE UPGRADE – ROUTE MAP AND SCOPE

INTEGRATED RAIL PLAN: BREAKDOWN OF PROPOSED SPEND

Integrated Rail Plan core pipeline	Provision (£ billion, 2019 prices)
Completion of HS2 Phase One and 2a (March 2020 onwards)	42.5
HS2 Phase 2b Western Leg (including Golborne link)	17.0
Smaller rail schemes in the North and Midlands until 2025	1.5
Transpennine Route Upgrade (TRU) base scope, including full electrifcation (Option F)	5.4
HS2 East Core Network (including HS2 Eastern Leg, Midland main line and East Coast upgrade)	12.8
NPR Core Liverpool–York (including TRU Option G enhancement)	17.2
Total provision	96.4
Previous spend on HS2	8.3

Source: IRP

Crossrail landmark as central section opens

Elizabeth Line launches with full service to follow in May 2023

2022 was a historic year for London's railways, with the opening of the new Elizabeth Line on 24 May. This date marked the launch of passenger services on the central section between Paddington and Abbey Wood, with the services east from Liverpool Street and west from Paddington rebranded from TfL Rail to the Elizabeth Line at the same time.

This was followed by two further milestones in autumn 2022: the opening of Bond Street on 24 October, this station being the only one not ready to open with the rest of the line in May, and then the launch of through running from Shenfield, Reading and Heathrow through the central section on 6 November. This comprises two overlapping services: Reading/Heathrow to Abbey Wood and Paddington to Shenfield, with a service of 16 trains per hour (tph) through the central section at off-peak times and 22tph at peak periods. The full Elizabeth Line timetable, with an increase to a 24tph peak service and additional direct through services, is scheduled to be introduced in May 2023.

This represented a revised opening plan. Originally the intention was to launch the Paddington to Abbey Wood service, and then to introduce in separate stages services from the Shenfield line to the east of the capital and from Heathrow and Reading in the west. The revision brought forward

Getting on board: passengers join an Elizabeth Line train at Paddington. **COURTESY CROSSRAIL**

the benefits of the project by introducing services from the east and west sides simultaneously.

BOOST

The successful opening is a welcome boost for Transport for London following a difficult period for Crossrail since a delay to the original schedule for opening the line was first declared in summer 2018. Since that point, the budget has grown by around £4 billion and the completion date has continually slipped back.

The good news is that usage through 2022 was ahead of TfL's budget, although the budgeted figures had been revised downward in the light of the pandemic's impact on people's lifestyles and the increasing propensity to work from home. Between 24 May and early October there were 54 million journeys across the whole Elizabeth Line, with 27 million on the new central section. YouGov polling indicated 24% of Londoners had used the Elizabeth Line since it opened.

Arriving at TfL in 2020, Commissioner Andy Byford stated his commitment to open the Elizabeth Line during the first half of 2022 and to deliver the project for no more than the £1.1 billion of additional funding the Crossrail board had declared was needed (on top of the funding envelope at the time). The Government provided an additional £825 million to Crossrail in December 2020, and while Mr Byford's aim was achieved there was still an additional requirement for funding to close the gap in autumn 2022. However, with these aims achieved, Mr Byford left TfL in October 2022, his last day at work being the opening day for Bond Street station.

DIRECT MANAGEMENT

One of Mr Byford's first moves was to integrate Crossrail Ltd into Transport for London in October 2020. Previously a subsidiary organisation, the change transferred direct management of the project

to TfL, with Crossrail CEO Mark Wild (who left after the 24 May 2022 opening) reporting directly to Mr Byford. The former Crossrail Ltd board was disbanded at this point, with new governance arrangements implemented.

Trial running began in May 2021, with a gradual build-up in frequency. In November 2021 this gave way to trial operations, the final phase prior to opening, which involved the testing of more than 150 scenarios in which volunteers helped validate emergency evacuation processes in the train, tunnels, shafts and stations.

The Crossrail project also included a range of upgrades to surface level stations, with this work mostly carried out by Network Rail. The last remaining upgrades, at Ilford and Romford, were completed in 2022, meaning step-free access from street level to platform was available at all 41 Elizabeth Line stations.

New Class 345 trains, built by Alstom, were initially introduced as seven-car reduced length units due to infrastructure limitations, seven-car versions also operating with simpler software than the full length nine-car variants. By spring 2022 just three reduced length units remained, due to the need for some services to use platform 14 at Paddington, which cannot accommodate a nine-car train. With the start of through running in November 2022 these three units were lengthened, creating a uniform fleet of 70x9-car trains. ∎

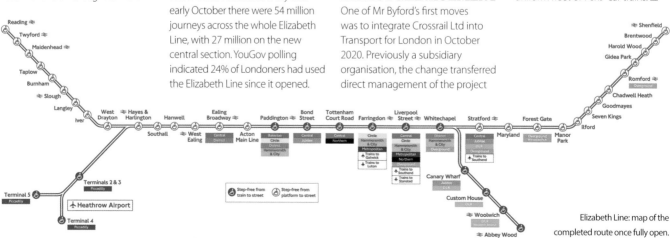

Elizabeth Line: map of the completed route once fully open.

INFRASTRUCTURE ENHANCEMENT AND RENEWAL

Uncertainty over enhancement funding

Delivery has continued despite the lack of a pipeline looking ahead

Infrastructure delivery in 2022 provided something of a contrast. Future enhancements on the railway remain somewhat uncertain; in 2019, the Government published the Rail Network Enhancements Pipeline (RNEP) with the intention of providing an annual update. The pandemic and continuing uncertainty put paid to this, and by autumn 2022 three years had passed since the sole publication, despite campaigning from organisations such as the Railway Industry Association. By contrast, renewals are funded within Network Rail's Control Period settlement, for which funding is fixed until 2024.

This does not mean the railway has stood still, and there have been successes in 2022. But some schemes which looked certain to feature before the pandemic arrived are on ice, either due to changed travel patterns (the major remodelling around Croydon is a notable example) or due to funding constraints (the Ely Area Capacity Upgrade being a case in point). Hopes of a rolling programme of electrification have also been dashed, with the proposals in Network Rail's Traction Decarbonisation Network Strategy (TDNS) declared unaffordable and the Great British Railways Transition Team working on a less ambitious approach.

WIRES ON MML AND TRU

This does not mean electrification has stopped completely. Following completion of the Bedford to Corby project and the launch of London to Corby electric services by East Midlands Railway in May 2021, work is progressing on extending electrification north from Kettering to Wigston South Junction with the same contractor, SPL Powerlines. The original intention had been to extend to Market Harborough, providing a connection to the power supply feed at Braybrooke, but Kettering to Wigston is now being treated as a single project.

A market briefing event for the remaining electrification north

Making space for overhead wires: work in progress to construct a new bridge at Nithsdale Road in Glasgow's Southside as part of the Glasgow to Barrhead electrification project. **COURTESY NETWORK RAIL**

from Wigston to Nottingham and Sheffield set out Network Rail's plans, with the route divided into seven sections. This project, although confirmed in the Government's Integrated Rail Plan (IRP), will not see contracts awarded until 2024.

England's other major committed electrification scheme is also within the IRP – the Transpennine Route Upgrade. This scheme is described in more detail in the 'Major Projects' section.

Also in progress is electrification from Wigan to Lostock Junction, west of Bolton. Although a small scheme at just 21 single track kilometres, it has been progressed because of its strategic importance in the North West. Work to reduce electrical clearances has cut the cost of this scheme, part of a general drive within Network Rail to reduce electrification costs.

Masts at Market Harborough: East Midlands Railway's No 180110 calls on 9 June 2022 with the 09.05 St Pancras to Nottingham. **PHILIP SHERRATT**

SCOTS SHOW THE WAY

When it comes to electrification, Scotland's Railway is leading the way. Following the publication of the Scottish Government's Rail Decarbonisation Action Plan in July 2020, the intention is to electrify most routes north of the border,

leaving only long rural routes served by alternative traction. Scotland's Railway is working hard to drive down the cost of electrification, and although current rates of around £2 million per single track kilometre are lower than elsewhere in the UK, the aim is to reduce this further.

Work is in progress on the Glasgow to Barrhead electrification and due for completion in December 2023, with East Kilbride planned to follow by December 2024. Plans to provide the infrastructure to increase capacity on the East Kilbride branch have been dialled down, given the changed travel patterns post-Covid.

Elsewhere, the focus is on Fife and the Borders Railway. Partial electrification is planned, covering Bowshank Tunnel to Tweedbank on the Borders route to make provision for battery EMUs to be deployed, with wiring due for completion by December 2024. Similarly, in Fife the initial plan is for partial electrification, with Haymarket to Dalmeny (at the south end of the Forth Bridge) coming first, followed by routes radiating from Thornton North, the junction with the Levenmouth branch.

That branch, which is being reopened, will also be electrified; although it will initially be served by diesel trains, provision is being made for electric operation when the rolling stock is available. The 5½-mile branch will feature new stations at Cameron Bridge and Leven, with opening planned for 2024.

Beyond that, the most advanced scheme is the Aberdeen to Central Belt enhancement. Likely to be completed in two phases, the aim first is to reduce journey times and provide additional capacity (scheduled for December 2026), followed by

electrification by 2029, tying in with the planned date for removal of ScotRail's Inter7City diesel High Speed Trains.

Supporting this electrification is a £120 million investment in power supply enhancements in Scotland, delivered by SPL Powerlines. Six new feeder stations will be built and a further nine sites upgraded. Phase one is due for completion in 2026.

CORE VALLEY LINES MODERNISATION

Electrification is also progressing in Wales as part of the Core Valley Lines upgrade, covering routes radiating from Cardiff. This scheme has faced numerous challenges since its inception in 2018, and the target date for completion is now May 2025 and the original £738 million budget will not be met.

Transport for Wales and its infrastructure delivery partners have formed the Craidd Alliance, which includes businesses contracted by TfW's partners: Amey Infrastructure Wales, Alun Griffiths Contractors, Balfour Beatty Rail and Siemens Mobility.

'Smart' electrification is being rolled out, with sections of permanently earthed overhead wire or sections which are not electrified at all to reduce the cost. A staged energisation is now planned, with the first energisation planned to Aberdare in March 2023, followed by the Merthyr Tydfil and Treherbert routes in July. Work is less advanced on the Rhymney and Coryton lines, where a two-week blockade is planned in March 2023 followed by shorter closures over the summer.

July 2024 is the target for testing and commissioning the new infrastructure in the Cardiff area, including remodelled junctions at both ends of Cardiff Queen

Street station. All being well, the wires will be energised in August 2024 from Queen Street to Coryton and along the Rhymney line as far as Lisvane & Thornhill, where the wires will end before the southern portal of Caerphilly Tunnel. The remainder of the Rhymney line, northwards from Caerphilly, is due to go electric in September 2024.

This will leave the Cardiff Bay branch, where the original ambition was to extend on-street to a new station closer to the bay. This plan is on hold for now – a new station at Butetown will be built and the existing station at Cardiff Bay enlarged. Tramway lineside signalling is due to be introduced from 2024, with the track redoubled. Cardiff Council is considering options for on-street running, with the present work making provision for on-street extensions from two places on the branch.

Meanwhile, on the Ebbw Vale branch work is in progress to enhance capacity to enable a second train per hour to run, providing a link to Newport in addition to the current service to Cardiff. The aim is to launch the enhanced service in 2023; a shuttle from Newport as far as Crosskeys has been introduced as an interim measure. Two miles of additional track is being laid, along with additional platforms at Newbridge and Llanhilleth stations.

RESTORING YOUR RAILWAY

Work on the Dartmoor line from Exeter to Okehampton has been completed. This was the first of the Government's Restoring your Railway initiatives to be completed, and the initial stage was delivered in less than nine months from its first formal funding announcement and under budget, with the application of the 'Project Speed' approach.

After a two-hourly service was launched in November 2021, a 15-day closure in spring 2022 enabled a linespeed increase to permit an hourly service to be introduced by Great Western Railway with the May 2022 timetable. In November 2022 Rail Minister Huw Merriman visited Okehampton station to hail the line's success as the number of journeys since reopening passed 250,000.

The next Restoring your Railway scheme being progressed is the Northumberland line. The aim is to reinstate passenger services on the freight-only line between Newcastle, Blyth and Ashington, with reopening targeted for December 2023. A major milestone was achieved in 2022 with the granting of a Transport and Works Act Order for the scheme. Network Rail is leading on track, signalling and level crossing upgrades, with Northumberland County Council responsible for the construction of the six stations on the line. The aim is to provide two services per hour with an Ashington to Newcastle journey time of 35 minutes.

The Restoring your Railway fund has a total value of £500 million. The headline element is an 'Ideas' fund, providing support to consultancy studies into reopening and enhancement projects; submissions must be backed by an MP. Three rounds of schemes have been awarded development funding through this element, the last being announced in October 2021. In June 2022 nine schemes were awarded further funding: the Barrow Hill line between Sheffield and Chesterfield; the Ivanhoe line between Leicester and Burton-on-Trent; new stations at Meir in Staffordshire, Haxby in Yorkshire, Devizes in Wiltshire, Ferryhill in County Durham; Aldridge station and line upgrade in Walsall; reinstating the Fleetwood line; and the Mid Cornwall Metro scheme for services between Newquay and Falmouth.

Aside from these, perhaps the best opportunity is the Waterside line scheme to reinstate passenger services on the Fawley branch in Hampshire. Network Rail has revised the scheme to be slightly less ambitious than previously planned, featuring an upgraded station at Marchwood and a new station at Hythe, although plans to run through to a station at Hythe & Fawley Parkway have been abandoned for now. A consultation on the scheme ran in summer 2022.

Wires in south Wales: overhead electrification equipment being installed at Radyr as part of the Core Valley Lines upgrade. **COURTESY TFW**

Another potential reopening in the south of England is to Hoo on the freight-only Isle of Grain branch, where Medway Council plans to build 12,000 new homes. A Housing Infrastructure Fund allocation included provision for a reinstated rail service, but it is thought more than the £63 million allocated will be needed to deliver the scheme.

EAST WEST RAIL

Construction of the East West Rail route from Oxford to Bletchley and Milton Keynes is well advanced, with opening targeted for December 2024. Whether the remainder of the scheme, which involves upgrading the Marston Vale line to Bedford and building a new line east from there to Cambridge, would be taken forward was in some doubt during 2022, but the Chancellor confirmed the Government's commitment to the project in the Autumn Statement. The Government's arm's length East West Rail Company had targeted starting Oxford to Cambridge services by the end of the

Upgrading for passenger services: work in progress on North Seaton viaduct on the Northumberland line from Newcastle to Blyth and Ashington. **COURTESY NETWORK RAIL**

decade. Target journey times are 45 minutes for Oxford to Milton Keynes, 60 minutes for Oxford to Bedford and 95 minutes for Oxford to Cambridge.

Delivery of the Oxford to Milton Keynes stretch is by Network Rail in an alliance with Atkins, Laing O'Rourke and VolkerRail. The work carried out by the EWR Alliance to revive the Bicester to Bletchley railway includes construction of 17 new bridges, reconstruction of 26 others, the installation of 63km of new track and a range of earthworks. Bletchley flyover has been partially rebuilt, construction is well in hand on platforms on the flyover and a new station at Winslow, and tracklaying is progressing. The aim is to have the infrastructure ready for testing to begin in May 2024.

Helping facilitate EWR is an upgrade at Oxford station. In August 2022 the Department for Transport confirmed further funding for the project and a Transport and Works Act Order has been granted. Changes include provision of a new track and platform on the west side of the station, a new western station entrance next to Botley Road, road network improvements and replacement of Botley Road bridge, and three new crossovers at Oxford North Junction. Completion is set for 2024, in time to provide the additional capacity for terminating EWR services.

In 2022 Network Rail also published proposals for reinstating passenger services on the two-mile Cowley freight branch from Oxford. New stations are proposed at Oxford South (near Oxford Science Park) and Oxford East (near Oxford Business Park), along with provision of a third track at Hinksey on the main line and an upgrade of the track on the branch.

HS2 IMPACT

While HS2 is a huge scheme in its own right, it will have a major impact on the operational railway too. HS2 works on the classic network are largely the responsibility of the On Network Works (ONW) team, a joint entity of Network Rail and HS2.

This starts at Euston, where platforms 17 and 18 at the western edge of the station have already been taken out of use to make space for the HS2 worksite. This will be followed in May 2023 by platform 16, which will be out of use for two years; platform 15 will also be unavailable for a short time during this period. Meanwhile, development is in progress on a major upgrade to the conventional station at Euston to ensure it matches the new high-speed station next door. The aim is to create a larger concourse, with the concourse to be moved down to street and platform level, rather than being raised as at present.

In west London, the Great Western main line will be affected by the construction of platforms to serve the new station at Old Oak Common, with four platforms each to be built on the main and relief lines. This will involve some significant disruption, with major Christmas works pencilled in for 2026 and 2028.

Another major focus is Crewe, the northern extent of Phase 2a of HS2. The station will be modified to accommodate HS2 trains, with the preferred option being to modify the two central islands for use by high-speed services; these will need to be extended, prompting a remodelling of the layout. With signalling renewal imminent, this will also feature.

Then there is the question of the northern stretch of the West Coast main line – HS2 trains will run on a shiny new main line from Euston, but the infrastructure on the conventional route here is in need of a significant upgrade, and the challenge will be making a case for this in a constrained funding environment.

HS2 impact: Avanti West Coast's No 390049 at Euston on 1 February 2022. Platform 16, on the left, will be taken out of use in May 2023 for two years to assist with construction of the high-speed station. **PHILIP SHERRATT**

BRISTOL BENEFITS

Progress has been slow on the MetroWest scheme to enhance services around Bristol, promoted by the West of England Combined Authority. Services on the Severn Beach line were enhanced in December 2021 to a half-hourly service as far as Avonmouth and hourly throughout. However, further frequency upgrades have stalled.

So too has the scheme to reopen the railway to Portishead, although it appears a series of setbacks have been overcome after a further funding gap for the project was finally filled. A £35.5 million gap had emerged, with combined resources from the Department for Transport, North Somerset Council and the West of England Combined Authority provided to fill this, and a Development Consent Order application was finally approved in November 2022.

Reopening of the Henbury line is the final aspect of MetroWest and includes new stations at North Filton and Henbury, plus a third new station on the Filton bank at Ashley Down.

A major programme of improvements is also in progress at Temple Meads station. This includes a rewire of the station and a renewal of the station roof by Taziker, the latter due for completion in 2023. In 2022 the Government confirmed a £95 million investment in station

East West Rail makes tracks: ballast is unloaded from an engineering train on 10 November 2022 at the site of old Swanbourne station ready for the installation of the second track as part of works on the Bicester to Bletchley stretch of EWR. **KEN BRUNT**

improvements, including a new eastern entrance serving the Temple Quarter.

WEST MIDLANDS SCHEMES PRESS ON

There are several projects of note in the West Midlands, all related to stations. The new station facilities at Wolverhampton were completed in June 2021 with the opening of the second phase. The project is part of the city's £150 million interchange scheme which improves bus, tram, cycle and rail connectivity. The final rail-related project is the extension of the West Midlands Metro to the station plaza to create a fully integrated transport hub with the neighbouring bus station, now due for completion in 2023.

Two major station rebuild schemes were associated with the Commonwealth Games at Perry Barr and University. Perry Barr served the Alexander Stadium, and the station closed in May 2021 for a year-long rebuild to create a much-improved

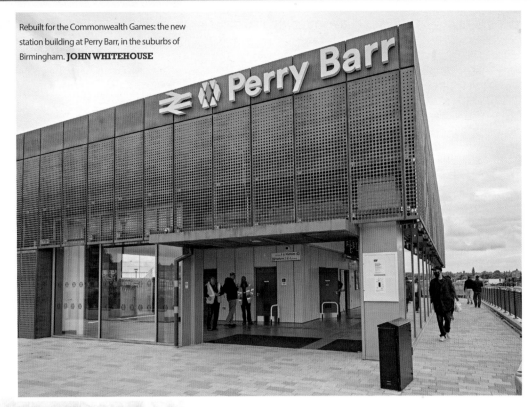

Rebuilt for the Commonwealth Games: the new station building at Perry Barr, in the suburbs of Birmingham. **JOHN WHITEHOUSE**

facility. Some of the new facilities at University station, also being rebuilt to provide a major capacity boost, were opened in time for the Games, but the full project will not be completed until 2023.

New stations are in prospect on the Camp Hill and Walsall to Wolverhampton lines. On the former, local services calling at Moseley Village, Kings Heath and Pineapple Road stations will be introduced, while on the Walsall to Wolverhampton line the intention is to introduce a two trains per hour service calling at new stations at Darlaston and Willenhall.

Longer-term ambitions for improvements include the Midlands Rail Hub enhancements. In December 2022 Midlands Connect proposed £1.5 billion of new and improved infrastructure to be completed between 2025 and 2030. The subnational transport body says this would make space for 100 additional trains on the network every day, and would cut journey times. It submitted an Outline Business Case and was seeking funding for a Full Business Case.

A pair of chords would be built at Bordesley, allowing access into Birmingham Moor Street from both the South West and Wales and from the East Midlands. The Government's Integrated Rail Plan, published in 2021, had cast doubt on whether the east chord would be built. Other upgrades include the revival of platform 4 at Birmingham Snow Hill station and platform 5 at Moor Street, and other new infrastructure and remodelling.

GATWICK UPGRADE

In May 2020 Network Rail began the major element of the £150 million station enhancement project at Gatwick Airport. Costain is delivering the project, which is creating a new station concourse so arriving and departing passengers can be segregated. A phased approach has seen platforms taken out of use in stages, with the fully upgraded station due to open in 2023.

Schemes on commuter routes have dropped down the list of priorities following the pandemic, which has changed travel patterns, potentially for good. Thus the major Croydon Area Remodelling Scheme (CARS) which Network Rail had been developing to remove the bottleneck north of East Croydon station is less of a priority now, as is the case for the Woking Area Capacity Enhancement (WACE) on the South Western main line. However, renewals are proceeding, one example being a £250 million scheme at Lewisham in south east London.

A notable feature post-pandemic, particularly on Southern Region, is the use of longer blockades to upgrade the railway in a more productive way. Numerous week-long closures have taken place throughout 2021 and 2022 for various activities, mostly renewals, but also some enhancements; the view is that a well-publicised blockade is better than a series of weekend closures, especially given passengers are now more likely to be able to amend their travel to work from home for such a period.

ELY STALLS

One of the railway's most notorious bottlenecks is Ely, but despite development work there is no funding at present for the Ely Area Capacity Enhancement (EACE).

Two consultations were held during 2021 on aspects of Network Rail's proposals, but no further funding has yet been released. The aim is to provide capacity through Ely for up to 10 trains per hour, compared to 6½tph at present, including an additional London to King's Lynn path, an additional hourly Felixstowe to Midlands freight path and an extra passenger path whose use is yet to be determined.

A major constraint on the layout at Ely North is that all trains using the Norwich and King's Lynn line share a single track for a short distance. Under EACE, Network Rail is proposing to remodel the junction to provide a second track here, while major changes to level crossings are also proposed, with various upgrades or closures.

RESILIENCE FOCUS

More frequent extreme weather events have sharpened the focus on resilience of the railway.

The impact of record temperatures in July 2022 prompted Network Rail to launch a taskforce to make recommendations on how the railway can develop its approach to resilience during hot weather. The review will consider four key areas, each led by an independent expert in their field. Dame Julia Slingo, an expert in climatology, will examine the likelihood of more frequent extreme hot weather events in the UK and how high-quality, detailed and timely weather forecasting can be maximised by Network Rail to mitigate the impact of heat on its infrastructure. Sir Douglas Oakervee will investigate options to ensure the railway infrastructure can continue to function safely and reliably during very hot weather. Simon Lane will explore operational standards, policies and practices which could allow

services to continue to operate safely and without highly limiting speed restrictions in extreme heat. Transport Focus Chief Executive Anthony Smith will examine how Network Rail communicates with passengers in the run-up to and during periods of extreme weather, as well as in its planning for disruptive events.

Likewise, the publication in March 2022 of the Rail Accident Investigation Branch report into the Carmont derailment has prompted a focus on drainage installation as well as record-keeping within Network Rail.

A significant scheme to improve the resilience of the railway alongside the river Severn between Lydney and Gloucester was completed in summer 2022, carried out by Network Rail and Taziker, with a further phase planned for summer 2023. This is alongside extensive work in Wales on the Marches, Cambrian and Conwy Valley routes to improve resilience.

The established South West Rail Resilience Programme, concentrating

on the coastal section of railway between Exeter and Newton Abbot, continues to make progress. The first phase, comprising construction of a new sea wall between Dawlish station and Kennaway Tunnel alongside Marine Parade, was completed in 2020. Work is now well under way on a second phase, covering the 415-metre stretch between Coastguards and Colonnade Breakwaters. For the third phase, Morgan Sindall is building an extended rockfall shelter at the entrance to Parsons Tunnel to protect trains, while Bam Nuttall has been awarded a contract to undertake design and surveys, cliff stabilisation, installation of rock anchors and netting of cliffs at Holcombe. Revised plans for the section between Holcombe and Teignmouth are expected to be presented in 2023.

NEW STATIONS

Excluding the new Elizabeth Line in London, several new stations opened on the main line network in 2022.

Making the railway more resilient: work in progress on the latest stage of work at Dawlish as part of the South West Rail Resilience programme. **COURTESY NETWORK RAIL**

Gatwick station upgrade: the project to rebuild the airport station is due to be completed in 2023. **COURTESY NETWORK RAIL**

Two of these were in Scotland. First up was Reston, on the East Coast main line, which opened on 23 May. The £20 million station was built by Bam Nuttall and has two 270-metre platforms, an accessible footbridge and a 70-space car park. It is served mostly by TransPennine Express services between Newcastle and Edinburgh, with less regular calls by LNER services. Work on a second new station on the ECML at East Linton in East Lothian began in February 2022, with completion due in 2023.

The second new station in Scotland was Inverness Airport station, near Dalcross on the line east of the city towards Aberdeen. An 11-day closure in October 2022 allowed Network Rail to install a new passing loop serving the station's two platforms. Opening was due to take place in December 2022.

The third new station was Barking Riverside, which opened on 18 July 2022 along with the extension to the London Overground network. This was achieved ahead of the planned autumn 2022 opening. A new 1.6km line entirely on viaduct was built by a joint venture of Morgan Sindall and VolkerFitzpatrick from a junction with the Barking to Grays line at Ripple Lane to the station. The branch serves a new town being built on the former Barking power station site, which will eventually incorporate more than 10,000 new homes. London Overground's Gospel Oak to Barking services have been extended

to the new station, providing a quarter-hourly service as the main public transport provision to the site.

PIPELINE

There are many new stations in the pipeline, either under construction or in the development phase – in addition to the new stretches of railway such as East West Rail, the Northumberland line and Levenmouth branch which will of course feature new stations.

Balfour Beatty is building a new station at Reading Green Park on the Reading to Basingstoke line, while also on the Western a new station at Portway Parkway on the Severn Beach line will serve a major park and ride site. Both should open during 2023.

Travellers on the Midland main line will have noticed good progress with the £40 million station at Brent Cross West in north London. Barnet Council is leading this project and has appointed VolkerFitzpatrick as the construction contractor for the five-platform station; opening is scheduled for 2023.

Six stations have been funded as part of the Restoring your Railway initiative, and three should open during 2023. Work is well advanced on a new station in Devon at Marsh Barton, on the main line south of Exeter St Thomas, serving a major trading estate and one of the largest employment centres in the region. Also in the South West, Restoring your Railway funding has been awarded for studies into reopening Cullompton and Wellington stations, both between

Taunton and Exeter, the former in Devon and the latter in Somerset.

The £35 million station at Thanet Parkway in Kent, between Minster and Ramsgate, is due to open in May 2023. The high capital cost also accounts for linespeed and level crossing work, ensuring calls at the new station can be accommodated without increasing journey times or having to do a major rewrite of the timetable.

White Rose station, between Leeds and Dewsbury on the trans-Pennine route in West Yorkshire, is also due to open in 2023. The £26.5 million station is being built by Spencer Group and will be located 750 metres from the current Cottingley station, which is planned to close. Another West Yorkshire scheme is Thorpe Park, east of Leeds, serving a major business park, due for opening in 2024, while still in the development phase is a proposed Leeds Bradford Airport Parkway station on the Harrogate line, on which construction could start in 2024.

Other Restoring your Railway funded new stations are Edginswell on the Torbay branch in Devon, which may be named 'Torquay Gateway', aimed at improving access to the area around Torbay hospital. This, along with St Clears in Carmarthenshire, is due to open in 2024.

Work continues to develop a new station at Cambridge South, serving the adjacent biomedical campus. A public enquiry on the Transport and Works application was held in 2022, with a decision awaited; the station could open in 2025.

On the Great Eastern main line, a new station is in prospect at Beaulieu Park, north of Chelmsford. Housing Infrastructure Fund support was awarded to Essex County Council in 2019, supporting a new development of up to 14,000 homes. The station is planned to include loops where fast trains can overtake slower services. A consultation exercise to inform designs was held in 2022, and opening could be in 2026.

In east London, a new station at Beam Park was planned on c2c's Tilbury branch between Dagenham Dock and Rainham, serving a major new housing development, but this now appears in doubt following a row regarding funding.

Merseyrail services are due to extend to a new station at Headbolt Lane in 2023. Kirkby branch services will be extended, with the interchange with Northern services from Wigan moving from Kirkby to the new three-platform station which will serve residents in the Northwood and Tower Hill areas of Kirkby. The extension will not be electrified, with seven of

New station in Scotland: celebrations marked the opening of Reston station on 23 May 2022. **COURTESY NETWORK RAIL**

Merseyrail's new Class 777s being fitted with batteries for the short stretch beyond Kirkby; the first of these was displayed by Stadler at the InnoTrans trade show in September 2022.

Meanwhile, the Liverpool City Region Combined Authority is progressing the reopening of the former Liverpool St James station on Merseyrail's Northern line as Liverpool Baltic, serving one of the fastest growing areas of the city. Costing between £80 and £100 million, opening could be before the end of 2025.

On the South Wales main line, studies are being undertaken

for five proposed new stations: Newport Road (Cardiff), Newport West, Newport East, Llanwern and Magor. The Welsh Government had awarded capital funding for a station at Llanwern, serving developments on the former steelworks site, but this has slipped and opening is not expected until 2029. Planning approval is awaited for a new Cardiff Parkway station, east of the city, which could be built in 2024. Further west, Grand Union Trains' new open access service could kickstart the construction of a new station at Felindre, adjacent to junction 46 of the M4 motorway near Swansea. ■

Brent Cross West: this new station on the Midland main line in north London is due to open in 2023. **COURTESY NETWORK RAIL**

SIGNALLING AND CONTROL

ETCS installation starts as lower-cost alternatives emerge

While the European Train Control System is the focus of Network Rail's signalling renewals strategy, other systems are available, explains *Modern Railways* Industry and Technology Editor **ROGER FORD**

As funding for future rail infrastructure enhancements remains unclear, installation of the European Train Control System (ETCS) on the southern end of the East Coast main line (ECML) has already begun. Funding was authorised by the Treasury before the current financial crisis and the release of over £1 billion was confirmed in July 2022.

Being carried out by the East Coast Digital Partnership (EDCP) with Siemens as the prime contractor, the programme will see cab signalling replace the existing multiple-aspect colour light signals over the 100 miles between King's Cross and Stoke Tunnel.

Work funded by a previously committed £350 million has already seen ETCS installed on the Northern City line (NCL) between Finsbury Park and Moorgate. This was commissioned in May 2022.

TRAINING

Driver training is expected to run through 2023, with ETCS overlaid on the existing signalling. This overlay enables the signalling to be switched between the two systems.

When the training programme is complete, the conventional signalling will be removed. This is expected to be early in 2024, after which all trains will run under cab signalling.

NCL will be one of the first commercial applications of ETCS on the UK network. Previously, the Thameslink core was the world's first installation of ETCS Level 2 incorporating Automatic Train Operation (ATO). The first train in passenger service ran through the central core under ATO five years ago.

ECDP will be adopting the NCL approach to driver training for the ECML signalling renewal, but only over a short section. The first tranche of ETCS will be installed as an overlay on the 10 miles between Welwyn and Hitchin.

Around 3,000 drivers will be trained, highlighting the scale of the programme. Although both the Govia Thameslink Railway (GTR) Siemens Class 700 and 717 outer-

and inner-suburban fleets are ETCS fitted, as are the LNER Hitachi Azuma trains, a cab fitment programme is already under way for other traction and rolling stock using the route.

Examples range in age from the ex-British Rail Class 43 power cars of the Network Rail New Measurement Train, used for track inspection, to Grand Central's Class 180 diesel multiple-units and the relatively new Class 387 EMUs operated by GTR. The ECML is an important freight route, and work on the first-in-class Class 66 cab fitment – the most widely used diesel locomotive – is also under way.

Current plans see Welwyn to Hitchin commissioning over the 2023 Christmas/New Year period, with driver training and migration starting after Easter 2024. The project is due to be completed by 2029.

One of the drivers of the ETCS programme is the cost of 'conventional' signalling renewals. This has been a concern dating back to Railtrack in the late 1990s, when renewal was deemed unaffordable.

For signalling the standard affordability metric is cost per Signalling Equivalent Unit (SEU). An SEU is a single item of signalling equipment, such as a set of points or a signal head.

MODULAR

Ways of reducing the cost per SEU have been on Network Rail's agenda since the company brought Railtrack out of administration in 2002. With typical costs for main line signalling of around £200,000/SEU, in 2011 Siemens (then Invensys) and Alstom were awarded contracts for pilot Modular Signalling (ModSig) renewal schemes with the target of £150,000/SEU – around £190,000 at today's prices.

With the target met on the Crewe – Shrewsbury and Norwich – Ely pilot schemes, by 2014 Network Rail was looking for further reductions from ModSig to around £125,000/ SEU (£160,000/SEU today). However, ModSig was not followed up, in part because it was seen as intended only for replacing mechanical signalling on lightly used lines.

Set to become a 'no signals' railway: Great Northern unit No 717020 arrives at Drayton Park on the Northern City line with the 18.17 Moorgate to Welwyn Garden City on 1 August 2022. **PHILIP SHERRATT**

FUNCTIONALITY

This resulted in Siemens applying a similar philosophy to that of ModSig but providing greater functionally. Known as Low-Cost Digital Ready (LoCoDR), it includes a wider range of signalling principles, such as four aspect signalling, more routes per signal and flashing aspects.

So, where ModSig was intended for routes such as Settle to Carlisle and Oxford to Worcester, its successor could provide low-cost signalling for Marylebone to Birmingham Snow Hill and most of the lines from Bristol to Penzance.

What it isn't designed to handle is signalling for complex and dense areas requiring facilities such as swinging overlaps and comprehensive approach locking. In more complex areas, a more conventional local solution would 'top-up' LoCoDR.

DISCIPLINE

Central to the cost benefits of LoCoDR is the customer committing to a disciplined process. For example, using standard interlocking templates for each island of signalling means the interlocking data is ready a couple of weeks after the project starts. With conventional signalling of complex locations, data preparation will take months.

For another example, if a potential client specifies cable troughing or similar 'extras', the cost soon approaches that of a conventional signalling scheme. The first application of LoCoDR was the North Wales coast resignalling.

When the contract was signed in 2016 the cost was £15 million, about one-third less than a conventional scheme. With 99 SEU, that gave £150,000/SEU, well under Network Rail's original 2011 target after allowing for inflation.

Currently Siemens is using LoCoDR for its Devon and Cornwall resignalling contract plus sections of the Transport for Wales Core Valley Lines. Where renewals can't wait for ETCS, and in a cash constrained industry, Siemens believes its digital-ready low-cost solution will become increasingly attractive.

190+

How do the costs of LoCoDR compare with ETCS? Currently the ECDP is expected to cost between £220,000 and £280,000 per SEU. But once the programme starts running and the renewal process becomes established costs are likely to settle at the bottom of the range.

In the hotseat: Rail Minister Huw Merriman at LNER's Azuma driver simulator at King's Cross during a visit to mark progress with the East Coast Digital Programme during 2022. **COURTESY NETWORK RAIL**

This is approaching the aspiration of Network Rail's Target 190+ programme. Launched in 2020, Target 190+ is a research and development programme aimed at reducing the whole life cost of signalling from a unit rate of £419,000/SEU when the programme was launched to £190,000/SEU by 2029. This is the level of cost Network Rail considers it will need if the ETCS Long-Term Deployment Plan is to be achieved.

Put in simple terms, over the next 15 years Network Rail needs to deliver an increase of over 50% of the forecast signalling renewals work at half the current price to achieve a sustainable, affordable railway.

SATNAV

However, there will remain some single-track rural routes where ETCS is unlikely to be affordable. For such lines, signal engineers at Comms Design Ltd (CDL) are developing a 21st century upgrade of the proven Radio Electronic Token Block (RETB) system. Advanced-RETB (A-RETB) offers digital in-cab signalling and train control with minimal trackside infrastructure. It combines Global Navigation Satellite Systems (GNSS) with other positioning systems, such as odometry and trackside beacons, to provide a positioning system sufficiently accurate for safety signalling.

A-RETB is not the only system using GNSS to provide cab signalling at lower cost than full ETCS. Network Rail has been developing the concept of Radio Based Limited Supervision (RBLS). Out of 65 options investigated, five were considered worth taking forward.

Like A-RETB, the Thales proposal is based on an upgrade to a proven safety signalling system, in this case the Train Protection and Warning System (TPWS).

ATP

Following the major accidents around the turn of the century, the Uff-Cullen joint inquiry into train protection systems recommended the rapid introduction of Automatic Train Protection (ATP). This assumed the availability of ETCS, but when this was shown to be premature, the railway industry came up with a simpler alternative.

TPWS measures the speed of a train approaching a signal at danger. If it is travelling too fast to stop, the brakes are applied, bringing the train to a halt within the 'overlap' after the signalling.

Thales, which supplies TPWS equipment, has responded to the RBLS requirement with TPWS-Continuous Supervision (TPWS-CS). The system has three core elements: continuous positioning sensors, including radar, GNSS and inertial measurement; the existing TPWS display; and access to the emergency braking system, also through the train's existing TPWS equipment.

INFRASTRUCTURE

While the train fitment is relatively straightforward, additional infrastructure equipment and associated data links will also be required. A 'State of the Railway Compiler' (SoRC) interrogates the local signalling interlockings. This is being developed by Park Signalling under a £217,000 'First of a Kind' innovation funding award made in 2022.

Additional trackside processors will link the local SoRC and communicate with the on-board systems through the standard GSM-R train radio. Data from the interlockings will enable a movement authority to be generated. However, unlike ETCS

this will not be displayed in the cab, since the driver will continue to observe the lineside signals.

However, the movement authority will take account of signal aspects, train speed, speed restrictions and other factors. And, as is the case with ATP, if the driver does not observe the required speed, a warning will first be shown on the modified TPWS display. If there is no response to the warning, the brakes will be applied.

BUSINESS CASE

In effect the continuous supervision provided by TPWS-CS provides the same ATP benefit as ETCS. However, basic TPWS proved so successful that it destroyed the business case for ATP based on safety benefits.

To justify the costs of the SoRC and other infrastructure equipment, TPWS-CS will need to be justified on the opportunities from having continuous background supervision against a movement authority. The key will be the ability to improve train performance, and this is being modelled under another research contract.

ETCS had its beginnings in 1996 when the European Commission became concerned about the lack of interoperability between the various national high-speed rail networks. As a concept it is now over 25 years old. The first trains on Network Rail's Cambrian line ETCS Early Deployment Programme ran over 10 years ago and the 100 miles of the UK's first main line installation on ECML South are not due to be fully operational for another six years.

What happens after that remains to be seen. But it is a fair bet that alternatives such as A-RETB and TPWS-CS will have a part to play. ∎

Signalling: horses for courses approach

Conventional schemes and advancement of new technologies are combining

Signalling technologies continue to develop to suit a range of scenarios. But not all technologies are applicable in all situations, and this is influencing resignalling projects across the network.

The European Train Control System (ETCS) solution being pursued on the East Coast main line will clearly not be suitable for a rural branch line. And, in any case, ETCS is not sufficiently well established in the UK to be feasible for all renewal schemes.

Thus the approach is something resembling horses for courses. But renewals do bring the opportunity to introduce new technology, including enhancements to existing systems.

VICTORIA PROGRESS

Progress continues with the Victoria resignalling project, which concerns a recontrol from Victoria Area Signalling Centre (which is actually located at Clapham Junction) to Three Bridges Rail Operating Centre. Phase 2 was completed in 2016-18, covering the Sutton and Streatham areas.

A major commissioning was due at Christmas 2022, marking Phase 3 of the project. This takes in the Brighton main line as far as Balham and the West London line from Clapham Junction to North Pole depot, where there is a boundary with Wembley Mainline Signal Control Centre. 1980s equipment has been renewed, with new signal heads and Frauscher axle counters installed. Trackwork associated with the project has mainly concerned the renewal of junctions, but there has also been a realignment of the ladder between the Brighton fast and slow lines, enabling linespeeds to increase. Installation of some new signals and repositioning of banner repeaters on platforms 12 to 15 at Clapham Junction will reduce headways and speed up platform reoccupation times. Also helping operationally will be new turnback facilities in platform 15 at Clapham Junction and platform 2 at Balham, making it easier to introduce shuttle services at times of engineering work or during disruption.

Siemens has been NR's delivery partner on the Phase 3 signalling work, with Westlock interlockings installed at TBROC. As part of the contract, Automatic Route Setting is being installed at Three Bridges for Victoria Phases 2 and 3.

There is a change of contractor for Phase 4, with Alstom awarded a £37 million contract under its Major Signalling Framework Agreement for Southern Region. This phase includes a stretch through Peckham Rye to Queens Road Peckham already under the control of Three Bridges ROC but due for resignalling, and a resignalling and recontrol from Streatham through Tulse Hill to East Dulwich and a targeted renewal and recontrol around Crystal Palace. The aim is to commission Phase 4 in February 2024.

New track layout: Govia Thameslink Railway's No 377211 on a Selhurst-bound service at Clapham Junction on 12 May 2022, passing an old signal box that is now used as a Mobile Operations Manager's office. Fresh ballast in the background shows where work has been undertaken on the track ladder as part of the Victoria resignalling scheme. **JAMIE SQUIBBS**

Alstom also has a £69 million contract to deliver Phase 5, in tandem with Phase 4. This covers a host of routes across south London and includes a switch and crossing renewal at Voltaire Road Junction at Wandsworth Road. This phase includes the recontrol to Three Bridges of 319 new signal equivalent units (SEUs), 494 new axle counters and 82 new Train Protection and Warning System (TPWS) units linked by 86,500 metres of signalling cable, with commissioning due at Christmas 2023.

The final stage, Phase 6, is yet to be authorised, and covers the lines through Bromley South. Given the geographical location and where the lines in Phase 6 go to, this area may be recontrolled to the East Kent Signalling Centre at Gillingham rather than Three Bridges. Network Rail hopes this will proceed in Control Period 7 (2024-29), leaving Victoria ASC redundant.

RETB enhancement: the pilot 'Request to Stop' kiosk installed on the Far North line at Scotscalder station. **COURTESY NETWORK RAIL**

WESSEX SCHEMES

Two significant resignalling projects feature on Network Rail's Wessex Route.

The £375 million Feltham resignalling scheme is an asset renewal covering a significant area of south west London and out into Surrey and Berkshire. The project has been split into six phases. The area concerned is that covered by the Feltham Area Signalling Centre (comprising four panels, although one is already redundant) plus the box at Wokingham. At 500 SEUs, this is one of the largest conventional resignalling schemes being undertaken by Network Rail.

Atkins' ElectroLogIXS equipment, made by Alstom, is the chosen technology for this scheme. After the resignalling of the Wherry lines from Norwich to Great Yarmouth/Lowestoft, completed in 2020, Feltham is the second scheme to deploy this technology on the main line. Track circuits are being replaced with Frauscher axle counters, NR's preferred train detection system, while cables, electrical and plant equipment and signals are all being renewed, meaning the scheme represents a complete system upgrade.

First to be commissioned in 2019 was Phase 0, covering the Shepperton branch. This was followed by Phase 1, mostly covering the Kingston loop but also a section of the Windsor lines. Phase 2 west of Staines followed at Easter 2022, while Phases 3 and 4 on the Hounslow loop and Windsor branch will follow together in August 2023. By this point all the route controlled by Feltham ASC will have been covered, and the ASC will close. The last commissioning, Phase 5, covers the area controlled by Wokingham box, with the transfer to Basingstoke Rail Operating Centre planned in February 2024.

The £94.5 million Portsmouth Direct upgrade is a condition-based renewal covering the stretch between Farncombe and Petersfield. Commissioning is in a single phase, planned in October 2024, with control to transfer to Basingstoke ROC and signal boxes at Farncombe, Haslemere and Petersfield to close. The contract has been awarded to Alstom, using the company's Smart Lock 400GP computer-based interlocking.

The project involves the installation of 90 new signals, 17 relocatable equipment buildings (REBs), more than 30km of new signalling cable and six new principal supply points (PSPs). Track circuits will be replaced with axle counters, and the current mix of three- and four-aspect signals will be upgraded to all four-aspect signals.

There is also significant work to level crossings: three footpath crossings will be upgraded with red/green stoplights, while nine road level crossings will be upgraded – two with CCTV control and seven with provision of obstacle detection equipment. This includes the use of the Mk 2 version of the obstacle detection system, one of the first schemes to adopt this.

LOW-COST APPROACH

Part of the shift in thinking within Network Rail has been the recognition that a more affordable signalling solution is needed for secondary lines, where the likes of ETCS will not be affordable.

A review by Network Rail has prompted three differing approaches. The Siemens solution, to be rolled out as part of a contract for resignalling in Devon and Cornwall, is described as low-cost digital ready (LoCoDR), an enhanced version of modular signalling which offers additional functionality. Siemens therefore believes LoCoDR could be applicable to a wider range of routes, for example bringing low-cost signalling to routes such as the Chiltern main line. Digital-ready implies that the system will be future-proof, foreseeing the eventual adoption of ETCS.

A different approach has been taken by Thales, which is increasing the functionality of Train Protection and Warning System (TPWS). Known as TPWS Continuous Supervision, the

CBTC to come here: a Metropolitan Line train of 'S' stock heads south at Neasden on 31 October 2022. **PHILIP SHERRATT**

system uses virtual balises to track the progress of a train, in the same way as fixed ETCS balises would.

A third system is under development for use on branch lines, including a new type of token instrument. Having developed an updated version of Radio Electronic Token Block (RETB) for use in Scotland, Park Signalling and Comms Design Ltd have now developed Advanced Radio Electronic Token Block (ARETB). This provides more accurate train position information using an augmented version of the Global Navigation Satellite System, plus a host of other day-to-day operational advantages such as automated warnings of temporary speed restrictions or, for example, trespassers or animals on the line. An upgrade on the Far North line is reducing the time taken to issue a token, with provision of new radio communication masts and antennae and installation of new equipment at Muir of Ord and Wick stations to enhance radio coverage.

An associated feature is the 'Request to Stop' system, devised in conjunction with the Highlands and Islands Transport Partnership and launched as a trial at Scotscalder station on the Far North line in summer 2022. Rather than trains slowing down for any intending passengers on the platform, those on the platform must push a button which would alert the driver of their presence. If there are no intending passengers

(and nobody on board wishes to alight), trains can maintain linespeed, saving time and helping provide a buffer to recover from delays. A further benefit is that the system gives passengers at rural stations better and more accurate train running information.

METRO SIGNALLING

2022 brought further progress with Transport for London's Four Lines Modernisation (4LM) programme, which is equipping the London Underground's Circle, District, Hammersmith & City and Metropolitan Lines with new Communications Based Train Control (CBTC) equipment supplied by Thales. Introduction is progressive across a series of Signalling Migration Areas (SMAs).

By the end of the year the whole of the Circle Line was operating under CBTC, with SMAs 1 to 5 all having gone live. Two timetable changes have exploited the improved capacity of the system: in September 2021 there were running time improvements on the north side of the Circle Line plus an extra train in the morning and evening peaks, while in September 2022 journey times were shortened on the south side of the Circle.

Next up will be extension eastwards along the District Line from Stepney Green to Upminster in two stages (SMAs 6 and 7), due in early 2023. SMA8, north from Finchley Road on the Metropolitan Line, brings

the complication of the interface with Neasden depot, which has its own control system and also interfaces with the slightly different Thales system on the Jubilee Line. This is pencilled in for 2024.

There have been changes to later stages of the programme on the grounds of cost and complexity. The western extremities of the District Line will no longer migrate to CBTC: this covers SMAs 10 to 12, west of Barons Court and Fulham Broadway, although it is planned to still introduce CBTC within parts of SMAs 10 and 12, meaning the new signalling will reach Stamford Brook and East Putney.

These areas feature a number of shared stretches of railway – with Network Rail on the Wimbledon and Richmond branches and with the Piccadilly Line west of Hammersmith. TfL had proposed an overlay solution, which would have seen the existing interlocking retained and controlling the railway, with a CBTC overlay for District trains. This contrasts with the outer stretches of the Metropolitan Line, shared with Chiltern Railways and with the Piccadilly Line on the Uxbridge branch, where an underlay solution is planned through which CBTC will control trains but with lineside signals retained for Chiltern and Piccadilly trains.

The cutting of scope eliminates technical risk with the overlay solution, while on these sections CBTC does

not provide any extra timetable capacity, although there will be a small impact on journey times. Resignalling of these stretches is now likely to be led by Network Rail, which is the infrastructure owner of the Richmond branch and of the Wimbledon branch south of East Putney.

These changes in scope notwithstanding, overall programme completion is scheduled for autumn 2025.

Meanwhile, CBTC is also coming to the Glasgow Subway. Strathclyde Partnership for Transport contracted a joint venture of Ansaldo (now Hitachi) and Stadler to provide new signalling and trains respectively. The original plan was that the new trains would run under the new signalling system from the outset, but this has now been revised and a software modification will allow them to operate under the legacy signalling until the new system is ready to go live. Installation of equipment for the new system is in progress. The current signalling on the Subway already uses automatic control but with a fixed block system.

The eventual plan on the Subway is for unattended train operation to be introduced. The new Stadler trains will initially have a temporary driver's cab at the end of the vehicle, but this can be removed later once the new signalling system is live and ready for a shift to unattended operation. ∎

LIGHT RAIL AND METRO

Transport for London

Transport for London (TfL) is a statutory body created under the Greater London Authority Act 1999. This Act gives the Mayor of London a general duty to develop policies for safe, integrated and efficient transport in London. TfL's role is to deliver the Mayor's strategy and to manage the services concerned. Currently there are around 9.5 million people living in Greater London, a figure which is expected to rise by 12% or so by the 2030s.

TFL COMPANIES

London Underground Ltd is the principal TfL rail operator and is a wholly-owned subsidiary; it serves 272 stations. It became part of TfL on 15 July 2003. The table shows how much Underground traffic has varies following Covid; it would seem 2022-23 will show continued improvement, though that also depends of what might happen regarding industrial action.

TfL is responsible for running the trains, stations and control centres, maintaining and renewing the infrastructure (except that of Network Rail), making sure the Underground is safe and secure, and collecting and protecting fares revenue. Other TfL companies include Docklands Light Railway Ltd, which owns the land on which the DLR is built and is responsible for the operation of the railway, and London Transport Museum.

The principal office of TfL is Palestra House, 197 Blackfriars Road, London SE1 8NJ, opposite Southwark Jubilee Line station.

Large scale passenger growth over time was resulting in the system becoming ever more crowded; very exceptionally the Underground was carrying over five million passengers a day. Pre-Covid projections have suggested the regular carriage of four million a day in future is a possibility for which plans should be made.

Covid prompted large scale reductions in passenger numbers; in the spring of 2020 carryings were down to 4-5% of what might usually have been expected. Since then, numbers have climbed, rather unsteadily, to around 80% of 'normal' levels by late 2022. One cause of reduced numbers was politicians imploring people, wherever they could, to work from home.

The key requirement for the Underground is to deliver a safe and reliable service day-in, day-out, irrespective of the performance of the ageing and often obsolete assets. The investment programme thus needs to make good the deficiencies in asset quality, and to build in sufficient new capacity to meet future demand. There also needs to be an ability to recover from the delays that do occur and customers need to be broadly satisfied with the overall results.

FINANCE AND FARES

The Mayor of London, Sadiq Khan, pledged as part of his election manifesto that fares would be kept unchanged for his term of office. Due to the Covid-19 emergency, his term was extended by an additional year to 2022. As a condition of further support, the Government required a 2.8% fares rise (RPI+1%). This was delayed, but eventually took place on 1 March 2022. In exchange for supporting TfL in 2023, a further fare rise of RPI+1% is being imposed from March 2023.

The Government's final extraordinary funding settlement for TfL expired on 3 August 2022 and the then Transport Secretary Grant Shapps MP agreed with Mayor Sadiq Khan a longer-term settlement. This is to last until 31 March 2024, or until TfL reaches financial sustainability.

Major upgrades are being delivered in terms of new trains for the Piccadilly Line, modernisation of the sub-surface lines, improvements to Elephant & Castle station and the Barking Riverside extension (of London Overground). In return, the Mayor is required to continue work on the possible introduction of driverless trains on the Underground. This is a Department for Transport (DfT) led joint programme which, according to the DfT, 'has the

LONDON UNDERGROUND KEY STATISTICS

	2019-20	2020-21	2021-22
Passenger journeys (millions)	1,337	296	748
Passenger kilometres (millions)	11,754	2,662	6,680
Passenger revenue (£ million, 2019-20 prices)	2,924	664	1,547

potential to offer a more punctual, reliable, customer responsive and safer service that is less susceptible to human error'. TfL will continue to modernise and control operating costs to provide an effective, efficient and financially stable operation.

The DfT claims the settlement 'is fair and proportionate to London, whilst also taking account of funding provided elsewhere in the country and the cost to the national taxpayer'.

Passenger payments for all TfL services are dominated by Oyster cards and contactless payments. Oyster card acts as a prepaid credit card, topped up by the user as necessary. The scheme is nearly 20 years old.

Staffed Underground ticket offices are now all but extinct. Cash fares are available from ticket machines, but these are priced to discourage their usage. Typically, the charge is about twice Oyster/contactless levels.

Momentous day for TfL: then Commissioner Andy Byford (left) and Mayor of London and Chair of TfL Sadiq Khan at the opening of the Elizabeth Line on 24 May 2022. **COURTESY TFL**

NEW PICCADILLY TRAINS

As part of line asset renewals generally, Siemens Mobility has been awarded the Stage 1 contract to design and build 94 new generation Inspiro 2024 stock trains for the Piccadilly Line. These will replace the increasingly unreliable 1973 stock. The new trains will be walk through and air-cooled and complemented by investment in supporting infrastructure. This includes the modernisation and extension of depot facilities at Cockfosters and Northfields, as well as power upgrades. Intermediate driving cabs are no longer required, as all trains on all lines now run at full length. Capital costs are thus saved, with the space made available for passenger use. With the first trains expected to enter service in 2025, train frequencies are expected to increase to 27 trains per hour (tph) by 2027.

More capacity at Bank: a Northern Line train of 1995 stock arrives at the new wider southbound platform on 30 August 2022. **PHILIP SHERRATT**

New trains taking shape: a 2024 stock vehicle for the Piccadilly Line in the assembly hall at Siemens' plant in Vienna. **COURTESY TFL**

Stage 2 of this programme, as yet unfunded, is intended to see a signalling upgrade for the entire line, a further 15 trains provided and the possibility of running a 36tph service.

OTHER ROLLING STOCK

In the queue for replacement are the Bakerloo's 1972 stock, plus the Central and Waterloo & City Lines' 1992 stock. The 1995 stock for the Jubilee Line and the 1996 stock for the Northern are already 25 years old. A more nearly uniform fleet would allow trains to be transferred between lines should requirements change over time, though differing platform (and hence train) lengths and signal spacing are just two of the many items that would have to be considered. Of the deep tube lines, only the 2009 stock for the Victoria Line is of fairly recent build.

FOUR LINES MODERNISATION

The Circle, Hammersmith & City, District and Metropolitan Lines are now operated exclusively by Alstom (formerly Bombardier) 'S' stock. The 192 air-conditioned trains consist of eight-car sets for the Metropolitan (S8) and seven-car very similar sets for the remainder (S7).

The original intention was that all signalling equipment on the sub-surface railway would be replaced.

This is roundly 40% of the total Underground network. The digital signalling and train control systems are being installed by Thales.

However, it was later decided to reduce financial and technical risks by retaining the existing signalling south of East Putney and west of Stamford Brook on the District Line. Parts of these routes also see the operation of National Rail trains, with the infrastructure owned by Network Rail, while there is a shared section with the Piccadilly Line west of Hammersmith and almost as far as Ealing Broadway.

Line capacities are being increased by around one-third. An example target is 32tph on both north and south sides of the traditional Circle Line. The new Service Control Centre for all four lines uses seven desks at Hammersmith.

Under the new signalling, trains are driven automatically. The train operator in the cab opens and closes the doors and is responsible for managing customer information and safety. The completion date is likely to be 2025.

The introduction of regenerative braking has allowed a reduction in the overall power consumption on the District. Other work has included strengthening power supplies generally, lengthening platforms, laying new track, and rebuilding the rolling stock depots.

BANK/MONUMENT

Bank/Monument might be termed a combined station. The 10 platforms there are served, at various levels, by the Central, Circle, District, Northern and Waterloo & City Lines, plus the Docklands Light Railway.

This station complex (more than 120 million passengers in a normal year) has been extensively reconstructed, with the target of increasing this multi-level station's capacity by 40%. That includes two new lifts, 20 new escalators, and new station entrances in Wallbrook and another in Cannon Street. More than 1,000 metres of new tunnel have been bored. The physical works started in April 2016.

A prolonged closure of the Northern Line City branch between Moorgate and Kennington took place from 15 January to 15 May 2022. This enabled the southbound line to be diverted further westwards in a new tunnel with a new platform. The space vacated is now occupied by a long concourse. Moving walkways speed passengers from one end of the station (District/Circle Lines at Monument) to the other (Central Line at Bank), with the Northern Line platforms in between on each side of the more southerly part. The DLR platforms, with enhanced access, are at the level below.

HEATHROW TERMINAL 4

Heathrow Terminal 4 station (on the terminal loop from Hatton Cross) was closed on 9 May 2020 because the Airport Authority closed the airport's Terminal 4 itself due to the Covid pandemic. Both reopened on 14 June 2022.

BUSY STATIONS

London Underground's network is at its busiest between the hours of 05.45 to 09.15 and 16.00 to 17.30.

Entry/exit hotspots in terms of passenger volumes, in descending order of passenger numbers, are King's Cross St Pancras, Waterloo, Oxford Circus, Victoria, London Bridge and Liverpool Street. All see between 70 million and 100 million entries and exits in a normal year. Of this group, only Oxford Circus is not directly connected to a main line station. This indicates the very real pressures that passengers to and from National Rail put on the Underground in its role as urban distributor of commuters and others.

ESCALATORS

The Otis company holds a contract for the procurement and maintenance of new escalators throughout their 30-year life. At least 50 heavy duty metro-type will be installed on London Underground over the next 10 years, not counting those for the Elizabeth Line. A major aim is to improve reliability, given that most operate for 20 hours a day and each runs for an average of 46 days between failures. The whole life cost of a single escalator is around £2.5 million, and there are a lot of them!

NIGHT TUBE

The Night Tube and London Overground night services were suspended during the coronavirus pandemic but have been restored.

UNFUNDED EXTENSIONS

There are a number of unfunded proposals for system extensions of the London Underground; how likely they are to take place, and in what timescale, is another matter. One of these is for the Bakerloo, taking it south from Elephant & Castle (new platforms), in tunnel, via the Old Kent Road (two stations) to New Cross Gate (reconstructed) and Lewisham (new integrated station). Another is the diversion of the Metropolitan's Watford branch via a new connection to Watford High Street and Watford Junction.

LONDON OVERGROUND

London Overground services are operated by Arriva Rail London for TfL. These run largely on the National Rail network, with additions such as the former East London Underground line. All are now electrified, some with AC overhead, others DC third rail. The routes are:
- Euston to Watford Junction;
- Stratford to Highbury & Islington and via Willesden Junction to Richmond/Clapham Junction;
- Dalston Junction via Wapping to New Cross/Clapham Junction;

Extension in east London: Class 710s at the new London Overground station at Barking Riverside on 21 July 2022. **PHILIP SHERRATT**

- Highbury & Islington via Wapping to New Cross Gate and Crystal Palace/West Croydon;
- Gospel Oak via Walthamstow Queen's Road to Barking Riverside;
- Liverpool Street to Enfield Town;
- Liverpool Street via Southbury to Cheshunt;
- Liverpool Street to Chingford;
- Romford to Upminster.

The Enfield Town, Cheshunt and Romford to Upminster services operate at a basic 2tph, the rest at a minimum 4tph.

A recent addition is the 74-chain double track branch off the London, Tilbury & Southend line, east of Barking. This was opened to the new station at Barking Riverside on 18 July 2022. The purpose is to serve a housing estate presently under construction and is operated by London Overground as an extension of the Gospel Oak to Barking service.

There are a large number of potential additions to the London Overground network, such as West Ealing to Greenford (presently operated by GWR) and a largely new West London Orbital from the Hendon area to Acton Central and Hounslow, but these all remain as planning aspirations.

ELIZABETH LINE

The Elizabeth Line was officially opened by Queen Elizabeth II on 17 May 2022, with public services beginning a week later on 24 May. This was over

New signalling coming: a Metropolitan Line train of 'S' stock on a southbound service at Dollis Hill on 31 October 2022. **PHILIP SHERRATT**

the 10 stations from Abbey Wood to Paddington, inclusive. The intermediate stations are Woolwich, Custom House, Canary Wharf, Whitechapel, Liverpool Street, Farringdon and Tottenham Court Road, plus Bond Street, which opened later on 24 October. Initially, services ran at up to 12tph on Mondays to Saturdays only.

More extensively, 6 November saw the physical connections of the Elizabeth Line with the stations on the Great Eastern line to Shenfield and to the Great Western line to Reading, plus Heathrow, brought into use. This did not preclude certain services finishing

at the main line termini. The Elizabeth Line serves 41 stations in total.

Services from that date, over a longer operating day, consist of Abbey Wood to Reading, Abbey Wood to Heathrow, and Shenfield to Paddington. Cross-platform interchange is available where needed. Provided by a fleet of 70 Class 345 nine-car Aventra units built at Derby by Alstom, services operate at up to 22tph over the central section. Sunday services also began at this point.

Further enhancements are to follow with a full timetable to be introduced in May 2023, raising peak frequencies to 24tph.

Operation is by MTR, which will run Elizabeth Line services for Transport for London until May 2025. This follows agreement of a two-year extension to the Crossrail (original name) operating concession. This originally began on 31 May 2015, when MTR took over the Liverpool Street to Shenfield services, followed in stages by Paddington local services in 2018-19.

With services fully operational on the Elizabeth Line as well as Thameslink, there is likely to be further growth in Underground traffic. From where these lines intersect, at Farringdon, there are direct services to the airports at Heathrow, Gatwick and Luton and, with a single change of train at Liverpool Street, to Stansted and Southend airports. Reaching London City Airport requires a further change to the Docklands Light Railway.

OUTSTANDING PROJECT

The Crossrail 2 proposal envisages a route in new tunnels between Wimbledon and Tottenham Hale, with a branch to New Southgate.

Elements of the route remain undetermined, but in general it would serve Clapham Junction, King's Road Chelsea, Victoria, Tottenham Court Road, a combined station with exits to both Euston and St Pancras main line stations, Angel and Dalston.

At the southern end, it would extend over Network Rail lines to Epsom, Chessington South, Hampton Court and Shepperton, and in the north over what would become a newly four-tracked Lea Valley line to Broxbourne.

Various cost saving measures have been suggested, such as dispensing with the New Southgate branch. A less ambitious but wholly self-contained version of Crossrail 2, which did not extend onto Network Rail tracks at either Tottenham or Wimbledon, might also be possible.

This approach is similar to that of both the Elizabeth Line and Thameslink.

The National Infrastructure Commission has endorsed the project, but construction powers and funding are lacking. This scheme is presently paused and is unlikely to be built before 2040 at the earliest.

LONDON TRAVELWATCH

London Travelwatch is the statutory organisation representing transport users in and around the capital. It is sponsored and funded by the London Assembly. It promotes integrated transport policies and presses for higher standards of quality, performance and accessibility. It also considers user complaints, which the operator has failed to deal with adequately in the opinion of the passenger.

Chief Executive Officer:
Michael Roberts

Light Rail and Metro

The light rail sector was hit as hard as National Rail by the Covid outbreak. Passenger numbers fell fast, but service provision cutbacks were much more limited. Table 1 summarises the overall situation to the end of the years 2019-20, 2020-21 and 2021-22. These figures are derived from national statistics issued by the Department for Transport. They cover the 10 major systems operating in Britain as set out in this chapter, but exclude London Underground. All except Edinburgh Trams and the Glasgow Subway are in England.

Journeys made by light rail were seriously affected by Covid restrictions. These were eased gradually, but the level of patronage in 2020-21 was only 30% of that recorded a year earlier. The 2021-22 results showed a substantial further recovery; the schools returned, but there was still a long way to go. Government financial support for operators was forthcoming.

How many staff are needed on a vehicle? With unsegregated systems, which includes most tramways, the post of at least the driver would seem to be secure. Elsewhere, the duties of on-train staff may be confined

to commercial roles. Who or what else is needed? How necessary might it be on various systems to purchase a ticket before boarding?

What will happen with patronage and hence revenue? As light rail and metro are essentially urban operations, this will be a function of the extent to which people have become accustomed to home working and how acceptable businesses find it. To what extent will employees opt for four-day weeks, maybe working longer hours to compensate? On the other hand, home working is hardly possible for shop staff or production line work, for example.

Answers will become apparent as time progresses, but not perhaps for four or five years.

NETWORKS

The statistics which follow under each undertaking summarise the year-by-year effects of the Covid pandemic. Thus the 2019-20 financial year figures are a little lower than might have been expected, but the full force of it was felt in 2020-21. The following 2021-22 year saw considerable improvements for most operations, but with quite

a bit of growth still needed to return them to the levels of 2019-20.

In the table which appears at the beginning of each section, key statistics give the numbers of journeys made, kilometres travelled and passenger revenues at constant fare levels for each system, for the three most recent years available.

That still leaves the period since April 2022 outstanding, for which the indications are that pre-Covid levels of traffic are continuing to improve for the rail-based systems.

Blackpool Transport

KEY STATISTICS		
2019-20	2020-21	2021-22
Passenger journeys (millions)		
4.8	1.1	4.2
Passenger kilometres (millions)		
21.0	4.9	18.3
Passenger revenue (£ million, 2021-22 prices)		
7.1	1.9	5.3

Only one of the original routes of Blackpool trams survives from the early days, the 18km from Blackpool, Starr Gate to Fleetwood, Ferry Terminus. This is a 600V DC overhead system. Operation is by the municipally-owned Blackpool Transport Services Ltd under contract to Blackpool Borough Council.

The 18 Bombardier 'Flexity 2' trams are housed at Starr Gate depot. Each has five articulated sections. These 32.2-metre-long vehicles have 74 seats

plus a standing capacity of 148. They are fully accessible, with level access at the 37 stops. End-to-end journey times are about 58 minutes, and all trams carry conductors. There are also some vintage double-deckers and a heritage fleet based at Bispham.

Operations are subject to the vagaries of the weather and storms can result in heavy reductions in both service levels and patronage. These are particular problems in seaside locations such as this.

The £22 million extension of the tramway system from North Pier to an additional terminus at Blackpool North station has been funded by the Local Enterprise Partnership and Blackpool Council. This sum included the cost of two additional 'Flexity 2' trams (nos 017/018). Work on the extension started in 2017 and completion is now anticipated by 2023.

KEY STATISTICS		
2019-20	2020-21	2021-22
Passenger journeys (millions)		
116.8	39.7	77.2
Passenger kilometres (millions)		
620.7	206.5	398.2
Passenger revenue (£ million, 2021-22 prices)		
178.0	54.2	104.9

The Docklands Light Railway dates from 1982 when the London Docklands Development

TABLE 1: LIGHT RAIL IN BRITAIN (EXCLUDING LONDON UNDERGROUND)

	2019-20	2020-21	2021-22
Passenger journeys (millions)	283.3	85.1	182.3
Passenger kilometres (millions)	1,909.1	546.2	1,206.6
Passenger revenue (£ million, 2021-22 prices)	435.6	138.3	274.5

New train for the DLR: one of the first CAF trains for the light rail network on test in Spain. **COURTESY TFL**

Corporation was formed to co-ordinate the redevelopment of the extensive and very run-down area. The docks themselves had already moved downstream.

One of the very many requirements was a new transport system. The existence of the river Thames itself, its curvaceous nature and the water area represented by the docks all made access difficult.

The 12km first stage of the Docklands Light Railway opened in 1987 with two routes, from both Tower Gateway and Stratford to Island Gardens. There were 15 stations and a fleet of 11 two-section articulated cars. Extensions have since taken the system to its present length of 38km with 45 stations and three-car length trains. These are operated automatically with no driver, but the Passenger Service Agent on board is responsible for closing the doors.

The third rail 750V DC electrification uses underside contact. There are many grade-separated junctions, keeping operational conflicts to a minimum. Alcatel Seltrac moving block signalling is used.

The system is operated by KeolisAmey Docklands, the contract now continuing until April 2025. The company is paid a fixed fee for operating the railway to agreed levels and standards of service, with adjustments for performance.

An order for 43 new 87-metre-long trains has been placed with CAF of Spain, for delivery from 2023. Of these, 33 are for replacing the B90/B92 fleets, with the other 10 catering for traffic growth. As a consequence, Beckton depot is being enlarged.

TfL is also finalising an agreement with Government for Housing Infrastructure Funding to support future growth. This covers an extra 11 new CAF trains, further expansion at Beckton depot and an oversite development at the DLR's original depot at Poplar.

The newer B07 vehicles will remain in service; these have been converted to all-longitudinal seating. This is to increase unit capacity, as can be seen in more builds of Underground trains.

To serve the Royal Docks development, infrastructure and service enhancements are planned. Under consideration is a new cross-river branch of the DLR to serve Thamesmead, though this is presently paused.

A Network Rail Thameside study has suggested that passenger growth at Fenchurch Street makes a six (instead of four) platform station highly desirable. This might mean moving the station site 350m further east, which would result in the forced closure of the DLR's Tower Gateway terminus.

KEY STATISTICS

	2019-20	2020-21	2021-22
Passenger journeys (millions)			
	7.1	0.9	2.8
Passenger kilometres (millions)			
	57.3	7.3	25.6
Passenger revenue (£ million, 2021-22 prices)			
	16.7	2.1	7.3

Edinburgh Trams is the operator and infrastructure manager of the city's tramway. Transport for Edinburgh is the holding company for the local authority owned operator.

Services commenced on the 14km line from Edinburgh Airport to York Place (presently St Andrew Square) on 31 May 2014. End-to-end journey time is about 35 minutes for the 15 stops. There is a core service frequency of a tram every 7½ minutes, enhanced at peak.

The 27 seven-section 42.8-metre Urbos 3 trams built by CAF are based at Gogar depot and are the longest in use in Britain. Ticketing Services Assistants on trams check but do not issue tickets. Penalty fares are in operation.

The project had a difficult construction period involving cost overruns, construction delays and the delivery of a lesser system than was planned. A public inquiry was established in June 2014 to ascertain why matters went so badly wrong, but eight years later there is still no report. The cost of that inquiry has meanwhile risen to £12 million.

Work is nearing completion on the original proposal for Line 1a, a 5km extension from York Place to Leith and Newhaven, with eight additional stops. The existing fleet is sufficient to provide the enhanced service. The budgeted cost is £207 million and opening is expected in spring 2023.

KEY STATISTICS

	2019-20	2020-21	2021-22
Passenger journeys (millions)			
	12.7	2.5	8.0
Passenger kilometres (millions)			
	40.7	8.0	25.7
Passenger revenue (£ million, 2021-22 prices)			
	21.2	4.0	13.0

The circular 10.6km route of the Glasgow Subway has 15 stations, eight on the north side of the river Clyde and seven on the south. Apart from Broomloan depot, reached by ramps between Ibrox and Govan stations, it is wholly underground. The busiest stations are Buchanan Street and St Enoch, followed by Hillhead and Kelvinbridge.

Presently, a round trip will take 24 minutes, with a train every four minutes in each direction at peak. Two separate running tunnels (Inner Circle and Outer Circle) are built to the restrictive diameter of 3.35 metres, and track gauge is a unique 1,220mm (4ft). The present three-car trains dating from 1980 are a mere 38.3 metres long.

This 600V DC third rail system is owned and operated by Strathclyde Passenger Transport (SPT). It opened with cable traction in 1896, was electrified in 1935 and totally refurbished in 1980.

Transport Scotland and SPT have made grants for system modernisation. The 17 new trains from Stadler are in course of delivery. Each is of four cars, formed of two articulated pairs of the same total length as the present three-car units. Wide inter-car gangways are available for passenger use. All seating is longitudinal.

This £288 million contract includes the associated signalling, communication and control systems in a consortium with Ansaldo. Tunnel linings and water ingress problems have also been addressed; notably, the tunnels vary in depth between seven and 115 feet below the Clyde's high water mark. All stations have now been modernised, with 28 new escalators installed, plus lifts at St Enoch and Govan. Platforms will be equipped with half-height screen doors.

Trains in daily operation will be increased from 12 to 16. Later, Unattended Train Operation (UTO) is planned and the temporary drivers' cabs on the new trains will then be removed.

KEY STATISTICS

	2019-20	2020-21	2021-22
Passenger journeys (millions)			
	27.2	11.6	19.1
Passenger kilometres (millions)			
	141.3	60.2	99.5
Passenger revenue (£ million, 2021-22 prices)			
	24.0	11.5	16.9

The core of London Trams' operation is a one-way street level loop around central Croydon. This includes both East and West Croydon stations, and the bus station. From this, lines diverge to Wimbledon, Beckenham Junction, Elmers End and New Addington. Most of the branches are for the large part former heavy rail lines on a reserved formation, but that to New Addington was new construction on or beside existing roads. Inevitably, there are road level crossings.

The system is 26km long and became operational on various dates in May 2000. There are 39 stops. Electrification is at 750V DC overhead and the maximum speed 70km/h. The original 24 three-section CR4000 trams were built by Bombardier, later supplemented by 12 Variobahn trams from Stadler; TfL has begun market engagement about replacing the CR4000 vehicles. Selective double-tracking has been undertaken with the aim of offering more reliable and delay resilient services.

Operation is by FirstGroup subsidiary Tram Operations Ltd; tram maintenance is undertaken in-house at Therapia Lane depot. The assets are owned by Transport for London.

Extensive changes have been made to both systems and operations since the Sandilands derailment in 2016. This caused seven deaths and injured at least 50 people. Traffic volumes are still depressed, though some of this can be ascribed to Covid.

Making tracks for Newhaven: work in progress on Leith Walk in August 2022 with the project to extend the Edinburgh Trams route. **COURTESY CITY OF EDINBURGH COUNCIL**

The most likely route for system extension is an on-road route from Colliers Wood to Sutton, crossing the existing Tramlink branch from Wimbledon at Belgrave Walk. This remains unfunded and has been paused.

Metrolink

KEY STATISTICS		
2019-20	2020-21	2021-22
Passenger journeys (millions)		
44.3	10.3	26.0
Passenger kilometres (millions)		
463.0	107.8	272.2
Passenger revenue (£ million, 2021-22 prices)		
87.1	26.7	52.6

Manchester's Metrolink began operation in 1992 using the rail infrastructure on the radial Bury and Altrincham lines, both electrified, albeit on different systems, and combining them with the use of street running through the city centre. This is a 750V DC high floor system.

Subsequent extensions have taken Metrolink to Ashton-under-Lyne, East Didsbury, Eccles, Manchester Airport, MediaCity, Rochdale and the Trafford Centre. The Second City Crossing via Exchange Square rather than Market Street was opened in 2015, enhancing capacity but also giving some operating flexibility and benefits to reliability. The expanding network has resulted in a substantial growth in passenger usage, though subject to the effects of Covid.

A fleet of 147 Bombardier M5000 'Flexity Swift' trams provides all services. These are 28.4-metre six-axle trams in two sections, each with a capacity of 206 passengers. Depots are at Queen's Road and Trafford.

Metrolink is owned by the Greater Manchester Combined Authority (GMCA) and the system is operated and maintained by Keolis/Amey. Metrolink now has 99 stops, more than on any other British light rail network. Future opportunities include an extension to Manchester Airport Terminal 2 and beyond. Other work is to examine the opportunities for reliability upgrades and the practicalities of capacity increases.

In 2022, the Department for Transport accepted the GMCA's bid for funding for its Pathfinder North scheme. This proposes to introduce tram-train operation on the route from Oldham to Rochdale (presently Metrolink) and continuing to Bury (formerly railway but now disused). The funding is for both the seven vehicles needed and the infrastructure.

Further such schemes are on the drawing board, notably Manchester to Hale and Manchester Airport to Wilmslow.

KEY STATISTICS		
2019-20	2020-21	2021-22
Passenger journeys (millions)		
18.7	3.4	9.1
Passenger kilometres (millions)		
123.3	22.4	60.0
Passenger revenue (£ million, 2021-22 prices)		
22.5	5.4	12.0

The 32km Nottingham Express Transit (NET) system has 51 stops. It consists of three lines, and all trams serving the city centre call at Nottingham station. Line 1 to Hucknall and Phoenix Park opened in 2004, with Line 2 to Clifton South and Line 3 to Toton Lane in 2015.

The original fleet consisted of 15 articulated five-section 33.0-metre Bombardier vehicles, later supplemented by a further 22 five-section Alstom Citadis 302 trams. Each pair of cars has around 56 seats. The depot is at Wilkinson Street. Overhead electrification is at 750V DC.

NET serves a number of Park & Ride sites, together accommodating around 5,400 parking spaces.

The Tramlink Nottingham consortium holds a Private Finance Initiative concession to finance, build, operate and maintain NET Lines 2 and 3, as well as the continuing operation and maintenance of Line 1, until the end of 2033.

It was planned that NET's Line 3 to Toton Lane could be extended by around 2km to the site of the planned HS2 Toton station, though the HS2 scheme is not now to proceed beyond East Midlands Parkway. That would however permit HS2 trains to use the existing rail system to reach the former Midland station at Nottingham or continue to Sheffield via Derby and Chesterfield.

Stagecoach SUPERTRAM

KEY STATISTICS		
2019-20	2020-21	2021-22
Passenger journeys (millions)		
10.5	2.8	6.9
Passenger kilometres (millions)		
68.2	18.4	30.0
Passenger revenue (£ million, 2021-22 prices)		
14.6	6.4	10.9

The 750V DC Supertram network was opened in 1994-95. About half the 29 route kilometres of the original system are fully segregated, with on-street running for the rest. Curvature is tight, with maximum gradients of 10%.

Services are operated by Stagecoach from the city centre to Middlewood, Meadowhall Interchange, Halfway and Herdings Park.

Operation is by 25 three-section Siemens/Duewag cars, each of 34.8 metres in length and based at Nunnery Square. These 86-seat vehicles can accommodate around 115 standing passengers.

The Citylink tram-train project is testing the operation of specialist tramway-type vehicles on both a conventional tram network and the national rail system. Inaugurated on 25 October 2018, tram-trains run at 3tph from Sheffield Cathedral over the existing tram line to Meadowhall South, thence by the Tinsley chord to the freight-only railway to Rotherham Central and a terminus beyond at Parkgate Retail Centre. Operation is by seven Class 399 three-section 37.2m Citylink tram-train vehicles, built by Vossloh (now Stadler) in 2015-16. They have 25kV AC as well as 750V DC capability, but the present application uses DC only.

Passenger journeys reached 15 million in 2010-11 but have since declined substantially. The present operating contract with Stagecoach continues until 2024 and at some stage the replacement of the Siemens/Duewag tram vehicles, now approaching 30 years of age, will be necessary. In October 2022 the South Yorkshire Mayoral Combined Authority agreed that when the current concession finishes an arm's length body of the authority will be established to take over the operation, rather than going out to the private sector again.

KEY STATISTICS		
2019-20	2020-21	2021-22
Passenger journeys (millions)		
33.1	9.4	24.3
Passenger kilometres (millions)		
289.1	80.0	211.8
Passenger revenue (£ million, 2021-22 prices)		
52.6	20.4	41.4

The core of the Tyne and Wear Metro is the former British Rail third rail electrified network, linked by underground construction in Newcastle city centre and a new bridge over the river Tyne. Services started in 1980 and successive enhancements have taken the system to its present length of 78km. There are 60 stations and electrification is at 1,500V DC overhead.

Substantial early patronage with a high of 59.1 million in 1985-86 dwindled, reaching a low of 32.5

million passengers in 2000-01. Usage subsequently recovered to around 40 million, but the later effects of Covid have been felt here as elsewhere.

The Green line runs from Airport to South Hylton, the Yellow line from St James to South Shields via Whitley Bay. They overlap in the central area. The section from Pelaw towards Sunderland and South Hylton is on Network Rail infrastructure, which is in part shared with National Rail trains.

Nexus is the public body delivering local transport services for Tyne and Wear on behalf of the North East Joint Transport Committee. Metro is an in-house operation. Nexus has always owned the Metro, set fares and determined services.

The original Metrocar fleet is being replaced with new trains built by Stadler, delivery of which is under way. This 46-strong fleet has all longitudinal seating, air-conditioning and dual-voltage capability. The five-section trains are 60 metres long and the contract covers both their supply and their maintenance for 35 years.

The three single track sections of the branch from Pelaw to South Shields, totalling 2.8km, have been converted to double track by the Buckingham Group and electrified. This will increase line capacity and enable full sharing between passenger and freight services. Work was due for completion in early 2023.

Stadler is leading the total rebuilding of the South Gosforth depot, which dates from 1923. This is a four-year project. Meanwhile, a new satellite depot for Metrocars

has been built at Howden in North Tyneside and a skills centre for staff training established at South Shields.

KEY STATISTICS		
2019-20	2020-21	2021-22
Passenger journeys (millions)		
8.0	3.4	4.7
Passenger kilometres (millions)		
84.3	35.2	50.1
Passenger revenue (£ million, 2021-22 prices)		
11.9	5.8	12.0

Midland Metro's 20.4km Line 1 between Birmingham Snow Hill and Wolverhampton opened in 1999, mostly over the reserved formation of the Great Western Railway.

At the Birmingham end, Line 1 has now been diverted away from Snow Hill station to a new on-street tram stop of St Chads, as part of the Birmingham Westside Metro extension. This ran to Bull Street, Corporation Street, Grand Central, Library and Town Hall. The final phase, opening on 17 July 2022, took the line to Brindleyplace, Five Ways and the terminus at Edgbaston Village.

Trams on the section through Victoria Square and sections of the route on to Edgbaston are powered by on-board rechargeable batteries, largely on environmental grounds. This means neither catenary nor its supports are needed here. The batteries are charged on the preceding overhead sections.

This development has been led by Transport for the West Midlands,

part of the West Midlands Combined Authority, working with construction and design partner Midland Metro Alliance, operator Midland Metro Ltd, and Birmingham City Council.

At Wolverhampton, a second Midland Metro terminal is being created at Wolverhampton National Rail station and following delays is due to open in spring 2023.

An Eastside extension is under construction from a new junction at Bull Street to reach New Canal Street (for HS2 at Curzon Street) and High Street Deritend.

The first phase of the 11km Wednesbury to Brierley Hill Metro extension over the former heavy rail route from Stourbridge towards Walsall is currently under construction. It is due to open in 2024 and will link with Dudley Town Centre, where a combined bus station and Metro stop is being built. The second phase is due to see the route continue to Brierley Hill, with a stop at the Merry Hill Shopping Centre, although there is uncertainty about funding for this.

The Midland Metro Alliance is planning, designing and delivering the extensions for the West Midlands Combined Authority. Services are operated by West Midlands Metro Ltd, a company wholly owned by the Combined Authority.

The whole Metro system has been divided into four fare zones. These replace traditional point-to-point fares.

The original fleet of 21 CAF Urbos 3 trams has suffered extensive bodywork cracks, which forced the temporary withdrawal of these vehicles and

New train for the Metro: newly completed Tyne and Wear Metro Class 555 unit. **COURTESY NEXUS**

Edgbaston extension: tram No 42 heads over the new section of West Midlands Metro from Edgbaston Village towards Birmingham centre and Wolverhampton on 10 October 2022. This is a catenary-free section, with the tram running on battery power. **TONY MILES**

service curtailment during 2022. Repairs are in progress to rectify the issue. A delivery of 21 new Urbos 100 trams is to be completed in 2023, with an option for CAF to build further vehicles for the expanding network.

Electrification is at 750V DC overhead and the operations centre and depot are at Wednesbury.

SOUTH WALES METRO

Transport for Wales is pushing ahead with its South Wales Metro scheme, which is based on major improvements to the rail infrastructure and services in the Valleys area north of Cardiff. TfW already owns the infrastructure north of Cardiff and that to Cardiff Bay, transferred from Network Rail to the Welsh Government in March 2020.

Rolling stock will be completely replaced. 36x3-car Stadler Class 398 Citylink tram-trains, with both electric and traction battery power, will operate services from Cardiff to Treherbert, Aberdare and Merthyr Tydfil, Cardiff Bay, and on the City line to Radyr. A further 7x3-car and 17x4-car Stadler Class 756 Flirts, with tri-mode capability (electric/battery/diesel) will operate from Rhymney/Coryton and south of Grangemouth to Penarth, Barry Island and the Vale of Glamorgan.

Briefly, the scheme will see partial electrification of the routes from Cardiff to Treherbert, Aberdare, Merthyr Tydfil, Coryton, Cardiff Bay and Rhymney. West of Cardiff, electrification will include the City line to Radyr and that to Grangetown (on the lines to Barry and Penarth). The tram-trains will also operate on yet to be built street tramway sections.

Generally, infrastructure is being improved and sections of single

track line are having new loops put in, existing loops extended, or even converted to double-track operation.

The control centre and the Metro infrastructure hub are both at Treforest. The rolling stock depot for the new tram-train fleet is at Taff's Well.

STOURBRIDGE SHUTTLE

Pre-Metro Operations Ltd (PMOL) operates the 1.2km self-contained single-track Network Rail branch between Stourbridge Junction and Stourbridge Town stations. This is the shortest branch line in Britain, run by the smallest Train Operating Company. The track was relaid in 2021. The only pointwork is that connecting it to the main line via a ground frame, which is not in regular use. There are six services an hour in each direction, reducing to four on Sundays. End-to-end running time is three minutes and service reliability is better than 99%.

PMOL operates on behalf of West Midlands Trains, employs the operating staff and maintains the vehicles.

The majority of branch passengers interchange with other rail services towards Birmingham or Worcester at Stourbridge Junction National Rail station.

A four-wheeled Class 139 Parry People Mover has been used since 2009, with a second as a spare. Only one vehicle is in use at any one time. These hybrids have a small Ford engine powered by LPG and flywheel stored energy. The vehicles are 8.7m long and weigh 12.5 tonnes, with a maximum speed of 45mph. These have 21 seats and a total carrying capacity of around 50. West Midlands Trains has indicated that the vehicles are becoming increasingly unreliable and is to start investigation of options for replacement.

UK TRAM

UK Tram is a not-for-profit trade body for all light rail and other guided transport systems in the British Isles. The principal aims of UK Tram are:
- to promote the adoption of light rail through the benefits it offers;
- to reduce the time and costs in developing new tramways;
- to increase technical standardisation and promote good practice;
- to deliver a single pool of expertise, accessible to interested parties.

The purpose of UK Tram is to provide a single industry voice in dealing with Government and statutory bodies and to help develop a co-ordinated and structured approach to regulation, procurement and standardisation.

UK Tram's investigations include those which could speed up and/or reduce the cost of network construction, or result in lower energy and/or operating costs. There are advisory groups on safety, operations, engineering, heritage systems and the promotion of light rail.
Managing Director: James Hammett

LIGHT RAIL SAFETY & STANDARDS BOARD (LRSSB)

A subsidiary of UK Tram, the LRSSB is the sector body responsible for co-ordinating advances in tramway safety and setting recognised industry standards. It has developed a Tram Accident and Incident Reporting database as part of its general purpose to develop tram standards and good practice, and to provide authoritative and impartial advice.

LRSSB was established following the RAIB report on the major derailment at Sandilands, Croydon in 2016.
Chief Executive: Carl Williams

VERY LIGHT RAIL (VLR)

Light rail is costly in terms of both vehicles and infrastructure. Could cheaper forms be developed? A Very Light Rail research and development programme aims to deliver the benefits of trams, but at a fraction of the cost. Funding of £14.7 million from the West Midlands Combined Authority and the Coventry & Warwickshire Local Enterprise Partnership has been secured.

A Very Light Rail vehicle is intended to weigh less than one tonne per linear metre, to be self-powered and have between 20 and 60 seats. A key feature will be low-cost prefabricated track, quickly installed and designed to minimise the need to relocate utilities. A lightweight zero-emission battery powered guided demonstrator vehicle, which has the ability for autonomous operation, is now under test at the National Innovation Centre in Dudley. With no need for overhead current collection, it can carry 56 passengers.

A permanent 7km tracked route is planned for the City of Coventry as a starter, between the National Rail station and the University Hospital. Around 80% of the route would operate in mixed traffic.

REVOLUTION VLR

Revolution VLR has been conceived to provide a modern, attractive and cost-effective lightweight railcar for use on heavy rail infrastructure. It might thus allow enhanced services on poorly served branch lines, facilitate the reopening of disused lines, and also encourage rail network extensions. These could enhance connectivity, particularly in the context of new residential and business developments.

A test vehicle is undergoing validation tests. The 18-metre-long demonstrator has a Cummins engine and a diesel-electric power train adapted from automotive technology, giving a maximum speed of 105km/h. There is a lithium titanate battery pack for regenerative braking, enabling zero emission operation at up to 30km/h in stations and in built-up areas.

It is designed primarily for short routes, where the operation of heavy rail or tram vehicles is uneconomic. It might include mixed operation with heavy rail. The aim is to produce a significantly cheaper and lower emission vehicle for such lines. The Rail Safety & Standards Board (RSSB) has identified 35 routes for which it might be suitable. ∎

INTO EUROPE

Europe's railways seek stability

Modern Railways' Europe Editor **KEITH FENDER** reviews a turbulent year for railways on the Continent

Europe's rail industry will be hoping 2023 turns out to be more stable than 2022. The combined effects of the Covid pandemic, the war in Europe following Russia's invasion of Ukraine and the consequent energy price shock which fed existing post-pandemic price inflation led to major cost increases for rail, as in most other industries.

Whether inflation across Europe will peak in 2023 and whether peace will return in Ukraine are both major influencers on the state of the economy, but outside the scope of *Modern Railways'* forecasting ability. Even if headline inflation falls, prices are unlikely to fall back to 2021 levels, so European economies will have to cope with higher operating costs for existing rail concession contracts. Labour represents a significant proportion of these costs, and substantial (if below headline inflation) pay increases will have changed the cost base for the medium-term. Energy cost increases, especially electricity prices, have led to calls for intervention by national or European authorities as rising traction current prices threaten the viability of rail freight.

Industry supply costs have increased, partly due to the overall inflationary pressures but also due to supply chain disruption. Causes include China's strict approach to Covid, shutting down factories and in some cases whole cities, and Russia's invasion of Ukraine, which has limited exports from Ukraine, while international sanctions mean most raw materials previously exported from or via Russia are no longer available.

Inflationary pressure led several governments to offer free or significantly discounted fares in 2022, at the cost of substantial additional funding to train operators to make up revenue shortfalls. These will continue in Spain throughout 2023, whilst in Germany a new national low fare ticket priced at €49 a month will be introduced (funded by €3 billion of additional Government support to operators) – although on a subscription basis like previous season tickets (most of which it will replace) but not as a walk-up fare, as seen during the €9 monthly ticket promotion in summer 2022.

2023 will see the first large scale use of new technology, with both battery and hydrogen powered multiple-units entering daily service in Germany, whilst in Italy new Hitachi-built 'Blues' tri-mode (diesel/electric/battery) units will enter service,

replacing older DMUs and the few remaining diesel loco-hauled services.

OPEN ACCESS EXPANSION

In Spain significant expansion of high-speed services is planned, with three operators offering services. From late 2022 Spanish Government owned RENFE was competing with two other operators on the key high-speed route from Madrid to Barcelona. New operator Iryo, part-owned by Trenitalia with investors Globalvia and Air Nostrum, began operating in late 2022, while new entrant French state operator SNCF has offered Ouigo low-cost high-speed services since mid-2021. In response to this competition, RENFE has also started its own low-cost operation, branded Avlo, using dedicated former AVE high-speed trains. Services from Madrid to both Valencia and Seville are also planned by the new entrants and Avlo in 2023.

Open access daytime services expanded in Germany in 2021-22,

New freight locos: use of Stadler's Eurodual and Euro 9000 locos is spreading across many EU countries. Eurodual No 159 222 passes Gemünden (Main) on 3 October 2022 with a northbound train. Retrack is the brand name for the freight logistics business of wagon leasing company VTG. VTG was owned by US bank Morgan Stanley from mid-2019 until July 2022, when a 72.5% share was sold to Global Infrastructure Partners and the Abu Dhabi Investment Authority. **KEITH FENDER**

Entering service in 2023: Stadler BEMU for NAH SH in Schleswig-Holstein on display at InnoTrans 2022. **KEITH FENDER**

with Flixtrain adding multiple routes, thanks to track access charges being funded by government as a Covid support measure (for all long-distance operators). Whether expansion will continue in 2023 is unclear.

In France, plans for open access operation by Railcoop and new high-speed operator 'Le Train' have been delayed by rolling stock and regulatory issues; whether these will be overcome in 2023 is unclear. Open access competition in France by Italian state operator Trenitalia utilising Hitachi-built ETR1000 high-speed EMUs began in late 2021.

In central Europe, Czech operator Regiojet will launch services from Prague to cities in Poland, although its plans for Polish domestic open access services in 2023 were rejected by regulators. Regiojet also plans to extend its seasonal overnight Prague – Zagreb/Split service to start in Berlin.

Open access domestic services in the Netherlands began in late 2022, with Arriva operating an overnight service to and from Schiphol Airport, serving cities in the north of the country; the service is operated with a Flirt EMU used in daylight hours for tendered services.

Austrian open access operator Westbahn is planning to use its new Chinese (CRRC) built double-deck EMUs for a new Vienna to Budapest route during 2023, assuming the trains, which it will lease from CRRC, gain approval for use in the EU.

OVERNIGHT TRAIN EXPANSION CONTINUES

Several new overnight train services were launched during late 2022, although new services between Stockholm and Hamburg operated by Swedish national operator SJ

on a part-subsidised basis under a contract let by the Swedish Government were initially unable to offer sleeping cars due to delays in preparing the stock to be used.

Problems with availability of rolling stock also led to delays in the planned launch of Dutch start-up 'European Sleeper', which plans to offer services from Brussels/Amsterdam to Berlin and Prague. These services will be operated by Czech open access company Regiojet on behalf of European Sleeper, and all necessary track access agreements were in place for a 2022 launch; however, it was delayed by a lack of rolling stock, which is being modernised to offer various levels of comfort.

Europe's biggest overnight train operator Austrian Federal Railways (ÖBB) will expand its fleet of overnight trains during 2023, introducing the first of 33 new 'Nightjet' trainsets being built by Siemens using the Viaggio coach design (also used for ÖBB's daytime 'Railjet' trains). ÖBB will introduce the new 230km/h seven-car 'Nightjet' trains (each with two seating cars, three couchettes and two sleeping cars) on routes from Vienna to Italian cities during 2023.

NEW HIGH-SPEED TRAINS

In Germany the new Class 408 'Velaro Neo' 320km/h EMU being supplied by Siemens was due to enter service in December 2022, with more of the 73 trains on order to be introduced during 2023. Siemens also expects to deliver the last of 137 ICE4 trains to Deutsche Bahn in April 2023, completing an order placed in 2011. DB has announced plans to tender for a new generation of ICE trains.

New high-speed train deliveries elsewhere in Europe should include the new Talgo 'Avril' Class 106 design for Spanish state operator RENFE, which will feature 2+3 seating in second class and will be used to replace older AVE trains. In France, testing of the first TGV-M for SNCF will begin in 2023; these are due to enter service in 2024.

INFRASTRUCTURE DEVELOPMENTS

In Germany the Wendlingen – Ulm high-speed line was due to open with the December 2022 timetable change. This is the eastern end of the future Stuttgart – Ulm route using the new underground Stuttgart Hauptbahnhof station, although the station is not due to open before December 2025. Construction work on multiple other new sections of new infrastructure nearing completion in the Stuttgart region should continue in 2023. In the area around Stuttgart 59km of new tunnels are being fitted out with European Train Control System Level 2.

In Norway, the long-running Follo line project creating a new high-speed route between Ski and Oslo was due to open in December 2022.

The new Pajares base tunnel in northern Spain should open in 2023, although given previous delays to this long-running project it is possible the opening will be postponed again. In advance of the route opening, Spanish state-owned freight operator RENFE Mercancías will introduce the first of 12 Stadler-built Class 256 1,668mm gauge tri-voltage Euro 6000 locos for use on the Pajares route.

On the border between Slovenia and Austria, the new 1.53km Pekel Tunnel and a new 3.7km realignment of part of the Maribor to Graz line

Spanish low-cost service: operated by state rail company RENFE, a Class 112 train branded 'Avlo' arrives at Llerida with a Barcelona – Madrid service on 10 November 2021. RENFE uses identical trains on several routes, but in its white 'AVE' livery. **KEITH FENDER**

should be completed in 2023; whether these will open before 2024 is unclear.

In the Baltic states, construction at multiple sites will be under way in 2023 on the planned Tallinn – Kaunas (– Poland) 'Rail Baltica' electrified standard gauge line. In Italy and Spain construction of several additional sections of high-speed line to expand the national networks should continue in 2023. In south eastern Europe, further major progress in updating the Serbian main line network is expected, and further east construction work on the new line from Kumanovo connecting Bulgaria and North Macedonia should begin in earnest after three decades of planning and discussion.

In several countries, detailed planning for new high-speed lines will continue or commence. In France this includes planned lines between Bordeaux and Toulouse plus Montpellier and Perpignan, with planning approval for the new Montpellier to Béziers section expected in mid-2023. Construction will take until the early 2030s. Planning for the proposed 1,668mm 'Iberian' gauge Lisbon to Porto high-speed line will get under way following a decision in late 2022 by the Portuguese Government to restart work.

In Poland, planning for several new sections of high-speed line is well advanced, although whether construction will begin is unclear due to ongoing disputes between the Polish Government and the European Commission; much of the funding required will come from EU sources.

REGIONAL RAIL SERVICES

Whilst tendering of regional services is now well established and legally required, the level of tendering

activity varies considerably between countries. In Slovakia, one of the few routes to be tendered multiple times, the regional service from Bratislava to Komárno, was awarded to its third operator, Czech firm Leo Express (since 2021 part-owned by Spanish rail operator RENFE) for operation from 2023, although the handover date was brought forward to late 2022. In the Netherlands the decision of the Government in 2022 to award a single national concession contract for the 'core network' to state-owned operator NS is likely to be challenged in the courts and possibly by the European Commission during 2023.

In Germany major changes to the tendered regional rail market in 2022 included the complete withdrawal of French company Keolis (selling its Eurobahn business to a German investment company) and the removal of Abellio from most routes following an insolvency process. British firm National Express gained significant additional 'Rhein Ruhr Express' contracts in the Ruhr region as a result of Abellio losing its contracts, leading to its German business growing revenues by nearly two-thirds. Go-Ahead began operation in Bavaria in December 2021 and a further major contract centred on Augsburg using fleets of new Siemens Desiro HC and Mireo EMUs began in December 2022. Go-Ahead was bought by a consortium of investors Kinetic and Globalvia in late 2022.

Arriva, owned by DB since 2010, sold several country subsidiaries in 2022, with rail operations in both Sweden and Denmark sold. It is unclear if further disposals will be announced in 2023.

NEW TRAINS, NEW TECHNOLOGIES

In Switzerland, after a delay partly due to the pandemic, the introduction of

through trains between Interlaken and Montreux began in December 2022 with a single train pair operated using new Stadler-built gauge changing coaches; the Interlaken to Zweisimmen section is standard gauge and the line from there to Montreux is metre gauge. Locomotives from the two operators – standard gauge BLS Lötschbergbahn (BLS) and metre gauge Montreux Oberland Bahn (MOB) – work the trains in push-pull mode via a gauge changer (for the carriages only) in the station at Zweisimmen. From mid-2023 the service will increase to three train pairs daily.

Other Swiss regional operators will receive new EMU fleets in 2023, mostly also built by Stadler. The metre gauge Matterhorn Gotthard Bahn will introduce new 'Orion' EMUs, replacing loco-hauled trains on regional routes, especially those radiating from Andermatt. Further east, the Rhätische Bahn will receive more 'Capricorn' EMUs, allowing withdrawal of most of its remaining loco-hauled trains. Swiss mountain railways are also investing in new rolling stock – the unique Pilatus Bahn near Luzern, the only railway in the world using the Locher rack system, will open in May 2023 with a completely new fleet of Stadler/ Calag made EMUs replacing the old fleet, some dating from the 1930s.

In France, introduction of substantial numbers of (ex-Bombardier) Omneo/ R2N EMUs ordered by regional governments will continue in 2023, with the trains replacing loco-hauled sets of Corail coaches on regional routes from Paris to Dijon/Lyon, Tours/ Orleans and long-distance regional services from Paris Gare du Nord. Similar trains have already replaced loco-hauled intercity and regional trains from Paris to Normandy. Construction work will continue in the Paris area

for both the RER E extension west of Hausmann-St Lazare, which will open in stages from 2024, and the new CDG Express Paris Est – Charles de Gaulle airport link, due to open in 2027.

In the Czech Republic, Regiojet will begin operation of brand new Pesa-built 'Elf' EMUs on local services around Usti nad Labem, whilst in Latvia Czech builder Škoda will deliver 32 EMUs to replace 1980s Soviet-built trains. In Sweden, seven Class ER1 double-deck Stadler 'Kiss' EMUs ordered by Transitio for Tåg i Bergslagen (TiB) will enter service on the on the Ludvika – Västerås route, whilst in Luxembourg the first of 34 new 'Coradia Stream High Capacity' EMUs (22x3-car Class 2400 EMUs and 12x6-car Class 2450) being built in Spain by Alstom will replace older EMUs.

NEW TECHNOLOGY FLEETS ENTERING SERVICE

The first of the fleet of Flirt 'Akku' battery EMUs (BEMUs) being built for use by north German regional transport authority NAH.SH in Schleswig-Holstein will enter service in mid-2023. The trains are fitted with lithium-ion traction batteries and can operate as normal EMUs under 15kV AC catenary; they feature one powered bogie at one end (with two 500kW motors) and two non-powered bogies (including the central articulated bogie). Fast

battery charging using 15kV catenary is also possible, and to allow recharging away from the existing electrified network 'electrification islands' are being built, with electrified branch termini and wires at key junctions on otherwise unelectrified lines.

NAH.SH tendered for non-diesel trains to operate networks comprising 10 million train kilometres annually in 2018-19, initially anticipating hydrogen-powered trains would be viable. However, NAH.SH left the choice of technology to potential suppliers and after evaluating several offers chose Stadler's BEMU option. The state of Schleswig-Holstein has set itself the target of becoming climate neutral by 2040 and sees transition in transport emissions as a key part of that effort; the BEMU fleet is part of this strategy.

The network to be BEMU-operated represents around 40% of the state's passenger rail system and is only partially electrified, with non-electrified sections as long as 40km to be operated before either an electrified line or an 'electrification island' rapid charge area is encountered. All 55 trains should be in service from May 2024. In the 2019 order Stadler also won a 30-year maintenance contract for the new BEMU fleet. The depot will be built in Rendsburg in the centre of the state's network and should open in 2023.

Both fleets of Alstom iLint hydrogen-powered units ordered for use in Germany will fully enter service in 2023. The first fleet of 14 trains owned by Lower Saxony state-owned ROSCO LNVG entered service between Cuxhaven and Bremerhaven/ Buxtehude in mid-2022, whilst the bigger fleet of 27 trains owned by the state of Hessen via its leasing company Fahma entered initial service from Frankfurt on lines to the Taunus region in December 2022.

In Italy, national operator Trenitalia will introduce its Hitachi-built tri-mode 'Blues' unit equipped for 3kV DC, battery and diesel operation. In addition to use in both Sicily and Sardinia, the new hybrid trains will replace 1970s/1980s vintage loco-hauled sets and DMUs in Tuscany and elsewhere in Italy.

FREIGHT – DISRUPTION, NEW LOCOS AND DIGITISATION

Russia's invasion of Ukraine early in 2022 has redrawn the map for some freight flows, with previously buoyant volumes between China and Europe falling dramatically although not ceasing completely. Some traffic has been rerouted to avoid Russia altogether, although this requires a time-consuming transhipment from trains to Black Sea or Caspian Sea shipping.

For countries bordering Russia, the loss of some or all cross-border traffic represents a major reduction in overall volumes. From 2023 Finland's railways will no longer handle any traffic to or from Russia, whilst major reductions in volume have impacted freight operators in the Baltic states too.

In Estonia, national rail freight company Operail reported volumes in 2022 had halved, leaving the long-term viability of the Estonian rail network, until now reliant on transit freight, in doubt. The impact of sanctions and the overall economic situation has led to some retrenchment by national operators which had expanded into neighbouring countries; Estonia's Operail has decided to cease operation in Finland, and further west Swedish national rail freight company Green Cargo has announced it will cease operation in Norway.

The growth in export traffic by rail, especially agricultural products from Ukraine, was one of the least expected outcomes following Russia's invasion. This has enabled grain and other foodstuffs to be exported from ports in the EU, some near Ukraine and others further away, such as the Baltic coast ports in Poland and even Barcelona on the Mediterranean.

Ukrainian Railways (Ukrzaliznytsia or UZ) has proactively reopened several lines into neighbouring countries that had fallen into disuse over the last three decades, sometimes in advance of the rail infrastructure on the opposite side of the border being ready for reopening work.

Multiple major EU-based rail freight companies including DB Cargo, PKP Cargo and Austrian national operator ÖBB have been heavily involved in rail logistics for Ukrainian exports, and this has included the use of containers to carry grain rather than traditional hopper wagons. It is likely the same partners, plus others from across Europe, will be involved in post-war reconstruction for Ukraine's railways, although exactly when that will occur is unclear.

At InnoTrans in September 2022 DB Chief Executive Dr Richard Lutz agreed a memorandum of understanding guaranteeing UZ support from DB for reconstruction after the war, including collaboration on expanding freight services.

FREIGHT 'DIGITISATION' PROGRESS

Decisions on pan-EU standards for the new digital automatic couplings (DAC) should be finalised in 2023. Previous practical trials in multiple countries, largely funded

New route opening and deliveries ending: a DB ICE4 high-speed train on the classic Geislingen (Steige) route between Stuttgart and Ulm on 26 September 2022. Most long-distance services on this route were due to switch to the new Wendlingen – Ulm line in December 2022. All 137 of the ICE4 trains on order from Siemens will have been delivered by mid-2023. **KEITH FENDER**

by the German Government, have led to the Scharfenberg digital coupler design being agreed as the new standard, although several important technical details such as coupler height and electrical connections need to be agreed.

German operator DB Cargo has announced plans to establish 150 'pop-up' temporary workshops across Europe to retrofit wagons with the new digital automatic couplers from 2023 onwards. Over 460,000 wagons across Europe will potentially be fitted with DAC equipment at a cost of around €8 to €12 billion; exactly how this will be financed remains unclear.

In France, state railway SNCF has proactively disposed of several major (and profitable) subsidiaries in recent years, including wagon leasing firm Ermewa and rolling stock company Akiem. These disposals have given the rail freight business Fret SNCF a short-term boost in profitability, whilst SNCF has continued to invest in its large logistics business, Geodis, adding acquisitions in both the USA and Asia in 2022. It appears likely the German Government intends to follow a different route, with a sale of all or part of the DB Schenker logistics business likely to be attempted. DB has already begun disposing of its Arriva contracted passenger operating business with piecemeal sale of Arriva units in Sweden and Denmark during 2022.

NEW LOCOS FROM MULTIPLE BUILDERS

Loco manufacturers, especially Siemens with its four-axle Vectron range and Stadler with its Eurodual and new Euro 9000 six-axle heavy freight bi-mode locomotives, will deliver large numbers of new locos in 2023, most bought by leasing companies or major state-owned rail freight operators. Other manufacturers such as Alstom (with the ex-Bombardier Traxx range), and Polish builders Pesa and Newag will also deliver new locos, primarily for freight operators.

Thirty of Stadler's powerful new six-axle 9MW Euro 9000s were ordered by leasing firm ELP in 2019; many will enter service in 2023. They are designed as a 120km/h four-voltage electric for use in multiple countries and are also equipped with two CAT32 Euro V 950kW diesel engines and an 1,800-litre diesel tank for operation away from catenary. ELP has also ordered 64 'Eurodual' electro-diesel bi-modes, and deliveries of the remaining locos should follow in 2023; these are now in service with multiple operators, mostly in Germany.

Also in Germany, DB Cargo will begin introduction of 100 new Class 249 'Vectron dual-mode' locos designed to replace older diesel shunting and trip locos. The first of an order for 100 battery-diesel hybrid locos being built by Toshiba at a DB site in Rostock should also appear in 2023.

LIGHT RAIL AND METROS

In Greece the new automated metro system in Thessaloniki is due to finally open during 2023; construction has been delayed multiple times due to unexpected archaeological discoveries in one of Europe's oldest port cities. Hitachi has supplied 18 trains from its Italian factories, based on those in use in Copenhagen. In the Greek capital Athens, where the final section of the new Line 3 opened in late 2022, construction work is now under way on a fourth line; initially a 12.8km section of the planned 38.5km line is being built.

In Paris, the western extension of Metro Line 11, adding six more stations between Mairie des Lilas and Rosny-Bois-Perrier, is due to open in 2023. A further western extension as part of the Grand Paris Express metro expansion programme is also planned, and substantial construction work for this project will continue in 2023 with the aim of opening some sections of new line serving Orly Airport before the 2024 Paris Olympic Games.

Introduction of new metro trains to replace older fleets is under way in several cities across Europe. In Berlin the new 'small profile' type JK trains will enter service alongside more of the 'IK' large profile version. In Warsaw Czech manufacturer Škoda is introducing 37 six-car metro EMUs, which will replace Soviet-built trains dating from the metro system's opening.

Across central Europe renewal of older tram fleets with new vehicles is under way, with large numbers of vehicles likely to enter service in German, Czech, Polish and Romanian cities from builders located all over Europe, plus others from Turkey and South Korea.

In Germany Stadler will deliver the first of its new 'Tina' range of light rail vehicles to Darmstadt operator HEAG, whilst in the Polish capital Warsaw Hyundai Rotem will deliver most of the 123 low-floor trams on order, although operation with them began in 2022. In Poland domestic tram specialist Modertrans Poznań will supply an additional 21 'Moderus Gamma' trams to the tram operator in Wrocław; an initial order for 25 vehicles was completed in late 2022. Three single-car versions of the Moderus Gamma will be also delivered to the Woltersdorf tram route in Germany east of Berlin in 2023, replacing 1950s/1960s vintage 'Gotha' cars. In the far west of Europe, in the Portuguese city of Porto the first of 18 new four-section light rail vehicles made in China by CRRC will begin testing in 2023. The order, originally placed in 2020, was delayed by the Covid pandemic, and the first vehicles were shipped from China in late October 2022. ■

New tram fleet: Pesa Gamma vehicle No 3317 near Wrocław Główny station 26 June 2022. The tram sports a Ukrainian flag, and Wrocław operator MPK Wrocław has employed several Ukrainian tram drivers who became refugees in the city earlier in 2022. **KEITH FENDER**

DIRECTORY

THE UK RAIL INDUSTRY IN YOUR HANDS

IN ASSOCIATION WITH

1Spatial Group
Tennyson House, Cambridge Business Park, Cambridge, CB4 0WZ
T: 01223 420414
W: https://1spatial.com/

1stinrail
1D North Crescent, Cody Road, London, E16 4TG
T: 0845 527 8440
F: 0845 527 8441
W: www.1stinrail.co.uk/

21st Century Technology plc
12 Charter Point Way, Ashby-de-la-Zouch, Leicestershire, LE65 1NF
T: 0844 871 7990
E: info@21stplc.com
W: www.21stplc.com

345 Rail Leasing
10-11 Charterhouse Square, London, EC1M 6EH

360 Vision Technology Ltd
Unit 7, Seymour Court, Manor Park, Runcorn, Cheshire, WA7 1SY
T: 0870 903 3601
F: 0870 903 3602
E: info@ipx360solutions.com
W: www.360visiontechnology.com

3A Composites Mobility AG
Park Altenrhein, CH-9423 Altenrhein, Switzerland
T: 0071 858 4848
F: 0071858 4858
E: contact.mobility@3acomposites.com
W: 3acompositesmobility.com

3D Laser Mapping
1a Church St, Bingham, Nottingham, NG13 8AL
T: 0870 442 9400
F: 0870 121 4605
E: info@3dlasermapping.com
W: www.3dlasermapping.com

3DVSL (3D Visual Simulations Ltd)
Suite 5.9 Techcube, 1 Summerhall, Edinburgh, EH9 1PL
M: 07730 417111
E: hello@3dvsl.com
W: www.3dvsl.com

3M CPPD
Standard Way, Northallerton, N.Yorks, DL6 2XA
T: 01609 780170
F: 01609 780438
W: www.copon.co.uk

3M United Kingdom PLC
3M Centre, Cain Rd, Bracknell, Berks, RG12 8HT
T: 01344 858704
E: railsolutions@mmm.com
W: www.3m.co.uk/railsolutions

3Squared
Fountain Precinct, Balm Green, Sheffield, S1 2JA
T: 0333 121 3333
E: info@3squared.com
W: www.3squared.com

42 Technology
Meadow Lane, St Ives, Cambridgeshire, PE27 4LG
T: 01480 302700
F: 01480 302701
E: answers@42technology.com
W: www.42technology.com/

4Silence
Vliegveldstraat 100-C38, 7524 PK Enschede, Netherlands
T: +31 53 303 4888
E: info@4silence.com
W: www.4silence.com

50026 Indomitable

A&J Electrical Services
3 Greenshields Industrial Estate, Bradfield Road, London, E16 2AU
T: 020 7366 6519
F: 020 7476 3638
W: www.ajeltd.com/

Aalco Metals Ltd
25 High Street, Cobham, KT11 3DH
T: 01932 576820
E: info@aalco.co.uk
W: www.aalco.co.uk

Aardvark Site Investigations Ltd
See Screwfast Foundations Ltd

Aaron Rail
Pepper House, Pepper Road, Hazel Grove, Stockport, SK7 5DP
T: 0161 638 3283
E: enquiries@aaronrail.co.uk
W: www.aaronrail.co.uk

AATI Rail Ltd
11 Swinborne Drive, Springwood Ind. Est, Braintree, Essex, CM7 2YP
T: 01376 346278
F: 01376 348480
E: info@aati.co.uk
W: www.aati.co.uk

AB Connectors Ltd
Abercynon, Mountain Ash, Rhondda Cynon Taff, CF45 4SF
T: 01443 743403
F: 01443 741676
E: sales@ttabconnectors.com
W: www.ttabconnectors.com

AB Hoses & Fittings Ltd
Units 5-7, Warwick Street Industrial Estate, Chesterfield, Derbyshire, S40 2TT
T: 01246 208831
F: 01246 209302
E: sales@abhoses.com
W: www.abhoses.com

ABA Surveying
Lansbury Est., Lower Guildford St, Knaphill, Woking, Surrey, GU21 2EP
T: 01483 797111
F: 01483 797211
E: info@abasurveying.co.uk
W: www.abasurveying.co.uk

Abacus Lighting Ltd
Oddicroft Lane, Sutton-in-Ashfield, Notts, NG17 5FT
T: 01623 511111
F: 01623 552133
E: sales@abacuslighting.com
W: www.abacuslighting.com

ABB Ltd
Tower Court, Foleshill Enterprise Park, Courtaulds Way, Coventry, CV6 5NX
T: 02476 368500
E: lv.enquiries@gb.abb.com
W: www.abb.com/railway

Abbey Pynford Foundation Systems Ltd
IMEX, First Floor, West Wing, 575-599 Maxted Road, Hemel Hempstead, Herts, HP2 7DX
T: 0870 085 8400
F: 0870 085 8401
E: info@abbeypynford.co.uk
W: www.abbeypynford.co.uk

Abbeydale Training Ltd
26 Stonewood Grove, Sheffield, S10 5SS
T: 0114 230 4400
E: abbeydale.training@btconnect.com
W: www.abbeydaletraining.co.uk

Abbi Access Services Ltd
Clwyd Close, Hawarden Industrial Estate, Manor Lane, Hawarden, CH5 3PZ
T: 01244 629919
F: 01244 676557
M: 07733 216036
E: admin@abbiaccess.com
W: www.abbiaccess.com

Abbott Risk Consulting Ltd
Audley House, 13 Palace Street, London, SW1E 5HX
M: 07789 176401
E: rail@consultarc.com
W: www.consultarc.com

ABC Electrification
Myson House, Rugby, Warks, CV21 3HT
T: 01788 545654
W: abcel.co.uk/

Abellio
5th Floor, The Culzean Building, 36 Renfield Street, Glasgow, G2 1LU
T: 020 7430 8270
F: 020 7430 2239
E: info@abellio.com
W: www.abellio.com

ABET Ltd
70 Roding Rd, London Ind. Park, London, E6 4LS
T: 020 7473 6910
F: 020 7476 6935
E: sales@abet.ltd.uk
W: www.abetuk.com

Abloy UK
Portobello Works, School St, Willenhall, West Midlands, WV13 3PW
T: 01902 364500
F: 01902 364501
E: sales@abloy.co.uk
W: www.abloy.co.uk

ABM Precast Solutions Ltd
Ollerton Rd, Tuxford, Newark, Notts, NG22 0PQ
T: 01777 872233
E: precast@abmeurope.com
W: www.abmprecast.co.uk

Abracs Ltd
Abracs House, Unit 3, George Cayley Drive, Clifton Moor, York, YO30 4XE
T: 01904 789997
F: 01904 789996
E: abracs@abracs.com
W: www.abracs.com

ABS Consulting
EQE House, The Beacons, Warrington Rd, Birchwood, Warrington, WA3 6WJ
T: 01925 287300
F: 01925 287301
E: enquiriesuk@absconsulting.com
W: www.eqe.co.uk

Abtus Ltd
Falconer
Rd, Haverhill, Suffolk, CB9 7XU
T: 01440 702938
F: 01440 702961
E: chris.welsh@abtus.com
W: www.abtus.com

Acal BFI UK Limited
3 The Business Centre, Molly Millars Lane, Wokingham, RG41 2EY
T: 01189788878
E: sales-uk@acalbfi.co.uk
W: www.acalbfi.co.uk

Access Design & Engineering Ltd
Marsh Road, Middlesbrough, TS1 5JS
T: 01642 245151
E: sales@access-design.co.uk
W: www.access-design.co.uk

Access IS
18 Suttons Business Park, Reading, Berks, RG6 1AZ
T: 0118 966 3333
F: 0118 926 7281
E: carol.harraway@access-is.com
W: www.access-is.com

Acciona Infrastructure
Avda. Europa 18, Parque Empresarial La Moraleja, 28108 Alcobendas (Madrid), Spain
T: +34 91 663 28 50
F: +34 91 663 30 99
E: webmail-infraestructuras@acciona.es
W: www.acciona-infrastructure.com/

Acetech Personnel Ltd
See Morson International

Achilles Information Ltd (Link-Up)
30 Park Gate, Milton Park, Abingdon, Oxon, OX14 4SH
T: 01235 820813
F: 01235 838156
E: link-up@achilles.com
W: www.achilles.com

ACIC International Ltd
14 Blacknest Business Park, Blacknest, Nr Alton, Hants, GU34 4PX
T: 01420 23930
F: 01420 23921
E: sales@acic.co.uk
W: www.acic.co.uk

ACM Bearings Ltd
Derwent Way, Wath West Ind Est, Rotherham, S Yorks, S63 6EX
T: 01709 874951
F: 01709 878818
E: sales@acmbearings.co.uk
W: www.acmbearings.co.uk

ACO Technologies Plc
ACO Business Park, Hitchin Rd, Shefford, Beds, SG17 5TE
T: 01462 816666
F: 01462 815895
E: technologies@aco.co.uk
W: www.aco.co.uk

ACOREL S.A.S
Technopar Pole 2000, 3 Rue Paul Langevin, 07130 St Peray, France
T: 0033 475 405979
F: 0033 475 405771
E: info@acorel.com
W: www.acorel.com

Acorn People
7 York Rd, Woking, Surrey, GU22 7XH
T: 01483 654463
F: 01483 723080
E: sarah.griffiths@acornpeople.com
W: www.acornpeople.com

ACT Informatics Ltd
One St Peters Rd, Maidenhead, Berks, SL6 1QU
T: 0870 114 9800
F: 0870 114 9801
E: admin@act-consultancy.com

Actavo
Unit C, Cedar Court Office Park, Denby Dale Road, Calder Grove, Wakefield, WF4 3QZ
E: info@actavo.com
W: actavo.com

Acumen Design Associates Ltd
1 Sekforde St, Clerkenwell, London, EC1R 0BE
T: 020 7107 2900
F: 020 7107 2901
E: info@acumen-da.com
W: www.acumen-da.com

AD Engineering
Unit 1, Saxon Shore Business Park, Castle Road, Eurolink Industrial Estate, Sittingbourne, Kent, ME10 3EU
T: 01795 435900
F: 01795 435940
W: www.adengineering.co.uk

Adamson Associates
6th Floor, One Canada Square, Canary Wharf, London, E14 5AB
T: 020 7418 2068
F: 020 7418 2517
E: mroyston@adamson-associates.com
W: www.adamson-associates.com/

Adaptaflex
Station Rd, Coleshill, Birmingham, B46 1HT
T: +44 (0) 2476 368500
F: 01675 464276
E: lv.customerservice@gb.abb.com
W: www.adaptaflex.com

ADAS UK Ltd
Woodthorn, Wergs Rd, Wolverhampton, WV6 8TQ
T: 01902 754190
E: sam.lowe@adas.co.uk
W: www.adas.co.uk

THE 2023 MODERN RAILWAY DIRECTORY - THE MOST COMPREHENSIVE DIRECTORY OF BUSINESSES INVOLVED IN THE OPERATION OF THE UK RAIL INDUSTRY

KEY TO SYMBOLS

TRAIN OPERATORS
Passenger and Freight Train Operators, TOC Owning Groups, Light Railway, Metro and Tramway Operators, Rail Tour Operators, Passenger Transport Authorities/Executives, Freight Forwarders/Brokers.

ROLLING STOCK MANUFACTURE, SUPPLY AND DELIVERY
Locomotive, Light Rail, Metro, Carriage and Wagon Manufacture, Locomotive, Wagon and Coaching Stock Hire, Chartering, Rolling Stock Leasing Companies, Rolling Stock Delivery.

INFRASTRUCTURE
Infrastructure Maintenance and Renewal, Lineside Equipment, Construction Projects, Electrification, Electrical Components Misc.,Trackwork, Ground Protection and Safety, Workshop Equipment, Fencing & Security, Lighting (except rolling stock), Platforms, Access Systems, Walkways & Gantries, Cable Management, Power Supply, Carriage Washing, Freight Terminals, Level Crossings and Associated Components, Passenger Information Displays, Signs and Notifications, Car Parking, Cleaning, Weighing & Lifting, Grafitti Removal, Pest Control, Ticketing, CCTV, Public Address, Test Facilities, Fares and Collection. Customer Accessibility, Route Management and Ownership, Noise and Vibration Control.

INFRASTRUCTURE MATERIAL SUPPLIES
Buildings & Building Refurbishment, Plant, Tools, Welding, Paints & Coatings, Clothing & Boots, Chemicals and Lubricants, Scaffolding and Safety Netting, Temporary Bridges, Roads, Buildings and Containers, Flooring, Weighing & Lifting.

ON TRACK PLANT & MISCELLANEOUS
On Track Plant Manufacturers, Misc.

ROLLING STOCK MAINTENANCE/PARTS
Locomotive, Carriage and Wagon Maintenance, Component Supply, Lighting and Cabling, Decals and Transfers, De-Icing, Sanding, Upholstery, Disposal, Textiles, Fuel Technology, In Train Entertainment, Train Monitoring Systems, Train Branding, Vinyls and Wraps, Depot Equipment, Carpeting & Insulation.

HUMAN RESOURCES INCLUDING CATERING, TRAINING & HEALTH
Recruitment and Training Companies/ Consultancies, Personnel Supply, Retirement and Convalescence, Catering.

SIGNAL & TELECOMMUNICATION
S&T Installation and Equipment, Wireless Technology and Datacoms, Training Simulators.

PROFESSIONAL ADVICE, CONSULTANCY AND SERVICES
Consultants, Legal Services, Economists, Industry Reporting, Insurance, Accreditation & Compliance, Verification & Validation, Assessment, Test & Development, Systems & Software, IT Services, Architects and Design Agencies, Surveying, Data Management, Financial Services, Property, Solutions and Turnkey Providers, Mapping, Vehicle Acceptance, Video & Film Production, Photography, Journey Planning, Conferences & Exhibitions, Specialist Media, Project Management, Marketing, PR & Branding, Weather Forcasting, Simulation, Drugs and Alcohol Testing, Research Organisations.

INDUSTRY AND REGULATORY BODIES
Trade Associations, Alliances and Authorities, Advisory Boards, Government Departments, Customer Organisations, Accident Investigators, Campaigning Organisations, Passenger Watchdogs, Trade Unions, Port Authorities and Development Agencies.

ROAD TRANSPORT SERVICES
Fleet Management, Heavy Haulage, Replacement Buses and Vehicle Hire

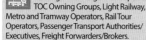

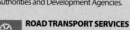

ADComms
Unit 11, Billet Lane, Normanby Enterprise
Park, Scunthorpe, DN15 9YH
T: 01724 292200
E: info@adcomms.eu.panasonic.com
W: adcomms.ltd

Addleshaw Goddard
Milton Gate, 60 Chiswell Street, London, EC1Y 4AG
T: 020 7606 8855
F: 020 7606 4390
W: www.addleshawgoddard.com/

Adeo Construction Consultants
Unit 16, Oakhurst Business Park, Wilberforce Way, Southwater, Horsham, RH13 9RT
T: 01403 821770
F: 01403 733405
E: enquiries@adeo.uk.com
W: www.adeo.uk.com

Adey Steel Group
Falcon Industrial Park, Meadow Lane, Loughborough, Leicestershire, LE11 1HL
T: 01509 556677
F: 01509 828622
E: mail@adeysteel.co.uk
W: www.adeysteelgroup.co.uk/

Adien Ltd
Unit 5 Third Avenue, Delta Court, Sky Business Park, Doncaster, DN9 3GN
T: 01302 802200
E: info@adien-utility-detection.com
W: www.adien-utility-detection.com/

ADT Fire & Security
Security House, The Summit, Hanworth Rd, Sunbury on Thames, TW16 5DB
T: 01932 743229
F: 01932 743047
W: www.adt.co.uk/

Advance Consultancy Ltd
St Mary's House, Church St, Uttoxeter, ST14 8AG
T: 01889 561510
F: 01889 561591
W: www.advance-consulting.com

Advance Training & Recruitment Services
2nd Floor, Stamford House, 91 Woodbridge Rd, Guildford, GU1 4QD
T: 01483 361061
F: 01483 431958
E: info@advance-trs.com
W: www.advance-trs.com

Advanced Handling Ltd
Northfields Ind. Est, Market Deeping, Peterborough, PE6 8LD
T: 01778 345365
F: 01778 341654
E: sales@advancedhandling.co.uk
W: www.advancedhandling.co.uk

Advanced Micro Peripherals
1 Harrier House, Sedgeway Business Park, Witchford, Cambridge, CB6 2HY
T: 01353 659500
F: 01353 659600
E: sales@ampltd.com
W: www.ampltd.com

Advanced Selection Ltd
39 Mitchell Point, Ensign Way, Hamble, Hampshire, SO31 4RF
T: 02380 744455
F: 01794 518549
E: office@advancedselect.co.uk
W: www.advancedselect.co.uk

Advantage Resourcing
No 1 Poultry, London, EC2R 8EJ
T: 0207 390 7000
E: complianceteam@advantagegroup.co.uk
W: www.advantageresourcing.co.uk

Advantage Technical Consulting
See Atkins

Advante Strategic Site Services
4th Floor, Phoenix House, Christopher Martin Rd, Basildon, SS14 3HG
T: 01268 280500
F: 01268 293454
E: sales@advante.co.uk
W: www.advante.co.uk

Advantech
Unit 3 Gunnery Terrace, Duke of Wellington Avenue, Royal Arsenal, Woolwich, London, SE18 6SW
T: 02083197683
F: 02088369732
E: brian.lin@advantech.com
W: www.advantech.eu

Adventis Consulting
3 Chiswick Park, 566 Chiswick High Rd, Chiswick, London, W4 5YA
T: 020 8878 3454
W: adventis.co.uk

AE Petsche
Unit 8, Suttons Business Park, Sutton Park Avenue, Earley, Reading, Berkshire, RG6 1AZ
T: 0118 969 3230
E: contactaep@aepetsche.com
W: www.aepetsche.com/

AECOM
AECOM House, 63-77 Victoria St, St Albans, Herts, AL1 3ER
T: 0141 3545722
E: ian.hay@aecom.com
W: www.aecom.com

Aedas Group Ltd
5-8 Hardwick St, London, EC1R 4RG
T: 020 7837 9789
F: 020 7837 9678
E: london@aedas.com
W: www.aedas.com

AEG Power Solutions Ltd
Suite 16, Wenta Business Centre, 1 Electric Avenue, Enfield, Middx, EN3 7XU
T: 01992 719200
F: 01992 702151
E: kevin.pateman@aegps.com
W: www.aegps.com

Aegis Certification Services Ltd
29 Brunel Parkway, Pride Park, Derby, DE24 8HR
T: 01332 384302
E: info@aegis-cert.co.uk
W: www.aegis-cert.co.uk

AEGIS Engineering Systems Ltd
29 Brunel Parkway, Pride Park, Derby, DE24 8HR
T: 01332 384302
E: sales@aegiseng.co.uk
W: www.aegisengineering.co.uk

AEI Cables Ltd
Durham Rd, Birtley, Chester-le-Street, Co. Durham, DH3 2RA
T: 0191 410 3111
F: 0191 410 8312
E: info@aeicables.co.uk
W: www.aeicables.co.uk

Aerco Ltd
16-17 Lawson Hunt Ind. Park, Broadbridge Heath, Horsham, West Sussex, RH12 3JR
T: 01403 260206
F: 01403 259760
M: 07767 002298
E: chenderson@aerco.co.uk
W: www.aerco.co.uk

Aerosystems International
See BAE Systems

AES
The Old Warehouse, Park St, Worcester, WR5 1AA
T: 01905 363520
E: contact@aesco.co.uk
W: www.aesco.co.uk

Aether
Oxford Centre for Innovation, New Road, Oxford, OX1 1BY
T: 01865 261466
E: enquiries@aether-uk.com
W: www.aether-uk.com

AGC AeroComposites Derby
Unit 10a, Sills Rd, Willow Farm Business Park, Castle Donington, DE74 2US
T: 01332 818000
F: 01332 818089
E: sales@paulfabs.co.uk
W: www.agcaerocomposites.com

AGD Equipment Ltd
Avonbrook House, 198 Masons Rd, Stratford Enterprise Park, Stratford upon Avon, Warks, CV37 9LQ
T: 01789 292227
F: 01789 268350
E: info@agd-equipment.co.uk
W: www.agd-equipment.co.uk

Aggregate Industries UK Ltd
Bardon Hill, Bardon Hill Quarry, Coalville, Leics, LE67 1TL
T: 01530 510066
F: 01530 510123
E: corporate.communications@aggregate.com
W: www.aggregate-uk.com

Aggreko UK Ltd
2 Voyager Drive, Cannock, Staffs, WS11 8XP
T: 08458 247365
F: 01543 437772
E: enquiries@aggreko.co.uk
W: www.aggreko.co.uk

AGH Engineering Ltd
Mill House, North Street, York, North Yorkshire, YO1 6JQ
T: 01904 545040
E: info@aghengineering.co.uk
W: www.aghengineering.co.uk/

Agilia
71 Central Street, Clerkenwell, London, EC1V 3AR
T: 020 7971 1014
E: info@agilia.co.uk
W: www.agilia.co.uk

Agility Trains
7th Floor, 40 Holborn Viaduct, London, EC1N 2PB
T: 020 7970 2700
E: enquiries@agilitytrains.com
W: www.agilitytrains.co.uk

Ainscough
Bradley Hall, Bradley Lane, Standish, Lancs, WN6 0XQ
T: 0800 272 637
F: 01257 473286
E: heavy.cranes@ainscough.co.uk
W: www.ainscough.co.uk

Airedale International Air Conditioning Ltd
Leeds Road, Rawdon, Leeds, LS19 6JY
T: 0113 239 1000
F: 0113 250 7219
E: connect@airedale.com
W: https://airedale.com/

Airquick (Newark) Ltd
Brunel Business Park, Jessop Close, Newark, Notts, NG24 2AG
T: 01636 640480
F: 01636 701216
E: info@airquick.co.uk
W: www.airquick.co.uk

Airtec International Ltd
40 Couper St, Glasgow, G4 0DL
T: 0141 552 5591
F: 0141 552 5064
E: akilpatrick@airtecintl.co.uk
W: www.airtecinternational.com

AJT Engineering
Craigshaw Crescent, West Tullos, Aberdeen, AB12 3TB
T: 01224 871791
F: 01224 890251
E: info@ajt-engineering.co.uk
W: www.ajt-engineering.co.uk/

Akiem Group
W: www.akiem.com/

AKS Training
Goodwill Solutions Buildings, Deer Park Road, Moulton Park Ind Est, Northampton, Northamptonshire, NN3 6RX
T: 01604 247800
E: info@akstraining.com
W: https://akstraining.com/

AKT II
100 St John Street, London, EC1M 4EH
T: 020 7250 7777
F: 020 7250 5555
W: www.akt-uk.com/

Alan Baxter
75 Cowcross Street, London, EC1M 6EL
T: 020 7250 1555
E: aba@alanbaxter.co.uk
W: alanbaxter.co.uk

Alan Murray Architects
9 Harrison Gardens, Edinburgh, EH11 1SJ
T: 0131 313 1999
E: ama@ama-ltd.co.uk
W: www.ama-ltd.co.uk

Alandale Group
9 Selsdon Way, City Harbour, London, E14 9GL
T: 020 7005 0050
F: 020 7005 0051
W: www.alandaleuk.com

Albion Economics
Sandpiper, Kingston Road, Lewes, East Sussex, BN7 3ND

Alcad
1st Floor, Unit 5, Astra Centre, Edinburgh
Way, Harlow, Essex, CM20 2BN
T: 01279 772555
E: carter.sarah@alcad.com
W: www.alcad.com

Alcatel-Lucent
Voyager Place, Shoppenhangers Rd, Maidenhead, SL5 2PJ
T: 01628 428221
F: 01628 428785
E: phil.cottom@alcatel-lucent.com
W: www.alcatel-lucent.com/railways

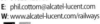

Alcontrol
Units 7&8, Hawarden Business Park, Manor Rd, Hawarden, Deeside, Flintshire, CH5 3US
T: 01244 528700
F: 01244 528701
W: www.alcontrol.com

Alere Healthcare Connections
Nashleigh Court, 188 Severalls Avenue, Chesham, Bucks, HP5 3EN
T: 01235 861483
W: www.alerehealthcareconnections.com/

Alertive Workforce Management
15 St Christophers Way, Pride Park, Derby, DE24 8JY
T: 01332 368 500
E: info@alertive.co.uk
W: www.alertiveworkforce.com

The Alexander Partnership
Suite 47, 34 Buckingham Palace Road, Belgravia, London, SW1W 0RH
T: 0845 643 0824
E: info@thealexanderpartnership.com
W: www.thealexanderpartnership.com/

Alfatronix Ltd
29-30 Newtown Business Park, Dorset, Poole, BH12 3LL
T: 01202 715517
F: 01202 715122
E: sales@alfatronix.com
W: www.alfatronix.com

Alfred Bagnall & Sons (North)
6, Manor Lane, Shipley, West Yorks, BD18 3RD
T: 01274 714800
F: 01274 530171
E: info@bagnalls.co.uk
W: www.bagnalls.co.uk

Alfred McAlpine Plc
See Carillion Rail

All Clothing & Protection Ltd
Units 6&7, Manor Park Ind Est, Station Rd South, Totton, Hants, SO40 9HP
T: 02380 428003
F: 02380 869333
E: sales@allclothing.co.uk
W: www.allclothing.co.uk

Allan Webb Limited
Bonds Mill, Stonehouse, GL10 3RF
T: 01453824581
E: info@smartditch.co.uk
W: www.allanwebb.co.uk

Allbatteries UK Ltd
Unit 20, Monkspath Business Park, Highlands Road, Solihull, West Midlands, B90 4NZ
T: 0121 506 8619
E: customerservice@allbatteries.co.uk
W: www.allbatteries.co.uk/

Allelys Heavy Haulage
The Slough, Studley, Warks, B80 7EN
T: 01527 857621
F: 01527 857623
E: robert@allelys.co.uk
W: www.allelys.co.uk

Allen & Douglas Corporate Clothing
See Sartoria Corporatewear

Allerton Steel
Thurston Road, Northallerton, North Yorkshire, DL6 2NA
T: 01609 774471
F: 01609 780364
E: contactus@allertonsteel.co.uk
W: https://www.allertonsteel.co.uk/

Allford Hall Monaghan Morris (AHMM)
Morelands, 5-23 Old Street, London, EC1V 9HL
T: 020 7251 5261
F: 020 7251 5123
W: www.ahmm.co.uk/

Alliance Rail Holdings
See Grand Central Railway Co. Ltd.

Allies & Morrison
85 Southwark St, London, SE1 0HX
T: 020 7921 0100
F: 020 7921 0101
E: newprojects@alliesandmorrison.com
W: www.alliesandmorrison.com

Allstar Business Solutions
PO Box 1463, Windmill Hill, Swindon, Wiltshire, SN5 6PS
T: 0870 182 8489
W: www.allstarcard.co.uk/

Alltask Ltd
Alltask House, Commissioners Rd, Rochester, Kent, ME2 4EJ
T: 01634 298000
E: enquiries@alltask.co.uk
W: www.alltask.co.uk

Alltype Fencing Specialists Ltd
Ye Wentes Wayes, High Rd, Langdon Hills, Essex, SS16 6HY
T: 01268 545192
F: 01268 545260
E: sales@alltypefencing.com
W: www.alltypefencing.com

Alonyx Ltd
The Mills, Canal St, Derby, DE1 2RJ
E: alexbrain@alonyx.com
W: www.alonyx.com

Alphatek Hyperformance Coatings Ltd
Head Office & Works, Unit A5, Cuba Ind. Est, Bolton Rd North, Ramsbottom, Lancs, BL0 0NE
T: 01706 821021
F: 01706 821023
E: railcoatings@alphatek.co.uk
W: www.alphatek.co.uk

Alstom Transport
The Place, 175 High Holborn, London, WC1V 7AA
T: 020 7438 9230
M: 07739 009 575
W: www.alstom.com

Altius
Wyvern Court, Stanier Way, Wyvern Business Park, Derby, DE21 6BF
T: 01332 960320
E: enquiries@altiusva.com
W: www.altiusva.com

Altpro
Velika cesta 41, 10020 Zagreb – Odra, Croatia
T: +385 1 6011 700
E: altpro@altpro.hr
W: altpro.com

Altran UK Ltd
2nd Floor Offices, 22 St Lawrence St, Southgate, Bath, BA1 1AN
T: 01225 466991
F: 01225 496006
E: info-uk@altran.com
W: www.altran.co.uk

Altro Ltd
Works Road, Letchworth Garden City, Hertfordshire, SG6 1NW
T: 01462 480480
F: 01462 480010
E: enquiries@altro.com
W: www.altro.com

Alucast Ltd
Western Way, Wednesbury, W. Midlands, WS10 7BW
T: 0121 556 6111
F: 0121 505 1302
E: aes@alucast.co.uk
W: www.alucast.co.uk

Aluminium Lighting Company (ALC)
Croeserw Industrial Estate, Eastern Avenue,
Crymmer, Port Talbot, SA13 3PB
T: 01639852502
E: sales@alulight.co.uk
W: www.aluminium-lighting.com

Aluminium Special Projects Ltd (ASP Group)
Unit 39, Second Ave, The Pensnett Estate, Kingswinford, W.Midlands, DY6 7UW
T: 01384 291900
F: 01384 400344
E: david@aspgroup.co.uk
W: www.aspgroup.co.uk

Alun Griffiths Ltd
Waterways House, Merthyr Road, Llanfoist, Abergavenny, NP7 9PE
T: 01873 857211
F: 01873 857679
E: enquiries@alungriffiths.co.uk
W: www.alungriffiths.co.uk/

Alvey & Towers
Bythorn House, 8 Nether St, Harby, Leics, LE14 4BW
T: 01949 861894
E: office@alveyandtowers.com
W: www.alveyandtowers.com

AM1 Projects Ltd
8 Second Avenue, Chatham, Kent, ME4 5AU
T: 01634 400033
E: info@am1projects.co.uk
W: www.am1projects.co.uk/

Amaro Group Ltd
Unit J2, Knights Park Industrial Estate, Knights Road, Strood, Rochester, Kent, ME2 2LS
T: 0845 207 1190
E: info@amarogroup.co.uk
W: amarogroup.co.uk/

Ambersil (CRC UK)
Ambersil House, Wylds Road, Bridgewater, TA6 4DD
T: 01278727272
E: marketing.uk@ambersil.com
W: www.ambersil.com

Ambirad Ltd
Fens Pool Avenue, Brierley Hill, West Midlands, DY5 1QA
T: 01384 489700
F: 01384 489707
E: ambiradsales@nordyne.com
W: www.ambirad.co.uk

AMCL Systems Engineering Ltd
221 St John St, Clerkenwell, London, EC1V 4LY
T: 020 7688 2828
F: 020 7688 2829
E: enquiries@amcl.com
W: www.amcl.com

AMCO Giffen
Whaley Road, Barugh, Barnsley, South Yorkshire, S75 1HT
T: 01226 243413
F: 01226 320202
E: info@amco.co.uk
W: www.amcogiffen.co.uk/

AMEC Environment & Infrastructure UK
Atlantic House, Imperial Way, Reading, RG2 0TP
T: 0800 371733
E: info.ukenvironment@amec.com
W: www.amec-ukenvironment.com/

Amery Construction Ltd
Flannery House, Third Way, Wembley, Middlesex, HA9 0RZ
T: 020 8903 1020
F: 020 8903 1560
E: reception@ameryconstruction.co.uk
W: www.ameryconstruction.co.uk

Ametek Airtechnology Group Ltd
111 Windmill Road, Sunbury-on-Thames, Middlesex, TW16 7EF
T: 01932 765822
E: paul.hammond@ametek.co.uk
W: www.airscrew.co.uk/

Amey
The Sherard Building, Edmund Halley Rd, Oxford, OX4 4DQ
T: 01865 713100
F: 01865 713357
E: ais@amey.co.uk
W: www.amey.co.uk

Amicus
See Unite - The Union

AMOT
Western Way, Bury St Edmunds, Suffolk, IP33 3SZ
T: 01284 762222
F: 01284 760256
E: info@amot.com
W: www.amot.com

Amphenol Ltd
Thanet Way, Whitstable, Kent, CT5 3JF
T: 01227 773200
F: 01227 276571
E: info@amphenol.co.uk
W: www.industrial-amphenol.com

AMPL Ltd
See Carillion Rail

Amplicon Liveline Ltd
Centenary Industrial Estate, Hollingdean Rd, Brighton, BN2 4AW
T: 01273 570220
F: 01273 570215
E: sales@amplicon.com
W: www.amplicon.com

AMT Sybex Ltd
The Spirella Building, Bridge Rd, Letchworth Garden City, Herts, SG6 4ET
T: 01462 476400
F: 01462 476401
E: info@amt-sybex.com
W: www.amt-sybex.com

Amtrain Midlands Ltd
A38 Southbound, Fradley, Lichfield, Staffs, WS13 8RD
T: 01283 792633
F: 01283 792622
E: info@amtrain.co.uk
W: www.amtrain.co.uk

Anchor Systems (Europe) Ltd
Unit 45, Rowfant Business Centre, Wallage Lane, Rowfant, West Sussex, RH10 4NQ
T: 01342 719362
F: 01342 719436
E: info@anchorsystems.co.uk
W: www.anchorsystems.co.uk

AndersElite Ltd
Adamson House, 2 Centenary Way, Salford, M50 1RD
T: 0161 832 7577
F: 020 7256 9898
E: contactus@anderselite.com
W: www.anderselite.com

Anderton Concrete Products Ltd
Units 1 & 2, Cosgrove Business Park, Soot Hill, Anderton, Northwich, Cheshire, CW9 6AA
T: 01606 79436
F: 01606 871590
E: sales@andertonconcrete.co.uk
W: www.andertonconcrete.co.uk

Andrew Muirhead & Son Ltd
273-289 Dunn St, Glasgow, G40 3EA
T: 0141 554 3724
F: 0141 554 3724
E: sales@muirhead.co.uk
W: www.muirhead.co.uk

Andrews Signs and Engravers
Units 5 & 6, Rawcliffe Industrial Estate, Manor Lane, York, YO30 5XY
T: 01904 658322
E: sales@andrewssigns.co.uk
W: www.railsigns.com

Andromeda Engineering Ltd
14 Hurricane Court, Estuary Boulevard, Liverpool, L24 8RL
T: 0151 427 3802
E: info@andromedauk.com
W: www.andromedauk.com

Andy Waters Rail Safety
Cwm Elan, Cherry Tree Lane, Botesdale, Diss, Norfolk, IP22 1DL
T: 01379 898918
M: 07713656355
E: andy@watersrailsafety.co.uk
W: www.watersrailsafety.co.uk/

Angel Trains Limited
123 Victoria St, London, SW1E 6DE
T: 020 7592 0500
F: 020 7592 0520
E: communications@angeltrains.co.uk
W: www.angeltrains.co.uk

Anixter
See Anixter (UK) Ltd

Anixter (UK) Ltd
Unit A, The Beacons, Birchwood Park, Birchwood, Warrington, Cheshire, WA3 6GP
T: 0870 242 2822
F: 01925 850292
E: 021team@anixter.com
W: www.anixter.com

Ansaldo STS
2.04 The Euston Office, One Euston Square, 40 Melton Street, London, NW1 2FD
T: 020 3574 4980
E: info@ansaldo-sts.com
W: www.ansaldo-sts.com/

Anstee & Ware Ltd - Midlands
Unit 15, Willow Rd, Trent Lane Industrial Est, Castle Donington, Derbys, DE74 2NP
T: 01332 850346
M: 01332 850686
E: john.alden@ansteeware.co.uk
W: www.ansteeware.co.uk

Antagrade Electrical Ltd
6 Verity Court, Middlewich, Cheshire, CW10 0GW
T: 01606 833299
F: 01606 836959
E: enquiries@antagrade.co.uk
W: www.antagrade.co.uk

Antal International Network
170 Lanark Rd West, Currie, Edinburgh, EH14 5NY
T: 0870 428 1745
F: 0870 428 1745
E: edinburgh@antal.com
W: www.antal.com

Antislip Antiwear Treads Int.
See AATI Rail Ltd

Anturas Consulting
83 Princes Street, Edinburgh, EH2 2ER
T: 0131 247 6771
E: info@anturasconsulting.com
W: www.anturasconsulting.com

AP Diesels Ltd
25a Victoria Street, Englefield Green, Egham, Surrey, TW20 0QY
T: 01784437228
E: office@apdiesels.com
W: www.apdiesels.com

AP Webb Plant Hire Ltd
Common Rd, Stafford, ST16 3DQ
T: 01785 241335
F: 01785 255178
W: www.apwebbplanthire.co.uk

APB Group Ltd
Ryandra House, Ryandra Business Park, Brookhouse Way, Cheadle, Stoke-on-Trent, Staffordshire, ST10 1SR
T: 01538 755377
F: 01538 755010
E: apbgroup@aol.com
W: www.apbgroup.co.uk

APC Technology Group
6 Stirling Park, Laker Road, Rochester Airport Estate, Rochester, Kent, ME1 3QR
T: 0330 313 3220
E: info@apcplc.com
W: apcplc.com

APCOA
Wellington House, 4-10 Cowley Road, Uxbridge, Middlesex, UB8 2XW
T: 01895 272500
W: www.apcoa.co.uk/

APD Communications Ltd
Minster Corner, South Church Side, Hull, HU1 1RR
T: 01482 808300
F: 01482 803901
E: marketing@apdcomms.com
W: www.apdcomms.com

Aperio Ltd
See Fugro

Apex Cables Ltd
St Johns Rd, Meadowfield Ind Est, Durham, DH7 8RJ
T: 0191 378 7908
F: 0191 378 7809
E: apex@apexcables.co.uk
W: www.apexcables.co.uk

API Capacitors Ltd
Leyden Works, Station Road, Great Yarmouth, NR31 0HB
T: 01493 652752
F: 01493 655433
E: info@api-capacitors.com
W: www.api-capacitors.com

Application Solutions (Safety & Security) Ltd
Unit 17, Cliffe Ind. Est, Lewes, E Sussex, BN8 6JL
T: 01273 405411
F: 01273 405415
E: contactus@asl-control.co.uk
W: www.asl-control.co.uk

Applied Card Technologies Ltd
Langley Gate, Kington Langley, Chippenham, Wilts, SN15 5SE
T: 01249 751200
F: 01249 751201
E: info@weareact.com
W: www.weareact.com

Applied Inspection Ltd
Mosley Business Park, Mosley Street, Burton upon Trent, DE14 1DW
T: 01283 515163
F: 01283 539729
E: mark@appliedinspection.co.uk
W: www.appliedinspection.co.uk

APT Skidata Ltd
The Power House, Chantry Place, Headstone Lane, Harrow, Middlesex, HA3 6NY
T: 020 8421 2211
F: 020 8421 3951
E: d.murphy@aptskidata.co.uk
W: www.aptcontrols-group.co.uk

Aqua Fabrications Ltd
Belmont House, Garnett Place, Skelmersdale, Lancs, WN8 9UB
T: 01695 51933
F: 01695 51891
E: sales@aquafab.co.uk
W: www.aquafab.co.uk

Aquaforce Jetting Ltd
Innovation House, Euston Way, Telford, TF3 4LT
T: 01952 201790
W: www.aquaforcejetting.co.uk/

Aquarius Railroad Technologies Ltd
Old Slenningford Farm, Mickley, Ripon, N Yorks, HG4 3JB
T: 01765 635021
F: 01765 635022
E: enquiries@railrover.com
W: www.railrover.com

Arbil Lifting Gear
Providence St, Lye, Stourbridge, West Midlands, DY9 8HS
T: 01384 424006
F: 01384 898814
E: info@arbil.co.uk
W: www.arbil.co.uk

Arcadia Alive Ltd
8 The Quadrant, 99 Parkway Avenue, Sheffield, S9 4WG
T: 0845 260 0126
E: talk@arcadiaalive.com
W: www.arcadiaalive.com

Arcadis LLP
Arcadis House, 34 York Way, London, N1 9AB
T: 020 7812 2000
W: www.arcadis.com

Archer Safety Signs
Unit 6 Daniels Way, Hucknall, Nottingham, NG15 7LL
T: 0115 968 1152
F: 0115 976 1110
E: sales@archersigns.co.uk
W: www.archersafetysigns.co.uk

Archerdale Ltd
Hirstwood Works, Hirstwood Road, Shipley, West Yorkshire, BD18 4BU
T: 01274595783
E: sales@archerdale.com
W: www.archerdale.com

Arco Ltd
Head Office, PO Box 21, Waverley St, Hull, HU1 2SJ
T: 01482 222522
F: 01482 218536
E: sales@arco.co.uk
W: www.arco.co.uk

Arcola Energy
24 Ashwin Street, Dalston, London, E8 3DL
T: 020 7503 1386
E: sales@arcolaenergy.com
W: www.arcolaenergy.com

Arentis Limited
2 Wortley Road, Deepcar, Sheffield, S36 2UZ
T: 0114 218 0470
E: sales@arentis.co.uk
W: www.arentis.co.uk

Areva Risk Management Consulting Ltd
Suite 7, Hitching Court, Abingdon Business
Park, Abingdon, Oxon, OX14 1RA
T: 01235 555755
F: 01235 525143
E: abingdon@arevarmc.com
W: www.arevarmc.com

Ark Signalling Consultancy
Lower Granary, Cornwells Farm, Marden, Kent, TN12 9NS
T: 01622 902880
M: 07917 697185
E: enquiries@arksignalling.co.uk
W: www.arksignalling.co.uk

Arlington Fleet Services Ltd
Railway Works, Campbell Rd, Eastleigh, Hants, SO50 5AD
T: 02380 696789
F: 02380 629118
E: info@arlington-fleet.co.uk
W: www.arlington-fleet.co.uk

ARM Engineering
Langstone Technology Park, Langstone Rd, Havant, Hants, PO9 1SA
T: 02392 228283
F: 02036 978 434
E: ibe@arm.co.uk
W: www.arm.co.uk

Arriva CrossCountry
See CrossCountry

Arriva plc
1 Admiral Way, Doxford International Business Park, Sunderland, SR3 3XP
T: 0191 520 4000
F: 0191 520 4001
E: enquiries@arriva.co.uk
W: www.arriva.co.uk

Arriva Rail London (London Overground)
Customer Services Centre, Overground House, 125 Finchley Rd, London, NW3 6HY
T: 0203 031 9315
E: overgroundinfo@tfl.gov.uk
W: www.arrivaraillondon.co.uk/

Arriva TrainCare
Crewe Carriage Shed, Off Weston Road, Crewe, Cheshire, CW1 6NE
T: 01270 508000
E: info@arrivatc.com
W: www.arrivatc.com

Arrow Cleaning & Hygeine Solutions
Rawdon Rd, Moira, Swadlincote, Derbys, DE12 6DA
T: 01283 221044
F: 01283 225731
E: sales@arrowchem.com
W: www.arrowchem.com

Artel Rubber Company
Unit 11, Waterloo Park, Wellington Rd, Bidford on Avon, Warks, B50 4JH
T: 01789 774099
F: 01789 774599
W: www.artelrubber.com

Artelia International
26-28 Hammersmith Grove, Hammersmith, London, W6 7HA
T: +44 20 8237 1800
F: +44 20 8237 1810
W: www.uk.arteliagroup.com

Artemis Intelligent Power
Unit 3, Edgefield Industrial Estate, Loanhead, Midlothian, EH20 9TB
T: 0131 440 6260
E: enquiries@artemisip.com

Arthur D Little Ltd
Unit 18, Science Park, Milton Rd, Cambridge, CB4 0FH
T: 01223 427100
F: 01223 427101
E: info.adl@adlittle.com
W: www.adl.com

Arthur Flury (UK) Ltd
Unit 218, Milton Keynes Business Centre, Foxhunter Drive, Linford Wood, Milton Keynes, MK14 6GD, Switzerland
T: 01908 686766
E: info@aflury.co.uk
W: www.aflury.co.uk

Arthur J Gallagher
International Division, The Walbrook Building, 25 Walbrook, London, EC4N 8AW
T: +44 (0)20 7204 6000
E: ukenquiries@ajg.com
W: www.ajginternational.com

Arup
The Arup Campus, Blythe Gate, Blythe Valley Park, Solihull, West Midlands, B90 8AE
T: 0121 213 3412
F: 0121 213 3001
E: rail@arup.com
W: www.arup.com/rail

ASCO Numatics
Pit Hey Place, West Pimbo, Skelmersdale, Lancs, WN8 9PG
T: 01695 713600
F: 01695 713633
E: enquiries.asconumatics.uk@emerson.com
W: www.asconumatics.eu

Ashley Group
8 Kimpton Link, 40 Kimpton Road, Sutton, Surrey, SM3 9QP
T: 020 8644 4416
F: 020 8644 4417
E: info@ashleygroup.co.uk
W: www.ashleygroup.co.uk

Ashurst
Broadwalk House, 5 Appold St, London, EC2A 2HA
T: 020 7859 1897
F: 020 7638 1112
E: email@ashurst.com
W: www.ashurst.com

ASL Contracts
See Pitchmastic PmB Ltd

ASL Control
Unit 17, Cliffe Industrial Estate, Lewes, East Sussex, BN8 6JL
T: 01273 405411
F: 01273 405415
E: sales@asl-control.co.uk
W: www.asl-control.co.uk/

ASLEF
75-77 St Johns St, Clerkenwell, London, EC1M 4NN
T: 020 7324 2400
F: 020 7490 8697
E: info@aslef.org.uk
W: www.aslef.org.uk

Aspire Rail Consultants
See Keltbray Aspire Rail Ltd

Assenta Rail
Suite 30 Bonnington Bond, 2 Anderson Place, Edinburgh, EH6 5NP
T: 0131 516 7110
E: contact@assenta.co.uk
W: www.assentarail.co.uk/

Assertis
150 Minories, London, EC3N 1LS
T: 0207 347 5280
E: info@assertis.co.uk
W: www.assertis.co.uk

Asset International Structured Solutions
Suite 5, Brecon House, William Brown Close, Llantarnam Ind Park, Llantarnam, Cwmbran, Torfaen, NP44 3AB
T: 01633 499830
E: david.mason@assetint.co.uk
W: www.assetint.co.uk

Asset VRS
Springvale Business & Ind. Park, Bilston, Wolverhampton, West Midlands, WV14 0QL
T: 01902 499400
F: 01902 402104
E: assetvrs@hill-smith.co.uk
W: www.asset-vrs.co.uk/

Asset-Pro Ltd
Concorde House, 24 Cecil Pashley Way, Shoreham Airport, W.Sussex, BN43 5FF
T: 0845 120 2046
F: 01444 448071
E: info@asset-pro.com
W: www.asset-pro.com

Associated British Ports
Aldwych House, 71-91 Aldwych, London, WC2B 4HN
T: 020 7406 7853
F: 020 7430 1384
E: pr@abports.co.uk
W: www.abports.co.uk

Associated Rewinds (Ireland) Ltd
Tallaght Business Park, Whitestown, Dublin 24, Republic of Ireland
T: 00353 1 452 0033
F: 00353 1 452 0476
E: sales@associatedrewinds.com
W: www.associatedrewinds.com

Associated Train Crew Union
DBH Serviced Business Centres Ltd, Longfields Court, Middlewoods Way, Carlton, Barnsley, S71 3GN
T: 01226 630166
E: headoffice@atcu.org.uk
W: www.atcu.org.uk

Associated Utility Supplies Ltd
1 Dearne Park Ind Est, Park Mill Way, Clayton West, Huddersfield, HD8 9XJ
T: 01484 860575
F: 01484 860576
E: sales@aus.co.uk
W: www.aus.co.uk

Association for Project Management
150 West Wycombe Rd, High Wycombe, Bucks, HP12 3AE
T: 01494 460246
F: 01494 528937
E: info@apm.org.uk
W: www.apm.org.uk

Association of Railway Training Providers (ARTP)
Kelvin House, RTC Business Park, London Rd, Derby, DE24 8UP
T: 01332 360033
F: 01332 366367
E: info@artp.co.uk
W: www.artp.co.uk

Association of Train Operating Companies (ATOC)
See Rail Delivery Group

AST Language Services Ltd
Unit 8, Ayr st, Nottingham, NG7 4FX
T: 0115 970 5633
F: 0845 051 8780
E: office@astls.co.uk
W: www.astlanguage.com

AST Recruitment Ltd
First Floor, Chase House, Park Plaza, Heath Hayes, Cannock, Staffs, WS12 2DD
T: 01543 331331
E: iperry@ast-recruit.com
W: www.astrecruitment.co.uk

Ast Signs
The Box, Eden Business Park, Penrith, Cumbria, CA11 9FB
T: 01768 892292
M: 07725 888029
E: gareth.livingstone@astsigns.com
W: https://www.astsigns.com

Astutis
6 Charnwood Court, Parc Nantgarw, Cardiff, CF15 7QZ
T: 0345 241 3685
E: enquiries@astutis.com
W: www.astutis.com

At Source QX Ltd
18 Eve St, Louth, Lincs, LN11 0JJ
T: 01507 604322
F: 01507 608513
E: mick@sourceqx.com
W: www.protecthear.co.uk

ATA Rail
See TQ Training

ATEIS UK Ltd
10 Hacche Lane Business Park, Pathfields, South Molton, Devon, EX36 3LH
T: 0845 652 1511
F: 0845 652 2527
E: neil.voce@ateis.co.uk
W: www.ateis.co.uk

Atkins
Euston Tower, 286 Euston Road, London, NW1 3AT
T: 020 7121 2000
F: 020 7121 2111
E: rail@atkinsglobal.com
W: www.atkinsglobal.com

ATL Transformers Ltd
Hanson Close, Middleton, Manchester, M24 2HD
T: 0161 653 0902
F: 0161 653 4744
E: sales@atltransformers.co.uk
W: www.atltransformers.co.uk

Atlantic Design Projects Limited
Branch Hill Mews, Branch Hill, London, NW3 7LT
T: 020 7435 1777
E: cg@atlanticdesign.uk.com
W: www.atlanticdesign.uk.com

Atlantis International Ltd
See Karcher Vehicle Wash

Atlas Copco Compressors Ltd
Swallowdale Lane, Hemel Hempstead, Herts, HP2 7HA
T: 01442 261201
F: 01442 234791
E: general.enquiries@uk.atlascopco.com
W: www.atlascopco.co.uk

Atlas Rail Components Ltd
See Associated Utility Supplies Ltd

ATOS Origin
4 Triton Square, Regents Place, London, NW1 3HG
T: 020 7830 4447
E: ukwebenquiries@atos.net
W: www.atos.net/transport

Auctus Management Group
Tech Block, Gee Business Park, Holborn Hill, Aston, Birmingham, B7 5JR
T: 0121 366 8800
E: info@auctusmg.co.uk
W: www.auctusmg.co.uk/

Aura Brand Solutions
Freemantle Road, Lowestoft, Suffolk, NR33 0EA
T: 0845 052 5241
E: info@aurabrands.com
W: www.aurabrands.com

Austin Reynolds Signs
Augustine House, Gogmore Lane, Chertsey, Surrey, KT16 9AP
T: 01932 568888
F: 01932 566600
M: 07831 465491
E: austin.reynolds@austinreynolds.co.uk
W: www.austinreynolds.com

Autobuild Ltd
See Pelma Services and Autobuild Ltd

Autoclenz Holdings Plc
See REACT Specialist Cleaning

Autodrain
Wakefield Rd, Rothwell Haigh, Leeds, LS26 0SB
T: 0113 205 9332
F: 0113 288 0999
E: mark@autodrain.net
W: www.autodrain.net

Autoglass
1 Priory Business Park, Cardington, Bedford, MK44 3US
T: 01234 273636
E: debbie.barnes@autoglass.co.uk
W: www.autoglass.co.uk

Autoglym PSV
Works Road, Letchworth Garden City, Herts, SG6 1LU
T: 01462 677766
F: 01462 686565
E: npro@autoglym.com
W: www.autoglymprofessional.com/psv/trains.asp

Autolift GmbH
Mayrwiesstasse 16, 5300 Hallwang, Salzburg, Austria
T: 0043 662 450588 11
F: 0043 662 450588 18
E: office@autolift.info
W: www.autolift.info

Automotive Trim Developments (ATD)
Priory Mill, Charter Avenue, Coventry, West Midlands, CV4 8AF
T: 02476 695150
F: 02476 695156
E: info@autotrimdev.com
W: www.autotrimdev.com/

AV Dawson
Riverside Park Road, Middlesbrough, TS2 1UT
T: 01642 219271
F: 01642 222636
W: www.av-dawson.com

Avanti West Coast
North Wing Offices, Euston Station, London, NW1 2HS
T: 03331 031 031
W: https://www.avantiwestcoast.co.uk/

Avery Weigh-Tronix
Foundry Lane, Smethwick, West Midlands, B66 2LP
T: 0845 3070314
F: 0870 9050085
E: info@awtxglobal.com
W: www.awtxglobal.com

Avondale Environmental Services Ltd
Fort Horsted, Primrose Close, Chatham, Kent, ME4 6HZ
T: 01634 823200
F: 01634 844485
E: info@avondaleuk.com
W: www.avondaleuk.com

AWW Architects
Rivergate House, 70 Redcliff Street, Bristol, BS1 6LS
T: 0117 923 2535
E: info@aww-uk.com
W: aww-uk.com/

Axiom Rail
Whieldon Road, Stoke on Trent, ST4 4HP
T: 07801 905 799
E: sales@axiomrail.com
W: www.wabteccorp.com

Axis Communications (UK) Ltd
Ground Floor, Gleneagles, Belfry Business Park, Colonial Way, Watford, WD24 4WH
T: 01923 211417
F: 01923 205589
E: pressoffice@axis.com
W: www.axis.com/trains

Axminster Carpets Ltd
Woodmead Rd, Axminster, Devon, EX13 5PQ
T: 01297 630686
F: 01297 35241
E: sales@axminster-carpets.co.uk
W: www.axminster-carpets.co.uk

Axon Bywater
See Bywater Training Ltd

AZPML
55 Curtain Road, London, EC2A 3PT
T: 020 7033 6480
F: 020 7033 6481
E: lon@azpml.com
W: www.azpml.com

Aztec Chemicals
Gateway, Crewe, CW1 6YY
T: 01270 655500
F: 01270 655501
E: info@aztecchemicals.com
W: www.aztecchemicals.com

BA Events
156 Great Charles Street, Queensway, Birmingham, B3 3HN
T: 0121 728 2193
E: info@baevents.co.uk
W: www.baevents.co.uk/

Babcock Rail
Kintail House, 3 Lister Way, Hamilton International Park, Blantyre, G72 0FT
T: 01698 203005
F: 01698 203006
E: shona.jamieson@babcock.co.uk
W: www.babcock.co.uk/rail

Bache Pallets Ltd
Bromley St, Lye, Stourbridge, West Midlands, DY9 8HU
T: 01384 897799
F: 01384 891351
E: sales@bache-pallets.co.uk
W: www.bache-pallets.co.uk

Bachy Soletanche
Henderson House, Langley Place, Higgins Lane, Burscough, Lancashire, L40 8JS
T: 01704 895686
W: www.bacsol.co.uk/

Baker Bellfield Ltd
Display House, Hortonwood 7, Telford, Shropshire, TF1 7GP
T: 01952 677411
F: 01952 670188
E: sales@bakerbellfield.co.uk
W: www.bakerbellfield.co.uk

BakerHicks
20 Timothy's Bridge Road, Stratford-upon-Avon, Warks, CV37 9NJ
T: 01789 204288
E: contact@baker-hicks.com
W: baker hicks.com/

Baldwin & Francis Ltd
President Park, President Way, Sheffield, S4 7UR
T: 0114 286 6000
F: 0114 286 6059
E: sales@baldwinandfrancis.com
W: www.baldwinandfrancis.com

Balfour Beatty Ground Engineering
2430 The Quadrant, Aztec West, Almondsbury, Bristol, BS32 4aq
T: 01454 877 555
E: enquiries-bristol@bbge.com
W: www.balfourbeatty.com

Balfour Beatty Rail
Kingsgate, 62 High Street, Redhill, Surrey, RH1 1SH
T: 01737 854400
E: info@bbrail.com
W: balfourbeatty.com

Balfour Kilpatrick Ltd
See Balfour Beatty Rail

Ballard Power
Majsmarken 1, DK-9500 Hobro, Denmark
E: marketing@ballard.com
W: www.ballard.com

Ballast Tools (UK) Ltd
7 Pure Offices, Kembrey Park, Swindon, SN2 8BW
T: 01793 697800
M: 07703 608551
E: sales@btukltd.com
W: www.btukltd.com

Ballyclare Ltd
The Forum, Hercules Business Park, Bird Hall Lane, Cheadle Heath, Stockport, Cheshire, SK3 0UX
T: 0844 493 2808
F: 0844 493 2801
E: info@ballyclarelimited.com
W: www.ballyclarelimited.com

BAM Nuttall Ltd
St James House, Knoll Rd, Camberley, Surrey, GU15 3XW
T: 01276 63484
F: 01276 66060
E: headoffice@bamnuttall.co.uk
W: www.bamnuttall.co.uk

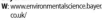

Bam Ritchies
Glasgow Rd, Kilsyth, Glasgow, G65 9BL
T: 01236 467000
F: 01236 467030
E: ritchies@bamritchies.co.uk
W: www.bamritchies.co.uk

R Bance & Co
Cockrow Hill House, St Mary's Rd, Surbiton, Surrey, KT6 5HE
T: 020 8398 7141
F: 020 8398 4765
E: admin@bance.com
W: www.bance.com

Bank of Scotland Corporate
155 Bishopsgate, London, EC2M 3YB
T: 020 7012 8001
F: 020 7012 9455
W: www.bankofscotland.co.uk/corporate

Baqus Group Plc
2/3 North Mews, London, WC1N 2JP
T: 020 7831 1283
F: 020 7242 9512
E: enquiries@baqus.co.uk
W: www.baqus.co.uk

Barat Group
France
W: www.barat.com/en

Barcodes For Business Ltd
Buckland House, 56 Packhorse Rd, Gerrards Cross, SL9 8EF
T: 01753 888833
F: 01753 888834
E: info@barcodesforbusiness.co.uk
W: www.barcodesforbusiness.co.uk

Bardon Aggregates
See Aggregate Industries UK Ltd

Barhale Construction Plc
Unit 3, The Orient Centre, Greycaine Rd, Watford, Herts, WD24 7GP
T: 01923 474500
F: 01923 474501
E: samantha.davis@barhale.co.uk
W: www.barhale.co.uk

Barker Ross Recruitment
24 De Montford St, Leicester, LE1 7GB
T: 0800 0288 693
F: 0116 2550 811
E: people@barkerross.co.uk
W: www.barkerross.co.uk

Barnbrook Systems Ltd
25 Fareham Park Rd, Fareham, Hants, PO15 6LD
T: 01329 847722
F: 01329 844132
E: sales@barnbrook.co.uk
W: www.barnbrook.co.uk

Barnshaw Section Bending Ltd
Tipton Rd, Tividale, Oldbury, West Midlands, B69 3HY
T: 0121 557 8261
F: 0121 557 5323
E: info@barnshaws.com
W: www.barnshaws.com

Barrier Electrical Engineering
Pearl Buildings, Stephenson Street, Willington Quay, Wallsend, Tyne and Wear, NE28 6UE
T: 0191 262 0510
E: recruitment@barrierltd.co.uk
W: www.barriergroup.com/

Basic Solutions Ltd
See LNT Solutions Ltd

H S Bassett
Coronet Way, Enterprise Park, Morriston, Swansea, SA6 8RH
T: 01792 790022
F: 01792 790033
E: info@hsbassett.co.uk
W: www.hsbassett.co.uk

BATT Cables
The Belfry, Fraser Rd, Erith, Kent, DA8 1QH
T: 01322 441165
F: 01322 443681
E: battindustrial.sales@batt.co.uk
W: www.batt.co.uk

Bauer Consumer Media
Media House, Peterborough Business Park, Lynch Wood, Peterborough, PE2 6EA
T: 01733 468000
E: rail@bauermedia.co.uk
W: www.bauermedia.co.uk

BaxterStorey
9th Floor, 140 London Wall, London, EC2Y 5DN
T: 020 7600 3838
F: 020 7600 3121
W: www.baxterstorey.co.uk/

Bayer Environmental Science
W: www.environmentalscience.bayer.co.uk/

BCM Construction
6 Blenheim Centre, Locks Lane, Mitcham, Surrey, CR4 2JX
T: 020 8640 7887
F: 020 8640 3437
W: www.bcmconstruction.co.uk/

BCM Glass Reinforced Concrete
Unit 22, Civic Industrial Unit, Whitchurch, Shropshire, SY13 1TT
T: 01948 665321
F: 01948 666381
E: info@bcmgrc.com
W: www.bcmgrc.com/railhome

BDP (Building Design Partnership)
16 Brewhouse Yard, Clerkenwell, London, EC1V 4LJ
T: 020 7812 8000
F: 020 7812 8399
E: london@bdp.com
W: www.bdp.com/en/

Beacon Rail Leasing Ltd
111 Buckingham Palace Road, Victoria, London, SW1W 0SR
T: 0207 340 8500
E: rail@beaconrail.com
W: www.beaconrail.com

Beakbane Bellows Ltd
Stourport Rd, Kidderminster, Worcs, DY11 7QT
T: 01562 820561
F: 01562 820560
E: info@beakbane.co.uk
W: www.beakbane.co.uk

Bearward Engineering Ltd
Main Road, Far Cotton, Northampton, Northamptonshire
T: 01604 762851
F: 01604 766168
E: sales@bearward.com
W: www.bearward.com

Beaver Sports (Yorkshire) Ltd
Flint Street, Fartown, Huddersfield, HD1 6LG
T: 01484 512354
E: sales@beaversports.co.uk
W: www.royalscotsgrey.com

Bechtel Ltd
11 Pilgrim Street, London, EC4V 6RN
T: 020 7651 7777
F: 020 7651 7972
E: jgreen2@bechtel.com
W: www.bechtel.com

Beck & Pollitzer
Burnham Rd, Dartford, Kent, DA1 5BD
T: 01322 223494
F: 01322 291859
E: info@beck-pollitzer.com
W: www.beck-pollitzer.com

Becorit GmbH
PO Box 189, Congleton, Cheshire, CW4 7FB
F: 01270 269000
E: becorit@btinternet.com
W: www.becorit.de

Beeswift
Delta House, Delta Point, Greets Green Road, West Bromwich, West Midlands, B70 9PL
T: 0121 524 2323
F: 0121 524 2325
E: marketing@beeswift.com
W: www.beeswift.com

Belden Solutions
Suite 13, Styal Rd, Manchester, M22 5WB
T: 0161 498 3724
F: 0161 498 3762
E: info@belden.com
W: www.belden.com

Bell & Pottinger
E: info@bell-pottinger.com

Bell & Webster Concrete Ltd
Alma Park Rd, Grantham, Lincs, NG31 9SE
T: 01476 562277
F: 01476 562944
E: bellandwebster@eleco.com
W: www.bellandwebster.co.uk/

Bellvedi
Suite 2, Berkhamsted House, 121 High St, Berkhamsted, Hertfordshire, HP4 2DJ
T: 01442 861041
E: info@bellvedi.com
W: bellvedi.com/

Belmond Luxury Trains
Shackleton House, 4 Battle Bridge Lane, London, SE1 2HP
T: 020 3117 1300
F: 020 7921 4708
E: help@belmond.com
W: www.belmond.com/luxury-trains

Belvoir Rail
Unit 13, High Hazles Road, Cotgrave, Nottingham, NG12 3GZ
T: 0115 989 2760
E: enquiries@belvoir-rail.com
W: www.belvoir-rail.com

Bemrose Booth Paragon
Stockholm Rd, Hull, HU7 0XY
T: 01482 826343
E: rfarmer@bemrosebooth.com
W: www.bemrosebooth.com/

Bender UK Ltd
Low Mill Business Park, Ulverston, Cumbria, LA12 9EE
T: 01229 480123
F: 01229 480345
E: info@bender-uk.com
W: www.bender-uk.com

Bentley Systems International Limited
2 Park Place, Upper Hatch Street, Dublin 2, Republic of Ireland
T: (+353) 1 436 4600
W: www.bentley.com

Bentley Systems UK Ltd
North Heath Lane, Horsham, W Sussex, RH12 5QE
T: 01403 259511
W: www.bentley.com

Bernstein Ltd
Unit One, Tintagel Way, Westgate, Aldridge, West Midlands, WS9 8ER
T: 01922 744999
F: 01922 457555
E: sales@bernstein-ltd.co.uk
W: www.bernstein-ltd.co.uk

Berry Systems
Springvale Business & Industrial Park, Bilston, Wolverhampton, WV14 0QL
T: 01902 491100
F: 01902 494080
E: sales@berrysystems.co.uk
W: www.berrysystems.co.uk

Best Impressions
15 Starfield Rd, London, W12 9SN
T: 020 8740 6443
F: 020 8740 9134
E: talk2us@best-impressions.co.uk
W: www.best-impressions.co.uk

Bestchart Ltd
6A Mays Yard, Down Rd, Horndean, Waterlooville, Hants, PO8 0YP
T: 023 9259 7707
F: 023 9259 1700
W: www.bestchart.co.uk

Beta Technology
Barclay Court, Heavens Walk, Doncaster Carr, Doncaster, South Yorkshire, DN4 5HZ
T: 01302 322633
E: info@betatechnology.co.uk
W: www.betatechnology.co.uk

BHSF Occupational Health Ltd
Banham Court, Hanbury Rd, Stoke Prior, Bromsgrove, Worcs, B60 4JZ
T: 01527 577242
F: 01527 832618
E: admin@bhsfoh.co.uk
W: www.bhsf.co.uk

Bijur Delimon International
Wenta Business Centre, 1 Electric Ave, Innova Science Park, Enfield, EN3 7XU
T: 01432 262107
F: 01432 365001
E: chris.riley@bijurdelimon.co.uk
W: www.bijurdelimon.co.uk

Bilfinger
Carl-Reiß-Platz 1-5, 68165 Mannheim, Germany
T: +49 621 459-0
F: +49 621 459-2366
W: www.bilfinger.com/en/

Bingham Rail
Barrow Rd, Wincobank, Sheffield, S9 1JZ
T: 0870 774 2341
F: 0870 774 5423
E: info@binghamrail.com
W: www.trainwash.co.uk

Bircham Dyson Bell LLP
50 Broadway, London, SW1H 0BL
T: 020 7227 7000
F: 020 7222 3480
E: enquirieslondon@bdb-law.co.uk
W: www.bdb-law.co.uk

Birchwood Price Tools
Birch Park, Park Lodge Rd, Giltbrook, Nottingham, NG16 2AR
T: 0115 938 9000
F: 0115 938 9010
W: www.birdwoodpricetools.com

Birley Manufacturing Ltd
Birley Vale Ave, Sheffield, S12 2AX
T: 0114 280 3200
F: 0114 280 3201
E: info@birleyml.com
W: www.birleyml.com

Birmingham Centre for Railway Research and Education (BCRRE)
University of Birmingham, Gisbert Kapp Building, Edgbaston, Birmingham, B15 2TT
T: 0121 414 2626
F: 0121 414 4291
E: j.grey@bham.ac.uk
W: www.birmingham.ac.uk/railway

Birse Rail Ltd
See Balfour Beatty Rail

Black Country Innovative Manufacturing Organisation (BCIMO)
c/o Clegg Construction Site Office, Zoological Way, off Tipton Road, Dudley, DY1 4SQ
M: 07769 586893
E: info@bcimo.co.uk
W: www.verylightrail.com/

Blackpool Transport Services
Rigby Rd, Blackpool, Lancs, FY1 5DD
T: 01253 473001
F: 01253 473101
E: enquiries@blackpooltransport.com
W: www.blackpooltransport.com

Blu Wireless
5th Floor, 1 Temple Way, Bristol, BS2 0BY
W: www.bluwireless.com

Blue I UK Ltd
See Peli Products (UK) Ltd

BMAC Ltd
Units 13-14, Shepley Ind. Est. South, Shepley Road, Audenshaw, Manchester, M34 5DW
T: 0161 304 5644
F: 0161 336 5691
E: enquiries@bmac.ltd.uk
W: www.bmac.ltd.uk

BMAC Ltd
Units 13 & 14 Shepley Industrial Estate South, Shepley Road, Audenshaw, M34 5DW
T: +44(0)161 337 3070
F: 01457 878887
E: enquiries@bmac.ltd.uk
W: www.bmac.ltd.uk

BMI UK & Ireland
2 Pitfield, Kiln Farm, Milton Keynes, MK11 3LW
E: sales.admin@bmigroup.com
W: www.bmigroup.com

BMT Group
Goodrich House, 1 Waldegrave Road, Teddington, Middlesex, TW11 8LZ
T: 020 8943 5544
F: 020 8943 5347
E: enquiries@bmtmail.com
W: www.bmt.org/

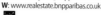

BNP Paribas Real Estate
One Redcliff St, Bristol, BS1 6NP
T: 0117 984 8480
F: 0117 984 8401
E: realestate.press@bnpparibas.com
W: www.realestate.bnpparibas.co.uk

BOC
Customer Service Centre, Priestley Rd, Worsley, Manchester, M28 2UT
T: 0800 111 333
F: 0800 111 555
E: custserv@boc.com
W: www.bocindustrial.co.uk

Boddingtons Electrical
Prospect House, Queenborough Lane, Great Notley, Essex, CM77 7AG
T: 01376 567490
F: 01376 567495
E: info@boddingtons-electrical.com
W: www.boddingtons-electrical.com/

Boden Rail Engineering
16 Taplin Close, Holmcroft, Stafford, ST16 1NW

Bodycote Materials Testing
See Exova (UK) Ltd

Bodyguard Workwear Ltd
Adams St, Birmingham, B7 4LS
T: 0121 380 1308
E: sales@bodyguardworkwear.co.uk
W: www.bodyguardworkwear.co.uk / www.railclothing.co.uk

Bonar Floors Ltd
See Forbo Flooring Ltd

Bonatrans AS
Revoluční 1234, 735 81 Bohumín, Czech Republic
T: +420 597 083 112
W: www.bonatrans.cz/

Bond Dickinson LLP
4 More London Riverside, London, SE1 2AU
T: 0345 415 0000
F: 0345 415 6200
W: www.bonddickinson.com/

Bond Insurance Services
Salisbury House, 81 High St, Potters Bar, Herts, EN6 5AS
T: 01707 291200
F: 01707 291202
E: info@bond-insurance.co.uk
W: www.bond-insurance.co.uk

C F Booth Ltd
Clarence Metal Works, Armer St, Rotherham, S. Yorks, S60 1AF
T: 01709 559198
F: 01709 561859
E: info@cfbooth.com
W: www.cfbooth.com

Bosch Rexroth Ltd
15 Cromwell Rd, St Neots, Cambs, PE19 2ES
T: 01480 223253
E: info@boschrexroth.co.uk
W: www.boschrexroth.co.uk

Bosch Security Systems
PO Box 750, Uxbridge, Middx, UB9 5ZJ
T: 01895 878094
F: 01895 878098
E: uk.securitysystems@bosch.com
W: www.boschsecurity.co.uk

Boss Cabins Limited
BCS House, Pinfold Road, Bourne, Lincolnshire, PE10 9HT
T: 0845 1801616
F: 01778 395265
M: 07854008955
E: rburchell@bosscabins.co.uk
W: www.bosscabins.co.uk

Botany Weaving Mill Ltd
Vauxhall Avenue, Cork Street, Dublin 8, Republic of Ireland
T: +353 1 453 2278
E: marek@botanyweaving.com
W: www.botanyweaving.com

Bott Ltd
Bude-Stratton Business Park, Bude, Cornwall, EX23 8LY
T: 01288 357788
F: 01288 352692
E: i-sales@bottltd.co.uk
W: www.bott-group.com

Bowden Bros Ltd
Brickworks House, Spook Hill, North Holmwood, Dorking, Surrey, RH5 4HR
T: 01306 743355
F: 01306 876768
E: ian.bowden@bowden-bros.com
W: www.bowden-bros.com

Bowen Projects Ltd
203 Torrington Ave, Coventry, CV4 9UT
T: 02476 695550
F: 02476 695040

Bowmer & Kirkland Ltd
High Edge Court, Heage, Belper, Derbys, DE56 2BW
T: 01773 853131
F: 01773 856710
E: general@bandk.co.uk
W: www.bandk.co.uk/

Bradgate Containers
Leicester Rd, Shepshed, Leics, LE12 9EG
T: 01509 508678
F: 01509 504350
E: sales@bradgate.co.uk
W: www.bradgate.co.uk

The Bradley Group
Junction 21 Business Park, Gorse Street, Chadderton, Oldham, Greater Manchester, OL9 9QH
T: 01706 621421
F: 01706 366154
E: web@bradleymanufacturing.com
W: www.bradleymanufacturing.com/

Brady UK
Wildmere Industrial Estate, Banbury, Oxon, OX16 3JU
T: 01295 228288
E: csuk@bradycorp.com
W: www.bradyeurope.com

Branch Line Society
10 Sandringham Rd, Stoke Gifford, South Gloucestershire, BS34 8NP
E: general.secretary@branchline.uk
W: www.branchline.uk

Brandauer
235 Bridge Street West, Birmingham, B19 2YU
T: 0121 359 2822
E: sales@brandauer.co.uk
W: https://brandauer.co.uk/

Bratts Ladders
Abbeyfield Rd, Lenton Industrial Estate, Nottingham, NG7 2SZ
T: 0115 986 6851
F: 0115 986 1991
E: stephen@brattsladders.com
W: www.brattsladders.com

Braybrook Ltd
Harvey Road, Burnt Mills Industrial Estate, Basildon, Essex, SS13 1DF
T: 01268 763399
E: admin@braybrookltd.co.uk
W: braybrookltd.co.uk/

Brecknell, Willis & Co Ltd
PO Box 10, Chard, Somerset, TA20 2DE
T: 01460 260700
F: 01460 66122
E: sales@brecknellwillis.com
W: www.brecknellwillis.com

Brentto Industry
See Onyxrail Ltd

Briben Products
Unit 29, Braintree Business Park, Blackwell Drive, Springwood Industrial Estate, Braintree, Essex, CM7 2PU
T: 01376 335119
E: sales@briben.com
W: https://www.briben.com

Bridgeway Consulting Ltd
Bridgeway House, 2 Riverside Way, Nottingham, NG2 1DP
T: 0115 919 1111
F: 0115 919 1112
E: enquiries@bridgeway-consulting.co.uk
W: www.bridgeway-consulting.co.uk

Briggs Equipment
Orbital Way, Cannock, Staffordshire, WS11 8XW
T: 0330 123 9814
W: www.briggsequipment.co.uk/

BriggsAmasco
Amasco House, 101 Powke Lane, Cradley Heath, B64 5PX
T: 0121 502 9600
F: 0121 502 9601
W: www.briggsamasco.co.uk/

Bright Bond (BAC Group)
Stafford Park 11, Telford, Shropshire, TF3 3AY
T: 01952 290321
F: 01952 290325
E: sales@bacgroup.com
W: www.bacgroup.com

Britannia Washing Systems
See Smith Bros & Webb Ltd

RMS Locotec Ltd
Stanhope Station, Stanhope, Bishop Auckland, Co Durham, DL13 2YS
T: 01388 526203
E: sales@rmslocotec.com
W: www.rmslocotec.com

British Geological Survey
Kingsley Dunham Centre, Keyworth, Nottingham, NG12 5GG
T: 0115 936 3100
F: 0115 936 3200
E: enquiries@bgs.ac.uk
W: www.bgs.ac.uk

British Springs
See GME Springs

British Steel
Rail Service Centre, PO Box 1, Brigg Road, Scunthorpe, North Lincolnshire, DN16 1BP
T: 01724 404040
E: rail@britishsteel.co.uk
W: britishsteel.co.uk/rail

British Transport Police (BTP)
25 Camden Rd, London, NW1 9LN
T: 020 7830 8800
F: 020 7023 6952
E: first_contact@btp.pnn.police.uk
W: www.btp.police.uk

Briton Fabricators Ltd
Fulwood Rd South, Huthwaite, Sutton-in-Ashfield, Notts, NG17 2JW
T: 0115 963 2901
F: 0115 968 0335
E: sales@britonsltd.co.uk
W: www.britonsltd.co.uk

Brixworth Engineering Co Ltd
Creaton Rd, Brixworth, Northampton, NN6 9BW
T: 01604 880338
F: 01604 880252
E: sales@benco.co.uk
W: www.benco.co.uk

Broadland Rail
7 York Rd, Woking, Surrey, GU22 7XH
T: 01483 725999
W: www.broadlandrail.com

Broadway Malyan
Holmes House, 4 Pear Place, London, SE1 8BT
T: 020 7261 4200
W: https://www.broadwaymalyan.com/

Brockhouse Forgings Ltd
Howard St, West Bromwich, West Midlands, B70 0SN
T: 0121 556 1241
F: 0121 502 3076
W: www.brockhouse.co.uk

Brodie Engineering Ltd
Bonnyton Rail Depot, Bonnyton Industrial Estate, Munro Place, Kilmarnock, Ayrshire, KA1 2NP
T: 01563 546280
F: 01563 546281
E: sales@brodie-engineering.co.uk
W: www.brodie-engineering.co.uk/

Brodie Leasing Ltd
C/O Mr Gerry Hilferty, Montgreenan House Offices, Montgreenan, Kilwinning, Ayrshire, KA13 7QZ

Brown & Mason Ltd
Anson House, Schooner Court, Crossways Business Park, Dartford, DA2 6QQ
T: 01322 277731
F: 01322 284152
E: b&m@brownandmason.ltd.uk
W: www.brownandmason.com

Browse Bion Architectural Signs
Unit 19/20, Lakeside Park, Medway City Est, Rochester, Kent, ME2 4LT
T: 01634 710063
F: 01634 290112
E: sales@browsebion.com
W: www.browsebion.com

BRP Ltd
See Keltbray

Brush Switchgear
Unit 3, Blackwood Ind. Estate, Newport Rd, Blackwood, S.Wales, NP12 2XH
T: 01495 223001
F: 01495 225674
W: https://www.brush.eu/switchgear

Brush Traction
PO Box 17, Falcon Works, Meadow Lane, Loughborough, Leics, LE11 1HS
T: 01302 340700
F: 01302 790058
E: sales@brushtraction.com
W: www.brushtraction.com

Brush Transformers Ltd
Falcon Works, Loughborough, LE11 1EX
T: 01509 611511
E: salesuk@brush.eu
W: www.brush.eu/en/38/home/products/transformers

Bruton Knowles
Greybrook House, 28 Brook St, London, W1K 5DH
T: 0845 200 6489
F: 020 7499 8435
E: patrick.downes@brutonknowles.co.uk
W: www.brutonknowles.co.uk

Bryn Thomas Cranes Ltd
421 Chester Rd, Flint, CH6 5SE
T: 01352 733984
F: 01352 733990
E: dylan.thomas@brynthomascranes.com
W: www.brynthomascranes.com

BSP Consulting
12 Oxford St, Nottingham, NG1 5BG
T: 0115 840 2227
F: 0115 840 2228
E: info@bsp-consulting.co.uk
W: www.bsp-consulting.co.uk

BT Fleet
Parkside Business Park, Mile Lane, Coventry, CV1 2TR
T: 0800 032 0012
W: www.btfleet.com/

BTMU Capital Corporation
See Beacon Rail Leasing Ltd

BTRoS Interiors & Cabling
Litchurch Lane, Derby, Derbyshire, DE24 8AD
T: 01332 257 500
E: jshelton@btros.co.uk
W: www.btros.co.uk

C Buchanan
See SKM Colin Buchanan

Buck and Hickman
Siskin Parkway East, Middlemarch Business Park, Coventry, CV3 4FJ
T: 02476 306444
F: 02476 514214
E: enquiries@buckandhickman.com
W: www.buckandhickman.com

Buckingham Group Contracting Ltd
Silverstone Rd, Stowe, Bucks, MK18 5LJ
T: 01280 823355
F: 01280 812830
E: bd@buckinghamgroup.co.uk
W: www.buckinghamgroup.co.uk

Buildbase
Gemini One, 5520 Oxford Business Park, Cowley, Oxford, OX4 2LL
F: 01865 871700
E: tony.newcombe@buildbase.co.uk

Bupa – Health Care Service Delivery
Battle Bridge House, 300 Grays Inn Rd, London, WC1X 8DU
T: 0808 271 4818
F: 0207 800 6461
W: www.bupa.co.uk/

Bureau Veritas Weeks
Tower Bridge Court, 224-226 Tower Bridge Rd, London, SE1 2TX
T: 020 7550 8900
F: 020 7403 1590
E: transport.logistics@bureauveritas.com
W: www.bureauveritas.com

Burges Salmon LLP
Narrow Quay House, Narrow Quay, Bristol, BS1 4AH
T: 0117 939 2000
F: 0117 902 4400
E: email@burges-salmon.com
W: www.burges-salmon.com

Burgess Rail Solutions Ltd
M: 07798 858494
E: robbie@burgessrailsolutions.co.uk
W: www.burgessrailsolutions.co.uk

Burns + Nice
70 Cowcross Street, London, EC1M 6EJ
T: 020 7253 0808
F: 020 7253 0909
E: info@burnsnice.com
W: www.burnsnice.com/

Business Moves Group
4 Acre Road, Reading, Berkshire, RG2 0SX
T: 0118 933 6600
F: 0118 975 1358
W: www.businessmoves.com/

Butler & Young (BYL) Ltd
Unit 3-4 Jansel House, Hitchin Road, Luton, LU2 7XH
T: 01582 404113
F: 01582 483420
E: debbie.clark@byl.co.uk
W: www.byl.co.uk

M Buttkereit Ltd
Unit 2, Britannia Rd Ind. Estate, Sale, Cheshire, M33 2AA
T: 0161 969 5418
F: 0161 969 5419
E: sales@buttkereit.co.uk
W: www.buttkereit.co.uk

Blending forward-thinking design with unrivalled manufacturing expertise, we create textiles which transform rail interiors and deliver an exceptional passenger experience.
Explore our collection at www.camirafabrics.com
camira

BWB Consulting
5th Floor, Waterfront House, Station Street, Nottingham, NG2 3DQ
T: 0115 924 1100
E: nottingham@bwbconsulting.com
W: www.bwbconsulting.com/

BWCS
6 Worcester Road, Ledbury, Herefordshire, HR8 1PL
T: 01531 634326
F: 01531 631443
E: ross.parsons@bwcs.com
W: www.bwcs.com/

Bywater Training Ltd
Couchmore House, Littleworth Road, Esher, Surrey, KT10 9TN
T: 0333 123 9001
E: contact@bywater.co.uk
W: www.bywater.co.uk

C & S Equipment Ltd
15 Wingbury Courtyard, Leighton Rd, Wingrave, Bucks, HP22 4LW
T: 0843 504 4011
E: info@candsequipment.co.uk
W: www.candsequipment.co.uk

C A P Productions Ltd
The Crescent, Hockley, Birmingham, B18 5NL
T: 0121 554 9811
F: 0121 554 3791
E: sales@capproductions.co.uk
W: www.capproductions.co.uk

C P Plus Ltd
10 Flask Walk, Camden, London, NW3 1HE
T: 020 7431 4001
F: 020 7435 3280
E: info@cp-plus.co.uk
W: www.cp-plus.co.uk

C2C Rail Ltd
2nd Floor, Cutlers Court, 115 Houndsditch, London, EC3A 7BR
T: 020 7444 1800
F: 020 7444 1803
W: www.c2c-online.co.uk

C2e Consulting
Ludlow House, The Avenue, Stratford upon Avon, Warks, CV37 0RH
E: ed.sharman@c2econsulting.co.uk
W: www.c2econsulting.co.uk

Cable & Wireless UK
Lakeside House, Cain Rd, Bracknell, Berks, RG12 1XL
T: 01908 845000
F: 01344 713961
E: companysecretary@cwc.com
W: www.cwc.com

Cable Detection Ltd
Unit 1, Blythe Park, Sandon Rd, Cresswell, Stoke on Trent, ST11 9RD
T: 01782 384630
F: 01782 388048
W: www.cabledetection.co.uk

Cable Dynamics Ltd
Unit 15, Binghams Park Business Centre, Potten End Hill, Water End, Hemel Hempstead, Hertfordshire, HP1 3BN
T: 01442 234808
W: www.cabledynamics.co.uk/

Cable Management Products Ltd - Thomas & Betts Ltd
See ABB Ltd

Cablecraft Ltd
Cablecraft House, Unit 3, Circle Business Centre, Blackburn Rd, Houghton Regis, Beds, LU5 5DD
T: 01582 606033
F: 01582 606063
E: claire@cablecraft.co.uk
W: www.cablecraft-rail.co.uk

Cabletec ICS Ltd
Sunnyside Rd, Weston Super Mare, BS23 3PZ
T: 01934 424900
F: 01934 636632
E: sales@cabletec.com
W: www.cabletec.com

Cadenza Transport Consulting Ltd
8-10 South Street, Epsom, KT18 7PF
M: 07786 430420
E: info@cadenza.co.uk
W: www.cadenza.co.uk

CADFEM
Suite 173-177, Airport House Business Centre, Purley Way, Croydon, Surrey, CR0 0XZ
T: 0844 212 5900
F: 0844 212 5910
E: info@cadfemuk.com
W: cadfemukandireland.com/

Cairn Cross Civil Engineering
1 Cadman Court, Morley, Leeds, LS27 0RX
T: 0113 284 2415
E: info@cairncross.uk.com
W: www.cairncross.uk.com

Calco Services Ltd
Melrose House, 42 Dingwall Rd, Croydon, CR0 2NE
T: 020 8655 1600
F: 020 8655 1588
E: careers@calco.co.uk
W: www.calco.co.uk

Caledonian Rail Leasing
99 Queen Victoria Street, London, EC4V 4EH

Caledonian Sleepers Rail Leasing Ltd

Calmet Laboratory Services
Hampton House, 1 Vicarage Rd, Hampton Wick, Kingston upon Thames, KT1 4EB
T: 0208 977 8455
F: 020 8614 8048
E: sales@calmet.co.uk
W: www.calmet.co.uk

Camira Fabrics Ltd
The Watermill, Wheatley Park, Mirfield, West Yorks, WF14 8HE
T: 01924 490591
F: 01924 495605
E: info@camirafabrics.com
W: www.camirafabrics.com/transport

Camlin Rail
31 Ferguson Drive, Knockmore Hill Ind. Park, Lisburn, County Antrim, BT28 2EX, Northern Ireland
T: 028 9262 6982
E: mail@camlinrail.com
W: www.camlingroup.com

Campaign for Better Transport
First Floor, 10 Queen Street Place, London, EC4R 1BE
E: communications@bettertransport.org.uk
W: www.bettertransport.org.uk

CAN Geotechnical
Smeckley Wood Close, Chesterfield Trading Est., Chesterfield, S40 3JW
T: 01246 261111
F: 01246 261626
E: info@can.ltd.uk
W: www.can.ltd.uk

Cannon Technologies Ltd
Head Office, Queensway, Stem Lane, New Milton, Hants, BH25 5NU
T: 01425 638148
F: 01425 619276
E: sales@cannontech.co.uk
W: www.cannontech.co.uk

Capel (CS) Ltd
638 Cranbrook Road, Ilford, Essex, IG6 1HJ
T: 020 8518 5354
F: 020 8518 6454
E: info@capelcsltd.com
W: www.capelcsltd.com

Capgemini UK
Forge End, Woking, Surrey, GU21 6DB
T: 01483 764764
F: 01483 786161
W: www.uk.capgemini.com

Capita Property and Infrastructure Ltd
Capita House, Wood St, East Grinstead, W. Sussex, RH19 1UU
T: 01342 327161
F: 01342 315927
E: john.mayne@capita.co.uk
W: www.capitasymonds.co.uk

Capita Architecture
90-98 Goswell Rd, London, EC1V 7DF
T: 020 7251 6004
F: 020 7253 3568
E: mervyn.franklin@capita.co.uk
W: www.capitaarchitecture.co.uk

Capital & Counties Properties plc (Capco)
15 Grosvenor Street, London, W1K 4QZ
T: 020 3214 9150
F: 020 3214 9151
E: feedback@capitalandcounties.com
W: www.capitalandcounties.com/

Capital Project Consultancy Ltd (CPC)
See CPC Project Services LLP

Capitol Industrial Batteries
22 Napier Court, Wardpark North Industrial Estate, Cumbernauld, Glasgow, G62 6HU
T: 01236 731982
W: www.capitolbatteries.co.uk/

Captec Ltd
11 Brunel Way, Segensworth, Fareham, Hants, PO15 5TX
T: 01489 866066
F: 01489 866088
E: sales@captec.co.uk
W: www.captec.co.uk

Cardev International
See Environmental Technologies Ltd.

Carlbro Group
See Sweco

Carlisle Support Services
800 The Boulevard, Capability Green, Luton, Beds, LU1 3BA
T: 01582 692692
E: info@carlislesupportservices.com
W: www.carlislesupportservices.com

Carlow Concrete Tanks
Regus Express, Ground Floor, The Comet Building, Birmingham Airport, Birmingham, B26 3QJ
T: 0121 661 4471
F: 07595 076617
E: sales@carlowtanks.com
W: carlowtanks.co.uk

Carlton Technologies Ltd
Unit 4, Church View Business Park, Coney Green Rd, Clay Cross, Chesterfield, Derbys, S45 9HA
T: 01246 861330
F: 01246 251466
E: sales@carltontech.co.uk
W: www.carltontech.co.uk

Carrickarory Consulting Ltd
1 Bell Meadow, Dulwich Wood Avenue, London, SE19 1HP

Carter Jonas
One Chapel Place, London, W1G 0BG
T: 020 3733 6767
F: 020 7408 9238
E: chapelplace@carterjonas.co.uk
W: www.carterjonas.co.uk/

Carver Engineering Services Ltd
11 Brunel Close, Brunel Ind. Est, Blyth Rd, Harworth, Doncaster, DN11 8QA
T: 01302 751900
F: 01302 757026
E: sales@carverengineering.com
W: www.carverengineering.com

Cass Hayward LLP
York House, Welsh St, Chepstow, Monmouthshire, NP16 5UW
T: 01291 626994
F: 01291 626306
E: office@casshayward.com
W: www.casshayward.com

Castle Precision Engineering
241 Drakemire Drive, Glasgow, G45 9SZ
T: 0141 634 1377
F: 0141 634 3678
E: sales@castleprecision.com
W: www.castleprecision.com

Catalis
See TQ Training

Cats Solutions Ltd
Two Rushy Platt, Caen View, Swindon, Wilts, SN5 8WQ
T: 01793 432913
F: 01793 490270
E: sales@cats-solutions.co.uk
W: www.cats-solutions.com

Caunton Engineering Ltd
Caunton House, 2 Coombe Road, Moorgreen Industrial Park, Moorgreen, Nottingham, NG16 3SU
T: 01773 531111
W: www.caunton.co.uk

CB Frost & Co Ltd
Green St, Digbeth, Birmingham, B12 0NE
T: 0121 773 8494
F: 0121 772 3584
E: info@cbfrost-rubber.com
W: www.cbfrost-rubber.com

CCD Design and Ergonomics
Northdown House, 11-21 Northdown St, London, N1 9BN
T: 0207 593 2900
E: info@ccd.org.uk
W: www.ccd.org.uk

CCL Rail Training
Scope House, Weston Rd, Crewe, CW1 6DD
T: 01270 252400
E: info@ccltraining.com
W: www.ccltraining.com

CDC Draincare Ltd
Unit 1, Chatsworth Ind. Est, Percy St, Leeds, LS12 1EL
T: 0845 644 6130
E: enquiries@cdc-draincare.co.uk
W: www.cdc-draincare.co.uk

CDL (Collinson Dutton Ltd)
See GHD Ltd (Gutteridge, Haskins & Davey Ltd)

CDM-UK
PO Box 7035, Melton Mowbray, Leics, LE13 1WG
T: 01664 482486
F: 01664 482487
E: info@cdm-uk.co.uk
W: www.cdm-uk.co.uk

CDS Rail Ltd
Unit 1, Fulcrum 4, Solent Way, Whiteley, Hants, PO15 7FT
T: 01489 571771
F: 01489 571985
E: sales@cdsrail.com
W: www.cdsrail.com

Cecence
Unit 6, Bunas Business Park, Hollom Down Road, Lopcombe Corner, Hampshire, SP5 1BP
T: 01264 781115
E: info@cecence.com
W: www.cecence.com

Cembre Ltd
Dunton Park, Kingsbury Rd, Curdworth, Sutton Coldfield, B76 9EB
T: 01675 470440
F: 01675 470220
E: sales@cembre.co.uk
W: www.cembre.co.uk

Cemex Rail Products
Aston Church Rd, Washwood Heath, Saltley, Birmingham, B8 1QF
T: 0121 327 0844
F: 0121 327 7545
W: www.cemex.co.uk

Censol Ltd
Forbes Close, Long Eaton, Nottingham, NG10 1PX
T: 0115 972 7070
F: 0115 973 6722
E: info@censol.co.uk

Centinal Group
The Brook Works, 174 Bromyard Rd, St Johns, Worcester, WR2 5EE
T: 01905 748569
F: 01905 420700
E: les@mfhhydraulics.co.uk
W: www.centinalgroup.co.uk/

Central Engineering & Hydraulic Services Ltd
See Centinal Group

Centre for Economics and Business Research (CEBR)
Unit 1, 4 Bath Street, London, EC1V 9DX
T: 020 7324 2850
E: enquiries@cebr.com
W: cebr.com

Centregreat Rail Ltd
Ynys Bridge, Heol yr Ynys, Tongwynlais, Cardiff, CF15 7NT
T: 02920 815662
F: 02920 813598
E: rail@centregreat.net
W: www.centregreatrail.co.uk

Centric Rail Limited
Oxford House, Robin Hood Airport, Sixth Ave, Doncaster, South Yorkshire, DN9 3GG
T: 01302 590624
M: +44 (0)7769 169 504
E: info@centricrail.com
W: www.centricrail.com

Centrus MDT
10 Queen Street Place, London, EC4R 1BE
T: 020 3846 5670
E: jacqui.nelson@centrusadvisors.com
W: www.centrusadvisors.com

CGI IT UK Ltd
Kings Place, 90 York Way, 7th Floor, London, N1 9AG
T: 0845 070 7765
W: www.cgi-group.co.uk/

CH2M
2nd Floor, Quarnmill House, Stores Rd, Derby, DE21 4XF
T: 01332 222620
F: 01332 222621
E: robert.kaul@ch2m.com
W: www.ch2m.com

Chapman Taylor
10 Eastbourne Terrace, London, W2 6LG
T: 020 7371 3000
E: london@chapmantaylor.com
W: www.chapmantaylor.com

Charcon
See Aggregate Industries UK Ltd

Charcroft Electronics Ltd
Dol-y-Coed, Llanwrtyd Wells, Powys, LD5 4TH
T: 01591 610408
F: 01591 562013
E: chris.leek@charcroft.com
W: www.charcroft.com

Charles Endirect Ltd
Wessex Way, Wincanton Business Park, Wincanton, Somerset, BA9 9RR
T: 01963 828400
F: 01963 828401
E: info@charlesendirect.com
W: www.charlesendirect.com

Charles Rayner Ltd
12 Drakes Mews, Crownhill, Milton Keynes, Buckinghamshire, MK8 0ER
T: 01908 565904
E: info@charlesraynerltd.co.uk
W: www.charlesraynerltd.co.uk

Charter Security Plc
Suite 6, Ensign House, Admirals Way, London, E14 9XQ
T: 020 7515 0771
E: info@charter-security.co.uk
W: www.charter-security.co.uk

Chartered Institute of Logistics and Transport (UK) (CILT)
Logistics and Transport Centre, Earlstrees Court, Earlstrees Rd, Corby, NN17 4AX
T: 01536 740100
F: 01536 740101
E: enquiry@ciltuk.org.uk
W: www.ciltuk.org.uk

Chartered Institution of Railway Operators (CIRO)
The Moat House, 133 Newport Rd, Stafford, ST16 2EZ
T: 03333 440523
E: info@railwayoperators.co.uk
W: https://www.ciro.org/

Chela Ltd
68 Bilton Way, Enfield, Middx, EN3 7NH
T: 020 8805 2150
F: 020 8443 1868
E: tony.philippou@chela.co.uk
W: www.chela.co.uk

Chester le Track Ltd
See Trainline

CHG Electrical
2 Wortley Road, Deepcar, Sheffield, S36 2UZ
T: 0114 218 0470
F: 0114 283 1874
E: info@chgelectrical.co.uk
W: www.chgelectrical.co.uk/

Chieftain Trailers Ltd
207 Coalisland Rd, Dungannon, Co Tyrone, BT71 4DP
T: 028 8774 7531
F: 028 8774 7530
E: sales@chieftaintrailers.com
W: www.chieftaintrailers.com

Chiltern Railways
2nd Floor, Western House, Rickfords Hill, Aylesbury, Bucks
T: 03456 005165
F: 01296 332126
W: www.chilternrailways.co.uk

Chloride Power Protection
See Emerson Network Power

Chrome Angel Solutions
3A Market Place, Woodstock, Oxfordshire, OX20 1SY
M: 07891 296370
E: mark@chromeangel.eu
W: chromeangel.co

Chrysalis Rail
Electra House, Electra Way, Crewe, Cheshire, CW1 6GL
T: 01270 534683
E: info@chrysalisrail.com
W: chrysalisrail.com

Chubb Systems Ltd
Shadsworth Rd, Blackburn, BB1 2PR
T: 0844 561 1316
F: 01254 667663
E: systems-sales@chubb.co.uk
W: www.chubbsystems.co.uk

MJ Church Plant Ltd
Star Farm, Marshfield, Nr Chippenham, Wiltshire, SN14 8LH
T: 01225 891591
F: 01225 891173
E: info@mjchurch.com
W: mjchurch.com/

Cintec International Ltd
Cintec House, 11 Gold Tops, Newport, S.Wales, NP20 4PH
T: 01633 246614
F: 01633 246110
E: johnbrooks@cintec.co.uk
W: www.cintec.co.uk

CIRAS
4th Floor, The Helicon, One South Place, London, EC2M 2RB
T: 0203 142 5367
E: info@ciras.org.uk
W: www.ciras.org.uk

CITI
Lovat Bank, Silver St, Newport Pagnell, Bucks, MK16 0EJ
T: 01908 283600
F: 01908 283601
E: bdu@citi.co.uk
W: www.citi.co.uk

Civil Water Management Ltd
Unit 9 Offices, Leeds Bradford Airport Industrial Estate, Harrogate Road, Yeadon, Leeds, LS19 7WP
T: 020 3189 1468
E: patrick@civilwater management.com
W: www.civilwatermanagement.com

CJ Associates Ltd
26 Upper Brook St, London, W1K 7QE
T: 020 7529 4900
F: 020 7529 4929
E: info@cjassociates.co.uk
W: www.cjassociates.co.uk

Clancy Docwra
Clare House, Coppermill Lane, Harefield, Middx, UB9 6HZ
T: 01895 823711
F: 01895 825263
E: enquiries@theclancygroup.co.uk
W: www.theclancygroup.co.uk

Clarabridge
EMEA - London, 6th Floor, 95 Aldwych, London, WC2B 4JF
T: 020 3142 8615
W: www.clarabridge.com/

Clarke Chapman Group
PO Box 9, Saltmeadows Road, Gateshead, Tyne & Wear, NE8 1SW
T: 0191 477 2271
E: info@clarkechapman.co.uk
W: www.clarkechapman.co.uk/

Clarks Vehicle Conversions
Unit 16A, Carcroft Enterprise Park, Station Road, Carcroft, Doncaster, DN6 8DD
T: 01302 784490
E: sales@cvcltd.co.uk
W: www.van-conversion.co.uk/

Class 40 Preservation Society (CFPS)
The East Lancashire Railway, Bolton St, Bury, Lancs, BL9 0EY
T: 07500 040145
M: 07818 040135
E: chairman@cfps.co.uk
W: www.cfps.co.uk

Class 50 Alliance Limited
Severn Valley Railway, Number One, Comberton Place, Kidderminster, DY10 1QR
T: 01562 757900
W: www.class50alliance.co.uk

Clayton Equipment
Second Avenue, Centrum 100 Business Park, Burton Upon Trent, Staffordshire, DE14 2WF
T: 01283 524470
E: contact@claytonequipment.co.uk
W: claytonequipment.co.uk/

CLD Fencing Systems
Unit 11, Springvale Business Centre, Millbuck Way, Sandbach, Cheshire, CW11 3HY
T: 01270 764751
F: 01270 757503
E: sales@cld-fencing.com
W: www.cld-fencing.com

CLD Services
170 Brooker Rd, Waltham Abbey, Essex, EN9 1JH
T: 01992 702300
F: 01992 702301
E: contact@cld-services.co.uk
W: www.cld-services.co.uk

Clements Technical Recruitment Ltd t/a Clemtech
7 Falcon Court, Parklands Business Park, Denmead, Waterlooville, Hants, PO7 6BZ
T: 023 9224 2690
F: 023 9224 2692
E: rail@clemtech.co.uk
W: www.clemtech.co.uk

Clemtech
See Clements Technical Recruitment Ltd t/a Clemtech

Cleshar Contract Services Ltd
Heather Park House, North Circular Rd, Stonebridge, London, NW10 7NN
T: 020 8733 8888
F: 020 8733 8899
E: info@cleshar.co.uk
W: www.cleshar.co.uk

Cleveland Bridge Uk
PO Box 27, Yarm Rd, Darlington, DL1 4DE
T: 01325 381188
F: 01325 382320
E: info@clevelandbridge.com
W: www.clevelandbridge.com

Cleveland Cable Company
Riverside Park Road, Middlesbrough, Cleveland, TS2 1QW
T: 01642 241133
F: 01642 226171
E: sales@clevelandcable.com
W: www.clevelandcable.com/

Clifford Marker Associates
9 Warners Close, Woodford Green, Essex, IG8 0TF
T: 020 8504 2570
W: www.cliffordmarkerassociates.com

Clifton Rubber Company Ltd
Edison Road, Industrial Estate, St Ives, Cambs, PE27 3FF
T: 01480 496161
E: sales@cliftonrubber.co.uk
W: www.cliftonrubber.co.uk/

Cloud Cycle
W: cloudcycle.com

Clyde & Co LLP
St Botolph Building, 138 Houndsditch, London, EC3A 7AR
T: 020 7876 5000
E: robert.meakin@clydeco.com
W: www.clydeco.com

CML
See Construction Marine Ltd

CMS Cameron McKenna
Cannon Place, 78 Cannon Street, London, EC4N 6AF
T: 020 7367 2113
F: 020 7367 2000
E: jonathan.beckitt@cms-cmck.com
W: www.cmslegal.com

Cnection Ltd
Nottingham Geospatial Building, Triumph Rd, Nottingham, NG7 2TU
T: 0115 778 6442
E: contact@cnection.co.uk
W: www.cnection.co.uk

CNNCT Ltd
2 The Court, Bohortha, St Anthony, Truro, Cornwall, TR2 5EY
T: 01872 581978
E: enq@cnnctconsultancy.com
W: https://www.cnnct consultancy.com/

Co Channel Electronics
Victoria Rd, Avonmouth, Bristol, BS11 9DB
T: 0117 982 0578
F: 0117 982 6166
E: sales@co-channel.co.uk
W: www.co-channel.co.uk

Cobham Technical Services (ERA Technology Ltd)
Cleeve Rd, Leatherhead, Surrey, KT22 7SA
T: 01372 367030
F: 01372 367102
E: era.rail@cobham.com
W: www.cobham.com/ technicalservices

Coffey Geotechnics
Atlantic House, Atls Business Park, Simonsway, Manchester, M22 5PR
T: 0161 499 6800
F: 0161 499 6802
E: andrew_smith@coffey.com
W: www.coffey.com

Cogitamus
11 Woodfield Road, Peterborough, PE3 6HD
T: 01733 767244
F: 01733 313492
E: info@cogitamus.co.uk
W: https://cogitamus.co.uk/

COLAS Rail
Dacre House, 19 Dacre Street, London, SW1H 0DH
T: 020 7593 5353
F: 020 7593 5343
E: enquiries@colasrail.co.uk
W: www.colasrail.co.uk

Coleman and Company
The Coleman Group, Shady Lane, Great Barr, Birmingham, B44 9ER
T: 0121 325 2424
F: 0121 325 2425
E: contracts@coleman-co.com
W: www.coleman-co.com/

Colin Buchanan
See SKM Colin Buchanan

Collaborative Project Management Services (CPMS)
Office 113B, New Broad Street House, 35 New Broad Street, London, EC2M 1NH
T: 0203 009 3119
E: info@cpmsrail.co.uk
W: www.cpmsrail.co.uk

Collis Engineering Civils Division
Salcombe Rd, Meadow Lane Ind. Est, Alfreton, Derbys, DE55 7RG
T: 01773 833255
F: 01773 836525
E: sales@collis.co.uk
W: www.signalhousegroup.co.uk

Collis Engineering Ltd
Salcombe Rd, Meadow Lane Ind. Est, Alfreton, Derbys, DE55 7RG
T: 01773 833255
F: 01773 520693
E: sales@collis.co.uk
W: www.collis.co.uk

Colman Rail Services
8 Fort House Business Centre, Primrose Close, Chatham, Kent, ME4 6HZ
T: 01634 888620
E: office@colmanrailservices.co.uk
W: www.colmanrailservices.co.uk

Colour-Rail
558 Birmingham Road, Bromsgrove, Worcs, B61 0HT
E: colourrail@aol.com
W: www.colourrail.com/

Colt Industrial
Colt Business Park, Witty Street, Hull, HU3 4TT
T: 01482 214244
F: 01482 215037
W: www.colt-industrial.co.uk/

Coltraco Ultrasonics
46 Mount Street, Mayfair, London, W1K 2SA
T: 020 7629 8475
F: 020 7629 8477
E: info@coltraco.co.uk
W: www.coltraco.com/

Comech Metrology Ltd
Castings Rd, Derby, DE23 8YL
T: 01332 867700
F: 01332 867707
E: sales@comech.co.uk
W: www.comech.co.uk

Commend UK Ltd
Commend House, Unit 20, M11 Business Link, Parsonage Lane, Stansted, Essex, CM24 8GF
T: 01279 872020
F: 01279 814735
E: sales@commend.co.uk
W: www.commend.co.uk

Comms Design Ltd
40 Freemans Way, Harrogate Business Park, Wetherby Road, Harrogate, North Yorkshire, HG3 1DH
T: 01423 895071
E: sales@commsdesign.net
W: commsdesign.ltd.uk/

Community Rail Network
The Old Water Tower, Huddersfield Railway Station, Huddersfield, HD1 1JF
T: 01484 548926
E: info@communityrail.org.uk
W: communityrail.org.uk

Competence Assurance Solutions Ltd
40 Bowling Green Lane, London, EC1R 0NE
T: +44 (0) 774 904 3607
E: info@cas-ukcn.com
W: www.cas-ukcn.com

Compin-Fainsa
Horta, 08107 Martorelles, Spain
T: (34) 93 5796970
E: fainsa@fainsa.com
W: www.compin.com/?lang=en

Complete Drain Clearance
Unit 17G, Raleigh Hall Industrial Estate, Eccleshall, Stafford, ST21 6JL
T: 01785 851444
E: enquiries@completedrainclearance.co.uk
W: www.completedrainclearance.co.uk

Complus Teltronic
See Commend UK Ltd

Composites UK
Innovation House, 39 Mark Road, Hemel Hempstead, Herts, HP2 7DN
T: 01442275365
E: info@compositesuk.co.uk
W: www.composites.co.uk

CompoTech
Nová 1316, Sušice 34201, Czech Republic
T: +420 376 526 839
F: +420 376 522 350
E: enquire@compotech.com
W: www.compotech.com/

Comtest Wireless
Badgemore House, Gravel Hill, Henley on Thames, Oxfordshire, RG9 4NR
T: 01491 579512
F: 01491 576377
E: contact@comtestwireless.eu
W: www.comtestwireless.eu/

Comtrol
Unit 6/7 Bignell Park Barns, Chesterton, Bicester, Oxon, OX26 1TD
T: 01908 929300
F: 01869 351848
E: sales@comtrol.co.uk
W: www.comtrol.co.uk

Concrete Canvas Ltd
Unit 3, Block A22, Pontypridd, CF37 5SP
T: 0845 680 1908
E: info@concretecanvas.com
W: www.concretecanvas.com

Conductix-Wampfler Ltd (Insul 8)
1 Michigan Ave, Salford, M50 2GY
T: 0161 848 0161
F: 0161 873 7017
E: info.uk@conductix.com
W: www.conductix.co.uk

Confederation of Passenger Transport UK
Drury House, 34-43 Russell St, London, WC2B 5HA
T: 020 7240 3131
F: 020 7240 6565
E: admin@cpt-uk.org
W: www.cpt-uk.org

Consillia Ltd
See Donfabs and Consillia Ltd

Construcciones y Auxiliar de Ferrocarriles SA (CAF)
The TechnoCentre, Puma Way, Coventry, CV1 2TT
T: 02476 158195
F: 0034 914 366008
E: caf@caf.net
W: www.caf.net

Construction Marine Ltd
The Coach House, Mansion Gate Drive, Chapel Allerton, Leeds, LS7 4SY
T: 0113 262 4444
F: 0113 262 4400
E: info@cml.uk.com
W: www.cml-civil-engineering.co.uk

Containerlift
PO Box 582, Great Dunmow, Essex, CM6 3QX
T: 0800 174 546
F: 0800 174 547
E: joostbaker@containerlift.co.uk
W: www.containerlift.com

Continental Contitech
Chestnut Field House, Chestnut Field, Rugby, Warks, CV21 2PA
T: 01788 571482
F: 01788 542245
W: www.contitech.co.uk

Cook Rail
See William Cook Rail

Cooper and Turner Ltd
Templeborough Works, Sheffield Rd, Sheffield, S9 1RS
T: 0114 256 0057
F: 0114 244 5529
E: sales@cooperandturner.co.uk
W: www.cooperandturner.com

Cooper B-Line
See Eaton Electrical Ltd

Cooper Bussmann (UK) Ltd
Melton Road, Burton-on-the-Wolds, Leics, LE12 5TH
T: 01509 882737
F: 01509 882786
E: bule.sales@cooperindustries.com
W: www.cooperbussmann.com

Cooper Handling
Holly Farm Business Park, Honiley, Kenilworth, Warwickshire, CV8 1NP
T: 01926 658900
F: 01926 484310
E: info@cooperhandling.com
W: www.cooperhandling.com/

Copon E Wood Ltd
See 3M CPPD

Corbett Keeling
8 Angel Court, London, EC2R 7HP
T: 020 7626 6266
F: 020 7626 7005
E: info@corbettkeeling.com
W: www.corbettkeeling.com/

Cordek Ltd
Spring Copse Business Park, Slinfold, West Sussex, RH13 0SZ
T: 01403 799600
F: 01403 791718
E: sales@cordek.com
W: www.cordek.com

Corehard Ltd
Viewpoint, Babbage Rd, Stevenage, Herts, SG1 2EQ
T: 01438 225102
F: 01438 213721
E: info@corehard.com
W: www.corehard.com

Corelink Rail Infrastructure
Suite 1, 3rd Floor, 11-12 St James's Square, London, SW1Y 4LB

Coronet Rail Ltd
See LB Foster Europe

Corporate College
Derby College, Prince Charles Ave, Derby, DE22 4LR
T: 01332 520145
E: enquiries@derby-college.ac.uk
W: www.corporatecollege.co.uk

Correl Rail Ltd
See SGS UK Ltd

Corus Cogifer
See Vossloh Cogifer UK Ltd

Corus Rail Infrastructure Services
See Tata Steel Projects

Corys
44 Rue des Berges, 38024 Grenoble, France
T: 0033 476 288200
F: 0033 476 288211
E: coryscom@corys.fr
W: www.corys.com

Cosalt Ltd
See Ballyclare Ltd

Costain Ltd - Rail Sector
Costain House, Vanwall Business Park, Maidenhead, Berks, SL6 4UB
T: 01628 842310
E: gren.edwards@costain.com
W: www.costain.com

Covanburn Contracts Ltd
91 Bothwell Road, Hamilton, Lanarkshire, ML3 0DW
T: 01698 200057
E: enquiries@covanburncontracts.co.uk
W: www.covanburn.com/

Covtec Ltd
Allens West, Eaglescliffe Logistics Centre, Durham Rd, Eaglescliffe, Stockton on Tees, TS16 0RW
E: info@covtec.co.uk
W: www.covtec.co.uk

Cowans Sheldon
The Clarke Chapman Group Ltd, PO Box 9, Saltmeadows Rd, Gateshead, NE8 1SW
T: 0191 477 2271
F: 0191 478 3951
E: martin.howell@clarkechapman.co.uk
W: www.cowanssheldon.co.uk

COWI
Eastfield, Church Street, Uttoxeter, Staffordshire, ST14 8AA
T: 01889 563680
E: info_uk@cowi.com
W: https://www.cowi.com/

Coyle Personnel Plc
Hygeia, 66-68 College Rd, Harrow, Middx, HA1 1BE
T: 020 8901 6619
F: 020 8901 6706
E: roger@coyles.co.uk
W: www.coylerail.co.uk

CP Films Solutia (UK) Ltd
13 Acorn Business Centre, Northarbour Rd, Cosham, PO6 3TH
T: 02392 219112
F: 02392 219102
W: www.llumar.eu.com

CPC Project Services LLP
7th Floor, 100 Wood Street, London, EC2V 7AN
T: 020 7539 4750
M: 07734 052747
E: andy.norris@cpcprojectservices.com
W: www.cpcprojectservices.com

CPR
Millburn Roads Depot, Main Street, Renton, West Dunbartonshire, G82 4PZ
T: 01389 751797
W: www.cpr-resurfacing.co.uk/

Craig & Derricott Ltd
Hall Lane, Walsall Wood, Walsall, WS9 9DP
T: 01543 375541
F: 01543 361619
E: sales@craiganddericott.com
W: www.craiganddericott.com

Cranfield University
College Rd, Cranfield, Beds, MK43 0AL
T: 01234 750111
E: info@cranfield.ac.uk
W: www.cranfield.ac.uk/soe/rail-investgation

Creactive Design (Transport)
Unit 2 Trojan Business Centre, Tachbrook Park Drive, Warwick, CV34 6RS
T: 01926 290450
E: design@creactive-design.co.uk
W: www.creactive-transport.co.uk

Creative Rail Dining
PO Box 10375, Little Waltham, Chelmsford, Essex, CM1 9JW
T: 01245 364051
E: enquiries@crdltd.co.uk
W: www.crdltd.co.uk

Crécy Publishing Ltd
1a Ringway Trading Estate, Shadowmoss Road, Manchester, M22 5LH
T: 0161 499 0024
F: 0161 499 0298
E: enquiries@crecy.co.uk
W: www.crecy.co.uk/

Credit360 Ltd
Compass House, Vision Park, Cambridge, CB24 9BZ
T: 01223 237 200
W: https://cr360.com/en-gb/

Critical Power Supplies Ltd
The Malthouse, Mill Lane, Scotsgrove, Thame, Oxon, OX9 3RP
T: 01844 340122
W: www.criticalpowersupplies.co.uk

Critical Project Resourcing Ltd
116a, High St, Sevenoaks, Kent, TN13 1UZ
T: 01732 455300
F: 01732 458447
E: rail@cpresourcing.co.uk
W: www.cpresourcing.co.uk

Cross London Trains
210 Pentonville Road, London, N1 9JY

CrossCountry
5th Floor, Cannon House, 18 Priory Queensway, Birmingham, B4 6BS
T: 0344 736 9123
F: 0121 200 6001
E: customer.relations@crosscountrytrains.co.uk
W: www.crosscountrytrains.co.uk

Crossrail 2
E: crossrail2@tfl.gov.uk
W: crossrail2.co.uk/

Crossrail Ltd
25 Canada Square, Canary Wharf, London, E14 5LQ
T: 0845 602 3813
E: helpdesk@crossrail.co.uk
W: www.crossrail.co.uk

CrossTech
Hack Partners, 10 Market Place, Devizes, Wiltshire, SN10 1HT
W: https://crosstech.co.uk/

Crouch Waterfall & Partners Ltd
15 Apex Court, Woodlands, Bradley Stoke, Bristol, BS32 4JT
T: 01454 270707
E: bristol@crouchwaterfall.co.uk
W: crouchwaterfall.co.uk

Crowd Dynamics
21 Station Rd West, Oxted, Surrey, RH8 9EE
T: 01883 718690
F: 08700 516196
E: enquiries@crowddynamics.com
W: www.crowddynamics.com

Crowle Wharf Engineers Ltd (CWE)
Unit 1 & 2, Woodland Court, Coach Road, Shireoaks Triangle, Worksop, S81 8AD
T: 01909 498641
E: info@cwelimited.com
W: cwelimited.com/

Crown International
Old Mill Road, Portishead, Bristol, BS20 7BX
T: 01275 818008
F: 01275 818288
W: www.crown-international.co.uk/

Croylek Ltd
23 Ullswater Cres, Coulsdon, Surrey, CR5 2UY
T: 020 8668 1481
F: 020 8660 0750
E: sales@croylek.co.uk
W: www.croylek.co.uk

CRRC Corporation Ltd
No.16 West 4th-Ring Mid Road, Haidian District, Beijing, 100036, China
T: 01522 502757
F: +86-10-63984785
M: 07836 500382
E: paul.taylor@dynexsemi.com
W: www.crrcgc.cc/en

Ctrack
Park House, Headingley Office Park, 8 Victoria Road, Leeds, LS6 1PF
T: 0345 055 8555
F: 0113 203 6771
E: info@ctrack.co.uk
W: www.ctrack.co.uk/

Cubic Transportation Systems
AFC House, Honeycrock Lane, Salfords, Redhill, Surrey, RH1 5LA
T: 01737 782362
F: 01737 789759
W: www.cubic.com/cts

Cubis Industries
Lurgan, Co Armagh, BT66 6LN
T: 0151 548 7900
F: 0151 548 7184
E: info@cubisindustries.com
W: www.cubisindustries.com

Cubris
Cubris ApS, Ebertsgade 2, 2, DK-2300, Copenhagen S, Denmark
T: 0330 2230 460
E: info@cubris.dk
W: www.cubris.dk/

Cudis Ltd
Power House, Parker St, Bury, BL9 0RJ
T: 0161 765 3000
F: 0161 705 2900
E: sales@cudis.co.uk
W: www.cudis.co.uk

Cummins
Yarm Rd, Darlington, DL1 4PW
T: 01327 886464
F: 0870 241 3180
E: cabo.customerassistance@cummins.com
W: www.everytime.cummins.com

Cundall
One Carter Lane, London, EC4V 5ER
T: 020 7438 1600
W: www.cundall.com

Cyient
Apex, Forbury Road, Reading, RG1 1AX
T: +44 118 3043720
W: www.cyient.com

D&D Rail Ltd
Time House, Time Square, Basildon, Essex, SS14 1DJ
T: 01268 520000
F: 01268 520011
E: info@ddrail.com
W: www.ddrail.com

D2 Rail and Civils
1st Floor, Langton House, Bird St, Lichfield, WS13 6PY
T: 0161 817 5022
F: 0161 817 8006
E: info@d2rc.co.uk
W: www.d2railandcivils.co.uk

D5 Architects LLP
71-77 Coventry Street, Birmingham, B5 5NH
T: 0121 633 4663
F: 0121 633 0540
M: 0794697305
E: info@d5architects.net
W: d5architects.net

DAC Ltd
Union Mill, Watt Street, Sabden, Lancashire, BB7 9ED
T: 01282 447000
F: 0845 280 1915
E: sales@daclimited.co.uk
W: www.daclimited.co.uk

Dailys UK Ltd
See Novah Ltd

Dallmeier Electronic UK Ltd
Dallmeier House, 3 Beaufort Trade Park, Pucklechurch, Bristol, BS16 9QH
T: 0117 303 9303
F: 0117 303 9302
E: dallmeieruk@dallmeier-electronic.com
W: www.dallmeier-electronic.com

Danburykline
1A, The Old Fire Station, 150 Waterloo Road, London, SE1 8SB
M: 07747 180180
W: www.danburykline.co.uk

Danny Sullivan Group
22 Barretts Green Rd, Park Royal, London, NW10 7AE
T: 020 8961 1900
F: 020 8961 1965
E: enquiries@dannysullivan.co.uk
W: www.dannysullivan.co.uk

Darran Jacobs Limited
PO Box 7254, Wednesbury, WS10 1DU
M: 07903 999901
E: djhodgetts@darranjacobs.co.uk

Dartford Composites Ltd
Unit 1, Ness Rd, Erith, Kent, DA8 2LD
T: 01322 350097
F: 01322 359438
E: sales@dartfordcomposites.co.uk
W: www.dartfordcomposites.co.uk

Data Acquisition & Testing Services Ltd
Unit 4, Gainsborough Close, Gainsborough Business Park, Long Eaton, Nottingham, NG10 1PX
T: 01332 875450
F: 05603 137103
E: enquiries@datsltd.com
W: www.datsltd.com

Data Systems & Solutions
See Optimized Systems & Solutions Ltd

Datasys Ltd
See Tracsis Plc

Datum - Composite Products
22 Longbridge Lane, Derby, DE24 8UJ
T: 01332 751503
F: 01332 385487
E: composites@datum-patterns.co.uk
W: www.datum-patterns.co.uk

David Brice Consultancy
11 Sebastian Ave, Shenfield, Brentwood, Essex, CM15 8PN
T: 01277 221422
M: 07721 657521
E: davidpbrice@aol.com
W: www.bricerail.co.uk

David Brown Gear Systems Ltd
Park Gear Works, Lockwood, Huddersfield, HD4 5DD
T: 01484 465634
F: 01484 465587
E: steve.oldroyd@dbsantasalo.com
W: www.dbsantasalo.com

David Keay Railway & Tramway Engineering
16 Willoughby Close, Penkridge, Staffs, ST19 5QT
M: 07904 011079
E: david.keay@outlook.com

David Lane Publishing
62 North Street, Bourne, Lincolnshire, PE10 9NB
T: 01778 420888
F: 01778 421550
M: 07795 031051
E: dave@davidlanepublishing.co.uk

David Simmonds Consultancy
112 George Street, Edinburgh, EH2 4LH
T: 01223 316098
E: admin@davidsimmonds.com
W: www.davidsimmonds.com

DB Cargo (UK)
Lakeside Business Park, Carolina Way, Doncaster, DN4 5PN
T: 01302 575000
E: uk.dbcargo@deutschebahn.com
W: uk.dbcargo.com

DB ESG
Derwent House, RTC Business Park, London Rd, Derby, DE24 8UP
T: 01332 483800
E: enquiries@dbesg.com
W: www.deutschebahn.com/dbesg

DB Symmetry
Grange Park Court, Roman Way, Northampton, NN4 5EA
T: 01604 330630
W: www.dbsymmetry.com/

DB Systemtechnik
Weserglacis 2, 32423 Minden, Germany
T: +49 571 3935500
W: www.deutschebahn.com/en/business/engineering_services

dBD Communications
4 Furlongs, Basildon, Essex, SS16 4BW
T: 01268 449871
F: 01268 442390
E: npurcell@dbdcom.co.uk
W: www.dbdcom.co.uk

DBK Technitherm Ltd
Unit 11, Llantrisant Business Park, Llantrisant, CF72 8LF
T: 01443 237927
F: 01443 237867
E: info-uk@dbk-group.com
W: www.dbktechnitherm.ltd.uk

DC Airco
Opaalstraat 18, 1812 RH Alkmaar, Netherlands
T: 0031 72533 6540
E: info@dcairco.com
W: www.dcairco.com

DCA Design International
19 Church St, Warwick, CV34 4AB
T: 01926 499461
E: transport@dca-design.com
W: www.dca-design.com/

DCRail
Offices 9 & 10, Days Space Business Centre, Litchurch Lane, Derby, DE24 8AA
T: 01332 977008
E: ahickling@dcrail.com
W: www.dcrail.com

Dedicated Micros
1200 Unit, Daresbury Park, Daresbury, Warrington, WA4 4HS
T: 0845 600 9500
F: 0845 600 9504
E: customerservices@dmicros.com
W: www.dedicatedmicros.com/uk

DEG Signal Ltd
Aspect House, Crusader Park, Warminster, Wilts, BA12 8BT
T: 01985 212020
F: 01985 212053
E: info@degsignal.co.uk
W: www.degsignal.co.uk

Delay Attribution Board
1 Eversholt St, 8th Floor, London, NW1 2DN
E: admin@delayattributionboard.co.uk
W: www.delayattributionboard.co.uk

Delimon Denco Lubrication
See Bijur Delimon International

Delkor Rail
74 Harley Cres, Condell Park, NSW, Australia
T: 61 2 9709 2918
F: 61 2 9709 5934
E: george@delkorrail.com
W: www.delkorrail.com

Dellner Couplers UK Ltd
Hearthcote Rd, Swadlincote, Derbys, DE11 9DX
T: 01283 221122
E: ukinfo@dellner.com
W: www.dellner.com

Dellner Romag
Leadgate Ind. Est., Leadgate, Consett, Co Durham, DH8 7RS
T: 01207 500000
F: 01207 591979
E: sales@dellner-romag.co.uk
W: www.romag.co.uk

Delmatic
The Power House, 6 Power Rd, Chiswick, London, W4 5PY
T: 020 8987 5900
F: 020 8987 5957
E: sales@delmatic.com
W: www.delmatic.com

Deloitte LLP
2 New Street Square, London, EC4A 3BZ
T: 020 7936 3000
F: 020 7583 1198
W: www2.deloitte.com/uk/en/

Delta Plus
Unit 1, Point 5, Walker Ind. Park, Blackburn, Lancs, BB1 2QE
T: 01254 686100
F: 01254 686111
E: enquiries@deltaplus.co.uk
W: www.deltaplus.co.uk

Deltic Preservation Society ltd
Barrow Hill Roundhouse, Railway Centre Campbell Drive, Barrow Hill, Chesterfield, Derbyshire, S43 2PR
E: secretary@thedps.co.uk
W: www.http://thedps.co.uk

Deltix Transport Consulting
4 Church Hill Drive, Edinburgh, EH10 4BT
T: 0131 447 7764
M: 07917 877399
E: david@deltix.co.uk
W: www.deltix.co.uk

Demco
Heyford Close, Aldermans Green Ind. Est., Coventry, CV2 2QB
T: 02476 602323
F: 02476 602116
E: info@mgs.co.uk
W: www.demco.co.uk

Denchi Power Ltd
Denchi House, Thurso, Caithness, KW14 7XW
T: 01847 808000
W: www.denchipower.com

Dentons UKMEA LLP
One Fleet Place, London, EC4M 7WS
T: 020 7242 1212
F: 020 7246 7777
W: www.dentons.com/en/

Department for Transport
Great Minster House, 33 Horseferry Road, London, SW1P 4DR
T: 020 7944 5409
F: 020 7944 2158
W: www.dft.gov.uk

Deploy UK Rail
The Podium, 1 Eversholt St, London, NW1 2DN
T: 020 7434 0300
E: info@deployuk.com
W: www.deployuk.com

Depot Rail Ltd
Mercury House, Willoughton Drive, Foxby Lane Business Park, Gainsborough, Lincs, DN21 1DY
T: 01427 619512
F: 01427 619501
E: sales@drail.co.uk
W: www.depotrail.co.uk

Derby Engineering Unit Ltd
Unit 22, Riverside Park, East Service Rd, Raynesway, Derby, DE21 7RW
T: 01332 660364
F: 01332 675191
E: enquiries@derbyengineeringunit.co.uk
W: www.derbyengineeringunit.co.uk

The Deritend Group Ltd
Cyprus St, Off Upper Villiers St, Wolverhampton, WV2 4PB
T: 01902 426354
F: 01902 711926
E: sales@deritend.co.uk
W: www.deritend.co.uk

Design & Projects Int. Ltd
2 Manor Farm, Flexford Rd, North Baddesley, Hants, SO52 9FD
T: 02380 277910
F: 02380 277920
E: colin.brooks@designandprojects.com
W: www.railwaymaintenance.com

Design and Analysis Ltd
Unit 1 H2O, Lake View Drive, Sherwood Business Park, Nottingham, NG15 0HT
T: 0115 888 2666
E: info@design-and-analysis.co.uk
W: www.designandanalysis.co.uk/

Design Triangle Ltd
The Maltings, Burwell, Cambridge, CB25 0HB
T: 01638 743070
F: 01638 743493
E: mail@designtriangle.co.uk
W: www.designtriangle.com

Designplan Lighting
16 Kimpton Park Way, Sutton, Surrey, SM3 9QS
T: 020 8254 2000
F: 020 8644 4253
E: sales@designplan.co.uk
W: www.designplan.co.uk

Det Norske Veritas
See DNV (Det Norske Veritas)

Deustche Bahn UK
DB Vertrieb GmbH, Suite 6/7, The Sanctuary, 23 Oakhill Grove, Surbiton, Surrey, KT6 6DU
W: www.bahn.co.uk

Deuta-Werke GmbH
Paffrather Str. 140, D-51465 Bergisch Gladbach, Germany
T: 0049 2202 958 100
F: 0049 2202 958 145
E: support@deuta.de
W: www.deuta.de

DEUTZ AG - UK & Ireland
Unit 3, Willow Park, Burdock Close, Cannock, Staffs, WS11 7FQ
T: 01543 438901
F: 01543 438931
E: brocklebank.s@deutz.com
W: www.deutz.de/

Devol Engineering Ltd
Unit 2, Faulds Park Industrial Estate, Faulds Park Road, Gourock, PA19 1FB
T: 01475 657360
F: 01475 787873
E: sales.devol.uk@jameswalker.biz
W: www.devol.com

Devon & Cornwall Rail Partnership
School of Geography Earth & Environmental Science, University of Plymouth, Plymouth, PL4 8AA
T: 01752 584777
E: railpart@plymouth.ac.uk
W: www.greatscenicrailways.com

Dewalt
210 Bath Rd, Slough, SL1 3YD
T: 01753 567055
F: 01753 521312
E: reply@dewalt.com
W: www.dewalt.co.uk

DEWESoft
Meadow Brook, Summerside Road, Buckland, Faringdon, Oxfordshire, SN7 8QY
T: 01367 871000
F: 01367 871001
E: sales.uk@dewesoft.com
W: www.dewesoft.com

Dewhurst Plc
Unit 9, Hampton Business Park, Hampton Road West, Feltham, Middx, TW13 6DB
T: 020 8744 8200
F: 020 8744 8299
E: info@dewhurst.co.uk
W: www.dewhurst.co.uk

Dexeco Ltd
Brickfields Business Park, Gillingham, Dorset, SP8 4PX
T: 01747 858100
F: 01747 858153
E: sales@dexeco.co.uk
W: www.dexeco.co.uk/

DfT OLR Holdings Ltd
Albany House, 94-98, Petty France, London, SW1H 9AE
E: enquiries@olrholdings.co.uk
W: www.olrholdings.co.uk/

DG Design
Friar Gate Studios, Ford Street, Derby, DE1 1EE
T: 01332 258360
E: design@davidgordonltd.co.uk
W: www.davidgordonltd.co.uk/

DG8 Design and Engineering Ltd
Room 7, The College Business Centre, Uttoxeter New Rd, Derby, DE22 3WZ
T: 01332 869351
F: 01332 869350
E: jenny.hughes@dg8design.com
W: www.dg8design.com

DGauge Ltd
Unit 5, 11 Brunel Parkway, Pride Park, Derby, DE24 8HR
T: 01332 546905
E: colin.johnson@dgauge.co.uk
W: www.dgauge.co.uk

DGP Logistics
Station House, Station Road, Southfleet, Kent, DA13 9PA
T: 01474 833388
E: enquiries@dgplogisticsplc.com
W: www.dgplogisticsplc.com

dhp11 Ltd
The Barn, Overlees, Barlow, Dronfield, Derbyshire, S18 7SN
T: 0114 289 9393
F: 0114 289 9400
E: info@dhp11.com
W: www.dhp11.com/

Diamond Seating Ltd
Unit 3, Butterthwaite Lane, Ecclesfield, Sheffield, S35 9WA
T: 0114 257 0909
F: 0114 245 7950
E: info@diamondseating.co.uk

DIEM Ltd
11 Jubilee Rd, Formby, Merseyside, L37 2HN
T: 01704 870461
M: 07737 194686
E: davidinman@diemltd.co.uk
W: www.diemltd.co.uk

Diesel Traction Group
E: info@westernchampion.co.uk
W: westernchampion.co.uk

Difuria Ltd
West Stockwith Business Park, Stockwith Road, Misterton, Doncaster, DN10 4ES
T: 01427 848712
F: 01427 848056
E: sales@difuria.co.uk
W: www.difuria.co.uk

Digitals Barriers
Enterprise House, 1-2 Hatfields, London, SE1 9PG
T: 020 7940 4740
F: 020 7940 4746
E: info@digitalbarriers.com
W: www.digitalbarriers.com/

Digital Technology International (DTI)
31 Affleck Rd, Perth Airport WA 6105, Western Australia, Australia
T: 01913 854803
F: +61 8 9479 1190
E: dti@dti.com.au
W: www.dti.com.au/

Dilax Systems UK Ltd
Unit 1, Knowlhill Business Park, Roebuck Way, Milton Keynes, MK5 8HL
T: 01908 607340
F: 020 7223 2011
E: sales.uk@dilax.com
W: www.dilax.co.uk

Dimension Data
Dimension Data House, Building 2, Waterfront Business Park, Fleet Road, Fleet, Hampshire, GU51 3QT
T: 01252 779000
W: www2.dimensiondata.com/en-uk

The Direct Group
Unit 2, Churnet Court, Churnetside Business Park, Harrison Way, Cheddleton, Staffs, ST13 7EF
T: 01538 360555
F: 01538 369100
E: dpl@direct-group.co.uk
W: www.direct-group.co.uk

Direct Rail Services (DRS)
Regents Court, Baron Way, Carlisle, CA6 4SJ
T: 01228 406600
E: salesenquiries@drsl.co.uk
W: www.directrailservices.com

Direct Track Solutions Ltd
Unit C Midland Place, Midland Way, Barlborough Links, Barlborough, Chesterfield, S43 4FR
T: 01246 810198
F: 01246 570926
E: info@directtracksolutions.co.uk
W: www.directtracksolutions.co.uk

Directly Operated Railways
4th Floor, Chancery Lane, London, EC4A 1BL
T: 020 7904 5043
E: enquiries@directlyoperatedrailways.co.uk
W: www.directlyoperatedrailways.co.uk

Direx Solutions
1 Fulwith Close, Harrogate, North Yorkshire, HG2 8HP

Discover LEDs
PO Box 222, Evesham, Worcs, WR11 4WT
T: 0844 578 1000
F: 0844 578 1111
E: sales@mobilecentre.co.uk
W: www.mobilecentre.co.uk

DLA Piper UK LLP
Princes Exchange, Princes Square, Leeds, LS1 4BY
T: 0113 369 2468
F: 0113 369 2999
W: www.dlapiper.com

DMC Group
Unit 17, The Capstan Centre, Thurrock Park Way, Tilbury, Essex, RM18 7HH
T: 01375 845070
F: 01375 841333
E: office@dmccontracts.co.uk
W: www.dmccontracts.co.uk

DML Group
See Babcock Rail

DMS Technologies
Unit 1 Belbins Business Park, Cupernham Lane, Romsey, Hampshire, SO51 7JF
M: 07718 577059
E: sales@dmstech.co.uk
W: dmstech.co.uk/

DNH WW Ltd
31 Clarke Rd, Mount Farm, Bletchley, Milton Keynes, MK1 1LG
T: 01908 275000
F: 01908 275100
E: dnh@dnh.co.uk
W: www.dnh.co.uk

DNV (Det Norske Veritas)
30 Stamford Street Vivo Building, 4th Floor, London, SE1 9LQ
T: +44203816 4000
F: 020 7716 6738
E: ulrike.haugen@dnv.com
W: www.dnv.com

Docklands Light Railway
Castor Lane, Poplar, London, E14 0DX
T: 020 7363 9898
F: 020 7363 9708
E: enquire@tfl.gov.uk
W: www.dlr.co.uk

Docmate Services Ltd
18 Alder Tree Rd, Banchory, Aberdeenshire, AB31 4FW
T: 01330 822620
F: 01330 822620
E: info@docmates.co.uk
W: www.docmates.co.uk

Dold Industries Ltd
11 Hamberts Rd, Blackall Ind Est, South Woodham Ferrers, Essex, CM3 5UW
T: 01245 324432
F: 01245 325570
E: admin@dold.co.uk
W: www.dold.co.uk

Dominium Bierrum Ltd
Seebeck House, 1 Seebeck Place, Knowlhill, Milton Keynes, Buckinghamshire, MK5 8FR
T: 01582 845745
F: 01582 845746

Domnick Hunter Industrial Operations
Dukesway, Team Valley Trading Est., Gateshead, Tyne & Wear, NE11 0PZ
T: 0191 402 9000
F: 0191 482 6296
E: dhindsales@parker.com
W: www.domnickhunter.com

Donaldson Associates
See COWI

Donfabs and Consillia Ltd
The Old Iron Warehouse, The Wharf, Shardlow, Derby, DE72 2GH
T: 01332 792483
F: 01332 799209
E: ian.moss@consillia.com
W: www.donfabsandconsillia.com

Donyal Engineering Ltd
Unit 7, Hobson Ind Est, Burnopfield, Newcastle upon Tyne, NE16 6EA
T: 01207 270909
F: 01207 270333
E: mike@donyal.co.uk
W: www.donyal.co.uk

Dormakaba
Lower Moor Way, Tiverton, Devon, EX16 6SS
T: 01884 256464
F: 01884 234415
E: info.gb@dormakaba.com
W: www.dormakaba.com

Dorset Woolliscroft
Falcon Road, Sowton Industrial Estate, Exeter, Devon, EX2 7LB
T: 01392 473037
F: 01392 473003
E: info@dorsetwoolliscroft.com
W: www.dorsetwoolliscroft.co.uk

Dow
Station Rd, Birch Vale, High Peak, Derbyshire, SK22 1BR
T: 01663 746518
F: 01663 746605
W: www.dow.com

Downer Group
Triniti Business Campus, 39 Delhi Road, North Ryde NSW 2113, Sydney, Australia
T: +61 2 9468 9700
F: +61 2 9813 8915
W: www.downergroup.com/

DP Consulting
Unit 4, Tygan House, The Broadway, Cheam, Surrey
T: 0845 094 2380
F: 0700 341 8557
E: info@dpconsulting.org.uk
W: www.dpconsulting.org.uk

DPSS Cabling Services Ltd
Unit 16, Chiltern Business Village, Arundel Rd, Uxbridge, UB2 2SN
T: 01895 251010
F: 01895 813133
E: airon.duke@dpsscabling.co.uk
W: www.dpsscabling.co.uk

Dragados S.A.
Regina House, 2nd Floor, 1-5 Queen St, London, EC4N 1SW
T: 020 7651 0900
F: 020 7248 9044
E: jcruzd@dragados.com
W: www.grupoacs.com

DRail
See Depot Rail Ltd

Drum Cussac
8 Hill St, St Helier, Jersey, JE4 9XB
T: 0870 429 6944
E: risk@drum-cussac.com
W: www.drum-cussac.com

DSM Demolition Group
Arden House, Arden Road, Heartlands, Birmingham, B8 1DE
T: 0121 322 2225
F: 0121 322 2227
E: info@dsmgroup.info
W: www.dsmdemolitiongroup.co.uk/

Dual Inventive Ltd
Unit 2, Kestrel Court, First Avenue, Doncaster, DN9 3RN
T: 03300 169033
E: info@dualinventive.com
W: www.dualinventive.com

DuPont (UK) Ltd
Wedgwood Way, Stevenage, Herts, SG1 4QN
T: 01438 734061
F: 01438 734836
W: www.rail.dupont.com

Dura Composites
Dura House, Telford Rd, Clacton-on-Sea, Essex, CO15 4LP
T: 01255 423601
F: 01255 435426
E: info@duracomposites.com
W: www.duracomposites.com

Durapipe
Walsall Rd, Norton Canes, Cannock, Staffs, WS11 9NS
T: 01543 279909
E: enquiries@durapipe.co.uk
W: www.durapipe.co.uk

DW Windsor UK
Pindar Rd, Hoddesden, Herts, EN11 0DX
T: 01992 474600
F: 01992 474600
E: light@dwwindsor.co.uk
W: www.dwwindsor.co.uk

DWG Timber Components Ltd
2 Burrough Court, Burrough-on-the-Hill, Melton Mowbray, Leicestershire, LE14 2QS
T: 0115 939 5992
E: info@dwguk.com
W: www.dwguk.com

DXC Technology
3rd Floor, 1 St Pancras Square, One Pancras Road, King's Cross, London, N1C 4AG
T: 020 3882 4422
W: www.dxc.technology

Dyer & Butler Ltd
Mead House, Station Rd, Nursling, Southampton, SO16 0AH
T: 02380 742222
F: 02380 742200
E: enquiries@dyerandbutler.co.uk
W: www.dyerandbutler.co.uk

Dyer Engineering Ltd
Solution House, Morrison Road Industrial Estate, Annfield Plain, Stanley, County Durham, DH9 7RU
T: 01207 234315
F: 01207 282834
E: lee.farms@dyer.co.uk
W: www.dyer.co.uk

Dynex Semiconductor Ltd
Doddington Rd, Lincoln, LN6 3LF
T: 01522 500500
F: 01522 500020
E: power_solutions@dynexsemi.com
W: www.dynexsemi.com

Dywidag-Systems International Ltd
Northfield Rd, Southam, Warks, CV47 0FG
T: 01926 813980
F: 01926 813817
E: sales@dywidag.co.uk
W: www.dywidag-systems.co.uk

E A Technology
Capenhurst Technology Park, Capenhurst, Chester, CH1 6ES
T: 0151 339 4181
F: 0151 347 2404
W: www.eatechnology.com

E C Harris
ECHQ, 34 York Way, London, N1 9AB
T: 020 7812 2000
F: 020 7812 2001
W: www.echarris.com

EAL
Unit 2, The Orient Centre, Greycaine Rd, Watford, WD24 7GP
T: 01923 652400
F: 01923 652401
E: customercare@eal.org.uk
W: www.eal.org.uk

EAO Ltd
Highland House, Albert Drive, Burgess Hill, West Sussex, RH15 9TN
T: 01444 236000
F: 01444 236641
E: sales.euk@eao.com
W: www.eao.com

East Anglian Sealing Co Ltd
Units 3-6, Goldingham Hall, Bulmer, Sudbury, Suffolk, CO10 7ER
T: 01787 880433
F: 01787 880442
E: sales@easeals.co.uk
W: easeals.co.uk/

East Lancashire Railway
Bolton St Station, Bury, Lancs, BL9 0EY
T: 0161 764 7790
E: admin@eastlancsrailway.co.uk
W: www.eastlancsrailway.org.uk

East Midlands Railway
Locomotive House, Locomotive Way, Derby, DE24 8PU
T: 03457 125678
F: 01738 643648
W: https://www.eastmidlandsrailway.co.uk/

East West Main Line Partnership
E: aking@englandseconomicheartland.com
W: https://www.eastwestrail.org.uk/

East West Rail (EWR)

Eaton Electrical Ltd
270 Bath Road, Slough, Berkshire, SL1 4DX
T: 08700 545 333
W: https://uk.eaton.com/

Ebeni Ltd
Hartham Park, Corsham, Wilts, SN13 0RP
T: 01249 700505
F: 01249 700001
M: 07776 532131
E: matthew.pearson@ebeni.com
W: www.ebeni.com

EcarbonUK
See Electrical Carbon UK Ltd

ECR Retail Systems
Church House, Church Lane, Kings Langley, WD4 8JP
T: 020 8205 7766
E: sales@ecr.co.uk
W: www.ecr.co.uk

ECT Group
See RMS Locotec Ltd

Ecus Environmental Consultants
Brook Holt, 3 Blackburn Road, Sheffield, S61 2DW
T: 0114 2669292
E: contactus@ecusltd.co.uk
W: www.ecusltd.co.uk/

Ede and Wilkinson
Inntel House, 85 London Road, Marks Tey, Colchester, Essex, C06 1EB
T: 01206 213279
F: 01206 213055
E: enquiries@ewgltd.com
W: www.edewilkinson.co.uk/

Eden Brown
222 Bishopsgate, London, EC2M 4QD
T: 020 7422 7300
F: 0845 434 9573
E: london@edenbrown.com
W: www.edenbrown.com

Eden Lea Rail
Meteor House, First Avenue, RHADS Business Park, Finningley, Doncaster, DN9 3GA
T: 01302 791750
E: info@edenlearail.co.uk
W: www.edenlearail.co.uk

Edenred
50 Vauxhall Bridge Road, London, SW1V 2RS
T: 0843 453 0206
W: www.edenred.co.uk/

EDF Energy
See UK Power Networks Services

Edgar Allen
See Balfour Beatty Rail

Edilon Sedra
See Tiflex Ltd

Edinburgh Trams Limited
55 Annandale Street, Edinburgh, EH7 4AZ
T: 0131 475 0177
W: edinburghtrams.com

Edmund Nuttall Ltd
See BAM Nuttall Ltd

Edward Barber & Jay Osgerby
37-42 Charlotte Road, London, EC2A 3PG
T: 020 7033 3884
E: info@barberosgerby.com
W: www.barberosgerby.com/

EFD Corporate
41 Caxton Court, Garamonde Drive, Wymbush, Milton Keynes, MK8 8DD
T: 0845 1285172 / 01908 560669
F: 01908 565672
M: 07827 891705
E: enquiries@efd-corporate.com
W: www.efd-corporate.com

Efficio
22 Long Acre, London, WC2E 9LY
T: 020 7550 5677
F: 020 7550 5679
E: info@efficioconsulting.com
W: www.efficioconsulting.com/

EFI Heavy Vehicle Brakes, part of EBC Brakes
EBC Brakes World Headquarters, Upton Valley Way East, Pineham, Northampton, NN4 9EF
T: +44 (0)1604 583344
F: +44 (0)1604 585679
E: sales@ebcbrakesdirect.com
W: www.efiltd.co.uk

Egis Rail
15 avenue du Centre, CS 20538 Guyancourt, 78286 Saint-Quentin-en-Yvelines CEDEX, France
T: +33 (0)1 39 41 40 00
W: www.egis-group.com/

EHS Holdings Ltd t/a EHS Roofing
627 Kingsbury Road, Erdington, Birmingham, West Midlands, B24 9PP
T: 0845 634 3131
E: info@ehsroofing.net
W: www.ehsroofing.co.uk

Eiffage
163 Quai du Docteur-Dervaux, 92601 Asnières-sur-Seine, Paris, France
T: 0001 4132 8000
F: 0001 4132 8113
W: www.eiffage.com/en/

EKE Electronics
Piispanportti 7, 02240 Espoo, Finland
T: +358 9 6130 30
F: +358 9 6130 3300
E: sales@eke.com
W: https://www.eke-electronics.com/

Eland Cables
120 Highgate Studios, 53-79 Highgate Rd, London, NW5 1TL
T: 020 7241 8787
F: 020 7241 8700
E: sales@eland.co.uk
W: www.eland.co.uk

Elastacloud
138-142 Holborn, London, EC1N 2SW
M: 07918 638492
E: info@elastacloud.com

Elcot Environmental
The Nursery, Kingsdown Lane, Blunsdon, Swindon, Wilts, SN25 5DL
T: 01793 700100
F: 01793 722221
E: peterw@elcotenviro.com
W: www.elcotenviro.com

Eldapoint Ltd
Charleywood Rd, Knowsley Ind. Prk North, Knowsley, Merseyside, L33 7SG
T: 0151 548 9838
F: 0151 546 4120
E: paul.wyatt@eldapoint.co.uk
W: www.eldapoint.co.uk

E-Leather Ltd
Kingsbridge Centre, Sturrock Way, Peterborough, PE3 8TZ
T: 01733 843939
F: 01733 843940
M: 07500 609351
E: carl.watkins@eleathergroup.com
W: www.eleathergroup.com

Electren UK
2nd Floor, Regina House, 1-5 Queen Street, London, EC4N 1SW
T: 020 3542 8281
E: electrenuk@electren.co.uk
W: www.electren.co.uk

Electric Railway Improvement Company (ERICO)
See Pentair

Electrification Solutions Ltd
Floor 5, Building 4, Exchange Quay, Manchester, M5 3EE
T: 0161 875 1341
E: info@electrificationsolutions.co.uk
W: www.electrificationsolutions.co.uk

Electro Motive
See Progress Rail Services

Electromagnetic Testing Services Ltd (ETS)
Pratts Fields, Lubberhedges Lane, Stebbing, Dunmow, Essex, CM6 3BT
T: 01371 856061
F: 01371 856144
E: info@etsemc.co.uk
W: www.etsemc.co.uk

Element Materials Technology
100 Frobisher Business Park, Leigh Sinton Road, Malvern, Worcs, WR14 1BX
T: 01684 571700
F: 01684 571701
W: www.element.com

ELG Carbon Fibre
Cannon Business Park, Darkhouse Lane, Coseley, West Midlands, WV14 8XQ
T: 01902 406010
E: contactus@elgcf.com
W: www.elgcf.com/

Elite KL Ltd
19A Sandy Way, Amington Industrial Estate, Tamworth, Staffordshire, B77 4DS
T: 01827 300100
F: 01827 300111
E: sales@elitekl.co.uk
W: www.elitekl.co.uk/

Elite Precast Concrete
Halesfield 9, Telford, Shropshire, TF9 4QW
T: 01952 588885
F: 01952 582011
E: sales@eliteprecast.co.uk
W: www.eliteprecast.co.uk

Ellis Patents Ltd
High Street, Rillington, Malton, North Yorkshire, YO17 8LA
T: 01944 758395
F: 01944 758808
E: sales@ellispatents.co.uk
W: www.ellispatents.co.uk/

Elmatic
Wentloog Road, Rumney, Cardiff, CF3 1XH
T: 029 2077 8727
F: 029 2079 2297
E: petercrisp@elmatic.co.uk
W: www.elmatic.co.uk

Eltek Valere UK Ltd
Cleveland Road, Hemel Hempstead, Herts, HP2 7EY
T: 01442 219355
F: 01442 245894
E: sales.gb@eltek.com
W: www.eltek.com/

Eltherm UK Ltd
Liberta House, Scotland Hill, Sandhurst, Berks, GU47 8JR
T: 01252 749910
E: sales@eltherm.uk.com
W: www.eltherm.uk.com

Embed Ltd
Viscount Centre Two, University of Warwick Science Park, Millburn Hill Road, Coventry, Warks, CV4 7HS
T: 02476 323251
E: webenquiries@embeduk.com
W: www.embeduk.com

Embedded Rail Technology Ltd
Rosehill House, Derby, DE23 8GG
M: 07967 667020
E: cp@charlespenny.com

EMEG Electrical Ltd
Unit 3, Dunston Place, Dunston Road, Whittington Moor, Chesterfield, Derbys, S41 8NL
T: 01246 268678
F: 01246 268679
E: enq@emeg.co.uk
W: www.emeg.co.uk

Emergency Power Systems
See Emerson Network Power

Emergi-Lite - Thomas & Betts Ltd
Bruntcliffe Lane, Morley, Leeds, LS27 9LL
T: 0113 281 0600
F: 0113 281 0601
E: emergi-lite.sales@tnb.com
W: www.emergi-lite.co.uk

Emerson Crane Hire
Emerson House, Freshwater Road, Dagenham, Essex, RM8 1RX
T: 020 8548 3900
F: 020 8548 3999
E: liam@emersoncranes.com
W: www.emersoncranes.com

Emerson Network Power
Ebury Gate, 23 Lower Belgrave Street, London, SW1W 0NR
T: 020 7881 1440
F: 020 7730 5085
E: uk.rail@emerson.com
W: www.emersonnetworkpower.com

Emerson Network Power Chloride Products & Services
See Emerson Network Power

Emico Ltd
Innovation House, 39 Mark Rd, Hemel Hempstead, Herts, HP2 7DN
T: 01442 213111
F: 01442 236945
E: contact@emico.co
W: www.emico.co

Eminox
Miller Road, Corringham Road Industrial Estate, Gainsborough, Lincolnshire, DN21 1QB
T: 01427 810088
E: enquiries@eminox.com
W: www.eminox.com/

Emission Solutions Ltd (EMSOL)
Sustainable Workspaces, 25 Lavington Street, London, SE1 0NZ
T: 020 3982 9440
E: info@emsol.io
W: www.emsol.io

EMKA
Patricia House, Bodmin Road, Coventry, CV2 5DG
T: 02476 616505
F: 02476 612837
E: enquiries@emka.co.uk
W: www.emka.com/uk_en/

Enable Access
Marshmoor Works, Great North Road, North Mymms, Hatfield, AL9 5SD
T: 0208 2750375
F: 02084490326
E: technical@enable-access.com
W: www.enable-access.com

Enable ID
10-12 The Courtyard, Timothys Bridge Road, Stratford-upon-Avon, CV37 9NP
T: 020 8102 9541
E: hello@enableid.com
W: enableid.com/

Encocam Ltd
5 Stukeley Business Centre, Blackstone Road, Huntingdon, Cambridgeshire, PE29 6EF
T: 01480 435302
W: www.encocam.com/industries/rail

Enerpac
Bentley Rd South, Darlaston, West Midlands, WS10 8LQ
T: 0121 505 0787
F: 0121 505 0799
E: info@enerpac.com
W: www.enerpac.com

EnerSys Ltd
Oak Court, Clifton Business Park,
Wynne Ave, Swinton, Manchester,
M27 8FF
T: 0161 794 4611
F: 0161 727 3809
E: enersys.rail@uk.enersys.com
W: www.enersys.com

Engineered Composites Ltd
Unit 4, Borders 2 Industrial Park, River
Lane, Saltney, Chester, CH4 8RJ
T: 01244 676000
E: info@engineered-composites.co.uk
W: www.engineered-composites.co.uk

Engineering Support Group
See DB ESG

**England's Economic
Heartland (EEH)**
c/o Buckinghamshire County Council,
Walton Street, Aylesbury, HP20 1UA
T: 01296 382703
E: englandseconomicheartland@
buckscc.gov.uk
W: www.englands
economicheartland.com/

Ennstone Johnston
See FP McCann Ltd

ENOTRAC UK Ltd
Chancery House, St Nicholas Way,
Sutton, Surrey, SM1 1JB
T: 020 8770 3501
F: 020 8770 3502
W: www.enotrac.com

Entech Technical Solutions Ltd
1st Floor, Hamilton House, 111
Marlowes, Hemel Hempstead, Herts,
HP1 1BB
T: 01442 898900
F: 01442 898990
E: info@entechts.com
W: www.entechts.com

Enterprise
See Amey

**Enterprise Managed
Services Ltd**
See Amey

**Environmental Management
Solutions Group Holdings Ltd
(EMS)**
Sigeric Business Park, Holme Lacey
Road, Rotherwas, Hereford, HR2 6BQ
T: 01432 263333
F: 01432 263355
W: www.ems-asbestos.co.uk/

**Environmental
Technologies Ltd.**
Grimbald Crag Road, Environmental
Technologies Ltd. Grimbald Crag
Road Knaresborough, HG5 8PY
T: 01423 817200
F: 01423 817400
E: admin@ecolube.co.uk
W: www.etlfluidexperts.com

Envirotech
See LH Group Services

EPC Global
See Talascend Ltd

EQE International
See ABS Consulting

Equib Ltd
Fold House, The Green, Finningley,
Doncaster, DN9 3BP
T: 01200 449709
E: bob.hide@equib.co.uk
W: www.equib.co.uk/

E-Rail
T: 0121 285 2622
E: comms@e-rail.co.uk
W: www.e-rail.co.uk

ERG Transit Systems (UK) Ltd
See Vix Technology

**Ergonomics & Safety Research
Institute (ESRI)**
Holywell Building, Holywell Way,
Loughborough, Leics, LE11 3UZ
T: 01509 226900
F: 01509 226960
E: dsoffice@lboro.ac.uk
W: www.lboro.ac.uk

Eric Wright Group
Sceptre House, Sceptre Way, Bamber
Bridge, Preston, PR5 6AW
T: 01772 698822
F: 01772 628811
E: info@ericwright.co.uk
W: www.ericwright.co.uk

Erlau AG
John Wilson Business Park, Units
10-14, Thanet Way, Whitstable, Kent,
CT5 3QT
T: 01227 276611
W: www.erlauuk.co.uk/

ERM Ltd
2nd Floor, Exchequer Court, 33 St Mary
Axe, London, EC3 8LL
T: 020 3206 5200
F: 020 3206 5440
W: www.erm.com

Ernst & Young LLP
1 More London Place, London,
SE1 2AF
T: 020 7951 1113
F: 020 7951 3167
E: gfavaloro@uk.ey.com
W: www.ey.com/uk

ESAB (UK) Ltd
Hanover House, Queensgate,
Britannia Rd, Waltham Cross, EN8 7TF
T: 01992 768515
F: 01992 788053
E: info@esab.co.uk
W: www.esab.com

ESP Group
68-74 Holderness Rd, Hull, HU9 1ED
T: 01482 384500
W: www.the-espgroup.com

ESR Technology Ltd
202 Cavendish Place, Birchwood Park,
Warrington, Cheshire, WA3 6WU
T: 01925 843400
F: 01925 843500
E: info@esrtechnology.com
W: www.esrtechnology.com

Essempy
1 Phoebe Lane, Church End,
Wavendon, Milton Keynes, MK17 8LR
T: 01908 582491
M: 07967 398431
E: norman.price@essempy.co.uk
W: www.essempy.co.uk

E-T-A Engineering Technology
Telford Close, Aylesbury,
Buckinghamshire, HP19 8DG
T: 01296 420336
F: 01296 488497
E: info@e-t-a.co.uk
W: www.e-t-a.co.uk

ETL Fluid Experts
Grimbald Crag Road, Knaresborough,
North Yorkshire, HG5 8PY
T: 01423 522911
F: 01423 530043
W: www.etlfluidexperts.com

ETS Cable Components
Units 4-6, Red Lion Business Park, Red
Lion Rd, Tolworth, Surrey, KT6 7QD
T: 020 8405 6789
F: 020 8405 6790
E: sales@etscc.co.uk
W: www.etscc.co.uk

Eurailscout GB Ltd
Unit 2, Kimberley Court, Kimberley Rd,
Queens Park, London, NW6 7SL
T: 020 7372 2973
F: 020 7372 5444
E: info@eurailscout.com
W: www.eurailscout.com

Euro Cargo Rail SAS
Immeuble Euralille, 25-29 Place de la
Madelaine, 75008 Paris, France
T: 0033 977 400 000
F: 0033 977 400 200
E: info@eurocargorail.com
W: www.eurocargorail.com

Eurochemi
Kingsbury Park, Midland Rd,
Swadlincote, Derbys, DE11 0AN
T: 01283 222111
F: 01283 550177
E: info@hkw.co.uk
W: www.eurochemi.co.uk

Eurocom Ltd
W013 to W015, Westminster Business
Square, Durham Street, Vauxhall,
London, SE11 5JH
T: 020 7820 8344
F: 020 7820 8355
E: comms@eurocomltd.co.uk
W: www.eurocomlimited.com/

Eurofins York
Unit 1 Ground Floor, Arabesque
House, Monk Cross Drive, York,
YO32 9GW
T: +44 (0) 330 430 3456
E: enquiryyork@eurofins.com
W: www.yorkemc.co.uk

Eurolog Ltd
Orlando House, 3 High St, Teddington,
TW11 8NP
T: 020 8977 4407
F: 020 8977 3714
E: info@eurolog.co.uk
W: www.eurolog.co.uk

**European Association of
Railway Personnel**
32 Greet Road, Lancing, Sussex,
BN15 9NS
T: 01903 521850
E: fam.andrews@yahoo.com

European Investment Bank (EIB)
1 Royal Exchange Buildings, London,
EC3V 3LF
T: 020 7375 9660
F: 020 7375 9699
W: www.eib.org

European Union

Europhoenix
Registered Address, 58a High Street,
Stony Stratford, Milton Keynes,
Buckinghamshire, MK11 1AQ
W: www.europhoenix.eu

Eurostar International Ltd
Times House, Bravingtons Walk,
Regent Quarter, London, N1 9AW
E: press.office@eurostar.co.uk
W: www.eurostar.com

Eurotech Ltd
3 Clifton Court, Cambridge, CB1 7BN
T: 01223 403410
F: 01223 410457
E: sales.uk@eurotech.com
W: www.eurotech.com/en/

Eurox
Aqua House, Buttress Way,
Smethwick, B66 3DL
T: 0121 555 7167
F: 0121 555 7168
E: sales.orders@eurox.co.uk
W: www.eurox.co.uk

Eve Trakway Ltd
Bramley Vale, Chesterfield, Derbys,
S44 5GA
T: 08700 767676
F: 08700 737373
E: mail@evetrakway.co.uk
W: www.evetrakway.co.uk

Everdelta
Rua Mar da China, 1, Office 1.3,
1990-137 Lisbon, Portugal
T: (+351) 210 200 000
E: info@everdelta.com
W: https://everdelta.com/

Evergrip Ltd
Unit 4, Flaxley Rd, Selby, YO8 4BG
T: 01757 212744
F: 01757 212749
E: sales@evergrip.com
W: www.evergrip.com

Eversheds
1 Royal Standard Place, Nottingham,
NG1 6FZ
T: 0845 497 9797
F: 0845 497 4919
W: www.eversheds.co.uk

Eversholt Rail (UK) Ltd
Ground Floor, WeWork 1 Warehouse
Square, 138-142 Holborn, London,
EC1N 2ST
T: 020 7380 5051
E: enquiries@eversholtrail.co.uk
W: www.eversholtrail.co.uk

evo rail
4th Floor, Capital House, 25 Chapel
Street, London, NW1 5DH
E: enquiries@evo-rail.com
W: www.evo-rail.com/
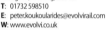

Evolvi Rail Systems Ltd
2nd Floor, Reading Bridge House,
George St, Reading, RG1 8Is
T: 01732 598510
E: peter.koukoularides@evolvirail.com
W: www.evolvi.co.uk

EWS
See DB Cargo (UK)

Excalibur Screwbolts Ltd
Gate 3, Newhall Nursery, Lower Rd,
Hockley, Essex, SS5 5JU
T: 01702 206962/207909
F: 01702 207918
E: charles.bickford@screwbolt.com
W: www.excaliburscrewbolts.com

Exide Technologies
See GNB Industrial Power (UK) Ltd

Exled ITD
Phoenix Mill, London Rd, Stroud, Glos,
GL5 2BU
T: 01453 456361
F: 01453 756505
E: sales@exled.co.uk
W: www.exled.co.uk

Exova (UK) Ltd
6 Coronet Way, Centenary Park,
Salford, M50 1RE
T: 0161 787 3291
F: 0161 787 3251
E: steve.hughes@exova.com
W: www.exova.com

Expamet Security Products
PO Box 14, Longhill Ind. Est. (North),
Hartlepool, TS25 1PR
T: 01429 867366
F: 01429 867355
E: sales@exmesh.co.uk
W: www.expandedmetalfencing.com

Expedition Engineering
Hamilton House, 1 Temple Avenue,
London, EC4Y 0HA
T: 020 7307 1000
F: 020 7307 1001
E: info@expedition.uk.com
W: expedition.uk.com/

Express Electrical
37 Cable Depot Rd, Riverside Ind Est,
Clydebank, G81 1UY
T: 0141 941 3689
F: 0141 952 8155
E: sales@expresselectrical.co.uk
W: www.expresselectrical.co.uk

Express Medicals Ltd
8 City Business Centre, Lower Rd,
London, SE16 2XB
T: 020 7500 6900
F: 020 7500 6910
E: workhealth@expressmedicals.co.uk
W: www.expressmedicals.co.uk

Fabric Architecture Ltd
Unit B4 Nexus, Gloucester Business
Park, Brockworth, GL3 4AG
T: 01452 612800
E: info@fabarc.co.uk
W: fabricarchitecture.com/

Factair Ltd
49 Boss Hall Rd, Ipswich, Suffolk,
IP1 5BN
T: 01473 746400
F: 01473 747123
E: enquiries@factair.co.uk
W: www.factair.co.uk

Faithful & Gould
Euston Tower, 286, Euston Rd, London,
NW1 3AT
T: 020 7121 2121
F: 020 7121 2020
E: info@fgould.com
W: www.fgould.com
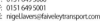

Faiveley Transport Ltd
Morpeth Wharf, Twelve Quays,
Birkenhead, Wirral, CH41 1LF
T: 0151 649 5000
F: 0151 649 5001
E: nigel.lavers@faiveleytransport.com
W: www.faiveleytransport.com

Falcon Electrical Engineering Ltd
Falcon House, Main St, Fallin,
Stirlingshire, FK7 7HT
T: 01786 819920
F: 01786 814381
E: sales@falconelectrical.com
W: www.falconelectrical.com

Farrans
99 Kingsway, Dunmurry, Belfast, Co
Antrim, BT17 9NU
T: 02890 551300
W: https://www.farrans.com/

**Fastrack (Expamet
Security Products)**
PO Box 14, Longhill Ind. Est.(North),
Hartlepool, TS25 1PR
T: 01429 867366
F: 01429 867355
E: sales@exmesh.co.uk
W: www.expanded
metalcompany.co.uk

FCC Construcción
Federico Salmón, 13. 28016, Madrid,
Spain
T: 34 913 595 400
F: 34 913 594 923
W: www.fcc.es/

**Federal Mogul Friction Products
(Ferodo)**
Hayfield Road, Chapel-en-le-Frith,
Derbys, SK23 0JP
T: 01298 811689
F: 01298 811580
W: www.federalmogul.com

Feilden Fowles
8 Royal Street, London, SE1 7LL
T: 020 7033 4594
E: info@feildenfowles.co.uk
W: www.feildenfowles.co.uk

Fenbrook Consulting Ltd
22 Fenbrook Close, Hambrook, Bristol,
BS16 1QJ
T: 0117 970 1773
E: trevor@fenbrook.com
W: www.fenbrook.com

**Fencing
& Lighting Contractors Ltd**
Unit 21, Amber Drive, Bailey Brook Ind
Est, Langley Mill, Derbys, NG16 4BE
T: 01773 531383
F: 01773 531921
E: info@fencingandlighting.co.uk
W: www.fencingandlighting.co.uk/

Fenix Rail Systems
18 Shottery Brook Office Park,
Timothys Bridge Road, Stratford upon
Avon, CV37 9NR
T: 03300 580180
E: enquiries@fenixrailsystems.com
W: www.fenixrailsystems.com

Feonic Technology
3e Newlands Science Park, Inglemire
Lane, Hull, HU6 7TQ
T: 01482 806688
F: 01482 806654
E: info@feonic.com
W: www.feonic.com

Fereday Pollard
30 Kings Bench Street, London,
SE1 0QX
T: 020 7253 0303
E: admin@fereday-pollard.co.uk
W: https://www.fereday-pollard.co.uk/

Ferrabyrne Ltd
Fort Rd Ind. Est, Littlehampton, West
Sussex, BN17 7QU
T: 01903 721317
F: 01903 730452
E: sales@ferrabyrne.co.uk
W: www.ferrabyrne.co.uk

Ferrograph Ltd
Unit 1, New York Way, New York Ind
Park, Newcastle Upon Tyne, NE27 0QF
T: 0191 280 8800
F: 0191 280 8810
E: info@ferrograph.com
W: www.ferrograph.com

Ferrovial Agroman
10th Floor, BSI Building 389, Chiswick
High Road, London, W4 4AL
E: pressheadoffice@ferrovial.com
W: www.faukie.com/

FGD Ltd
Smestow Bridge, Bridgnorth Road,
Wombourne, Wolverhampton,
Staffordshire, WV5 8AY
T: 01902 893226
F: 01902 895283
E: info@fgdltd.co.uk
W: www.fgdltd.co.uk

**Fibergrate
Composite Structures**
5151 Beltline Rd, Ste 1212, Dallas, TX
75254, United States
T: 00 800 527 4043
F: 00 972 250 1530
E: info@fibergrate.com
W: www.fibergrate.com

Fibrelite Composites Ltd
Snaygill Ind. Est, Keighley Rd, Skipton,
N Yorks, BD23 2QR
T: 01756 799773
F: 01756 799539
E: covers@fibrelite.com
W: www.fibrelite.com

EVERSHOLT
UK RAILS GROUP

Owners of UK passenger and freight
rolling stock with more than 25 years'
of experience in the rail industry.

Tel: **+44 20 7380 5051**
www.eversholtrail.co.uk

Fieldfisher LLP
Riverbank House, 2 Swan Lane, London, EC4R 3TT
T: 020 7861 4000
F: 020 7488 0084
M: 07795 267789
E: nicholas.thompsell@fieldfisher.com
W: www.fieldfisher.com

Fifth Dimension Associates Ltd (FDAL)
Suite 18411, 20-22 Wenlock Road, London, N1 7GU
T: 020 7060 2332
F: 020 7060 3325
E: london@fdal.co.uk
W: www.fdal.co.uk

Findlay Irvine Ltd
Bog Rd, Penicuik, Midlothian, EH26 9BU
T: 01968 671200
F: 01968 671237
E: sales@findlayirvine.com
W: www.findlayirvine.com

Finning (UK) Ltd
Unit 3, Triangle Business Park, Oakwell Way, Birstall, Batley, West Yorks, WF17 9LU
T: 0113 201 2065
E: oillab@finning.co.uk
W: www.fluid-analysis.com

Fircroft
Trinity House, 114 Northenden Rd, Sale, Cheshire, M33 3FZ
T: 0161 905 2020
F: 0161 969 1743
E: hq@fircroft.co.uk
W: www.fircroft.co.uk

The Fire Service College
Moreton-in-Marsh, Glos, GL56 0RH
T: 01608 812130
F: 01608 651790
E: dluff@fireservicecollege.ac.uk
W: www.fireservicecollege.ac.uk

Fireclad Ltd
5th Floor, 120 Old Broad Street, London, EC2N 1AR
T: 020 7628 6500
W: www.fireclad.com/

First Call Building Services Ltd
PO Box 45544, 1 Barnby Street, London, NW1 2WB
T: 020 7383 2002

First Choice Protection
See Portwest Clothing Ltd

First Components Ltd
Wallows Ind Est, Wallows Rd, Brierley Hill, DY5 1QA
T: 01384 262068
F: 01384 482383
E: info@firstcomponents.co.uk
W: www.firstcomponents.co.uk

First Engineering Ltd
See Babcock Rail

First Procurement Associates
See FPA Consulting Ltd

First Rail Support Ltd
Unit 20, Time Technology Park, Blackburn Rd, Simonstone, Lancs, BB12 7TG
T: 01282 688110
F: 01282 688141
E: rail.support@firstgroup.com
W: www.firstgroup.com/firstrailsupport

FirstClass Safety & Control Ltd
Unit 1, Industrial Estate, Steeple Road, Mayland, CM3 6AX
T: 01621 743743
M: 07849 896270
E: info@firstclass-safety-control.co.uk
W: www.firstclass-safety-control.co.uk

Firstco Ltd
4 Celbridge Mews, Royal Oak, London, W2 6EU
T: 020 7034 0833
F: 020 7229 8002
E: info@firstco.uk.com
W: www.firstco.uk.com

FirstGroup Plc
395 King St, Aberdeen, AB24 5RP
T: 01224 650100
E: corporate.comms@firstgroup.com
W: www.firstgroupplc.com

FISA (Fabbrica Italiana Sedili Autoferroviari Srl)
Via Giovanni De Simon, 6, 33010 Rivoli di Osoppo (UD), Italy
T: +39 0432 986 071
F: +39 0432 986 086
W: www.fisaitaly.com/

Fishbone Solutions Ltd
7 Pride Point Drive, Pride Park, Derby, DE24 8BX
T: 01332 899190
F: 01332 898560
E: go-fish@fishbonesolutions.co.uk
W: www.fishbonesolutions.co.uk

Fitzpatrick Contractors Ltd
See VolkerFitzpatrick Ltd

FKI Switchgear
See Brush Switchgear

Flash Forward Consulting
M: 07771 828 644
E: enquiries@flashforwardconsulting.co.uk
W: www.flashforwardconsulting.co.uk/

Flexible & Specialist (FS) Cables
Alban Point, Alban Park, Hatfield Rd, St Albans, AL4 0JX
T: 01727 840841
F: 01727 840842
E: sales@fscables.com
W: www.fscables.com

Flexicon Ltd
Roman Way, Coleshill, Birmingham, B46 1HG
T: 01675 466900
F: 01675 466901
E: rail@flexicon.uk.com
W: www.flexicon.uk.com

FLI Structures
Francis & Lewis International, Waterwells Drive, Waterwells Business Park, Gloucester, GL2 2AA
T: 01452 722200
F: 01452 722244
E: m.jones@fli.co.uk
W: www.fliscrewpiles.co.uk

Flint Bishop Solicitors
St Michaels Court, St Michaels Lane, Derby, DE1 3HQ
T: 01332 340211
E: info@flintbishop.co.uk
W: www.flintbishop.co.uk

Flir Systems Ltd (UK)
2 Kings Hill Ave, West Malling, Kent, ME19 4AQ
T: 01732 220011
F: 01732 843707
E: flir@flir.com
W: www.flir.com

Flotec Rail Division
Unit 8, Pavilion Way, Loughborough, Leicestershire, LE11 5GW
T: 01509 230100
E: rail@floteconline.com
W: www.flotecindustrial.com

Flowcrete UK Ltd
The Flooring Technology Centre, Booth Lane, Sandbach, Cheshire, CW11 3QF
T: 01270 753000
F: 01270 753333
E: uk@flowcrete.com
W: www.flowcrete.com

Fluke UK Ltd (Tracklink)
52 Hurricane Way, Norwich, NR6 6JB
T: 020 7942 0700
F: 020 7942 0701
E: industrial@uk.fluke.nl
W: www.fluke.co.uk

Fluor Ltd
Fluor Centre, 140 Pinehurst Road, Farnborough, Hants, GU14 7BF
T: 01252 291000
F: 01252 292222
W: www.fluor.com

Focus 2000 Infrared Ltd
5a Lodge Hill Business Park, Westbury-sub-Mendip, Somerset, BA5 1EY
T: 01749 870620
F: 01749 870622
E: sales@focus2k.co.uk
W: www.focus2k.co.uk

Fone Alarm Installations Ltd
59 Albert Rd North, Reigate, RH2 9EL
T: 01737 223673
F: 01737 224349
E: enquiries@fonealarm.co.uk
W: www.fonealarm.co.uk

Forbo Flooring Ltd
High Holborn Rd, Ripley, Derbys, DE5 3NT
T: 01773 744121
F: 01773 744142
E: bob.summers@forbo.com
W: www.forbo-flooring.co.uk

Ford & Stanley Ltd
44 Royal Scot Rd, Pride Park, Derby, DE24 8AJ
T: 01332 344443
M: 07720 678521
E: rail@fordandstanley.com
W: www.fordandstanley.com

Ford Engineering Group
East Side, Tyne Dock, South Shields, Tyne & Wear, NE33 5ST
T: 0191 454 0141
E: contactus@ford-engineering.com
W: www.ford-engineering.com

ForgeTrack Ltd
Thistle House, St Andrew St, Hertford, SG14 1JA
T: 01992 500900
F: 01992 589495
E: sales@forgetrack.co.uk
W: www.forgetrack.co.uk

ForPeople
1 Pickle Mews, London, SW9 0FJ
T: 020 7820 6070
E: hello@forpeople.com
W: https://forpeople.com/

Forte Engineering
2 Rankine Avenue, East Kilbride, Glasgow, G75 0QF
T: 0141 212 0836
E: info@forte-engineering.co.uk
W: www.forte-engineering.co.uk/

Forwardis Ltd
102-116 rue Victor Hugo, Levallois-Perret, Paris, 92300, France
T: +33 (0)1 85 64 18 00
E: contact@forwardis.com
W: www.forwardis.com

Fosroc Ltd
Drayton Manor Business Park, Coleshill Rd, Tamworth, Staffs, B78 3XN
T: 01827 262222
F: 01827 262444
E: enquiryuk@fosroc.com
W: www.fosroc.com

Fourth Friday Club
Key Publishing, PO Box 100, Stamford, Lincolnshire, PE9 1XQ
T: 01780 755131
W: www.modernrailways.com/fourth-friday-club

Fourway Communication Ltd
Delamere Rd, Cheshunt, Herts, EN8 9SH
T: 01992 629182
F: 01992 639227
E: enquiries@fourway.co.uk
W: www.fourway.co.uk

FP McCann Ltd
Cadeby Depot, Brascote Lane, Cadeby, Nuneaton, Warks, CV13 0BE
T: 01455 290780
F: 01455 292189
E: scarson@fpmccann.co.uk
W: www.fpmccann.co.uk

FPA Consulting Ltd
1 St Andrew's House, Vernon Gate, Derby, DE1 1UJ
T: 01332 604321
F: 01332 604322
E: johnb@fpaconsulting.co.uk
W: www.fpaconsulting.co.uk

Frankham Consultancy Group Ltd
Irene House, 7b Five Arches Business Estate, Maidstone Rd, Sidcup, Kent, DA14 5AE
T: 020 8309 7777
F: 020 8306 7890
E: enquire@frankham.com
W: www.frankham.com

Franklin + Andrews
Sea Containers House, 20 Upper Ground, London, SE1 9LZ
T: 020 7633 9966
F: 020 7928 2471
E: enquiries@franklinandrews.com
W: www.franklinandrews.com

Frauscher UK
Abbey House, 282 Farnborough Road, Farnborough, Hampshire, GU14 7NA
T: 01276 534700
E: office@uk.frauscher.com
W: www.frauscher.com

Frazer-Nash Consultancy Ltd
Stonebridge House, Dorking Business Park, Station Rd, Dorking, Surrey, RH4 1JH
T: 01306 885050
F: 01306 886464
E: t.myall@fnc.co.uk
W: www.fnc.co.uk

Freeman Williams Language Solutions Ltd
College Business Centre, Uttoxeter New Rd, Derby, DE22 3WZ
T: 01332 869342
F: 01332 869344
E: abi@freemanwilliams.co.uk
W: www.freemanwillams.co.uk

Freeths LLP
Cardinal Square, 2nd Floor, West Point, 10 Nottingham Rd, Derby, DE1 3QT
T: 0845 634 9791
F: 0845 634 9804
E: mike.copestake@freeths.co.uk
W: www.freeths.co.uk

Freight Europe (UK) Ltd
See Forwardis Ltd

Freight Systems Express Wales (FSEW)
South Wales International FL Terminal, Newlands Road, Wentloog, Cardiff, CF3 2EU
T: 02920 020900
E: info@fsew.com
W: www.fsew.com

Freight Transport Association (FTA)
Hermes House, St John's Road, Tunbridge Wells, Kent, TN4 9UZ
T: 03717 112 222
F: 01892 552360
E: enquiry@fta.co.uk
W: https://fta.co.uk

FreightArranger Ltd
West View, Brownshill, Stroud, Glos, GL6 8AQ
T: 01453 367150
W: www.freightarranger.co.uk

Freightliner Group Ltd
3rd Floor, 90 Whitfield Street, Fitzrovia, London, W1T 4EZ
T: 03330 169545
F: 020 7200 3975
E: info@gwrr.co.uk
W: www.freightliner.co.uk

Frequentis UK Ltd
Regal House, 70 London Road, Twickenham, TW1 3QS
T: 020 8891 1518
E: marketing@frequentis.com
W: www.frequentis.com

Freshfields Bruckhaus Deringer LLP
65 Fleet St, London, EC4Y 1HT
T: 0207 936 4000
F: 0207 832 7001
E: digitalcommunications@freshfields.com
W: www.freshfields.com

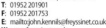

Freshwater
Raglan House, Cardiff Gate Business Park, Cardiff, CF23 8BA
T: 02920 304050
E: hello@freshwater-uk.com
W: www.freshwater-uk.com/

Freyssinet Ltd
Innovation House, Euston Way, Town Centre, Telford, Shropshire, TF3 4LT
T: 01952 201901
F: 01952 201753
E: mailto:john.kennils@freyssinet.co.uk
W: www.freyssinet.co.uk

Frontier Economics
71 High Holborn, London, WC1V 6DA
T: 0207 031 7000
E: hello@frontier-economics.com
W: www.frontier-economics.com/

FS Cables
See Flexible & Specialist (FS) Cables

Fuchs Lubricants (UK) Plc
New Century St, Hanley, Stoke on Trent, ST1 5HU
T: 08701 203700
F: 01782 202072
E: contact-uk@fuchs-oil.com
W: www.fuchslubricants.com

Fuel Integrated
E: hello@fuelintegrated.com
W: fuelintegrated.com

Fuelcare Ltd
Suite 1, The Hayloft, Blakenhall Park, Barton under Needwood, Staffs, DE13 8AJ
T: 01283 712263
F: 01283 262263
E: sales@fuelcare.com
W: www.fuelcare.com

Fugro
Fugro House, Hithercroft Road, Wallingford, OX10 9RB
T: 01491 820700
W: www.fugro.com

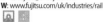

Fujikura Europe Ltd
C51 Barwell Business Park, Leatherhead Rd, Chessington, Surrey, KT9 2NY
T: 020 8240 2000
F: 020 8240 2010
E: sales@fujikura.co.uk
W: www.fujikura.co.uk

Fujitsu
22 Baker Street, London, W1U 3BW
T: 0843 354 7998
E: askfujitsu@uk.fujitsu.com
W: www.fujitsu.com/uk/industries/rail

Fullmen
Fullmen Industrial Park, Kings Road, Canvey Island, Essex, SS8 0SF
T: 01268 683530
W: www.fullmen.com/

Funkwerk Information Technologies York Ltd
See Trapeze Group Rail Ltd

Furneaux Riddall & Co Ltd
Alchorne Place, Portsmouth, Hants, PO3 5PA
T: 02392 668624
F: 02392 668625
E: info@furneauxriddall.com
W: www.furneauxriddall.com

Furrer + Frey
1st Floor, Winchester House, 19 Bedford Row, London, WC1R 4EB
T: 020 3740 5455
M: 07825 258397
E: ndolphin@furrerfrey.ch
W: www.furrerfrey.ch

Furse - Thomas & Betts Ltd
Wilford Rd, Nottingham, NG2 1EB
T: 0115 964 3700
F: 0115 986 0538
E: enquiry@furse.com
W: www.furse.com

Furtex
See Camira Fabrics Ltd

Fuse Rail
Unit D, Concept Court, Shearway Business Park, Folkestone, Kent, CT19 4RG
T: 01233 877780
E: info@fuserail.com
W: fuserail.com

Fusion People Ltd
3700 Parkway, Solent Business Park, Whiteley, PO15 7AW
T: 01489 865200
F: 023 8062 6556
W: www.fusionpeople.com

Future Rail (formerly Future Welding)
The Rowe, Stableford, Staffs, ST5 4EN
T: 01782 411800
E: futureraildesign@gmail.com
W: www.futurerail.co.uk

GAI-Tronics (Hubbell Ltd)
Brunel Dr., Stretton Business Park, Burton upon Trent, DE13 0BZ
T: 01283 500500
F: 01283 500400
E: sales@gai-tronics.co.uk
W: www.gai-tronics.co.uk

Galldris
Galldris House, Pavilion Business Centre, Kinetic Crescent, Innova Science Park, Enfield, EN3 7FJ
T: 01992 763000
E: info@galldris.co.uk
W: https://galldris.co.uk/

Galliford Try Rail
Crab Lane, Fearnhead, Warrington, WA2 0XR
T: 01925 822821
F: 01925 812323
E: babita.pawar@gallifordtry.co.uk
W: www.gallifordtry.co.uk

Gamble Rail
See Keltbray

Ganymede Solutions Ltd
The Derby Conference Centre, London Road, Derby, DE24 8UX
T: 0333 011 2048
E: info@ganymedesolutions.co.uk
W: www.ganymedesolutions.co.uk

Gardiner & Theobald
10 South Crescent, London, WC1E 7BD
T: 020 7209 3000
F: 020 7209 1840
E: p.armstrong@gardiner.com
W: www.gardiner.com

Gardner Denver Ltd
Claybrook Drive, Washford Ind. Est, Redditch, Worcs, B98 0DS
T: 01527 838200
F: 01527 521140
E: hydrovane-info.uk@gardnerdenver.com
W: www.gardnerdenver.com/

Garic Ltd
Kingfisher Park, Aviation Rd, Pilsworth, Bury, BL9 8GD
T: 0844 417 9780
F: 0161 766 8809
E: sales@garic.co.uk
W: www.garic.co.uk

GarrettCom Europe Ltd
See Belden Solutions

Gatecare
Unit N, Tyson Courtyard, Weldon South Industrial Est, Corby, Northamptonshire, NN18 8AZ
T: 01536 266211
F: 01536 261491
E: sales@gatecare.co.uk
W: www.gatecare.co.uk/

Gates Power Transmission
Tinwald Downs Rd, Heath Hall, Dumfries, DG1 1TS
T: 01387 242000
F: 01387 242010
W: www.gates.com

Gatwick Express
See Southern/Gatwick Express

Gauge Communication
Suite S1, Unit 1, Verulam industrial Estate, 224 London Road, St Albans, Herts, AL1 1JB
T: 01727 853952
E: info@gauge-communication.com
W: www.gauge-communication.com/

GAV Access Covers
PO Box 2282, Nuneaton, Warks, CV11 9ZT
T: 02476 381090
F: 02476 373577
E: gavmet@aol.com
W: www.gav-solutions.com

GB Electronics
Ascot House, Mulberry Close, Woods Way, Goring-by-Sea, West Sussex, BN12 4QY
T: 01903 244500
F: 01903 700715
E: matt.s@gbelectronics.com
W: www.gbelectronics.uk

GB Railfreight
3rd Floor, 55 Old Broad Street, London, EC2M 1RX
T: +44 (0)20 7904 3393
F: 020 7983 5113
E: info@gbrailfreight.com
W: www.gbrailfreight.com

GBR-Rail Ltd
Dartmouth House, Bawtry Road, Wickersley, Rotherham, S66 2BL
T: 0800 949 9575
E: sales@gbr-rail.com
W: www.gbr-rail.com

GCRE Ltd
Tramshed Facility, One Central Square, Cardiff, CF10 1FS
W: gov.wales/gcre

GDS Technology Ltd
Unit 6, Cobham Centre, Westmead Industrial Est, Westlea, Swindon, SN5 7UJ
T: 01793 498020
E: sales.gdstechnology@gds.com
W: www.gdstechnology.co.uk

Geatech S.p.A
Via Del Palazzino 6/B, 40051 Altedo (BO), Italy
T: 0039 051 6601514
F: 0039 051 6601309
E: info@geatech.it
W: www.geatech.it

Geismar UK Ltd
Salthouse Rd, Brackmills Ind. Est., Northampton, NN4 7EX
T: 01604 769191
F: 01604 763154
E: sales-uk@geismar.com
W: www.geismar.com

Geldards LLP
Number One, Pride Place, Pride Park, Derby, DE24 8QR
T: 01332 331631
F: 01332 294295
E: michelle.craven-faulkner@geldards.com
W: www.geldards.co.uk

Gemini Rail Services Ltd
Wolverton Works, Stratford Road, Wolverton, Milton Keynes, MK12 5NT
T: 01908 574400
E: info@geminirg.co.uk
W: www.geminirailgroup.co.uk

Gemini Rail Technology Ltd
2 Priestley Wharf, Holt Street, Birmingham, B7 4BN
T: 0121 359 7777
E: info@geminirg.co.uk
W: www.geminirailgroup.co.uk

Gemma Lighting
Unit 3, Marshlands Spur, Farlington, Portsmouth, Hampshire, PO6 1RX
T: 0844 856 5201
F: 0844 856 5209
E: marketing@gemmalighting.com
W: www.gemmalighting.com

GenQuip Plc
Aberafan Rd, Baglan Ind. Park, Port Talbot, SA12 7DJ
T: 01639 823484
F: 01639 822533
E: sales@genquip.co.uk
W: www.genquip.co.uk

Gensler
Aldgate House, 33 Aldgate High Street, London, EC3N 1AH
T: 020 7073 9600
F: 020 7539 1917
W: www.gensler.com/

Genwork Ltd
See Bache Pallets Ltd

Geodesign Barriers Ltd
2 Montgomery Ave, Pinehurst, Swindon, SN2 1LE
T: 01793 538565
E: britt.warg@palletbarrier.com
W: www.geodesignbarriers.com

Geoff Brown Signalling Ltd
The Cottage, Old Lodge, Minchinhampton, Stroud, GL6 9AQ
M: 07977 265721
E: geoffbrownsignalling@btinternet.com

GeoRope
Arumindarrich, West Laroch, Ballachulish, Argyll, PH49 4JG
T: 01855 811224
E: kam@geo-rope.com
W: www.geo-rope.com

Geosynthetics Ltd
Fleming Rd, Harrowbrook Ind.Est., Hinckley, Leics, LE10 3DU
T: 01455 617139
F: 01455 617140
E: sales@geosyn.co.uk
W: www.geosyn.co.uk

Geotechnical Engineering Ltd
Centurion House, Olympus Park, Quedgeley, Glos, GL2 4NF
T: 01452 527743
F: 01452 729314
E: geotech@geoeng.co.uk
W: www.geoeng.co.uk

Geotechnics Ltd
The Geotechnical Centre, 203 Torrington Ave, Tile Hill, Coventry, CV4 9UT
T: 02476 694664
F: 02476 694642
E: mail@geotechnics.co.uk
W: www.geotechnics.co.uk

Getlink
The Channel Tunnel Group Ltd, UK Terminal, Ashford Rd, Folkestone, Kent, CT18 8XX
T: 08443 353535
F: 01303 288784
W: www.eurotunnel.com

Getzner Werkstoffe GmbH
Herrenaus, A-6706 Burs, Austria
T: 0043 5552 2010
F: 0043 5552 201899
W: www.getzner.at

GEW 2 Ltd
Unit 4, Office Village, Keypoint, Keys Road, Alfreton, Derbyshire, DE55 7FQ
T: 0345 508 2057
E: commercialteam@gew2ltd.co.uk
W: www.gew2.co.uk/

Gewiss UK Ltd
2020 Building, Cambourne Business Park, Cambourne, Cambridge, CB23 6DW
T: 01954 712757
F: 01954 712753
E: marketing@gewiss.co.uk
W: www.gewiss.co.uk

GGB UK
Wellington House, Starley Way, Birmingham Int. Park, Birmingham, B37 7HB
T: 0121 767 9100
F: 0121 781 7313
E: greatbritain@ggbearings.com
W: www.ggbearings.com/en

GGR Group Ltd
Broadway Business Park, Broadgate, Chadderton, Oldham, OL9 0JA
T: 0161 683 2580
F: 0161 683 4444
E: info@ggrrail.com
W: www.ggrrail.com

GGS Engineering (Derby) Ltd
Atlas Works, Litchurch Lane, Derby, DE24 8AQ
T: 01332 299345
F: 01332 299678
E: sales@ggseng.com
W: www.ggseng.com

GHD Ltd (Gutteridge, Haskins & Davey Ltd)
Level 6, 10 Fetter Lane, London, EC4A 1BR
T: 020 3077 7900
W: www.ghd.com

Giffen Group
See AMCO Giffen

Gifford
See Ramboll UK Ltd

Giken Europe BV
15 Manchester Mews, London, W1U 2DX
T: 0845 260 8001
F: 0845 260 8002
E: info@giken.co.uk
W: www.giken.com

Gilbarco Veeder-Root
Gilbert Barker House, Burnt Mills Road, Basildon, Essex, SS14 3BA
T: 01268 533090
F: 01268 524214
E: uksales@gilbarco.com
W: www.gilbarco.com

Gillespies
1 St John's Square, London, EC1M 4DH
T: 020 7253 2929
W: www.gillespies.co.uk/

Gioconda Limited
Unit 10, Woodfalls, Gravelly Ways, Laddingford, Maidstone, Kent, ME18 6DA
T: 01622 872512
E: mail@gioconda.co.uk
W: www.gioconda.co.uk

GKD Technik Ltd
17 Cobham Rd, Ferndown Industrial Estate, Wimborne, Dorset, BH21 7PE
T: 01202 861961
F: 01202 861361
E: nick@gkdtechnik.com
W: www.gkdtechnik.com

GKN Hybrid Power
Po Box 55, Ipsley House, Ipsley Church Lane, Redditch, Worcs, B98 0TL
T: 01527 517715
W: www.gkn.com/landsystems/brands/hybrid-power/pages/default.aspx

Glasdon UK Ltd
Preston New Rd, Blackpool, Lancs, FY4 4UL
T: 01253 600410
F: 01253 792558
E: sales@glasdon-uk.co.uk
W: www.glasdon.com

Gleeds
95 New Cavendish St, London, W1W 6XF
T: 020 7631 7000
F: 020 7631 7001
E: london@gleeds.co.uk
W: www.gleeds.com

Glenair UK Ltd
40 Lower Oakham Way, Oakham Business Park, Mansfield, Notts, NG18 5BY
T: 01623 638100
F: 01623 638111
E: sales@glenair.com
W: www.glenair.com

Glendale
The Coach House, Duxbury Hall Road, Duxbury Park, Chorley, Lancs, PR7 4AT
T: 01257 460461
F: 01257 460421
E: info@glendale-services.co.uk
W: www.glendale-services.co.uk/

Glenn Howells Architects
321 Bradford Street, Birmingham, B5 6ET
T: 0121 666 7640
E: mail@glennhowells.co.uk
W: glennhowells.co.uk

Global Centre of Rail Excellence (GCRE)
E: enquiries@gcre.wales
W: https://gov.wales/global-centre-rail-excellence-wales

Global Crossing (UK) Telecommunications Ltd
See Level 3 Communications

Global House Training Services Ltd
1 Cotswold Close, Bexleyheath, Kent, DA7 6ST
T: 01322 331617
F: 01322 341817
E: contact@globalhouse.co.uk
W: www.globalhouse.co.uk

Global Rail Construction Ltd
Unit 20, The IO Centre, Hatfield Business Park, Hearle Way, Hatfield, Hertfordshire, AL10 9EW
T: 0870 990 4074
E: enquiries@grcl.co.uk
W: www.grcl.co.uk/

Global Rail Support
8 Curzon Lane, Alvaston, Derby, DE24 8QS
T: 01332 601596
F: 01332 727494
E: ask@globalrailsupport.com
W: www.globalrailsupport.com

Global Transport Forum
3rd Floor, Petersham House, 57A Hatton Garden, London, EC1N 8JG
T: 020 7045 0900
E: marketing@globaltransportforum.com

GlobalReach Technology
110 Cannon Street, London, EC4N 6EU
T: 020 7831 5630
E: sales@globalreachtech.com
W: globalreachtech.com/

GLS Coatings
Units 1-2 Broncoed Court, Broncoed Business Park, Mold, Flintshire, CH7 1HP
T: 0800 231 5260
E: info@glscoatings.co.uk
W: glscoatings.co.uk/

GME Springs
Unit C, GME Industrial Estate, Coventry, CV6 5NN
T: 02476 664911
F: 02476 663020
E: sales@gmesprings.co.uk
W: www.gmesprings.co.uk

GMI Construction Group
Middleton House, Westland Road, Leeds, West Yorkshire, LS11 5UH
T: 0113 276 0505
E: build@gmicon.co.uk
W: gmiconstructiongroup.co.uk/

GMT Rubber-Metal-Technic Ltd
The Sidings, Station Rd, Guiseley, Leeds, LS20 8BX
T: 01943 870670
F: 01943 870631
E: sales@gmtrubber.com
W: www.gmtrubber.com

GNB Industrial Power (UK) Ltd
Mansell House, Aspinall Close, Middlebrook, Horwich, Bolton, BL6 6QQ
T: 0845 606 4111
F: 0845 606 4112

Go-Ahead Group plc
Head Office, 4 Matthew Parker St, Westminster, London, SW1H 9NP
T: 020 7799 8999
F: 020 7799 8998
E: communications@go-ahead.com
W: www.go-ahead.com

GOBOTiX Ltd
140B Longden Coleham, Shrewsbury, SY3 7DN
T: 01743 387030
E: sales@gobotix.co.uk
W: www.gobotix.co.uk/

Golder Associates (UK) Ltd
1 Alie Street, London, E1 8DE
T: (0)20 7423 0940
F: (0)20 7423 0941
W: www.golder.co.uk

Goldwing Cable Ltd
Unit 8A, Ellough Ind Est, Beccles, Suffolk, NR34 7TD
T: 01502 713161
F: 01502 717773
E: jon@goldwingcable.com
W: www.goldwingcable.com

GoMedia
Evergreen House North, Grafton Place, London, NW1 2DX
T: 020 3691 1873
E: enquiries@gomedia.io
W: www.gomedia.io/

GO-OP Co-operative Ltd
10 East Reach, Taunton, TA1 3EW
E: info@go-op.coop
W: www.go-op.coop

Gordon Services Ltd
Unit 8, Dawes Farm, Ivy Barn Lane, Ingatestone, Essex, CM4 0PX
T: 01277 352895
F: 01277 356115
E: enquiries@gordonservicesltd.co.uk
W: www.gordonservicesltd.co.uk

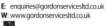

GOS Tool & Engineering Services Ltd
Heritage Court Rd, Gilchrist Thomas ind. Est, Blaenavon, NP4 9RL
T: 01495 790230
F: 01495 792757
E: enquiries@gosengineering.co.uk
W: www.gosengineering.co.uk

Goskills
See People 1st

Go-Tel Communications Ltd
See Samsung Electronics Hainan Fibreoptics

Govia
Go-Ahead Group Rail, Go-Ahead House, 26-28 Addiscombe Rd, Croydon, Surrey, CR9 5GA
E: contact@go-ahead-rail.com
W: www.govia.info

Govia Thameslink Railway (GTR)
1st and 2nd Floor, Monument Place, 24 Monument Street, London, EC3R 8AJ
T: 0345 026 4700
W: www.gtrailway.com/

Gradus Ltd
Park Green, Macclesfield, Cheshire, SK11 7LZ
T: 01625 428922
F: 01625 433949
E: imail@gradusworld.com
W: www.gradusworld.com

GRAHAM
1 Seaward Place, Centurion Business Park, Glasgow, G41 1HH
T: 0141 418 5550
E: glasgow@graham.co.uk
W: www.graham.co.uk

Gramm Barrier Systems Ltd
18 Clinton Place, Seaford, East Sussex, BN25 1NP
T: 01323 872243
F: 01323 872244
E: info@grammbarriers.com
W: www.grammbarriers.com

Gramm Interlink
17-19 High St, Ditchling, East Sussex, BN6 8SY
F: 01275 846397
M: 07827 947086
W: www.gramminerlinkrail.co.uk

Grammer Seating Systems Ltd
Willenhall Lane Ind. Est., Bloxwich, Walsall, WS3 2XN
T: 01922 407035
F: 01922 710552
E: david.bignell@grammer.com
W: www.grammer.com

Gramos Applied Ltd
Orapi Applied Ltd, Spring Rd, Smethwick, West Midlands, B66 1PT
T: 0121 525 4000
F: 0121 525 4950
E: info@gramos-applied.com
W: www.gramos-applied.com

Grand Central Railway Co. Ltd.
Third Floor, Northern House, Rougier Street, York, YO1 6HZ
T: 0345 603 4852
F: 01904 466066
E: customer.services@grandcentralrail.com
W: www.grandcentralrail.co.uk

Grand Union Trains
Fulford Lodge, 1 Heslington Lane, Fulford, York, YO10 4HW

Grant Rail Group
See VolkerRail

Grant Thornton UK LLP
Melton St, Euston Square, London, NW1 2EP
T: 0141 223 0731
E: taylor.ferguson@uk.gt.com
W: www.grant-thornton.co.uk

Grants of Shoreditch
Grant House, Prospect Way, Hutton, Brentwood, Essex, CM13 1XD
T: 01277 236190
F: 01277 212849
E: office@grantsint.com
W: www.grantsint.com/

Grass Concrete Ltd
Duncan House, 142 Thornes Lane, Thornes, Wakefield, WF2 7RE
T: 01924 379443
F: 01924 290289
E: info@grasscrete.com
W: www.grasscrete.com

GrayBar Ltd
10 Fleming Close, Park Farm Ind. Est, Wellingborough, Northants, NN8 6UF
T: 01933 676700
F: 01933 676800
E: sales@graybar.co.uk
W: www.graybar.co.uk

Great British Railways Transition Team (GBRTT)
Waterloo Station General Offices, London, SE1 8SW
E: enquiries@gbrtt.co.uk
W: gbrtt.co.uk

Great Western Railway
Milford House, 1 Milford St, Swindon, SN1 1HL
T: 0345 7000 125
E: fgwfeedback@firstgroup.com
W: www.gwr.com/

Greater Anglia
11th Floor, One Stratford Place, Montfitchet Rd, London, E20 1EJ
T: 020 7904 4031
F: 020 7549 5999
E: contactcentre@greateranglia.co.uk
W: https://www.greateranglia.co.uk/

Green Leader Ltd
21 Foxmoor Close, Oakley, Basingstoke, Hants, RG23 7BQ
T: 01256 781739

Green Light Signalling
1 Bedford Court, Bawtry, Doncaster, South Yorkshire, DN10 6RU

Greenbrier Europe/Wagony Swidnica SA
Ul Strzelinska 35, 58-100 Swidnica, Poland
T: 0048 74 856 2000
F: 0048 74 856 2035
E: europeansales@gbrx.com
W: www.gbrx.com

Greenfold Systems
Pitreavie Drive, Pitreavie Business Park, Dunfermline, Fife, KY11 8UN
T: 01383 731363
W: www.greenfoldsystems.co.uk/

Greengauge 21
28 Lower Teddington Road, Kingston-upon-Thames, Surrey, KT1 4HJ
E: co-ordinator@greengauge21.net
W: www.greengauge21.net

GreenMech Ltd
The Mill Ind. Park, Kings Coughton, Alcester, Warks, B49 5QG
T: 01789 400044
F: 01789 400167
E: sales@greenmech.co.uk
W: www.greenmech.co.uk

Grimshaw Architects
57 Clerkenwell Rd, London, EC1M 5NG
T: 0207 291 4141
E: info@grimshaw.global
W: www.grimshaw.global

Grinsty Rail
Arrow Business Park, Shawbank Road, Lakeside, Redditch, Worcestershire, B98 8YN
T: 01527 514151
E: sales@grinstyrail.co.uk
W: www.grinstyrail.co.uk

GripDeck UK
Unit 1, Chancers Farm, Fossett Lane, Colchester, Essex, CO6 3NY
T: 01206 242494
F: 01206 242496
E: mail@gripdeck.co.uk
W: www.gripdeck.co.uk

Groeneveld Uk Ltd
The Greentec Centre, Gelders Hall Rd, Gelders hall Ind. Est, Shepshed, Leics, LE12 9NH
T: 01509 600033
F: 01509 602000
E: info-uk@groeneveld-group.com
W: www.groeneveld-group.com

Ground Control Ltd
1st Floor, Kingfisher House, Radford Way, Billericay, Essex, CM12 0EQ
T: 01277 650697
F: 01277 630746
E: info@ground-control.co.uk
W: www.ground-control.co.uk/

Groundwise Searches Ltd
Suite 8, Chichester House, 45 Chichester
Rd, Southend on Sea, SS1 2JU
T: 01702 615566
F: 01702 460239
E: mail@groundwise.com
W: www.groundwise.com

GroupCytek
The Oast House, 5 Maed Lane, Farnham, Surrey, GU9 7DY
T: 01252 715171
F: 01252 713271
E: projects@groupcytek.com
W: www.groupcytek.com

GT Engineering (Markyate) Ltd
Unit 4, Pulloxhill Business Park, Greenfield Rd, Pulloxhill, MK45 5EU
T: 01525 718585
E: sales@gtengineering.co.uk
W: www.gtengineering.co.uk

Gummiwerk
See STRAIL (UK) Ltd

Gunnebo UK Ltd
First Floor, Kennicott House, Well Lane, Wednesfield, WV11 1XR
T: +44 (0)370 224 0294
F: 01902 351961
E: enquiries.uk@gunnebo.com
W: www.gunnebo.com

Gutteridge, Haskins & Davey Ltd
See GHD Ltd (Gutteridge, Haskins & Davey Ltd)

G-volution
Trym Lodge, 1 Henbury Road, Bristol, BS9 3HQ
T: 0117 959 6470
F: 0845 052 9345
E: sales@g-volution.co.uk
W: www.g-volution.co.uk

H&M Security Services
476-478 Larkshall Road, London, E4 9HH
T: 020 8523 2227
F: 020 8523 5595
E: info@hmsecurityservices.co.uk
W: www.hmsecurityservices.co.uk/

H.A. Marks Construction Ltd
T: 020 8659 6918
E: info@hamarks.com
W: www.hamarks.co.uk

h2gogo Ltd
The Heights, 59-65 Lowlands Rd, Harrow, Middx, HA1 3AW
T: 01494 817174
E: info@h2gogo.com
W: www.h2gogo.com

HackTrain powered by Hack Partners
Hack Partners, WeWork Old St, 41 Corsham Street, London, N1 6DR
E: hello@hackpartners.com
W: hacktrain.com/

HaCon (UK)
Luminous House, 300 South Row, Milton Keynes, MK9 2FR
T: 0845 835 8688
F: 0049 511 33699-99
E: info@hacon.de
W: www.hacon.de

Hadleigh Castings Ltd
Pond Hall Rd, Hadleigh, Ipswich, Suffolk, IP7 5PW
T: 01473 827281
F: 01473 827879
E: data@hadleighcastings.com
W: www.hadleighcastings.com

Hafren Security Fasteners
Unit 23, Mochdre Industrial Park, Newtown, Powys, SY16 4LE
T: 01686 621300
F: 01686 621800
E: sales@hafrenfasteners.com
W: www.hafrenfasteners.com

Haigh Rail Ltd
Unit 35, Roundhouse Court, Barnes Wallis Way, Buckshaw Village, Chorley, Lancs, PR7 7JN
T: 01772 458000
E: chris@haighrail.com
W: www.haighrail.com

A W Hainsworth & Sons Ltd
See Replin Fabrics

Haki Ltd
Magnus, Tame Valley Ind. Est, Tamworth, Staffs, B77 5BY
T: 01827 282525
F: 01827 250329
E: info@haki.co.uk
W: www.haki.co.uk

Hako Machines Ltd
Eldon Close, Crick, Northants, NN6 7UD
T: 01788 825600
F: 01788 823969
E: sales@hako.co.uk
W: www.hako.co.uk

Halfen Ltd
A1/A2 Portland Close, Houghton Regis, Dunstable, Beds, LU5 5AW
T: 01582 470300
F: 01582 470304
E: info@halfen.co.uk
W: www.halfen.co.uk

HallRail
See Trackwork Ltd

Halo Rail
See Stewart Signs Rail

Hammond (ECS) Ltd
Canal Road, Cwmbach, Aberdare, CF44 0AG
T: 01685 884813
F: 01685 888187

Hanson and Hall Rail Services Solutions
Office 12, Days Space Business Centre, Litchurch Lane, Derby, DE24 8AA
T: 01332 631760
E: info@hansonhallrail.co.uk
W: www.hansonhallrail.co.uk

Hanson Springs
Hanson Place, Gorrells Way, Rochdale, Lancs, OL11 2PX
T: 01706 510600
M: 07780 496290
E: sales@hanson-springs.co.uk
W: www.hanson-springs.co.uk/

Hardstaff Barriers
Hillside, Gotham Road, Kingston on Soar, Nottingham, NG11 0DF
T: 0115 983 2304
E: enquiries@hardstaffbarriers.com
W: www.hardstaffbarriers.com/

Harmill Systems Ltd
Unit P, Cherrycourt Way, Leighton Buzzard, Beds, LU7 4UH
T: 01525 851133
F: 01525 850661
W: www.harmill.co.uk

Harmonic Ltd
The Hatchery, Eaglewood Park, Ilminster, TA19 9DQ
T: 01460 256500
F: 01460 200037
W: www.harmonicltd.co.uk

Harp Visual Communications Ltd
Unit C4, Segensworth Business Centre, Segensworth Road, Fareham, Hants, PO15 5RQ
T: 01329 844005
E: sales@harpvisual.co.uk
W: www.harpvisual.co.uk

Harrington Generators International (HGI)
Ravenstor Rd, Wirksworth, Derbys, DE4 4FY
T: 01629 824284
F: 01629 824613
E: sales@hgigenerators.com
W: www.hgigenerators.com

Harry Fairclough Construction
Howley Lane, Howley, Warrington, Cheshire, WA1 2DN
T: 01925 628300
F: 01925 628301
E: post@harryfairclough.co.uk
W: www.harryfairclough.co.uk

Harry Needle Railroad Company
Rail Maintenance Depot, Babbage Way (off Sandy Lane), Worksop, S80 1UQ
T: 01909 509671
E: harrycneedle@aol.com
W: https://www.harry-needle.co.uk/

Harsco Rail Ltd
Unit 1, Chewton St, Eastwood, Notts, NG16 3HB
T: 01773 539480
F: 01773 539481
E: uksales@harsco.com
W: www.harscorail.com/

Harting Limited
Caswell Rd, Brackmills Ind. Est, Northampton, NN4 7PW
T: 01604 827500
F: 01604 706777
E: gb@harting.com
W: www.harting.co.uk

Harvard Engineering plc
Tyler Close, Normanton, Wakefield, West Yorks, WF6 1RL
T: 0113 383 1000
F: 0113 383 1010
E: johncharles@harvardeng.com
W: www.harvardeng.com

Haskoll
39 Harrington Gardens, London, SW7 4JU
T: 020 7835 1188
F: 020 7373 7230
W: www.haskoll.co.uk/

HaslerRail
Unit A2, Brookside Business Park, Greengate, Middleton, Manchester, M24 1GS
T: 0161 655 6614
E: tim.allard@haslerrail.com
W: www.haslerrail.com

Hawkgrove Ltd
The Rural Enterprise Centre, The Showground, Shepton Mallet, Somerset, BA4 6QN
T: 01373 710777
E: mike.duberry@hawkgrove.co.uk
W: www.hawkgrove.co.uk

Hawkins\Brown
159 St John Street, London, EC1V 4QJ
T: 020 7336 8030
F: 020 7336 8851
E: mail@hawkinsbrown.com
W: www.hawkinsbrown.com/

Hawsons
Pegasus House, 463a Glossop Road, Sheffield, S10 2QD
T: 0114 266 7141
E: email@hawsons.co.uk
W: www.hawsons.co.uk/

Hayley Group Ltd.
Shelah Road, Halesowen, West Midlands, B63 3XL
E: phil.mccabe@hayley-group.co.uk
W: www.hayley-group.co.uk

Haywood and Jackson Fabrication
Denton Drive, Northwich, Cheshire, CW9 7LU
T: 01606 47777
F: 01606 41234
E: info@haywoodandjackson.co.uk
W: www.haywoodandjackson.co.uk/

HBC-radiomatic (UK) Ltd
50 Avenue Road, Aston, Birmingham, B6 4DY
T: 0121 503 6930
F: 0121 333 3996
E: sales@hbc-radiomatic.co.uk
W: www.hbc-radiomatic.co.uk

HBM Test & Measurement
1 Churchill Court, 58 Station Rd, North Harrow, Middx, HA2 7SA
T: 020 8515 6000
F: 020 8515 6002
E: info@uk.hbm.com
W: www.hbm.com

HComm
2b Kettlestring Lane, Clifton Moor, York, YO30 4XF
T: 01904 692790
E: info@hcommrail.co.uk
W: www.hcommrail.co.uk

Health, Safety & Engineering Consultants Ltd (HSEC)
70 Tamworth Rd, Ashby de la Zouch, Leics, LE65 2PR
T: 01530 412777
F: 01530 415592
E: hsec@hsec.co.uk
W: www.hsec.co.uk

Healthcare Connections Ltd
Nashleigh Court, 188 Severalls Ave, Chesham, Bucks, HP5 3EN
T: 08456 773002
F: 08456 773004
E: sales@healthcare-connections.com
W: www.healthcare-connections.com

Heat Trace Ltd
Mere's Edge, Chester Rd, Helsby, Frodsham, Cheshire, WA6 0DJ
T: 01928 726451
F: 01928 727846
E: neil.malone@heat-trace.com
W: www.heat-trace.com

Heathrow Express
The Compass Centre, Nelson Road, Hounslow, Middlesex, TW6 2GW
T: 0345 600 1515
W: www.heathrowexpress.com

Heathrow Hub Ltd
60-62, Old London Road, Kingston on Thames, KT2 6QZ
T: 020 3642 1310
E: heathrowhub@boscobelandpartners.com
W: www.heathrowhub.com

Heathrow Southern Railway
Connect House, 133-137 Alexandra Road, London, SW19 7JY
T: 01733 767244
W: heathrowrail.com/

Heavy Haul Power International GmbH
Steigerstrasse 9, 99096 Erfurt, Germany
T: 0049 361 43046714
F: 0049 361 2629971

Hedra
See WSP UK

Hegenscheidt MFD GmbH & CO KG
Hegenscheidt Platz, D-41812 Erkelenz, Germany
T: 0049 2431 86279
F: 0049 2431 86480
E: info@niles-simmons.de
W: www.hegenscheidt-mfd.de

Heimdall UK Ltd
BCS House, Pinfold Road, Bourne, Lincolnshire, PE10 9HT
T: 0843 855 0068
F: 01778 395265
E: info@heimdalluk.co.uk
W: www.heimdalluk.co.uk

Hellermann Tyton
Sharston Green Business Park, 1 Robeson Way, Altrincham Rd, Wythenshawe, Manchester, M22 4TY
T: 0161 947 2200
F: 0161 947 2220
E: sales@hellermanntyton.co.uk
W: www.hellermanntyton.co.uk

Henkel Loctite
Technologies House, Wood Lane End, Hemel Hempstead, Herts, HP2 4RQ
T: 01442 278100
F: 01442 278293
W: www.loctite.com

Henry Williams Ltd
Dodsworth St, Darlington, Co. Durham, DL1 2NJ
T: 01325 462722
F: 01325 245220
E: info@hwilliams.co.uk
W: www.hwilliams.co.uk

Hepworth Rail International
4 Merse Road, Moons Moat North Industrial Estate, Redditch, Worcestershire, B98 9HL
T: 01527 61243
F: 01527 66836
E: rail.web@b-hepworth.com
W: www.b-hepworth.com

Hering UK LLP
Wessex House, Oxford Rd, Newbury, Berks, RG14 1PA
T: 01635 814490
F: 01635 814491
W: www.heringinternational.com

Herrenknecht AG
Schlehenweg 2, 77963 Schwanau, Germany
T: 0049 7824 3020
F: 0049 7824 3403
E: info@herrenknecht.com
W: www.herrenknecht.com

Hertford Controls Ltd
14 Ermine Point, Gentlemens Field, Westmill Rd, Ware, Herts, SG12 0EF
T: 01920 467578
F: 01920 487037
E: info@hertfordcontrols.co.uk
W: www.hertfordcontrols.co.uk

Hevertech
Unit 2, Treefield Industrial Estate, Gildersome, Leeds, LS27 7JU
T: 0113 238 3355
F: 0113 253 5443
E: enquiries@hevertech.co.uk
W: www.hevertech.co.uk/

Hexagon Metrology Ltd
Halesfield 13, Telford, Shropshire, TF7 4PL
T: 0870 446 2667
F: 0870 446 2668
E: enquiry.uk@hexagonmetrology.com
W: www.hexagonmetrology.com/uk

Hiflex Fluidpower
Howley Park Rd, Morley, Leeds, LS27 0BN
T: 0113 281 0031
F: 0113 307 5918
E: sales@hiflex-europe.com
W: www.dunlophiflex.com

High Speed 1 Ltd
See HS1 Ltd

High Speed 2 Ltd
See HS2 Ltd

High Voltage Maintenance Services Ltd
Unit A, Faraday Court, Faraday Rd, Crawley, West Sussex, RH10 9PU
T: 0845 604 0336
F: 01293 537739
E: enquiries@hvms.co.uk
W: www.hvms.co.uk

Highlands and Islands Transport Partnership (HITRANS)
2nd Floor, Rear, 7 Ardross Terrace, Inverness, IV3 5NQ
T: 01463 719002
E: info@hitrans.org.uk
W: https://www.hitrans.org.uk/

Hill Cannon (UK) LLP
Business Centre, Hartwith Way, Harrogate, HG3 2XA
T: 01423 813522
F: 01423 530018
E: harrogate@hillcannon.com
W: www.hillcannon.com

Hill McGlynn
See Randstad CPE

Hilti (GB) Ltd
1 Trafford Wharf Rd, Trafford Park, Manchester, M17 1BY
T: 0800 886 100
F: 0800 886 200
E: gbsales@hilti.com
W: www.hilti.co.uk

HIMA Paul Hildebrandt GmbH
Albert-Bassermann-Str. 28, 68782 Bruehl, Germany
T: +49 06202 709-405
E: hima-uk@hima.com
W: www.hima.com

Hird Rail Services Ltd
Head Office & Factory, Barton Lane, Armthorpe, Doncaster, DN3 3AB
T: 01302 831339
F: 01302 300031
E: info@hirds.co.uk
W: www.hirdrail.com/

Hire Station
Fields Farm Road, Long Eaton, Nottingham, NG10 3FZ
T: 0845 604 5337
F: 0845 668 8999
W: www.hirestation.co.uk/

Hiremasters
See Quickbuild (UK) Ltd

Hitachi ABB Power Grids
Wells House, 65 Boundary Road, Woking, Surrey, GU21 5BS
T: 01483 722777
E: power-grids@hitachi-powergrids.com
W: www.hitachiabb-powergrids.com/

Hitachi Capital Vehicle Solutions Ltd
Kiln House, Kiln Rd, Newbury, Berks, RG14 2NU
T: 01635 574640
W: www.hitachicapitalvehiclesolutions.co.uk

Hitachi Information Control Systems Europe
Manvers House, Kingston Rd, Bradford-on-Avon, Wilts, BA15 1AB
T: 01225 860140
F: 01225 867698
E: contact_us@hitachi-infocon.com
W: www.hitachi-infocon.com/

Hitachi Rail Ltd
7th Floor, 1 New Ludgate, 60 Ludgate Hill, London, EC4M 7AW
T: 020 3904 4000
F: 020 7970 2799
E: rail.enquiries@hitachirail-eu.com
W: www.hitachirail-eu.com

HJ Skelton & Co Ltd
9 The Broadway, Thatcham, Berks, RG19 3JA
T: 01635 866877
E: email@hjskelton.com
W: www.hjskelton.co.uk

HOCHTIEF (UK) Construction Ltd
Epsilon, Windmill Hill Business Park, Whitehill Way, Swindon, Wilts, SN5 6NX
T: 01793 755555
F: 01793 755556
E: enquiries@hochtief.co.uk
W: www.hochtief-construction.co.uk/

Hodge Clemco Ltd
36 Orgreave Drive, Handsworth, Sheffield, South Yorks, S13 9NR
T: 0114 254 8811
F: 0114 254 0250
E: sales@hodgeclemco.co.uk
W: www.hodgeclemco.co.uk

Hogia Transport Systems Ltd
24 Old Queen Street, London, SW1H 9HP
E: info@hogia.se
W: www.hogia.se

HOK International Ltd
Qube, 90 Whitfield St, London, W1T 4EZ
T: 020 7636 2006
F: 020 7636 1987
E: hokcontact@hok.com
W: www.hok.com

Holdtrade UK
No. 1, The Rubicon, 51 Norman Road, Greenwich, London, SE10 9QB
T: 020 8293 5999
F: 020 8293 7123
E: holdtrade@holdtrade.co.uk
W: www.holdtrade.co.uk/

Holland Company
1000 Holland Drive, Crete, Illinois, 60417 USA, United States
T: 001 708 672 2300
F: 001 708 672 0119
E: sales@hollandco.com
W: www.hollandco.com

Holmar Rail Services
Kendal House, The Street, Shadoxhurst, Ashford, Kent, TN26 1LU
T: 01233 731007
F: 01233 733221
W: www.holmar.co.uk

Holmatro Group
Lissenveld 30, P.O. Box 66, 4940 AB, Raamsdonksveer, Netherlands
T: +31 (0) 162 751 480
E: info@holmatro.com
W: www.holmatro.com/

Holophane Rail Solutions
Bond Avenue, Bletchley, Milton Keynes, Bucks, MK1 1JG
T: 01908 649292
F: 01908 367618
E: info@holophane.co.uk
W: www.holophane.co.uk

Homegrown Timber (Rail) Ltd
Courtlands, Antlands Lane, Shipley Br, Surrey, RH6 9TE
T: 01293 821321
F: 01293 772319
E: rail@homegrowntimber.com
W: www.homegrowntimber.com

Hook-up Solutions Ltd (Hooka)
Unit 1, Royston Road, Baldock, Herts, SG7 6PA
T: 01462 499642
M: 07788 594796
E: charles.sterling@hookup-solutions.com
W: www.thehooka.co.uk

Hoppecke Industrial Batteries Ltd
Unit 2, Centre 500, Lowfield Drive, Wolstanton, Newcastle-under-Lyme, Staffs, ST5 0UU
T: 01782 667306
F: 01782 667314
E: sales@hoppecke.co.uk
W: www.hoppecke.co.uk

Horizon Utility Supplies Ltd
Unit 1, Windmill Business Park, Windmill Road, Clevedon, North Somerset, BS21 6SR
T: 01275 342700
E: enquiries@hor-i-zon.com
W: www.horizonutilitysupplies.com

Hosiden Besson Ltd
11 St Josephs Close, Hove, East Sussex, BN3 7EZ
T: 01273 861166
F: 01273 777501
E: info@hbl.co.uk
W: www.hbl.co.uk

Houghton International
Ronnie Mitten Works, Shields Road, Newcastle upon Tyne, NE6 2YL
T: 0191 234 3000
E: info@houghton-international.com
W: www.houghton-international.com

House of Commons Transport Commitee
7th Floor, 14 Tothill Street, House of Commons, London, SW1H 9NB
T: 020 7219 3266
E: transcom@parliament.uk
W: www.parliament.uk/business/committees/committees-a-z/commons-select/transport-committee

Howarth & Co Consultancy Ltd
39 Ordnance Hill, St John's Wood, London, NW8 6PS
T: 020 7586 5770
F: 020 7586 6556
W: www.howarthandco.com

Howells Railway Products Ltd
Longley Lane, Sharston Ind. Est., Wythenshawe, Manchester, M22 4SS
T: 0161 945 5567
F: 0161 945 5597
E: info@howells-railway.co.uk
W: www.howells-railway.co.uk

Howmet Fastening Systems
Johnson Lane, Ecclesfield, Sheffield, S35 9XH
T: 01952 290011
E: enquiries@hfsindustrial.com
W: www.hfsindustrial.com

HPR Consult
See Rendel Limited

HR Kilns Ltd
Unit 5 & 7, Gorsey Place, Gillibrands, Skelmersdale, Lancs, WN8 9UP
T: 01695 557711
E: sales@hrkilns.com
W: www.hrfibreglass.co.uk/

HRD Rail Fabrications
3 Acorn Business Centre, Northarbour Road, Portsmouth, PO6 3TH

HS Carlsteel Engineering Ltd
Suite B, Hailey Road Industrial Estate, 68 Hailey Road, Erith, Kent, DA18 4AU
T: 020 8312 1879
F: 020 8320 9480
E: admin@hscarlsteel.co.uk
W: www.hscarlsteel.co.uk

HS1 Ltd
5th Floor, Kings Place, 90 York Way, London, N1 9AG
T: 020 7014 2700
E: wendy.spinks@highspeed1.co.uk
W: https://highspeed1.co.uk/

HS2 Ltd
One Canada Square, London, E14 5AB
T: 020 7944 4908
E: hs2enquiries@hs2.org.uk
W: www.hs2.org.uk

HSBC Rail (UK)
See Eversholt Rail (UK) Ltd

HSS Training Ltd
Circle House, Lostock Rd, Davyhulme, Manchester, M41 0HS
T: 0845 766 7799
F: 0161 877 9074
E: training@hss.com
W: www.hsstraining.com

Huber + Suhner (UK) Ltd
Telford Rd, Bicester, Oxon, OX26 4LA
T: 01869 364100
F: 01869 249046
E: info.uk@hubersuhner.com
W: www.hubersuhner.co.uk

Hull Trains
Floor 4 Europa House, 184 Ferensway, Hull, HU1 3UT
T: 0345 071 0222
E: customer.services@hulltrains.co.uk
W: www.hulltrains.co.uk

Human Reliability
1 School House, Higher Lane, Dalton, Lancs, WN8 7RP
T: 01257 463121
F: 01257 463810
E: dembrey@humanreliabilty.com
W: www.humanreliability.com

Hunslet Barclay
See Brush Barclay

Hunslet Engine Co
See LH Group Services

John F Hunt
London Road, Grays, Essex, RM20 4DB
T: 01375 366700
W: www.johnfhunt.co.uk

HurleyPalmerFlatt
NWS House, 1e High Street, Purley, Surrey, CR8 2AF
T: 020 8763 5900
W: www.hurleypalmerflatt.com/

Husqvarna Construction Products
Unit 4, Pearce Way, Bristol Rd, Gloucester, GL2 5YD
T: 0844 844 4570
E: husqvarna.construction@husqvarna.co.uk
W: www.husqvarna.co.uk

Hutchinson Team Telecom Ltd
See Indigo Telecom Group

HV Wooding Ltd
Range Rd Industrial Estate, Hythe, Kent, CT21 6HG
T: 01303 264471
F: 01303 262408
E: sales@hvwooding.co.uk
W: www.hvwooding.co.uk

HW Martin (Fencing Contractors) Ltd
Fordbridge Lane, Blackwell, Alfreton, Derbys, DE55 5JY
T: 01773 813214
F: 01773 813339
E: fencing@hwmartin.com
W: www.hwmartin.com

Hyder Consulting (UK) Ltd
Manning House, 22 Carlisle Place, London, SW1P 1JA
T: 020 3014 9000
F: 020 7828 8428
E: mahmoud.alghita@hyderconsulting.com
W: www.hyderconsulting.com

HydraPower Dynamics Ltd
St Marks Street, Birmingham, B1 2UN
T: 0121 4565 656
F: 0121 4565 668
E: salesoffice@hdl.uk.net
W: www.hydrapower-dynamics.com

Hydraulic Pumps (UK) Ltd
Summit 2, Mangham Rd, Barbot Hill Ind. Est, Rotherham, S61 4RJ
T: 01709 360370
F: 01709 372913
E: sales@hydraulicpumps.co.uk
W: www.hydraulicpumps.co.uk

Hydrex Equipment UK Ltd
See TXM Plant Ltd

Hydro
Pantglas Ind. Est., Bedwas, Caerphilly, CF83 8DR
T: 01773 549300
E: marketing.extrusion.uk@hydro.com
W: www.hydro.com/en-us

Hydrotech Europe Ltd
Beaufort Court, 11 Roebuck Way, Knowlhill, Milton Keynes, MK5 8HL
T: 01908 675244
F: 01908 397513
E: enquiries@hydro-usl.com
W: www.hydro-usl.com

Hydrotechnik UK Ltd
1 Central Park, Lenton Lane, Nottingham, NG7 2NR
T: 01159 003550
F: 01159 868875
E: sales@hydrotechnik.co.uk
W: www.hydrotechnik.co.uk

Hyperdrive Innovation
Future Technology Centre, Barmston Court, Nissan Way, Sunderland, Tyne and Wear, SR5 3NY
T: 0191 640 4586
E: info@hyperdriveinnovation.com
W: https://hyperdriveinnovation.com

Hypertac UK
36-38 Waterloo Rd, London, NW2 7UH
T: 020 8450 8033
F: 020 8208 4114
E: info@hypertac.co.uk
W: www.hypertac.com

I C Consultants Ltd
58 Prince's Gate, Exhibition Rd, London, SW7 2QA
T: 020 7594 6565
F: 020 7594 6570
E: consultants@imperial.ac.uk
W: www.imperial-consultants.co.uk

IAD Rail Systems
See Network Rail Infrastructure Ltd

Ian Catling Consultancy
Ash Meadow, Bridge Way, Chipstead, CR5 3PX
T: 01737 552225
F: 01737 556669
E: ic@catling.com
W: www.catling.com

Ian Riley
See Riley & Son (E) Ltd

IBI Group (UK) Ltd
One Didsbury Point, 2 The Avenue, Didsbury, Manchester, M20 2EY
T: 0161 696 4980
F: 0844 7440 5012
E: ukandirelandcontactus@ibigroup.com
W: www.ibigroup.com

IBM UK Ltd
PO Box 41, North Harbour, Portsmouth, PO6 3AU
T: 0870 542 6426
W: www.ibm.com

ICEE
20 Arnside Rd, Waterlooville, Hants, PO7 7UP
T: 02392 230604
F: 02392 230605
E: sales@icee.co.uk
W: www.icee.co.uk

Icomera UK
2nd Floor, Victory House, Quayside, Chatham Maritime, Chatham, Kent, ME4 4QU
T: 0870 446 0461
E: sales@icomera.com
W: www.icomera.com

Icon Aerospace Technology
Retford, Nottinghamshire, DN22 6HH
T: 01777 714300
F: 01777 709739
E: info@iconaerotech.com
W: www.iconaerotech.com

Iconsys
Technology House, Hortonwood 33, Telford, TF1 7EX
T: 01952 607300
E: info@iconsys.co.uk
W: www.iconsys.co.uk

ID Computing Ltd
Marble Hall, 80 Nightingale Road, Derby, DE24 8BF
M: 07734 602800
E: info@idcomputing.co.uk
W: www.idcomputing.co.uk

Ideagen
Ergo House, Mere Way, Ruddington Fields Business Park, Nottinghamshire, NG11 6JS
T: 01629 699100
W: www.ideagen.com/

Ideas Limited (Integration Design Ergonomics Applications Solutions)
PO Box 193, Thame, Oxon, OX9 0BR
T: 01844 216896
F: 0970 460 6190
E: info@ideas.ltd.uk
W: www.ideas.ltd.uk

IET
See Institution of Engineering & Technology

IETG Ltd
Cross Green Way, Cross Green Ind. Est., Leeds, LS9 0SE
T: 0113 201 9700
F: 0113 201 9701
E: ietg-info@ietg.co.uk
W: www.ietg.co.uk

IFE (Innovation for Entrance Systems)
See Knorr-Bremse Platform Screen Doors

IFPL
Elm Lane, Calbourne, Newport, Isle of Wight, PO30 4JY
T: 01983 555900
F: 01983 531608
E: enquiries@ifpl.com
W: www.ifpl.com/

igus UK
Caswell Road, Northampton, NN4 7PW
T: 01604 677240
F: 01604 677242
E: sales@igus.co.uk
W: www.igus.co.uk/

Igus UK Limited
Caswell Road, Northampton, Northamptonshire, NN4 7PW
T: 01604 677240
E: sales@igus.co.uk
W: www.igus.co.uk

iGuzzini Illuminazione UK Ltd
Astolat Business Park, Astolat Way, off Old Portsmouth Rd, Guildford, GU3 1NE
T: 01483 468000
F: 01483 468001
E: info@iguzzini.co.uk
W: www.iguzzini.co.uk

Ilecsys Rail
1 Kites Park, Summerleys Road, Princes Risborough, Buckinghamshire, HP27 9PX
T: 01844 397300
E: info@ilecsysrail.co.uk
W: www.ilecsysrail.co.uk

iLine Technologies Ltd/ Channeline International
KG House, Kingsfield Way, Northampton, NN5 7QS
T: 01443 743402
E: hello@i-group.uk.com
W: www.iline.uk.com/

ILME UK Ltd
50 Evans Rd, Venture Point, Speke, Merseyside, L24 9PB
T: 0151 336 9321
F: 0151 336 9326
E: sales@ilmeuk.co.uk
W: www.ilmeuk.co.uk

IM Kelly Rail
The Moorings Business Park,, Channel Way,, Exhall, Coventry, CV6 6RH
T: 02476 644026
F: 02476 367841
E: kgriffiths@imkra.co.uk
W: www.imkelly.co.uk/

Imagerail
Reservoir House, Wetheral Pasture, Carlisle, CA4 8HR
T: 01768 800208
E: andrew@imagerail.com
W: www.imagerail.com

Imetrum Ltd
Unit 4, Farleigh Court, Old Weston Road, Flax Bourton, Bristol, BS48 1UR
T: 01275 464443
E: sales@imetrum.com
W: www.imetrum.com/

IMI Precision Engineering
Blenheim Way, Fradley Park, Lichfield, Staffordshire, WS13 8SY
T: 01543 265000
E: advantage@imi-precision.com
W: www.imi-precision.com/

Impact Reporting
2nd Floor, 24-26 Lever St, Manchester, M1 1DW
T: 0161 660 7949
W: impactreporting.co.uk/

Impreglon UK Limited
Kingsbury Link, Trinity Road, Piccadilly, Tamworth, West Midlands, B78 2EX
T: 01827 871400
F: 01827 871401
E: info@impreglon.co.uk
W: https://www.impreglon.co.uk/

Imtech
TWENTY, 20 Kingston Road, Staines-upon-Thames, Middlesex, TW18 4LG
T: 01784 411600
W: www.imtech.co.uk

In2rail Ltd
Hobbs Hill, Rothwell, Northants, NN14 6YG
F: 01536 711804

Inabensa
1 Lyric Square, London, W6 0NB
T: 0203 5427832
W: www.inabensa.com/web/en/

Inbis Ltd
Club St, Bamber Bridge, Preston, Lancs, PR5 6FN
T: 01772 645000
F: 01772 645001
W: www.inbis.com

Inchmere Design
Swan Close Studios, Swan Close Way, Banbury, Oxon, OX16 5TE
T: 01295 661000
F: 01295 277939
E: mark@inchmere.co.uk
W: www.inchmere.co.uk

Incorporatewear
Edison Rd, Hams Hall National Distribution Park, Coleshill, B46 1DA
T: +44 (0) 1675 432 200
F: 0844 257 0591
E: enquiries@icwuk.com
W: www.incorporatewear.co.uk

Incremental Solutions
York Science Park, Innovation Centre, Innovation Way, York, YO10 5DG
T: 01904 435100
E: contact@incrementalsolutions.co.uk
W: www.incrementalsolutions.co.uk/

Independent Glass Co Ltd
540-550 Lawmoor St, Dixons Blazes Ind. Est, Glasgow, G5 0UA
T: 0141 429 8700
F: 0141 429 8524
E: toughened@independentglass.co.uk
W: www.independentglass.co.uk

Independent Transport Commission (ITC)
70 Cowcross Street, London, EC1M 6EJ
T: 0207 253 5510
E: independenttransportcommission@gmail.com
W: www.theitc.org.uk/

Indigo Telecom Group
Field House, Uttoxeter Old Rd, Derby, DE1 1NH
T: 01332 375570
F: 01332 375673
E: sales@indigotelecomgroup.com
W: www.indigotelecomgroup.com

Industrial Communication Products
The Angel Business Centre, 1 Luton Road, Toddington, Bedfordshire, LU5 6DE
T: 020 3086 9569
F: 020 3002 5648
E: sales@industrialcomms.com
W: www.industrialcomms.co.uk/

Industrial Door Services Ltd
Adelaide St, Crindau Park, Newport, Gwent, NP20 5NF
T: 01633 853335
F: 01633 851989
E: enquiries@indoorserv.co.uk
W: www.indoorserv.co.uk

Industrial Flow Control Ltd
3 Ryder Way, Basildon, Essex, RM17 5XR
T: 01268 596900
F: 01268 728435
E: sales@inflow.co.uk
W: www.inflow.co.uk

Ineco
Southern Cross, Bramble Bill, Balcombe, Haywards Heath, RH17 6HR
T: 01444 811090
W: www.ineco.com/webineco/en

Inflow
See Industrial Flow Control Ltd

Infodev EDI Inc.
1995 Rue Frank-Carrel, Suite 202, Quebec G1N 4H9, Canada
T: 001 418 681 3539
F: 001 418 681 1209
E: info@infodev.ca
W: www.infodev.ca

Infor
1 Lakeside Rd, Farnborough, Hants, GU14 6XP
T: 0800 376 9633
F: 0121 615 8255
E: ukmarketing@infor.com
W: www.infor.co.uk

informatica Software Ltd
6 Waltham Park, Waltham Rd, White Waltham, Maidenhead, Berks, SL6 3JN
T: 01628 511311
F: 01628 511411
E: ukinfo@informatica.com
W: www.informatica.com

Informatiq
Gresham House, 53 Clarendon Rd, Watford, WD17 1LA
T: 01923 224481
F: 01923 224493
E: permanent@informatiq.co.uk
W: www.informatiq.co.uk

Infotec Ltd
The Maltings, Tamworth Rd, Ashby De La Zouch, Leics, LE65 2PS
T: 01530 560600
F: 01530 560111
E: sales@infotec.co.uk
W: www.infotec.co.uk

Infra Safety Services
See ISS Labour

Infrastructure Measurement Solutions Ltd
22 Mallard Way, Pride Park, Derby, DE24 8GX
E: info@bumpbox.eu
W: www.bumpbox.eu/

Infrata
One Fetter Lane, London, EC4A 1BR
T: 020 3440 5920
E: info@infrata.com
W: www.infrata.com/

Instrumentel is a world leading manufacturer of electronics systems for Condition Based Maintenance and precision measurement in extreme environments.

Technology & Products Solutions

instrumentel
MEASURING SUCCESS

Ingersoll Engineers
1 Northumberland Avenue, Trafalgar Square, London, WC2N 5BW
T: 020 7872 5666
E: info@ingersollengineersuk.com
W: www.ingersollengineersuk.com/

INIT Innovations in Transportation Ltd
49 Stoney St, The Lace Market, Nottingham, NG1 1LX
T: 0870 890 4648
F: 0115 989 5461
W: www.init.co.uk

Initiate Consulting Ltd
Edinburgh House, 40 Great Portland Street, London, W1W 7LZ
T: 020 7357 9600
F: 020 7357 9604
E: info@initiate.uk.com
W: www.initiate.uk.com

Inline Track Welding Ltd
Ashmill Business Park, Ashford Rd, Lenham, Maidstone, ME17 2GQ
T: 01622 854730
F: 01622 854731
E: david.thomson@fsmail.net

InnoTrans
Messe Berlin GmbH, Messedamm 22, D-14055 Berlin, Germany
T: 0049 303038 0
F: 0049 303038 2325
E: innotrans@messe-berlin.de
W: www.innotrans.com

Innovative Railway Safety Ltd
Ty Penmynydd, Llangennith, Swansea, SA3 1DT
M: 07974 065798
E: paul@inrailsafe.co.uk
W: www.inrailsafe.co.uk

Innovative Support Systems Ltd (ISS)
15 Fountain Parade, Mapplewell, Barnsley, S Yorks, S75 6FW
T: 01226 381155
F: 01226 381177
E: enquiries@iss-eng.com
W: www.iss-eng.com

The Input Group
Input House, 101 Ashbourne Road, Derby, DE22 3FW
T: 01332 348830
F: 01332 296342
E: info@inputgroup.co.uk
W: www.inputgroup.co.uk

Inside Out Group (Europe) Limited
190 North Gate, Nottingham, NG7 7FT
T: 0115 979 1719
E: info@insideoutgroup.co.uk
W: www.insideoutgroup.co.uk/

Insight Security
Units 1 & 2, Cliffe Ind. Est, South Street, Lewes, E Sussex, BN8 6JL
T: 01273 475500
F: 01273 478800
E: info@insight-security.com
W: www.insight-security.com

Insituform Technologies Ltd
4-8 Brunel Close, Park Farm Industrial Estate, Wellingborough, Northants, NN8 6QX
T: 01933 670500
F: 01933 689249
E: jwatson@insituform.com
W: www.insituform.co.uk

Inspectahire Instrument Co. Ltd
Badentoy Road, Badentoy Industrial Estate, Portlethen, Aberdeen, AB12 4YA
T: 01224 789692
F: 01224 789462
E: enquiries@inspectahire.com
W: www.inspectahire.com

Install CCTV Ltd
10 Rochester Court, Anthonys Way, Rochester, Kent, ME2 4NW
T: 01634 717784
F: 01634 718085
W: www.installcctv.co.uk

Installation Project Services Ltd
53 Ullswater Crescent, Coulsdon, Surrey, CR5 2HR
T: 020 8655 6060
F: 020 8655 6070
E: sales@ips-ltd.co.uk
W: www.ips-ltd.co.uk

Institute of Rail Welding
Granta Park, Great Abington, Cambridge, CB21 6AL
T: 01223 899000
E: iorw@twi.co.uk
W: www.iorw.org

Institute of Railway Research
University of Huddersfield, Queensgate, Huddersfield, HD1 3DH
T: 01484 472030
E: irr.info@hud.ac.uk
W: www.hud.ac.uk/irr

Institute Of Transport Studies, University Of Leeds
34-40 University Road, University of Leeds, Leeds, LS2 9JT
T: 0113 343 5325
F: 0113 343 5334
W: www.its.leeds.ac.uk

Institution of Civil Engineers (ICE)
One Great George St, Westminster, London, SW1P 3AA
T: 020 7222 7722
E: communications@ice.org.uk
W: www.ice.org.uk

Institution of Engineering & Technology
Michael Faraday House, Six Hills Way, Stevenage, Herts, SG1 2AY
T: 01438 313311
F: 01438 765526
E: postmaster@theiet.org
W: www.theiet.org

Institution of Mechanical Engineers (IMechE)
1 Birdcage Walk, Westminster, London, SW1H 9JJ
T: 020 7222 7899
F: 020 7222 4557
E: railway@imeche.org.uk
W: www.imeche.org/

Institution of Railway Signal Engineers (IRSE)
4th Floor, 1 Birdcage Walk, Westminster, London, SW1H 9JJ
T: 020 7808 1180
F: 020 7808 1196
E: hq@irse.org
W: www.irse.org

Instrumentel Ltd
Leeds Innovation Centre, 103 Clarendon Road, Leeds, LS2 9DF
T: 0113 346 6223
E: enquiries@instrumentel.com
W: www.instrumentel.com/

Intamech Ltd
See Arbil Lifting Gear

Intec (UK) Ltd
York House, 76-78 Lancaster Rd, Morecambe, Lancs, LA4 5QN
T: 01524 426777
F: 01524 426888

Integrated Transport Planning Ltd
50 North Thirtieth St, Milton Keynes, MK9 3PP
T: 01908 259718
F: 01908 605747
E: wheway@itpworld.net
W: www.itpworld.net

Integrated Utility Services
Unit 8, Brindley Way, 41 Industrial Estate, Wakefield, West Yorks, WF2 0XQ
T: 0800 0737373
E: enquiries@ius.co.uk
W: www.ius.co.uk

Integrated Water Services Ltd
Green Lane, Walsall, WS2 7PD
T: 01543 445700
F: 01543 445717
E: contact@integrated-water.co.uk
W: www.integrated-water.co.uk

Intelligent Data Collection Ltd
4 Pocketts Yard, Cookham, Berks, SL6 9SL
T: 0845 003 8747
E: info@intelligent-data-collection.com
W: www.intelligent-data-collection.com

Intelligent Glass Protection (IGP)
16 Hillbottom Rd, High Wycombe, Bucks, HP12 4HJ
T: 0800 448 8855
F: 01494 462675
E: sales@igpsolutions.com
W: www.igpsolutions.com

Intelligent Locking Systems
Bordesley Hall, Alvechurch, Birmingham, B48 7QA
T: 01527 68885
F: 01527 66681
E: info@ilslocks.co.uk
W: www.ilslocks.co.uk

InterCity RailFreight
T: 0845 125 9659
E: info@intercityrailfreight.com
W: intercityrailfreight.com/

Interface Fabrics Ltd
See Camira Fabrics Ltd

Interfaces
2 Valley Close, Hertford, SG13 8BD
T: 01992 422042
E: reg.harman@ntlworld.com

Intermodality Ltd
Owlsbrook House, New Pond Lane, Heathfield, East Sussex, TN21 0NA
T: 0845 130 4388
F: 01435 867637
E: info@intermodality.com
W: www.intermodality.com

International Engineering
314 W. Pitkin Ave, Pueblo, Colorado 81004, United States
E: info@i-engr.com
W: www.i-engr.com/

International Institute of Obsolescence Management (IIOM)
Unit 3, Curo Park, Frogmore, St Albans, Herts, AL2 2DD
T: 01727 876029
E: admin@theiiom.org
W: www.theiiom.org

International Rail
PO Box 153, Alresford, Hants, SO24 4AQ
T: 0871 231 0790
F: 0871 231 0791
E: sales@internationalrail.com
W: www.internationalrail.com

International Transport Intermediaries Club Ltd
See ITIC

Interserve plc
Interserve House, Ruscombe Park, Twyford, Berks, RG10 9JU
T: 0118 932 0123
F: 0118 932 0206
E: info@interserve.com
W: www.interserve.com

Intertek NDT
Unit 10A, Victory Park, Victory Road, Derby, DE24 8ZF
T: 01332 275700
E: ndt@intertek.com
W: www.intertek.com

Intertrain (UK) Ltd
Balby Court Business Campus, Balby Carr Bank, Doncaster, DN4 8DE
T: 0844 800 3397
E: sales@intertrain.biz
W: www.intertrain.biz

Intoware
The Ingenuity Centre, Jubilee Campus, University of Nottingham, Nottingham, NG7 2TU
T: 0115 977 8969
E: hello@intoware.com
W: https://www.intoware.com/

Intuitive Interim & Executive Search
22 Top o'th Lane, Brindle, Chorley, Lancashire, PR6 8PA
M: 07801 995094
E: nina.lockwood@intuitiverecruitment.com
W: www.intuitiverecruitment.com

Invensys Rail Ltd
See Siemens Mobility Ltd

Invertec Interiors Ltd
Trimdon Grange Industrial Estate, Trimdon Grange, County Durham, TS29 6PE
T: 01429 882210
E: sales@invertec.co.uk
W: www.invertec.co.uk

Ionbond Ltd
Unit 36, Number One Ind Est, Medomsley Rd, Consett, Co Durham, DH8 6TS
T: 01207 500823
F: 01207 590254
E: maria.beadle@ionbond.com
W: www.ionbond.com

Ipex Consulting Ltd
Liberty House, 222 Regent Street, London, W1B 5TR
T: 020 3642 5893
E: accounts@ipexconsulting.com
W: www.ipexconsulting.com

IPPR
4th Floor, 14 Buckingham Street, London, WC2N 6DF
T: 020 7470 6100
F: 020 7470 6111
W: www.ippr.org/

IQM Software
Unit 2, Hove Technology Centre, St Josephs Close, Hove, East Sussex, BN3 7ES
T: 01293 226136
E: support@iqmsoftware.co.uk
W: www.iqmsoftware.co.uk

IQPC
129 Wilton Road, London, SW1V 1JZ
T: 020 7368 9300
F: 020 7368 9301
E: enquire@iqpc.co.uk
W: www.iqpc.co.uk

Iridium Onboard
Clue House, Petherton Rd, Hengrove, Bristol, BS14 9BZ
T: 01275 890140
W: www.iridiumonboard.com

iris-GMBH
Ostendstraße 1-14, Berlin, 12459, Germany
E: mail@irisgmbh.de
W: www.irisgmbh.de

Irish Traction Group
31 Hayfield Rd, Bredbury, Stockport, SK6 1DE
M: 07713 159869
E: info@irishtractiongroup.com
W: www.irishtractiongroup.com

IRL Group Ltd
Unit C1, Swingbridge Rd, Loughborough, Leics, LE11 5JD
T: 01509 217101
F: 01509 611004
E: info@irlgroup.com
W: www.irlgroup.com

Ironside Farrar
111 McDonald Rd, Edinburgh, EH7 4NW
T: 0131 550 6500
E: mail@ironsidefarrar.com
W: www.ironsidefarrar.com

Irvine-Whitlock
Brickstone House, Priory Business Park, Bedford, MK44 3JW
T: 01234 832300
F: 01234 832400
W: www.irvine-whitlock.co.uk/en

ISC
Best Practice Consultancy Ltd
Lower Market Hall Offices, Market St, Okehampton, Devon, EX20 1HN
T: 01837 54555
E: isc@ischq.com
W: www.isc-bestpractice consultancy.co.uk

Ischebeck Titan
John Dean House, Wellington Rd, Burton upon Trent, Staffordshire, DE14 2TG
T: 01283 515677
F: 01283 516126
E: sales@ischebeck-titan.co.uk
W: www.ischebeck-titan.co.uk

IS-Rayfast Ltd
2 Lydiard Fields, Great Western Way, Swindon, Wilts, SN5 8UB
T: 01793 616700
F: 01793 644304
E: sales@israyfast.com
W: www.israyfast.com

ISS Labour
Unit 5, Sidney Robinson Business Park, Ascot Drive, Derby, DE24 8EH
T: 01332 37082
E: info@isslabour.co.uk
W: www.isslabour.co.uk

ITAL Group Ltd
Unit 2-3, Ridgeway Office Park, Bedford Road, Petersfield, Hampshire, GU32 3QF
T: 0844 544 7449
E: info@ital-uk.com
W: www.ital-uk.com/

ITIC
90 Fenchurch St, London, EC3M 4ST
T: 020 7338 0150
F: 020 7338 0151
E: itic@thomasmiller.com
W: www.itic-insure.com

itmsoil Group Ltd
Bell Lane, Uckfield, E Sussex, TN22 1QL
T: 01825 765044
F: 01825 744398
E: sales@itmsoil.com
W: www.itmsoil.com

ITS United Kingdom
Suite 312, Tower Bridge Business Centre, 46-48 East Smithfield, London, E1W 1AW
T: 020 7709 3003
F: 020 7709 3007
E: mailbox@its-uk.org.uk
W: www.its-uk.org.uk

ITSO Ltd
Aurora House, Deltic Ave, Milton Keynes, MK13 8LW
T: 01908 255455
F: 01908 255450
E: info@itso.org.uk
W: www.itso.org.uk

ITT Water & Wastewater UK Ltd
Colwick, Nottingham, NG4 2AN
T: 0115 940 0111
F: 0115 940 0444
W: www.itwww.co.uk

IXC UK Ltd
Innovation Birmingham Campus, Faraday Wharf, Holt St, Birmimgham, B7 4BB
T: 0121 250 5717
E: connect@ixc-uk.com
W: www.ixc-uk.com

Ixthus Instrumentation Limited
The Stables, Williams Barns, Tiffield Road, Towcester, Northants, NN12 6JR
T: 01327 353437
F: 01327 353564
E: info@ixthus.co.uk
W: www.ixthus.co.uk

IXYS Westcode
Langley Park Way, Langley Park, Chippenham, Wilts, SN15 1GE
T: 01249 444524
F: 01249 659448
W: www.ixysuk.com/

J.Boyle Associates Ltd
Bunch Meadows, Woodway, Princes Risborough, Bucks, HP27 0NW
F: 0870 460244
E: info@jba.uk.net
W: www.jba.uk.net

Jabero Consulting Ltd
22 Church Rd, Tunbridge Wells, TN1 1JP
T: 01892 535730
W: www.jaberoconsulting.com

Jacobs Consultancy UK Ltd
See LeighFisher

Jacobs UK Ltd
1180 Eskdale Rd, Winnersh, Wokingham, RG41 5TU
T: 0118 946 7000
F: 0118 946 7001
W: www.jacobs.com

Jactron
Northdown Business Park, Ashford Road, Lenham, Maidstone, Kent, ME17 2DL
T: 01622 852848
W: www.jactron.co.uk/

Jafco Tools Ltd
Anchor Lane, Bliston, Wolverhampton, West Midlands, WV14 9NE
T: 0121 556 7700
F: 0121 556 7788
E: sales@jafcotools.com
W: www.jafcotools.com

James Fisher and Sons plc
Fisher House, PO Box 4, Michaelson Road, Barrow-in-Furness, Cumbria, LA14 1HR
T: 01229 615400
F: 01229 836761
W: www.james-fisher.com

Jasper Products Ltd
Stamford Works, Queens Lane, Bromfield Industrial Estate, Mold, Flintshire, CH7 1JR
T: 01244 531889
E: sales@jasperproducts.co.uk
W: jasperproducts.co.uk

JB Corrie & Co Ltd
Frenchmans Rd, Petersfield, Hants, GU32 3AP
T: 01730 237129
F: 01730 264915
E: mhickman@jbcorrie.co.uk
W: www.jbcorrie.co.uk

JBA Management Consultants
See J.Boyle Associates Ltd

JC Decaux UK
991 Great West Road, Brentford, Middlesex, TW8 9DN
T: 020 8326 7777
W: www.jcdecaux.co.uk

JCB
World Headquarters, Rocester, Staffs, ST14 5JP
T: 01889 590312
F: 01889 593455
W: www.jcb.co.uk

JCPii Ltd
69 Chadwick Way, Hamble, Hampshire, SO31 4FD
T: 02380 197116
E: office@jcpii.co.uk
W: www.jcpii.co.uk/

Jeanette Bowden, Network PR
PO Box 173, Harrogate, North Yorkshire, HG2 8YX
T: 01423 538699
E: jeanette@networkpr.co.uk
W: www.networkpr.co.uk

Jefferson Sheard Architects
Fulcrum, 2 Sidney St, Sheffield, S1 4RH
T: 0114 276 1651
F: 0114 279 9191
E: contactus@jeffersonsheard.com
W: www.jeffersonsheard.com

Jestico + Whiles
1 Cobourg St, London, NW1 2HP
T: 020 7380 0382
E: jw@jesticowhiles.com
W: www.jesticowhiles.com/

Jewers Doors Ltd
Normandy Lane, Stratton Business Park, Biggleswade, Beds, SG18 8QB
T: 01767 317090
F: 01767 312305
E: mjewers@jewersdoors.co.uk
W: www.jewersdoors.co.uk

Jigsaw M2M Ltd
Pemberton Business Centre, Richmond Hill, Pemberton, Wigan, Lancashire, WN5 8AA
T: 01942 621786
E: sales@jigsawm2m.com
W: www.jigsawm2m.com

JLL
30 Warwick Street, London, W1B 5NH
T: 020 7493 4933
W: www.jll.co.uk/

JMJ Laboratories
See Synergy Health Plc

JMP Consultants Ltd
See Systra UK

Jnction
Unit 1, 33 Waterson Street, London, E2 8HT
T: 020 3011 1008
E: hello@jnction.uk
W: https://jnction.uk/

Jobson James - Specialist Rail Supply Chain Insurance
148 Leadenhall Street, London, EC3V 4QT
T: 020 7983 9039
E: rail@jobson-james.co.uk
W: www.jobson-james-rail.co.uk

John McAslan + Partners
7-9 William Road, London, NW1 3ER
T: 020 7313 6000
F: 020 7313 6001
E: marketing@mcaslan.co.uk
W: www.mcaslan.co.uk/

Johnson Rail
Orchard Ind Est, Toddington, Gloucestershire, GL54 5EB
T: 01242 621362
F: 01242 621554
E: sales@obelixsys.co.uk
W: www.johnson-security.co.uk/

Jonathan Lee Recruitment
3 Sylvan Court, Southfield Business Park, Basildon, Essex, SS15 6TU
T: 01268 455520
F: 01268 455521
E: southfields@jonlee.co.uk
W: www.jonlee.co.uk

Jonathan Roberts Consulting (JRC)
Bridge House, Wanstrow, Somerset, BA4 4TE
M: 07545 641204
E: jrc@jrc.org.uk
W: www.jrc.org.uk

Jones Garrard Move Ltd
7 Beaker Close, Smeeton Westerby, Leics, LE8 0RT
E: michael-rodber@jonesgarrardmove.com
W: www.jonesgarrardmove.com

Jotun Paints (Europe) Ltd
Stather Rd, Flixborough, Scunthorpe, N. Lincs, DN15 8RR
T: 01724 400000
F: 01724 400100
E: csd.flixborough@jotun.co.uk
W: www.jotun.com

Journey4
Blake House, 18 Blake Street, York, YO1 8QG
T: 01823 451199
W: www.journey4.co.uk/

Journeycall Ltd
3 James Chalmers Road, Arbroath Enterprise Park, Kirkton Industrial Estate, Arbroath, DD11 3RQ
T: 01241 730300
E: journeycall@the-espgroup.com
W: www.journeycall.com

JourneyPlan c/o Logan Interactive Ltd
2 Frances Street, Langholm, DG13 0BQ
T: 01387 381046
F: 01387 381046
E: iain@logan.co.uk
W: www.journeyplan.co.uk

JR East (East Japan Railway Company)
1st Floor, Boston House, 63-64 New Broad Street, London, EC2M 1JJ
T: 020 7786 9900
W: www.jreast.co.jp/e/

JSD Research & Development Ltd
14-15 Globe Park, Moss Bridge Road, Rochdale, OL16 5EB
T: 01706 646959
F: 01904 352412
E: info@jsdrail.com
W: www.jsdrail.com

J-Trec (Japan Transport Engineering Company)
3-1 Okawa, Kanazawa-ku, Yokohama 236-0043, Japan
W: https://www.j-trec.co.jp/eng/

Judge 3d
Bellingham House, 2 Huntingdon Street, St Neots, Cambs, PE19 1BG
T: 01480 211080
F: 05601 152019
E: mary.morahan@judge3d.com
W: judge3d.com/

JUMO Instrument Co Ltd
Temple Bank, Riverway, Harlow, Essex, CM20 2DY
T: 01279 635533
F: 01279 625029
E: info.uk@jumo.net
W: www.jumo.co.uk/

Junction 9 Network Ltd
Parkgate House, Ickleton Road, Elmdon, Saffron Walden, Essex, CB11 4LT
T: 01763 838288
M: 07971 498113
E: jhall@j9imaging.co.uk
W: www.j9network.co.uk/

Jura Consultants
7 Straiton View, Straiton Business Park, Loanhead, EH20 9QZ
T: 0131 440 6750
E: admin@jura-consultants.co.uk
W: www.jura-consultants.co.uk

Kaicer Building Envelope Solutions
The Ring Tower Centre, Moorside Rd, Winnall, Winchester, Hants, SO23 7RZ
T: 01962 826500
E: enquiries@kaicer.com
W: www.kaicer.com

Kalmar UK Limited
2 Clayton Way, Oxon Business Park, Shrewsbury, SY3 5AL
T: 01743 298300
E: barry.roberts@kalmarglobal.com
W: www.kalmarglobal.co.uk

Kapsch Group
Unit 2 espace, 26 St Thomas Place, Ely, Cambs, CB7 4EX
T: 01353 644010
F: 01353 611001
E: ktc.uk.info@kapsch.net
W: www.kapsch.net/uk

Karcher Vehicle Wash
Karcher UK Ltd, Karcher House, Beaumont Rd, Banbury, Oxon, OX16 1TB
T: 01295 752172
F: 01295 752040
E: enquiries@karcher.co.uk
W: www.karchervehiclewash.co.uk

Kavia Moulded Products Ltd
Rochdale Rd, Walsden, Todmorden, West Yorks, OL14 6UD
T: 01706 816696
F: 01706 813822
E: enquiries@kavia.info
W: www.kavia.info

Kaymac Marine & Civil Engineering Ltd
Osprey Business Park, Byng Street, Landore, Swansea, SA1 2NX
T: 01792 301818
F: 01792 645698
E: enquiries@kaymacltd.co.uk
W: www.kaymacmarine.co.uk

Kee Systems
Thornsett Works, Thornsett Rd, Wandsworth, London, SW18 4EW
T: 0208 874 6566
F: 0208 874 5726
E: sales@keesystems.com
W: www.keesystems.com

Kelly Integrated Transport Services Ltd
Unit 21, Kynock Rd, Eley Ind. Est, Edmonton, London, N18 3BD
T: 020 8884 6605
F: 020 8884 6633
E: kitsenquiries@kelly.co.uk
W: www.kelly.co.uk

Keltbray
St Andrews House, Portsmouth Rd, Esher, Surrey, KT10 9TA
T: 020 7643 1000
F: 020 7643 1001
E: enquiries@keltbray.com
W: www.keltbray.com

Keltbray Aspire Rail Ltd
Unit 4a/5b, Crewe Hall Enterprise Park, Weston Lane, Crewe, CW1 6UA
T: 01270 254176
F: 01270 253267
W: www.keltbray.com

Kelvatek Ltd
Bermuda Innovation Centre, St David's Way, Bermuda Park, Nuneaton, Warks, CV10 7SD
T: 02476 320100
F: 02476 641172
E: mail@kelvatek.com
W: www.kelvatek.com/

Kendall Poole Consulting
Pinewood Business Park – TS2, Coleshill Rd, Marston Green, Solihull, B37 7HG
T: 0121 779 0934
E: scm@kendallpoole.com
W: www.kendallpoole.com

Kennedy Solutions
1 Bromley Lane, Chislehurst, Kent, BR7 6LH
T: 020 8468 1016
F: 01689 855261
E: martin@kennedy-solutions.com
W: www.kennedy-solutions.com

Kent Modular Electronics Ltd (KME)
621 Maidstone Rd, Rochester, Kent, ME1 3QJ
T: 01634 830123
F: 01634 830619
E: sales@kme.co.uk
W: www.kme.co.uk

Kent PHK Ltd
Kent House, Lower Oakham Way, Mansfield, Notts, NG18 5BY
T: 01623 421202
F: 01623 421302
E: enquiries@kentphk.co.uk
W: www.kentphk.com/

Kent Stainless (Wexford) Ltd
Ardcavan, Wexford, Republic of Ireland
T: 0800 376 8377
F: 00353 53914 1802
E: info@kentstainless.com
W: www.kentstainless.com

Keolis (UK) Ltd
Evergreen Building North, 160 Euston Rd, London, NW1 2DX
T: 020 3691 1715
E: comms@keolis.co.uk
W: www.keolis.co.uk

KeTech Ltd
Glaisdale Drive East, Bilborough, Nottingham, NG8 4GU
T: 0115 900 5600
F: 0115 900 5601
E: info@ketech.com
W: www.ketech.com

Key Fasteners
Cavalry Hill Industrial Estate, Weedon Bec, Northants, NN7 4PP
T: 01332 207342
E: enquiries@keyfasteners.co.uk
W: www.keyfasteners.co.uk/

Key Publishing
Units 1-4, Gwash Way Industrial Estate, Ryhall Road, Stamford, Lincolnshire, PE9 1XP
T: 01780 755131
F: 01780 757261
W: www.keypublishing.com/

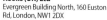

Keyline Builders Merchants
Grove Road, Northfleet, Kent, DA11 9AX
T: 020 7473 5288
F: 020 7473 5171
E: rail@keyline.co.uk
W: www.keyline.co.uk

Keysight Technologies
610 Wharfedale Rd, IQ Winnersh, Wokingham, Berks, RG41 5TP
T: 0800 0260637
F: 01189 276855
E: contactcentre_uk@keysight.com
W: www.keysight.com

Kiel Seating UK Ltd
Regents Pavilion, 4 Summerhouse Road, Moulton Park, Northampton, NN3 6BJ
T: 01604 641148
F: 01604 641149
E: p.scott@kiel-seating.co.uk
W: www.kiel-sitze.de

Kiepe Electric Ltd
Kiepe-Platz 1, 40599 Düsseldorf, Germany
T: +49 (0) 211 74 97-0
F: +49 (0) 211 74 97-300
E: info.kiepe@knorr-bremse.com
W: www.kiepe.knorr-bremse.com

Kier Rail
Tempsford Hall, Station Road, Tempsford, Sandy, Beds, SG19 2BD
T: 01767 355000
F: 01767 355633
E: contact.us@kier.co.uk
W: www.kier.co.uk

Kilborn Consulting Ltd
6th Floor, South Suite, 12 Sheep Street, Wellingborough, Northants, NN8 1BL
T: 01933 279909
F: 01933 276629
E: pmcsharry@kilbornconsulting.co.uk
W: www.kilbornconsulting.co.uk

Kilbride Rail
Bury House, 1-3 Bury Street, Guildford, Surrey, GU2 4AW
T: 01483 569263
F: 01483 577379
E: info@kilbridegroup.com
W: kilbridegroup.com/

Kilfrost Ltd
Albion Works, Haltwhistle, Northumberland, NE49 0HJ
T: 01434 320332
F: 0191 230 0426
E: info@kilfrost.com
W: www.kilfrost.com

Kilnbridge Construction Services Ltd
McDermott House, Cody Rd. Business Park, South Crescent, London, E16 4TL
T: 020 7511 1888
F: 020 7511 1114
E: sales@kilnbridge.com
W: www.kilnbridge.com

Kimberley-Clark Professional
1 Tower View, Kings Hill, West Malling, Kent, ME19 4HA
T: 01732 594000
F: 01732 594060
E: marta.longhurst@kcc.com
W: www.kcprofessional.com/uk

King Rail
King Trailers Ltd, Riverside, Market Harborough, Leics, LE16 7PX
T: 01858 467361
F: 01858 467161
E: info@kingtrailers.co.uk
W: www.kingtrailers.co.uk

Kingfisher Productions
Losinga, PO Box 110, Cullompton, Devon, EX15 9AZ
T: 0333 121 0707
E: roger@kingfisher-prods.demon.co.uk
W: www.railwayvideo.com

Kingston Engineering Co (Hull) Ltd
Pennington St, Hull, HU8 7LD
T: 01438 325676
F: 01438 216438
E: sales@kingston-engineering.co.uk
W: www.kingston-engineering.co.uk

Kirow
Spinnereistraße 13, 04179 Leipzig, Germany
T: 49 341 4953 0
F: 49 341 477 3274
W: www.kranunion.de/nc/en/

KIT Design
International House, Nunnery Drive, Sheffield, S2 1TA
T: 0114 279 8136
E: sales@kitdesignworks.co.uk
W: kitdesignworks.co.uk

KJ Hall Chartered Land & Engineering Surveyors
22 Bower Hinton, Martock, Somerset, TA12 6JY
T: 01935 823423
E: admin@kjhsurvey.co.uk
W: www.kjhsurvey.co.uk

Klauke UK Ltd
Hillside Road East, Bungay, Suffolk, NR35 1JX
T: 01986 891519
E: klauke-info@emerson.com
W: www.klauke.com

Klaxon Signals Ltd
Bradwood Court, St Crispin Way, Haslingden, Lancs, BB4 4PW
T: 01706 234800
E: sales@klaxonsignals.com
W: www.klaxonsignals.com

Kluber Lubrication GB Ltd
Longbow Close, Pennine Business Park, Bradley, Huddersfield, HD2 1GQ
T: 01422 205115
F: 01422 206073
E: sales@uk.klueber.com
W: www.klueber.com

KLW - Wheelco SA
Via San Salvatore 13, PO Box 745, CH-6902 Paradiso-Lugan, Switzerland
T: 0041 91261 3910
F: 0041 91261 3919
E: info@klw-wheelco.ch
W: www.klw.biz

KM&T Ltd
The Techno Centre, Coventry University Technology Park, Puma Way, Coventry, CV1 2TT
T: 02476 236275
E: info@kmandt.com
W: www.kmandt.com

KME
See Kent Modular Electronics Ltd (KME)

KN Network Services
4 Chancerygate Business Centre, South Ruislip, Middlesex, HA4 0JA
T: 020 8845 9292
F: 020 8845 9287
W: knnetworkservices.com/

Knight Architects
Thame House, 9 Castle Street, High Wycombe, Buckinghamshire, HP13 6RZ
T: 01494 525 500
E: info@knightarchitects.co.uk
W: knightarchitects.co.uk

Knorr-Bremse Platform Screen Doors
Knorr-Bremse Rail Systems (UK) Ltd, Westinghouse Way, Hampton Park East, Melksham, Wilts, SN12 6TL
T: 01225 898700
F: 01225 898705
E: david.jeske@knorr-bremse.com
W: www.platformscreendoors.com

Kone UK
Global House, Station Place, Fox Lane North, Chertsey, Surrey, KT16 9HW
T: 0870 770 1122
F: 0870 770 1144
E: sales.marketinguk@kone.com
W: www.kone.com

Konecranes UK Ltd
Unit 1B, Sills Road, Willow Farm Business Park, Castle Donington, Leics, DE74 2US
T: 0844 3246 599
F: 01332 697755
E: sales.uk@konecranes.com
W: www.konecranes.co.uk/

Kontron AG
Units 5&7, Sussex Business Village, Lake Lane, Barnham, West Sussex, PO22 0AL
T: 01243 533900
E: uksales@kontron.com
W: www.kontron.com

Korec Group
Blundellsands House, 34-44 Mersey View, Brighton-le-Sands, Liverpool, L22 6QB
T: 0845 603 1214
F: 0151 931 5559
E: info@korecgroup.com
W: www.korecgroup.com

KPMG
15 Canada Square, Canary Wharf, London, E14 5GL
T: 020 7311 1000
F: 020 7311 3311
W: https://home.kpmg.com/uk/en/home.html

Kroy (Europe) Ltd
Unit 2, 14 Commercial Rd, Reading, Berks, RG2 0QJ
T: 0118 986 5200
F: 0118 986 5205
E: sales@kroyeurope.com
W: www.kroyeurope.com

KS Terminals Inc
21F-2, No 6, Lane 256, Sec 2, Xitun Road, Xitun District, 407 Taichung City, Taiwan
T: 886 2706 6260
M: 886 4758 2786
E: exp@ksterminals.com.tw
W: www.ksterminals.com.tw

KV Mobile Systems Division
See Parker KV Division

Kwik-Step Ltd
Unit 5, Albion Dockside, Hanover Place, Bristol, BS1 6UT
T: 0117 929 1400
F: 0117 929 1404
E: info@kwik-step.com
W: www.kwik-step.com

L&S Waste Management
Pegham Industrial Park, Laveys Lane, Fareham, Hampshire, PO15 6SD
T: 01329 840000
F: 01329 840001
E: info@lswaste.co.uk
W: www.lswaste.co.uk/

L.C. Switchgear Ltd
Unit 16, St Josephs Business Park, St Josephs Close, Hove, East Sussex, BN3 7ES
T: 01273 770540
E: sales@lcswitchgear.com
W: www.lcswitchgear.com/

Laboursite Group Ltd (Rail)
See Wyse Rail Ltd

Lafarge Aggregates (UK) Ltd
Portland House, Bickenhill Lane, Solihull, West Midlands, B37 7BQ
T: 01530 510066
F: 0870 336 8602
E: enquiries@lafargetarmac.com
W: www.aggregate.com

Lagan Construction Group
Rosemount House, 21 – 23 Sydenham Road, Belfast, BT3 9HA, Northern Ireland
T: 028 9045 5531
F: 028 9045 8940
W: www.laganconstructiongroup.com/

Laing O'Rourke Infrastructure
Bridge Place, Anchor Blvd., Admirals Park, Crossways, Dartford, Kent, DA2 6SN
T: 01322 296200
F: 01322 296262
E: info@laingorourke.com
W: www.laingorourke.com

Laing Rail
Western House, 14 Rickfords Hill, Aylesbury, Bucks, HP20 2RX
T: 01296 332108
F: 01296 332126
E: enquiries@laing.com
W: www.laing.com/

Lambert Smith Hampton
UK House, 180 Oxford Street, London, W1D 1NN
T: 020 7198 2000
F: 020 7198 2001
W: www.lsh.co.uk/

Lamifil
Frederic Sheidlaan, B-2620 Hemiksem, Belgium
T: 32 (0)3 8700 611
F: 32 (0)3 8878 059
W: lamifil.be/

Land Sheriffs
Bencroft, Dassels, Braughing, Ware, Hertfordshire, SG11 2RW
T: 0845 257 4567
E: info@landsheriffs.co.uk
W: www.landsheriffs.co.uk/

Landolt + Brown
Unit 13.2.2 The Leathermarket, 11-13 Weston Street, London, SE1 3ER
T: 020 7357 9547
W: https://landoltbrownportfolio.wordpress.com/

Lanes Group Plc - Lanes For Drains
17 Parkside Lane, Parkside Ind. Est, Leeds, LS11 5TD
T: 0800 526488
F: 0161 788 2206
E: sales@lanesfordrains.co.uk
W: www.lanesfordrains.co.uk

Lankelma Limited
Cold Harbour Barn, Cold Harbour Lane, Iden, East Sussex, TN31 7UT
T: 01797 280050
F: 01797 280195
E: info@lankelma.co.uk
W: www.lankelma.com

Lantern Engineering Ltd
Unit 4, Globe Court, Coalpit Road, Denaby Main, Doncaster, DN12 4LH
T: 01709 861008
F: 01709 863623
E: info@lantern.co.uk
W: www.lantern.co.uk

Largam
Unit 9, Oak Industrial Park, Great Dunmow, Essex, CM6 1XN
T: 01371 876121
E: plant@largam.co.uk
W: www.largam.co.uk

Laser Rail
See Balfour Beatty Rail

LB Foster Europe
Stamford St, Sheffield, S9 2TX
T: 0114 256 2225
E: sales@lbfoster.com
W: www.lbfoster.eu

Leadec Limited
2 Academy Drive, Warwick, CV34 6QZ
T: 01926 623550
F: 01926 623551
E: info-uk@leadec-services.com
W: www.leadec-services.com/uk

Leda Recruitment
See McGinley Support Services

Leewood Projects
38 Deacon Rd, Kingston upon Thames, Surrey, KT2 6LU
T: 020 8541 0715
F: 020 8546 4260
E: david.cockle@leewoodprojects.co.uk
W: www.leewoodprojects.co.uk

Legioblock (A Jansen B.V.)
Kanaaldojk Zuid 24, 5691 NL SON, Netherlands
T: 0845 689 0036
F: 0845 689 0035
E: sales@legioblock.com
W: www.legioblock.com

Legion Limited
Hamilton House, Mabledon Place, London, WC1H 9BB
T: 020 7793 0200
E: info@legion.com
W: www.legion.com

Legrand Electric Ltd
Great King St. North, Birmingham, B19 2LF
T: 0121 515 0522
E: legrand.sales@legrand.co.uk
W: www.legrand.co.uk

Leica Geosystems Ltd
Hexagon House, Michigan Drive, Tongwell, Milton Keynes, MK15 8HT
T: 01908 513400
F: 01908 513401
E: uk.sales@leica-geosystems.com
W: www.leica-geosystems.co.uk

Leidos
Skypark 1, 8 Elliot Place, Glasgow, G3 8EP
W: www.leidos.com

LeighFisher
New City Court, 20 St Thomas Street, London, SE1 9RS
T: 0118 946 8152
E: david.bradshaw@leighfisher.com
W: www.leighfisher.com

LEK Consulting
40 Grosvenor Place, London, SW1X 7JL
T: 020 7389 7200
F: 020 7389 7440
E: surfacetransport@lek.com
W: www.lek.com/

LEM UK Ltd
West Lancs Investment Centre, Suite 10, Maple View, White Moss Business Park, Skelmersdale, Lancs, WN8 9TG
T: 01942 388440
F: 01942 388441
E: luk@lem.com
W: www.lem.com

Lemon Consulting
See AMCL Systems Engineering Ltd

Lendlease Consulting
20 Triton St, Regents Place, London, NW1 3BF
T: 020 3430 9000
F: 020 3430 9001
W: www.lendlease.com

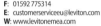

Lesmac (Fasteners) Ltd
73 Dykehead St, Queenslie Ind. Est, Queenslie, Glasgow, G33 4AQ
T: 0141 774 0004
F: 0141 774 2229
E: sales@lesmac.co.uk
W: www.lesmac.co.uk

Level Crossing Installations Ltd
Suite 9, Canterbury Business Centre, 18 Ashchurch Rd, Tewkesbury, Glos, GL20 8BT
T: 01684 278022
W: www.levelcrossinginstallations.co.uk

Leviton Network Solutions
Viewfield Industrial Estate, Glenrothes, KY6 2RS
T: 01592 772124
F: 01592 775314
E: customerserviceeu@leviton.com
W: www.levitonemea.com

Lexicraft Ltd
2 Bromborough Pool Business Park, Price's Way, Bromborough, Wirral, CH62 4LP
T: 0151 647 9281
F: 0151 666 1079
E: rfewtrell@lexicraft.co.uk
W: www.lexicraft.co.uk

Ley Hill Solutions
Beech House, 9 Cheyne Walk, Chesham, Bucks, HP5 1AY
T: 01494 772327
F: 0870 169 5984
E: graham.hull@leyhill.com
W: www.leyhill.com

LGM (UK) Ltd
Unit 18, Apex Court, Woodlands, Bradley Stoke, Bristol, BS32 4JT
T: 0117 321 0827
M: 07547 912197

LH Group Services
Graycar Business Park, Barton-under-Needwood, Burton upon Trent, Staffs, DE13 8EN
T: 01283 722600
F: 01283 722622
E: lh@lh-group.co.uk
W: www.lh-group.co.uk

Liebherr Transportation Systems UK
Liebherr Sunderland Works Ltd, Ayres Quay, Deptford Terrace, Sunderland, SR4 6DD
T: e+44 191 514-3001
F: x+44 191 514-4191
E: info.lsw@liebherr.com
W: www.liebherr.com

Life Environmental Services
4 Ducketts Wharf, South Street, Bishop's Stortford, Hertfordshire, CM23 3AR
T: 01279 503117
F: 01279 503162
W: www.lifeenvironmental.co.uk/

Light Rail Transit Association (LRTA)
138 Radnor Ave, Welling, Kent, DA16 2BY
T: 01179 517785
E: office@lrta.org
W: www.lrta.org

Linbrooke Services Ltd
Sheffield Business Park, Churchill Way, Chapeltown, Sheffield, S35 2PY
T: 0114 232 8290
F: 0844 800 0984
E: info@linbrooke.co.uk
W: www.linbrooke.co.uk

Lindapter International
Lindsay House, Brackenbeck Rd, Bradford, BD7 2NF
T: 01274 521444
F: 01274 521130
E: enquiries@lindapter.com
W: www.lindapter.com

Line Worx Ltd
2nd Floor, Afon Building, Worthing Road, Horsham, West Sussex, RH12 1TL
T: 0333 9000 939
W: www.lineworx.co.uk

Lineside Structure Maintenance
Works Depot, Lilac Grove, Beeston, Nottingham, NG9 1PF
T: 0115 922 5218
F: 0115 967 7516
E: info@lineside.co.uk
W: www.lineside.co.uk/

Liniar Retaining Systems
Flamstead House, Denby Hall Business Park, Denby, Derbyshire, DE5 8JX
T: 01332 883900
E: info@liniar.co.uk
W: www.liniar.co.uk

Link2 Ltd
2 Wortley Road, Deepcar, Sheffield, S36 2UZ
T: 0114 2180475
E: marketing@link-2.biz
W: www.link-2.biz

Linklite Systems Ltd
29 Waterloo Road, Wolverhampton, WV1 4DJ
T: 0345 862 0236
E: sales@linklite.co.uk
W: www.linklite.co.uk

Link-up
See Achilles Information Ltd (Link-Up)

LINSINGER Maschinenbau GmbH
Dr-Linsinger-Strasse 24, A-466 Steyrermühl, Austria
T: 0043 7613 8840 140
F: 0043 7613/8840-951
E: maschinenbau@linsinger.com
W: www.linsinger.com

Liquid Management Solutions Ltd
Creative Industries Centre, Wolverhampton Science Park, Glashier Drive, Wolverhampton, WV10 9TG
T: 0845 450 7373
E: client.services@liquidms.co.uk
W: www.liquidms.co.uk

Lista (UK) Ltd
14 Warren Yard, Wolverton Mill, Milton Keynes, MK12 5NW
T: 01908 222333
E: info@lista.com
W: www.lista.com

Llumar Anti-Grafitti Coating
See CP Films Solutia (UK) Ltd

LML Products Ltd
13 Portemarsh Rd, Calne, Wilts, SN11 9BN
T: 01249 814271
F: 01249 812182
E: sales@lmlproducts.co.uk
W: www.lmlproducts.co.uk

LNT Solutions Ltd
Helios 47, Leeds, LS25 2DY
T: 0113 385 4187
F: 0113 385 3854
E: info@lntsolutions.com
W: www.lntsolutions.com

LoatesHR
32 Friar Gate, Derby, DE1 1BX
T: 01332 890345
E: hello@loates.net
W: https://loateshr.net/

LUSO electronics
EN50155 approved rail power solutions for onboard and trackside applications.
AC/DC and DC/DC offerings in multiple formats.
Contact Luso Electronics – The Power Specialists
www.lusoelectronics.com

Lobo Systems Ltd
Centurion Way Business Park, Alfreton Rd, Derby, DE21 4AY
T: 01332 365666
F: 01332 365661
E: sales@lobosystems.com
W: www.lobosystems.com

Locomotive Services Ltd
Railway Yard, Collett Way, Great Western Industrial Park, Southall, Middlesex, UB2 4SE
W: www.locomotiveservices.co.uk/

Logic Engagements Ltd
45-47 High St, Cobham, Surrey, KT11 3DP
T: 01932 869869
F: 01932 864455
E: info@logicrec.com
W: www.logicrec.com

LogiKal Ltd
27-29, Cursitor St, London, EC4A 1LT
T: 020 7404 4826
E: admin@logikal.co.uk
W: www.logikalprojects.co.uk

Lombard Finance
PO Box 520, Rotherham, South Yorkshire, S63 3BR
T: 0345 877 8888
W: https://www.lombard.co.uk/

London & Continental Railways (LCR)
4th Floor, One Kemble Street, London, WC2B 4AN
T: 020 7391 4300
F: 020 7391 4401
E: rwillis@lcrhq.co.uk
W: www.lcrhq.co.uk/

London North Eastern Railway (LNER)
East Coast House, 25 Skeldergate, York, YO1 6DH
T: 03457 225 333
W: https://www.lner.co.uk/

London Overground
See Arriva Rail London (London Overground)

London Rail
See Transport for London

London TravelWatch
169 Union Street, London, SE1 0LL
T: 020 3176 2999
E: enquiries@londontravelwatch.org.uk
W: www.londontravelwatch.org.uk

London Underground Limited
See Transport for London

Lonsdale Rail
22-24 Cowper Street, London, EC2A 4AP
T: 01753 588750
W: https://www.michaellonsdale.com/divisions/lonsdale-rail/

Look CCTV
Fleetwood Road North, Blackpool, Lancs, FY5 4QD
T: 01253 490399

Loram
3900 Arrowhead Dr., P.O. Box 188, Hamel, MN 55340, United States
T: 1-800-328-1466
W: www.loram.com/

Loram UK
Loram House, 7 Mallard Way, Pride Park, Derby, DE24 8GX
T: 01332 293035
F: 01332 331210
E: enquiries@loram.co.uk
W: https://www.loram.co.uk/

Lordgate Engineering
1 Stonehill, Stukeley Meadows Ind Est, Huntingdon, Cambs, PE29 6ED
T: 01480 455600
F: 01480 454972
E: sales@lordgate.com
W: www.lordgate.com

Lorne Stewart Plc
Stewart House, Orford Park, Greenfold Way, Leigh, Lancs, WN7 3XJ
T: 01942 683333
E: andy.vickers@lornestewart.co.uk
W: www.lornestewart.co.uk

Lowery Ltd
Ashley Place, Hanworth Lane, Chertsey, Surrey, KT16 9JX
T: 01932 564248
E: info@lowery.co.uk
W: www.lowery.co.uk/

LPA Group
Light & Power House, Shire Hill, Saffron Walden, Essex, CB11 3AQ
T: 01799 512800
F: 01799 512826
E: enquiries@lpa-group.com
W: www.lpa-group.com

LPDN - Luhn & Pulvermacher, Dittmann & Neuhaus
See Sogefi Rejna SpA

LSC Group
See Babcock Rail

Lucy Zodion Ltd
Chestnut Lodge, 3 Meeres Lane, Kirton, Lincs, PE20 1PS
T: 01422 317337
E: pwpsales@lucyzodion.com
W: www.lucyzodion.com

Luminator Technology Group
Lanciavej 12C, 7100 Vejle, Denmark
T: 0045 721 93500
F: 0045 721 93501
W: luminator.com

Lumo
4th Floor, Central Square South, Orchard Street, Newcastle-upon-Tyne, NE1 3PG
T: 0345 528 0409
E: customerexperience@lumo.co.uk
W: https://www.lumo.co.uk/

Lundy Projects Ltd
195 Chestergate, Stockport, Cheshire, SK3 0BQ
T: 0161 476 2996
F: 0161 476 3760
E: mail@lundy-projects.co.uk
W: www.lundy-projects.co.uk

LUR - Lucchini Unipart Rail Ltd
Ashburton Road West, Trafford Park, Manchester, M17 1GU
T: 0161 872 0492
F: 0161 872 2895
W: www.lur.co.uk

Luso Electronic Products Ltd
595 Salisbury House, London Wall, London EC2M 5QQ
T: 020 7588 1109
F: 0207 638 7674
E: sales@lusoelectronics.com
W: www.lusoelectronics.com

Luxfer Gas Cylinders
Colwick Industrial Estate, Nottingham, NG4 2BH
T: 0115 980 3800
F: 0115 980 3899
W: www.luxfercylinders.com

Luxfer Superform
Cosgrove Close, Blackpole, Worcester, WR3 8UA
T: 01905 874300
F: 01905 874301
E: superform@luxfer.com
W: www.superforming.com

Luxury Train Club
See Train Chartering (Luxury Train Club)

Lynch Plant Hire
Lynch House, Parr Rd, Stanmore, Middx, HA7 1LE
T: 020 8900 0000
F: 020 8733 2020
E: brucel@l-lynch.com
W: www.l-lynch.com

Lyndon Scaffolding
Valepits Road, Garretts Green, Birmingham, B33 0TD
T: 0121 789 7979
F: 0121 789 7034
E: enquiries@lyndonscaffolding.co.uk
W: www.lyndonscaffolding.co.uk/

M H Southern & Co Ltd
Church Bank Sawmills, Jarrow, Tyne & Wear, NE32 3EB
T: 0191 489 8231
F: 0191 428 0146
E: timber@mhsouthern.co.uk
W: www.mhsouthern.co.uk

M.A.C. Solutions (UK) Ltd
Unit 6-7, Kingfisher Business Park, Arthur St, Lakeside, Redditch, Worcs, B98 8LG
T: 01527 529774
F: 01527 838131
E: sales@mac-solutions.co.uk
W: www.mac-solutions.net

Maber Architects
85 Tottenham Court Rd, London, W1T 4TQ
T: 020 3402 2065
F: 020 7268 3100
E: info@maber.co.uk
W: www.maber.co.uk

Mabey Hire Ltd
Scout Hill, Ravensthorpe, Dewsbury, West Yorkshire, WF13 3EJ
T: 01942 460601
E: marketing@mabeyhire.co.uk
W: www.mabeyhire.co.uk

Mac Roberts LLP
Capella, 60 York St, Glasgow, G2 8JX
T: 0141 303 1100
F: 0141 332 8886
E: carly.mason@macroberts.com
W: www.macroberts.com

Mace Group
155 Moorgate, London, EC2M 6XB
T: 020 3522 3000
E: info@macegroup.com
W: www.macegroup.com

Macemain + Amstad Ltd
Boyle Rd, Willowbrook Ind. Est., Corby, Northants, NN17 5XU
T: 01536 401331
F: 01536 401298
E: sales@macemainamstad.com
W: www.macemainamstad.com

Machines with Vision
CodeBASE, 3 Lady Lawson Street, Edinburgh, EH3 9DR
M: 07481 245147
E: jan.wessnitzer@machineswithvision.com
W: www.machineswithvision.com

Mack Brooks Exhibitions Ltd
Romeland House, Romeland Hill, St Albans, Herts, AL3 4ET
T: 01727 814400
F: 01727 814401
E: railtex@mackbrooks.co.uk
W: www.railtex.co.uk/

Maclay Murray & Spens LLP
One London Wall, London, EC2Y 5AB
T: 0330 222 0050
F: 0330 222 0054
W: www.mms.co.uk/

MacRail Systems Ltd
Units One & Two, Morston Court, Aisecome Way, Weston Super Mare, BS22 8NG
T: 01934 319810
F: 01934 424139
E: info@macrail.co.uk
W: www.macrail.co.uk

Macrete Precast Concrete Engineers
50 Creagh Rd, Toomebridge, Co. Antrim, BT41 3SE
T: 02879 650471
F: 02879 650084
E: info@macrete.com
W: www.macrete.com

Maddox Consulting Ltd
34 South Molton Street, London, W1K 5RG
M: 0788 7575 254
E: info@maddoxconsulting.com
W: www.maddoxconsulting.com

MagDrill
Unit 11, Unthank Road, Bellshill, North Lanarkshire, ML4 1DD
T: 01698 333200
F: 01698 749294
E: sales@magdrill.com
W: www.magdrill.com/

Mainframe Communications Ltd
Network House, Journeymans Way, Temple Farm Ind Est, Southend on Sea, Essex, SS2 5TF
T: 01702 443800
F: 01702 443801
E: info@mainframecomms.co.uk
W: www.mainframecomms.co.uk

Mainline Resourcing Ltd
Suite 214, Business Design Centre, 52 Upper St, London, N1 0QH
T: 0845 083 0245
F: 020 7288 6685
E: info@mainlineresourcing.com
W: www.mainlineresourcing.com

Majorfax Ltd
Charles Street, Walsall, West Midlands, WS2 9LZ
T: 01922 645815
E: castings@majorfax.co.uk
W: www.majorfax.co.uk/

Majorlift
Arnolds Field Estate, Wickwar, Wotton-Under-Edge, Gloucestershire, GL12 8JD
T: 01454 299299
F: 01454 294003
E: info@majorlift.com
W: www.majorlift.co.uk/

Malcolm Rail
Fouldubs, Laurieston Rd, Grangemouth, Falkirk, FK3 8XT
T: 01324 668329
F: 01324 668312
E: turnerd@whm.co.uk
W: www.malcolmgroup.co.uk

Mallatite
Unit 5, Clarendon Drive, The Parkway, Tipton, West Midlands, DY4 0QA
T: 0121 506 4770
F: 0121 506 4771
E: groupsales@mallatite.co.uk
W: www.mallatite.co.uk

Mammoet (UK) Ltd
The Grange Business Centre, Belasis Ave, Billingham, Cleveland, TS23 1LG
T: 0800 111 4449
E: saleseurope@mammoet.com
W: www.mammoet.com

MAN Energy Solutions UK Ltd
Hythe Hill, Colchester, Essex, CO1 2HW
T: 01206 875536
F: 01206 794325
E: phil.hoskins@man-es.com
W: uk.man-es.com / vp185enquiries@man-es.com

Managed Transport Maintenance Solutions (MTMS)
23-25 Hartshorne Road, Woodville, Swadlincote, Derbyshire, DE11 7GT
E: sales@mtms.co.uk
W: www.mtms.co.uk

Manbat Ltd
Lancaster House, Lancaster Road, Shrewsbury, SY1 3NJ
T: 01743 218500
F: 01743 218511
E: sales@manbat.co.uk
W: www.manbat.co.uk

Mane Rail
UCB House, 3 St George St, Watford, WD18 0UH
T: 01923 470720
E: rail@mane.co.uk
W: www.mane.co.uk

Mansell Recruitment Group
Mansell House, Priestley Way, Crawley, West Sussex, RH10 9RU
T: 01293 404050
F: 01293 404122
E: recruitment@mansell.co.uk
W: www.mansell.co.uk

Maple Resourcing
Black Sea House, 72 Wilson Street, London, EC2A 2DH
T: 020 7048 0775
F: 0845 052 9357

Marcroft Engineering Services
See Axiom Rail

Maritime and Rail
E-Business Centre, Consett Business Park, Villa Real, Consett, DH8 6BP
T: 01207 693616
F: 01207 693917
W: www.maritimeandrail.com

Maritime Transport
Clickett Hill Road, Felixstowe, Suffolk, IP11 4AX
T: 01394 617300
F: 01394 617299
E: enquiries@maritimetransport.com
W: www.maritimetransport.com/

Marl International Ltd
Marl Business Park, Morcambe Road, Ulverston, Cumbria, LA12 9BN
T: 01229 582430
F: 01229 585155
E: sales@marl.co.uk
W: www.leds.co.uk

Marsh Bellofram Europe Ltd
9 Castle Park, Queens Drive, Nottingham, NG2 1AH
T: 0115 993 3300
F: 0115 993 3301
E: bellofram@aol.com
W: www.marshbellofram.eu

Marsh Commercial
Hillside Court, Bowling Hill, Chipping Sodbury, Bristol, BS37 6JX
T: 01454 272 727
W: www.marshcommercial.co.uk

Marshalls plc
Landscape House, Premier Way, Lowfields Business Park, Elland, West Yorkshire, HX5 9HT
T: 01422 312000
E: info@marshalls.co.uk
W: www.marshalls.co.uk/commercial

Martek Power Ltd
Glebe Farm Technical Campus, Knapwell, Cambridge, CB23 4GG
T: 01954 267726
F: 01954 267626
E: pippa.keane@martekpower.co.uk
W: www.martekpower.com

Martifer
26 - 28 Hammersmith Grove, London, W6 7BA
T: 020 8834 1348
E: info@martifer.com
W: www.martifer.com/en/

Martin Higginson Transport Research & Consultancy
5 The Avenue, Clifton, York, YO30 6AS
T: 01904 636704
M: 07980 874126
E: mhrcgm@gmail.com
W: www.martinhigginson.co.uk

Martineau
See SGH Martineau LLP

Marubeni-Komatsu
Padgets Lane, Redditch, Worcestershire, B98 0RT
T: 01527 512512
E: customerfeedback@mkl.co.uk
W: www.marubeni-komatsu.co.uk/

Masabi
56 Ayres St, London, SE1 1EU
T: 020 7089 8860
E: kevin@masabi.com
W: www.masabi.com

Matchtech Group
1450 Park Way, Solent Business Park, Whiteley, Fareham, Hants, PO15 7AF
T: 01489 898989
F: 01489 898290
E: info@matchtech.com
W: www.matchtech.com

Matisa (UK) Ltd
PO Box 202, Dawes Lane, Scunthorpe, North Lincolnshire, DN15 6XR
T: +44-1724 786 160
F: +44-1724 786 159
E: matisa@matisa.co.uk
W: www.matisa.ch

Mattei Compressors Ltd
Admington Lane, Admington, Shipston-on-Stour, Warwickshire, CV36 4JJ
T: 01789 450577
F: 01789 450698
E: info@mattei.co.uk
W: https://www.mattei.co.uk/

Maxim Power Tools (Scotland) Ltd
40 Couper St, Glasgow, G4 0DL
T: 0141 552 5591
F: 0141 552 5064
E: akilpatrick@maximpower.co.uk
W: www.maximpower.co.uk

May & Scofield
Stroudley Road, Basingstoke, Hants, RG24 8UG
T: 01256 306800
F: 01256 306810
E: philj@may-scofield.co.uk
W: www.may-scofield.co.uk

May Gurney Rail Services
See Kier Rail

Mayflower Engineering Ltd
Coleridge Road, Sheffield, South Yorkshire, S9 5DA
T: 0114 244 1353
F: 0114 2445977
E: info@mayflower-engineering.co.uk
W: www.mayflower-engineering.co.uk/

Maynard Design Consultancy
5 Baldwin Terrace, London, N1 7RU
T: 020 7724 9500
E: info@maynard-design.com
W: https://www.maynard-design.com/

M-Brain Ltd
County House, 3rd Floor, Friar St, Reading, RG1 1DB
T: 0118 956 5836
F: 0118 956 5850
E: response@esmerk.com
W: www.m-brain.com

MC Electronics
61 Grimsdyke Rd, Hatch End, Pinner, Middlesex, HA5 4PP
T: 020 8428 2027
F: 020 8428 2027
E: info@mcelectronics.co.uk
W: www.mcelectronics.co.uk

Sir Robert McAlpine Ltd
Eaton Court, Maylands Avenue, Hemel Hempstead, Herts, HP2 7TR
T: 01442 233444
F: 01442 230024
E: information@srm.com
W: www.srm.com

McAuley Engineering
21 Ballymena Rd, Ballymoney, County Antrim, Northern Ireland
T: 02827 666646
F: 02827 665150
M: 07730 136660
E: wesley@mcauleyengineering.co.uk
W: mcauleyengineering.co.uk

McCulloch Rail
Craigiemains, Main St, Ballantrae, Girvan, Ayrshire, KA26 0NB
T: 01465 831350
F: 01465 831350
E: enquiries@mccullochrail.com
W: www.mccullochrail.com

McGee Group Ltd
340-342 Athlon Rd, Wembley, Middx, HA0 1BX
T: 020 8998 1001
F: 020 8997 7689
E: mail@mcgee.co.uk
W: www.mcgee.co.uk

McGeoch LED Technology
86 Lower Tower Street, Birmingham, B19 3PA
T: +44 121 687 5850
F: 0121 333 3089
E: sales@mcgeoch.co.uk
W: www.mcgeoch.co.uk

McGinley Support Services
Ground Floor, Edward Hyde Building, 38 Clarendon Rd, Watford, Herts, WD17 1JW
T: 0845 543 5953
F: 0845 543 5956
E: info@mcginley.co.uk
W: www.mcginley.co.uk

B&M McHugh Ltd
429a Footscray Rd, New Eltham, London, SE9 3UL
T: 020 8859 7706
F: 020 8859 9999
E: msg@mchughltd.co.uk
W: www.mchughltd.co.uk

MCL (Martin Childs Ltd)
1 Green Way, Swaffham, Norfolk, PE37 7FD
T: 01760 722275
E: enquiries@martinchilds.com
W: www.martinchilds.com

McLaughlin & Harvey
15 Trench Road, Mallusk, Newtownabbey, BT36 4TY
T: +44 28 9034 2777
E: mclh@mclh.co.uk
W: www.mclh.co.uk/

McNealy Brown Limited - Steelwork
Prentis Quay, Mill Way, Sittingbourne, Kent, ME10 2QD
T: 01795 470592
F: 01795 471238
E: info@mcnealybrown.co.uk
W: www.mcnealybrown.co.uk

McNicholas Rail
Lismirrane Industrial Park, Elstree Road, Elstree, Herts, WD6 3EA
T: 020 8953 4144
F: 01302 380591
E: infrastructure@mcnicholas.co.uk
W: www.mcnicholas.co.uk

MCT Brattberg Ltd
Commerce St, Carrs Ind. Est, Haslingden, Lancs, BB4 5JT
T: 01706 244890
F: 01706 244891
E: info@mctbrattberg.co.uk
W: www.mctbrattberg.co.uk

MDA Rail Ltd
Millbank House, Northway, Runcorn, Cheshire, WA7 2SX
T: 01928 751000
F: 01928 751555
E: railresource@mdarail.com
W: www.mdarail.com

MDL Laser Measurement Systems
See Trimble UK

MDS Transmodal Ltd
5-6 Hunters Walk, Canal St, Chester, CH1 4EB
T: 01244 348301
F: 01244 348471
W: www.mdst.co.uk

Mechan Ltd
Sir John Brown Building, Davy Industrial Park, Prince of Wales Road, Sheffield, S9 4EX
T: 0114 257 0563
F: 0114 245 1124
E: info@mechan.co.uk
W: www.mechan.co.uk

Mechan Technology Ltd
See Zonegreen

MEDC Ltd
Unit B, Sutton Parkway, Oddicroft Lane, Sutton in Ashfield, Notts, NG17 5FB
T: 01623 444400
F: 01623 444531
E: medcadmin@eaton.com
W: www.medc.com

MegaTech Projects
20 Forrestfield Gardens, Newton Mearns, Glasgow, G77 6DZ
T: 0141 778 5165
E: info@megatechprojects.co.uk
W: www.megatechprojects.co.uk/

Melford Technologies Ltd
Units 3 & 4, St Georges Industrial Estate, White Lion Road, Amersham, Buckinghamshire, HP7 9JQ
T: 01494 638069
F: 01494 463358
E: info@melfordtechnologies.com
W: www.melfordtechnologies.com

Mendip Rail Ltd
See Aggregate Industries UK Ltd

Mennekes Electric Ltd
Unit 4, Crayfields Ind. Park, Main Rd, St Pauls Cray, Orpington, Kent, BR5 3HP
T: 01689 833522
F: 01689 833378
E: sales@mennekes.co.uk
W: www.mennekes.co.uk

The Mental Wealth Company Limited
40 Hazelwood Road, Duffield, Belper, Derbyshire, DE56 4AA
M: 07305 843993
E: wendy@thementalwealthcompany.co.uk
W: www.thementalwealthcompany.co.uk

Meon LLP
Railside, Northarbour Spur, Portsmouth, PO6 3TU
T: 02392 200606
F: 02392 200707
E: mail@meonuk.com
W: www.meonuk.com

Merak
Parque Empresarial La Carpetania, C/ Miguel Faraday, 1, 28906 GETAFE - Madrid, Spain
T: +34 911 459 400
F: +34 911 459 444
W: www.merak-hvac.com/en/

Merc Engineering UK Ltd
Lower Clough Hill, Pendle St, Barrowford, Lancs, BB9 8PH
T: 01282 694290
F: 01282 613390
E: sales@merceng.co.uk
W: www.merceng.co.uk

Mercia Charters
PO Box 1926, Coventry, CV3 6ZL
T: 07535 759344
E: team@merciacharters.co.uk
W: www.merciacharters.co.uk

Merebrook Consulting Ltd
Suite 2B, Bridgefoot, Belper, Derbys, DE56 2UA
T: 01773 829988
F: 01773 829393
E: consulting@merebrook.co.uk
W: www.merebrook.co.uk

Meridian Generic Rail
8 Westerdale Road, Greenwich, London, SE10 0LW
W: www.meridian-generic-rail.co.uk/

Mermec
Via Oberdan 70, I-70043 Monopoli (Bari), Italy
T: 0039 080 9171
F: 0039 080 9171 112
E: mermec@mermecgroup.com
W: www.mermecgroup.com

Merseyrail
Rail House, Lord Nelson St, Liverpool, L1 1JF
T: 0151 702 2534
F: 0151 702 3074
W: www.merseyrail.org

Merseytravel
PO Box 1976, Liverpool, L69 3HN
T: 0151 227 5181
E: comments@merseytravel.gov.uk
W: www.merseytravel.gov.uk

Merson Signs
2 Young Place, Kelvin Ind. Est., East Kilbride, Glasgow, G75 0TD
T: 01355 243021
E: web@merson-signs.com
W: www.railsignage.com

Met Systems Ltd
Cottis House, Locks Hill, Rochford, Essex, SS4 1BB
T: 020 3246 1000
F: 020 7712 2146
E: info@metsystems.co.uk
W: www.metsystems.co.uk

Metalweb
Unit 1, Stargate Business Park, Cuckoo Road, Nechells, Birmingham, B7 5SE
T: 0121 326 2900
F: 0121 328 3421
E: info@metalweb.co.uk
W: www.metalweb.co.uk

MeteoGroup UK Ltd
292 Vauxhall Bridge Rd, London, SW1V 1AE
T: 020 7963 7575
F: 020 7963 7599
E: uk@meteogroup.com
W: www.meteogroup.com

Meteor Power Limited
Unit 2245, Silverstone Technology Park, Towcester, Northamptonshire, NN12 8GX
E: mike.edwards@meteorpower.com
W: www.meteorpower.com/

Metham Aviation Design ltd (MADCCTV Ltd)
Unit 5, Station Approach, Four Marks, Alton, Hants, GU34 5HN
T: 01420 565618
F: 01420 565628
E: stuart@madcctv.com
W: www.madcctv.com

Metrail Construction Ltd
Unit 1, 70 Bell Lane, Bellbrook Ind. Est., Uckfield, TN22 1QL
T: 01825 761360
E: nadia@metrail.co.uk
W: www.metrail.co.uk

Metroline
ComfortDelGro House, 3rd Floor, 329 Edgware Road, Cricklewood, London, NW2 6JP
T: 020 8218 8888
F: 020 8218 8899
W: https://www.metroline.co.uk/

Metrolink (Manchester)
Metrolink House, Queens Road, Manchester, M8 0RY
T: 0161 205 8665
E: customerservices@metrolink.co.uk
W: www.metrolink.co.uk

Mettex Electronic Co Ltd
Beaumont Close, Beaumont Road Ind Est, Banbury, Oxon, OX16 1TG
T: 01295 250826
F: 01295 268643
E: sales@mettex.com
W: www.mettex.com

MF Hydraulics
See Centinal Group

MGB Electrical Ltd
See Ilecsys Rail

MGB Engineering Ltd
MGB House, Unit D, Eagle Rd, Langage Business Park, Plympton, Plymouth, PL7 5JY
T: 0845 070 2490
F: 0845 070 2495
E: enquiries@mgbl.co.uk
W: www.mgbl.co.uk

MGF Trench Construction Ltd
Foundation House, Wallwork Road, Astley, Manchester, M29 7JT
T: 01942 402700
E: enquiries@mgf.ltd.uk
W: www.mgf.ltd.uk

Michael Evans & Associates Ltd
34 Station Rd, Draycott, Derbys, DE72 3QB
T: 01332 871840
F: 01332 871841
E: mike@mevans.co.uk
W: www.mevans.co.uk

Mick George Ltd
6 Lancaster Way, Ermine Business Park, Huntingdon, Cambridgeshire, PE29 6XU
T: 01480 498099
F: 01480 498077
E: sales@mickgeorge.co.uk
W: www.mickgeorge.co.uk/rail

Micro-Epsilon UK Ltd
Dorset House, West Derby Rd, Liverpool, L6 4BR
T: 0151 260 9800
F: 0151 261 2480
E: info@micro-epsilon.co.uk
W: www.micro-epsilon.co.uk

Micro-Mesh Engineering Ltd
Innovation House, Dabell Ave, Blenheim Industrial Estate, Nottingham, NG6 8WA
T: 01159 752929
F: 01159 751175
E: enquiries@micro-mesh.co.uk
W: www.micro-mesh.co.uk

Middle Peak Railways Ltd
PO Box 71, High Peak, Derbys, SK23 7WL
T: 0870 881 6743
F: 0870 991 7350
E: info@middlepeak.co.uk
W: www.middlepeak.co.uk

Midland Metro Alliance
W: www.metroalliance.co.uk/

Midland Quarry Products
Leicester Road, Whitwick, Leicestershire, LE67 5GR
T: 01530 831000
F: 01530 832299
E: enquiries@mqp.co.uk
W: www.mqp.co.uk/

Midlands Connect
16 Summer Lane, Birmingham, B19 3SD
W: https://www.midlandsconnect.uk

Mid-West Services
44 Broadway, Stratford, London, E15 1XH
T: 020 3130 0466
F: 020 3070 0065
E: info@midwestservices.co.uk
W: www.midwestservices.co.uk

Mike Worby Survey Consultancy Ltd
37 Ramblers Way, Welwyn Garden City, Herts, AL7 2JU
T: 01707 333677
F: 01707 333677
M: 07767 456196
E: survey@mw-sc.co.uk
W: www.mw-sc.co.uk

Millar Bryce Ltd
5 Logie Mill, Beaverbank Office Park, Logie Green Rd, Edinburgh, EH7 4HH
T: 0131 556 1313
F: 0131 557 5960
E: marketing@millar-bryce.com
W: www.millar-bryce.com

Millcroft Services Plc
Salutation House, 1 Salutation Rd, Greenwich, London, SE10 0AT
T: 020 8305 1988
F: 020 8305 1986
E: sales@millcroft.co.uk
W: www.millcroft.co.uk

Millenium Site Services Ltd
Haydock Park Road, Derby, DE24 8HT
T: 01332 820003
E: lee.birkett@millenium siteservices.co.uk
W: www.milleniumsiteservices.co.uk

Miller Fabrications
Bartonhall Works, Overtown Road, Waterloo, Wishaw, ML2 8EW
T: 01698 373770
E: info@millerfabrications.com
W: www.millerfabrications.com

Mills Ltd
13 Fairway Drive, Fairway Industrial Estate, Greenford, Middlesex, UB6 8PW
T: 020 8833 2626
F: 020 8833 2600
E: sales@millsltd.com
W: www.millsltd.com

Minova
Unit 19, Redbrook Business Park, Wilthorpe Road, Barnsley, S75 1JN
T: 01226 280567
F: 01226 731563
E: globalmarketing@minovaglobal.com
W: www.minovaglobal.com

Mirror Technology Ltd
Redwood House, Orchard Ind Est, Toddington, Glos, GL54 5EB
T: 01242 621534
F: 01242 621529
E: malcolm@mirrortechnology.co.uk
W: www.mirrortechnology.co.uk

Mission Room Ltd
Kings Meadow Campus, Lenton Lane, Nottingham, NG7 2NR
T: 0115 951 6800
F: 0115 954 1002
E: info@missionroom.com
W: www.missionroom.com

DIRECTORY

Mita (UK) Ltd
See Schneider Electric Ltd

Mitchell Bridges Ltd
London Rd, Kingsworthy, Winchester, Hants, SO23 7QN
T: 01962 885040
F: 01962 885040
E: chris@mitchellbridges.com
W: www.temporarybridges.com

MITIE
1 Harlequin Office Park, Fieldfare, Emersons Green, Bristol, BS16 7FN
T: 0117 970 8800
E: info@mitie.com
W: www.mitie.com/

Mitsubishi Electric (Melco)
Travellers
Lane, Hatfield, Herts, AL10 8XB
T: 01707 276100
F: 01707 278693
W: www.mitsubishielectric.co.uk/

Mitsui & Co Europe plc
8th and 9th Floors, 1 St. Martin's Le Grand, London, EC1A 4AS
T: 020 7822 0321
W: www.mitsui.com/eu/

MLM Consulting Engineers Ltd
North Kiln, Felaw Maltings, 46 Felaw Street, Ipswich, Suffolk, IP2 8PN
T: 01473 231100
E: lee.bowker@mlmgroup.com
W: www.mlmgroup.com/

MLP Railway Maintenance Ltd
60 Brookhill Road, Pinxton, Notts, NG16 6NS
T: 01773 811977
W: https://www.mlprail.co.uk/

MMRA
4th Floor, 10 Fleet Place, London, EC4M 7RB
T: +44(0)207 651 0590
E: info@mmra-cert.com
W: www.mmra-cert.com

The Mobile Catering Group
The Monkey House, Kersoe, Pershore, Worcs, WR10 3JD
T: 01386 710123
F: 01386 710123
M: 07850 915959
E: fred@cateringcontracts.com
W: www.cateringcontracts.com

Modern Railways EXPO
Key Publishing, Units 1-4, Gwash Way Industrial Estate, Ryhall Road, Stamford, Lincolnshire, PE9 1XP
T: 01780 755131
W: www.modernrailways.com/expo

Mole Solutions
Alconbury, Huntingdon, Cambridgeshire, PE28 4DA
T: 01480 413141
E: info@molesolutions.co.uk
W: www.molesolutions.co.uk/

Mono Design
16 Scarsdale Avenue, Littleover, Derby, DE23 6ER
T: 01332 361616
E: info@monodesign.co.uk
W: www.monodesign.co.uk

Moore Concrete Products Ltd
Caherty House, 41 Woodside Rd, Ballymena, Co. Antrim, BT42 4QH, Northern Ireland
T: 028 2565 2566
F: 028 2565 8480
E: info@moore-concrete.com
W: www.moore-concrete.com

MoreVision ExcelWraps
T: 0113 815 2220
W: www.excelwraps.com/

Morgan Advanced Materials
Upper Fforest Way, Swansea Enterprise Park, Swansea, SA6 8PP
T: 01792 763052
F: 01792 763167
E: meclsales@morganplc.com
W: www.morganelectrical materials.com

Morgan Hunt
5th Floor, 16 Old Bailey, London, EC4M 7EG
T: 020 7419 8968
F: 020 7419 8999
E: rail@morganhunt.com
W: www.morganhunt.com

Morgan Marine Ltd
Llandybie, Ammanford, Carms, SA18 3GY
T: 01269 850437
F: 01269 850656
E: sales@morgan-marine.com
W: www.morgan-marine.com

Morgan Sindall Group
Corporation Street, Rugby, Warwickshire, CV21 2DW
T: 01788 534500
F: 01788 534579
E: info@morgansindall.com
W: https://www.morgansindall.com/

D Morgan plc
New Hey, Chester Road, Great Sutton, Ellesmere Port, CH66 2LS
T: 0151 339 8113
F: 0151 347 1254
E: contact@dmorgan.co.uk
W: www.dmorgan.co.uk/

Mornsun Guangzhou Science & Technology Co Ltd
No 5, Kehui St 1, Kehui Development Centre, Science Avenue, Guangzhou Science City 510660, Luogang District, China
T: 0086 203860 1850
F: 0086 203860 1272
E: info@mornsun.cn
W: www.mornsun-power.com

Morris Lubricants
Castle Foregate, Shrewsbury, Shropshire, SY1 2EL
T: 01743 232200
E: info@morris-lubricants.co.uk
W: www.morrislubricants.co.uk/

Morris Site Machinery
Station Rd, Four Ashes, Wolverhampton, WV10 7DB
T: 01902 790824
F: 01902 790355
E: info@morrismachinery.co.uk
W: www.morrismachinery.co.uk

Morrison Utility Services Ltd
Fitzwilliam House, Middle Bank, Doncaster, South Yorkshire, DN4 5NG
T: 01302 898303
E: chris.ford@morrisonus.com
W: www.morrisonus.com

Mors Smitt UK Ltd (A Wabtec Company)
Graycar Business Park, Barton-under-Needwood, Burton upon Trent, Staffordshire, DE13 8EN
T: 01283 357263
F: 01283 722651
E: msu_sales@wabtec.com
W: www.morssmitt.com

Morson International
Stableford Hall, Monton, Eccles, Manchester, M30 8AP
T: 0161 707 1516
F: 0161 788 8372
E: rail@morson.com
W: www.morson.com

Morson Projects Ltd
Adamson House, Centenary Way, Salford, Manchester, M50 1RD
T: 0161 707 1516
F: 0161 786 2360
E: andy.hassall@morson-projects.co.uk
W: www.morsonprojects.co.uk

Motorail Logistics
Quinton Rail Technology Centre, Station Road, Long Marston, Stratford upon Avon, Warks, CV37 8PL
T: 01789 721995
F: 01789 721396
E: ruth.dunmore@motorail.co.uk
W: www.motorail.co.uk

Mott MacDonald Group
Mott MacDonald House, 8-10 Sydenham
Rd, Croydon, Surrey, CR0 2EE
T: 020 8774 2000
F: 020 8681 5706
E: railways@mottmac.com
W: www.mottmac.com

Mouchel
See WSP UK

Movares
Mireille Ros, Leidseveer 10, 3511 SB Utrecht, Netherlands
T: 0031 30265 3101
F: 0031 30265 3111
E: info@movares.nl
W: www.movares.com

Movement Strategies
31-35 Kirby Street, Farringdon, London, EC1N 8TE
T: 020 3540 8520
E: info@movementstrategies.com
W: www.movementstrategies.com/

Moveright International Ltd
Dunton Park, Dunton Lane, Wishaw, Sutton Coldfield, B76 9QA
T: 01675 475590
F: 01675 475591
E: andrew@moverightinternational.com
W: www.moverightinternational.com

Moxa Europe GmbH
Einsteinstrasse 7, D-85716 Unterschleissheim, Germany
T: 0049 893700 3940
F: 0049 893700 3999
E: europe@moxa.com
W: www.moxa.com/rail

MPB Structures
4th Floor, Hamilton House, Mabledon Place, London, WC1H 9BB
T: 020 7554 8864
W: www.mpb.co.uk/

MPEC Technology Ltd
Wyvern House, Railway Terrace, Derby, DE1 2RU
T: 01332 363979
F: 08701 363958
E: andrew.whawell@mpec.co.uk
W: www.mpec.co.uk

MPH Construction
Bromfield House, Bromfield Industrial Estate, Queens Lane, Mold, Flintshire, CH7 1XB
T: 01352 755151
F: 01352 758892
E: info@mphconstruction.co.uk
W: mph.futurestudios.net/

MPI Ltd
International House, The Chase, Foxholes Business Park, Hertford, Hertfordshire, SG13 7NN
T: 01992 501111
F: 01992 583384
E: info@mpi.ltd.uk
W: www.mpi.ltd.uk

MPower Kernow C.I.C.
30 North Street, Tywardreath, Par, Cornwall, PL24 2PN
E: enquiries@mpowerkernow.org
W: https://www.mpowerkernow.org/

MR Site Services Ltd
Unit 6, Worcester Trading Estate, Blackpole, Worcester, WR3 8HR
T: 01905 755055
F: 01905 755053
E: welding@mrsiteservices.co.uk
W: www.mrsiteservices.co.uk

MRX Technologies Ltd
See Siemens Mobility Ltd

MSc Traction Oy
Alasniitynkatu 30, FIN-33560 Tampere, Finland
T: 358 050 532 1469
E: info@msc.eu
W: www.msc.eu

MSD Construction UK Ltd
Manvers House, Pioneer Close, Wath Upon Dearne, Rotherham, S63 7JZ
T: 01709 878988
F: 01709 878918
E: enquiries@msdconstruction.com
W: www.msdconstruction.com

Mtag Composites
Unit 4A, Cowbridge Business Park, Boston, Lincolnshire, PE22 7DJ
T: 01205 352992
W: www.mtagcomposites.co.uk/

MTM Power Messtechnik Mellenbach GmbH
Zirkel 3, 98744 Schwarzatal, Germany
T: 0049 69154 2628
E: info@mtm-power.com
W: www.mtm-power.com

MTR Corporation
Third floor, 123 Pall Mall, London, SW1Y 5EA
T: 020 7766 3500
F: 020 7839 6217
W: mtreurope.com/

MTR Elizabeth line
63 St Mary Axe, London, EC3A 8NH
T: 020 7444 0213
E: communications@mtrel.co.uk
W: www.mtrel.co.uk

MTR Training Ltd
See HSS Training Ltd

MTU UK Ltd
Unit 27 & 29, The Birches Industrial Estate, East Grinstead, West Sussex, RH19 1XZ
T: 01342 335450
F: 01342 335470
W: www.mtu-online.com

Multicell
Swannington Rd, Broughton Astley, Leicester, LE9 6TU
T: 01455 283443
F: 01455 284250
E: help@multicell.co.uk
W: www.multicell.co.uk

Multipulse
Units 1-2, Goldsworth Park Trading Est, Kestrel Way, Woking, Surrey, GU21 3BA
T: 01483 713600
F: 01483 729851
E: sales@multipulse.com
W: www.multipulse.com

J Murphy & Sons Ltd
Hiview House, 81 Highgate Rd, London, NW5 1TN
T: 020 7267 4366
F: 020 7428 3107
E: info@murphygroup.co.uk
W: www.murphygroup.co.uk

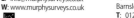

Murphy Surveys
Head Office UK, 39-41 North Road, London, N7 9DP
T: 020 3598 3775
E: info@murphysurveys.co.uk
W: www.murphysurveys.co.uk

MVA Consultancy
See Systra UK

MWH Treatment Ltd
Biwater Place, Gregge St, Heywood, Lancs, OL10 2DX
T: 01706 626258
F: 01706 626294
E: info@mwhglobal.com
W: www.mwhglobal.com

Nacco (UK) Ltd
See VTG Rail UK Ltd

Napier Turbochargers Limited
Ruston House, PO Box 1, Waterside South, Lincoln, Lincolnshire, LN5 7FD
T: 01522 516666
E: napier_enquiry@wabtec.com
W: www.napier-turbochargers.com

National Car Parks Ltd (NCP)
Saffron Court, 14B St Cross Street, London, EC1N 8XA
T: 0345 050 70 80
W: www.ncp.co.uk

National College for Advanced Transport & Infrastructure (NCATI)
2 Lister Street, Birmingham, B7 4AG
T: 0330 120 0375
E: enquiries@ncati.ac.uk
W: www.ncati.ac.uk

National Composites Centre
Feynman Way Central, Bristol & Bath Science Park, Emersons Green, Bristol, BS16 7FS
T: 0117 370 7600
E: info@nccuk.com
W: www.nccuk.com

National Express East Anglia
See Greater Anglia

National Express Group Plc
75 Davies St, London, W1K 5HT
T: 020 7529 2000
F: 020 7529 2100
E: info@natex.co.uk
W: www.nationalexpressgroup.com

National Infrastructure Commission (NIC)
E: enquiries@infrastructure-commission.gsi.gov.uk
W: www.nic.org.uk/

National Rail Enquiries
T: 08457 484950
W: www.nationalrail.co.uk

National Railway Museum
Leeman Rd, York, YO26 4XJ
T: 0800 047 8124
E: info@railwaymuseum.org.uk
W: www.railwaymuseum.org.uk

National Training Academy for Rail (NTAR)
Unit 5, Heathfield Way, Kings Heath, Northampton, NN5 7QP
T: 01604 594440
E: info@ntar.co.uk
W: www.ntar.co.uk

Nationwide Engineering
Units 19-20, The Bluestone Centre, Sun Rise Way, Amesbury, SP4 7YR
T: 01722 421625
E: enquiries@nationwide engineering.co.uk
W: www.nationwideengineering.co.uk

Nationwide Healthcare Connect
See Healthcare Connections Ltd

Native Land
The Pavilion, 118 Southwark Street, London, SE1 0SW
T: 020 7758 3650
F: 020 7437 4831
E: reception@native-land.com
W: www.native-land.com/

Natural Cement Distribution Ltd
10-11 Fountain Parade, Mapplewell, Barnsley, South Yorkshire, S75 6FW
T: 01226 381133
F: 01226 381177
E: enquiries@naturalcement.co.uk
W: www.naturalcement.co.uk

Navaho Technologies Ltd
8/9 Hayters Court, Grigg Lane, Brockenhurst, Hants, SO42 7PG
T: 02380 000010
F: 02380 988598
E: sales@navaho.co.uk
W: www.navaho.co.uk

Navigant Consulting
5th Floor, Woolgate Exchange, 25 Basinghall Street, London, EC2V 5HA
T: 020 7469 1111
F: 020 7469 1110
E: inquiries@navigant.com
W: www.navigant.com/

Nazeing Glass Works Ltd
Nazeing New Rd, Broxbourne, Herts, EN10 6SU
T: 01992 464485
F: 01992 450966
E: sales@nazeing-glass.co.uk
W: www.nazeing-glass.com

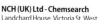

NCH (UK) Ltd - Chemsearch
Landchard House, Victoria St, West Bromwich, B70 8ER
T: 0121 524 7300
F: 0121 500 5386
W: www.chemsearch.co.uk

NDC Consultants
Unit 6, Berkeley Business Park, Wainwright Road, Worcester, WR4 9FA
T: 01905 756000
F: 01905 756010
E: info@ndcconsultants.co.uk
W: www.ndcconsultants.co.uk/

Neale Consulting Engineers Ltd
Highfield, Pilcot Hill, Dogmersfield, Fleet, Hants, RG27 8SX
T: 01252 629199
F: 01252 815625
E: ncel@tribology.co.uk
W: www.tribology.co.uk

Neary Rail
9 Coal Pit Lane, Atherton, Manchester, M46 0RY
T: 01942 881470
F: 01942 884147
E: info@neary.co.uk
W: www.neary.co.uk

NedRailways
See Abellio

Nedtrain BV
Kantorencentrum Katereine 9, Stationshal 17, 3511 ED, Utrecht, Netherlands
T: 0031 30 300 4929
F: 0031 30 300 4647
W: www.nedtrain.nl

Nelsons Solicitors
Sterne House, Lodge Lane, Derby, DE1 3WD
T: 01332 372372
E: enquiries@nelsonslaw.co.uk
W: www.nelsonslaw.co.uk

Nemesis Rail Ltd
Burton Rail Depot, Derby Rd, Burton
upon Trent, Staffordshire, DE14 1RS
T: 01283 531562
E: enquiries@nemesisrail.com
W: www.nemesisrail.com

Nenta Traintours
Railtour House, 10 Buxton Rd, North
Walsham, Norfolk, NR28 0ED
T: 01692 406153
F: 01692 406152
E: ray.davies@nentatraintours.co.uk
W: www.nentatraintours.co.uk

Neon Hire Services Ltd
Unit 27, Icknield Way Farm, Tring Road,
Dunstable, Bedfordshire, LU6 2JX
T: 01582 478000
F: 01582 668006
W: www.neonhire.co.uk/

Neopul UK
Beaufort House, 11th Floor, 15 St
Botolph Street, Aldgate, London,
EC3A 7BB
W: www.neopul.pt

NES Track
Station House, Stamford New Rd,
Altrincham, Cheshire, WA14 1EP
T: 0161 942 4016
F: 0161 942 7969
E: nestrack.manchester@nes.co.uk
W: www.nestrack.co.uk

Network Certification Body Ltd
Ground Floor, Caldecotte, The
Quadrant, Eldergate, Milton Keynes,
MK9 1EN
T: 01908 784002
E: ncbenquiries@networkrail.co.uk
W: www.net-cert.co.uk

**Network
Construction Services Ltd**
Ercall House, Pearson Rd, Central Park,
Telford, Shropshire, TF2 9TX
T: 01952 210243
F: 01952 290168
E: sales@ncsjob.co.uk
W: www.ncsjob.co.uk

Network Rail Consulting Ltd
42 Upper Berkeley Street, London,
W1H 5PW
T: 020 3356 0454
E: contactnrc@networkrail.co.uk
W: www.networkrailconsulting.co.uk

Network Rail Infrastructure Ltd
1 Eversholt Street, London, NW1 2DN
T: 020 7557 8000
W: www.networkrail.co.uk

Network Rail Property
1 Eversholt Street, London, NW1 2DN
T: 0800 916 8895
E: property@networkrail.co.uk
W: property.networkrail.co.uk

Neway Training Solutions Ltd
Kelvin House, RTC Business Park,
London Rd, Derby, DE24 8UP
T: 01332 360033
F: 01332 366367
E: enquiries@neway-training.com
W: www.neway-training.com

Newbury Data Recording Ltd
T: 0870 224 8110
F: 0870 224 8177
E: ndsales@newburydata.co.uk
W: www.newburydata.co.uk

Newby Foundries Ltd
Smith Road, Wednesbury, West
Midlands, WS10 0PB
T: 0044 (0) 121 556 4451
F: 0044 (0) 121 505 3626
E: sales@newbyfoundries.co.uk
W: www.newbyfoundries.co.uk

**NewRail Centre for
Railway Research**
Stephenson Building, Newcastle
University, Claremont Rd,
Newcastle-upon-Tyne, NE1 7RU
T: 0191 208 8575
F: 0191 208 8600
E: newrail@ncl.ac.uk
W: www.newrail.org

Newton Europe
2 Kingston Business Park, Kingston
Bagpuize, Oxon, OX13 5FE
T: 01865 601 300
F: 01865 601 348
E: info@newtoneurope.com
W: www.newtoneurope.com

Nexans
Nexans House, Chesney Wold, Bleak
Hall, Milton Keynes, MK6 1LF
T: 01908 250840
F: 01908 250841
E: iandi.sales@nexans.com
W: www.nexans.com

Nexus (Tyne & Wear Metro)
Nexus House, 33 St James Blvd,
Newcastle upon Tyne, NE1 4AX
T: 0191 203 3333
F: 0191 203 3180
E: contactmetro@nexus.org.uk
W: www.nexus.org.uk/metro

Nexus Alpha Group
London House, 7 Prescott Place,
Clapham, London, SW4 6BS
T: 020 7652 2051
F: 020 7622 6817
E: commercialdept@nexusalpha.com
W: www.nexusalphagroup.com

NFM Technologies
5, place Jules Ferry, 69456 LYON Cedex
06, France
T: +33 (0)4 26 84 87 00
F: +33 (0)426 848 710
W: www.nfm-technologies.com/

NG Bailey
Denton Hall, Ilkley, West Yorkshire,
LS29 0HH
T: 01943 601 933
E: enquiries@ngbailey.co.uk
W: www.ngbailey.co.uk

Nichols Group Ltd
7-8 Stratford Place, London, W1C 1AY
T: 020 7292 7000
F: 020 7292 5200
E: operations@nichols.uk.com
W: www.nicholsgroup.co.uk

Nigel Nixon Consulting
Suite 1, AD Business Centre,
Hithercroft Rd, Wallingford, Oxon,
OX10 9EZ
T: 01491 824030
F: 01491 824078
E: nigel@nigelnixon.com
W: www.nigelnixon.com

Nightsearcher Ltd
Unit 4, Applied House, Fitzherbert
Spur, Farlington, Portsmouth, PO6 1TT
T: 023 9238 9774
F: 023 9238 9788
E: sales@nightsearcher.co.uk
W: www.nightsearcher.co.uk

Nimble Media
Unit 6, Old Station Yard, Ashwell,
Oakham, Rutland, LE15 7SP
T: 01780 432930
E: info@nimblemedia.co.uk
W: www.nimblemedia.co.uk

BME Nitech Ltd
Unit 2A Nevis Business Park,
Balgownie Road, Bridge of Don,
Aberdeen, AB22 8NT
T: 01224 825320
E: sales@bmenitech.co.uk
W: www.bmenitech.co.u

NMB Minebea UK Ltd
Doddington Rd, Lincoln, LN6 3RA
T: 01522 500933
F: 01522 500975
W: www.nmb-minebea.co.uk

No1 Scaffolding Ltd
Woolshots Farm, Church Road,
Ramsden Bellhouse, Billericay, Essex,
CM11 1RH
T: 01268 724793
F: 01268 725606
E: infono1scaffolding@gmail.co.uk
W: no1-scaffolding.co/

Nomad Digital Limited
5th Floor, One Trinity, Broad Chare,
Newcastle-upon-Tyne, NE1 2HF
T: 020 7096 6966
F: 0191 221 1339
E: experts@nomad-digital.com
W: www.nomad-digital.com

**Nomix Enviro Ltd - A division of
Frontier Agriculture Ltd**
The Grain Silos, Weyhill Rd, Andover,
Hants, SP10 3NT
T: 01264 388050
F: 01522 866176
E: nomixenviro@frontierag.co.uk
W: www.nomix.co.uk

Nord-Lock Ltd
Kingsgate House, Newbury Road,
Andover, Wilts, SP10 4DU
T: 01264 355557
F: 01264 369555
E: enquiries@nord-lock.co.uk
W: www.nord-lock.com
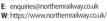

Norgren Ltd
See IMI Precision Engineering

Nortek Global HVAC
Fens Pool Avenue, Brierley Hill, West
Midlands, DY5 1QA
T: 01384 489250
E: info.reznor@nortek.com
W: https://www.nortekhvac.com/

North East Railtours
See SRPS Railtours

North Highland Consulting
8th Floor, 120 Holborn, London,
EC1N 2TD
T: 020 7812 6460
E: info@northhighland.com
W: www.northhighland.com/

North Star Consultancy Ltd
78 York St, London, W1H 1DP
T: 020 7692 0936
F: 020 7692 0937
E: enquiries@northstar
consultancy.com
W: www.northstarconsultancy.com

Northern
Northern House, 9 Rougier St, York,
YO1 6HZ
T: 0333 222 0125
F: 0113 247 9059
E: enquiries@northernrailway.co.uk
W: https://www.northernrailway.co.uk/

Northern Ireland Railways
See Translink NI Railways

**Northston Engineering
Consultancy Ltd**
18 Market Place, Brackley,
Northamptonshire, NN13 7DP

Northwood Railway Eng. Ltd
9 Scot Grove, Pinner, Middx, HA5 4RT
T: 020 8428 9890
E: davidnbradley@btopenworld.com

Norton & Associates
32a High St, Pinner, Middx, HA5 5PW
T: 020 8869 9237
F: 07005 964635
E: mail@nortonweb.co.uk
W: www.nortonweb.co.uk

Norton Rose Fulbright LLP
3 More London, Riverside, London,
SE1 2AQ
T: 020 7283 6000
F: 020 7283 6500
E: tim.marsden@
nortonrosefulbright.com
W: www.nortonrose.com

Norwest Holst Construction
See Saba Park Services Ltd

Nottingham Trams Ltd
NET Depot, Wilkinson St, Nottingham,
NG7 7NW
T: 0115 942 7777
E: info@thetram.net
W: www.thetram.net

NOV Fiber Glass Systems
Pipex Ltd, Devon Enterprise Facility, 1
Belliver Way, Roborough, Plymouth,
Devon, PL6 7BP
T: 01752 581200
F: 01752 581209
E: fgssales@nov.com
W: pipexltd.com

Novacroft
Lakeside House, 9 The Lakes, Bedford
Road, Northampton, NN4 7HD
T: 0333 103 3330
E: getmore@uk.novacroft.com
W: www.novacroft.com

Novah Ltd
Unit 12, Jensen Court, Astmoor
Industrial Estate, Runcorn, Cheshire,
WA7 1SQ
T: 01928 242918
F: 01928 567838
E: sales@novah.co.uk
W: www.novah.co.uk

Novograf
10 Langlands Place, East Kilbride,
Glasgow, G75 0YF
T: 01355 202740
E: contactus@novograf.co.uk
W: www.novograf.co.uk

Novus Rail Ltd
Solaris Centre, New South Prom,
Blackpool, FY4 1RW
T: 01253 478027
F: 01253 478037
E: mmcm@novusrail.com
W: www.novusrail.com

NR Engineering Ltd
Duckworth Mill, Skipton Road, Colne,
Lancs, BB8 0RH
T: 01282 868500
F: 01282 868157
E: sales@nrengineering.co.uk
W: www.nrengineering.co.uk

NRL
Second Floor, Atlas House, Caxton
Close, Marus Bridge, Wigan, Lancs,
WN3 6XU
T: 01942 326727
F: 01942 829729
E: rail@nrl.co.uk
W: www.nrl.co.uk/rail

**NSAR (National Skills Academy
for Rail)**
11 Carteret Street, London, SW1H 9DJ
T: 0203 021 0575
E: enquiries@nsare.org
W: www.nsar.co.uk

NTM Sales & Marketing Ltd
PO Box 2, Summerbridge, Harrogate,
HG3 4XN
T: 01423 781010
F: 01423 593953
E: info@xl-lubricants.com
W: www.xl-lubricants.com

**NTRS (Network Training &
Resource Solutions)**
Unit 3&4, Churchill Way, Chapeltown,
Sheffield, S35 2PY
T: 0844 809 9902
F: 0844 809 9903
E: info@ntrs.co.uk
W: www.ntrs.co.uk

Nu Star Material Handling
Lakeside, Ednaston Business Centre,
Ednaston, Derby, DE6 3AE
T: 0115 880 0070
F: 0115 880 0071
E: matt@nu-starmhl.com
W: www.nu-starmhl.com

Nucleus VP Group
The Oasts, Charmans Farm,
Westerham, Kent, TN16 1QP
T: 0844 775 0000
E: info@nucleusvp.ccom
W: www.nucleusvp.com

Nufox Rubber Ltd
Unit 1, Bentley Ave, Middleton,
Manchester, M24 2GP
T: 0161 655 0303
F: 0161 655 8801
E: info@nufox.com
W: www.nufox.com/

Nusteel Structures
Lympne, Hythe, Kent, CT21 4LR
T: 01303 268112
F: 01303 266098
E: general@nusteelstructures.com
W: www.nusteelstructures.com

Nuttall Finchpalm
See BAM Nuttall Ltd

NVR Fleet UK
See Hitachi Capital Vehicle
Solutions Ltd

Oakland Consulting
West One, 114 Wellington Street,
Leeds, West Yorkshire, LS1 1BA
T: 0113 234 1944
F: 0113 234 1988
E: contactus@oaklandconsulting.com
W: www.oaklandconsulting.com/

OakTec
Hill House Farm, Cockerham,
Lancaster, LA2 0DZ
T: 01524 751373
E: paul.andrews@oaktec.net
W: www.oaktec.net

Oce UK Ltd
Oce House, Chatham Way, Brentwood,
Essex, CM14 4DZ
T: 0870 600 5544
F: 0870 600 1113
E: info@oce.com
W: www.oce.com

Odgers Ray & Berndtson
20 Cannon Street, London, EC4M 6XD
T: 020 7529 1111
F: 020 7529 1000
E: information@odgersberndtson.com
W: www.odgersberndtson.com

Office of Rail and Road
25 Cabot Square, London, E14 4QZ
T: 020 7282 2000
F: 020 7282 2040
E: contact.cct@orr.gsi.gov.uk
W: www.orr.gov.uk

Ogier Electronics Ltd
Unit 13, Sandridge Park, Porters Wood,
St Albans, Herts, AL3 6PH
T: 01727 845547
F: 01727 852186
E: david.sproule@ogierelectronics.com
W: www.ogierelectronics.com
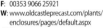

Oil Analysis Services Ltd
Unit 6/7, Blue Chalet Ind. Park, London
Rd, West Kingsdown, Kent, TN15 6BQ
T: 01474 854450
F: 01474 854408
E: ihbrown@oas-online.co.uk
W: www.oas-online.co.uk

Oilaway
Wakefield Road, Rothwell Haigh,
Leeds, West Yorkshire, LS26 0SB
T: 0113 205 9332
E: info@oilaway.net
W: www.oilaway.net

Oldcastle Enclosure Solutions
IDA Industrial Est., Racecourse Rd,
Roscommon, Republic of Ireland
T: 00353 9066 25922
F: 00353 9066 25921
W: www.oldcastleprecast.com/plants/
enclosures/pages/default.aspx

Oldham Engineering
Castle Iron Works, Overens Street,
Oldham, Lancashire, OL4 1LA
T: 0161 627 5822
F: 0161 626 3500
E: sales@oldham-eng.com
W: https://oldham-eng.com/

Oleo International
Grovelands, Longford Rd, Exhall,
Coventry, CV7 9NE
T: 02476 645555
F: 02476 645900
E: sales@oleo.co.uk
W: www.oleo.co.uk

Omega Red Group Ltd
Dabell Ave, Blenheim Ind.Est., Bulwell,
Nottingham, NG6 8WA
T: 0115 877 6666
F: 0115 876 7766
E: enquiries@omegaredgroup.com
W: www.omegaredgroup.com

Omnicom Balfour Beatty Ltd
Eboracum House, Clifton Park Avenue,
York, YO30 5PB
T: 01904 778100
F: 01904 778200
E: info@omnicomengineering.co.uk
W: www.omnicomengineering.co.uk

On Track Design Solutions Ltd
1st Floor Suite, 11 Pride Point Drive,
Pride Park, Derby, DE24 8BX
T: 01332 204450
F: 01332 204458
E: brianchadwick@
ontrackdesign.co.uk
W: www.ontrackdesign.co.uk

ON Train Limited
Orchard Rise, 173 Yardley Fields,
Yardley, Birmingham, B33 8RP
T: 0121 783 9480
M: 07527 811700
E: sales@on-train.co.uk
W: www.on-train.co.uk

Onboard Retail Solutions
See Iridium Onboard

One Big Circle
The Engine Shed, Station Approach, Bristol, BS1 6QH
T: 0845 838 7178
E: info@onebigcircle.co.uk
W: onebigcircle.co.uk

One Way
26 Basepoint, Andersons Road, Southampton, Hampshire, SO14 5FE
T: 0845 644 8843
W: www.oneway.co.uk/

One-On Ltd
7 Home Farm Courtyard, Meriden Rd, Berkswell, West Midlands, CV7 7SH
T: 0845 505 1955
F: 0845 505 1977
E: info@one-on.co.uk
W: www.one-on.co.uk

OnTrac Ltd
Floor 1, Baltimore House, Baltic Business Quarter, Gateshead, Tyne and Wear, NE8 3DF
T: 0191 477 4951
W: www.on-trac.co.uk/

Open Technology Ltd
1 Woodlands Court, Albert Drive, Burgess Hill, West Sussex, RH15 9TN
T: 0845 680 4004
F: 0845 680 4005
E: info@opentechnologyuk.com
W: www.opentechnologyuk.com

Opentree Ltd
Cabinet House, Ellerbeck Court, Stokesley Business Park, North Yorkshire, TS9 5PT
T: 01642 714471
F: 01642 714451
E: info@opentree.co.uk
W: www.opentree.co.uk

Opinsta
Suites 35-37, The White House, 111 New Street, Birmingham, B2 4EU
M: 07375 812874
E: info@opinsta.com
W: www.opinsta.com

OptaSense
Building A8, Room 1005, Cody Technology Park, Ively Road, Farnborough, Hampshire, GU14 0LX
T: 01252 392000
W: www.optasense.com/

Optilan Communication Systems
Sibree Rd, Stonebridge Ind. Est, Coventry, CV3 4FD
T: 01926 864999
F: 01926 851818
E: sales@optilan.com
W: www.optilan.com

Optimas Solutions
Waterwells Drive, Quedgeley, Gloucester, GL2 2FR
T: 01452 880500
W: optimas.com

Optimized Systems & Solutions Ltd
SIN D-7, PO Box 31, Derby, DE24 8BJ
T: 01332 771700
F: 01332 770921
W: www.o-sys.com

Optimum Consultancy Ltd
Spencer House, Mill Green Rd, Haywards Heath, West Sussex, RH16 1XQ
T: 0800 009 6329
E: info@optimum.uk.com
W: www.optimum.uk.com

Opus International Consultants Ltd
Yale Business Village, Wrexham Technology Park, Wrexham, LL13 7YL
T: 01978 368100
F: 01978 368101
E: mark.valentine@opusinternational.co.uk
W: www.opusinternational.co.uk

Oracle Recruitment
See Acorn People

Orchard Consulting
See Optimum Consultancy Ltd

Ordnance Survey
Romsey Rd, Southampton, SO16 4GU
T: 02380 305030
F: 02380 792615
E: customerservice@ordnancesurvey.co.uk
W: www.ordnancesurvey.co.uk

Orient Express
T: [illegible]
F: 020 7805 5908
W: www.orient-express.com

Orion Electrotech
4 Danehill, Lower Earley, Reading, RG6 4UT
T: 0118 923 9239
F: 0118 975 3332
E: rail@orion-group.co.uk
W: www.orionelectrotech.com

Orion High Speed Logistics
Wyvern House, Railway Terrace, Derby, DE1 2RU
T: 01332 343295
E: orion@railopsgroup.co.uk
W: orion.railopsgroup.co.uk/

Orion Rail Services Ltd
40 Holmethorpe Avenue, Redhill, RH1 2NL
T: 01795 591919
E: info@orionrail.com
W: orionrail.com

Osborne Clarke
One London Wall, London, EC2Y 5EB
T: 020 7105 7000
E: enquiries@osborneclarke.com
W: www.osborneclarke.com

Osborne Rail
Fonteyn House, 47-49 London Rd, Reigate, Surrey, RH2 2PY
T: 01737 378200
F: 01737 378295
E: enquiries@osborne.co.uk
W: www.osborne.co.uk

OSL Rail
The Railway Exchange, Weston Road, Crewe, Cheshire, CW1 6AA
T: 0845 271 9171
F: 08701 236249
E: enquiries@o-s-l.uk.com
W: oslglobal.com/service/rail/

Otis Ltd
Chiswick Park, Building 5 Ground Floor, 566 Chiswick High Road, London, W4 5YF
T: 020 8495 7750
W: www.otis.com/site/gb/

OTN Systems
Industrielaan 17b B-2250, B-2250 Olen, Belgium
T: 003214252847
F: 003214252023
E: info@otnsystems.com
W: www.otnsystems.com

Overhead Line Engineering Ltd
4B Mallard Way, Pride Park, Derby, DE24 8GX
T: 01332 342122
M: 07501 467095
E: contact@ole-limited.co.uk
W: www.ole-limited.co.uk/

Owen Williams
See Amey

Oxera Consulting
Park Central, 40/41 Park End Street, Oxford, OX1 1JD
T: 01865 253000
E: enquiries@oxera.com
W: www.oxera.com/

Oxford Archaeology
Janus House, Osney Mead, Oxford, OX2 0ES
T: 01865 980700
E: dan.poore@oxfordarch.co.uk
W: oxfordarchaeology.com/

Oxford Architects
Bagley Croft, Hinksey Hill, Oxford, OX1 5BS
T: 01865 329100
E: info@oxford-architects.com
W: www.oxford-architects.com

Oxford Economics
Abbey House, 121 St Aldates, Oxford, OX1 1HB
T: 01865 268 900
E: mailbox@oxfordeconomics.com
W: www.oxfordeconomics.com/

Oxford Hydrotechnics Ltd
Suite 2, The Great Barn, Baynards Green, Bicester, Oxon, OX27 7SR
T: 01869 346001
F: 01869 345455
E: info@h2ox.net
W: www.h2ox.net

PA Consulting
123 Buckingham Palace Road, London, SW1W 9SR
T: 020 7333 5865
W: www.paconsulting.com/

Padacar UK
1 Chamberlain Square, Birmingham, B3 3AX
W: www.pacadar.com/

Palfinger AG
Lamprechtshausener Bundesstraße 8, 5101 Bergheim, Austria
T: +43 (0)662 2281-0
F: +43 (0)662 2281-81077
E: info@palfinger.com
W: https://www.palfinger.com/en/

Palmers Scaffolding
331 Charles Street, Royston, Glasgow, G21 2QA
T: 0141 553 4040
F: 0141 552 6463
W: www.palmersgroup.co.uk

Panasonic Computer Products Solutions
Panasonic House, Willoughby Road, Bracknell, Berks, RG12 8FP
T: 01344 853366
W: www.toughbook.eu

Panasonic Electric Works UK Ltd
Sunrise Parkway, Linford Wood, Milton Keynes, MK14 6LF
T: 01908 231555
F: 01908 231599
W: www.panasonic-electric-works.co.uk

Pandrol UK Ltd
63 Station Road, Addlestone, Surrey, KT15 2AR
T: 01932 834500
E: info@pandrol.com
W: www.pandrol.com

Pantrak Transportation Ltd
John G. Russell Building WKR, Container Base, Gartsherrie Road, Coatbridge, North Lanarkshire, ML5 2DY
T: 01292 442457
M: 07974 724173
E: gavinroser@pantrak.com
W: www.pantrak.com

Parallel Project Training
Davidson House, Forbury Sq, Reading, RG1 3EU
T: 0845 519 2305
F: 0118 900 0501
E: withyouallttheway@parallelprojecttraining.com
W: www.parallelprojecttraining.com

Parallel Studios
22 Balmoral Ave, Bedford, MK40 2PT
F: 01234 217200
E: rick@parallelstudios.co.uk
W: ricktks.magix.net/website/about_us.30.html#home

PARK SIGNALLING
a Unipart Company

We utilise our **specialist engineering skills** and **knowledge** to deliver a range of **products, services** and **systems**.

We **listen** to your **needs, understand** your **challenges** and **implement practical solutions** for operational maintenance and life extension of critical equipment for railway Signalling & Telecomms.

Design ● Develop ● Integrate ● Investigate

Park Signalling Limited
T: +44 (0) 161 219 0161 E: sales@park-signalling.co.uk **www.park-signalling.co.uk**

Park Signalling Ltd
3rd Floor, Houldsworth Mill Business Centre, Houldsworth St, Reddish, Stockport, SK5 6DA
T: 0161 219 0161
E: sales@park-signalling.co.uk
W: www.park-signalling.co.uk

Parkeon Ltd
10 Willis Way, Fleets Ind Est, Poole, Dorset, BH15 3SS
T: 01202 339339
F: 01202 339369
E: sales_uk@parkeon.com
W: www.parkeon.com

Parker Hannifin (UK) Ltd
Tachbrook Park Drive, Tachbrook Park, Warwick, CV34 6TU
T: 01926 317878
F: 01926 317855
E: filtrationinfo@parker.com
W: www.parker.com

Parker KV Division
Presley Way, Crownhill, Milton Keynes, MK8 0HB
T: 01908 561515
F: 01908 561227
E: saleskv@parker.com
W: www.parker.com

Parry People Movers Ltd
Overend Rd, Cradley Heath, West Midlands, B64 7DD
T: 01384 569553
E: info@parrypeoplemovers.com
W: www.parrypeoplemovers.com

Parsons Brinckerhoff
WSP House, 70 Chancery Lane, London, WC2A 1AF
T: 020 7314 5000
F: 020 7314 5111
E: railandtransit@pbworld.com
W: www.wsp-pb.com/en/

Parsons Transportation Group
Holborn Gate, High Holborn, London, WC1V 7QT
T: 020 8326 5621
F: 020 3102 6906
E: enquiries.pgil@parsons.com
W: www.parsons.com

Partex Marking Systems (UK) Ltd
Unit 61-64, Station Road, Coleshill, Birmingham, B46 1JT
T: 01675 463670
E: sales@partex.co.uk
W: www.partex.co.uk

Partsmaster Ltd (NCH Europe)
NCH House, Springvale Avenue, Bilston, West Midlands, WV14 0QL
T: 01902 510335
E: victoria.summerfield@nch.com
W: www.partsmaster.com

Passcomm Ltd
Unit 24, Tatton Court, Kingsland Garage, Warrington, Cheshire, WA1 4RR
T: 01925 821333
F: 01925 821321
E: info@passcomm.co.uk
W: www.passcomm.co.uk

Passenger Transport Intelligence Services
M: 07972 213486
E: info@passtrans.co.uk
W: www.passtrans.co.uk

Passenger Transport Networks
Castlegate House, Castlegate, York, YO1 9RP
T: 01904 611187
E: ptn@btconnect.com
W: www.passengertransportnetworks.co.uk

Pathfinder Systems UK PTY Ltd
Unit 6, Bighams Park Farm, Waterend, Hemel Hempstead, HP1 3BN
T: 07711 189366
F: 020 7328 8818
E: cel@pathfindersystems.com.au
W: www.pathfindersystems.com.au

Pathfinder Tours
Stag House, Gydynap Lane, Inchbrook, Woodchester, Glos, GL5 5EZ
T: 01453 835414/834477
F: 01453 834053
E: office@pathfindertours.co.uk
W: www.pathfindertours.co.uk

Pauley Interactive
Bletchley Leys Farm, Whaddon Road, Milton Keynes, MK17 0EG
T: 01908 522532
E: info@pauley.co.uk
W: www.pauley.co.uk

A J Paveley
416 Goldon Hillock Road, Sparkbrook, Birmingham, B11 2QH
T: 01217721739
E: sales@ajpaveley.com
W: www.ajpaveley.com

Paypoint
1 The Boulevard, Shire Park, Welwyn Garden City, Herts, AL7 1EL
T: 08457 600633
E: enquiries@paypoint.com
W: www.paypoint.com

PB – Consult GmbH
Am Plaerrer 12, 90429 Nuremburg, Germany
T: 0049 911 32239 0
F: 0049 911 32239 10
E: info@pbconsult.de
W: www.pbconsult.eu

PB Design & Development
Unit 9/10, Hither Green Ind. Est., Clevedon, Bristol, BS21 6XT
T: 01275 874411
F: 01275 874428
E: sales@pbdesign.co.uk
W: www.pbdesign.co.uk

PBH Rail Ltd
The Old Coach House, 4a Custance Walk, York, YO23 1BX
T: 01904 655666
F: 01904 655667
E: darren.pudsey@pbhrail.com
W: www.pbhrail.com

PD Devices Ltd
Unit 1, Old Station Yard, South Brent, Devon, TQ10 9AL
T: 01364 649248
E: marketing@pddevices.co.uk
W: www.pddevices.co.uk

PDG Helicopters
The Heliport, Dalcross, Inverness, IV2 7XB
T: 01667 462740
F: 01667 462376
E: enquiries@pdghelicopters.com
W: www.pdghelicopters.com/

Peacock Salt Ltd
North Harbour, Ayr, KA8 8AE
T: 01292 292000
F: 01292 292001
E: info@peacocksalt.co.uk
W: www.peacocksalt.co.uk

Pearsons Engineering Services Ltd
17 Ilkeston Road, Heanor, Derbys, DE75 7DR
T: 01773 763508
F: 01773 763508
E: nathan@pearsonsengineeringservices.co.uk
W: www.pearsonsengineeringservices.co.uk

A S Peck Engineering Ltd
116 Whitby Rd, Ruislip, Middlesex, HA4 9DR
T: 01895 621398
M: 07850 826003
E: info@aspeckeng.co.uk
W: www.aspeckeng.co.uk

Peeping Ltd
See Tracsis Plc

PEI Genesis UK Ltd
George Curl Way, Southampton, SO18 2RZ
T: 02380 621260
F: 02380 621270
E: peiuk@peigenesis.com
W: www.peigenesis.com

Peli Products (UK) Ltd
Peli House, Peakdale Rd, Brookfield, Glossop, Derbys, SK13 6LQ
T: 01457 869999
F: 01457 869966
E: sales@peliproducts.co.uk
W: www.peliproducts.co.uk

Pell Frischmann
5 Manchester Square, London, W1A 1AU
T: 020 7486 3661
F: 020 7487 4153
E: pflondon@pellfrischmann.com
W: www.pellfrischmann.com

Pelma Services and Autobuild Ltd
Chestnut Tree Cottage, One Pin Lane, Farnham Common, Bucks, SL2 3QY
T: 01753 648484
E: pelma@btconnect.com
W: www.autobuildltd.co.uk

Peninsula Rail Task Force
c/o Plymouth City Council, Transport Strategy, Ballard House, Plymouth, PL1 3BJ
E: info@peninsulatransport.org.uk
W: www.peninsulatransport.org.uk/

Penna plc
5 Fleet Place, London, EC4M 7RD
T: 0800 028 1715
E: corporate@penna.com
W: www.penna.com/

Pennant Consulting Ltd
1 Sopwith Crescent, Wickford Business Park, Wickford, Essex, SS11 8YU
T: 01268 493495
E: office@pennant-consult.com
W: www.pennant-consult.com

Pennant International Ltd
Pennant Court (Head Office),
Staverton Technology Park,
Cheltenham,
Gloucestershire, GL51 6TL
T: 01452 714914
F: 01452 714920
E: john.churchman@pennantplc.co.uk
W: www.pennantplc.co.uk

Pentair
Postbus 487, 5000 AL Tilburg,
Netherlands
T: 0808 234 1670
F: 0808 234 4676
W: www.erico.com/

Pentalver
T: 0333 150 8280
W: www.pentalver.com

Pentaxia
40-44 Longbridge Lane, Ascot
Business Park, Derby, DE24 8UJ
T: 01332 574 870
F: 01332 573 568
E: enquiries@pentaxia.co.uk
W: www.pentaxia.co.uk

People 1st
Hospitality House, 11-59 High Road,
London, N2 8AB
T: 020 3074 1222
E: info@people1st.co.uk
W: www.people1st.co.uk

Perco Engineering Services Ltd
The Old Nurseries, Nottingham Rd,
Radcliffe
on Trent, Nottingham, NG12 2DU
T: 0115 933 5000
F: 0115 933 4692
E: info@perco.co.uk
W: www.perco.co.uk

Permali Gloucester Ltd
Permali Park, Bristol Rd, Gloucester,
GL1 5TT
T: 01452 528282
F: 01452 507409
E: fraser.rankin@permali.co.uk
W: www.permali.co.uk

Permalok Fastening Systems Ltd
Plumtree Industrial Estate, Harworth,
Doncaster, S Yorks, DN11 8EW
T: 01302 711308
F: 01302 719823
E: info@permalokfastening.co.uk
W: www.permalokfastening.co.uk

Permanent Way Institution
5 Mount Crescent, Warley, Brentwood,
Essex, CM14 5DB
T: 01277 230031
E: info@thepwi.org
W: www.thepwi.org

Permaquip Ltd
Brierley Industrial Park, Stanton Hill,
Sutton-in-Ashfield, NG17 3JZ
T: 01623 513349
F: 01623 517742
E: sales@permaquip.co.uk
W: www.permaquip.co.uk

Perpetuum Ltd
Unit 2, Strategic Park, Comines Way,
Hedge End, Southampton, SO30 4DA
T: 02380 765888
F: 02380 765889
E: info@perpetuum.com
W: www.perpetuum.com/rail

PESA
Zygmunta Augusta 11, PL-85 082
Bydgoszcz, Poland
T: 0048 52339 1360
E: marketing@pesa.pl
W: www.pesa.pl

Petards Joyce-Loebl Ltd
390 Princesway North, TVTE,
Gateshead, Tyne & Wear, NE11 0TU
T: 0191 420 3000
E: rail@petards.com
W: www.petards.com

Peter Brett Associates
Caversham Bridge House, Waterman
Place, Reading, RG1 8DN
T: 0118 950 0761
F: 0118 959 7498
E: reading@peterbrett.com
W: peterbrett.com/

Peter Davidson Consultancy
Brownlow House, Ravens Lane,
Berkhamsted, Herts, HP4 2DX
T: 01442 891665
F: 01442 879776
E: mail@peter-davidson.com
W: www.peter-davidson.com

Peter Staveley Consulting
247 Davidson Rd, Croydon, CR0 6DQ
T: 07973 168742
E: peter@peterstaveley.co.uk
W: www.peterstaveley.co.uk

Pfisterer
Unit 9, Ellesmere Business Park, off
Swingbridge Rd, Grantham, Lincs,
NG31 7XT
T: 01476 578657
F: 01476 568631
E: info.uk@pfisterer.com
W: www.pfisterer.co.uk

Pfleiderer
See RAIL.ONE GmbH

PFS Ltd
Unit 2-3, Wheaton Court, Wheaton
Road, Witham, Essex, CM8 3UJ
T: 01376 535260
F: 01376 535268
E: trevor.mason@pfsfueltec.com
W: www.pfsfueltec.com

Phi Group Ltd
Hadley House, Bayshill Road,
Cheltenham, Glos, GL50 3AW
T: 01242 707600
F: 0870 333 4127
E: marketing@phigroup.co.uk
W: www.phigroup.co.uk

Phoenix Contact Ltd
Halesfield 13, Telford, Shropshire,
TF7 4PG
T: 0845 881 2222
F: 0845 881 2211
E: info@phoenixcontact.co.uk
W: www.phoenixcontact.co.uk

Phoenix Systems UK Ltd
Unit 48, Standard Way, Fareham
Industrial
Park, Fareham, Hants, PO16 8XQ
T: 0845 658 6111
F: 0845 658 6222
E: neills@phoenixsystemsuk.com
W: www.phoenixsystemsuk.com

PHS Besafe incorporating Hiviz Laundries Ltd
PHS Group, Western Industrial Estate,
Caerphilly, CF83 1XH
T: 02920 809120
F: 02920 863288
E: enquiries@phs.co.uk
W: www.phs.co.uk

Pickersgill-Kaye Ltd
Pepper Road, Hunslet, Leeds, West
Yorkshire, LS10 2PP
T: 0113 277 5531
F: 0113 276 0221
E: enquiries@pkaye.co.uk
W: www.pkaye.co.uk/

Picow Engineering Group
1 Station House, Lowlands Road,
Runcorn, Cheshire, WA7 5TQ
T: 01928 567337
F: 01928 575401
W: www.picow.co.uk/

Pilkington Glass Ltd
Prescot Rd, St Helens, Merseyside,
WA10 3TT
T: 01744 28882
F: 01744 692660
E: classics@pilkington.com
W: www.pilkington.com

Pilz Automation Technology
Pilz House, Little Colliers Field, Corby,
Northants, NN18 8TJ
T: 01536 460766
F: 01536 460866
E: sales@pilz.co.uk
W: www.pilz.co.uk

Pinsent Masons
City Point, One Ropemaker St, London,
EC2Y 9AH
T: 020 7418 7000
F: 020 7418 7050
W: www.pinsentmasons.com

Pipeline Drillers Ltd
10 Kirkford, Stewarton, Kilmarnock,
KA3 5HZ
T: 01560 482021
F: 01560 484809
E: info@pipelinedrillers.co.uk

Pirtek (UK) Ltd
199 The Vale, Acton, London, W3 7QS
T: 020 8749 8444
F: 020 8749 8333
E: info@pirtek.co.uk
W: www.pirtek.co.uk/

Pitchmastic PmB Ltd
Panama House, 184 Attercliffe Rd,
Sheffield, S4 7WZ
T: 0114 270 0100
F: 0114 276 8782
E: info@pitchmasticpmb.co.uk
W: www.pitchmasticpmb.co.uk

Plan Me Project Management
PO Box 281, Malvern, WR14 9EP
T: 07906 439055
F: 0800 471 5332
E: info@planme.com
W: www.planme.com

Planet Platforms
Brunel Close, Century Park, Wakefield
41 Ind. Est, Wakefield, WF2 0XG
T: 0800 085 4161
F: 01924 267090
E: info@planetplatforms.co.uk
W: www.planetplatforms.co.uk

A Plant
See Sunbelt Rentals

PlasmaTrack
Power Road Studios, 114 Power Road,
Chiswick, London, W4 5PY

Plasser Machinery, Parts & Services Ltd
Manor Rd, West Ealing, London,
W13 0PP
T: 020 8998 4781
F: 020 8997 8206
E: info@plasser.co.uk
W: www.plasser.co.uk

Platform 5 Publishing
52 Broadfield Road, Sheffield, S8 0XJ
T: 0114 255 2625
F: 0114 255 2471
E: andrew.dyson@platform5.com
W: www.platform5.com/

Platipus Anchors Ltd
Unit Q, Philanthropic Rd, Kingsfield
Business Centre, Redhill, Surrey,
RH1 4DP
T: 01737 762300
F: 01737 773395
E: info@platipus-anchors.com
W: www.platipus-anchors.com

Playle Consultancy Ltd
1579 London Road, Leigh-On-Sea,
Essex, SS9 2SG

Plettac Security UK Ltd
Unit 39, Sir Frank Whittle Business
Centre, Great Central Way, Rugby,
Warks, CV21 3XH
T: 0844 800 1725
F: 01788 544549
E: info@plettac.co.uk
W: www.plettac.co.uk

Plextek
The Plextek Building, London Road,
Great Chesterford, Saffron Walden,
CB10 1NY
T: 01799 533200
E: hello@plextek.com
W: www.plextek.com

Plexus
Bay 150, Shannon Industrial Estate,
Shannon, Co. Clare, Republic of Ireland
T: 353 61 771 500
F: 00 353- (0) 61- 474446
E: mail@itwep.com
W: www.itwplexus.co.uk

Plowman Craven Ltd
2 Lea Business Park, 141 Lower Luton
Rd, Harpenden, Herts, AL5 5EQ
T: 01582 765566
F: 01582 765370
E: post@plowmancraven.co.uk
W: www.plowmancraven.co.uk

PM Safety Consultants Ltd
Suite D, 3rd Floor, Saturn Facilities, 101
Lockhurst Lane, Coventry, CV6 5SF
T: 02476 665770
F: 02476 582401
E: info@pmsafety.com
W: www.pmsafety.com

PMProfessional Learning
See Aikona Management Ltd

Pneumatrol
West End Business Park, Blackburn
Road, Oswaldtwistle, Accrington,
Lancs, BB5 4WZ
T: 01254 872277
F: 01254 390133
E: sales@pneumatrol.com
W: www.pneumatrol.com/

Pochins Ltd
Brookes Lane, Middlewich, Cheshire,
CW10 0JQ
T: 01606 833333
F: 01606 833331
W: www.pochins.plc.uk/

Pod-Trak Ltd
Crove House, 14 Aintree Road,
Perivale, Middx, UB6 7LA
T: 0845 450 4190
F: 020 998 6901
E: enquiries@pod-trak.com
W: www.pod-trak.com

Poise Group Ltd
Fleet House, 8-12 New Bridge Street,
London, EC4V 6AL
T: 020 3086 9400
E: info@poisegroup.uk
W: www.poisegroup.uk/

Polyamp AB
Box 229, Atvidaberg, 597 25, Sweden
T: 0046 120 85410
F: 0046 120 85405
E: info@polyamp.se
W: www.polyamp.com

Polydeck Ltd
Unit 14, Burnett Ind Est, Cox's Green,
Wrington, Bristol, Somerset, BS40 5QS
T: 01934 863678
F: 01934 863683
E: sales@gripfast.co.uk
W: www.polydeck.co.uk/

Polyflor Ltd
Transport Flooring Division, PO Box 3,
Radcliffe New Rd, Whitefield,
Manchester, M45 7NR
T: 0161 767 1111
F: 0161 767 1100
E: transport@polyflor.com
W: www.polyflor.com

Polynt
Laporte Road, Stallingborough, Near
Grimsby, Lincolnshire, DN41 8DR,
France
T: 01469 552571
E: contact@polynt.com
W: www.polynt.com

Polypipe
Charnwood Business Park, North
Road, Loughborough, Leicestershire,
LE11 1LE
T: 01509 615100
E: civilsenquiries@polypipe.com
W: www.polypipe.com

Polyrack Tech-Group
Steinbeisstrasse 4, D-75334
Straubenhardt, Germany
T: 0800 7659 7225
E: sales@polyrack.com
W: www.polyrack.com

Polysafe Level Crossings
25 King St. Ind. Est., Langtoft,
Peterborough, PE6 9NF
T: 01778 560555
F: 01778 560773
E: sales@polysafe.co.uk
W: www.polysafe.co.uk

Pontoonworks
The Old Glove Factory, Bristol Road,
Sherborne, Dorset, DT9 4HP
T: 01935 814950
F: 01935 815131
E: office@pontoonworks.co.uk
W: www.pontoonworks.co.uk

PORR AG
Absberggasse 47, A-1100 Wien, Austria
T: 43 (0)50 626-0
W: www.porr.at/

Portaramp UK Ltd
Units 3&4, Dolphin Business Park,
Shadwell, Thetford, Norfolk, IP24 2RY
T: 01953 681799
F: 01953 688153
E: sales@portaramp.co.uk
W: www.portaramp.co.uk

Portastor
New Lane, Huntington, York,
YO32 9PR
T: 01904 656869
F: 01904 611760
M: 07710 313301
E: action@portastor.com
W: www.portastor.com

Portec Rail Group
See LB Foster Europe

Porterbrook
Ivatt House, 7 The Point, Pinnacle Way,
Pride Park, Derby, DE24 8ZS
T: 01332 285050
F: 01332 285051
E: enquiries@porterbrook.co.uk
W: www.porterbrook.co.uk

Portwest Clothing Ltd
Commercial Rd, Goldthorpe Ind. Est.,
Goldthorpe, S.Yorks, S63 9BL
T: 01709 894575
F: 01709 880830
E: info@portwest.com
W: www.portwest.com

Portwest Construction Ltd
Unit 3, Whitworth Court, Manor Park,
Runcorn, Cheshire, WA7 1WA
T: 01928 597818
E: info@portwestconstruction.com
W: www.portwestconstruction.com/

PoS Insights
50 Liverpool Street, London,
EC2M 7PY
T: 020 8914 7914
W: pos-insights.com

Postfield Systems
53 Ullswater Cres., Coulsdon, Surrey,
CR5 2HR
T: 020 8655 6080
F: 020 8655 6082
E: demo@postfield.co.uk
W: https://postfieldsystems.wixsite.com/postfield

Potensis Ltd
7th Floor, Froomsgate House, Rupert
St, Bristol, BS1 2QJ
T: 0117 910 7999
F: 0117 927 2722
E: office@potensis.com
W: www.potensis.com

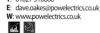

Potter Logistics Ltd
Melmerby Ind. Est, Green Lane,
Melmerby,
Ripon, North Yorks, HG4 5HP
T: 01353 646703
E: sales@potterlogistics.co.uk
W: www.potterlogistics.co.uk

Powdertech (Corby) Limited
Cockerell Road, Phoenix Parkway,
Corby, Northants, NN17 5DU
T: 01536 400890
E: richard.b@powdertech.co.uk
W: www.powdertechcorby.co.uk

Powelectrics
12 Ninian Park, Tamworth, Staffs,
B77 5ES
T: 01827 310666
E: dave.oakes@powelectrics.co.uk
W: www.powelectrics.co.uk

Powell Dobson
Suite 1F Building One, Eastern
Business Park, Wern Fawr Lane, Old St.
Mellons, Cardiff, CF3 5EA
T: 03333 201001
M: 029 2079 1212
W: www.powelldobson.com/en/

Power 4 from Fox & Cooper
See Stuart Group

Power Electrics Generators Ltd
St. Ivel Way, Warmley, Bristol, BS30 8TY
T: 0117 947 9700
F: 0117 947 9702
E: sales@powerelectrics.com
W: www.powerelectrics.com

Power Electronics (PE Systems Ltd)
Victoria St, Leigh, Lancs, WN7 5SE
T: 01942 260330
F: 01942 261835
E: sales@pe-systems.co.uk
W: www.pe-systems.co.uk

Power Jacks Ltd
Balmacassie Commercial Park, Ellon,
Aberdeenshire, AB41 8BX
T: 01358 285100
E: sales@powerjacks.com
W: www.powerjacks.com

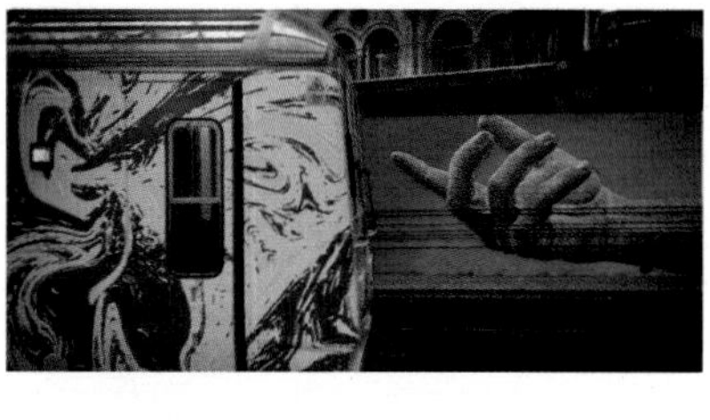
At the heart of
Britain's railway
for over 25 years
porterbrook.co.uk porterbrook

Powerbox Group
Bennett House, The Dean, Alresford, Hants, SO24 9BH
E: info.uk@prbx.com
W: www.prbx.com/

Powernetics Systems Ltd
Jason Works, Clarence St, Loughborough, Leics, LE11 1DX
T: 01509 214153 x205
F: 01509 262460
E: jag@powernetics.co.uk
W: www.powernetics.co.uk

Powertron Convertors Ltd
See Martek Power Ltd

Praxis
See Altran UK Ltd

Praybourne Ltd
Unit 2c, Eagle Road, North Moons Moat, Redditch, Worcs, B98 9HF
T: 0844 669 1860
F: 01527 543 752
E: enquiries@praybourne.co.uk
W: www.praybourne.co.uk

PRB Consulting
167 London Rd, Hailsham, E.Sussex, BN27 3AN
T: 0845 557 6814
E: paul.brace@prbconsulting.co.uk
W: www.prbconsulting.co.uk

PRC Rail Consulting
7 Hunters Rise, Kirby Bellars, Melton Mowbray, Leics, LE14 2DT
T: 01664 810118
E: piers.connor@railway-technical.com
W: www.railway-technical.com

Pre Metro Operations Ltd
Regent House, 56 Hagley Road, Stourbridge, West Midlands, DY8 1QD
T: 01384 441325
F: 01384 396587
E: premetro@aol.com
W: www.premetro.co.uk/

Preformed Markings Ltd
Unit 6, Oyster Park, 109 Chertsey Rd, Byfleet, Surrey, KT14 7AX
T: 01932 359270
F: 01932 340936
E: info@preformedmarkings.co.uk
W: www.preformedmarkings.co.uk

Premier Calibration Ltd
Unit 3K/L, Lake Enterprise Park, Sandall Stores Rd, Kirk Sandall, Doncaster, DN3 1QR
T: 01302 888448
F: 01302 881197
E: enquiries.premcal@btconnect.com
W: www.premiercalibration.co.uk/

Premier Rail Pits
Town Drove, Quadring, Spalding, Lincs, PE11 4PU
T: 01775 821222
E: info@premierpits.com
W: www.premierpits.com

Premier Stampings
Station St, Cradley Heath, West Midlands, B64 6AJ
T: 01384 353100
F: 01384 353101
E: ashleyh@premierstampings.co.uk
W: www.premierstampings.co.uk

Premier Train Catering
See Creative Rail Dining

Preserved Traction Technical Services
3 No4 Pembroke Rd, London, N15 4NW
E: markb754@aol.com
W: www.preservedtractiontechservice.com

Preston Trampower Ltd
Preston Office, 1 Navigation Way, Preston, Lancashire, PR2 2YP
T: 01772 730290
F: 01772 730291
E: lincoln.shields@trampower.co.uk
W: www.prestontrampower.co.uk

Price Tool Sales Ltd
See Birchwood Price Tools

Price Waterhouse Coopers LLP
1 Embankment Place, London, WC2N 6RH
T: 020 7583 5000
F: 020 7822 4652
W: www.pwc.co.uk

PriestmanGoode
150 Great Portland St, London, W1W 6QD
T: 020 7580 3444
M: 07376 286884
E: studio@priestmangoode.com
W: www.priestmangoode.com

Primat Recruitment
Lingfield Point, Darlington, DL1 1RW
T: 01325 744400
W: www.primatrecruitment.com

Prime Rail Solutions Ltd
Dartford Road, March, Cambridgeshire, PE15 8AE
T: 01733 462420
E: peter@primerailsolutions.com
W: www.primerailsolutions.com

Priority Vehicle Hire Ltd
Unit 1, Bestmans Lane Ind. Estate, Bestmans Lane, Kempsey, Worcester, WR5 3PZ
T: 01905 821843
E: enquiries@priorityhire.co.uk
W: www.priorityhire.co.uk/

Pro Rail Services Ltd
Unit 2-4, Little Ridge, The Ridgeway, Welwyn Garden City, AL7 2BH
T: 01707 927400
E: info@prorailservices.co.uk
W: www.prorailservices.co.uk/

ProActive Rail
78 York Street, London, W1H 1DP
T: 020 7993 6049
F: 020 7625 4530
W: www.proactiverail.co.uk/

Product Innovation Ltd
39 St Gabriels Road, London, NW2 4DT
T: 020 8452 3968
F: 020 8452 5665
E: peter.frank@productinnovation.com
W: www.productinnovation.com

Professional Lifting Services (PLS)
Unit 7, Parkview Works, 870 Penistone Road, Sheffield, S6 2DL
T: 0114 285 5488
F: 0114 285 4553
W: www.plsltd.co.uk/

Progress Rail Services
Eastfield, Peterborough, PE1 5NA
T: 01159 218 218
E: prsuk.sales@progressrail.com
W: www.progressrail.com

Project Leaders Ltd
Sarre House, Canterbury Road, Sarre, Kent, CT7 0JY
T: 01843 847848
F: 01843 842463
W: projectleaders.co.uk/

Project7 Consultancy
Westpoint House, 5 Redwood Place, Peel Park, East Kilbride, G74 5PB
T: 0844 568 6840
F: 0844 568 6850
W: www.project7consultancy.com/

Prolec Ltd
25 Benson Rd, Nuffield Ind. Est., Poole, Dorset, BH17 0GB
T: 01202 681190
F: 01202 677909
E: info@prolec.co.uk
W: www.prolec.co.uk

Pro-Link Europe
Irene House, Five Arches Business Park, Maidstone Rd, Sidcup, Kent, DA14 5AE
T: 020 8309 2700
F: 020 8309 7890
E: enquire@prolink-europe.com
W: www.prolink-europe.com

Prostaff Rail Recruitment
172 Buckingham Ave, Slough, Bucks, SL1 4RD
T: 01753 575888
W: www.prostaff.com

Protec Fire Detection Plc
Protec House, Churchill Way, Nelson, Lancs, BB9 6RT
T: 01282 717171
F: 01282 717273
E: sales@protec.co.uk
W: www.protec.co.uk

Proteq
Head Office, The Pinnacle Works, Station Road, Epworth, Doncaster, DN9 1JU
T: 01427 872572
F: 01427 875094
E: info@proteq.co.uk
W: www.proteq.co.uk

Provertha
21 Tarrant Wharf, Arundel, West Sussex, BN18 9NY
E: service@provertha.com
W: www.provertha.com

PRV Engineering
Pegasus House, Polo Grounds, New Inn, Pontypool, Gwent, NP4 0TW
T: 01495 769697
F: 01495 769776
E: enquiries@prv-engineering.co.uk
W: www.prv-engineering.co.uk

Prysm Rail
See Archer Safety Signs

Prysmian Cables & Systems
Chickenhall Lane, Eastleigh, Hants, SO50 6YU
T: 023 8029 5029
F: 023 8060 8769
E: marketing.telecom@prysmian.com
W: www.prysmiangroup.com

PSV Glass and Glazing Ltd
Hillbottom Rd, High Wycombe, Bucks, HP12 4HJ
T: 01494 533131
F: 01494 462675
E: rail@psvglass.co.uk
W: www.psvglass.com

PSV Wipers Ltd
18 Kempton Road, Keytec 7 Business Park, Pershore, WR10 2TA
T: 01905 350500
F: 01905 763928
E: sales@psvwipers.com
W: www.psvwipers.com/

PTH Group Ltd
See BHSF Occupational Health Ltd

PTM Design Ltd
Unit B2, Sovereign Park Ind Est, Lathkill St, Market Harborough, LE16 9EG
T: 01858 463777
F: 01858 463777
E: sales@ptmdesign.co.uk
W: www.ptmdesign.co.uk/

PTP Associates
The Lodge, 21 Harcourt Rd., Dorney Reach, Berks, SL6 0DT
T: 01628 776059
E: ces@ptpassociates.co.uk
W: www.ptpassociates.co.uk

Publica
10 Clerkenwell Green, London, EC1R 0DP
T: 020 7490 3986
E: mail@publica.co.uk

Pullman Rail
Train Maintenance Depot, Leckwith Rd, Cardiff, CF11 8HP
T: 02920 368850
F: 02920 368874
E: info@pullmanrail.co.uk
W: www.pullmanrail.co.uk

PULS UK Ltd
Unit 10, Ampthill Business Park, Station Road, Ampthill, Beds, MK45 2QW
T: 01525 841001
E: sales@puls.co.uk
W: www.puls.co.uk

Pulsarail
See Praybourne Ltd

Pulsarail Workwear
108 Manchester Road, Carrington, Manchester, M31 4BD
T: 0161 777 4230
W: www.pulsarailworkwear.co.uk/

Pyeroy Group
Kirkstone House, St Omers Rd, Western Riverside Route, Gateshead, Tyne & Wear, NE11 9EZ
T: 0191 493 2600
F: 0191 493 2601
E: mail@pyeroy.co.uk
W: www.pyeroy.co.uk

Pym & Wildsmith (Metal Finishers) Ltd
Bramshall Ind. Est, Bramshall, Uttoxeter, Staffs, ST14 8TD
T: 01889 565653
F: 01889 567064
E: enquiries@pymandwildsmith.co.uk
W: www.pymandwildsmith.co.uk

Q'Straint
Unit 72-76, John Wilson Business Park, Whitstable, Kent, CT5 3QT
T: 01227 773035
F: 01227 770035
E: info@qstraint.co.uk
W: www.qstraint.com

QA-Aikona Ltd
Rath House, 55-65 Uxbridge Rd, Slough, SL1 1SG
T: 0845 757 3888
E: info@qa.com
W: www.qa.com

QC Data Ltd
Park House, 14 Kirtley Drive, Castle Marina, Nottingham, NG7 1LD
T: 0115 941 5806
F: 0115 947 2901
E: rjohnson@qcdata.com
W: www.qcdata.com

QED Scaffolding
Lock Street, St Helens, Merseyside, WA9 1HS
T: 01744 751117
F: 01744 755779
E: enquiries@qedscaffolding.com
W: www.qedscaffolding.com/

QikServe
Randolph House, 2nd Floor, 4 Charlotte Lane, Edinburgh, EH2 4QZ
E: hello@qikserve.com
W: https://www.qikserve.com/

QinetiQ
Cody Technology Park, Ively Road, Farnborough, Hampshire, GU14 0LX
T: 0117 952 8442
E: railservices@qinetiq.com
W: www.qinetiq.com

Qmatic Ltd
Derwent House, Ground Floor, University Way, Cranfield Technology Park, Bedfordshire, MK43 0AZ
T: 01234 757110
F: 0845 123 0201
E: info.uk@qmatic.com
W: www.qmatic.com/

Qognify
Tallis House, 2 Tallis Street, London, EC4Y 0AB
E: info.emea@qognify.com
W: https://www.qognify.com/

The QSS Group Ltd
2 St Georges House, Vernon Gate, Derby, DE1 1UQ
T: 01332 221400
F: 01332 221401
E: enquiries@theqssgroup.co.uk
W: www.theqssgroup.co.uk

QTS Plant
QTS Group, Rench Farm, Drumclog, Strathaven, S. Lanarks, ML10 6QJ
T: 01357 440222
F: 01357 440364
E: enquiries@qtsgroup.com
W: www.qtsgroup.com

Qualitrain Ltd
Bridge House, 12 Mansfield Rd, Tibshelf, Derbys, DE55 5NF
F: 01773 590671
E: richard.bates@qualitrain.co.uk
W: www.qualitrain.co.uk

Qualter Hall & Co Ltd
PO Box 8, Johnson St, Barnsley, South Yorkshire, S75 2BY
T: 01226 205761
F: 01226 286269
E: admin@qualterhall.co.uk
W: www.qualterhall.co.uk

Quantexa
10 York Road, London, SE1 7ND
E: info@quantexa.com
W: www.quantexa.com

Quartzelec
Castle Mound Way, Central Park, Rugby, Warwickshire, CV23 0WB
T: 01788 512512
E: info.uk@quartzelec.com
W: www.quartzelec.com/

Quattro Plant Ltd
Greenway Court, Canning Rd, Stratford, London, E15 3ND
T: 020 8519 6165
F: 020 8503 0505
E: sales@quattroplant.co.uk
W: www.quattroplant.co.uk

Qube Global Software
9 King Street, London, EC2V 8EA
T: 020 7726 3200
F: 020 7726 3201
E: info@qubeglobal.com
W: www.qubeglobal.co.uk/

Quest Diagnostics
Unit B1, Parkway West, Cranford Lane, Heston, Middlesex, TW5 9QA
T: 020 8377 3378
F: 020 8377 3350
W: www.questdiagnostics.com

Quickbuild (UK) Ltd
Imperial House, 1 Factory Rd, Silvertown, London, E16 2EL
T: 020 7473 2712
F: 020 7476 2713
E: davidbrowne@hiremasters.co.uk
W: www.hiremasters.co.uk/www.quickbuild.uk.com

Quickway Buildings
Hardy's Yard, London Rd, Riverhead, Sevenoaks, Kent, TN13 2DN
T: 01304 612284
F: 01304 620012
E: sales@quickway-wingham.co.uk
W: www.quickway-wingham.co.uk

Quinn Infrastructure
Minster House, 42 Mincing Lane, London, EC3R 7AE
T: 020 7993 0731
E: info@quinninfrastructure.co.uk
W: www.quinninfrastructure.co.uk

QW Rail Leasing
12 Plumtree Court, London, EC4A 4HT

R E Cooke Limited
Brunel Drive, Stretton Business Park, Burton Upon Trent, Staffordshire, DE13 0BY
T: 01283 561671
F: 01283 510960
E: sales@recooke.co.uk
W: www.recooke.co.uk/

R&B Switchgear Group
Switchgear House, The Courtyard, Green Lane, Heywood, Lancs, OL10 2EX
T: 01706 369933
F: 01706 364564
E: info@rbswitch.co.uk
W: www.rbswitch.co.uk

R&W Rail
Cheriton Mill Offices, Alresford, Hampshire, SO24 0NG
T: 02380 845379
W: https://www.rwcivilengineering.co.uk/what-we-do/rail/

R.S. Clare & Co Ltd
8-14 Stanhope St, Liverpool, L8 5RQ
T: 0151 709 2902
F: 0151 709 0518
E: info@rsclare.co.uk
W: www.rsclare.com

r2p UK Systems Ltd
Unit 1, Merlin Centre, Charlwood Court, County Oak Way, Crawley, RH11 7XA, Germany
M: 07747 460509
E: balvinder.chana@r2p.com
W: www.r2p.com/our-solutions

Ra'alloy Ramps Ltd
A3 Stafford Park 15, Telford, Shropshire, TF3 3BB
T: 01952 291224
E: enquiries@raalloy.co.uk
W: www.raalloy.co.uk/

Racon
2nd Floor, Mercantile Chambers, 53 Bothwell Street, Glasgow, G2 6TS
T: 0141 248 3038
E: info@racon-ms.com
W: www.racon-ms.com/

RAICS
See R&I Consulting

Rail & Road Protec GmbH
Lise-Meitner-Strasse 4, D-24941 Flensburg, Germany
T: 01293 8873 08
E: info@r2p.com
W: www.r2p.com

Rail Academy
Newcastle College Rail Academy, William St, Felling, Gateshead, Tyne & Wear, NE10 0JP

Rail Accident Investigation Branch
The Wharf, Stores Rd, Derby, DE21 4BA
T: 01332 253300
E: enquiries@raib.gov.uk
W: www.raib.gov.uk

Rail Alliance
The Control Tower, Quinton Rail Technology Centre, Station Rd, Long Marston, Stratford upon Avon, Warks, CV37 8PL
T: 01789 720026
E: info@railalliance.co.uk
W: www.railalliance.co.uk

Rail Aspects
M: 07917 763321
W: railaspects.com/

Rail Audit & Assurance Services (RAAS)
54 Highfield Rd, Cheadle Hulme, Stockport, SK8 6EP
T: 0161 486 1237
E: stockport@raas.co.uk
W: www.raas.co.uk

Rail Charter Services
Craven House, 16 Northumberland Avenue, London, WC2N 5AP
W: www.railcharterservices.co.uk/

Rail Delivery Group
2nd Floor, 200 Aldersgate Street, London, EC1A 4HD
T: 020 7841 8000
E: info@raildeliverygroup.com
W: www.raildeliverygroup.com

Rail Forum
Lonsdale House, Quaker Way, Derby, DE1 3HD
T: 01332 593550
E: karen@railforum.uk
W: www.railforum.uk

Rail Freight Group
7 Bury Place, London, WC1A 2LA
T: 020 3116 0007
F: 020 3116 0008
E: phillippa@rfg.org.uk
W: www.rfg.org.uk

Rail Freight Services
Stone Terminal, Horn Lane, Acton, London, W3 9EH
T: 0208 896 9192
F: 0208 869 6829
E: enquiries@railfreightservices.co.uk
W: www.railfreightservices.co.uk/

Rail Gourmet Group
169 Euston Road, London, NW1 2AE
T: 020 7529 8330
F: 020 7922 6596
E: jfleet@railgourmetuk.com
W: www.railgourmet.com

Rail Images & Rail Images Video
5 Sandhurst Crescent, Leigh on Sea, Essex, SS9 4AL
T: 01702 525059
F: 01702 525059
E: info@railimages.co.uk
W: www.railimages.co.uk

Rail Industry Contractors Association Ltd (RICA)
Gin Gan House, Thropton, Morpeth, Northumberland, NE65 7LT
T: 01669 620569
E: enquiries@rica.uk.com
W: www.rica.uk.com

Rail Industry First Aid Association (RIFAA)
Po Box 1152, Doncaster, DN1 9NL
T: 01302 329 729
F: 01302 320 590
E: bookings@rifaa.com
W: www.rifaa.com

The Rail Innovation Group
W: www.railinnovationgroup.com/

Rail Innovations
Ashbourne, Derbyshire, DE6 1GY
T: 07730 303799
E: greg@railinnov.com
W: https://railinnov.com/

Rail Insights Ltd
Highlands, St Andrews Rd, Henley-on-Thames, RG9 1PG
T: 01491 414218
E: roger.mcdonald@railinsights.com
W: www.railinsights.com

Rail Manche Finance EEIG
Times House, Bravingtons Walk, Regent Quarter, London, N1 9AW
T: 020 7042 9961
F: 020 7833 3896
E: david.hiscock@rmf.co.uk
W: www.rmf.co.uk

Rail North
See Transport for the North (TfN)

Rail Op UK Ltd
Gowers Farm, Tumblers Green, Braintree, Essex, CM77 8AZ
T: 0845 450 5232
F: 01376 388295
E: info@railop.co.uk
W: www.railop.co.uk

Rail Operations Developments Ltd
Electra House, Electra Way, Crewe Business Park, Crewe, CW1 6GL
T: 01270 588500
F: 01270 588500
E: enquiries@rodl.co.uk
W: www.railoperationaldevelopment.co.uk/

Rail Operations Group
6 Snow Hill, London, EC1A 2AY
E: info@railopsgroup.co.uk
W: www.railopsgroup.co.uk

Rail Order
Unit 11, Billet Lane, Normanby Enterprise Park, Scunthorpe, DN15 9YH
T: 01724 292860
F: 01724 292242
E: sales@rail-order.co.uk
W: www.rail-order.co.uk

Rail Partners
1 Northumberland Avenue, London, WC2N 5BW
T: 020 3821 1478
E: contactus@railpartners.co.uk
W: railpartners.co.uk

Rail Personnel Ltd
Level 13, 141 Thomson Road, Wanchai, Hong Kong, China
T: 00 852 2753 5636
F: 00 852 2305 4512
E: info@railpersonnel.com
W: www.railpersonnel.com

Rail Positive Relations
The Bothy, 18 Holloway Road, Duffield, Derbyshire, DE56 4FE
T: 07973 950923
E: rupert@railpr.com
W: www.railpr.com

Rail Products UK
Mountcairn, 22 Cairneymount Road, Carluke, ML8 4EN
T: 01555 773027
E: derek@railproducts.uk.com
W: www.railproducts.uk.com

Rail Professional Development
Cranes House, 5 Paycocke Rd, Basildon, Essex, SS14 3DP
T: 01268 822842
F: 01268 822841
E: info@rpd.co.uk
W: www.rpd.co.uk

Rail Research UK Association (RRUKA)
See UK Rail Research and Innovation Network (UKRRIN)

Rail Safety Solutions
Unit 27, Royal Scot Rd, Pride Park, Derby, DE24 8AJ
T: 01332 989593
F: 020 3142 5301
E: info@railsafetysolutions.com
W: www.railsafetysolutions.com

Rail Safety Systems BV
See Innovative Railway Safety Ltd

Rail Settlement Plan Ltd
See Rail Delivery Group

Rail Supply Group
E: secretariat@railsupplygroup.org
W: www.railsupplygroup.org

Rail Tech Group (Railway & Signalling Engineering) Ltd
91 Dales Rd, Ipswich, Suffolk, IP1 4JR
T: 01473 242344
F: 01473 242379
W: www.rttrainingsolutions.co.uk/railway-courses/

The Rail Technology Unit (RTU) at Manchester Metropolitan University
Rail Technology Unit, Manchester Metropolitan University, John Dalton Building, Chester St, Manchester, M1 5GD
T: 0161 247 6247
F: 0161 247 6840
E: j.grey@bham.ac.uk
W: www.mmu.ac.uk/business/our-expertise/expertise.php?area=sustainability_and_climate_change&expertise=railway_research_and_consultancy

Rail Training International Ltd
North Suite, Parsonage Offices, Church Lane, Canterbury, Kent, CT4 7AD
T: 01227 769096
F: 01227 479435
E: andrewrussell@rti.co.uk
W: www.rti.co.uk

Rail Vac
4 Sarum Place, Hemel Hempstead, HP2 6DP
T: 01442 244970
E: info@railvac.com
W: www.railvac.com/

Rail Vision
2 Cygnus Court, Beverley Rd, Pegasus Business Park, East Midlands Airport, Castle Donnington, Leics, DE74 2UZ
T: 01509 672211
E: enquiries@rail-vision.com
W: www.rail-vision.com

Rail Waiting Structures
Unit 60, Dyffryn Business Park, Llantwit Major Rd, Llandow, Vale of Glamorgan, CF71 7PY
T: 01446 795444
F: 01446 773344
E: rail@shelters.co.uk
W: www.railwaitingstructures.com/

RAIL.ONE GmbH
Ingolstaedter Strasse 51, 92318 Neumarkt, Germany
T: 0049 9181 8952-0
F: 0049 9181 8952-5001
E: info@railone.com
W: www.railone.com

Rail-Ability Ltd
Tilcon Ave, Baswich, Stafford, ST18 0YJ
T: 01785 214747
F: 01785 214717
E: skelly@railability.co.uk
W: www.railability.co.uk

Railcare Ltd
See Knorr-Bremse Platform Screen Doors

Railcare Sweden Ltd
Unit 1, Derwent Park, 214-216 London Road, Derby, DE1 2SX
T: 01332 647388
E: info@railcare.co.uk
W: www.railcare.co.uk/

Raileasy
10 Station Parade, High St, Wanstead, London, E11 1QF
T: 0906 2000 500
E: admin@raileasy.co.uk
W: www.raileasy.co.uk

Railex Global Ltd
Unit 19, Howard Road, Park Farm Ind. Est, Redditch, Worcestershire, B98 7SE
T: 01564 700372
F: 07709 837909
E: tony@railexglobal.com
W: www.railexglobal.com

Railfuture
14 Ghent Field Circle, Thurston, Suffolk, IP31 3UP
E: info@railfuture.org.uk
W: www.railfuture.org.uk

Railscape Ltd
15 Totman Cresc, Brook Rd Ind Est, Rayleigh, Essex, SS6 7UY
T: 01268 777795
F: 01268 777762
E: info@railscape.com
W: www.railscape.com

Railsite Telecom
10 The Street, West Horsley, Surrey, KT24 6AX
T: 01483 286456
W: https://railsitetelecom.co.uk/

Railtex/Infrarail
See Mack Brooks Exhibitions Ltd

Railtourer Ltd
See West Coast Railway Co.

Railway Approvals Ltd
Derwent House, RTC Business Park, London Rd, Derby, DE24 8UP
T: 01332 483800
F: 01332 483800
E: sales@railwayapprovals.com
W: www.railwayapprovals.co.uk

Railway Benefit Fund (RBF)
1st Floor, Millennium House, 40 Nantwich Road, Crewe, CW2 6AD
T: 0345 241 2885
E: info@railwaybenefitfund.org.uk
W: www.railwaybenefitfund.org.uk

Railway Brake Services Ltd
Unit 2, Sidings Industrial Estate, Wetmore Road, Burton On Trent, Staffordshire, DE14 1SB
T: 01283 440102
F: 01538 340051
E: support@railwaybrakeservices.co.uk
W: www.railwaybrakeservices.co.uk/

Railway Children
1 The Commons, Sandbach, Cheshire, CW11 1EG
T: 01270 757596
E: hello@railwaychildren.org.uk
W: www.railwaychildren.org.uk/

Railway Civil Engineers Association
One Great George St, Westminster, London, SW1P 3AA
T: 020 7665 2238
E: rcea@ice.org.uk
W: www.rcea.org.uk/

The Railway Consultancy Ltd
1st Floor, South Tower, Crystal Palace Station, London, SE19 2AZ
T: 020 8676 0395
F: 020 8778 7439
E: info@railwayconsultancy.com
W: www.railwayconsultancy.com

Railway Convalescent Home (RCH)
Bridge House, 2 Church St, Dawlish, Devon, EX7 9AU
T: 01626 866850
F: 01626 866676
E: bookings@rch.org.uk
W: www.rch.org.uk

Railway Electrical Services
St Bartholomews Church, Hallam Fields Road, Ilkeston, Derbyshire, DE7 4AZ
T: 0115 944 4608
W: www.railwayelectricalservices.co.uk/

Railway Employees & Public Transport Association
See REPTA (Railway Employees and Public Transport Association)

Railway Engineering Associates Ltd
125 Boden St, Glasgow, G40 3QF
T: 0141 556 0415
E: henry@rea.uk.com
W: www.rea.uk.com

Railway Engineers Forum (REF)
T: 020 7651 7910
W: www.theref.org.uk

Railway Finance Ltd
2 Rutland Park, Sheffield, S10 2PD
T: 01223 891300
F: 01223 891302

Railway Heritage Trust
1 Eversholt St, London, NW1 2DN
T: 020 7904 7354
E: rht@railwayheritagetrust.co.uk
W: www.railwayheritagetrust.co.uk

Railway Industry Association
Kings Building, 16 Smith Square, London, SW1P 3HQ
T: 020 7201 0777
F: 020 7235 5777
E: ria@riagb.org.uk
W: www.riagb.org.uk

The Railway Mission
Rugby Railway Station, Station Approach, Rugby, Warwickshire, CV21 3LA
T: 020 3887 7000
M: 07718 971918
E: office@railwaymission.org
W: www.railwaymission.org

Railway Study Forum (within CILT)
PO Box 375, Burgess Hill, West Sussex, RH15 5BX
W: https://ciltuk.org.uk/about-us/professional-sectors-forums/forums/rsa-main

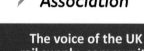

Railway Support Services
Montpellier House, Montpellier Drive, Cheltenham, Glos, GL50 1TY
T: 0870 803 4651
F: 0870 803 4652
E: info@railwaysupportservices.co.uk
W: www.railwaysupportservices.co.uk

Railway Systems Engineering & Integration Group
Birmingham Centre for Railway Reasearch & Education College of Engineering Sciences, University of Birmingham, Edgbaston, Birmingham, B15 2TT
T: 0121 414 4342
F: 0121 414 4291
E: j.grey@bham.ac.uk
W: www.eng.bham.ac.uk/civil/study/postgrad/railway.shtml

Railway Touring Company
14a Tuesday Market Place, Kings Lynn, Norfolk, PE30 1JN
T: 01553 661500
F: 01553 661800
E: enquiries@railwaytouring.co.uk
W: www.railwaytouring.co.uk

Railways Pension Scheme
2nd Floor, Camomile Court, 23 Camomile St, London, EC3A 7LL
T: 0800 234 3434
E: csu@rpmi.co.uk
W: www.railwayspensions.co.uk

Railweight
Foundry Lane, Smethwick, Birmingham, B66 2LP
T: 0845 246 6714
F: 0845 246 6715
E: sales@railweight.co.uk
W: www.averyweigh-tronix.com/railweight

Ramboll UK Ltd
240 Blackfriars Road, London, SE1 8NW
M: 07799 864156
E: steve.brown@ramboll.co.uk
W: www.ramboll.co.uk

Rambus Ecebs Ltd
The Torus Building, Rankine Ave, Scottish Enterprise Technology Park, East Kilbride, G75 0QF
T: 01355 272911
F: 01355 272993
E: enquiries@ecebs.com
W: www.ecebs.com

Ramtech Electronics Ltd
Abbeyfield House, Abbeyfield Rd, Nottingham, NG7 2SZ
T: 0115 957 8282
F: 0115 957 8299
E: solutions@ramtechglobal.com
W: www.ramtechglobal.com

Randstad CPE
6th Floor, 10 Colmore Row, Birmingham, B3 2QD
T: 0121 212 7790
W: www.randstad.co.uk

RASIC
W: www.rasic.co.uk/

Raspberry Software Ltd
9 Deben Mill Business Centre, Old Maltings Approach, Melton, Woodbridge, Suffolk, IP12 1BL
T: 01394 387386
F: 01394 387386
E: info@raspberrysoftware.com
W: www.raspberrysoftware.com

Ratcliff Palfinger
Bessemer Rd, Welwyn Garden City, Herts, AL7 1ET
T: 01707 325571
F: 01707 327752
E: info@palfinger.com
W: www.palfinger.com

Rayleigh Instruments
Raytel House, Brook Rd, Rayleigh, Essex, SS6 7XH
T: 01268 749300
F: 01268 749309
E: sales@rayleigh.co.uk
W: www.rayleigh.co.uk

RazorSecure
Suite 10, Innovation Centre, Basing View, Basingstoke, RG21 4HG
E: sales@razorsecure.com
W: www.razorsecure.com

RBC Schaublin
Rue De La Blancherie 9, Delemont, 2800, Switzerland
T: 0041324211300
M: 0041799176809
E: office.d@schaublin.ch
W: www.schaublin.ch

RDM Group
The Old Doctors House, 74 Grand Road, Dudley, West Midlands, DY1 2AW
M: 07810 791278
E: info.uk@rdmgroup.com
W: rdmgroup.com

RE: Systems
Systems House, Deepdale Business Park, Bakewell, Derbys, DE45 1GT
T: 01629 813961
F: 01629 813185
E: steve.england@re-systems.co.uk
W: www.re-systems.co.uk

REACT Specialist Cleaning
115 Hearthcote Road, Swadlincote, Derbys, DE11 9DU
T: 01283 550 503
F: 08707 510417
E: info@reactsc.co.uk
W: www.reactsc.co.uk

Reactec
Vantage Point, 3 Cultins Road, Edinburgh, EH11 4DF
T: 0131 221 0920
F: 0131 229 9051
W: www.reactec.com/

Readypower Rail Services
620 Wharfedale Road, Winnersh, Berks, RG41 5TP
T: 01189 774901
E: info@readypower.co.uk
W: www.readypower.co.uk

Real Time Consultants Plc
118-120 Warwick St, Royal Leamington Spa, Warks, CV32 4QY
T: 01926 313133
F: 01926 422165
E: contract@rtc.co.uk
W: www.rtc.co.uk

Realtime Trains
E: tom@swlines.co.uk
W: www.realtimetrains.co.uk

Rebo Systems
Beckeringhstraat 21, NL-3762 EV Soest, Netherlands
T: 0031 0356 016 941
E: info@rebo.nl
W: www.rebosystems.com

Recab UK
Suite 13, Ashford House, Beaufort Court, Sir Thomas Longley Rd, Rochester, ME2 4FA
T: 01634 300900
F: 01634 722398
E: sales@recabuk.com
W: www.recabuk.com

Record Electrical Associates Ltd
Unit C1, Longford Trading Est., Thomas St., Stretford, Manchester, M32 0JT
T: 0161 864 3583
F: 0161 864 3603
E: alanj@reauk.com
W: www.record-electrical.co.uk

Recruitrail (Recruit Engineers)
Bank Chambers, 36 Mount Pleasant Rd, Tunbridge Wells, Kent, TN1 1RA
T: 01909 540825
F: 0870 443 0453
W: www.recruitrail.com

Red Lion Controls
The News Building, 3 London Bridge Street, London, SE1 9SG
T: 020 3868 0909
E: info@redlion.net
W: www.redlion.net

Red Plant Ltd
Red House, The Corner, Parkside, Wootton, Canterbury, Kent, CT4 6RR
T: 0845 838 7584
E: info@redplant.co.uk
W: www.redplant.co.uk

Redman Fisher Engineering Ltd
Marsh Road, Middlesbrough, Teesside, TS1 5JS
T: 01952 685110
F: 01952 685117
E: sales@redmanfisher.co.uk
W: www.redmanfisher.co.uk

RedRay LLP
Lantern House, 39-41 High Street, Potters Bar, Hertfordshire, EN6 5AJ
T: 01707 662997
M: 07799 387741
E: enquiries@redray.co.uk
W: www.redray.co.uk/

Redstone Associates
T: 0161 848 9982
E: dave.carter@redstonerail.co.uk
W: www.redstoneassociates.co.uk

Reekie Steeltec Ltd
Baden-Powell Rd, Kirkton Industrial Estate, Arbroath, Angus, DD11 3LS
T: 01241 873841
E: sales@reekiesteeltec.com
W: reekiesteeltec.com

Rees Bradley Hepburn (RBH) Ltd
Diddington Farm, Diddington Lane, Meriden, West Midlands, CV7 7HQ
T: 01675 443939
F: 01675 443477
E: info@rbh.co.uk
W: www.rbh.co.uk/

Rehau Ltd
Hill Court, Walford, Ross-on-Wye, Herefordshire, HR9 5QN
T: 01989 762600
F: 01989 762601
E: enquiries@rehau.com
W: www.rehau.com

Reid Lifting Ltd
Unit 1, Severnlink, Newhouse Farm Ind. Est, Chepstow, Monmouthshire, NP16 6UN
T: 01291 620796
F: 01291 626490
E: enquiries@reidlifting.com
W: www.reidlifting.com

Reinforced Earth Company
Innovation House, Euston Way, Telford, Shropshire, TF3 4LT
T: 01952 204357
F: 01952 201753
E: info@reinforcedearth.co.uk
W: www.reinforcedearth.co.uk

Relec Electronics Ltd
Animal House, Justin Bus. Park, Sandford Lane, Wareham, Dorset, BH20 4DY
T: 01929 555700
F: 01929 555701
E: sales@relec.co.uk
W: www.relec.co.uk

Reliable Data Systems
March House, Lime Grove, West Clandon, Guildford, Surrey, GU4 7UH
T: 01483 225604
E: rdsintl@rdsintl.com
W: www.rdsintl.com

Renaissance Trains Ltd
4 Spinneyfield, Ellington, Cambs, PE28 0AT
M: 07767 643360

Rendel Limited
61 Southwark St, London, SE1 1SA
T: 020 7654 0500
F: 020 7654 0401
E: london@rendel-ltd.com
W: www.rendel-ltd.com

Rennsteig Werkzeuge GMBH
An der Koppel 1, D-98547 Viernau, Germany
T: 49 0368 474 410
E: info@rennsteig.com
W: www.rennsteig.com

Renown Railway Services
Brookside House, Brookside Business Park, Cold Meece, Staffs, ST15 0RZ
T: 01785 764484
F: 01785 760896
E: enquiries@renownrailway.co.uk
W: www.renownrailway.co.uk

REO (UK) Ltd
Units 2-4, Callow Hill Road, Craven Arms Business Park, Craven Arms, Shropshire, SY7 8NT
T: 01588 673411
F: 01588 672718
E: main@reo.co.uk
W: www.reo.co.uk/

Replin Fabrics
March St Mills, Peebles, EH45 8ER
T: 01721 724311
F: 01721 721893
E: enquiries@replin-fabrics.co.uk
W: www.replin-fabrics.co.uk

REPTA (Railway Employees and Public Transport Association)
c/o 4 Brackmills Close, Forest Town, Mansfield, Notts, NG19 0PB
T: 01623 646789
E: peter@24foxglove.co.uk
W: www.repta.co.uk

Resonate
Hudson House, 2 Hudson Way, Pride Park, Derby, DE24 8HS
T: 01332 221000
F: 01332 221008
E: hello@resonate.tech
W: www.resonate.tech/

Resourcing Solutions
Vector House, 5 Ruscombe Park, Ruscombe, Berks, RG10 9JW
T: 0118 932 0100
F: 0118 932 1818
E: info@resourcing-solutions.com
W: www.resourcing-solutions.com

Rethinking Transport
E: jon@rethinkingtransport.com
W: www.rethinkingtransport.com

Retro Railtours Ltd
2 Brookfield Grove, Ashton-under-Lyne, Lancashire, OL6 6TL
T: 0161 330 9055
E: info@retrorailtours.co.uk
W: www.retrorailtours.co.uk

Revitaglaze
Unit 2, Swanwick Business Centre, Bridge Road, Southampton, Hants, SO31 7GB
T: 020 3384 0220
F: 01372 200881
E: enquiries@revitaglaze.com
W: www.revitaglaze.com

Rexel UK Ltd
Eagle Court 2, Hatchford Brook, Hatchford, Sheldon, Birmingham, B26 3RZ
T: 0121 366 1000
F: 0121 366 1029
E: marc.roberts@rexel.co.uk
W: www.rexel.co.uk

Rexquote Ltd
Broadgauge Business Park, Bishops Lydeard, Taunton, Somerset, TA4 3RU
T: 01823 433398
F: 01823 433378
E: sales@rexquote.co.uk
W: www.rexquote.co.uk

Rhenus Lupprians (Romac)
Keiler House, Challenge Rd, Ashford, Middx, TW15 1AX
T: 01784 422900
F: 01784 423105
E: sales@lupprians.com
W: www.lupprians.com

Rittal - The System.
Faster - better - everywhere.

Rittal is the world's largest manufacturer of enclosures and associated products for both indoor and outdoor applications with an extensive stock holding here in the UK.

To find out more, please contact us:

RITTAL Ltd
Braithwell Way
Hellaby Industrial Estate
Hellaby
Rotherham
South Yorkshire
S66 8QY

01709 704000
01709 701217
information@rittal.co.uk
www.rittal.co.uk

Rhomberg Sersa UK Ltd
Unit 2, Sarah Court, Yorkshire Way, Doncaster, DN3 3FD
T: 0300 303 0230
E: info.uk@rsrg.com
W: www.uk.rhomberg-sersa.com

RIB Software (UK) Ltd
12 Floor, The Broadgate Tower, 20 Primrose St, London, EC2A 2EW
T: 020 7596 2747
F: 020 7596 2701
W: www.rib-software.co.uk

Ricardo Rail Ltd
Edward Lloyd House, 8 Pinnacle Way, Pride Park, Derby, DE24 8ZS
T: 01332 268700
F: 01332 268799
E: ricardorail@ricardo.com
W: rail.ricardo.com

Richmond Interior Supplies Ltd
Units 2 - 4, Chichester Business Centre, Chichester Street, Rochdale, Lancashire, OL16 2AU
T: 01706 525623
E: info@richmonds-ltd.co.uk
W: www.richmonds-ltd.co.uk/

Riding Sunbeams
20 Brewsters Corner, Pendicke Street, Southam, Warwickshire
W: www.ridingsunbeams.org/

Riello UPS Ltd
Unit 50, Clywedog Rd North, Wrexham Ind.Est., Wrexham, LL13 9XN
T: 01978 729297
F: 01978 729290
E: marketing@riello-ups.co.uk
W: www.riello-ups.co.uk

Riggotts & Co Ltd
Unit X, Lodge Lane Industrial Estate, Tuxford, Newark, Nottinghamshire, NG22 0NL
T: 01777 872525
W: www.riggott.co.uk/

Riley & Son (E) Ltd
Baron St, Bury, Lancs, BL9 0TY
T: 0161 764 2892
F: 0161 763 5191
E: rileys@btconnect.com
W: www.rileyandson.co.uk/

RINA Consulting Ltd
Cleeve Rd, Leatherhead, Surrey, KT22 7SA
T: 01372 367345
E: infolh@rina.org
W: www.rinaconsulting.org/

RIQC Ltd
2 St Georges House, Vernon Gate, Derby, DE1 1UQ
T: 01332 221421
F: 01332 221401
E: enquiries@riqc.co.uk
W: www.riqc.co.uk

Risk Solutions
Dallam Court, Dallam Lane, Warrington, WA2 7LT
T: 01925 413984
E: enquiries@risksol.co.uk
W: www.risksol.co.uk

Risktec Solutions
Wilderspool Park, Greenalls Ave, Warrington, WA4 6HL
T: 01925 611200
F: 01925 611232
E: enquiries@risktec.co.uk
W: www.risktec.co.uk

Ritelite Systems Ltd
Meadow Park, Bourne Rd, Essendine, Stamford, Lincs, PE9 4LT
T: 01780 765600
F: 01780 765700
E: sales@ritelite.co.uk
W: www.ritelite.co.uk

Rittal Ltd
Braithwell Way, Hellaby Ind Est, Hellaby, Rotherham, South Yorks, S66 8QY
T: 01709 704000
F: 01709 701217
E: information@rittal.co.uk
W: www.rittal.co.uk

Riviera Trains
116 Ladbroke Grove, London, W10 5NE
T: 020 7727 4036
F: 020 7727 2083
E: enquiries@riviera-trains.co.uk
W: www.riviera-trains.co.uk

RJ Power Group
Unit 24, Graylands Estate, Langhurstwood Road, Horsham, West Sussex, RH12 4QD
T: 0345 034 1480
E: info@rjpowergroup.co.uk
W: www.rjpowergroup.co.uk/

RMD Kwikform UK
Brickyard Road, Aldridge, Walsall, WS9 8BW
T: 01922 743743
F: 01922 743400
E: info@rmdkwikform.com
W: www.rmdkwikform.com/

RMS Locotec locomotive Hire
See RMS Locotec Ltd

RMT
National Union of Rail, Maritime & Transport Workers, Unity House, 39 Chalton St, London, NW1 1JD
T: 020 7387 4771
F: 020 7387 4123
E: information@rmt.org.uk
W: www.rmt.org.uk

RNA Recruitment Ltd
Mere House, Brook St, Knutsford, Cheshire, WA16 8GP
T: 01302 366003
W: www.marecruitment.net

IN ASSOCIATION WITH Nomad Digital
connected transport, intelligent solutions

Robel Bahnbaumaschmen GmbH
Industriestrasse 31, D 83395, Freilassing, Germany
T: 0049 8654 6090
F: 0049 8654 609100
E: info@robel.info
W: www.robel.info

Robert West Consulting
Delta House, 175-177 Borough High St, London, SE1 1HR
T: 020 7939 9916
F: 020 7939 9909
E: london@robertwest.co.uk
W: www.robertwest.co.uk

RoboK
28 Chesterton Road, Cambridge, CB4 3AZ
E: info@robok.ai
W: robok.ai

Röchling Composites and Engineering Plastics
Waterwells Business Park, Waterwells Drive, Gloucester, GL2 2AA
T: 01452 727900
F: 01452 728056
E: sales@roechling-plastics.co.uk
W: www.roechling-plastics.co.uk

Rock Rail Holdings Ltd
Capital Tower, 91 Waterloo Road, London, SE1 8RT
T: 020 3170 0870
E: london@rockrail.com
W: www.rockrail.com

ROCOL
Rocol House, Wakefield Rd, Swillington, Leeds, LS26 8BS
T: 0113 232 2600
F: 0113 232 2740
E: customer-service.safety@rocol.com
W: www.rocol.com

Rogers Stirk Harbour + Partners (RSHP)
The Leadenhall Building, 122 Leadenhall Street, London, EC3V 4AB
T: 020 7385 1235
F: 020 7385 8409
E: enquiries@rsh-p.com
W: www.rsh-p.com/

Rollalong Ltd
Woolsbridge Ind. Park, Three Legged Cross, Wimborne, Dorset, BH21 6SF
T: 01202 824541
F: 01202 826525
E: enquiries@rollalong.co.uk
W: www.rollalong.co.uk

Romic House
A1/M1 Business Centre, Kettering, Northants, NN16 8TD
T: 01536 414244
F: 01536 414245
E: sales@romic.co.uk
W: www.romic.co.uk

Ronfell Ltd
Challenge House, Pagefield industrial Est., Miry Lane, Wigan, WN6 7LA
T: 01942 492200
F: 01942 492233
E: sales@ronfell.com
W: www.ronfell.com

Rose Hill P&OD Ltd
35 Colworth House, Colworth Park, Sharnbrook, Bedfordshire, MK44 1LQ
M: 07771 612321
E: info@rose-hill.co.uk
W: www.rose-hill.co.uk

Rosehill Rail
Spring Bank Mills, Watson Mill Lane, Sowerby Bridge, West Yorks, HX6 3BW
T: 01422 317482
F: 01422 316952
E: stuart.wilson@rosehillrail.com
W: www.rosehillrail.com

Rosemor International Ltd
Unit F, Moses Winter Way, Hithercroft Trading Estate, Wallingford, Oxfordshire, OX10 9FE
T: 01491 838011
F: 01491 832010
E: info@rosemor.com
W: www.rosemor.com

Rosenqvist Rail AB
Hyggesvägen 4, 824 34 Hudiksvall, Sweden
T: 0046 650 16505
F: 0046 650 16501
E: info@rosenqvist-group.se
W: www.rosenqvistrail.se

Rothwell Electrical Services
Unit 3, Yorvale Business Park, Hazel Court, James Street, York, YO10 3DR
T: 01904 413172
F: 01904 413174
W: rothwellelect.co.uk/

Roughton Group
A2 Omega Park, Electron Way, Chandlers Ford, Hants, SO53 4SE
T: 023 8027 8600
F: 023 8027 8602
E: info@roughton.com
W: www.roughton.com

Rowe Hankins Ltd.
Power House, Parker St, Bury, Lancs, BL9 0RJ
T: 0161 765 3000
F: 0161 705 2900
E: sales@rowehankins.com
W: www.rowehankins.com

Roxtec Ltd
Unit C1, Waterfold Business Park, Bury, Lancs, BL9 7BQ
T: 0161 761 5280
F: 0161 763 6065
E: info@uk.roxtec.com
W: www.roxtec.com

Royal British Legion Industries (RBLI)
Royal British Legion Village, Hall Rd, Aylesford, Kent, ME20 7NL
T: 01622 795900
F: 01622 795978
E: sales.office@rbli.co.uk
W: www.rbli.co.uk/manufacturing/services/19/

Royal Haskoning Ltd
Rightwell House, Bretton, Peterborough, PE3 8DW
T: 01733 334455
F: 01733 262243
E: info@uk.rhdhv.com
W: www.royalhaskoning.com

RPS Consulting Services
Sherwood House, Sherwood Avenue, Newark, Nottinghamshire, NG24 1QQ
T: 01636 605700
F: 01636 827309
E: alan.skipper@rpsgroup.com
W: www.rpsgroup.com

RS Components Ltd
Birchington Rd, Corby, Northants, NN17 9RS
T: 0845 602 5226
W: www.rswww.com/purchasing

RSK STATS Health & Safety Ltd
Spring Lodge, 172 Chester Rd, Helsby, Cheshire, WA6 0AR
T: 01928 726006
F: 01928 725633
E: info@rskgroup.com
W: rskgroup.com

RSK Ltd
18 Frogmore Rd, Hemel Hempstead, Herts, HP3 9RT
T: 01442 437500
F: 01442 437550
E: info@rsk.co.uk
W: www.rsk.co.uk

RSL Cityspace
Unit 3, Fullwood Close, Aldermans Green Industrial Estate, Coventry, Warks, CV2 2SS
T: 02476 587894
E: support@rslcityspace.co.uk
W: www.rslcityspace.co.uk/

RSSB
Block 2, Angel Square, 1 Torrens St, London, EC1V 1NY
T: 020 3142 5300
E: enquirydesk@rssb.co.uk
W: www.rssb.co.uk

RT Infrastructure Solutions
91 Dales Road, Ipswich, Suffolk, IP1 4JR
T: 01473 242330
F: 01473 242379
E: reception@rt-is.co.uk
W: www.rt-is.co.uk/

RTC Group
The Derby Conference Centre, London Rd, Derby, DE24 8UX
T: 01332 861336
F: 0870 890 0034
E: info@rtcgroupplc.co.uk
W: www.rtcgroupplc.co.uk

RTS Infrastructure Services Ltd
The Rail Depot, Bridge Rd, Holbeck, Leeds, LS11 9UG
T: 01132 344899
E: info@rtsinfrastructure.com
W: www.rtsinfrastructure.com

RTS Solutions Ltd
Atlantic House, Imperial Way, Reading, RG2 0TD
T: 0118 903 6045
F: 0118 903 6100
E: stuart@rts-solutions.net
W: www.rts-solutions.net

Rubirail
Victoria Buildings, 27 Victoria Rd, Draycott, Derby, DE72 3PS
T: 01332 872483
E: info@rubirail.co.uk
W: www.rubirail.co.uk/

RUGGED MOBILE Systems Ltd
Park View Business Centre, Combermere, Whitchurch, Shropshire, SY13 4AL
T: 0845 652 0816
F: 0845 652 0817
E: info@rm-systems.co.uk
W: www.ruggedmobilesystems.co.uk

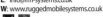

Rullion Engineering Personnel
Aldermary House, 10-15 Queen Street, London, EC4N 1TX
T: 0203 201 1217
E: justin.ayling@rullion.co.uk
W: www.rullion.co.uk

RWD Technologies UK Ltd
Furzeground Way, First Floor, Stockley Park, Uxbridge, UB11 1AJ
T: 020 8569 2787
F: 020 8756 3625
E: info@gpstrategies.com
W: www.rwd.com

Rydon Signs
Unit 3, Peek House, Pinhoe Trading Est, Exeter, Devon, EX4 8JN
T: 01392 466653
F: 01392 466671
E: sales@rydonsigns.com
W: www.rydonsigns.com

S and L Roberts (Railway Consulting) Ltd
W: sandlrobertsrailwayconsultingltd.wordpress.com

S H Lighting
Salcmbe Rd, Meadow Lane Ind. Est, Alfreton, Derbys, DE55 7RG
T: 01773 522390
F: 01773 520693
E: sales@shlighting.co.uk
W: www.shlighting.co.uk

S M Consult Ltd
3 High St, Stanford in the Vale, Faringdon, Oxon, SN7 8LH
T: 01367 710152
F: 01367 710152
E: info@smcsolar.co.uk
W: www.smconsult.co.uk

S&T Cover Ltd
Railway Goods Yard, Dutton Lane, Eastleigh, Hampshire, SO50 6AA
T: 023 8098 9545
E: enquiries@s-tcover.co.uk
W: www.s-tcover.co.uk/

S.E.T. Ltd
Atlas Works, Litchurch Lane, Derby, DE24 8AQ
T: 01332 346035
E: info@set-gb.com
W: www.set-gb.com

Saba Park Services Ltd
Second Floor, Building 4 Croxley Park, Hatters Lane, Watford, Herts, WD18 8YF
T: 01908 223500
F: 01923 231914
W: www.sabaparking.co.uk

Sabre Rail
Grindon Way, Heighington Lane Business Park, Newton Aycliffe, Co Durham, DL5 6SH
T: 01325 300505
F: 01325 300485
E: sales@sabrerail.com
W: www.sabrerail.com

Safeaid LLP
Signal House, 16 Arnside Rd, Waterlooville, Hants, PO7 7UP
T: 02392 254442
F: 02392 257444
E: sales@safeaidsupplies.com
W: www.safeaidsupplies.com

Safeglass (Europe) Ltd
Nasmyth Building, Nasmyth Ave, East Kilbride, G75 0QR
T: 01355 272438
F: 01355 272788
E: sales@safeglass.co.uk
W: www.safeglass.co.uk

Safeguard Pest Control Ltd
6 Churchill Business Park, The Flyers Way, Westerham, Kent, TN16 1BT
T: 0800 195 7766
F: 01959 565888
E: info@safeguardpestcontrol.co.uk
W: www.safeguardpestcontrol.co.uk

Safestyle Security Services
Exe. Suite 1, Cardiff International Arena, Mary Ann St, Cardiff, CF10 2EQ
T: 02920 221711
F: 02920 234592
E: office@safestylesecurity.co.uk
W: www.safestylesecurity.co.uk

Safetell Ltd
Unit 46, Fawkes Ave, Dartford Trade Park, Dartford, DA1 1JQ
T: 01322 223233
F: 01322 277751
E: sales@safetell.co.uk
W: www.safetell.co.uk

Safetrack Baavhammar AB
1 Moleberga, S-245 93 Staffanstorp, Sweden
T: 0046 4044 5300
F: 0046 4044 5553
E: sales@safetrack.se
W: www.safetrack.se

Safetykleen UK Ltd
2 Heath Road, Weybridge, Surrey, KT13 8AP
T: 01909 519300
E: skuk@sk-europe.com
W: www.safetykleen.co.uk

SAFT Ltd
1st Floor, Unit 5, Astra Centre, Edinburgh Way, Harlow, CM20 2BN
T: 01279 772550
F: 01279 420909
E: saftpress.contact@saftbatteries.com
W: www.saftbatteries.com

SAFT Power Systems Ltd
See AEG Power Solutions Ltd

Saint Gobain Abrasives Ltd
Doxey Rd, Stafford, ST16 1EA
T: 01785 279550
F: 01785 213487
W: www.saint-gobain.com

Saira Electronics
See HaslerRail

Salamander Fabrications Ltd
Salamander Works, Old Bank, Slathwaite, Huddersfield, West Yorkshire, HD7 5HB
T: 01484 843599
F: 01484 847105
E: sales@salamanderfabs.com
W: www.salamanderfabs.com

Saltburn Railtours
18 Oxclose Gardens, Saltburn-by-the-Sea, Cleveland, TS12 1PU
T: 01287 625956
M: 07813 841496
W: www.saltburnrailtours.co.uk

Samsung Electronics Hainan Fibreoptics
c/o Go Tel Communications Ltd, 4 Hicks Close, Wroughton, Swindon, SN4 9AY
T: 01793 813600
F: 01793 529380
E: robindash@gtcom.co.uk
W: www.samsungfiberoptics.com

Samuel James Engineering
21 Ashton Close, Beaumont Leys, Leicester, LE4 2BQ
T: 0116 235 0380
E: sales@samuel-james.co.uk
W: samuel-james.co.uk

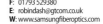

Samuel Taylor Ltd
Arthur Street, Redditch, Worcs, B98 8JY
T: 01527 504910
F: 01527 500869
E: sales@samueltaylor.co.uk
W: www.samueltaylor.co.uk

Santon Switchgear Ltd
Unit 9, Waterside Court, Newport, NP20 5NT
T: 01633 854111
F: 01633 854999
E: sales@santonswitchgear.co.uk
W: www.santonswitchgear.com

SAP (UK) Ltd
Clockhouse Place, Bedfont Road, Feltham, Middlesex, TW14 8HD
T: 0800 0852 631
W: https://go.sap.com/uk/

Sartoria Corporatewear
Gosforth Rd, Derby, DE24 8HU
T: 01332 342616
F: 01332 226940
W: www.sartorialtd.co.uk.co.uk

SAS International
31 Suttons Business Park, Reading, Berkshire, RG6 1AZ
T: 0118 929 0900
F: 0118 929 0901
W: sasintgroup.com/

Savigny Oddie Ltd
Wallows Ind. Est, Wallows Rd, Brierley Hill, West Midlands, DY5 1QA
T: 01384 481598
F: 01384 482383
E: keith@oddiefasteners.com
W: www.savigny-oddie.co.uk

SB Rail (Swietelsky Babcock)
Kintail House, 3 Lister Way, Hamilton International Park, Blantyre, G72 0FT
T: 01698 203005
F: 01698 203006
E: shona.jamieson@babcock.co.uk
W: www.babcock.co.uk/rail

Scantec
Spinnaker House, Morpeth Wharf, Twelve Quays, Wirral, CH41 1LF
T: 0151 666 8999
E: info@scantec.co.uk
W: www.scantec.co.uk/

SCCS
Hq1 Building, Phoenix Park, Eaton Socon, St Neots, Cambs, PE19 8EP
T: 01480 404888
F: 01480 404333
E: sales@sccssurvey.co.uk
W: www.sccssurvey.co.uk

SCG Solutions
335 Shepcote Lane, Sheffield, S9 1TG
T: 0114 221 1111
E: sales@scgsolutions.co.uk
W: www.scgsolutions.co.uk

Schaltbau Machine Electrics
335/336 Springvale Industrial Estate, Woodside Way, Cwmbran, NP44 5BR
T: 01633 877555
F: 01633 873366
E: sales@schaltbau-me.com
W: www.schaltbau-me.com

Scheidt & Bachmann (UK) Ltd
7 Silverglade Business Park, Leatherhead Rd, Chessington, Surrey, KT9 2QL
T: 01372 230400
F: 01372 722053
E: info@scheidt-bachmann.de
W: www.scheidt-bachmann.de

Schenck Process UK
Unit 3 Alpha Court, Capitol Park, Thorne, Doncaster, DN8 5TZ
T: 01302 321313
F: 01302 554400
E: enquiries@schenckprocess.co.uk
W: www.schenckprocess.co.uk

Schneider Electric Ltd
Stafford Park 5, Telford, Shropshire, TF3 3BL
T: 01952 209226
F: 01952 292238
E: gb-marcoms@gb.schneider.electric.com
W: www.se.com/uk

Schoenemann Design Ltd
Friar Gate Studios, Studio 26, Ford Street, Derby, DE1 1EE
T: 01332 258345
M: 07831 332790
E: andrew@schoenemann design.co.uk
W: https://schoenemanndesign.co.uk/

Schofield Lothian Ltd
Temple Chambers, 3-7 Temple Ave, London, EC4Y 0DT
T: 020 7842 0920
F: 020 7842 0921
E: enquiries@schofieldlothian.com
W: www.schofieldlothian.com

Schroff UK Ltd
Maylands Ave, Hemel Hempstead, Herts, HP2 7DE
T: 01442 240471
F: 01442 213508
E: schroff.uk@pentair.com
W: www.schroff.co.uk

Schweerbau GmbH & Co KG
UK Branch Office, 20 Beattyville Gardens, Ilford, IG6 1JN
F: 020 7681 3971
E: verheijen@schweerbau.de
W: www.schweerbau.de

Schweizer Electronic
Industriestrasse 3, CH-6260 Reiden, Switzerland
T: +41 62 749 07 07
F: +41 62 749 07 00
E: info@schweizer-electronic.com
W: www.schweizer-electronic.com

Schwihag AG
Lebernstrasse 3, CH-8274 Tägerwilen, Switzerland
T: 0041 71 666 8800
F: 0041 71 666 8801
E: info@schwihag.com
W: www.schwihag.com

The Modern Railway
197

Scisys
See CGI IT UK Ltd

Scot Seat Direct
Gainford Business Centre, Stewarton Road, Fenwick, Ayrshire, KA3 6AR
T: 01560 600100
E: sales@scotseats.co.uk
W: www.scotseats.co.uk

ScotRail
Atrium Court, 50 Waterloo St, Glasgow, G2 6HQ
T: 0344 811 0141
E: customer.relations@scotrail.co.uk
W: www.scotrail.co.uk/

Scott Bader
Wollaston, Wellingborough, Northants, NN29 7RL
T: 01933 663100
E: composites@scottbader.com
W: www.scottbader.com

Scott Brownrigg – Design Research Unit
77 Endell St, London, WC2H 9DZ
T: 020 7240 7766
F: 020 7240 2454
E: enquiries@scottbrownrigg.com
W: www.scottbrownrigg.com

Scott White & Hookins
Fountain House, 26 St Johns St, Bedford, MK42 0AQ
T: 01234 213111
F: 01234 213333
E: info@swh.co.uk
W: www.swh.co.uk

Scott Wilson Railways
See AECOM

Scotweld Employment Services
See SW Global Resourcing

SCP
Colwyn Chambers, 19 York Street, Manchester, M2 3BA
T: 0161 832 4400
E: info@scptransport.co.uk
W: scptransport.co.uk/

Screwfast Foundations Ltd
1st Floor, 4 Sandridge Park, Porters Wood, St. Albans, Herts, AL3 6PH
T: 01727 821282
F: 01727 828098
E: info@screwfast.com
W: www.screwfast.com

SCT Europe Ltd
See Wabtec Rail Ltd

SEA (Group) Ltd
Building 450, Bristol Business Park, Coldharbour Lane, Bristol, BS16 1EJ
T: 01373 852000
F: 01373 831133
E: info@sea.co.uk
W: www.sea.co.uk

Search Consultancy
198 West George St, Glasgow, G2 2NR
T: 0141 272 7777
F: 0141 272 7788
E: glasgow@search.co.uk
W: www.searchconsultancy.co.uk

Seaton Rail Ltd
Bridlington Business Centre, Enterprise Way, Bridlington, YO16 4SF
T: 01262 608313
F: 01262 604493
E: info@seaton-rail.com
W: www.seaton-rail.com

Secheron SA
Rue de pre-Bouvier 25, Zimeysa 1217 Meyrin, Geneva, Switzerland
T: 0041 22 739 4111
F: 0041 22 739 4811
E: info@secheron.com
W: www.secheron.com

Seed Architects
Parsonage Chambers, 3 Parsonage, Manchester, M3 2HW
T: 0161 832 5750
E: office@seedarchitects.co.uk
W: www.seedarchitects.co.uk

Seetru Ltd
Albion Dockside Works, Bristol, BS1 6UT
T: 0117 930 6100
E: info@seetru.com
W: www.seetru.com/

Sefac UK Ltd
Imex Business Centre, Oxleasow Road, Redditch, Worcestershire, B98 0RE
T: 0121 582 0367
W: www.sefac-lift.co.uk

Sekisui Chemical GmbH
Königsallee 106, 40215 Düsseldorf, Germany
T: +49 211 36977 0
F: +49 211 36977 31
E: contact@sekisui-rail.com
W: www.sekisui-rail.com

Scott Cables
Painter Close, Anchorage Park, Portsmouth, Hampshire, PO3 5RS
T: 02392 652552
F: 02392 655277
E: sales@scottcables.com
W: www.scottcables.com

Selectequip Ltd
Unit 7, Britannia Way, Britannia Enterprise Park, Lichfield, Staffs, WS14 9UY
T: 01543 416641
F: 01543 416083
E: sales@selectequip.co.uk
W: www.selectequip.co.uk

Selectrail (Australia) Pty Ltd
1/11 Trevi Crescent, Tullamarine, VIC 3043, Australia
T: 6103 9335 0600
E: info@selectrail.com
W: www.selectrail.com

Sella Controls
Carrington Field St, Stockport, Cheshire, SK1 3JN
T: 0161 429 4500
F: 0161 476 3095
E: sales@sellacontrols.com
W: www.sellacontrols.com

Selwood Ltd
Bournemouth Road, Chandler's Ford, Eastleigh, Hampshire, SO53 3ZL
T: 023 8026 6311
F: 023 8026 0906
W: www.selwood.co.uk/

Semikron Ltd
9 Harforde Court, John Tate Rd, Foxholes Business Park, Hertford, SG13 7NW
T: 01992 584677
F: 01992 503837
E: sales.skuk@semikron.com
W: www.semikron.com

Semmco Ltd
9 Kestrel Way, Goldsworth Park Trading Est, Woking, Surrey, GU21 3BA
T: 01483 757200
F: 01483 740795
E: sales@semmco.com
W: www.semmco.co.uk

Semperit Industrial Products Ltd
No 3 Caroline Court, 13 Caroline Street, St Pauls Square, Birmingham, B3 1TR
T: 01327 313144
F: 01327 313149
M: 07720 410655
E: sales.uk@semperitgroup.com
W: www.semperit.at

Senator Security Services Ltd
1 The Thorn Tree, Elmhurst Business Park, Lichfield, Staffs, WS13 8EX
W: www.senatorsecurity.co.uk

Senceive Ltd
Hurlingham Studios, Ranelagh Gardens, London, SW6 3PA
T: 020 7731 8269
E: info@senceive.com
W: www.senceive.com

SENER Group
1st Floor East, Adamson House, 2 Centenary Way, Salford, Manchester, M50 1RD
T: 0161 786 1950
W: www.sener.es/home/en

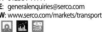

SenseAir AB
Flottiljgatan 49, SE-721 31, Vasteras, Sweden
T: 0046 21800099
E: mark.hawthorne@senseair.com
W: www.senseair.com/

Serco Caledonian Sleepers Ltd
Basement and Ground Floor, 1-5 Union Street, Inverness, IV1 1PP
T: 0330 060 0500
W: https://www.sleeper.scot/

Serco Transport Services
Serco House, 16 Bartley Wood Bus. Park, Bartley Way, Hook, Hants, RG27 9UY
T: 01256 745900
F: 01256 744111
E: generalenquiries@serco.com
W: www.serco.com/markets/transport

Serco Rail Technical Services
Derwent House, RTC Business Park, London Rd, Derby, DE24 8UP
T: 0330 109 8852
E: enquiries.srts@serco.com
W: www.serco.com/uk/sector-expertise/transport/rail-technical-services

Serfis Construction and Engineering Ltd
9a Church Street, Kidderminster, Worcestershire, DY10 2AD
T: 01562 822082
F: 01562 820813
E: info@serfis.co.uk
W: serfis.co.uk/

SES Security
The Barrows, Roydon Road, Harlow, Essex, CM19 5BL
T: 020 8804 5058
W: www.thesesgroup.co.uk/security/

Setec Ltd
11 Mallard Way, Derby, DE24 8GX
E: craig.king@setecltd.co.uk
W: www.setecltd.co.uk

Severfield
Severs House, Dalton Airfield Industrial Estate, Dalton, Thirsk, North Yorkshire, YO7 3JN
T: 01845 577896
F: 01845 577 411
W: www.severfield.com/

Severn Lamb
Tything Rd, Alcester, B49 6ET
T: 01789 400140
F: 01789 400240
E: sales@severn-lamb.com
W: www.severn-lamb.com

The Severn Partnership Ltd
Lambda House, Hadley Park East, Telford, Shropshire, TF1 6QJ
T: 01952 676775
E: info@severnpartnership.com
W: www.severnpartnership.com

Severn Valley Railway
Number One, Comberton Place, Kidderminster, Worcs, DY10 1QR
T: 01562 757900
E: contact@svrlive.com
W: www.svr.co.uk

Seymourpowell
The Factory, 265 Merton Rd, London, SW18 5JS
T: 020 7381 6433
E: hello@seymourpowell.com
W: www.seymourpowell.com

SGA (Stuart Gray Associates)
88 Spring Hill, Arley, Warks, CV7 8FE
T: 01676 541402
E: info@stuartgrayassociates.co.uk
W: www.stuartgrayassociates.co.uk

SGH Martineau LLP
No.1 Colmore, Birmingham, B4 6AA
T: 0800 763 1000
F: 0800 763 1001
E: andrew.whitehead@sghmartineau.com
W: www.sghmartineau.com

SGS Engineering (UK) Ltd
Unit 2, West Side Park, Belmore Way, Derby, DE21 7AZ
T: 01332 576850
F: 01332 753068
E: sales@sgs-engineering.com
W: www.sgs-engineering.com

SGS UK Ltd
Inward Way, Rossmore Business Park, Ellesmere Port, CH65 3EN
T: 0151 350 6666
F: 0151 350 6600
W: www.sgs.com

Shannon Rail Services Ltd
Orphanage Road Sidings, Reeds Crescent, Watford, Herts, WD17 1PG
T: 01923 254567
F: 01923 255678
E: info@shannonrail.co.uk
W: www.shannonrail.co.uk

Shay Murtagh Precast Ltd
Raharney, Mullingar, Co Westmeath, Republic of Ireland
T: 0844 202 0263
E: sales@shaymurtagh.co.uk
W: www.shaymurtagh.co.uk

SHB Hire Ltd
18 Premier Way, Abbey Park Industrial Estate, Romsey, Hampshire, SO51 9DQ
T: 01794 511458
E: enquiries@shb.co.uk
W: www.shb.co.uk/

Sheerspeed Shelters Ltd
Unit 3, Diamond House, Reme Drive, Heath Park Ind. Estate, Honiton, Devon, EX14 1SE
T: 01404 46006
F: 01404 45520
E: sales@sheerspeed.com
W: www.sheerspeed.com

Shell UK Oil Products Ltd
Brabazon House, Concord Business Park, Threapwood Rd, Manchester, M22 0RR
T: 08708 500924
F: 0161 499 8930
E: lubesenquiries-uk@shell.com
W: www.shell.co.uk/lubricants

Shere Ltd
See ATOS Origin

Sheridan Maine
Regus House, George Curl Way, Southampton, SO18 2RZ
T: 0871 218 0573
F: 0871 218 0173
E: southampton@sheridanmaine.com
W: www.sheridanmaine.com

Sherwin-Williams Protective & Marine Coatings
Tower Works, Kestor St, Bolton, Lancs, BL2 2AL
T: 01204 521771
F: 01204 382115
E: enquiries.uk@sherwin.com
W: protectiveemea.sherwin-williams.com/

Shield Batteries
277 Stansted Rd, Bishops Stortford, Herts, CM23 2BT
T: 01279 652067
F: 01279 758041
E: info@shieldbatteries.co.uk
W: www.shieldbatteries.co.uk

Shilcocks
Grosvenor House, 102 Beverley Road, Kingston-upon-Hull, HU3 1YA
T: 01482 221858
F: 01482 323269
E: admin@shilcocks.com
W: www.shilcocks.com/

Shilling Media Services
62 North St, Bourne, Lincs, PE10 9AJ
T: 01778 421550
M: 07736 635916
E: chris@shillingmedia.co.uk
W: www.shillingmedia.co.uk

Shoosmiths
1 St Martin's Le Grand, London, EC1A 4AS
T: 020 7205 7017
M: 07836 720537
E: martin.fleetwood@shoosmiths.co.uk
W: www.shoosmiths.co.uk

Shorterm Rail
The Barn, Philpots Close, Yiewsley, Middx, UB7 7RY
T: 01895 427900
E: info@shortermgroup.co.uk
W: www.shorterm.co.uk

Shotcrete Services Ltd
Old Station Yard, Hawkhurst Rd, Cranbrook, Kent, TN17 2SR
T: 01580 714747
E: stuart.manning@shotcrete.co.uk
W: www.shotcrete.co.uk

SICK (UK) Ltd
Waldkirch House, 39 Hedley Rd, St Albans, Herts, AL1 5BN
T: 01727 831121
F: 01727 856767
E: info@sick.co.uk
W: www.sick.co.uk

Sicut Enterprises Ltd
152 City Road, London, EC1V 2NX
T: 020 8123 6685
E: info@sicut.co.uk
W: sicut.co.uk

Siegrist-Orel Ltd
Pysons Rd Ind. Est., Broadstairs, Kent, CT10 2LQ
T: 01843 865241
F: 01843 867180
E: info@siegrist-orel.co.uk
W: www.siegrist-orel.co.uk

Siemens Mobility Ltd
Euston House, 24 Eversholt St, London, NW1 1AD
T: 020 7227 0722
F: 020 7227 4435
E: info.mobility.gb@siemens.com
W: www.siemens.co.uk/rail

Siemens Rail Automation
See Siemens Mobility Ltd

Siemens RUGGEDCOM UK
Princess Road, Princess Parkway, Manchester, M20 2UR
T: 0161 446 5000
F: 0161 446 5742
E: ianpoulett@ruggedcom.com
W: www.siemens.com/ruggedcom

SIG plc
Hillsborough Works, Landsett Road, Sheffield, S6 2LW
T: 0114 285 6327
E: sigri@sigplc.co.uk
W: www.sigri.co.uk

Sigma Coachair Group UK Ltd
Unit 1, Queens Drive, Newhall, Swadlincote, Derbys, DE11 0EG
T: 01283 559140
F: 01283 225253
W: www.sigmacoachair.com

Signal House Ltd
Cherrycourt Way, Stanbridge Rd, Leighton Buzzard, Beds, LU7 4UH
T: 01525 377477
F: 01525 850999
E: sales@signalhouse.co.uk
W: www.signalhousegroup.co.uk

Signalling Solutions Ltd
See Alstom Transport

Signature Aromas Ltd
Signature House, 65-67 Gospel End St, Sedgley, West Midlands, DY3 3LR
T: 01902 678822
F: 01902 672893
E: enquiries@signaturearomas.co.uk
W: www.signaturearomas.co.uk

Signet Solutions
Kelvin House, RTC Business Park, London Rd, Derby, DE24 8UP
T: 01332 343585
F: 01332 367132
E: enquiries@signet-solutions.com
W: www.signet-solutions.com

SigTech Rail
The Mount, Barrow Hill, Sellinge, Ashford, Kent, TN25 6JQ
T: 01303 764344
E: office@sigtechrail.co.uk
W: www.sigtechrail.co.uk

Sill Lighting UK
3 Thame Park Bus. Centre, Wenman Rd, Thame, Oxon, OX9 3XA
T: 01844 260006
F: 01844 260760
E: sales@sill-uk.com
W: www.sill-uk.com

Silver Atena
Cedar House, Riverside Business Park, Swindon Rd, Malmesbury, Wilts, SN16 9RS
T: 01666 580000
F: 01666 580001
E: info@silver-atena.de
W: www.silver-atena.com

Silver Fox Ltd
Swallow Court, Swallowfields, Welwyn Garden City, Herts, AL7 1SA
T: 01707 373727
F: 01707 372193
E: marketing@silverfox.co.uk
W: www.silverfox.co.uk

Silver Software
See Silver Atena

SilverRail
The Heal's Building, 22 Torrington Place, London, WC1E 7HJ
T: 0845 834 1069
E: info@silverrailtech.com
W: silverrailtech.com/

Simco External Framing Solutions
Leamore Lane, Bloxwich, Walsall, West Midlands, WS2 7DQ
T: 01922 494900
F: 01922 494982
E: webenquiry@simcoefs.com
W: www.simcoefs.com/

Simmons & Simmons
City Point, One Ropemaker St, London, EC2Y 9SS
T: 020 7628 2020
F: 020 7628 2070
E: juliet.reingold@simmons-simmons.com
W: www.simmons-simmons.com

Simona UK
Telford Drive, Brookmead Ind. Park, Stafford, ST16 3ST
T: 01785 222444
F: 01785 222080
E: mail@simona-uk.com
W: www.simona.de

SIMS
Fourth Floor, Roman Wall House, 1-2 Crutched Friars, London, EC3N 2HT
T: 020 7481 9798
F: 020 7481 9657
E: inbox@sims-uk.com
W: www.simsrail.co.uk

Simulation Systems Ltd
Unit 12, Market Ind. Est, Yatton, Bristol, BS49 4RF
T: 01934 838803
F: 01934 876202
W: www.simulation-systems.co.uk

Sinclair Knight Merz
See Jacobs UK Ltd

SIS Projects
Central House, Central Way, Winwick Street, Warrington, Cheshire, WA2 7TT
T: 01925 582960
F: 01424 215859
E: info@sis-projects.co.uk
W: www.sis-projects.co.uk

John Sisk & Sons Ltd
1 Curo Park, Frogmore, St Albans, Herts, AL2 2DD
T: 01727 875551
F: 01727 875642
W: www.johnsiskandson.com/uk

Site Eye Time-Lapse Films
Unit 8D, Top Lands, County Business Park, Cragg Road, Cragg Vale, Halifax, West Yorkshire, HX7 5RW
T: 01422 884477
E: info@site-eye.co.uk
W: www.site-eye.co.uk

Site Vision Surveys
19 Warwick St, Rugby, Warks, CV21 3DH
T: 01788 575036
F: 01788 576208
E: mail@svsltd.net
W: www.svsltd.net

SITECH UK & Ireland
Morgans Business Park, Norton Canes, Cannock, Staffs, WS11 9UU
T: 0845 600 5669
E: info@sitechukandireland.com
W: www.sitechukandireland.com

Skanska UK
Maple Cross House, Denham Way, Maple Cross, Rickmansworth, Herts, WD3 9SW
T: 01923 423100
F: 01923 423111
W: www.skanska.co.uk/

SKF UK Ltd
Railway Sales Unit, Sundon Park Rd, Luton, LU3 3BL
T: 01582 496490
F: 01582 496327
W: www.skf.com

SKM Colin Buchanan
New City Court, 20 St. Thomas Street, London, SE1 9RS
T: 020 7939 6160
W: www.skmcolinbuchanan.com

Škoda Transportation
Emila Škody 2922/1, 301 00 Plzeň, Czech Republic
T: +420 378 186 666
F: +420 378 186 455
E: transportation@skoda.cz
W: www.skoda.cz/en

Skymasts Antennas
Unit 2, Clayfield Close, Moulton Park Ind. Est, Northampton, NN3 6QF
T: 01604 494132
F: 01604 494133
E: info@skymasts.com
W: www.skymasts.com

SLC Rail
Suite 203, Guildhall Buildings, Navigation Street, Birmingham, B2 4BT
T: 0121 285 2622
E: enquiries@slcrail.com
W: www.slcrail.co.uk/

Slender Winter Partnership
The Old School, London Rd, Westerham, Kent, TN11 1DN
T: 01959 564777
F: 01959 562802
E: swp@swpltd.co.uk
W: www.swpltd.co.uk

Smart Component Technologies - Cambridge
Suite 19, Innovation Centre, 320 Cambridge Science Park, Cambridge, CB4 0WG
T: 01223 827160
E: info@smartcomptech.com
W: smartcomptech.com

SmartWater Technology Ltd
27 Queen Anne's Gate, London, SW1H 9BU
T: 0333 320 7797
F: 0333 320 7798
E: enquiry@smartwater.com
W: www.smartwater.com

SMBC Leasing (UK) Ltd
99 Queen Victoria Street, London, EC4V 4EH
T: 020 7786 1000
W: https://www.smbcgroup.com/emea/group-companies/smbc-leasing-(uk)-limited/

SMC Pneumatics Ltd
Vincent Ave, Crownhill, Milton Keynes, Bucks, MK8 0AN
T: 0845 121 5122
F: 01908 555064
E: sales@smcpneumatics.co.uk
W: www.smcpneumatics.co.uk

SME Ltd
Unit 1, Lloyd St, Parkgate, Rotherham, S62 6JG
T: 08444 930666
F: 08444 930667
W: www.sme-ltd.co.uk

SMI Conferences
SMI Group Ltd, Unit 122, Great Guildford Business Square, 30 Great Guildford St, London, SE1 0HS
T: 020 7827 6000
F: 020 7827 6001
E: events@smi-online.co.uk
W: www.smi-online.co.uk

Smith Bros & Webb Ltd
Britannia House, Arden Forest Ind.Est, Alcester, Warks, B49 6EX
T: 01789 400096
F: 01789 400231
E: sales@sbw-wash.com
W: www.sbw-wash.com

Smith Cooper
Wilmot House, St Helen's House, King St, Derby, DE1 3EE
T: 01332 332021
F: 01332 290439
E: janet.morgan@smithcooper.co.uk
W: www.smithcooper.co.uk

Smith Engineering (GB) Ltd
Solway Industrial Estate, Maryport, Cumbria, CA15 8NF
T: 01900 815831
E: r.smith@smith-eng.co.uk
W: www.smith-eng.co.uk/

Smiths Connectors
Research, Design & Development Centre, Centennial Park Unit 130, Centennial Avenue, Elstree, Hertfordshire, WD6 3SE
T: 020 8236 2400
F: 020 8208 4114
E: info@smithsconnectors.com
W: www.smithsconnectors.com

Smiths Rail
Stratton Business Park, London Road, Biggleswade, Bedfordshire, SG188QB
T: 01767 604706
E: info@smithmetal.com
W: www.smithmetal.com

SML Resourcing
Unit 3.07, New Loom House, 101 Back Church Lane, London, E1 1LU
T: 020 7423 4390
F: 020 7702 1097
E: jobs@sml-resourcing.com
W: www.sml-resourcing.com

SMP Electronics
Unit 6, Border Farm, Station Rd, Chobham, Woking, Surrey, GU24 8AS
T: 01276 855166
F: 01276 855115
E: sales@smpelectronics.com
W: www.samalite.com

Snap-On Rail Solutions
38A Telford Way, Kettering, Northants, NN16 8SN
T: 01536 413904
F: 01536 413874
E: rail@snapon.com
W: www.snapon.com/industrialuk

SNC-Lavalin
2 Roundhouse Road, Pride Park, Derby, DE24 8JE
T: 01332 223 000
F: 01332 223 001
W: www.snclavalin-railandtransit.com/

Society of Operations Engineers (SOE)
22 Greencoat Place, London, SW1P 1PR
T: 020 7630 1111
F: 020 7630 6677
E: soe@soe.org.uk
W: www.soe.org.uk

Socomec UPS (UK)
Units 7-9, Lakeside Business Park, Broadway Lane, South Cerney, Cirencester, Glos, GL7 5XL
T: 01285 863300
F: 01285 862304
E: info.uk@socomec.com
W: www.socomec.co.uk/

Socotec
ESG House, Bretby Business Park, Ashby
Rd, Burton upon Trent, DE15 0YZ
T: 01283 554400
F: 01283 554423
E: salesuk@socotec.com
W: www.socotec.co.uk

Softech Rail Ltd
Softech House, London Rd, Albourne, West Sussex, BN6 9BN
T: 01273 833844
F: 01273 833044
E: info@softechrail.com
W: www.softechrail.com

Sogefi Rejna SpA
Via Nazionale 7, Raffa di Puegnago (BS), I-25080, Italy
T: 39 365 526 213
E: giovannico.dore@sogefigroup.com
W: www.sogefigroup.com

SOLID Applications Ltd
Old Market Place, Market St, Oldbury, B69 4DH
T: 0121 544 1400
E: anton.plackowski@saplm.co.uk
W: www.solidapps.co.uk/

Solo Rail Solutions
Landor St, Saltley, Birmingham, B8 1AE
T: 0121 327 3378
E: robpugh@solorail.com
W: www.solorail.com

Solum Regeneration
6 Cavendish Place, London, W1G 0QA
T: 020 7462 2759
E: info@solum.co.uk
W: www.solum.co.uk

Solution Rail
22 Somers Way, Bushey, Herts, WD23 4HR
F: 0871 989 5700
E: enquiries@solutionrail.co.uk
W: www.solutionrail.co.uk

Solvay Solutions UK Ltd
Burrwood Way, Holywell Green, Halifax, HX4 9BH
T: 01422 898300
F: 01422 315945
W: www.solvay.com/en

Sonic Rail Service Ltd (SRS)
Unit 15, Springfield Ind. Est, Springfield Rd, Burnham-on-Crouch, Essex, CM0 8UA
T: 01621 784688
F: 01621 786594
E: stewart.robinson@sonicrail.co.uk
W: www.sonicrail.co.uk

Sotera Risk Solutions Ltd
22 Glanville Rd, Bromley, BR2 9LW
T: 01737 551203
F: 01737 551203
M: 07946 638424
E: chris.chapman@sotera.co.uk
W: www.sotera.co.uk

SOUNDEX Solutions
The Old Dairy, Southfield Avenue, Northampton, NN4 8AQ
T: 0800 814 4422
F: 0800 814 4423
E: enquiries@soundexsolutions.com
W: www.soundexsolutions.com

South Essex College
Basildon Campus, Luckyn Lane Entrance, Basildon, Essex, SS14 3AY
T: 0345 5212345
E: learning@southessex.ac.uk
W: www.southessex.ac.uk

South Western Railway
4th Floor, South Bank Central, 30 Stamford Street, London, SE1 9LQ
T: 0345 6000 650
W: www.southwesternrailway.com/

South Yorkshire Passenger Transport Executive
11 Broad St West, Sheffield, S1 2BQ
T: 0114 276 7575
F: 0114 275 9908
E: comments@sypte.co.uk
W: www.sypte.co.uk

Southco Manufacturing Ltd
Touch Point, Wainwright Rd, Warndon, Worcs, WR4 9FA
T: 01905 346722
F: 01905 346723
E: info@southco.com
W: www.southco.com

Southeastern
Floor 2, Four More London Riverside, London, SE1 2AU
T: 020 7620 5000
W: www.southeasternrailway.co.uk

Sovereign Planned Services On Line Ltd
Unit 9, Galveston Grove, Oldfields Business Park, Fenton, Stoke-on-Trent, Staffs, ST4 3PE
T: 01782 914274
E: sales@sovonline.co.uk
W: www.sovonline.co.uk

SPAL Automotive
Unit 3, Great Western Busisness Park, Worcester, Wr4 9PT
T: 01905 613714
E: matthew@spalautomotive.co.uk
W: www.spalautomotive.co.uk

Spartan Safety Ltd
Unit 3, Waltham Park Way, Walthamstow, London, E17 5DU
T: 020 8527 5888
F: 020 8527 5999
E: post@spartansafety.co.uk
W: www.spartansafety.co.uk

Specialist Engineering Services Ltd (SES)
Unit 3 Ses House, Carr Hill, Balby Rd, Doncaster, DN4 8DE
T: 01302 756800
F: 01302 756860
E: sales@ses-group.co.uk
W: www.ses-group.co.uk

Specialist Plant Associates
Airfield Rd, Hinwick, Wellingborough, Northants, NN29 7JG
T: 01234 781882
F: 01234 781992
E: info@specialistplant.co.uk
W: www.specialistplant.co.uk

Specialist Project Integration Ltd (SPI)
Bowback House, 299 Silbury Boulevard, Milton Keynes, MK9 1NR
T: 01908 671933
E: innovate@thinkspi.co.uk
W: www.thinkspi.com

Spectro
Palace Gate, Odiham, Hampshire, RG29 1NP
T: 01256 704000
F: 01256 704006
E: enquiries@spectro-oil.com
W: www.spectro-oil.com

Spectrum Freight Ltd
PO Box 105, Chesterfield, Derbys, S41 9XY
T: 01246 456677
F: 01246 456688
E: sales@spectrumfreight.co.uk
W: www.spectrumfreight.co.uk

Spectrum Technologies
Western Avenue, Bridgend, Mid Glamorgan, CF31 3RT
T: 01656 655437
F: 01656 655920
E: ehardy@spectrumtech.com
W: www.spectrumtech.com

Speedy Hire Plc
Chase House, 16 The Parks, Newton le Willows, Merseyside, WA12 0JQ
T: 01942 720000
F: 01942 720077
E: plc.admin@speedyservices.com
W: www.speedyservices.com

Spence Ltd
Parcel Deck, Barnby St, Euston Station, London, NW1 2RS
T: 020 7387 1268
F: 020 7380 1255
E: info@spenceltd.co.uk
W: www.spenceltd.co.uk

Spencer Group
One Humber Quays, Wellington Street West, Hull, East Yorkshire, HU1 2BN
T: 01482 766340
F: 01469 532233
E: mailbox@cspencerltd.co.uk
W: www.thespencergroup.co.uk

Speno International SA
Route du Nant-d'Avril 94, Case Postale 1, CH-1217 Meyrin 1, Switzerland
T: 0041 22906 4600
F: 0041 22906 4601
E: info@speno.ch
W: www.speno.ch

Sperry Rail International Ltd
Trent House, RTC Business Park, London Rd, Derby, DE24 8UP
T: 01332 262565
F: 01332 262541
E: jtansley@sperryrail.com
W: www.sperryrail.com

Sphera
Pavilion 3, Craigshaw Business Park, Craigshaw Road, West Tullos, Aberdeen, AB12 3QH
T: 01224 337200
F: 01224 337201
W: sphera.com

SPI Piling Ltd
See A E Yates Group

Spitfire Tours
PO Box 824, Taunton, TA1 9ET
T: 0870 879 3675
E: info@spitfirerailtours.co.uk
W: www.spitfirerailtours.co.uk

SPL Powerlines UK Ltd
Unit 3A, Hagmill Cres, East Shawhead Enterprise Park, Coatbridge, Lanarkshire, ML5 4NS
T: 01236 424666
F: 01236 426444
E: office@powerlines-group.com
W: www.powerlines-group.com

Spring
Millennium Bridge House, 2 Lambeth Hill, London, EC4V 4BG
E: london@spring.com
W: www.spring.com

SPX Rail Systems
Unit 7, Thames Gateway Park, Choats Rd, Dagenham, Essex, RM9 6RH
T: 020 8526 7100
F: 020 8526 7151
E: brian.cannon@spx.com
W: www.spx.com/en/spx-rail-systems/

SRPS Railtours
SRPS Office, 17-19 North Street, Bo'ness, West Lothian, EH51 0AQ
T: 0131 202 1033
E: railtours@srps.org.uk
W: www.srpsrailtours.com

SRS Rail System Ltd
Unit 3, Riverside Way, Gateway Business Park, Bolsover, Chesterfield, Derbyshire, S44 6GA
T: 01246 241312
F: 01246 825076
E: info@srsrailuk.com
W: www.srsrailuk.com/

SSDM
See Aura Brand Solutions

SSE Contracting
1 Forbury Place, 43 Forbury Road, Reading, Berkshire, RG1 3JH
W: www.ssecontracting.co.uk

SSE Enterprise Rail
Inveralmond House, 200 Dunkeld Road, Perth, PH1 3AQ
W: sse.com/whatwedo/sse-enterprise/rail/

SSP
169 Euston Rd, London, NW1 2AE
T: 020 7543 3300
F: 020 7543 3389
E: clare@templemerepr.co.uk
W: www.foodtravelexperts.com/uk/home/

St Leonards Railway Engineering Ltd
Bridgeway, St Leonards on Sea, E Sussex, TN38 8AP
T: 01233 617001

Stadler Pankow GmbH
Lessingstrasse 102, D-13158 Berlin, Germany
T: +49 30 91 91 16 16
F: +49 30 91 91 20 00
E: stadler.deutschland@stadlerrail.com
W: www.stadlerrail.com

Stadler Rail AG
Ernst-Stadler-Strasse 1, 9565 Bussnang, Switzerland
T: +41 (0)71 626 21 20
F: +41 (0)71 626 21 28
E: stadler.rail@stadlerrail.com
W: www.stadlerrail.com/en/

Stagecoach Group
10 Dunkeld Rd, Perth, PH1 5TW
T: 01738 442111
F: 01738 643648
E: info@stagecoachgroup.com
W: www.stagecoachgroup.com

Stagecoach Supertram
Nunnery Depot, Woodbourn Rd, Sheffield, S9 3LS
T: 0114 275 9888
F: 0114 279 8120
E: enquiries@supertram.com
W: www.supertram.com

Stahlwille Tools Ltd
Unit 2D, Albany Park Ind. Est, Frimley Rd, Camberley, Surrey, GU16 7PD
T: 01276 24080
F: 01276 24696
E: scottsheldon@stahlwille.co.uk
W: www.stahlwille.co.uk

Standish Engineering Co Ltd
Mayflower Works, Bradley Lane, Standish, Lancashire, WN6 0XF
T: 01257 422838
F: 01257 422381
E: nick@cnc-machining.co.uk
W: www.standishengineering.co.uk/

Stanley Tools
Sheffield Business Park, Sheffield City Airport, Europa Link, Sheffield, S3 9PD
T: 0114 244 8883
F: 0114 273 9038

Stannah Lifts
Anton Mill, Andover, Hants, SP10 2NX
T: 01264 339090
E: liftsales@stannah.co.uk
W: www.stannahlifts.co.uk

Stansted Express
See Greater Anglia

Stanton Precast Ltd
Littlewell Lane, Stanton by Dale, Ilkeston, Derbys, DE7 4QW
T: 0115 944 1448
F: 0115 944 1466
E: sbc@stanton-bonna.co.uk
W: www.stanton-bonna.co.uk

Stanway Consulting
91-97 Saltergate, Chesterfield, Derbyshire, S40 1LA

Star Fasteners (UK) Ltd
Unit 1, 44 Brookhill Road,, Pinxton, Nottinghamshire, NG16 6RY
T: 0115 932 4939
F: 0115 944 1278
E: sales@starfasteners.co.uk
W: www.starfasteners.co.uk

STARC Ltd
4a Mina Avenue, Slough, Berkshire, SL3 7BY
M: 07940 838842
E: enquiries@starcltd.co.uk
W: starcltd.co.uk/

Statesman Rail Ltd
PO Box 83, St Erth, Hayle, Cornwall, TR27 9AD
T: 0345 310 2458
F: 0115 944 1278
W: www.statesmanrail.com

STATS
See RSK Ltd

Stauff Ltd
500 Carlisle St East, Off Downgate Drive, Sheffield, S4 8BS
T: 01142 518518
F: 01141 518519
E: sales@stauff.co.uk
W: www.stauff.co.uk

Staytite Ltd
Staytite House, Coronation Rd, Cressex Bus. Park, High Wycombe, Bucks, HP12 3RP
T: 01494 462322
F: 01494 464747
E: fasteners@staytite.com
W: www.staytite.com

The Steam Dreams Rail Co
Albury Lodge, Albury, Guildford, Surrey, GU5 9AE
T: 01483 209888
E: info@steamdreams.co.uk
W: www.steamdreams.co.uk

Steatite Ltd
Ravensbank Business Park, Acanthus Rd, Redditch, Worcs, B98 9EX
T: 01527 512400
F: 01527 512419
E: sales@steatite.co.uk
W: www.steatite.co.uk

Steconfer
1 St. Peters Square, Manchester, M2 3DE
W: www.steconfer.com/en/

Steelteam Construction (UK) Ltd
46 Goods Station Rd, Tunbridge Wells, Kent, TN1 2DD
T: 01892 533677
F: 01892 511535
E: sales@steelteamconstruction.co.uk
W: www.steelteamconstruction.co.uk

Steelway Rail
Queensgate Works, Bilston Rd, Wolverhampton, West Midlands, WV2 2NJ
T: 01902 834911
F: 01902 452256
E: sales@steelway.co.uk
W: www.steelway.co.uk

Steer
28-32 Upper Ground, London, SE1 9PD
T: 020 7910 5000
F: 020 7910 5001
E: sdginfo@sdgworld.net
W: www.steerdaviesgleave.com

Stego UK Ltd
Unit 12, First Quarter Bus. Park, Blenheim Rd, Epsom, Surrey, KT19 9QN
T: 01372 747250
F: 01372 729854
E: info@stego.co.uk
W: www.stego.co.uk

Stemmer Imaging
The Old Barn, Grange Court, Tongham, Surrey, GU10 1DW
T: 01252 780030
F: 01252 780001
E: uk.info@stemmer-imaging.com
W: www.stemmer-imaging.co.uk/en/

Stent
See Balfour Beatty Ground Engineering

Step On Safety Ltd
Units 3-4, 122 Station Road, Lawford, Manningtree, Essex, CO11 2LH
T: 01206 396446
E: info@steponsafety.co.uk
W: www.steponsafety.co.uk

Stephenson Harwood LLP
1 Finsbury Circus, London, EC2M 7SH
T: 020 7329 4422
F: 020 7329 7100
E: info@shlegal.com
W: www.shlegal.com

Sterling Transport Consultancy
19 Aston Chase, Stone, Staffordshire, ST15 8SD
M: 07711 055825
E: lee@sterlingtransportconsultancy.com

Stewart Signs Rail
Trafalgar Close, Chandlers Ford Ind. Est, Eastleigh, Hants, SO53 4BW
T: 023 8025 4781
F: 023 8025 5620
E: sales@stewartsigns.co.uk
W: www.stewartsigns.co.uk

Stirling Maynard
Construction Consultants, Stirling House, Rightwell, Bretton, Peterborough, PE3 8DJ
T: 01733 262319
F: 01733 331527
E: enquiries@stirlingmaynard.com
W: www.stirlingmaynard.com

STM Security
1st Floor, Solar House, 1-9 Romford Road, Stratford, London, E15 4LJ
T: 020 3597 4264
F: 020 8555 8960
E: comms@stmsecurity.com
W: www.stmsecurity.com/

Stobart Rail
See XYZ Rail Ltd

Stock Redler Ltd
See Schenck Process UK

Stocksigns Ltd/ Burnham Signs
43 Ormside Way, Holmethorpe Ind Est, Redhill, Surrey, RH1 2LG
T: 01737 774072
F: 01737 763763
E: sales@stocksigns.co.uk
W: www.stocksigns.co.uk

Stockton Engineering Management Ltd
1 Warwick Row, London, SW1E 5ER
T: 020 7808 7808
F: 020 7117 5253
E: info@stocktonlondon.com
W: www.stocktonlondon.com

Stofl
131 Adventurers Quay, Cardiff, CF10 4NR
E: theproblemsolvers@stofl.net
W: www.stofl.net

Stored Energy Technology
See S.E.T. Ltd

Story Contracting
Burgh Rd Ind Est, Carlisle, Cumbria, CA2 7NA
T: 01228 590444
F: 01228 593359
E: feedback@storycontracting.com
W: www.storycontracting.com/

Strabag
Donau-City-Str. 9, 1220 Vienna, Austria
T: 0043 1 22422-0
E: pr@strabag.com
W: www.strabag.com/

STRAIL (UK) Ltd
Room 2, First Floor, 3 Tannery House, Tannery Lane, Send, Woking, Surrey, GU23 7EF
T: 01483 222090
F: 01483 222095
E: richard@srsrailuk.co.uk
W: www.strail.com

Strainstall UK Ltd
Unit 10, City Business Park, Easton Road, Bristol, BS5 0SP
T: 01761 414939
E: enquiries@strainstall.com
W: www.strainstall.co.uk

Strata Geotechnics
Summit Close, Kirkby-in-Ashfield, Nottinghamshire, NG17 8GJ
T: 01773 304056
E: info@stratageo.co.uk
W: www.stratageotechnics.com/

Strataform
See Technocover Limited

Stratasys Solutions Ltd
Suite 1, 3rd Floor, 11-12 St James's Square, London, SW1Y 4LB
W: www.stratasys.com

Strategic Team Group Ltd
Strategic Business Centre, Blue Ridge Park, Thunderhead Ridge, Glasshoughton, Castleford, West Yorks, WF10 4UA
T: 01977 555550
F: 01977 555509
E: contact@strategicteamgroup.com
W: www.strategicteamgroup.com

Strathclyde Partnership for Transport
131 St Vincent Street, Glasgow, G2 5JF
T: 0141 332 6811
E: enquiry@spt.co.uk
W: www.spt.co.uk

Street Crane Co. Ltd
Chapel-en-le-Frith, High Peak, Derbys, SK23 0PH
T: 01298 812456
F: 01298 814945
E: sales@streetcrane.co.uk
W: www.streetcrane.co.uk

Streets UK
Suite 411, Baltic Chambers, 50 Wellington Street, Glasgow, G2 6HJ
E: fiona.robertson@streets-uk.com
W: www.streets-uk.com/

Structural Fabrications Limited
2 Castings Road, Sir Francis Ley Industrial Park South, Derby, DE23 8YL
T: 01332 747400
F: 01332 747447
E: sales@structural-fabrications.co.uk
W: structuralfabrications.co.uk/

Strukton Rail
Westkanaaldijk 2, NL-3542 DA Utrecht, Netherlands
T: 31 30 248 66 94
E: info@struktonrail.com
W: www.struktonrail.com

STS Rail
See Mors Smitt UK Ltd (A Wabtec Company)

STS Signals
See Mors Smitt UK Ltd (A Wabtec Company)

Stuart Group
Middleplatt Road, Immingham, Lincs, DN40 1AH
T: 01469 551230
F: 01469 551239
E: enquiries@stuartgroup.info
W: www.stuartgroup.ltd.uk

Stuart Maher Ltd (SML)
Suite 112, 150 Minories, London, EC3N 1LS
T: +44 (0) 207 347 5450
F: +44 (0) 207 347 5451
E: enquiry@stuart-maher.co.uk
W: www.stuart-maher.co.uk

Studio Egret West
3 Brewhouse Yard, London, EC1V 4JQ
T: 020 7549 1730
E: hello@egretwest.com
W: egretwest.com/

Suez environnement
SITA House, Grenfell Road, Maidenhead, Berkshire, SL6 1ES
T: 01628 513100
W: www.sita.co.uk/

Sulzer Dowding & Mills
193 Camp Hill, Bordesley, Birmingham, B12 0JJ
T: 0121 766 6161
F: 0121 766 7247
E: engineering.birmingham@sulzer.com
W: www.sulzer.com

Sunbelt Rentals
102 Dalton Ave, Birchwood Park, Birchwood, Warrington, WA3 6YE
T: 01925 281000
F: 01925 281001
E: enquiries@sunbeltrentals.co.uk
W: www.sunbeltrentals.co.uk

Superjet London
Unit 5, Kennet Rd, Dartford, Kent, DA1 4QN
T: 01322 554595
F: 01322 557773
E: chris@superjet.co.uk
W: www.jetchem.com

Supersine Duramark
See Aura Brand Solutions

Surge Protection Devices Ltd
Unit 1, Ash Royd Farm, Royd Road, Meltham, Holmfirth, West Yorkshire, HD9 4BG
T: 01484 851747
F: 01484 852594
E: info@surgedevices.co.uk
W: www.surgedevices.co.uk

Survey Systems Ltd
Willow Bank House, Old Road, Handforth, Wilmslow, SK9 3AZ
T: 01625 533444
F: 01625 526815
E: enquiries@survsys.co.uk
W: www.survsys.co.uk/rail

Sustainable Transport Midlands
E: hey@transport-mids.com
W: transport-mids.com

SW Global Resourcing
270 Peters Hill Rd, Glasgow, G21 4AY
T: 0141 557 6133
F: 0141 557 6143
E: admin@sw-gr.com
W: sw-gr.com

Swallow Site Services Ltd
3 Hertford House, Hugo Gryn Way, Shenley, Hertfordshire, WD7 9AB
T: 020 8447 3727
E: john.cronin@swallow-site.biz
W: www.swallow-site.biz/

Sweco
Grove House, Mansion Gate Drive, Leeds, LS7 4DN
T: 0113 262 0000
E: info@sweco.co.uk
W: www.sweco.co.uk

Sweetnam & Bradley Ltd
Industrial Est, Gloucester Rd, Malmesbury, Wilts, SN16 0DY
T: 01666 823491
F: 01666 826010
E: sales@sweetnam-bradley.com
W: www.sweetnam-bradley.com

Sweett Group
60 Grays Inn Rd, London, W1X 8AQ
T: 020 7061 9000
F: 020 7430 0603
E: eryl.evans@sweettgroup.com
W: www.sweettgroup.com

Swietelsky Babcock
See SB Rail (Swietelsky Babcock)

Swietelsky Construction Company Ltd
7 Clairmont Gardens, Glasgow, G3 7LW
T: 0141 353 1915
E: office@swietelsky.at
W: www.swietelsky.com

SWLines Ltd
9 Wordsworth Avenue, Bournemouth, BH8 9NT
E: tom@swlines.co.uk

Sydac Ltd
Derwent Business Centre, Clarke St, Derby, DE1 2BU
T: 01332 299600
F: 01332 299624
E: sales@sydac.co.uk
W: www.sydac.co.uk

Sylmasta Ltd
Unit 1, Dales Yard, Lewes Rd, Scaynes Hill, W Sussex, RH17 7PG
T: 01444 831459
F: 01444 831971
W: www.sylmasta.co.uk

Synectic Systems Group Ltd
3-4 Broadfield Close, Sheffield, South Yorkshire, S8 0XN
T: 0114 2552509
F: 0114 2582050
E: sales@synx.com
W: www.synecticsystems.com

Synergy Health Plc
Gavenny Court, Brecon Rd, Abergavenny, Monmouthshire, NP7 7RX
T: 01873 856688
F: 01873 585982
E: enquiries@synergyhealthplc.com
W: www.synergyhealthplc.com

Syntax Conultancy
1 College Place, Derby, DE1 3DY
T: 01332 293605
F: 01332 296128
E: marketing@syntaxconsultancy.com
W: www.syntaxconsultancy.com

Systecon (UK) Ltd
PO Box 4612, Weymouth, Dorset, DT4 9YY
T: 0871 641 2202
F: 01305 768480
W: www.systecon.co.uk

System Store Solutions Ltd
Ham Lane, Lenham, Maidstone, Kent, ME17 2LH
T: 01622 859522
F: 01622 858746
E: sales@systemstoresolutions.com
W: www.system-store.com

Systra UK
Fourth Floor, Dukes Court, Duke St, Woking, Surrey, GU21 5BH
T: 01483 742941
F: 01483 755207
E: sgulyvasy@systra.com
W: www.systra.com

T & R Williamson Ltd
36 Stonebridgegate, Ripon, North Yorkshire, HG4 1TP
T: 01765 607711
F: 01765 607908
W: www.trwilliamson.co.uk

T & RS Engineering Ltd
Unit 8, Buccaneer Drive, Fountain Court, Doncaster, DN9 3QP
T: 01302 315011
E: mail@trsengineering.co.uk
W: www.trsengineering.co.uk

Talascend Ltd
First Floor, Broadway Chambers, Hammersmith Broadway, London, W6 7PW
T: 020 8600 1600
F: 020 8741 2001
W: www.talascend.com

Talentwise
44 Royal Scot Road, Pride Park, Derby, DE24 8AJ
T: 01332 344 443
E: daniel.taylor@fordandstanley.com
W: www.fordandstanley.com/employers/talentwise/

Talgo
Paseo del tren Talgo, 2, 28290 Las Matas, Madrid, Spain
T: (+34) 91 631 38 00
F: (+34) 91 631 38 93
E: marketing@talgo.com
W: https://www.talgo.com/en/

Tanfield Engineering Systems
Tanfield Lea Ind. Est. North, Stanley, Co Durham, DH9 9NX
T: 01207 521111
F: 01207 523355
W: www.tanfieldengineeringsystems.com/

Tangerine Ltd
Unit 9, Blue Lion Place, 237 Long Lane, London, SE1 4PU
T: 020 7357 0966
F: 020 7357 0784
E: mail@tangerine.net
W: www.tangerine.net

Tarmac
Portland House, Bickenhill Lane, Solihull, West Midlands, B37 7BQ
T: 0121 787 5001
W: www.tarmac.com/

Tasty Plant Sales
Unit 4, Asheridge Business Centre, Asheridge Road, Chesham, Bucks, HP5 2PT
T: 0845 677 4444
E: info@tastyplant.co.uk
W: www.tastyplant.co.uk

TATA Consultancy Services (TCS)
4th Floor, 33 Grosvenor Place, London, SW1X 7HY
T: 020 7245 1800
F: 020 7245 1875
E: uk.info@tcs.com
W: www.tcs.com/

Tata Steel Projects
Meridian House, The Crescent, York, YO24 1AW
T: 01904 454600
F: 01904 454601
E: tatasteelprojects@tatasteel.com
W: www.tatasteelrail.com/en/

Tata Steel Rail
See British Steel

Tate Rail Ltd
Station House, Station Hill, Cookham, Berks, SL6 9BP
T: 0844 381 9956
F: 0844 381 9957
E: info@taterail.com
W: www.taterail.com

Taylor Airey Ltd
2a Charing Cross Road, London, WC2H 0HF
T: 020 8017 4655
E: enquiries@taylorairey.com
W: www.taylorairey.com

Taylor Precision Plastics / Commercial Vehicle Rollers Ltd
Mile Oak Ind. Est, Maesbury Rd, Oswestry, Shropshire, SY10 8GA
T: 01691 679536
F: 01691 670538
E: sales@cvrollers.co.uk
W: www.cvrollers.co.uk

Taylor Technology Systems
Horizon Business Centre, Unit 25, Alder Close, Erith, Kent, DA18 4AJ
T: 020 8320 9944
E: sales@taylortechnologysystems.com
W: www.taylortechnologysystems.com/

Taylor Woodrow
Astral House, Imperial Way, Watford, Herts, WD24 4WW
T: 01923 233433
F: 01923 800085
E: info@taylorwoodrow.com
W: www.taylorwoodrow.com

Taylormade Fasteners Ltd
Units 4&5, Watery Lane Ind. Est, Willenhall, West Midlands, WV13 3SU
T: 01902 631222
F: 01902 601891
E: mlane@taylormadefasteners.co.uk
W: www.taylormadefasteners.co.uk

Taziker Industrial Ltd t/a TI Protective Coatings
Unit 6, Lodge Bank, Crown Lane, Horwich, Bolton, BL6 5HY
T: 01204 468080
F: 01204 695188
E: sales@taziker.com
W: https://taziker.com/

TBA Protective Technologies
Unit 3, Transpennine Trading Estate, Gorrells Way, Rochdale, OL11 2PX
T: 01706 647422
E: info@tba-pt.com
W: www.tba-pt.com

TBAT Innovation Limited
Unit 3, Bradley Court, Maple Road, Trent Lane, Castle Donington, Derby, DE74 2UT
T: 01332 819740
E: info@tbat.co.uk
W: www.tbat.co.uk/

TBI Consulting
7 Sunset Avenue, Woodford Green, Essex, IG8 0ST

TBM Consulting Group
Unit 8, H2O Business Complex, Sherwood Business Park, Annesley, Nottingham, NG15 0HT
T: 01623 758298
F: 01623 755941
E: nfletcher@tbmcg.com
W: www.tbmcg.com

TBM Rail
Unit B, The Quantum, Marshfield Bank, Crewe, Cheshire, CW2 8UY
T: 0844 8008577
E: enquiries@tbmrail.com
W: www.tbmrail.com

TCP Ltd
Quayside Industrial Park, Bates Road, Maldon, Essex, CM9 5FA
T: 01621 850777
F: 01621 843330
E: mail@tcp.eu.com
W: www.tcp.eu.com

TDK-Lambda UK
Kingsley Ave, Ilfracombe, Devon, EX34 8ES
T: 01271 856600
F: 01271 856741
E: powersolutions@emea.tdk-lambda.com
W: www.emea.tdk-lambda.com

TE Connectivity
1 rue Paul Martin, F-21220 Gervey-Chambertin, France
T: 33 03 80 58 32 13
E: rail@te.com
W: www.te.com/energy

TEAL Consulting Ltd
Deangate, Tuesley Lane, Godalming, Surrey, GU7 1SG
T: 01483 420550
E: info@tealconsulting.co.uk
W: www.tealconsulting.co.uk

Team Surveys Ltd
Team House, St Austell Bay Business Park, Par Moor Rd, St Austell, PL25 3RF
T: 01726 816069
F: 01726 814611

Tecalemit Garage Equipment Co Ltd
Eagle Rd, Langage Business Park, Plymouth, PL7 5JY
T: 01752 219111
F: 01752 219128
E: sales@tecalemit.co.uk
W: www.tecalemit.co.uk

Tecforce
Litchurch Lane, Derby, DE24 8AA
T: 01332 268000
F: 01332 268030
E: sales@tecforce.co.uk
W: www.tecforce.co.uk

Technical Cranes Ltd
Holmes Lock Works, Steel St, Holmes, Rotherham, S61 1DF
T: 01709 561861
F: 01709 556516
E: info@technicalcranes.co.uk
W: www.technicalcranes.co.uk

Technical Programme Delivery
10 Station Hill, Henley on Thames, RG9 1AY
T: 01932 228710
F: 01932 228710
E: pac@tpd.uk.com
W: www.tpd.uk.com

Technical Resin Bonders
See TRB Lightweight Structures Ltd

Technocover Limited
Henfaes Lane, Welshpool, Powys, SY21 7BE
T: 01938 555511
F: 01938 555527
E: sales@technocover.co.uk
W: www.technocover.co.uk

Technology Project Services Ltd
1 Warwick Row, London, SW1E 5LR
T: 020 7963 1234
F: 020 7963 1299

Technology Resourcing Ltd
The Technology Centre, Surrey Research Park, Guildford, GU2 7YG
T: 01483 302211
F: 01483 301222
E: railways@tech-res.co.uk
W: www.railwayengineeringjobs.co.uk

Tecton Ltd
186 Main Road, Fishers Pond, Eastleigh, Hants, SO50 7HG
T: 02380 695735
F: 02380 695702
E: sales@jthts.co.uk
W: www.tecton.co.uk

Tees Valley Combined Authority
Cavendish House, Teesdale Business Park, Stockton-on-Tees, Tees Valley, TS17 6QY
T: 01642 524400
E: info@teesvalley-ca.gov.uk
W: www.teesvalley-ca.gov.uk/

TEK Personnel Consultants Ltd
Norwich Union House, Irongate, Derby, DE1 3GA
T: 01332 360055
F: 01332 363345
E: derby@tekpersonnel.co.uk
W: www.tekpersonnel.co.uk

Telefonica O2 Ltd
260 Bath Road, Slough, Berkshire, SL1 4DX
W: www.o2.co.uk/

Telemecanique Sensors
T: 0870 608 8608
E: gb-customerservices@schneider-electric.com
W: www.tesensors.com/uk/en/

Telent Technology Services Ltd
Point 3, Haywood Rd, Warwick, CV34 5AH
T: 01926 693564
F: 01926 693023
E: services@telent.com
W: www.telent.com

Telerail Ltd
Royal Scot Suite, Carnforth Station Heritage Centre, Warton Rd, Carnforth, Lancs, LA5 9TR
T: 01524 735774
F: 01524 736386
E: info@telerail.co.uk
W: www.telerail.co.uk

Telerail Networks Ltd
Spaceworks, Benton Park Road, Newcastle Upon Tyne, NE7 7LX

Telespazio VEGA UK
350 Capability Green, Luton, Beds, LU1 3LU
T: 01582 399000
E: info@vegaspace.com
W: www.telespazio-vega.com

Televic Rail
Leo Bakaertlaan 1, B-8870 Izegem, Belgium
T: 0032 5130 3045
E: rail@televic.com
W: www.televic-rail.com

Temple Group Ltd
Devon House, 58-60 St Katharine's Way, London, E1W 1LB
T: 020 7394 3700
F: 020 7394 7871
E: enquiries@templegroup.co.uk
W: www.templegroup.co.uk

Ten 47 Ltd
Unit 2B, Frances Ind. Park, Wemyss Rd, Dysart, Kirkcaldy, KY1 2XZ
T: 01592 655725
F: 01592 651049
E: sales@ten47.com
W: www.ten47.com

TenBroeke Company Ltd
Dorset House, Refent Park, Kingston Rd, Leatherhead, Surrey, KT22 7PL
T: 01372 824722
F: 01372 824332
E: paul.tweedale@tenbroekco.com
W: www.tenbroekeco.com/

TenCate Geosynthetics UK Ltd
PO Box 773, Telford, Shropshire, TF7 9FE
T: 01952 588066
W: www.tencategeosynthetics.com

Tenconi SA
via della Stazione 50, CH-6780 Airolo, Italy
T: +41 91 873 30 00
F: +41 91 873 30 01
E: tenconi@tenconi.ch
W: www.tenconi.ch/en/

Tenmat Ltd (Railko Ltd)
Ashburton Road West, Trafford Park, Manchester, M17 1RU
T: 0161 872 2181
F: 0161 872 7596
W: www.tenmat.com

Tensar International
Cunningham Court, Shadsworth Business Park, Shadsworth, Blackburn, BB1 2QX
T: 01254 262431
F: 01254 266868
E: info@tensar-international.com
W: www.tensar.co.uk

Tension Control Bolts
TCB House, Clywedog Road South, Wrexham Industrial Estate, Wrexham, LL13 9XS
T: 01978 661122
E: info@tcbolts.co.uk
W: www.tcbolts.co.uk

Terram Ltd
Fiberweb Geosynthetics Ltd, Blackwater Trading Estate, The Causeway, Maldon, Essex, CM9 4GG
T: 01621 874200
E: info@terram.com
W: www.terram.com

Terrawise Construction Ltd
104 The Court Yard, Radway Green Business Centre, Radway Green, Crewe, Cheshire, CW2 5PR
T: 01270 879011
F: 01270 875079
E: info@terrawise.co.uk
W: www.terrawise.co.uk

TES 2000 Ltd
TES House, Heath Industrial Park, Grange Way, Colchester, CO2 8GU
T: 01206 799111
F: 01206 227910
E: info@tes2000.co.uk
W: www.tes2000.co.uk

TES Communication Solutions
Lancaster House, Bow Lane, Leyland, PR25 4YA
T: 0800 772 0090
F: 01772 901902
E: info@tesradio.com
W: www.tesradio.com

Testo Ltd
Newman Lane, Alton, Hants, GU34 2QJ
T: 01420 544433
F: 01420 544434
E: info@testo.co.uk
W: www.testo.co.uk

Tevo Ltd
Maddison House, Thomas Road, Wooburn Green Industrial Park, Wooburn Green, Bucks, HP10 0PE
T: 01628 528034
E: sales@tevo.eu.com
W: www.tevo.eu.com

Tew Engineering Ltd
See LB Foster Europe

Thales UK
The Quadrant, 4 Thomas More Square, 17 Thomas More Street, London, E1W 1YW
T: +44 118 943 4500
F: 020 3300 6994
E: greenpark.reception@uk.thalesgroup.com
W: www.thalesgroup.com/transportation

The Rail Logistics Company
John De Mierre House, Bridge Road, Haywards Heath, West Sussex, RH16 1UA
T: 01444 849375
W: theraillogisticscompany.com/

The Technical Strategy Leadership Group (TSLG)
Block 2, 1 Torrens St, Angel Square, London, EC1V 1NY
T: 0203 142 5300
E: innovations@futurerailway.org
W: www.futurerailway.org/leadership/pages

ThermaCom Ltd
Celsius House, Summit Close, Kirkby in Ashfield, Notts, NG17 8GJ
T: 01623 758777
E: sales@thermaqroup.com
W: www.thermagroup.com

Thermal Economics Ltd
Thermal House, 8 Cardiff Rd, Luton, Beds, LU1 1PP
T: 01582 450814
F: 01582 429305
E: info@thermal-economics.co.uk
W: www.thermal-economics.co.uk

Thermit Welding (GB) Ltd
87 Ferry Lane, Rainham, Essex, RM13 9YH
T: 01708 522626
F: 01708 553806
E: tw@goldschmidt.com
W: www.thermit-welding.com/

Thomas & Betts Ltd
See PMA UK Ltd (Thomas & Betts Ltd)

Thomas Vale Construction
See Bouygues Travaux Publics

Thomson Rail Equipment Ltd
Valley Rd, Cinderford, Gloucestershire, GL14 2NZ
T: 01594 826611
F: 01594 825560
E: sales@thomsondesignuk.com
W: www.thomsonrail.com

Threepwood Consulting
76 King Street, Manchester, M2 4NH
M: 07748 182460
E: ian.naylor@threepwoodconsulting.com
W: www.threepwoodconsulting.com

Threeshires Ltd
Piper Hole Farm, Eastwell Rd, Scalford, Leics, LE14 4SS
T: 01664 444604
F: 01664 444605
E: enquiries@threeshires.com
W: www.threeshires.com

Through Life Support Ltd
Red Lodge, Bonds Mill, Stonehouse, Gloucestershire, GL10 3RF
T: 01453 820376
M: 07803 698999
E: david.williams@throughlifesupport.com
W: www.throughlifesupport.com

Thurlow Countryside Management Ltd
2 Charterhouse Trading Est, Sturmer Rd, Haverhill, Suffolk, CB9 7UU
T: 01440 760170
F: 01440 760171
E: info@t-c-m.co.uk
W: www.t-c-m.co.uk

Thurrock Engineering Supplies Ltd
Unit 1, TES House, Motherwell Way, West Thurrock, Essex, RM20 3XD
T: 01708 861178
F: 01708 861158
E: info@thurrockengineering.com
W: www.thurrockengineering.com

TI Protective Coatings
See Taziker Industrial Ltd t/a TI Protective Coatings

TICS Ltd
Oxford House, Robin Hood Airport, Sixth Avenue, Doncaster, DN9 3GG
T: 01302 623074
F: 01302 623075
E: info@tics-ltd.co.uk
W: www.tics-ltd.co.uk

Tidyco Ltd
Unit 2, Pentagon Island, Nottingham Road, Derby, DE21 6BW
T: 01332 851300
E: enquiries@tidyco.co.uk
W: www.tidyco.co.uk

Tiflex Ltd
Tiflex House, Liskeard, Cornwall, PL14 4NB
T: 01579 320808
F: 01579 320802
M: 07967 343256
E: panderson@tiflex.co.uk
W: www.tiflex.co.uk

Time 24 Ltd
19 Victoria Gardens, Burgess Hill, West Sussex, RH15 9NB
T: 01444 257655
F: 01444 259000
E: sales@time24.co.uk
W: www.time24.co.uk

Timeplan Ltd
12 The Pines, Broad St, Guildford, Surrey, GU3 3BH
T: 01483 462340
F: 01483 462349
E: dave@timeplansolutions.com
W: www.timeplansolutions.com

TLT
One Redcliff Street, Bristol, BS1 6TP
T: 0333 006 0000
F: 0333 006 0011
W: www.tltsolicitors.com/

TMP Worldwide
Chancery House, Chancery Lane, London, WC2A 1QS
T: 020 7406 5075
E: contactus@tmpw.co.uk
W: www.tmpw.co.uk

Tolent Construction Ltd
Ravensworth House, 5th Avenue Business Park, Team Valley, Gateshead, Tyne & Wear, NE11 0HF
T: 0191 487 0505
F: 0191 487 2990
E: tyneside@tolent.co.uk
W: www.tolent.co.uk/

Tony Gee and Partners LLP
Hardy House, 140 High St, Esher, Surrey, KT10 9QJ
T: 01372 461600
F: 01372 461601
E: enquiries@tonygee.com
W: www.tonygee.com

Tony Miles Railway Writing and Photography
51 Braemar Avenue, Stretford, Manchester, M32 9WA
T: 0161 864 3396
M: 07973 619915
E: tonymiles61@btinternet.com

TopDeck Parking
Springvale Business & Industrial Park, Bilston, Wolverhampton, WV14 0QL
T: 01902 499400
F: 01902 494080
E: info@topdeckparking.co.uk
W: www.topdeckparking.co.uk

Topdrill
7 Deeping Gate, Stonebridge, Milton Keynes, MK13 0DE
T: 01908 321925
E: info@topdrill.co.uk
W: www.topdrill.co.uk

Toray Textiles Europe Ltd
Crown Farm Way, Forest Town, Mansfield, Notts, NG19 0FT
T: 01623 415050
F: 01623 415070
E: sales@ttel.co.uk
W: www.ttel.co.uk

Torrent Trackside Ltd
Network House, Europa Way, Britannia Enterprise Park, Lichfield, Staffs, WS14 9TZ
T: 01543 421900
F: 01543 421931
E: mail@torrent.co.uk
W: www.torrent.co.uk

Total Access (UK) Ltd
Unit 5, Raleigh Hall Ind. Est, Eccleshall, Staffs, ST21 6JL
T: 01785 850333
F: 01785 850339
E: enquiries@totalaccess.co.uk
W: www.totalaccess.co.uk

Total Rail Solutions
Crossway, Stephenson Road, Houndmills, Basingstoke, Hants, RG21 6XR
T: 01962 711642
F: 01962 717330
E: info@totalrailsolutions.co.uk
W: www.totalrailsolutions.co.uk/

TotalKare HDWS Ltd
Block G1, Dandy Bank Road, Pensnett Trading Estate, Kingswinford, DY6 7TD
T: 0121 585 2724
E: sales@totalkare.co.uk
W: www.totalkare.co.uk

Totectors (UK) Ltd
9 Pondwood Close, Moulton Park Ind. Estate, Northampton, NN3 6RT
T: 0870 600 5055
F: 0870 600 5056
E: sales@totectors.net
W: www.totectors.net

Touchstone Renard Ltd
152-160 City Road, London, EC1V 2NX
T: 020 3954 2576
M: 07768 366744
E: paustin@touchstonerenard.com
W: www.touchstonerenard.com

Tower Surveys Ltd
Opus House, 21 Vivian Avenue, Nottingham, NG5 1AF
T: 0115 960 1212
F: 0115 962 1200
E: info@towersurveys.co.uk
W: www.towersurveys.co.uk

TP Matrix Ltd
TP House, Prince Of Wales Industrial Units, Vulcan Street, Oldham, Greater Manchester, OL1 4ER
T: 0161 626 4067
F: 0161 627 1741
E: service@tpmatrix.co.uk
W: www.tpmatrixrail.co.uk/

TPA Portable Roadways Ltd
TPA Head Office, Dukeries Mill, Claylands Industrial Estate, Worksop, Notts, S81 7DJ
T: 0870 240 2381
F: 0870 240 2382
E: enquiries@tpa-ltd.co.uk
W: www.tpa-ltd.co.uk

TPGroup
Apex, Forbury Road, Reading, Berks, RG1 1AX
T: 01753 285800
E: enquiries@tpgroup.uk.com
W: www.tpgroupglobal.com

TPK Consulting Ltd (RPS Group)
Centurion Court, 85, Milton Park, Abingdon, Oxon, OX14 4RY
T: 01235 438151
F: 01235 438188
E: rpsab@rpsgroup.com
W: www.rpsplc.co.uk

TQ Training
Bragborough Farm, Welton Road, Braunston, Daventry, Northants, NN11 7JG
T: 01788 892050
W: www.tqtraining.co.uk/

TRAC Engineering Ltd
Dovecote Rd, Eurocentral, North Lanarkshire, ML1 4GP
T: 01698 831111
F: 01698 832222
E: engineering@trac.com
W: www.tracengineering.com

TRAC Training Ltd
5 Dovecote Road, Eurocentral, North Lanarkshire, ML1 4GP
T: 01698 748700
F: 01698 832222
E: training@trac.com
W: www.tractraining.com

Track Access Services Ltd
Unit 4, The Sidings, Station Road, Shepreth, Hertfordshire, SG8 6PZ
T: 01763 261708
E: mail@trackaccess.co.uk
W: www.trackaccess.co.uk

Track IQ, a Wabtec Company
17-19 King William St, Kent Town, South Australia, AUSTRALIA 5067, Australia
T: +61(0)8 7099 4600
E: tiqtrackiqinfo@wabtec.com
W: www.trackiq.com.au/

Track Maintenance Equipment Ltd
Witham Wood, Marley Lane, Haslemere, Surrey, GU27 3PZ
T: 01428 651114
F: 01428 644727
E: info@tmeltd.co.uk
W: www.tmeltd.co.uk

Track Safe Telecom (TST)
See Centregreat Rail Ltd

Tracklink UK Ltd
Unit 5, Miltons Yard, Petworth Rd, Witley, Surrey, GU8 5LH
T: 01428 685124
F: 01428 687788
E: enquiries@tklink.co.uk
W: www.tklink.co.uk

Tracksure
Wheelsure Holdings PLC, 8 Woburn Street, Ampthill, Beds, MK45 2HP
T: 01525 840557
F: 01525 403918
E: sales@wheelsure.co.uk
W: wheelsure.co.uk/tracksure/

Trackwork Ltd
PO Box 139, Kirk Sandall Lane, Kirk Sandall Ind. Est, Doncaster, DN31WX
T: 01302 888666
F: 01302 888777
E: sales@trackwork.co.uk
W: www.trackwork.co.uk

Tracsis Plc
Nexus, Discovery Way, Leeds, West Yorkshire, LS2 3AA
T: 01332 226860
E: info@tracsis.com
W: www.tracsisops.com

Tractel UK Ltd
Old Lane, Halfway, Sheffield, S20 3GA
T: 0114 248 2266
F: 0114 247 3350
E: tracteluk.info@tractel.com
W: www.tractel.com

TracTruc Bi-modal
See TruckTrain Developments Limited

Traditional Traction Ltd
100 Swan Street, Sible Hedingham, Essex, CO9 3HP

Traffic Management Services Ltd
PO Box 10, Retford, Notts, DN22 7EE
T: 01777 705053
F: 01777 709878
E: info@traffic.org.uk
W: www.traffic.org.uk/

Train Chartering (Luxury Train Club)
Benwell House, Preston, Chippenham, Wilts, SN15 4DX
T: 01249 890176
E: info@luxurytrainclub.com
W: www.luxurytrainclub.com/

Train Fleet (2019) Ltd
Great Minster House, 33 Horseferry Road, London, SW1P 4DR

TrainFX Ltd
4 Newmarket Court, Derby, DE24 8NW
T: 01332 366175
E: jacquit@trainfx.com
W: www.trainfx.com

Train'd Up
Elmbank Mill, Menstrie Business Centre, Menstrie, Clackmannanshire, FK11 7BU
T: 0845 602 9665
F: 0870 850 3397
E: enquiries@traindup.org
W: www.traindup.org

Trainline
Trainline Holdings Ltd, 498 Gorgie Rd, Edinburgh, EH11 3AF
T: 08704 111111
W: www.thetrainline.com

Trainpassenger.com Ltd
Suite 364, 12 South Bridge, Edinburgh, EH1 1DD
T: 0131 235 2358
E: info@trainpassenger.com
W: www.trainpassenger.com

Traka plc
30 Stilebrook Road, Olney, Bucks, MK46 5EA
T: 01234 712345
W: www.traka.com/

Trakside Systems Ltd
See High Voltage Maintenance Services Ltd

Traktionssysteme Austria GmbH (TSA)
Brown-Boveri-Straße 1, 2351 Wiener Neudorf, Austria
T: +43 (0)2236 8118-0
F: +43 (0)2236 8118-237
E: office@traktionssysteme.at
W: www.traktionssysteme.at/en/

TRAM Power Ltd
99 Stanley Rd, Bootle, Merseyside, L20 7DA
T: 0151 547 1425
F: 0151 521 5509
M: 07976 040618
E: lewis.lesley@trampower.co.uk
W: www.trampower.co.uk

Tramlink (Croydon)
See Transport for London

Tranect Ltd
Unit 4, Carraway Rd, Gilmoss Ind. Est, Liverpool, L11 0EE
T: 0151 548 7040
F: 0151 546 6066
E: sales@tranect.co.uk
W: www.tranect.co.uk

Transaction Systems Ltd
See Kiepe Electric Ltd

Transcal Ltd
Firth Rd, Houstoun Ind. Est, Livingston, West Lothian, EH54 5DJ
T: 01506 440111
F: 01506 442333
E: info@transcal.co.uk
W: www.transcal.co.uk

Transdek
Bryans Close, Harworth, Doncaster, DN11 8RY
T: 01302 752276
F: 01302 752434
E: info@transdek.com
W: www.transdek.com/

Translink NI Railways
Central Station, East Bridge St, Belfast, BT1 3PB
T: 02890 666630
F: 02890 899452
E: feedback@translink.co.uk
W: www.translink.co.uk

Transmission Dynamics
Unit 4, Arcot Court, Nelson Industrial Estate, Cramlington, Northumberland, NE23 1BB
T: 0191 580 0058
E: wsales@jrdltd.com
W: www.transmissiondynamics.co.uk

Transmitton
See Siemens Mobility Ltd

TransPennine Express
Bridgewater House, 60 Whitworth St, Manchester, M1 6LT
T: 0345 600 1671
F: 0161 228 8120
E: tpecustomer.relations@firstgroup.com
W: www.tpexpress.co.uk

TRL Ltd
Crowthorne House, Nine Mile Ride, Wokingham, Berkshire, RG40 3GA
T: 01344 773131
W: trl.co.uk

Transport 2000
See Campaign for Better Transport

Transport Benevolent Fund CIO
Suite 2.7, The Loom, 14 Gowers Walk, London, E1 8PY
T: 0300 333 2000 (ETD 00 38571)
F: 0870 831 2882
E: help@tbf.org.uk
W: www.tbf.org.uk

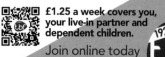

Transport Design International Ltd
Clifford Mill, Clifford Chambers, Stratford upon Avon, Warwickshire, CV37 8HW
T: 01789 205011
W: www.tdi.uk.com/

Transport Focus
Fleetbank House, 2-6 Salisbury Square, London, EC4Y 8JX
T: 0300 123 0860
F: 020 7630 7355
E: info@transportfocus.org.uk
W: www.transportfocus.org.uk

Transport for Edinburgh
55 Annandale Street, Edinburgh, EH7 4AZ
W: transportforedinburgh.com/

Transport for Greater Manchester
2 Piccadilly Place, Manchester, M1 3BG
T: 0161 244 1000
E: customer.relations@tfgm.com
W: www.tfgm.com/

Transport for London
55 Broadway, London, SW1H 0BD
T: 020 7222 5600
E: enquire@tfl.gov.uk
W: www.tfl.gov.uk/rail

Transport for the East Midlands
First Floor Offices, South Annexe, Pera Business Park, Nottingham Road, Melton Mowbray, Leicestershire, LE13 0PB
W: www.emcouncils.gov.uk/transport-for-the-east-midlands-tfem

Transport for the North (TfN)
2nd Floor, 4 Piccadilly Place, Manchester, M1 3BN
T: 0161 244 0888
E: mediarelations@transportforthenorth.com
W: www.transportforthenorth.com

Transport for the South East
County Hall, St Anne's Cresent, Lewes, BN7 1UE
T: 0300 3309474
E: tfse@eastsussex.gov.uk
W: transportforthesoutheast.org.uk/

Transport for Wales
South Gate House, Wood Street, Cardiff, CF10 1EW
T: 0300 200 6565
W: tfw.gov.wales/

Transport for Wales Rail
St Mary's House, 47 Penarth Rd, Cardiff, CF10 5DJ
T: 03333 211202
W: https://tfwrail.wales/

Transport for West Midlands (TfWM)
Customer Relations, 16 Summer Lane, Birmingham, B19 3SD
T: 0121 200 2787
E: customerrelations@centro.org.uk
W: www.centro.org.uk

Transport iNet
Loughborough University, Hazlerigg Building, Loughborough, Leicestershire, LE11 3TU
T: 01509 635270
F: 01509 635231
E: info@transport-inet.org.uk
W: www.transport-inet.org.uk/

Transport Investigations Ltd
Unit 65 The Oaks, Manston Business Park, Ramsgate, Kent, CT12 5FD
T: 01843 593595
E: info@transportinvestigations.co.uk
W: www.transportinvestigations.co.uk

Transport Scotland
Buchanan House, 58 Port Dundas Rd, Glasgow, G4 0HF
T: 0141 272 7100
E: info@transportscotland.gsi.gov.uk
W: www.transportscotland.gov.uk

Transport Systems Catapult
The Pinnacle, 170 Midsummer Boulevard, Milton Keynes, MK9 1BP
T: 01908 359 999
E: reception@ts.catapult.org.uk
W: https://ts.catapult.org.uk

Transreport
3 Shortlands, Hammersmith, London, W6 8DA
W: transreport.co.uk

Transsol Ltd
Unit 8, Marley House, Roseberry Place, Dalston, London, E8 3GD
T: 020 7923 4591
F: 0870 052 5838
E: enquiries@transsol.co.uk
W: www.transsol.co.uk/

Trans-Tronic Ltd
Whitting Valley Rd, Old Whittington, Chesterfield, Derbys, S41 9EY
T: 01246 264260
F: 01246 455281
E: sales@trans-tronic.co.uk
W: www.trans-tronic.co.uk

Transurb Technirail
Ravenstein Street 60/18, B-1000 Brussels, Belgium
T: 32 81 25 20 09
E: simulator@transurb.com
W: www.transurb.com/simulation

Transys Projects Ltd
See Kiepe Electric Ltd

Trapeze Group Rail Ltd
Jervaulx House, 6 St Mary's Court, Blossom Street, York, YO24 1AH
T: 01904 639091
F: 01904 639092
E: sales.railuk@trapezegroup.com
W: www.trapezegroup.com

Tratos Ltd
10 Eagle Court, Britton St, Farringdon, London, EC1M 5QD
T: 0845 413 9990
F: 020 3553 4815
E: john.light@tratos.co.uk
W: www.tratos.co.uk

Travel Info. Systems
71-75 Shelton Street, London, WC2H 9JQ
T: +44 (0)7967 562 190
F: 020 7267 1133
E: enquiries@travelinfosystems.com
W: www.travelinfosystems.com

TRB Lightweight Structures Ltd
12 Clifton Rd, Huntingdon, Cambs, PE29 7EN
T: 01480 447400
F: 01480 414992
E: info@trbls.com
W: www.trbls.com

TRE Ltd
See Hitachi Information Control Systems Europe

Treadmaster Flooring
See Tiflex Ltd

Trelleborg Industrial AVS
1 Hoods Close, Leicester, LE4 2BN
T: +44 116 2670 455
E: antivibration@trelleborg.com
W: www.trelleborg.com/industrialavs

Tremco Illbruck Limited
Coupland Rd, Hindley Green, Wigan, WN2 4HT
T: 01942 251400
F: 01942 251410
E: uk.info@tremco-illbruck.com
W: www.tremco-illbruck.com

Trenitalia UK Ltd
The Broadgate Tower, Third Floor, 20 Primrose Street, London, EC2A 2RS
W: www.trenitalia.com/

trenolab
Via Maniacco 7/A, 34170 Gorizia, Italy
T: +39 0481 30031
E: info@trenolab.com
W: www.trenolab.com/

Trent Instruments Ltd
Unit 39, Nottingham South and Wilford Ind. Est, Ruddington Lane, Nottingham, NG11 7EP
T: 0115 969 6188
F: 0115 945 5696
E: phillip@trentinstruments.co.uk
W: www.trentinstruments.co.uk

TRI Control Systems
Colham Green House, Colham Green Road, Uxbridge, Middlesex, UB8 3QQ
T: 01895 257500
W: tricontrols.com/

Tribo Rail
PO Box 676, Bury, BL8 9RR
T: 01298 214980
E: enquiries@triborail.com
W: www.triborail.com

Triforce Security Solutions Ltd
Westmead House, Westmead, Farnborough, Hants, GU14 7LP
T: 01252 373496
E: enquiries@triforcesecurity.co.uk
W: www.triforcesecurity.co.uk

Trimble UK
Trimble House, Meridian Office Park, Osborn Way, Hook, Hants, RG27 9HX
T: 01256 760150
F: 01256 760148
W: www.trimble.com

Triscan Systems Ltd
4 Petre Court, Clayton Business Park, Accrington, Lancs, BB5 5HY
T: 0845 225 3100
E: info@thetriscangroup.com
W: www.thetriscangroup.com

Tritech Rail/Tritech Rail Training
See AECOM

TRL (Transport Research Laboratory)
Crowthorne House, Nine Mile Ride, Wokingham, Berks, RG40 3GA
T: 01344 773131
F: 01344 770356
E: rail@trl.co.uk
W: www.trl.co.uk

Trojan Services Ltd
Curtis House, 34 Third Avenue, Hove, East Sussex, BN3 2PD
T: 0845 074 0407
F: 01243 783654
E: info@trojan-services.com
W: www.trojan-services.com

Trolex Ltd
Newby Rd, Hazel Grove, Stockport, SK7 5DY
T: 0161 483 1435
F: 0161 483 5556
E: sales@trolex.com
W: www.trolex.com

Trough-Tec Systems Ltd (TTS)
Bennetthorpe, Doncaster, DN2 6AA
T: 01302 343633
E: info@ttsrail.co.uk
W: www.ttsrail.co.uk

TRS Staffing Solutions
8th Floor, York House, Kingsway, London, WC2B 6UJ
T: 020 7419 5800
F: 020 7419 5801
E: info-uk@trsstaffing.com
W: www.trsstaffing.com

TruckTrain Developments Limited
4 Elfin Grove, Bognor Regis, West Sussex, PO21 2RX
T: 01243 869118
M: 07748 550964
E: pmtrucktrain@tiscali.co.uk
W: www.trucktrain.co.uk

Trueform Engineering Ltd
Unit 12, Pasadena Trading Estate, Pasadena Close, Hayes, Middlesex, UB3 3NQ
T: 020 8280 8800
F: 020 8848 1397
E: sales@trueform.co.uk
W: www.trueform.co.uk

Truflame Welding
Truflame House, 56 Newhall Rd, Sheffield, S9 2QL
T: 0114 243 3020
F: 0114 243 5297
E: sales@truflame.co.uk
W: www.truflame.co.uk

TS Components Ltd
Ladywood House, Ladywood Works, Lutterworth, Leics, LE17 4HD
T: 01455 550495
E: info@tscomponents.com
W: www.tscomponents.com

TSL Turton Ltd
PO Box 17, Effingham Street, Sheffield, S4 7YP
T: 0114 270 1577
F: 0114 275 6947
E: sales@tslturton.com
W: www.tslturton.com

TSO
Chemin du Corps de Garde, CS 80035, 77508 Chelles Cedex, France
T: (33) 01 64 72 72 00
F: (33) 01 64 26 30 23
E: info@tso.fr
W: www.tso.fr

TSP Projects
Meridian House, The Crescent, York, YO24 1AW
T: 01904 454600
F: 01904 454601
W: www.tspprojects.co.uk/

TSSA (Transport Salaried Staffs' Association)
Walkden House, 10 Melton St, London, NW1 2EJ
T: 020 7387 2101
F: 0141 3329879
E: enquiries@tssa.org.uk
W: www.tssa.org.uk

TT Electronics plc
Clive House, 12-18 Queens Rd, Weybridge, Surrey, KT13 9XB
T: 01932 825300
F: 01932 836450
E: info@ttelectronics.com
W: www.ttelectronics.com

TTCI UK
13 Fitzroy St, London, W1T 4BQ
T: 020 7755 4080
F: 020 7755 4203
E: michele_johnson@aar.com
W: www.ttc.aar.com

TTG Transportation Technology (Europe) Ltd
1st Floor, 6 Munro Road, Springkerse Industrial Estate, Stirling, FK7 7UU
T: 01786 488535
E: enquiries@ttgeurope.com
W: www.ttgtransportationtechnology.com

TTI Inc
Suite S06, Business & Technology Centre, Bessemer Drive, Stevenage, Herts, SG1 2DX
T: 01438 794170
F: 01438 791139
E: kasey.sweetlove@uk.ttiinc.com
W: www.ttieurope.com/page/campbell-collins

TTPP Construction Consultants
1st Floor, Crowne House, 56-58 Southwark Street, London, SE1 1UN
T: 020 7940 6500
F: 020 7378 0136
E: enquiries@ttpp.co.uk
W: www.ttpp.co.uk/

TTR
See TRL Ltd

Tube Lines
15 Westferry Circus, Canary Wharf, London, E14 4HD
T: 0845 660 5466
E: enquiries@tubelines.com
W: www.tubelines.com

Tufnol Composites Ltd
76 Wellhead Lane, Perry Barr, Birmingham, B42 2TN
T: 0121 356 9351
F: 0121 331 4235
E: sales@tufnol.co.uk
W: www.tufnol.com

Turbex Ltd
Unit 1, Riverwey Ind. Park, Newman Lane, Alton, Hants, GU34 2QL
T: 01420 544909
F: 01420 542264
E: sales@turbex.co.uk
W: www.turbex.co.uk

Turbo Power Systems Ltd
1 Queens Park, Queensway North, Team Valley Trading Est, Gateshead, Tyne & Wear, NE11 0QD
T: 0191 482 9200
F: 0191 482 9201
E: sales@turbopowersystems.com
W: www.turbopowersystems.com

Turkington Precast
James Park, Mahon Rd, Portadown, Co. Armagh, BT62 3EH, Northern Ireland
T: 028 38 332807
F: 028 38 361770
E: gary@turkington-precast.com
W: www.turkington-precast.com

Turnell & Odell Ltd
Sanders Road, Finedon Road Industrial Estate, Wellingborough, Northants, NN8 4NL
T: 01933 222061
E: sales@toengineering.co.uk
W: toengineering.co.uk/

Turner & Townsend
Low Hall, Calverley Lane, Horsforth, Leeds, LS18 4GH
T: 0113 258 4400
F: 0113 258 2911
E: gary.easton@turntown.co.uk
W: www.turnerandtownsend.com

Turner EPS
Unit 1, Millennium Way, High Carr Business Park, Newcastle-Under-Lyme, ST5 7XE
T: 01782 569190
E: sales@turner-eps.co.uk
W: turner-eps.co.uk

Tusp Ltd
Ground Floor, Unit 7, Highpoint Business Village, Henwood, Ashford, Kent, TN24 8DH
T: 01233 640257
E: enquiries@tusp.co.uk
W: www.tusp.co.uk

TUV Product Service Ltd
Octagon House, Concorde Way, Segensworth, North Fareham, Hants, PO15 5RL
T: 01489 558100
F: 01489 558101
E: info@tuvps.co.uk
W: www.tuvps.co.uk

TUV-SUD Rail GmbH
Westendstrasse 199, 80686, Munich, Germany
T: 0049 89519 03537
F: 0049 89519 02933
W: www.tuv-sud.co.uk

TVS Supply Chain Solutions
Logistics House, Buckshaw Avenue, Chorley, Lancashire, PR6 7AJ
T: 01257 265 531
E: info@tvsscs.com
W: https://www.tvsscs.com/

TXM Plant Ltd
Wood Lane, Beckingham, Doncaster, South Yorkshire, DN10 4NS
T: 01302 328900
E: sales@txmplant.co.uk
W: www.txmplant.co.uk

TXM Projects Ltd
1 St Peters Court, Church Lane, Bickenhill, Solihull, B92 0DN
T: 01675 446830
F: 01675 446839
E: simon.pitt@txmprojects.co.uk
W: www.txmprojects.co.uk

TXM Recruit Ltd
Blackhill Drive, Wolverton Mill, Milton Keynes, Bucks, MK12 5TS
T: 0845 2263454
F: 0845 2262453
E: info@txmrecruit.co.uk

Tyco Fire and Integrated Solutions
Tyco Park, Grimshaw Lane, Newton Heath, Manchester, M40 2WL
T: 0161 455 4400
W: www.tycofis.co.uk/

Tyne & Wear Metro
See Nexus (Tyne & Wear Metro)

Tyrolit
Eldon Close, Crick, Northants, NN6 7UD
T: 01788 824500
E: gborder@tyrolit.com
W: www.tyrolit.co.uk

Tyrone Fabrication Ltd (TFL)
87 Goland Rd, Ballygawley, Co Tyrone, BT70 2LA
T: 028 8556 7200
F: 028 8556 7089
E: info@tyrone.co.uk
W: www.tyronefabrication.co.uk

Tyseley Locomotive Works Limited
670 Warwick Rd, Tyseley, Birmingham, B11 2HL
T: 0121 708 4960
F: 0121 708 4960
E: office@vintagetrains.co.uk

UK Accreditation Service (UKAS)
2 Pine Trees, Chertsey Lane, Staines-upon-Thames, TW18 3HR
T: 01784 429000
E: info@ukas.com
W: https://www.ukas.com/

UK Power Networks Services
Newington House, 237 Southwark Bridge Rd, London, SE1 6NP
T: 0207 397 7695
E: rail@ukpowernetworks.co.uk
W: www.ukpowernetworks.co.uk/internet/en/infrastructure-services/rail/

UK Rail Leasing
Beal Street, Leicester, LE2 0AA
T: 0116 262 2783
E: info@ukrl.co.uk
W: www.ukrl.co.uk

UK Rail Research and Innovation Network (UKRRIN)
UKRRIN Coordinating Hub, Partnerships Team, RSSB The Helicon, One South Place, London, EC2M 2RB
T: 020 3142 5300
E: ukrrin@rssb.co.uk
W: www.ukrrin.org.uk/

UK Railtours
PO Box 350, Welwyn, AL6 0WG
T: 01438 715050
W: www.ukrailtours.com

UK Trade & Investment - Investment Services
1 Victoria St, London, SW1H 0ET
T: 0845 539 0419/020 7333 5442
E: enquiries@ukti-invest.com
W: www.ukti.gov.uk

UK Ultraspeed
Warksburn House, Wark, Hexham, Northumberland, NE48 3LS
T: 020 7861 2497
F: 020 7861 2497
E: alan.james@expall.com
W: www.500kmh.com

UKDN Waterflow
2480 Regents Court, The Crescent, Birmingham Business Park, Solihull, West Midlands, B37 7YE
T: 0333 344 2937
E: enquiries@ukdnwaterflow.co.uk
W: ukdnwaterflow.co.uk

UKRS Projects Ltd
See Bowen Projects Ltd

UKTram
Centro House, 16 Summer Lane, Birmingham, B19 3SD
E: info@uktram.co.uk
W: www.uktram.co.uk/

UKWSL
Alexander House, Cafferata Way, Newark-on-Trent, Nottinghamshire, NG24 2TN
T: 01636 640744
F: 01636 640745
W: www.ukwsl.co.uk/

Ultimate Hearing Protection
13 Moorfield Road, Orpington, Kent, BR6 0HG
T: 01689 876885
E: sales@ultimateear.com
W: www.ultimateear.com

Ultra Electronics PMES Ltd
Towers Business Park, Wheelhouse Rd, Rugeley, Staffs, WS15 1UZ
T: 01889 503300
F: 01889 572929
E: enquiries@ultra-pmes.com
W: www.ultra-pmes.com

Ultra Electronics-Electrics
Kingsditch Lane, Cheltenham, Glos, GL51 9PG
T: 01242 221166
F: 01242 221167
E: info@ultra-electrics.com
W: www.ultra-electrics.com

Ultrimax Coatings
Clayfield Industrial Estate, Tickhill Road, Doncaster, Yorkshire, DN4 8QG
T: 01302 856666
F: 01302 571510
E: sales@ultrimaxcoatings.co.uk
W: www.ultrimaxcoatings.co.uk/

Underground Pipeline Services Ltd
See Integrated Water Services Ltd

Unic Cranes Europe
See GGR Group Ltd

Unicard
Peartree Business Centre, Cobham Road, Wimborne, Dorset, BH21 7PT
T: 01202 850810
W: www.unicard-uk.com

UNIFE
Avenue Louise 221, B-1050 Brussels, Belgium
T: 0032 2642 2328
F: 0032 2626 1261
E: judit.sandor@unife.org
W: www.unife.org

Unilathe Ltd
Ford Green Business Park, Ford Green Road, Smallthorne, Stoke-on-Trent, Staffs, ST6 1NG
T: 01782 532000
F: 01782 532013
E: enquiries@unilathe.co.uk
W: www.unilathe.co.uk

Unilite International
The Lab, Moons Moat North Industrial Estate, Winyates Way, Redditch, B98 9FG
T: 01527 584344
F: 01527 584345
E: sales@unilite.co.uk
W: https://www.uni-lite.com/

Unilokomotive Ltd
Dunmore Rd, Tuam, Co. Galway, Republic of Ireland
T: 00353 93 52150
F: 00353 93 52227
E: omcconn@unilok.ie
W: www.unilok.ie

Unipart Dorman
Wennington Rd, Southport, Merseyside, PR9 7TN
T: 01704 518000
F: 01704 518001
E: dorman.enquiries@unipartdorman.co.uk
W: www.unipartdorman.co.uk

Unipart Rail Ltd
Jupiter Building, First Point, Balby Carr Bank, Doncaster, DN4 5JQ
T: 01302 731400
F: 01302 731401
E: enquiries@unipartrail.com
W: www.unipartrail.com

Unite - The Union
Unite House, 128 St Theobald's Road, Holborn, London, WC1X 8TN
T: 020 7611 2500
E: executive.council@unitetheunion.org
W: www.unitetheunion.com

United Kingdom Society for Trenchless Technology
Camden House, Warwick Road, Kenilworth, Warks, CV8 1TH
T: 01926 513773
E: admin@ukstt.org.uk
W: www.ukstt.org.uk

United Springs Ltd
Mandale Park, Norman Road, Rochdale, Lancs, OL11 4HP
T: 01706 644551
F: 01706 630516
E: sales@united-springs.co.uk
W: www.united-springs.com

Universal Boltforgers Ltd
28 Dudley Road West, Tividale, Oldbury, West Midlands, B69 2PJ
T: 0121 522 5950
F: 0121 520 5333
E: office@universal-boltforgers.co.uk
W: www.universalboltforgers.co.uk/

The Universal Improvement Company
First Floor, Millennium House, 40 Nantwich Road, Crewe, CW2 6AD
M: 07941 451021
E: info@theuic.com
W: www.theuic.com

Universal Railway Equipment Ltd
Princess Royal Buildings, Whitecroft Rd, Bream, Lydney, Glos, GL15 6LY
T: 01594 560555
E: unirail@btconnect.com
W: www.peeway.co.uk

University of Derby - Faculty of Arts, Design & Technology
Markeaton St, Derby, DE22 3AW
T: 01332 593216
E: adtenquiry@derby.ac.uk
W: www.derby.ac.uk

University of Sheffield AMRC
Factory of the Future, Advanced Manufacturing Park, Wallis Way, Catcliffe, Rotherham, S60 5TZ
T: 0114 222 9588
E: enquiries@amrc.co.uk
W: www.amrc.co.uk

Delivering Performance Improvement for the Rail Industry

Supply Chain Solutions

Technology & Products Solutions

Our solutions are designed to help our customers **improve performance, reduce risk** and **optimise cost.**

And with a focus on sustainability, we help to deliver on your Corporate Responsibility goals.

UNIPART RAIL

UP3
Hersham Place Technology Park, Molesey Road, Walton-on-Thames, KT12 4RZ
T: 020 3432 1432
E: hello@up3.co.uk
W: www.up3.co.uk

UR Group
Unit 12, Woodside Road, South Marston Park, Swindon, Wiltshire, SN3 4WA
T: 01793 756980
E: uk@ur-group.com
W: www.ur-group.com/

Urban Hygiene Ltd
Sky Business Park, Robin Hood Airport, Doncaster, South Yorks, DN9 3GN
T: 01302 623193
F: 01302 623167
E: enquiries@urbanhygiene.com
W: www.urbanhygiene.co.uk

Urban Transport Group
Wellington House, 40-50 Wellington Street, Leeds, LS1 2DE
T: 0113 251 7204
E: info@urbantransportgroup.org
W: www.urbantransportgroup.org/

Urbis Lighting Ltd
See Urbis Schreder Ltd

Urbis Schreder Ltd
Sapphire House, Lime Tree Way, Hampshire International Business Park, Chineham, Basingstoke, Hants, RG24 8GG
T: 01256 354446
F: 01256 841314
E: sales@urbis-schreder.com
W: www.urbis-schreder.com

Uretek UK Ltd
Unit 6, Peel Rd, Skelmersdale, Lancs, WN8 9PT
T: 01695 50525
F: 01695 555212
E: sales@uretek.co.uk
W: www.uretek.co.uk

URS
See AECOM

VA Rail Ltd
Level 37, One Canada Square, Canary Wharf, London, E14 5DY
M: 07802 549727
E: enquiries@varail.co.uk
W: www.varail.co.uk/

Vaisala Ltd
Elm House, 351 Bristol Rd, Birmingham, B5 7SW
T: 0121 683 1200
F: 0121 683 1299
E: liz.green@vaisala.com
W: www.vaisala.com

Valmont Stainton Ltd
Unit 5, Dukesway, Teesside Industrial Estate, Thornaby, Cleveland, TS17 9LT
T: 01642 766242
F: 01642 765509
E: stainton@valmont.com
W: www.valmont-stainton.com

Van der Vlist UK Ltd
Burma Drive, Kingston upon Hull, HU9 5SD
T: 01482 210100
F: 01482 216222
E: info@vandervlist.co.uk
W: www.vandervlist.com/en/european_offices/uk

Van Elle
Kirkby Lane, Pinxton, Notts, NG16 6JA
T: 01773 580580
F: 01773 862100
E: info@van-elle.co.uk
W: www.van-elle.co.uk

Vanguard Sustainable Transport Solutions
W: www.vanguardsts.com

Vapor Ricon Europe Ltd
Meadow Lane, Loughborough, Leicestershire, LE11 1HS
T: 01509 635920
F: 01509 261939
E: riconuk@wabtec.com
W: www.ricon.eu

Varamis Rail
Denison House, Hexthorpe Road, Doncaster, DN4 0BF
E: logistics@varamis.co.uk
W: www.varamis.co.uk

Variable Message Signs Ltd (VMS)
Unit 1, Monkton Business Park North, Mill Lane, Hebburn, Tyne & Wear, NE31 2JZ
T: 0191 423 7070
F: 0191 423 7071
E: sales@vmstech.co.uk
W: www.vmslimited.co.uk

Vector Management Ltd
Strathclyde House, Green Man Lane, London Heathrow Airport, Feltham, Middx, TW14 0NZ
T: 020 8844 0444
F: 020 8844 0666
E: ju-liang.trigg@vecman.com
W: www.vecman.com

Vector X-Cel Limited
Bessemer Way, Rotherham, S60 1FB
T: 01709 724260
F: 01709 839312
E: sales@vectorx-cel.com
W: www.vectorx-cel.com/

Vectra Group Ltd
See Arcadis LLP

Veea Systems
Cambridge House, Henry Street, Bath, BA1 1JS
T: 01225 618120
W: www.veea.com

Vendigital Ltd
91 Wimpole Street, London, W1G 0EF
T: 020 3871 2769
E: info@vendigital.com
W: https://vendigital.com/

Veolia
5 Limeharbour Court, Limeharbour, London, E14 9RH
T: 01784 496200
F: 01784 496222
E: carol.taylor@dalkia.co.uk
W: veolia.co.uk

Verint Systems
241 Brooklands Rd, Weybridge, Surrey, KT13 0RH
T: 01932 839500
F: 01932 839501
E: marketing.emea@verint.com
W: www.verint.com

Veritec Sonomatic Ltd
Ashton House, The Village, Birchwood Bus.Park, Warrington, WA3 6FZ
T: 01925 414000
F: 01925 655595
E: jl@vsonomatic.com
W: www.vsonomatic.com/

Versaperm Limited
10 Rawcliffe House, Howarth Road, Maidenhead, Berkshire, SL6 1AP
T: 01628 777668
E: webcontact@versaperm.com
W: www.versaperm.com/

Vertemax Limited
Spinney House, Wilcox Close, Aylesham, Kent, CT3 3EP
T: 01227 711072
E: info@vertemax.com
W: www.vertemax.com

Vertex Systems
See AMCL Systems Engineering Ltd

Vertex Systems Engineering
Soane Point, 6-8 Market Place, Reading, RG1 2EG
T: 0118 925 5462
F: 0118 925 5888
E: enquiries@vertex-se.com
W: www.vertex-se.com

Veryards Opus
See Opus International Consultants Ltd

VGC Group
Cardinal House, Bury St, Ruislip, Middx, HA4 7GD
T: 08456 201201
E: enq@vgcgroup.co.uk
W: www.vgcgroup.co.uk

Vi Distribution
Unit 7, Springvale Business Centre, Millbuck Way, Sandbach, Cheshire, CW11 3HY
T: 01270 750520
F: 01270 750521
E: sales@vidistribution.co.uk
W: www.vidistribution.co.uk

Victa Railfreight Ltd
51 Granville Road, Maidstone, Kent, ME14 2BJ
T: 01622 690978
F: 01622 692096
E: enquiries@victa-railfreight.com
W: www.victa-railfreight.com/

Video 125 Ltd
Glade House, High St, Sunninghill, Berks, SL5 9NP
T: 01344 628565
E: sales@video125.co.uk
W: www.video125.co.uk

VINCI Construction UK Ltd
See Taylor Woodrow

Vintage Trains Ltd
670 Warwick Rd, Tyseley, Birmingham, B11 2HL
T: 0121 708 4960
F: 0121 708 4963
E: vintagetrains@btconnect.com
W: www.vintagetrains.co.uk

Viper Innovations
Unit 3A, Marine View Office Park, 45 Martingale Way, Portishead, Bristol, BS20 7AW
T: 01275 787878
E: enquiries@viperinnovations.com
W: www.viperinnovations.com/

VIP-Polymers
15 Windover Road, Huntingdon, Cambridgeshire, PE29 7EB
T: 01480 411333
F: 01480 413991
W: www.vip-polymers.com/

Vision Infrastructure Ltd
Unit 7, Durham Lane, West Moor Park, Doncaster, DN3 3FE
T: 01302 831730
F: 01302 832671
W: www.visioninfrastructure services.com

Vistorm Ltd
See HP Information Security

Visual Security Services
1st Floor, Digital House, Stourport Road, Kidderminster, Worcestershire, DY11 7QH
T: 01562 747241
E: enquiries@visualsecurityltd.co.uk
W: www.visualsecurityltd.co.uk/

Visul Systems
Kingston House, 3 Walton Rd, Pattinson North, Washington, Tyne & Wear, NE38 8QA
T: 0191 402 1960
F: 0191 402 1906
E: info@visulsystems.com
W: www.visulsystems.com

Vita Safety Ltd
1 Gillingham Rd, Eccles, Manchester, M30 8NA
T: 0161 789 1400
F: 0161 280 2528
E: ian.hutchings@vitasafety.com
W: www.vitasafety.com

Vital Rail
Morson Group, Adamson House, Centenary Way, Salford, M50 1rd
T: (+44) 0 161 707 1516
E: enquiries@morson.com
W: www.morson.com/vital/

Vitec
3 Cae Gwrydd, Greenmeadow Springs Bus. Park, Cardiff, CF15 7AB
T: 02920 620232
F: 02920 624837
E: cardiff@vitecconsult.com
W: www.vitecwebberlenihan.com

Vitra Ltd
30 Clerkenwell Road, London, EC1M 5PG
T: 020 7608 6200
F: 020 7608 6201
W: www.vitra.com/en-gb/

Vivarail Ltd
Kineton Road Industrial Estate, Westfield Road, Southam, Warks, CV47 0JH
T: 01789 532230
E: info@vivarail.co.uk
W: www.vivarail.co.uk/

Vix Technology
8 The Irwin Centre, Dry Drayton, Cambridge, CB23 8AR
T: 01223 728700
E: emea@vixtechnology.com
W: www.vixtechnology.com

Viztek Ltd
North East Business & Innovation Centre, Wearfield, Enterprise Park East, Sunderland, SR5 2TA
T: 0191 516 6606
E: info@viztekltd.co.uk
W: www.viztekltd.co.uk

VMS
See Variable Message Signs Ltd (VMS)

Voestalpine Turnout Technology UK Ltd
2 Sir Harry Lauder Road, Edinburgh, EH15 1DJ
T: 0131 322 7210
F: 0131 550 2660
E: jim.gemmell@vae.co.uk
W: www.voestalpine.com/vae

Voestalpine UK Ltd
Voestalpine House, Albion Place, Hammersmith, London, W6 0QT
T: 020 8600 5800
E: catherine.crisp@voestalpine.com
W: www.voestalpine.com

Vogelsang Ltd
Crewe Gates Ind. Est, Crewe, Cheshire, CW1 6YY
T: 01270 216600
F: 01270 216699
E: sales@vogelsang.co.uk
W: www.vogelsang.co.uk

Voith Turbo Ltd
Unit 49, 6 Beddington Farm Road, Croydon, CR0 4XB
T: 020 8667 0333
F: 020 8569 1726
E: vtgbrailsales@voith.com
W: www.voith.com

VolkerFitzpatrick Ltd
Hertford Rd, Hoddesdon, Herts, EN11 9BX
T: 01992 305000
F: 01992 305001
E: enquiries@volkerfitzpatrick.co.uk
W: www.volkerfitzpatrick.co.uk

VolkerRail
Units 4 & 6, Carr Hill Road, Doncaster, South Yorks, DN4 8DE
T: 01302 791100
F: 01302 791200
E: marketing@volkerrail.co.uk
W: www.volkerrail.co.uk

Vortex Exhaust Technology
53 Tower Road, Globe Industrial Estate, Grays, Essex, RM17 6ST
T: 01375 372037
E: enq@vortexexhausttechnology.com
W: www.vortexexhaust technology.com/

Vossloh AG
Vosslohstrasse 4, 58791 Werdohl, Germany
T: 0049 2392 520
F: 0049 2392 520
W: www.vossloh.com

Vossloh Cogifer UK Ltd
80a Scotter Rd, Scunthorpe, North Lincs, DN15 8EF
T: 01724 862131
F: 01724 295243
E: info@vfs.vossloh.com
W: www.vossloh.com

Vossloh Fastening Systems GmbH
Vosslohstrasse 4, D-58791 Werdohl, Germany
T: 0049 2392 52 0
F: 0049 2392 52 375
E: info@vfs.vossloh.com
W: www.vossloh.com

Vp Group plc
Central House, Beckwith Knowle, Otley Road, Harrogate, North Yorkshire, HG3 1UD
T: 01423 533400
F: 01423 565657
W: www.vpplc.com

VTG Rail UK Ltd
Sir Stanley Clarke House, 7 Ridgeway, Quinton Business Park, Birmingham, B32 1AF
T: 0121 421 9180
F: 0121 421 9192
E: sales@vtg.com
W: www.vtg-rail.co.uk

VTS Track Technology Ltd
See Vossloh Cogifer UK Ltd

Vulcanite UK and Europe
PO Box 456, Newcastle, NE3 9DR
T: 0191 490 6203
M: 07554 447099
E: stuart.ramsay@contitech.uk
W: www.vulcanite.com

Vulcascot Cable Protectors Ltd
Unit 12, Norman-D-Gate, Bedford Rd, Northampton, NN1 5NT
T: 0800 035 2842
F: 01604 632344
E: sales@vulcascotcable protectors.co.uk
W: www.vulcascotcableprotectors.com

W A Developments Ltd
See XYZ Rail Ltd

Wabtec Rail Ltd
PO Box 400, Doncaster Works, Hexthorpe Rd, Doncaster, DN1 1SL
T: 01302 340700
F: 01302 790058
E: wabtecrail@wabtec.com
W: www.wabtecgroup.com

Wabtec Transportation Systems
3rd Floor, 1 Ashley Road, Altrincham, Cheshire, WA14 2DT
W: www.wabteccorp.com/

Wacker Neuson (GB) Ltd
Lea Rd, Waltham Cross, Herts, EN9 1AW
T: 01992 707228
F: 01992 707201
W: www.wackerneuson.com

WAGO Ltd
Triton Park, Swift Valley Industrial Estate, Rugby, CV21 1SG
T: 01788 568008
E: ukmarketing@wago.com
W: www.wago.com

A N Wallis & Co Ltd
Greasley St, Bulwell, Nottingham, NG6 8NG
T: 0115 927 1721
F: 0115 875 6630
E: mark.rimmington@an-wallis.com
W: www.an-wallis.com

Warner Surveys
Unit 22, Theale Lakes Business Park, Moulden Way, Reading, RG7 4GB
T: 0118 930 3314
E: paul.matthews@ warnersurveys.com
W: https://www.warnersurveys.com/

Warwick Manufacturing Group (WMG)
International Manufacturing Centre, University of Warwick, Coventry, CV4 7AL
T: 024 7652 4871
E: wmg@warwick.ac.uk
W: https://warwick.ac.uk/fac/sci/wmg

Wascosa AG
Werftestrasse 4, 6005 Lucerne, Switzerland
T: +41 41 727 67 67
F: +41 41 727 67 77
E: info@wascosa.ch
W: www.wascosa.ch

Washroom Washroom
Units 1-10, Hill Farm, Epping Lane, Abridge, Essex, RM4 1TU
T: 0845 470 3000
F: 0845 470 3001
E: contact@washroom.co.uk
W: www.washroom.co.uk

Washtec UK Ltd
Unit 14A, Oak ind. Park, Great Dunmow, Essex, CM9 1XN
T: 01371 878800
F: 01371 878810
W: www.washtec-uk.com

Waterflow
See UKDN Waterflow

Waterman Infrastructure & Environment Ltd
Pickfords Wharf, Clink St, London, SE1 9DG
T: 020 7928 7888
F: 020 7902 0992
M: 07880 554632
E: paul.worrall@watermangroup.com
W: www.watermangroup.com/

Wath Group
Pump House, Station Road, Wath Upon Dearne, Rotherham, South Yorkshire, S63 7DQ
T: 01709 876900
F: 01709 878863
E: info@wath.co.uk

Wavesight Ltd
Unit 13, Dencora Way, Sundon Business Park, Luton, Beds, LU3 3HP
T: 01582 578160
F: 01582 578298
E: sales@wavesight.com
W: www.wavesight.com

Waymap
E: info@waymap.org
W: www.waymap.org

WDS Component Parts Ltd
Richardshaw Road, Grangefield Industrial Estate, Pudsey, Leeds, LS28 6LE
T: 0113 290 9852
E: sales@wdsltd.co.uk
W: www.wdsltd.co.uk

Webasto AG
Kraillinger Strasse 5, 82131 Stockdorf, Germany
T: 0049 89 857 948 444
F: 0049 89 899 217 433
E: tac3@webasto.com
W: www.rail.webasto.com

Webro Cable & Connectors Ltd
Vision House, Meadow Brooks Business Park, Meadow Lane, Long Eaton, Nottingham, NG10 2GD
T: 0115 972 4483
F: 0115 946 1230
E: info@webro.com
W: www.webro.com

WEC Group Ltd
Spring Vale House, Spring Vale Rd, Darwen, Lancs, BB3 2ES
T: 01254 773718
F: 01254 771109
E: stevecooke@wecl.co.uk
W: www.welding-eng.com

Weedfree
Holly Tree Farm, Park Lane, Balne, Goole, DN14 0EP
T: 01405 860022
F: 01405 862283
E: sales@weedfree.net
W: www.weedfree.net

Weidmuller Ltd
Klippon House, Centurion Court Office Park, Meridian East, Meridian Business Park, Leicester, LE19 1TP
T: 0116 282 1261
F: 0116 289 3582
E: marketing@weidmuller.co.uk
W: www.weidmuller.co.uk

Weightmans
High Holborn House, 52-54 High Holborn, London, WC1V 6RL
T: 020 7822 1900
F: 020 7822 1901
E: sarah.seddon@weightmans.com
W: www.weightmans.com

Weighwell Engineering Ltd
Weighwell House, Woolley Colliery Road, Darton, Barnsley, South Yorkshire, S75 5JA
T: 0114 269 9955
F: 0114 269 9256
E: sales@weighwell.com
W: www.weighwell.com

Weir Waste Services Ltd
Fawdry House, 50 Cato Street, Waterlinks, Birmingham, B7 4TS
T: 0121 772 6726
F: 0121 773 1244
E: sales@weirwaste.co.uk
W: www.weirwaste.co.uk/

Weld-A-Rail Ltd
Lockwood Close, Top Valley, Nottingham, NG5 9JN
T: 0115 926 8797
F: 0115 926 4818
E: admin@weldarail.co.uk
W: www.weldarail.co.uk

The Welding Institute
See Institute of Rail Welding

Welfare Cabins UK (WCUK)
See Garic Ltd

A J Wells & Sons Vitreous Enamellers
Bishop's Way, Newport, IOW, PO30 5WS
T: 01983 537766
F: 01983 537788
E: enamel@ajwells.co.uk
W: www.ajwells.com

Wentworth House Rail Systems Ltd
Vale House, Aston Lane North, Preston Brook, Cheshire, WA7 3PE
T: 01270 448405
E: enquiries@railelectrification.com
W: www.railelectrification.com

Werther International SpA
Via F Brunelleschi 12F, 42124-Cadè (RE), Italy
T: 39 0522 9431
E: sales@wertherint.com
W: www.wertherint.com

West Coast Railway Co.
Jesson Way, Carnforth, Lancs, LA5 9UR
T: 01524 732100
F: 01524 735518
E: enquiries@westcoastrailways.net
W: www.wcrc.co.uk

West Midlands Metro
Travel Midland Metro, Metro Centre, Potters Lane, Wednesbury, West Midlands, WS10 0AR
T: 0121 502 2006
F: 0121 556 6299
W: https://westmidlandsmetro.com/

West Midlands PTE
See Transport for West Midlands (TfWM)

West Midlands Rail Executive (WMRE)
16 Summer Lane, Birmingham, B19 3SD
T: 0121 214 7423
E: contact@westmidlandsrail.com
W: www.westmidlandsrail.com/

West Midlands Trains
2nd Floor, 134 Edmund Street, Birmingham, B3 2ES
T: 0121 634 2040
F: 0121 654 1234
W: https://www.wmtrains.co.uk/

West of England Combined Authority (WECA)
3 Rivergate, Temple Way, Bristol, BS1 6ER
T: 0117 428 6210
E: info@westofengland-ca.gov.uk
W: www.westofengland-ca.org.uk/

West Yorkshire Combined Authority
Wellington House, 40-50 Wellington St, Leeds, LS1 2DE
T: 0113 251 7272
E: metroline@westyorks-ca.gov.uk
W: www.westyorks-ca.gov.uk/

Westcode UK
See IXYS Westcode

Westermo Data Communications Ltd
Talisman Business Centre, Duncan Rd, Park Gate, Southampton, SO31 7GA
T: 01489 580585
F: 01489 580586
E: sales@westermo.co.uk
W: www.westermo.com

Western Rail Services
Unit 5H, Cricket Street, Wigan, Lancs, WN6 7TP
T: 01942 245599
F: 01942 825544
E: info@railcable.co.uk
W: www.railcable.co.uk

Westinghouse Platform Screen Doors
Knorr-Bremse Rail Systems (UK) Ltd, Westinghouse Way, Hampton Park East, Melksham, Wilts, SN12 6TL
T: 01225 898700
F: 01225 898705
E: wpsd.enquiries@knorr-bremse.com
W: www.platformscreendoors.com

Westinghouse Rail Systems
See Siemens Mobility Ltd

Westley Engineering Ltd
120 Pritchett St, Aston, Birmingham, B6 4EH
T: 0121 333 1925
F: 0121 333 1926
E: g.dunne@westleyengineering.co.uk
W: www.westleyengineering.co.uk

Weston Williamson
12 Valentine Place, London, SE1 8QH
T: 020 7401 8877
F: 020 7401 8349
E: team@westonwilliamson.com
W: www.westonwilliamson.com

Westshield Ltd
Ashcroft House, Bredbury Park Way, Bredbury, Stockport, Cheshire, SK6 2SN
T: 0161 682 6222
F: 0161 682 6333
E: info@westshield.co.uk
W: www.westshield.co.uk

Wettons
Wetton House, 278-280 St James's Rd, London, SE1 5JX
T: 020 7237 2007
F: 020 7252 3277
E: sales@wettons.co.uk
W: www.wettons.co.uk

WG Specialist Coatings
Foston Depot, Woodyard Lane,
Foston, Derbyshire, DE65 5PY
T: 01283 584806
F: 01283 584901
E: simon.starmer@wgtanker.com
W: www.wgtanker.com/

WH Davis Ltd
Langwith Rd, Langwith Junction,
Mansfield, Notts, NG20 9SA
T: 01623 741600
F: 01623 744474
W: www.whdavis.co.uk

Wheelsets (UK) Ltd
Unit 4B, Denby Way, Hellaby Industrial
Estate, Rotherham, S66 8NZ
T: 01302 322266
F: 01302 322299
E: martin@wheelsets.co.uk
W: www.wheelsets.co.uk

White & Case LLP
5 Old Broad St, London, EC2N 1DW
T: 020 7532 1000
F: 020 7532 1001
E: cmillersmith@whitecase.com
W: www.whitecase.com

White Young Green
See Amey

Whiteley Electronics Ltd
See Gemma Lighting

Whitfield Construction Services
1-2 Paris Garden, London, SE1 8ND
T: 020 8938 3705
E: info@whitfieldconstruction
services.co.uk
W: www.whitfieldconstruction
services.co.uk/

Whitmore
City Park, Watchmead, Welwyn
Garden City, Herts, AL7 1LT
T: 01707 379870
E: info-uk@whitmores.com
W: www.whitmores.com

Whitmore Rail
Whitmore Europe, City Park,
Watchmead, Welwyn Garden City,
Herts, AL7 1LT
T: 01707 379870
E: info-uk@whitmores.com
W: www.whitmores.com

Whoosh Media
Spoken Ink Ltd, Suite 40-41, The Hop
Exchange, 24 Southwark Street,
London, SE1 1TY
T: 020 7403 6763
E: info@whooshmedia.co.uk
W: www.whooshmedia.co.uk

Wicek Sosna Architects
Unit 15, 21 Plumbers Row, London,
E1 1EQ
T: 020 7655 4430
E: office@sosnaarchitects.co.uk
W: www.sosnaarchitects.co.uk

WiFi Spark
5 Cranmere Court, Lustleigh Close,
Matford
Business Park, Exeter, EX2 8PW
T: 0344 848 9555
E: info@wifispark.com
W: www.wifispark.com/

Wilcomatic Ltd
Unit 5, Commerce Park, 19 Commerce
Way, Croydon, CR0 4YL
T: 020 8649 5760
F: 020 8680 9791
E: sales@wilcomatic.co.uk
W: www.wilcomatic.co.uk

Wilkinson Star Ltd
Shield Drive, Wardsley Ind Est,
Manchester, M28 2WD
T: 0161 728 7900
E: wilkinsonstar.sales@
wilkinsonstar.com
W: www.wilkinsonstar.com

WilkinsonEyre
33 Bowling Green Lane, London,
EC1R 0BJ
T: 020 7608 7900
F: 020 7608 7901
E: info@wilkinsoneyre.com
W: www.wilkinsoneyre.com/

WillB Brand Consultants
Somerset House, The Strand, London,
WC2R 1LA
W: www.willbaxter.com

William Bain Fencing Ltd
Lochin Works, 7 Limekilns Rd, Blairlinn
Ind. Est, Cumbernauld, G67 2RN
T: 01236 457333
F: 01236 451166
E: sales@lochrin-bain.co.uk
W: www.lochrin-bain.co.uk/

William Cook Rail
Cross Green, Leeds, LS9 0SG
T: 0113 249 6363
F: 0113 249 1376
E: castproducts@william-cook.co.uk
W: www.william-cook.co.uk

**Willie Baker Leadership &
Development Ltd**
Aggborough Farm, College Rd,
Kidderminster, Worcs, DY10 1LU
E: willie@williebaker.co.uk
W: www.williebaker.co.uk

Wilmat Ltd
Wilmat House, 43 Steward Street,
Birmingham, B18 7AE
T: 0121 454 7514
F: 0121 456 1792
E: sales@wilmat-handling.co.uk
W: www.wilmat-handling.co.uk/

Winckworth Sherwood
Minerva House, 5 Montague Close,
London, SE1 9BB
T: 020 7593 5000
F: 0207 593 5099
E: info@wslaw.co.uk
W: www.wslaw.co.uk

Wind River UK Ltd
Oakwood House, Grove Business Park,
White Waltham, Maidenhead, Berks,
SL6 3HY
T: 01793 831831
F: 01793 831808
E: sue.woolley@windriver.com
W: www.windriver.com

**Windhoff Bahn und
Anlagentechnik GmbH**
Hovestrasse 10, D-48431 Rheine,
Germany
T: 0049 5971 580
F: 0049 5971 58209
E: info@windhoff.de
W: www.windhoff.de

Window Seater
W: https://windowseater.com/

Windsor Link Railway
Suite 1, Unit A1, Tectonic Place,
Holyport Road, Maidenhead,
Berkshire, SL6 2YE
W: windsorlink.co.uk/

Winn & Coales (Denso) Ltd
Denso House, Chapel Rd, London,
SE27 0TR
T: 020 8670 7511
F: 020 8761 2456
E: mail@denso.net
W: www.denso.net

Winstanley & Co Ltd
See Transcal Ltd

Winsted Ltd
Units 7/8, Lovett Rd, Hampton Lovett
Ind Est, Droitwich, Worcs, WR9 0QG
T: 01905 770276
F: 01905 779791
E: info@winsted.co.uk
W: www.winsted.co.uk

Wintersgill
110 Bolsover St, London, W1W 5NU
T: 020 7580 4499
F: 020 7436 8191
E: info@wintersgill.net
W: www.wintersgill.net

Wireless CCTV Ltd
Mitchell Hey Place, College Road,
Rochdale, Lancs, OL12 6AE
T: 01706 631166
E: sales@wcctv.com
W: www.wcctv.com

Witt O'Brien's Ltd
Trent House, RTC Business Park,
London Rd, Derby, DE24 8UP
T: 01332 222299
F: 01332 222298
E: info@wittobriens.com
W: www.wittobriens.com

WM Plant Hire Ltd
Manor Farm Lane, Bridgnorth,
Shropshire, WV16 5HG
T: 01452 722200
F: 01452 769666
E: info@wmplanthire.com
W: www.wmplanthire.com

Woking Homes
Oriental Rd, Woking, Surrey, GU22 7BE
T: 01483 763558
F: 01483 721048
E: administration@woking-homes.
co.uk
W: www.woking-homes.co.uk

Woma (UK) Ltd
Davenport House, Davenport Gate,
Macadam Way, West Portway
Industrial Estate, Andover, SP10 3SQ
T: 01264 369828
E: sales@woma.uk.com
W: www.woma.uk.com/

Women in Rail
123 Victoria Street, London, SW1E 6DE
T: 020 7592 0796
E: womeninrail@angeltrains.co.uk
W: www.womeninrail.org

Wood & Wood Signs
Heron Rd, Sowton Estate, Exeter,
EX2 7LX
T: 01392 444501
F: 01392 252358
E: info@wwsigns.co.uk
W: www.wwsigns.co.uk

Woodward Diesel Systems
Lancaster Centre, Meteor Business
Park, Cheltenham Rd East, Gloucester,
GL2 9QL
T: 01452 859940
F: 01452 855758
W: www.woodward.com

WordNerds
Proto, Baltic Business Quarter,
Gateshead, NE8 3DF
T: 0191 300 9444
E: hello@wordnerds.ai
W: www.wordnerds.ai

Workmates Daniel Owen
1st Floor, Genesis House, 17 Godliman
St, London, EC4V 5BD
T: 0207 539 1660
W: www.wmdo.co.uk/sectors/rail

XiTRACK Ltd
See Dow

XL Lubricants Ltd
See NTM Sales & Marketing Ltd

Worldline
Triton Square, Regents Place, London,
NW1 3HG
T: 020 7830 4447
F: 020 7830 4445
W: www.uk.worldline.com

Worlifts Rail Division
Guild House, Sandy Lane, Wildmoor,
Bromsgrove, Worcs, B61 0QU
T: 0121 460 1113
F: 0121 460 1116
E: rail@worlifts.co.uk
W: www.worlifts.co.uk

WPB Contractors
Unit 1, Heron Business Centre,
Henwood, Ashford, Kent, TN24 8DH
T: 01233 643549
E: info@wpbcontractors.co.uk
W: https://www.wpbcontractors.co.uk/

Wrekin Circuits Ltd
29/30 Hortonwood 33, Telford,
Shropshire, TF1 7EX
T: 01952 670011
F: 01952 606565
E: sales@wrekin-circuits.co.uk
W: www.wrekin-circuits.co.uk

WRS Cable Ltd
MGB House, Langage Business Park,
Plympton, Plymouth, Devon, PL7 5JY
W: www.wrscables.com

The WS Group (Tracksure)
8 Woburn St, Ampthill, Beds,
MK45 2HP
T: 01525 840557
F: 01525 403918
E: sales@tracksure.co.uk
W: www.tracksure.co.uk

WSP UK
Mountbatten House, Basing View,
Basingstoke, Hants, RG21 4HJ
T: 01256 318802
F: 01256 318700
W: www.wspgroup.com

WVCO Railroad Solutions
990 Owen Loop North, PO Box 2280,
Eugene, OR 97402, United States
T: 001 541 484 9621
F: 001 541 284 2096
E: wvcorailroadsolutions@
wilvaco.com
W: www.wvcorailroad.com

WWP Consultants
5-15 Cromer St, London, WC1H 8LS
T: 020 7833 5767
F: 020 7833 5766
W: www.wwp.co.uk

Wynnwith Rail
See Morson International

Wyse Rail Ltd
Lincoln Road, Cressex Business Park,
High Wycombe, Bucks, HP12 3RH
T: 0808 168 1675
F: 0845 873 0965
E: info@wysegroup.com
W: www.wysegroup.co.uk

WyvernRail Plc
Wirksworth Station, Station Rd,
Wirksworth, Derbys, DE4 4FB
T: 01629 821828
E: wirksworth_station@
wwyvernrail.co.uk
W: www.mytesttrack.com

XEIAD
22 Lower Town, Sampford Peverill,
Tiverton, Devon, EX16 7BT
T: 01884 822899
E: info@bridgezoneltd.co.uk
W: www.xeiad.com/

X-Press Spares Ltd & Co KG
Daimlerstr. 49, 48432 Rheine,
Germany
T: +49 5971 - 800155-0
F: +49 5971 - 800155-9
E: info@xpress-spares.de
W: www.xpress-spares.de

XRail Group Limited
30th Floor, 40 Bank Street, Canary
Wharf, London, E14 5NR
T: 020 3102 9562
E: enquiries@xrailgroup.com
W: www.xrailgroup.com/

XYZ Rail Ltd
Castle View, Gillan Way, Penrith 40
Business Park, Penrith, CA11 9BP
T: 01228 882300
E: contactus@xyzrail.com
W: www.xyzrail.com

Yardene Engineering 2000 Ltd
Daux Rd, Billingshurst, West Sussex,
RH14 9SJ
T: 01403 783558
F: 01403 783104
E: sales@yardene.co.uk
W: www.yardene.co.uk

A E Yates Group
Cranfield Road, Lostock Industrial
Estate, Bolton, BL6 4SB
T: 01204 696175
E: tadmin@aeyates.co.uk
W: www.aeyates.co.uk

Yellow Group Limited
Yellow House, Haydock Park Road,
Derby, DE24 8HT
T: 01332 470214
F: 01332 258823
E: enquiries@yellow-group.com
W: www.yellow-group.com

Yeltech Ltd
Upper Unstead Farm Cottage,
Unstead Lane, Bramley, Guildford,
GU5 0BT
T: 0845 052 3860
E: sales@yeltech.co.uk
W: www.yeltech.co.uk

YJL Infrastructure Ltd
39 Cornhill, London, EC3V 3ND
T: 020 7522 3220
F: 020 7522 3261
W: www.yjli.co.uk

Young Rail Professionals (YRP)
E: info@youngrailpro.com
W: www.youngrailpro.com

Zarges (UK) Ltd
Holdom Ave, Saxon Park Ind. Est,
Bletchley, Milton Keynes, MK1 1QU
T: 01908 641118
F: 01908 648176
E: sales@zargesuk.co.uk
W: www.zargesuk.com

Zebraware
Chadwick House, Birchwood Park,
Cheshire, WA3 6AE
T: 01925 945470
E: contact@zebraware.com
W: zebraware.com

ZEDAS GMBH
A-Hennecke-Strasse 37, D-01968
Senftenberg, Germany
T: 0049 3573 7075 0
E: info@zedas.com
W: www.zedas.com

Zep UK
PO Box 12, Tanhouse Lane, Widnes,
Cheshire, WA8 0RD
T: 0151 422 1000
F: 0151 422 1011
E: info@zep.com
W: www.zep.co.uk

Zephir SpA
Via Salvador Allende N.85, I-41122
Modena, Italy
T: 39 059 25 25 54
E: zephir@zephir.eu
W: www.zephir.eu

Zeta Specialist Lighting Ltd
Telford Road, Bicester, OX26 4LB
T: 01869 322500
E: info@thezetagroup.com
W: zetaled.co.uk/

Zetica
Units 15/16, Hanborough Business
Park, Long Hanborough, Oxon,
OX29 8LH
T: 01993 886682
F: 01993 886683
E: rail@zetica.com
W: www.zeticarail.com

ZF Services UK Ltd
Abbeyfield Rd, Lenton, Nottingham,
NG7 2SX
T: 0333 240 1123
F: 0844 257 0666
M: 07803 626420
E: gavin.donoghue@zf.com
W: www.aftermarketzf.com

ZF UK Laser Ltd
9 Avacado Court, Commerce Way,
Trafford Park, Manchester, M17 1HW
T: 0161 871 7050
F: 0161 312 5063
E: info@zf-uk.com
W: www.zf-uk.com

TuffTrak Ground Solutions
County Farm, High Roding, Dunmow,
Essex, CM6 1NQ
T: +44 (0) 1279 647021
F: 0845 643734
E: sales@tufftrak-safety.com
W: www.tufftrak-safety.com

Zipabout
Northcliffe House, Young St, London,
W8 5EH
W: www.zipabout.com

Zircon Software Ltd
Bellefield House, Hilperton Rd,
Trowbridge, Wilts, BA14 7FP
T: 01225 764444
F: 01225 753087
E: info@zirconsoftware.co.uk
W: www.zirconsoftware.co.uk

Zollner UK Ltd
Clayton Business Ctr, Midland Rd,
Leeds, LS10 2RJ
T: 0113 270 3008
E: signal@zoellner.de
W: www.zoellner.de/

Zonegreen
Sir John Brown Building, Davy Ind.
Park, Prince of Wales Rd, Sheffield,
S9 4EX
T: 0114 230 0822
F: 0871 872 0349
E: info@zonegreen.co.uk
W: www.zonegreen.co.uk

**Zoppas Industries Heating
Element Technologies**
Via Podgora 26, I-31029 Vittorio
Veneto (TV), Italy
T: 39 0438 9101
E: rica@zoppas.com
W: www.zoppasindustries.com

Z-Tech Control Systems Ltd
Unit 4 Meridian, Buckingway Business
Park, Anderson Rd, Swavesey,
Cambridge, CB24 4AE
T: 01223 653500
F: 01223 653501
W: www.z-tech.co.uk/

ZTR Control Systems
8050 Country Rd, 101 East, Shakopee,
Minnesota, 55379, United States
T: 001 952 233 4340
F: 001 952 233 4375
E: railinfo@ztr.com
W: www.ztr.com/rail

Zuken
1500 Aztec West, Almondsbury,
Bristol, BS32 4RF
T: 01454 207800
E: sales-uk@zuken.com
W: www.zuken.com

Zwicky Track Tools
See Arbil Lifting Gear